LIZ

Also by C. David Heymann

Bobby and Jackie:
A Love Story

American Legacy:
The Story of John and Caroline Kennedy

The Georgetown Ladies' Social Club:
Power, Passion and Politics in the Nation's Capital

RFK:
A Candid Biography of Robert F. Kennedy

A Woman Named Jackie:
An Intimate Biography of Jacqueline Bouvier Kennedy Onassis

Poor Little Rich Girl:
The Life and Legend of Barbara Hutton

American Aristocracy:
The Lives and Times of James Russell, Amy and Robert Lowell

Ezra Pound:
The Last Rower

The Quiet Hours (poetry)

LIZ

An Intimate Biography of Elizabeth Taylor

C. DAVID HEYMANN

ATRIA PAPERBACK
New York London Toronto Sydney

ATRIA PAPERBACK
A Division of Simon & Schuster, Inc.
1230 Avenue of the Americas
New York, NY 10020

Originally published in 1995 by Carol Publishing Group

First Atria Paperback edition April 2011

ATRIA PAPERBACK and colophon are trademarks of Simon & Schuster, Inc.

For information about special discounts for bulk purchases, please contact Simon & Schuster Special Sales at 1-866-506-1949 or business@simonandschuster.com.

The Simon & Schuster Speakers Bureau can bring authors to your live event. For more information or to book an event, contact the Simon & Schuster Speakers Bureau at 1-866-248-3049 or visit our website at www.simonspeakers.com.

Manufactured in the United States of America

10 9 8 7 6 5 4 3

Library of Congress Cataloging-in-Publication Data is available.

ISBN 978-1-4391-9188-0
ISBN 978-1-4391-9190-3 (ebook)

To Kent Bruce Cunow

1945–1989

Very simply, my best friend

Her legs are too short for the torso, the head too bulky for the figure. But the face, with those lilac eyes, is a prisoner's dream, a secretary's self-fantasy: unreal, non-attainable, at the same time shy, overly vulnerable, very human with the flicker of suspicion constantly flaring behind the lilac eyes.

—Truman Capote

"Will you walk into my parlour?" said the Spider to
the Fly,
"'Tis the prettiest little parlour that ever you did spy;
The way into my parlour is up a winding stair,
And I've many curious things to show when you are
there."
—Oh no, no," said the little Fly, "to ask me is in vain,
For who goes up your winding stair can ne'er come
down again."

—Mary Howitt
"The Spider and the Fly"

Chapter 1

Elizabeth Taylor's eyes surveyed the surroundings of white tile and porcelain inside the main residential unit at the Betty Ford Center for drug and alcohol rehabilitation. Set on fourteen acres in a desert bowl ringed by jagged mountains, the institution at Rancho Mirage, California, had been founded in 1981 as part of the Eisenhower Medical Center by Leonard Firestone, former United States ambassador to Belgium and a recovering alcoholic, and by former President Gerald Ford's wife, Betty, after her recovery from drug and alcohol abuse. Elizabeth Taylor, a victim of decades of multiple addictions to alcohol and narcotic drugs, had entered the facility of her own volition on December 5, 1983.

The decision to commit herself to treatment had come about while the then fifty-one-year-old Taylor languished in a bed at St. John's Hospital in Santa Monica, California, ostensibly because of a bowel obstruction. While she lay there, her children, her brother and sister-in-law, and her closest friend, actor Roddy McDowall, visited her to initiate what has become known as a "family intervention."

"I was assured of their love while at the same time I was told how my behavior had altered them, and of their real fears that I was killing myself," the actress later wrote in *Elizabeth Takes Off,* an autobiographical meditation on weight loss and self-awareness. "I listened in total silence," she continued. "I remember being shocked. I couldn't believe what I had become. At the end, they said reservations had been made for me at the Betty Ford Center and they wanted me to go."

She went and soon found herself involved in a program as strict and rigorous as it was ascetic. They assigned her to a small bedroom with two single beds, two desks, two high-intensity desk lamps, two chairs, two dressers, and one female roommate. She wasn't pleased.

"When she entered the institution, Elizabeth thought she would receive special treatment," said Barnaby Conrad, a professor of English literature at the University of California at Santa Barbara and a patient at the Betty Ford Center. "When they told her she had to share a room with another woman, she said, 'I've never in my life shared a room with another woman, and I'm not about to start.' The powers that be at the center quickly cut her down to size. They made her spend the next night or two in the 'swamp'—a room shared not by two but by four women. Finally, they agreed to let her room with just one woman."

The boot-camp mentality of the Betty Ford Center did not exempt Taylor. Patients were barred from leaving the hospital grounds except under the direct supervision of a clinic-appointed chaperone. Use of telephones was prohibited during the first week of a patient's stay; thereafter patients were permitted a maximum of ten minutes on the telephone each evening. Visitors were banned during the first five days and were then permitted for only four hours each Sunday. Attendance was required at all meals, at evening lectures (the center sponsored an extensive drug-and-alcohol-education program), as well as at group therapy sessions in which participants were expected to confess to their faults—and to any wrongs they had done to others while "under the influence." For good reason, Elizabeth described her initial reaction to the regime as one of "dread and loathing."

"They'd never had a celebrity before," she subsequently informed an interviewer at *Vanity Fair.* "The counselors told me later, they didn't know what to do with me, whether they should treat me like an ordinary patient or whether they should give me sort of special isolated treatment. They decided to lump me in with everyone else, which of course was the only way to do it." (At the time of Elizabeth Taylor's

1983 stay at Betty Ford, the center housed forty-five patients divided among three glass-and-mortar residential units. Patients in one unit were not allowed to fraternize with patients from another.)

Part of being lumped in with the others entailed participation in a daily regimen that began at 6:00 A.M. with a meditation walk and ended fifteen hours later with an evening meeting of Alcoholics Anonymous. More demanding still had to be the requirement that all patients maintain and clean their own living quarters, including bathroom facilities, public rooms, and outdoor areas. Denied the servants that had always been such an integral part of her life as a major star, Elizabeth for once became her own maid, making her own bed, vacuuming her own room, washing her own laundry, carrying out her own garbage, sweeping and scrubbing, cleaning up sinks and hospital lounges.

At first, Elizabeth and her bunkmates accepted their fate with abject resignation. But within a few weeks of their projected five-week stay they began to register complaints about nearly everything, including the fact that their residential unit, North House, received but a single copy of the daily newspaper and by the time it reached them the paper would usually be crumpled beyond readability. Nor did they enjoy having to fill out forms; yet within their first week at "Camp Betty," they filled out nothing but forms. There were additional hardships. They had been body-searched during their first day and finally had their mouthwash confiscated because it contained an alcohol base. Their aspirin had been taken away because Betty Ford personnel considered it a "mind-altering" medication.

Used to having things her own way, Elizabeth bridled at the endless list of DON'TS: no television except on weekends; no smoking indoors; no sunglasses or tinted lenses because patients were required to look straight into each other's eyes when talking; no meals for a patient unless he or she took his or her turn waiting tables. Elizabeth, long an enemy of regimentation, did not care for the three-times-per-day meetings or the twice-a-day Truth Game sessions, in which participants recounted intimate and often embarrassing details concerning their private lives. She cared more for the farewell parties, at which those gathered had to make short speeches about what they thought of the departing guest. It was almost always complimentary, for each patient in turn would be exposed to the same procedure.

Another ritual Elizabeth eventually came to tolerate was the frequently held "chanting session," for which a group of patients would gather, suddenly huddle, link arms, and chant, their voices vibrating with emotion: "No more drugs and no more booze, no more booze and no more drugs. . . ." In a daily journal the center required each patient to keep, Elizabeth described these exercises as a kind of group prayer meeting that helped her to sustain her resolve, at least for the moment.

Elizabeth's journal detailed her first week of detoxification as one of "terrific withdrawals." It continued: "Nobody here wants anything from anybody else except to share and help. It's probably the first time since I was nine that nobody has wanted to exploit me. Now, the bad news. I feel like hell. I'm going through a withdrawal. My heart feels big and pounding. I can feel the blood rush through my body. I can almost see it, rushing like red water over the boulders in my pain-filled neck and shoulders, then through my ears and into my pounding head. My eyelids flutter. Oh God, I am so, so tired."

Not until her second week could she admit to herself—and to the other patients—what she had become: "My name is Elizabeth Taylor. I am an alcoholic and a drug abuser."

She later termed her confession, issued during a group therapy session, "the most difficult lines I've ever had to speak," then offered the group a more detailed explanation: "For thirty-five years, I couldn't go to sleep without at least two sleeping pills. I'm a genuine insomniac. And I'd always taken a lot of medication for pain. I'd had nineteen major operations, and drugs had become a crutch. I wouldn't take them only when I was in pain. I was taking a lot of Percodan. I'd take Percodan and a couple of drinks before I would go out. I just felt I had to get stoned to get over my shyness. I needed oblivion, escape."

Elizabeth Taylor's *mea culpa* omitted far more than it contained. Her drug and alcohol problems were deeply rooted in a kaleidoscopic past filled with broken dreams and disillusionments, men and marriages, and a film career that had long before lost its luster. In the words of New York film critic Daphne Davis, Elizabeth had become "a relic of her own past, a throwback, a veritable dinosaur." "No producer in Hollywood with a serious picture in mind will go near her," reported William H. Stadiem, the screenwriter of one of Taylor's latest major flops, the ill-fated *Young Toscanini,* produced in 1988 but never released in the United States.

The full truth regarding Elizabeth Taylor's drug and alcohol addictions would emerge only in 1990 during a more than two-year investigation by John K. Van de Kamp, attorney general of the state of California, who examined the prescription and pharmaceutical practices of three of Taylor's personal physicians. The attorney general's inquiry stated that over a period of less than ten years, the actress had been given thousands of prescriptions for opiates, hypnotics, pain killers, tranquilizers, antidepressants, and stimulants in powder, pill, and injection form—"enough medication," insisted one investigator in the attorney general's office, "to fuel an army."

The volume and variety of drugs and medications exceed commonly accepted standards of safety. According to the attorney general's charges, the list of drugs and pharmaceuticals given to Elizabeth Taylor included the following: Ativan, Dalmane, Darvocet-N, Demerol, Dilaudid, Doriden, Empirin with codeine, Halcion, Hycodan, Lomotil, methadone, morphine sulfate, paregoric, Percocet, Percodan, Placidyl, Prelu-2, Ritalin, Seconal, Sublimaze, Tuinal, Tylenol with codeine, Valium, Xanax.

The details of Elizabeth Taylor's medical history were often dismaying. There were those who surmised that she must be distributing the myriad medications either among friends or to gay men in Los Angeles who were suffering the pain of AIDS. Continuing its probe, the attorney general's office learned that in 1982, within one seventeen-day stretch centered around a gala birthday bash for Elizabeth Taylor's friend Michael Jackson, Taylor had been prescribed at least six hundred pills. In a period of less than a year, in 1981, she had been given more than three hundred individual prescriptions—nearly one a day—and often for as many as thirty pills per prescription.

Enjoying solid reputations among their peers, the three medical practitioners who eventually became involved in the saga of Elizabeth Taylor's self-abuse and punishment, were Dr. William Skinner, director of the clinical dependency unit at Santa Monica Hospital; Dr. Michael Gottlieb, a leading immunologist generally credited for diagnosing America's first case of AIDS; and Dr. Michael Roth, Elizabeth's personal physician for more than ten years and a prominent California-based internist with a list of high-profile patients.

According to the attorney general, Dr. William Skinner had written out prescription after prescription for the actress and then insisted she sign herself into the Betty Ford Center to break the habit he had helped to encourage. As a means of increasing the overall effect of the various medications he administered to his patient, Skinner recommended she use compound syringes, a method considered dangerous among certain physicians. Members of the actress's personal staff were often assigned to give their employer the injections.

The medical records reveal, according to the attorney general, that even after the decision had been made at St. John's Hospital to send Elizabeth to the Betty Ford Center, she received an unusually high daily dosage of drugs, which included large doses of Demerol, Tuinal, Valium, and Tylenol #4.

The physician who prescribed the drugs in all these instances was Dr. Michael Roth, according to the attorney general.

Although Elizabeth Taylor became the first celebrity to enter the portals of the Betty Ford Center, two others followed directly in her wake: country-and-western singer Johnny Cash and actor Peter Lawford. Lawford, a close friend of Elizabeth's since their childhood days together at M-G-M, checked into the facility on December 12, a week after Taylor.

Patricia Seaton, niece of the late Hollywood producer George Seaton (*Miracle on 34th Street*) and Lawford's last wife, had watched the television news with Peter the day after Elizabeth's admission to the

Betty Ford Center. The announcement of Elizabeth Taylor's internment at the center gave Patricia Seaton a flash of inspiration. "I decided then and there," she said, "that if this place could help Elizabeth, it could also help Peter, whose addictions, if anything, were even more acute than hers.

"We flew from Los Angeles to Palm Springs, California, the nearest airport to the center. Peter drank twenty of those miniature bottles of vodka they serve aboard airplanes. By the time we landed, he was sloshed, and when the white station wagon with the words BETTY FORD CENTER embossed on its side pulled up on the tarmac, Peter thought the car belonged to the former First Lady. 'Are we going to visit her?' he asked. 'I've always liked Betty.'

"I imagine each patient who enters a detox center must undergo a similar shock of discovery—like, 'This is it. I've sunk as far as I can in life. This is the bottom of the well.' And the initial reaction is invariably one of anger and resentment. 'Look at what they've done to me. They've stuck me out here like a jackrabbit in the middle of nowhere to dry out in the desert with the cactuses and coyotes.'

"I'm certain Elizabeth Taylor felt the same as Peter. They were both terrible patients. As soon as I returned home to Los Angeles, I learned Peter had made an attempt to escape into the desert to find a liquor store.

"While still at Betty Ford, he managed to contact a drug dealer who regularly supplied him with whatever he needed. The dealer leased a helicopter and landed near the center. Peter would sneak off, meet his contact behind the center in the desert, do a few lines of cocaine, then sneak back into the facility. He would charge the drugs on his American Express card."

On one of Lawford's first days at Betty Ford, he spied Elizabeth Taylor in an exercise group scattered about the outdoor swimming pool. Racing to her side, Lawford was intercepted by a pair of well-muscled hospital attendants who dutifully informed him of the center's restrictions against fraternization.

"But I've known this girl my entire life," Lawford protested.

Unimpressed, the hospital workers hauled him away.

Lawford and Taylor shared an aversion to almost every chore they were asked to perform at the Betty Ford Center. "The only activity Peter performed with any relish at all was vacuum cleaning," noted Patricia Seaton. "He'd never operated a vacuum cleaner before, and the appliance intrigued him. He would vacuum for hours, even after he left the hospital and returned home. But while at Betty Ford, he refused to do anything else. When he learned Elizabeth wouldn't do the swimming-pool exercises required of all patients, he, too, began to balk. "If she doesn't do them, I don't do them," Lawford told his instructor. "She's only a Hollywood actress, but I'm the former brother-in-law of President John F. Kennedy." (Lawford's marriage to Patrica Kennedy ended in divorce in 1966.)

"Whenever I visited Peter at Betty Ford," reported Patricia Seaton, "he would hand me a shopping list—or read it to me over the telephone before I arrived. He'd say, 'Liz wants you to stop at the Rexall Drug Store in Palm Springs. She wants pancake makeup and deep olive eyeliner by Max Factor and two cartons of Salem.'

"'Deep olive eyeliner—that can't be right,' I said. 'That's not her color. It's too dark for her.'

"So when I reached Rexall I found a telephone booth and called Elizabeth at Betty Ford, and she confirmed the color. In fact, she loves to look the vamp. She has abysmal taste.

"Victor Luna, the Mexican lawyer whom Elizabeth was dating at this stage, used to visit her at the center the same days I visited Peter. So, Victor and I soon became friends. He struck me as a perfect gentleman. He never uttered a negative word about Elizabeth, though he, too, must have wondered about all that dark eye makeup. I think he had the feeling, though he never admitted it, that for all the drug counselors, medics, and psychiatrists, nobody really got cured at the center. You can't reverse a lifetime of self-abuse with a few weeks of group therapy and a lot of hand-holding."

Several weeks after the admission of Elizabeth Taylor and Peter Lawford to the Betty Ford Center, Patricia Seaton participated in a bizarre scheme to sneak an acquaintance of hers, British journalist Tony Brenna, into the center. Brenna wanted to write a story on the two stars for the *National Enquirer.*

"The *Enquirer* paid Peter Lawford $4,000 or so to sneak me in there," recalled Brenna. "Peter told everybody, including Elizabeth, that he and I were cousins. He needed the money, but he also wanted to dispel tabloid rumors that a romance between them had sprung up at Betty Ford."

"Peter didn't really care about the rumors, but he knew that the stories about the two of them annoyed Liz because of her involvement at the time with Victor Luna.

"The main purpose of this assignment had to do with convincing Elizabeth Taylor to talk. So Peter brought me around to see her. In addition, we had posted our photographers in the desert, about half a mile away, armed with high-powered telephoto lenses trained on me while I spoke to Taylor. We needed proof of a meeting in the event she tried to deny it. In truth, I found her very obliging. We had met once before when she and Richard Burton married for a second time, and during that encounter there had been an angry exchange between us. Fortunately, she had no recollection of ever meeting me.

"What Elizabeth had to do at the center was surrender all pretensions of being a big star, all pretensions of being a celebrity, as much as she bloody hated doing it. At Betty Ford, Taylor had her daily assignments to do, just like any other person there, and they included toiling over kitchen sinks piled high with dirty dishes. She stuck to the program for a while but finally lost interest and gave up. Had she persevered, she might well have beaten drugs and alcohol her first time around."

Amy Porter, a bookkeeper from Spokane, Washington, visited her sister at Betty Ford during the period of Elizabeth's stay and derived an impression of the actress as a "still glamorous but slowly fading superstar."

"My sister had an acute drug problem and had been designated a room only a few doors down the corridor from Elizabeth Taylor," remarked Porter. "The problem with Elizabeth was her apparent moodiness. One never knew what to expect from her. Some mornings, according to my sister, she would greet everyone with a broad, toothy smile and a lot of friendly chatter; you would see her again in the afternoon, and she would pretend she didn't know you. You never knew which Elizabeth Taylor to expect, the gushy, friendly one or the ice princess."

"In addition, Elizabeth didn't look so well at the time. She still had the luminous violet eyes, but otherwise she appeared a bit pudgy and worn. The sight of her as an aging, overweight star reminded me of that famous joke Joan Rivers liked to tell: 'Elizabeth Taylor used to be the one woman in America every other woman wanted to look like, and now we all do.'"

Elizabeth Taylor's days at Betty Ford ended as abruptly and unceremoniously as they began. Her doctors wanted her to stay for an additional week, particularly Dr. William Skinner, who felt Elizabeth needed more time to detoxify.

According to journalist George Carpozi Jr., "Liz started screaming at Dr. Skinner. She told the doctor she held him to blame for the fact that she'd become dependent on so many pills. She added she had no intention of staying any longer at the center than the five weeks she had already been there."

The late Roger Wall, Elizabeth's longtime personal assistant, recalled that a few months after Elizabeth left the center, she threw a lavish party at her home in Bel Air, California, to which she invited all her friends and acquaintances from Betty Ford. She served everything but alcohol.

"She took her recovery very seriously at first," said Wall. "She went on a crash diet and lost twenty-four pounds. She had some plastic surgery. She held Alcoholics Anonymous meetings at her home and regularly attended meetings at other members' homes. Then, suddenly, something went wrong."

By late 1984, less than a year after her stay at Betty Ford, Elizabeth Taylor resumed not only her drinking habit but also her daily regimen of pill and drug abuse. As documented by the California attorney general's office, Elizabeth's medical records revealed that as early as October 1984 she had begun consulting with Dr. Skinner again, and he had prescribed large quantities of drugs such as Tylenol #4, Percodan, Hycodan, Demerol, Dilaudid, Prelu-2, morphine sulfate, Halcion, and codeine—often up to sixteen capsules or tablets of each per day.

"I don't know why she suffered a relapse," said Patricia Seaton. "I suspect it had more to do with her essentially unhappy and lonely life, coupled with the genuine pain she felt from her various surgeries, than with any real lack of willpower on her part.

"Generally speaking, it was a difficult time for Elizabeth, and those who knew her felt powerless in the face of so much emotional and physical pain. Elizabeth's physicians probably reacted the same way. Given Elizabeth Taylor's superannuated position in the world, when she told you she felt pain, you did what you could to help."

Chapter 2

Elizabeth Taylor always possessed a gift for survival and a flair for the dramatic. In her own *Elizabeth Taylor: An Informal Memoir* the actress presents a brief 1963 version of her formative years—she announces with some degree of mirth that her "earliest memory is of pain." The memory in question can be traced to Heathwood, the Hampstead home in London, where, at 2:00 A.M. on February 27, 1932, with Dr. Charles Huggenheim in attendance, Elizabeth Rosemond Taylor was born. In her English home, she writes, she had been crawling about in diapers when she inched near an electrical coil and placed her hand on it. The future actress badly seared a finger in the process. The harsh memory is soon followed by another—Elizabeth's first encounter with death, of which in the same book she notes: "I remember too—I must have been tiny—the sick feeling of seeing the dead body of a little bird that had just been born. It was near some steps—just pink skin and no feathers."

These dark observations are followed closely by Elizabeth's earnest announcement that she "had the most idyllic childhood in England."

In truth, events seemed to go wrong from the start for the family. Sara Taylor, Elizabeth's mother, would pen a 1954 article for *Ladies' Home Journal* describing her initial reaction to her newborn eight-and-a-half-pound infant daughter:

"As the precious bundle was placed in my arms, my heart stood still. There inside the cashmere shawl was the *funniest*-looking little baby I had ever seen! Her hair was long and black. Her ears were covered with thick black fuzz, and inlaid into the sides of her head; her nose looked like a tilt-tipped button, and her tiny face so tightly closed it looked as if it would never unfold."

The odd physical appearance of the infant confounded doctors and alarmed her mother. In addition to other shortcomings, Elizabeth did little but gurgle and sputter during her first year of life. "It looked for a while as if she needed dentures," writes Sara, convinced her daughter's baby teeth would never appear.

"Sara had performed on the stage as a young woman and had always been overly dramatic, forever inventing lives for the members of her family, especially for Elizabeth, through whom Sara lived vicariously once her daughter became a Hollywood star."

Sara Viola Warmbrodt was born on August 21, 1896. A slim, petite brunette with a pretty face and an engaging manner, whom friends described as "highly ambitious, smart, aggressive as hell, even tough," she left her mill-town birthplace, Arkansas City, Kansas, when her father, a German-trained engineer, received a job offer to manage a laundry in Cherokee, Oklahoma. There, in the small midwestern city, she met a native of Springfield, Illinois, Francis Taylor, whose father (a Presbyterian of Scottish and English ancestry) operated the local general store. At first, Sara's father opposed the friendship because Francis, while intelligent and ambitious, was more than a year younger than Sara and a year behind her in school. (He was born on December 18, 1897.)

Nona Smith, a female classmate of Francis's in Cherokee, remembered him as "very handsome . . . and all the girls thought him marvelous, but he seemed not to notice. We were all really just youngsters, but he was the first *boy* I was ever aware of. I could have eaten him like ice cream on a stick."

Smith noted that when Francis turned nineteen, "his wealthy uncle arrived from the East Coast to take him back to New York, where he was buying and selling art." The uncle, S. Howard Young, had married Francis's aunt Mabel Rosemond (the inspiration for Elizabeth's middle name) in St. Louis, where he had transformed a small family photography business into a lucrative art dealership with galleries in New York and London. Without children of his own, Young regarded Francis Taylor almost as a son. He wanted young Francis to join him in the art-gallery enterprise as eventual general manager of the London branch. Francis spent four years learning the trade before returning briefly to Cherokee and Arkansas City.

Meanwhile, Sara had departed the Midwest and embarked on her own career. With the encouragement of her mother, Elizabeth, who played both violin and piano and who had inspired her creative endeavors (and who would be paid homage to in her granddaughter's christened name), Sara decided to pursue an acting career. Adopting the stage name Sara Sothern, she made her acting debut with Edward Everett Horton's stock company in Los Angeles, playing the role of Mary Margaret, a poor crippled girl who is miraculously healed in the final act of *The Fool,* a four-act drama by Channing Pollock. The play moved to New York in October 1922 and opened on Broadway to capacity audiences. Two years later, it moved to London, and Sara moved with it. Although Sara Sothern boasted of her role for years to come, she had such a minor part that her name in the cast of characters rarely appeared in print. Even though the play succeeded both financially and critically, Sara failed to gain the kind of notice that might have helped her launch an enduring acting career.

She also failed on another account. At some point during the early Los Angeles run of the play, she had been offered a screen test with M-G-M. The test gained her no more recognition than her performance in *The Fool,* and by early 1925 she was back in New York wondering what to do with herself. She had been offered a minor role in *The Little Spitfire,* a Broadway play which closed shortly after it opened. Thus, at nearly thirty, she had all but given up hope for a successful stage career. She appeared distraught and depressed the night she and a girlfriend went to Manhattan's El Morocco nightclub. It was there she encountered her old acquaintance Francis Taylor and his uncle Howard. Within a year, she and Francis were husband and wife.

✦ ✦ ✦

"Francis Taylor appealed to Sara for two reasons," observed Thelma Cazalet-Keir. "In the first place, he was extremely presentable—tall, lean, bespectacled. He had dark hair, bright blue eyes, wore the finest English three-piece tailored suits. He looked the part of the English gentleman, and he played it—he appeared debonair, sophisticated, and confident, an Oxford don type.

"In addition, his uncle Howard, although at times insufferably obnoxious, happened to be extremely affluent. He continually talked about expanding the number of art galleries he already controlled and forever discussed investing in certain world-class artists. He owned homes all over the United States [including New York; Westport, Connecticut; Star Island, Florida; and the resort town of Minocqua, Wisconsin] and was obviously well connected. One of his great pals [from his early years] was Dwight David Eisenhower. Sara had a keen eye for such detail."

Howard Young condoned the union only after Sara reassured him she no longer sought an acting career for herself. His wedding present for the newlyweds was a European honeymoon and a new position for Francis as his European purchasing representative. For the next three years, the Taylors traveled the Old World art circuit. The couple visited galleries and museums and dropped in on private collectors in London, Paris, Berlin, Vienna, and Budapest.

Kurt Stempler, a German author of note and a collector of German expressionist art, met the couple in Berlin. "They struck me at once as ill-suited for one another," began Stempler. "Although their backgrounds were similar, their temperaments were not. Sara came across as loud, brash and pushy, whereas Francis seemed quiet and introverted. At the same time, they made a handsome couple and exuded a kind of naïve American charm.

"Their differences were far more telling than their similarities. At a certain point in our friendship, it became clear they were having sexual difficulties. One evening I accompanied Francis Taylor to dinner, and it was on this occasion he confessed he had homosexual leanings and often acted on those tendencies. He even used the word 'front' to describe his marriage. Francis said he liked Sara, even loved her, but he admitted they were physically incompatible.

"'We've been married only a few years, and I would have to say we've had sexual relations at most once every two to three months,' he admitted. Francis then confessed he had been on intimate terms with three or four men since his marriage. In time, he and I had an affair, and although it was short-lived, we remained on friendly terms. I later visited the couple in London, and it surprised me to learn Sara Taylor had become pregnant and that they had decided to start a family."

Despite a spate of personal problems, Francis proved adept at his chosen field. He made a series of excellent deals in Europe; he acquired well-recognized but inexpensive works of art and shipped them to Uncle Howard, who resold them at exorbitant prices to a clientele in the United States. In 1929, Howard Young asked his nephew to assume the management of his London art gallery at 35 Old Bond Street, in the center of the English art market.

With money advanced by Young, the Taylors purchased Heathwood, their "dream house" (as Sara described it in a letter to her father), a spacious 1926 red-brick villa at 8 Wildwood Road, Hampstead. Perched atop a hill, graced with multitiered rose gardens in the front yard and informal colorful beds of tulips, violets, and snapdragons to the rear, the house stood opposite Hampstead Heath, a dark, wooded area of roughly four square miles spotted and dotted with parklands, playing fields, and bridle paths. Heathwood was the perfect fairy-tale setting for a family on the rise.

Consisting of six bedrooms, three baths, a living room, a sitting room, a large kitchen, and living quarters for a family of servants, the residence eventually became known as "the Elizabeth Taylor House." Elizabeth's brother, imbued with his father's striking good looks and named after his wealthy great-uncle, arrived some two years before his sister. His birth in late 1929 was less traumatic for Sara than Elizabeth's. Apparently, the physical strain of childbirth led one physician to warn Sara against the danger of having another child after the birth of her son. She wanted a daughter, however, and as a result persuaded her husband to try their luck again. With Elizabeth's birth, Sara's wish was granted.

Being the child of American parents residing in England at the time of her birth, Elizabeth enjoyed the advantage of dual citizenship, appropriate insofar as her early upbringing represented a solid combination of both her American and British backgrounds. Ernest Lowy, a Viennese art dealer and friend of the family who was also living in London in the mid-1930s, considered Francis Taylor "an Anglophile, and while Sara, too, tried to play up her Anglophilia, she came off as distinctly American. Basically, she seemed a social climber, very eager to rub shoulders with the British elite. She even affected a British accent so as to appear more polished.

"Although there were two children, Sara and Francis's marriage didn't strike me as a particularly happy one. The couple argued a great deal. Francis Taylor had a drinking problem. He drank too much, and his alcoholism became a major source of contention between husband and wife.

"As for Elizabeth, she was a late bloomer; she was still crawling at fifteen months when her parents brought her to Florida to visit Howard Young. Finally, the child began to toddle around, and it was as if a gust of fresh air had blown into the Taylor household. From the outset, the tot seemed very independent; she was always going off by herself into some far corner of the house or garden. I remember her at age two—she had a large head and a plump body. She already had those deep, dark blue-violet eyes framed by the thickest, darkest, and longest eyelashes I had ever seen. She had ringlets of brunette hair which drooped over her eyes, and it made her look far older than her years. Even in infancy, Elizabeth had a noticeably older visage.

"Physically speaking, Elizabeth had only one major difficulty. She suffered from hypertrichosis, a glandular condition which can cause a heavy growth of body hair. Her arms, shoulders, and back were covered with a thick downy pelt. The infant looked like a little monkey.

Although doctors assured her mother the condition would correct itself, it continued to plague Elizabeth for years."

Lady Diana Cooper, the late British society doyenne, met Francis and Sara Taylor on several social occasions in London and, like everybody else, "felt the tension between them. Sara Taylor hoped to mix and mingle exclusively with the British upper class, whereas Francis preferred the local artists and bohemians, the likes of Laura Knight and Augustus John. Francis Taylor actually discovered Augustus John for an American audience.

"The story goes as follows: Francis was visiting Augustus John's Chelsea studio one day and saw in a waste bin a number of portraits and landscapes the artist had simply tossed away. Francis looked them over, found them to his liking, and asked if he might purchase them.

"'They're not for sale,' replied the painter. 'They're not any good.'

"'Then may I take them?' asked Taylor.

"'With my blessings!' replied the artist.

"Francis Taylor retrieved the canvases and gave them to Howard Young, who promptly found a market for them in the States. Thereafter, Francis Taylor and Howard Young became Augustus John's exclusive American representatives."*

Victor Cazalet and Francis Taylor grew so fond of one another that Victor soon began accompanying the Taylors on family outings around England. Well-to-do and without a wife or child of his own, Victor often gave the family expensive presents, including a shiny new red Buick for Francis in 1935. He played the role of devoted godfather to Elizabeth, and when she turned five, he presented her with Betty, a New Forest pony from which she fell on her first ride. Later, she learned to ride under the tutelage of Victor's brother Peter Cazalet, a racehorse trainer for the royal family.

Victor's influence on Sara Taylor was spiritual in nature. A devout Christian Scientist, he patiently introduced her to the teachings of the faith and frequently took her along to weekly meetings of a local group

*By coincidence, Augustus John had owned Heathwood prior to the Taylors and had left several of his paintings hanging on the walls when the house was sold.

he had helped to organize and for which he acted as a lay preacher. Sara became an overnight convert and made frequent generous donations to the group's leaders.

One example of Cazalet's influence as a spiritual champion can perhaps be seen in his behavior toward a sickly three-year-old Elizabeth. Infected abscesses in both of her ear canals had to be repeatedly lanced, a procedure that proved so painful that the child had to sleep while sitting up for fear of placing too much weight on one side of the head or the other. Sara Taylor, cognizant of her daughter's suffering, spent weeks sitting by Elizabeth's bedside. As Mrs. Taylor recalled, Elizabeth had implored her to get some rest and finally told her: "Mother, please call Victor and ask him to come and sit with me." Cazalet drove ninety miles that night through a dense fog to reach the Taylor's home.

Sara later wrote: "Victor sat on the bed and held Elizabeth in his arms and talked to her about God. Her great dark eyes searched his face; she absorbed every word and nodded her head in full agreement with him. A wonderful sense of peace filled the room. I laid down my head on the side of the bed and went to sleep for the first time in three weeks. When I awakened, Elizabeth was fast asleep. Her fever had broken."

Although no doubt largely colored by Sara's overactive imagination, the anecdote underlines the degree to which the Taylor family became dependent on Victor Cazalet and the rest of his family. Cazalet had innumerable acquaintances among the elite in British society and gave frequent parties at which the Taylors could fraternize with such celebrated figures as Winston Churchill, Sir Anthony Eden, and fellow Brit Henry "Chips" Channon III.

"Everybody who was anybody attended Victor Cazalet's parties," remarked Diana Cooper, "which is not to say that Teenie was necessarily greatly admired. He just happened to know interesting people and liked to throw parties. Victor was a dandy, a London clubman.

Thelma Cazalet-Keir recalled her brother Victor's "warm feelings" for Elizabeth Taylor. "As a child Elizabeth had a set of wooden block letters with which she first learned the alphabet—Victor and she spent hours together spelling out various words. Then he would read to her. She liked best *The Secret Garden* by Hodgson Burnett and insisted he read it aloud over and over again.

"Even as a youngster, Elizabeth never did anything halfway. She rode her wooden rocking horse so furiously that it finally gave out. She would never make one crayon drawing, but a dozen at a time. Being characteristically stubborn and insistent upon doing exactly what she wanted, Elizabeth came across as intense and motivated, intelligent and highly verbal."

Victor Cazalet's affinity for young Elizabeth was beneficial to the Taylor family in general. A few months after her ear infection, he took the child to watch King George V's silver jubilee parade through the streets of London. He next arranged for the Taylors to visit 11 Downing Street, then the official residence of Neville Chamberlain, chancellor of the exchequer. It was "Auntie Mollie," Maud Cazalet, Victor's mother, who asked Elizabeth to take a gift in her behalf to Buckingham Palace on the occasion of Queen Mary's sixty-ninth birthday. Likewise, Maud saw to it that the Taylors, including Elizabeth, attended Royal Ascot, horse racing's premier event, at which top hats and tails were de rigueur for the gentlemen, while ladies donned their most elegant dresses. For the occasion, Elizabeth and her mother wore matching blue lace originals by Mainbocher, the U.S. fashion designer.

"Elizabeth loved all the pomp and circumstance as much as her mother did," emphasized Thelma Cazalet-Keir. "Frankly, it was not the mother's idea, but the child at age four who insisted upon attending the noted Vacani Dance School, located on the top three floors of a building on Brompton Road near Harrods. Elizabeth wanted to join because she had heard the two little princesses—Elizabeth and Margaret Rose, later Queen Elizabeth and Princess Margaret—were students at the same school."

Betty Vacani, whose mother, Pauline, cofounded the school, recalled Elizabeth as a four-year-old and years later remembered the young student when she emerged as a movie star. Elizabeth, too, spoke afterward about her experience at the Vacani Dance School, but as

Miss Vaccani described, "Unfortunately, either Elizabeth had a faulty memory or M-G-M and her mother purposely constructed a totally false picture of Vacani. The story as Elizabeth and her mother had presented it suggested that she had taken classes with members of the royal family. In truth, we had two generations of royal family members, including Princesses Elizabeth and Margaret, but none of the royals ever attended the school; rather, we sent our instructors to them. Elizabeth Taylor took dance at Vacani with ten to twenty other students per class. The children signed on for ten sessions at a time, paying roughly one pound per session [which was extravagant by the standards of the day].

"Elizabeth had no contact whatsoever with the royal family, at least not at the Vacani Dance School, nor did she ever actually study ballet there. Ballet wasn't taught to our four-year-olds. The children's classes, which were held once a week, included exercise, elementary dance routines, some tap, polka, and social dance steps, such as the waltz. The informal name for the class was Hop, Skip and Polka."

In her 1963 memoir, Elizabeth Taylor describes a 1936 benefit dance recital performed by Vacani students at London's Hippodrome. The performance, she writes, was attended by the duchess of York (the future Queen Elizabeth, the late queen mother), "who brought her daughters, Elizabeth and Margaret Rose." She continues: "It was a marvelous feeling on that stage—the isolation, the hugeness, the feeling of space and no end to space, the lights, the music—and then the applause bringing you back into focus, the noise rattling against your face." Strangely enough, it was her sole appearance onstage until her poetry reading in New York with Richard Burton in 1964.

"Elizabeth had her share of problems," noted Olivia Raye-Williams. "She would be brought to her lessons by Gladys Culverson, her nanny, only to stand off to the side of the class with her face buried in the folds of her nanny's uniform. She was shy at first, but she also wanted more than anything to participate.

"For Christmas, she convinced her mother to make ballet costumes for herself and another girl in the same dance class. Elizabeth seemed to be highly motivated. Sadly, she lacked the consummate skill and overall form of a ballerina."

Jane Lynch, also a student at Vacani and a Hampstead neighbor of the Taylors, insisted that Elizabeth "had always been ultracompetitive no matter what the endeavor. One reason may have been Elizabeth's size. She wasn't skinny, but she always seemed shorter than other girls her own age. She perpetually needed to prove herself. Maybe because her parents were Americans in Britain and Elizabeth felt herself on the outside looking in?

"She would try anything. For instance, her brother, Howard, had been given a pair of boxing gloves for his seventh birthday. Elizabeth insisted upon having a pair as well so she could take him on. She threw punches from every direction and with every ounce of strength she could muster. She became enraged when she missed, but on one occasion she managed to bloody her brother's nose."

In 1936, Victor Cazalet purchased a vast estate near Cranbrooke, in Kent, consisting of a manor house called Great Swifts, several guest cottages, and a gamekeeper's lodge which had become dilapidated for lack of use. Cazalet offered the lodge to the Taylors as a holiday and weekend retreat.

Francis Taylor accepted Cazalet's latest gift and set to work painting, restoring, and refurbishing the tiny four-room house. He planted elm, linden, and fruit trees, cultivated gardens of herbaceous flowers, and reseeded a lawn that had grown brown and bare. He haunted the local auction houses in search of antique furniture. Among the items he acquired were brass beds and a captain's table that seated twenty. He installed plumbing and electricity (the original house contained neither), turned a stone fireplace into a barbecue pit, and transformed an old coal cellar into a wood-paneled den, at one end of which he built a bar with seats fashioned from used wooden beer kegs. With Victor Cazalet's more stately mansion in mind, Sara Taylor dubbed their new hideaway Little Swallows.

Charles R. Stephens, an English journalist and art critic, visited

Great Swifts soon after Francis Taylor had completed rebuilding Little Swallows. "Conversation over drinks," said Stephens, "centered around the abdication of King Edward VIII at the time he married the ubiquitous Wallis Warfield Simpson. That was the big news story out of Great Britain for much of 1936–1937. What struck me most, however, was the apparent closeness between Victor Cazalet and Francis Taylor. One of them would begin a sentence, and the other would deem to complete it. There were other little signs as well indicative of the intimate nature of their friendship. It became clear the two men were lovers.

"I next spotted Victor Cazalet and Francis Taylor together—they seemed to be inseparable—at a Covent Garden Mozart festival. Once again they were recklessly overt about their mutual affection. Others must have noticed as well, but in those days and within those vaunted circles nobody dared mention such arrangements. But it all made perfect sense—why else would Victor Cazalet have given Elizabeth Taylor's father the little house on his property? It provided the opportunity and excuse to be together."

A more direct witness to the Cazalet–Taylor "arrangement" was Allen T. Klots, a young Yale-educated, American-born book editor who was visiting England. "Now and again I spent weekends as a houseguest at Great Swifts," recalled Klots. "The toings and froings were unforgettable in that house. Victor and Francis were sloshed much of the time and spent long hours quietly ensconced in Victor's bedroom, occasionally emerging in the buff and racing to the pantry for a refill of scotch or gin. I had no inkling what, if anything, Sara Taylor thought about all this. She frequently appeared unannounced at the house and was often accompanied by her two small children. It appeared she, too, might have had a crush on Cazalet.

"I remember distinctly her once telling Sir Anthony Eden, also a weekend guest at Great Swifts, how ideally suited she felt Victor would be as the next British prime minister. The following morning, Sir Anthony, no doubt still in a state of shock, took a ride on Betty, Elizabeth's little mare, and promptly slid off into a large mud puddle.

"In subsequent weeks I accompanied Victor and Francis on a trip to Paris, where we joined up with Howard Young. Young, a hulking, raucous, boorish man, made constant references in public to his nephew's homosexuality. He suggested if Francis continued to be seen with Victor Cazalet, the Howard Young gallery in London would surely go under.

"Francis took little heed. He and Victor were hardly inconspicuous—drinking together, singing, holding hands, passing notes, whispering, giggling, exchanging long looks and private jokes—at such fashionable Paris nightspots as Monseigneur, L'Elephant Blanc, and Scheherazade. Both men had trouble holding their firewater, and when they drank, they were capable of almost anything. Victor Cazalet struck me as an extrovert whether inebriated or not, whereas Francis Taylor required the stimulation of alcohol to help him break out of his shell."

New York society photographer Jerome Zerbe dropped in on the Taylor household while touring London in early 1937: "I arrived at their Hampstead home and immediately found myself in a handsome oak-paneled sitting room sipping black currant tea with Sara Taylor and her two young children. She explained that Francis had been delayed by virtue of an unexpected business meeting with several clients at his uncle's art gallery. We sat there, making small talk for maybe an hour, when her husband finally came stumbling in, evidently drunk and in a vicious mood. As with many mild-mannered men, Francis apparently did a complete about-face whenever he had too much to drink.

"The incident that I happened to witness proved this point to a tee. At a certain moment, the children's nanny entered the sitting room and informed their father that neither Howard nor Elizabeth had tidied up their bedrooms that afternoon. Their clothes and toys were strewn across the floor and every piece of furniture.

"In a voice and tone befitting an army drill sergeant, Francis Taylor ordered Elizabeth to straighten up her bedroom posthaste. The poor child apparently didn't move quickly enough, because without another word her father drew back his hand and delivered a resounding slap to the side of her face. He then went after her brother, grabbing the youngster by the arm, dragging him out of the room, and locking him in a broom closet located at the bottom of a stairwell. He left him there for hours. It was a frightening exhibition of parental brutality."

At the age of five and a half, Elizabeth Taylor entered Byron House, a now-defunct coeducational kindergarten and prep school in Highgate, some twenty minutes by automobile from Heathwood. Her brother, Howard, attended the same institution. The part-time family chauffeur, a Welshman named Culver, drove the children to school in the family Buick every morning and then retrieved them at the end of the day.

Deborah Zygot, a Byron House classmate of Elizabeth's, thought she looked "like a tiny porcelain figurine with perfect facial features and alabaster skin. She was the tiniest child in a kindergarten class of fifteen, but she was by far the cutest. Her favorite subject in school had to be nature. She loved animals and kept a menagerie of pets at home—dogs, cats, hamsters, rabbits, white mice, guinea pigs. School itself appealed somewhat less to Elizabeth. Byron House was posh, selective, snobbish, and strict. The requisite school uniform for girls consisted of a fern-green cotton smock and matching kneesocks. Elizabeth loathed the uniform, or rather the idea of having to dress the same as every other girl in school.

"Her brother, Howard, likewise detested the school uniform, which for boys combined a single-breasted burgundy blazer and gray flannel slacks or shorts, depending on the season. He and Elizabeth were both rather rebellious at this stage. Howard had his share of fistfights with fellow students. He once blackened another boy's eye because the foolish fellow lifted one of Elizabeth's schoolbooks and refused to return it. Howard passed the next two days in the headmaster's office, but Elizabeth redeemed her book—together with a profound apology from the boy who took it."

In the late winter of 1937 word arrive that Sara Taylor's mother had suffered a crippling stroke. The Taylors journeyed to Arkansas

City, where Sara's parents had returned to live, and spent three months nursing the ill woman. Elizabeth and Howard attended the town's local elementary school. John Taylor, Francis's older brother, considered it a "dim period" during which time "Elizabeth and Howard became the butt of ongoing ribbing among classmates unaccustomed to their pronounced English accents and mannerisms. Francis and Sara spoke constantly of the virtues of life in Britain. They were convinced all Americans were heathens and that President Franklin D. Roosevelt was the greatest disaster that had ever befallen the country."

The family returned to London in time to view the coronation of King George VI and Queen Elizabeth, followed by a week of parties, capped by the Queen's Ball at Buckingham Palace. Although Francis and Sara attended a party at the American embassy, then located at Grosvenor Square, not even their highly valued ties to the Cazalets afforded them entrée to the climactic Buckingham Palace function.

"Sara Taylor took the offense not simply as a rejection but more as a personal affront," said Thelma Cazalet-Keir, who tried but failed to get the Taylors a proper invitation. "Her entire view of the British began to shift. She wasn't alone in her bitterness. After all, everyone with even the vaguest pretense of social accomplishment wanted to be invited to the Queen's Ball, and when the London *Times* ran the twenty-five-hundred-name guest list on its society pages, those excluded from it were further mortified."

Sara Taylor's change of heart about Great Britain and that nation's "insidious class system," as she referred to it, roughly coincided with the growing Nazi war scare in England in the following few years, the issuance of gas masks, the digging of trenches around Hyde Park, and the institution of a modernized citywide air-raid warning system. The American embassy in London had begun sending out alarming letters to all U.S. citizens residing in Great Britain, cautioning them of the strong possibility of war and telling them to pack up and return to their homeland. Instead of a letter, Francis Taylor received a personal telephone call from the office of Joseph P. Kennedy, the American ambassador to the Court of Saint James's. Kennedy spoke of the urgent political situation and encouraged Taylor to immediately send back to America his wife and children, to shut down the art gallery, then to follow his family on the next available boat.

Francis hired the international transport and storage firm of Pitt & Scott to crate and ship to the United States the gallery's large inventory of paintings. The final destination of the artwork was the aging Château Elysée Hotel, Hollywood, California, site of Howard Young's most recent art gallery. Francis had already agreed to assume the management of the new gallery, a decision prompted in part by his father-in-law's recent acquisition of a chicken farm in nearby Pasadena.

On April 3, 1939, just weeks after Adolf Hitler's takeover of Czechoslovakia, Sara Taylor, the two children, and their nanny, Gladys, traveled by train from Victoria Station in London to Southampton, where they boarded the liner *Manhattan.* Filled to capacity, mostly with German and Austrian Jews fleeing the murderous rising tide of Nazism, the boat made the Atlantic crossing in eight days.

Midway through the voyage a minor event occurred which may well have played a major role in Elizabeth Taylor's later decision to pursue an acting career. As part of the daily program of shipboard activities, a newly released Hollywood film, *The Little Princess,* starring Shirley Temple, had been scheduled to be shown. Seven-year-old Elizabeth attended the screening with her mother and brother. Having viewed few movies while growing up in London, Elizabeth sat in her seat without moving a muscle and without averting her gaze from the screen. She claimed in later years that she had been mesmerized by the force and power of the picture of the curly-haired child as the image flickered in tiny streams of fragmented light from movie projector to the vast backdrop of the white screen. When the houselights came on at film's end, Elizabeth turned to her mother and proclaimed her admiration for Shirley Temple. Then, in a tiny whisper, almost by way of an afterthought, she voiced the sentiment that one day she, too, might like to be a performer. "I don't want to be a movie star," she said. "I want to become an actress."

Chapter 3

As more than one historian has noted, America's gradual involvement in the European military effort during World War II had a noticeable effect on the social patterns of Hollywood's hyperactive gentry. Premieres, tent parties, and studio galas, once held to promote motion pictures, were now given under the guise of fund-raisers and bond drives. Hollywood's fashionable restaurants and nightspots—the Trocadero, Mocambo, Ciro's, Romanoff's, Players'—were all doing a glowing business. Even in the high-priced specialty shops along Rodeo Drive in Beverly Hills, sales had increased. One reason for the sudden upsurge was the arrival in Los Angeles of a new contingent, an international assemblage of social climbers, publicity seekers, heiresses, socialites, dethroned royalty, and ordinary, old-fashioned aristocrats whose permanent vacations abroad had been disrupted by the war.

The onslaught of adventures gave Hollywood's languishing social scene a much-needed boost. Formal wear came back into style, jewelry was removed from safe-deposit boxes, and expensive fur coats were brought out of storage, even when the climate frequently proved too temperate for them. William Randolph Hearst set the social risorgimento in motion. His fetes at San Simeon and at Marion Davies's Santa Monica beach house were more than grand. Mammoth circus tents were raised over sweeping lawns and gardens. Swimming pools were boarded over to serve as dance floors. Orchestras were flown in from Havana and New York. Fireworks showered the skies. Parties were attended by casts of thousands.

Others followed Hearst's example. Darryl F. Zanuck threw a majestic beach bash for silver-mining heiress Dolly O'Brien; Louis B. Mayer gave a glittering reception for the earl of Warwick; Samuel and Frances Goldwyn hosted a giant lawn party for British statesman Leslie Hore-Belisha; King and Elizabeth Vidor gave a Romanov costume ball for Grand Duchess Marie of Russia; Elsa Maxwell threw a dinner for Richard Gulley, an English-born bon vivant and cousin of Sir Anthony Eden. Elsa, sharing a house in Beverly Hills with Evelyn Walsh McLean, owner of the oversized Hope diamond, found herself shorthanded in the kitchen the night of the party. Instead of canceling, she decided to improvise: She gave paper plates and crayons to her guests and awarded a prize for the most originally decorated paper plate. First prize consisted of a china dinner setting, the only one permitted that evening. The other guests were required to eat their meals on the paper plates they had designed. The grand-prize winner happened to be Francis Taylor, who attended Elsa Maxwell's soiree with his wife, Sara.

The Taylors climbed the proverbial social ladder with far greater ease in Hollywood than they had in London. Sara and the two children had arrived at her father's Pasadena home on May 1, 1939. That summer, Sara learned to drive and bought a secondhand Chevrolet sedan. At the beginning of September she enrolled both children in the Willard School, a private day school near Pasadena. Francis Taylor, having spent his last six months in England with Victor Cazalet, rejoined his family in California in December. Shortly thereafter, he moved the art gallery from the Château Elysée to the more upscale Beverly Hills Hotel, leasing a space on the lower level of the main building within easy reach of the outdoor swimming pool. Among Taylor's earliest clientele were some of Hollywood's leading stars, among them Howard Duff, Vincent Price, James Mason, Alan Ladd, and Greta Garbo.

Another high-visibility client was Hollywood gossip columnist Hedda Hopper. Hedda's initial interest in visiting the gallery stemmed from a long-standing friendship she enjoyed with Thelma Cazalet-Keir.

Thelma, who hosted Hedda whenever the latter visited London, wrote to her and asked if she wouldn't mind boosting the new gallery in her widely read newspaper column. Hedda not only visited the gallery and mentioned it in print, she also purchased from Francis Taylor a small sketch by Augustus John. In her column she drew attention to Sara Taylor's ill-fated stage career as well as to her "beautiful eight-year-old daughter, Elizabeth." The columnist noted that David O. Selznick, the producer of *Gone With the Wind,* had not as yet cast all the minor roles in the picture. According to Hopper, although Elizabeth had never acted professionally, she seemed an excellent choice to play Bonnie Blue, the daughter of Scarlett O'Hara and Rhett Butler. The idea was immediately squelched by Francis Taylor, whose art gallery was doing well and who had no interest at this point in allowing his daughter to pursue an acting career.

The success of the art gallery was in large measure due to Francis Taylor's ability to spot promising young artists. Oscar De Mejo, a talented creator of naïve surrealistic art, had his first exhibit in the United States at the Taylor-managed art gallery.

"I remember my delight at Francis Taylor's willingness to show a then relatively unknown artist like myself," said De Mejo. "The art scene in Los Angeles was just beginning to develop, but there were many better-known artists to choose from. Still, Taylor seemed to have faith in my work and the ability to sell it.

"He visited my studio in West Los Angeles, and in tandem we decided which paintings to place on exhibit. There were some thirty large paintings and perhaps a dozen sketches in all. Taylor arranged for several well-established art critics to attend as well as denizens of the Hollywood screen set, stars such as Robert Stack, Edward G. Robinson, Fred Astaire, Valentina Cortese—an actress who bought my first two paintings.

"I recall the opening not so much for the sale of these and other paintings but rather because of the presence of tiny Elizabeth Taylor. Elizabeth and her mother both served hors d'oeuvres that evening. Elizabeth had absolutely the most exquisite features, the kind of face

Botticelli might have created had he painted her. She wore a light blue cotton dress that clung and crept about her legs. She emitted an air of ageless, inculpable eroticism, enhanced by the fact that she always called you by name, thus making you very aware of yourself. 'Won't you have another caviar on toast, Monsieur De Mejo?'

"She had a clipped, surprisingly pronounced British accent, and she spoke in a high, breathless voice. I had the distinct sense she idolized her father, because she seemed always to be seeking from him a nod of approval or encouragement. Her relationship to her mother seemed more within the realm of coequals."

A press agent, a friend of Hedda Hopper, attended the De Mejo opening and observed that "whenever she thought she wasn't being watched, Elizabeth would furtively slip another hors d'oeuvre into her mouth. By the end of the exhibit, she had devoured an entire tray of finger sandwiches.

"The De Mejo opening wasn't the first exhibit I'd attended at the Beverly Hills Hotel gallery. Hedda Hopper escorted me to an earlier Augustus John exhibition. Most noteworthy about the exhibit was that it eventually led to Elizabeth Taylor's cinematic debut.

"It happened that one of the other guests at the exhibition was Andrea Berens, member of an old and wealthy English family, who had known the Taylors briefly in London. When the war broke out in England, Andrea moved to the United States, where she soon met and became engaged to Cheever Cowden, chairman and major stockholder of Universal Pictures in Hollywood.

"Andrea Berens had reason to appreciate the work of Augustus John. Years earlier she had posed for a portrait by the artist, and they had apparently become involved if not in a romance, at least in a mild flirtation. At this particular exhibit at the Beverly Hills Hotel, Andrea purchased twenty thousand dollars' worth of Augustus John paintings and sketches.

"'Sara,' she said at the opening, 'I would love for Cheever to see your daughter. Elizabeth is such a beautiful child; she should be in the movies.'

"The Taylors had since moved into an oceanfront home in the Pacific Palisades. They invited Andrea and Cheever to tea the following Sunday. Cheever Cowden evidently shared his fiancée's enthusiasm for Elizabeth's alluring appearance. Over tea, he asked Sara Taylor if the child had ever taken acting lessons.

"'Not exactly,' admitted Sara, 'but she has studied at the Vacani Dance Academy in London, with all the royals, and she's now taking classes after school [a private day school in Pacific Palisades, the Town and Country School] at a dance studio in Hollywood. Her classmates there include John Gilbert's daughter Susan; Judy and Barbara Goetz, Louis B. Mayer's grandchildren; and Evan Considine, whose father, John Considine, is an M-G-M producer.'

"Cheever Cowden nodded attentively, and before departing that afternoon he made Sara promise she would bring Elizabeth to Universal Studios for the grand tour. The prospect of a potential screen test for the child might be discussed at some future date."

There were others in Hollywood who similarly appreciated Elizabeth's youthful looks, including Carmen Considine, the wife of producer John Considine. Carmen once asked Sara Taylor if her daughter could sing. If she could, M-G-M might well be interested in her. Metro had recently seen one of its former child singing stars, Deanna Durbin, sign on with Universal and within months become one of that studio's major box-office attractions. Although they still had Judy Garland under contract, M-G-M had put out the word they were trying to replace Deanna.

The possibility of seeing her daughter sign on with so prestigious a Hollywood studio as Metro-Goldwyn-Mayer excited Sara Taylor. She herself had once flunked M-G-M's stringent screen test. As for Elizabeth, she garnered compliments for her resplendence wherever she went, and as far as her mother could discern, the child possessed a sweet, if untrained, voice. Guests at the Taylor residence were frequently exposed to Elizabeth's medleys. "Sing, darling, sing," her mother would coax her. Elizabeth would sing, although not always on key.

Carmen Considine, never privy to one of these impromptu recitals, encouraged her husband to arrange an "informal audition" in his office at M-G-M. After considerable delay, John Considine finally gave in. Elizabeth and her mother appeared, as did Benny Thau, Metro's new production chief, who tried to calm the nervous child by slipping her a stick of chewing gum.

Helen Rosen, a part-time M-G-M pianist, sat at the keyboard to accompany Elizabeth. In a whiny, high-pitched voice, Elizabeth managed to warble her way through the "Blue Danube" waltz, while those in attendance did their utmost to stifle their laughter.

"It was pathetic," recalled Helen Rosen. "The child couldn't sing to save herself. Considine announced that although beautiful in appearance, Elizabeth and Deanna Durbin had nothing in common in the voice department—it made little sense to put her name to a contract."

Discouraged but not defeated, Sara Taylor dragged her daughter to Hedda Hopper's Beverly Hills home and told Hedda of the fiasco at M-G-M, insisting that Elizabeth could certainly sing. Hedda was shortly treated to yet another of Elizabeth's renditions of the "Blue Danube." Again, Elizabeth performed off-key and without the slightest degree of conviction. Describing the encounter years later in her autobiography, Hopper wrote: "In a quavering voice, half swooning with fright, this lovely creature with enormous . . . eyes piped her way through her song. It was one of the most painful ordeals I've ever witnessed."

Assured that her ambitious daughter had no future as a singer, Sara turned for a second time to Andrea Berens, who agreed to arrange a screen test for Elizabeth at Universal Pictures. This time the child wasn't asked to sing, but the meeting resulted in no greater eagerness than had previous ones. Casting director Dan Kelly commented on Elizabeth in a memo to Cheever Cowden. "This kid has nothing." Even her best features, her eyes, left him cold: "Her eyes are too old; she doesn't have the face of a child."

Elizabeth nonetheless was given a Universal contract, evidence that the boss's girlfriend had laid down the law. Andrea Berens insisted that Cheever Cowden, chairman of the board, hire the child actress; on September 18, 1941, the studio signed her to a six-month renewable option at $100 a week. Hedda Hopper broke the story of Elizabeth's first contract in her column, adding that "by all hereditary rights, Elizabeth Taylor should be a smash success."

She was anything but. The only work Universal offered the neophyte actress consisted of a few days' labor in a movie entitled *Man or Mouse,* later renamed *There's One Born Every Minute.* In addition to portraying the antics of a zany family, the motion picture represented a showcase production intended to transform Carl "Alfalfa" Switzer—a freckle-faced, tousled-haired truant from the *Our Gang* comedies—into a leading child star.* A duet between Elizabeth and Carl was performed in the film, although Elizabeth's words were dubbed and poorly lip-synced by her. Neither Universal, the critics, nor the viewing audience proved particularly receptive to the young actress or the production. Even Elizabeth had a negative reaction to the experience. Years later, on the *David Frost Show,* she described her role in *There's One Born Every Minute* as that of "a beastly child who runs around slinging rubber bands at fat ladies' bottoms."

Less than six months after she signed with Universal, her contract was reviewed by Edward Muhl, the studio's production chief. Muhl met with Elizabeth's agent, Myron Selznick (brother of David) and with Cheever Cowden. Muhl challenged Selznick's constant support of Elizabeth: "She can't sing, she can't dance, she can't perform. What's more, her mother has to be one of the most unbearable women it has been my displeasure to meet."

Universal canceled Elizabeth's contract just short of her tenth birthday. According to Jane Hodges Crest, a neighbor of the young actress, her friend Elizabeth "remained desolate for days, refused to eat, wouldn't even come out of her house to play." By canceling Elizabeth's contract, Universal had done itself an even greater disservice. As time would tell, it had committed one of the costliest misjudgments in cinematic history.

*As for Carl Switzer, he was shot and killed in a Los Angeles barroom brawl in 1959 and thus became one of the many Elizabeth Taylor costars to meet an untimely and unfortunate end.

✦ ✦ ✦

Shortly after her tenth birthday, Elizabeth's family moved again, this time to 307 North Elm Drive in Beverly Hills. The low-slung Spanish-style house had pink stucco walls, red roof tiles, and a large olive tree in the front yard. Francis Taylor chose the location because of its proximity to the Beverly Hills Hotel. A neighbor in the insurance business, Charles Whalens, remarked that "Francis Taylor was the only person in Beverly Hills I ever saw walk to work. Everybody else drove, no matter how close their place of business."

Elizabeth and Howard Taylor were both enrolled at the nearby Hawthorne School. Judith Craven, who knew the actress as a child, recalled Howard as "an average student who rarely worked" and Elizabeth as "a strange child with giant eyes who was somewhat plump—but she made up for it with that Helen of Troy visage. Anne Westmore, whose family had founded Hollywood's top makeup and cosmetics firm, was her closest friend and next-door neighbor. They would return from school and immediately strap on their roller skates and go reeling down the street together, playing daredevil tricks with oncoming traffic.

"Elizabeth was a tomboy, although she also loved to dress in her mother's clothing and wear her makeup. On one occasion when her parents had houseguests, she and Anne Westmore appeared and modeled for everybody. Elizabeth had on her mother's best maroon velvet spiked heels and a black evening dress; her hair was pinned high on top of her head. Anne wore a print formal belonging to her mother. The next moment, the girls changed clothes, raced outside, and climbed the branches of the large olive tree in front of the house. Anne Westmore played Tarzan, Liz impersonated Jane, and the two swung from limb to limb.

"On random Sundays, the Taylors, accompanied by Anne Westmore and another of Elizabeth's girlfriends, would drive to her grandfather's farm in Pasadena. We'd have a fine time playing 'gangsters' or 'spies'—it was usually something sinister—and we would race through the barns. A less favorite game of Liz's was 'flower shop,' for which we used to gather flowers from her grandfather's backyard and set up a booth in the back of his pickup truck.

"Elizabeth invariably played the leader of the pack and called the shots. She was bossy and self-absorbed, like her mother. Another friend in the neighborhood, Carole Jean Phillips, always had a huge jar of green olives in her kitchen. We often raided her cupboard, put on our roller skates, and raced down the street, each eating a handful of green olives.

"We haunted an antique doll shop, then located in Beverly Hills, which carried a fascinating, big 'grown-up' doll with real hair that could be washed. One Christmas, Mrs. Taylor bought us all miniatures of the 'grown-up' doll with the same genuine hair.

"Until she became a childhood movie star, her youth seemed not unlike that of most young girls. We had a kind of clothes-exchange club, and Elizabeth loved the idea of wearing hand-me-downs. A girlfriend of mine in Fresno, California, Janice Cole Young, would give me her old clothes as she outgrew them. Since Elizabeth was the smallest member of the group, she inherited everything last, by which time the clothes were rather worn. It didn't bother her if the garments were full of holes. She adored the idea of acting out roles, such as Little Orphan Annie. Later, after she became a well-known and successful child star, she dropped us like a sack of potatoes. Of course, it was also true she consequently lacked the time for normal friendships."

A more distant childhood acquaintance, Barbara Jackson, whose uncle and aunt, Dalzell and Ruth Hatfield, owned the Hatfield Gallery, Los Angeles's most prestigious 1940s art gallery, then located at the Ambassador Hotel, recalled: "I first met Elizabeth at the wedding reception of my uncle, Ernest Pumphrey, who managed the Hatfield Gallery. Elizabeth attended the wedding with her parents; she talked of nothing but wanting to make it in the movies. I had turned nine at the time, and she was maybe a year older. She had recently been dropped by Universal, but she had apparently recovered from the disappointment and had set her mind on new possibilities.

"Elizabeth's brother, Howard, also appeared at the wedding. As compelling in appearance as his sister, Howard emerged as the more reticent. Elizabeth looked obsessive by comparison—she never stopped talking except when Howard referred to her as 'Lizzie the Lizard.' Afterward, she would fume in silence. Howard's sobriquet eventually led her to detest the name Liz. Her closest friends always called her Elizabeth.

"I saw Elizabeth again a few years later during a Frank Sinatra concert at the Hollywood Bowl. All these girls and young women, including Elizabeth, were screaming and carrying on. I couldn't hear Sinatra sing, and I wanted to listen to his voice, but the boisterous group inadvertently drowned out the entertainer. I found the bobby-sox craze stupid, and it surprised me to see Elizabeth as much a faddist as the rest of the crowd.

"The irony, I suppose, is that at a young age she became just as popular and famous as Sinatra, and like him, she amassed an army of fans and followers. After she starred in *National Velvet,* every teenage girl in America dreamed of becoming Elizabeth Taylor."

Elizabeth Taylor's emergence as a child star after her dismissal by Universal was largely the result of one man's intervention. The man in question, Samuel Marx, a tall, lanky story editor and film producer at M-G-M, had started working in the studio as a protégé of the illustrious and brilliant Irving G. Thalberg.

"As a producer at M-G-M," Marx began, "I became involved with *Lassie Come Home,* the quintessential boy-loves-dog film in which we had cast a collie with more acting ability and sense of drama than most actors I have worked with. Although set in England and Scotland, the film had to be shot on locations in the lake and mountain region of interior Washington and along the rugged coast of Monterey, California. We hired Roddy McDowall, a fourteen-year-old British import, as the boy lead, and a girl named Maria Flynn, who had previously appeared in *Intermezzo,* as Roddy's female counterpart. The brass at M-G-M had chosen to shoot the film in Technicolor, though in those days the colors tended to be much harsher in tone—the reds, yellows, and greens stood out in vivid contrast. It also took much longer to process Technicolor film. We had to wait more than a week for the dailies to come back from the lab.

"When the dailies at last arrived, Fred M. Wilcox, the director of the film, and I reviewed them, and to our horror we discovered that Maria Flynn stood a good head taller than Roddy McDowall. For some reason, we never stood them side by side, and only by viewing the film did we realize what a terrible mistake had been made.

"I knew immediately Maria Flynn had to go. She struck me as a cute girl, between nine and ten years of age. She had acting talent, and it became a harrowing task for me to inform her we had to replace her to the film solely because of her height. I would have preferred to say to Roddy McDowall that he was too short. Unfortunately, we couldn't easily replace him because not only had he scored a major hit as a horse-loving boy in *My Friend Flicka,* but also he had been loaned out to us by Twentieth Century-Fox. We had paid a small fortune for the loan-out and would not have been entitled to a rebate had we fired him.

"I took Maria Flynn into my office and told her straight out. She didn't cry; I nearly did. I thought she might become upset, so I had asked the M-G-M nurse to be present. The precaution wasn't necessary.

"After the meeting I called Louis B. Mayer, as well as Pandro Berman, a fellow M-G-M producer, and I told them we needed a new girl for the part. Pandro suggested we choose from among the six or seven young English girls who had appeared in *Mrs. Miniver.*

"Then I remembered an acquaintance of mine named Francis Taylor. We were air-raid wardens in the same civil-defense unit, assigned the dubious task of making certain that the Japanese didn't invade Southern California. During lulls on our patrol, we chatted about our work and families. For months, Francis's wife had been badgering him to tell me about Elizabeth. He had resisted, but finally he brought up the subject of his daughter's beauty and how Universal had miscast her. Taylor related the circumstances, stressing the mother's anxiety over Elizabeth's film career.

"I didn't realize that M-G-M had already seen her. Had I known, I might never had telephoned Francis Taylor. As I was fond of Francis, I gave him a ring.

"'Now's your daughter's opportunity,' I said to him. 'We have a part for a young girl with an English accent. Can you bring her around?'

"He sounded disappointed. 'Elizabeth and her mother are in Pasadena visiting Elizabeth's grandfather,' he said.

" 'That's a pity,' I answered, 'because casting is about to send in a half-dozen girls from *Mrs. Miniver* and I have to make my decision today.'

" 'I'll contact them at once,' he promised. 'I'll try to get Elizabeth to your office as soon as possible.'

"Within hours the half-dozen young actresses from *Mrs. Miniver* stood before me. I had just about made my choice when my secretary interrupted and announced that Mrs. Taylor and her daughter, Elizabeth, were waiting in the outer office. I told her to show them in. Moments later, a vision stepped over the threshold. The child, dressed in blue velvet with white trim and matching hat, was breathtaking. I knew immediately we had to have her for the role of Priscilla, the daughter of a wealthy duke who buys Lassie from the penniless Carracloughs, whose son is played by Roddy McDowall. In the end, boy and dog are reunited.

"I called in Fred Wilcox, and we enacted a scene or two using a floor mop for the dog. Elizabeth improvised well and looked so splendid that we opted to forgo a screen test. I walked her to the casting office, and we drew up a contract."

Elizabeth Taylor's initial contract with M-G-M, dated October 15, 1942, allotted her a $100-per-week salary for a period of up to three months, or the anticipated production span of *Lassie Come Home.* The canine that played Lassie received $250 a week for the same period; the dog's stand-in commanded the same fee as Elizabeth.

"I became the one forever connected with having 'discovered' Elizabeth Taylor," said Marx. "The sad part of the story is I never again heard from or about Maria Flynn. I'm afraid my discovery of Elizabeth coincided with the termination of Maria Flynn's acting career."

Recounting his first impression of Elizabeth Taylor for the benefit of a television documentary on the actress, Roddy McDowall noted: "I was absolutely floored by her. Absolutely astounded. . . . It was like seeing a tiny adult walking up with this exquisite face. She was the most beautiful child I ever saw. Her coloring was amazing. Her eyes were so astounding that the cameraman asked if her mother would please have the mascara removed. Elizabeth said, 'I'm not wearing any.'"

Sam Marx recalled that "Sara Taylor remained on the set whenever Elizabeth had a scene to shoot. She used hand signals to coach Elizabeth—a finger to her lips when she wanted her daughter to speak a line softly; a clenched fist signified more emotion; a finger to the forehead meant she wanted a frown.

"The film itself may have been shamelessly sentimental, but it worked. It worked because it contained universal themes and had a top-rate cast of supporting actors, including Donald Crisp, Elsa Lanchester, and Dame May Whitty. It became a box-office blockbuster."

The film's only mishap took place on the final day of shooting when a horse stepped on Elizabeth's foot, breaking a metatarsal bone. It was the first of many accidents and injuries the actress would endure over the years.

A far greater tragedy took place several months after the completion of *Lassie Come Home.* Victor Cazalet was killed at the age of forty-six on July 4, 1943, when the Liberator bomber on which he had flown with Gen. Władysław Sikorski, prime minister of Poland and commander in chief of the Free Polish Forces, crashed at Gibraltar. The plane had been en route to London from the Middle East and had stopped in Gibraltar for refueling.

Victor Cazalet's death devastated Francis Taylor. Earlier in the year, Cazalet had been in New York on a wartime mission for the British government, at the end of which he went to Los Angeles to present a series of public lectures on the progress of the war abroad. During his Los Angeles visit, he stayed with the Taylors.

Cazalet's death unfortunately came at a time when Elizabeth's career had begun to prosper. On the basis of her performance in *Lassie Come Home,* M-G-M agreed to sign her to a conventional seven-year contract, starting at the same $100-per-week salary she had earned at

Universal but increasing at regular intervals until it reached a hefty $750 per week during the seventh year.* The major drawback of all studio contracts was that while they guaranteed a minimum of forty weeks of work annually, they also included a yearly option clause, which gave the studio the right at the end of each year to suspend or drop the performer without legitimate cause. Elizabeth's contract also allotted $100 a week to her mother for coaching and chaperoning services.

Having signed with M-G-M (which bragged that it had, in the words of Howard Dietz, its New York publicity director, "more stars than there are in the heavens"), Elizabeth had the opportunity to appear in endorsements, for which she would receive handsome compensation. Seizing the occasion, Elizabeth's mother prompted her daughter to appear in a quick succession of magazine and newspaper advertisements for Lux soap, Luster-Creme shampoo, Woodbury Creme, and Whitman's Sampler chocolates.

Despite her promising start at Metro, Elizabeth's next two films turned out to be distinct disappointments. M-G-M loaned out the eleven-year-old to Twentieth Century-Fox at a $50-per-week profit (M-G-M collected $150 weekly for Elizabeth's services, while the actress only earned her usual $100 a week); she appeared with Orson Welles and Joan Fontaine in a cinematic version of *Jane Eyre,* Charlotte Brontë's nineteenth-century gothic classic. Playing Helen, the overly sensitive friend of the more major character Jane (Peggy Ann Garner), Elizabeth dies early in the film, prophetically, perhaps, of pneumonia. Her role had been so modest, her lines so scanty, that her name rarely appeared on cast lists. In the mid-1960s, Elizabeth Taylor gathered her children around to watch her scenes in the film on British television; as the movie progressed, she was dismayed to learn that her part had been cut out entirely.

*During World War II, minors employed by major Hollywood studios like M-G-M were by law required to invest no less than 10 percent of their gross earnings in war bonds. Elizabeth's family decided to invest 25 percent of her earnings in such bonds, assuring her a formidable nest egg from which to draw on in later years.

Only Orson Welles seemed to have taken note of the young actress's performance. In an interview toward the end of his career, Welles reflected on his early impressions of Elizabeth Taylor: "When I read *Lolita* by Vladimir Nabokov, I understood his characterization because of my contact with Elizabeth Taylor as a child. I have never encountered anyone like her. She was unbelievable."

Welles saw Elizabeth again at the M-G-M commissary following her fifteenth birthday. "Unlike other figures in Hollywood, I have never found myself attracted to young girls," he said. "I considered them as being off limits. But Elizabeth Taylor had something which transcended age. I will never forget how she moved down the commissary aisle, holding her food tray. I lusted for that young girl and felt, for the first time in my life, like a dirty old man."

Before *Jane Eyre* was released in early 1944, Elizabeth returned to England to play another naïve, sweet English girl, who flirts with Roddy McDowall, in *The White Cliffs of Dover,* a moving chronicle spanning two world wars in which an American woman tours England, where she meets and marries a nobleman. After her husband's death, the protagonist remains in her adopted homeland. Irene Dunne plays the woman; Roddy McDowall, her son. Upon completion of the film, Elizabeth's footage had been reduced to one sequence, and once more her billing was negligible. Irene Dunne remembered that "the film was shot in the English countryside, and Elizabeth and Roddy were continually wandering off the set and frolicking in the woods. They would pick bouquets of wild flowers and present them to me in my dressing room.

"It took place years ago, but I remember one very bizarre aspect of Elizabeth Taylor, the child. She seemed to look straight through you. She was one of those mysterious children who could make any adult feel very insecure and ill at ease."

Clarence Brown, the director of *The White Cliffs of Dover,* remarked that "M-G-M had acquired the film rights—originally based on the epic poem by Alice Duer Miller—from actor Ronald Colman, who had first purchased it as a movie vehicle for himself.

"Otherwise, I have little recollection of the film, even less of Elizabeth Taylor, who played a flirtatious country girl with a crush on the Roddy McDowall character. The sequence in which she appeared was charming, if expendable. In real life, she seemed to have more of a crush on Peter Lawford, who also had a role in the film.

"I recall a Valentine's Day card Elizabeth sent me. You yanked a little string and a tiny white heart pulled back to reveal the words 'Especially for you.' On another occasion, she sent me a very tender handmade birthday card containing a poem she had penned in my honor. I soon recognized the reason for all this attention. For quite a while Elizabeth had wanted the lead in my next film, and she had set a course calculated to achieve her ends. The title of that film was *National Velvet.*"

Chapter 4

In 1939, Metro-Goldwyn-Mayer had acquired the screen rights to *National Velvet,* Enid Bagnold's 1935 novel, with little conviction that they would ever produce it. Sam Marx confirmed that "M-G-M frequently bought bestselling books—fiction mainly—without any plans to film them. Metro purchased these works primarily to prevent other competing studios from being able to make them."

Clarence Brown, the eventual director of *National Velvet,* remembered the first time Elizabeth Taylor confronted him about the project: "She had just become a contract player at M-G-M when she heard about our acquisition of the book. She realized the property had been placed in mothballs, but she also knew that I had taken a personal interest in it. One afternoon while I was walking down the alley in the Culver City studio, Elizabeth and her mother suddenly stood before me. The encounter took place shortly before she appeared in *The White Cliffs of Dover,* so I didn't know either of them very well.

"The *alley,* I should add, was a broad avenue dividing the main lot at M-G-M, through which coursed the lifeblood of the studio—a constant stream of actors and extras on their way to dressing rooms and soundstages."

"At the center of that crowded artery, mother and daughter—two diminutive but formidable females—stopped me to chat about—what else?—*National Velvet.*

"'It's my favorite book,' purred Elizabeth.

"'She's the right child actress to portray Velvet Brown,' added her mother."

Elizabeth and Sara Taylor trailed Brown as he wandered through M-G-M's enormous back lot, with its lifelike outdoor sets, including a village square with homes, shops, and a replica of a small church; a block of brownstone fronts reminiscent of 1920s New York; city slums; and tropical jungles teeming with rivers, ponds, and a rock-studded waterfall. "As we walked along," recalled Brown, "Sara and Elizabeth prattled on about the would-be movie.

"What impressed me most with regard to Elizabeth was her absolute conviction that the picture would be made and would provide a vehicle for her eventual stardom. Her few previous films had afforded her only minor roles; she correctly gauged that *National Velvet* would grant her a part which could catapult her career."

Clarence Brown listened to Elizabeth and then informed her that if *National Velvet* ever came to fruition, it would only be because Pandro S. Berman, the highly touted M-G-M producer, had taken an initial interest in the project and would not rest until it hit the screen.

Learning of Berman's involvement, Elizabeth and her mother made an appointment to see the producer. By the time the duo met with Berman, the studio had opted to proceed with the film. Casting director Bill Grady had been assigned the picture, along with Metro talent scout Lucille Ryman Carroll.

"Elizabeth Taylor and her mother made an appointment with Pandro Berman, Bill Grady, and myself," said Lucille Carroll. "Despite her mother's presence and persistence, I felt Elizabeth took an equal interest in advancing her future. That is not to say her mother wasn't an important catalyst. In fact, Sara Taylor began encouraging Elizabeth's brother, Howard, to enter the profession. After arranging a screen test for her son, she was shocked to learn that on the day of the test Howard arrived at M-G-M with a bald pate—he had shaved his head. Needless to say, the boy flunked the test." (Howard Taylor nevertheless netted a minor role in *National Velvet,* that of a nameless schoolboy, and continued over the years to make brief appearances in other Elizabeth Taylor films. Another minor role in *National Velvet* went to Virginia McDowall, the sister of Roddy McDowall.)

"As for Elizabeth, I don't believe I've ever seen a more beautiful girl in my life. She was short and her voice high-pitched, a trait she evidently inherited from Sara Taylor, who tended to screech rather than speak. The initial problem with casting Elizabeth as Velvet Brown had nothing to do, however, with either her voice or her height. Howard Strickling, director of publicity for M-G-M, initiated a story in the press that the youngster wasn't tall enough and that Pandro Berman told her she would have to grow some three inches to be considered for the part. The truth had more to do with shape than size."

Lucille Carroll had been preparing to tour the country in search of talent when Elizabeth Taylor nominated herself for the role. Bill Grady had already auditioned several hundred Canadian hopefuls without much luck. Even the young Katharine Hepburn had been briefly considered for the Taylor part.

"I remember Elizabeth's exact words," Lucille mused aloud. "She entered the office, looked at me, and announced that we need search no further."

"'I am going to play Velvet,' she declared.

"I had to give the girl credit for knowing what she wanted, but I explained in as delicate a manner as possible that the role of Velvet Brown was that of an adolescent girl who had already begun to develop breasts. At age eleven, Elizabeth was still flat-chested.

"'Don't worry,' she responded defiantly. 'You'll have your breasts.' With that, she wheeled around and stalked out of the office, her mother following close behind.

"Ninety days later, Elizabeth returned wearing a plaid skirt and a tight red sweater. 'Take a look,' she said, flaunting her newly acquired bust. 'I'm Velvet,' she said. Pandro Berman and I both stared. In three months, Elizabeth had graduated from a training bra to a size B cup."

✦ ✦ ✦

Elizabeth Taylor attempted to enhance her budding physique not only by using "fast-grow" creams, of greater psychological than physiological benefit, but also by following a rigorous course of exercises recommended to her by the late socialite Liz Whitney, then married to industrialist and sportsman Jock Whitney.

"I became surrogate 'aunt' to eleven-year-old Elizabeth Taylor," reflected Liz Whitney. "They called us 'Big Liz' and 'Little Liz.' Jock and I owned a ranch in Mandeville Canyon, and Elizabeth would come out for horseback-riding lessons and trail rides. She longed to play Velvet Brown in *National Velvet,* and she wanted to refine her riding technique. As a child, she had ridden a bit in London, but she had never been properly trained. Her seat wasn't elegant, and she couldn't jump. Frankly, she seemed more concerned with the development of her bustline than with horses, and to this end she tried a variety of cosmetic creams and followed special diets. She ate huge country breakfasts—eggs, pancakes, home fries—at a diner called Tibbs in the hope the added weight would increase her proportions. Finally, I lent her a book of chest-development exercises I found in my attic. That seemed to inspire her. She performed one painful-looking exercise using a pair of rolling pins.

"'I look fat, short, and frumpy,' she complained, 'and my voice is either too high or too gravelly.' More than anything, she desired longer legs. 'I'd like to be tall and slim,' Elizabeth exclaimed.

"'Why?' I asked.

"'Because I'm not tall enough.'

"'I thought you wanted to be curvy.'

"'If I can't be tall and thin,' she replied, 'then I want to have nice breasts.'"

Elizabeth Taylor's bustline seemed to increase on its own accord; riding entailed greater labor on her part. Liz Whitney wasn't Elizabeth's only teacher; Egon Merz, an instructor at the Riviera Country Club, also took her on as a student. Now in his eighties, Merz, who still manages his own horseback-riding academy, reminisced: "I found her shy around horses. Her mother, who was aggressive to a cloying degree, tried to convince me that Elizabeth had all the makings of a first-rate jockey. On the contrary, she lacked confidence and was an uncertain rider. Despite all the movie-magazine talk, Elizabeth Taylor was no equestrienne; she had difficulty remaining astride an active mount.

"Elizabeth and her mother bickered a great deal. At a certain point, Sara Taylor became concerned that her daughter might injure her hands while riding and might not be able to continue taking piano lessons. That statement annoyed Elizabeth, who said, 'Oh, Mother, how am I going to be Velvet Brown if I have to worry about playing piano?'

"On another occasion her mother expressed concern that Elizabeth at eleven had no interest in boys. They were terrified of her. 'Elizabeth's an actress, and *normal* boys won't be interested in her as she matures. The only boys she meets are her brother's friends, and you can imagine how that goes. An older brother's friends being fixed up with his baby sister—it doesn't work.'

"I never met Elizabeth's father. Her mother always delivered her and then fetched her after class. I had been told by friends of the Taylors that Mrs. Taylor wore the pants in the family.

"As for the horses, Sara chose the Riviera Country Club for her daughter because the ladies dressed in hats and white gloves for the weekend riding events. The atmosphere reeked of money and society affairs. The Taylors were basically a simple family, but Sara Taylor had her share of social pretensions. She wanted to belong, to be somebody, and she felt it would be beneficial to expose Elizabeth to such an environment.

"The assistant manager of the country club was a former prizefighter named Snowy Baker. A massive and gentle lug, Snowy would get down on hands and knees with a rope in his mouth for reins, a towel across his back for a saddle; he loved to give Elizabeth rides around the clubhouse. She would crack her crop across Snowy's back, and he would bolt like a racehorse."

Ann Straus, a publicist at M-G-M, thought Elizabeth "a complex child—extremely bright, but you could never tell what thoughts she harbored at any given moment. Yet everyone at M-G-M knew of her ambition to star in *National Velvet.* She told everyone, from the studio gatekeeper to L. B. Mayer himself. She would brag about her progress as a horsewoman—how they had built a steeplechase course for her at the Riviera, how she would do forty jumps every morning, how she loved to ride.

"If she hadn't yet developed into a full-blown teenager," continued Straus, "she was nonetheless eminently photogenic. She still attended the Hawthorne School at the time and hadn't yet enrolled at M-G-M's famous Little Red Schoolhouse. My young niece went to the same school, as did the sons of two close friends of mine; those two boys were crazy about Elizabeth. They would follow her home from school every afternoon, and one of the two, being a trifle shy, would pay the other a quarter to ring her doorbell; then they would run and hide. It was the usual social ritual enacted by children."

Viennese-born Fred Zinnemann was directing shorts at M-G-M when the final decision came down to proceed with the film version of *National Velvet.* "When not directing shorts," noted Zinnemann, "I frequently directed screen tests for the casting department. I happened to direct the test which yielded Elizabeth Taylor her role in *National Velvet.*"

The instant Clarence Brown and Pandro Berman viewed the test, they realized that Elizabeth had blossomed into the persona required for her first major film role. "Something quite magical happened between Elizabeth and the camera," claimed Brown. "George Cukor said once that it's the camera that chooses the star. There's no way of knowing in advance whom the camera will love. In *National Velvet,* the camera loved Elizabeth Taylor, and it would love her for decades to come."

The film's strongest selling point, aside from the presence of Elizabeth Taylor and the increasingly popular Mickey Rooney, had to be the script. While mercilessly dated in contemporary terms, it appealed greatly to a 1940s audience attracted to poignant drama. Set in Sussex, England, the story is about a butcher's daughter (Taylor) who wins a horse called Pi (for Pirate) in a raffle. She teams up with a former jockey down on his luck (Rooney), who trains the horse to run in England's highly coveted Grand National. Disguised as a male jockey, with hair cut short, Elizabeth rides her mount to victory, only to be disqualified when her gender is discovered. Nevertheless, she is pleased and proud that Pi is a great champion.

The picture—and particularly Elizabeth Taylor's performance in it—gained generally wide acclaim from the critics. Bosley Crowther of the *New York Times* wrote:

> Mr. Brown has . . . drawn some excellent performances from the cast, especially from little Elizabeth Taylor. . . . Her face is alive with youthful spirit, her voice has the softness of sweet song and her whole manner in this picture is one of refreshing grace.

In subsequent years, Elizabeth came to regard her appearance in *National Velvet* as one of her two most accomplished performances, the other being in *Who's Afraid of Virginia Woolf?* "Of course, in *National Velvet*," she asserted, "I clearly played myself. It wasn't a question of portraying a character. I was in real life an extension of Velvet Brown."

James Agee in the *Nation* emerged as one of her few early detractors: "I wouldn't say she [Elizabeth Taylor] is particularly gifted as an actress. She seems, rather, to turn things off and on, much as she is told, with perhaps a fair amount of natural grace and a natural-born female's sleep-walking sort of smile, but without much, if any, of an artist's intuition, perception or resource."

Other criticism was leveled by Anne Revere, winner of an Academy Award for her performance as Elizabeth's mother in the film. "While well suited to her part," said Revere, "Elizabeth Taylor was not yet an actress. At odd moments she reminded me of a mechanized midget with buck teeth content simply to go through the motions without the slightest hint of feeling."

What Elizabeth lacked in outright talent, she made up for in energy and an uncanny eagerness to learn and to succeed. "She was a fast study," Angela Lansbury would inform author Chris Andersen. "I played her older sister in *National Velvet,* and while we didn't socialize off the set, she would occasionally visit my dressing room and watch me apply my own makeup. She expressed dismay I didn't use a makeup artist.

"'It's my training from the theater,' I told her. 'You learn to take care of yourself, or you become a slave to other people.'

"She seemed dubious, but in later years I heard she, too, started doing her own makeup for the screen. It pleased me to think I might have served her as a positive influence."

Mickey Rooney served Elizabeth as a mentor of a different kind. On one occasion, Clarence Brown found the pair deeply engaged in a discussion concerning the craft of acting.

"Mickey was instructing her to listen to him while he spoke his lines before the camera.

"'Really listen,' he said, 'and then react to what you hear. It will help you deliver your lines with greater emotion.'"

Rooney, who turned twenty-three just as preproduction began on *National Velvet,* found that working with Elizabeth Taylor could be a trying experience. "M-G-M cooked up so much hype over the film," he confirmed, "that fact and fiction became indistinguishable one from another. For example, the horse Elizabeth rode in the film, King Charles, a grandson of Man O' War, was supposedly untamed and untamable; only Elizabeth could ride the monster, and Elizabeth and her mother—as well as M-G-M—gave credence to this exaggerated tale in sundry gossip columns. Actually, King Charles had a magnificent disposition and always behaved himself.

"An even grander fiction had to do with a supposed fall Elizabeth took while riding King Charles during the making of the film. The infamous tumble became Elizabeth's lifelong excuse for winding up in hospitals and clinics at the most inopportune times with what she considered a chronic back problem. 'My back, my poor throbbing back,' she would complain, tracing its origin to the fateful day during the *Na-*

tional Velvet shoot when she missed a jump and lurched to the ground. M-G-M even provided the press with film footage to document the mishap.

"Not a word of it was true. Whenever they shot the jump scenes, Elizabeth sat on the sidelines. Billy Cartlidge, a stuntman with long hair who looked like Elizabeth, rode the steeplechase. It was he—and not she—who was thrown and whose back was injured."*

A final postscript to the film was related by Pandro Berman at a 1972 roundtable discussion sponsored by the American Film Institute. "When we finished *National Velvet,*" stipulated Berman, "Elizabeth came to me and told me how much she loved the horse King Charles. She had grown close to him. She said, 'I would give anything in the world if I could only get that horse.' I went to Louis Mayer and said, 'Give her the horse.' And he gave her the horse. She was the happiest kid I ever saw. Now fade out and fade in about fifteen years later. We were making *Butterfield 8* in New York. She had once been the most delightful, sweet, angelic child, but she was now Elizabeth, the cold-eyed dame, whom I, as producer, had forced to fulfill her contract with M-G-M by appearing in *Butterfield 8* before allowing her to complete a million-dollar deal by signing on to make *Cleopatra.*

"One day she saw me in a Manhattan restaurant. She sauntered over to my table and leered at me. 'Aren't you the guy who gave me King Charles after *National Velvet*?' she asked. I replied, 'Yes, I am afraid I am.' She quipped, 'You son of a bitch, do you know I'm still paying for feed for that goddamned nag.'"

*For all his truthfulness, even Mickey Rooney seemed misinformed about some of the facts. For years he claimed to have cut off Elizabeth Taylor's hair in preparation for the climactic race scene. Bob Salvatore, a former director at Max Factor, made plain in an interview with the author that the Max Factor Company created a wig for Elizabeth and that Rooney had chopped up the wig and nothing more.

Chapter 5

The immediate and overwhelming success of *National Velvet* altered Elizabeth Taylor's life forever. She became a regular visitor to William Randolph Hearst's vast San Simeon castle by the sea, where she not only viewed a screening of *National Velvet* but other first-run Hollywood films provided by the newspaper baron for the enjoyment of his guests. She also attended the annual Thanksgiving and Christmas Day parties hosted by Louis B. Mayer at his Santa Monica beach house as well as his birthday celebration given each year on the studio's largest soundstage.

Ava Gardner depicted the Mayer birthday celebration as "intolerable exercises in self-aggrandizement. Short, fat, and badgerlike, Mayer gave strict orders that we all sing 'Happy Birthday' during the unveiling of his birthday cake. Then he gave his perennial speech. He would address the assemblage, 'You must think of me as your father. You must come to me—any of you—with any of your problems, no matter how slight they may seem to you, because you are all my children.'

"Heaven help anyone dumb enough to take the old man up on his invitation. But that's exactly what Sara Taylor did when she heard Elizabeth was to be cast in an awful movie called *Sally in Her Alley*. The results of their meeting were predictable, with Mayer admonishing Elizabeth's mother for daring to question his judgment. 'Don't tell me how to make motion pictures,' he fulminated. 'I took you and your daughter out of the gutter!'

"Elizabeth, who was also present at the meeting, jumped to her feet and yelled, 'Don't you dare speak to my mother like that. You and your damned studio can both go to hell.' She ran out of the office, down Metro's main street, and out the front gate. Sara remained behind with Mayer to smooth edges.

"Elizabeth vowed never to enter Mayer's office again, and as we all know, she never appeared in *Sally in Her Alley.* It was Mayer's decision. Mayer was Big Brother; he laid down the law, and you either obeyed him, or you were fed to the dogs.

"What people didn't know is Sara Taylor had a tremendous crush on Louis B. Mayer. Elizabeth must have been aware of it, because her mother never stopped talking about Mayer. I think it's the reason Elizabeth hated him so much. She referred to him as 'Rumplestiltskin.' 'What an unpleasant little man,' she used to say. Regardless, Sara was crazy about him and would have doubtless divorced her husband to be with him."

Elizabeth's uncle, John Taylor, discussed the effect Elizabeth's early success had on her immediate family. "There had often been talk between her parents of returning with the children to live in England after the war. This option no longer seemed feasible, although Elizabeth and her mother did visit London in 1946. They traveled aboard the *Queen Mary,* and one of their fellow passengers, Cary Grant, invited them to a shipboard supper. Sara was still chattering about the occurrence six months later.

"Another major factor in the continuation of Elizabeth's career had to do with the economics of the situation. The child had by then become the family's major wage earner. While this didn't necessarily please her father, it made a difference to her mother, who had grown accustomed to a more luxurious lifestyle than the one they had enjoyed earlier in California. Furthermore, Sara Taylor tended to look down on Francis because of his incessant and substantial financial dependence on Howard Young. Sara and Francis argued often about Francis's predicament;

over the years they were formally separated on more than one occasion.

"Not long after the completion of *National Velvet,* Francis Taylor and Elizabeth's brother, Howard, were residing in bungalow 3 at the Beverly Hills Hotel, while Elizabeth and her mother continued to live in Beverly Hills. The basic incompatibility between Francis and Sara may have had a greater effect on Howard than on Elizabeth, who had her acting to fall back on. Howard performed so poorly in school that several of his instructors began to consider him a slow learner; in the end, he proved to be an adequate student, with talent as an artist.

"To be honest," continued Elizabeth's uncle, "I always felt sorry for my niece. Not only did her childhood career become a point of contention between her parents, it necessitated a great deal of personal sacrifice. She lived the life of a freak. She may have been invited as part of a Hollywood contingent to visit President Harry S. Truman and his wife, Bess, at the White House in 1946, but she didn't attend her first baseball game until 1986. She never went to a senior prom. She wasn't a typical teenager, engaging in the same activities as her brother or the girl next door; although a bright child, Elizabeth's education at M-G-M's Little Red Schoolhouse hardly prepared her for Radcliffe."

Elizabeth's early film success did, on the other hand, ensure her the credibility and acceptance she had previously sought but failed to secure at M-G-M. Jean Porter, an M-G-M actress and the future wife of director Edward Dmytryk, remembered that after filming *National Velvet,* Elizabeth could be found at the commissary lunch table considered most prestigious among child actors. Gathered around her for the afternoon meal were Mickey Rooney, Judy Garland, Darryl Hickman, Jane Powell, Dickie Moore, among others. "I thought Elizabeth was the most gorgeous little creature I had ever seen," commented Jean Porter. "I would just sit there and gaze at this radiant little girl eating her lunch."*

*As a child, Elizabeth Taylor, who, in actor Robert Stack's words, went "gaga over fellow celebrities," often toted an autograph book with her whenever she ate in the commissary. She claims the only notable performer who refused to sign her book was Katharine Hepburn, who today denies the accusation. Hepburn writes: "I certainly would never be ass enough to refuse to give Elizabeth Taylor an autograph—for what? She's a damned good actress—a very nice girl."

The view of Elizabeth Taylor as a great beauty, a youthful Anglo-American version of Greta Garbo, became the shared opinion of nearly everyone who crossed her path. It was not so much a question of visceral or sexual attractiveness at the pubescent age of twelve; rather, that she possessed a luminous, enduring beauty that set her apart from others of her generation. Her mother added to her daughter's own conception of herself as a legend by lavishing constant praise on her. Actress Terry Moore, three years Liz's senior, agreed that Sara Taylor "extolled Elizabeth's beauty. She would say rhetorically to me and others, 'Have you ever seen a more beautiful face, more beautiful hair, more beautiful teeth?' Sara's constant flattery bolstered Liz's ego to the point where she became overconfident. 'I'm so bored by people telling me I'm beautiful,' she used to say.

"Her only unattractive feature, as I recall, were her feet, which were stubby and wide. Otherwise, it was true, she sparkled with perfection."

William Ludwig, chief writer of the Andy Hardy series, recalled, "One day . . . this little kid, Elizabeth Taylor, the most beautiful thing you've ever seen, walked into the commissary. Everybody stopped, turned, and looked. Somebody at [our] table said, 'Humph! She thinks she can get into pictures.' And we all broke up completely. She was the most exquisite thing you've ever seen."

Elizabeth Taylor's daily existence at M-G-M, like that of other child actors, became highly regimented. Laura Barringer, one of her teachers at M-G-M's Little Red Schoolhouse, to which Elizabeth transferred following the completion of *National Velvet,* noted that the child's "upbringing in a matriarchal household greatly stunted her development, particularly since she also had an artificial patriarchy imposed on her—namely, the studio.

"M-G-M took the place of her retiring father, who partially stepped away from her once she committed herself to a film career. The studio's predominance could be felt in almost every aspect of her life. All day long some official would be telling her what to do or what not to do. She spent her entire preadolescence and adolescence inside the four walls of Metro-Goldwyn-Mayer, working on the set every afternoon and attending school every morning, or vice versa, depending upon her shooting schedule. In the evenings, she would be forced to memorize her lines for the following day's scenes. Any hint of normalcy in her weekly routine—playtime, contact with other children—was by necessity limited. Childhood all but ended for Elizabeth Taylor with her appearance in *National Velvet.*"

The Little Red Schoolhouse consisted of a two-room bungalow (in reality it was white save for its red-tile roof) that had once housed the executive dining room and stood just outside the studio wall near the Thalberg Building. Students of every age and grade level received instruction simultaneously, the emphasis being placed on English and mathematics. ("My worst subject," Elizabeth complained of the latter.)

Taylor, who came to regret her lack of a formal education, passed much of her time daydreaming in the girls' lavatory—"the only place you could find a bit of privacy at Metro," she scoffed. Unhappy with the curriculum, she often amused herself by hiding hand mirrors among the pages of her notebooks. According to Laura Barringer, "She spent hours admiring her reflection. I once asked her which Hollywood actress she found most attractive. 'Vivien Leigh,' she replied without a pause. 'She's by far the world's most beautiful woman.'"

Mary MacDonald, director of Metro's Little Red Schoolhouse from 1932 to 1967, found Elizabeth "the most attractive girl in the class. I wouldn't put her in the same intellectual category as Einstein, but she wasn't stupid. However, I am surprised the way she turned out; she mishandled her personal relationships, especially with men.

"On the other hand, she gave every indication of being a tender and caring child. When the school's pet goldfish died, Elizabeth gave the fish a solemn funeral in the schoolyard, fashioning a cross from sticks and placing the crucifix over the little grave.

"She was a slender and highly active child. We had a high picket fence around the schoolhouse; it stood a good four feet high, almost as tall as Elizabeth. At recess one day, she and Darryl Hickman were playing catch, and Darryl accidentally threw the ball over the fence. Instead of going through the gate to retrieve the ball, Elizabeth hurdled the fence like a gazelle. It was such a graceful and acrobatic leap, it must have surprised even Elizabeth."

Actress Jane Powell, who for years sat next to Elizabeth in class, recalled her classmate in "dirndl skirts and lots of petticoats, always fastened with safety pins. Elizabeth came to school with pins everywhere; her mother evidently didn't have time for mundane activities like sewing. Our director, Miss MacDonald, kept a box of safety pins on her desk just for Elizabeth.

"Ironically, Sara Taylor also believed in living the good life. If Elizabeth desired a pair of shoes or a sweater, her mother would buy them by the dozen in every style and shade. She did this despite the fact that the studio encouraged us to borrow apparel and shoes from wardrobe, especially for a premiere or social affair. You would contact head designer Helen Rose, and she would make all the arrangements."

Actress Kathryn Grayson, also a student at the Little Red Schoolhouse, remembered Elizabeth "not only borrowing clothes from wardrobe but also retaining them—she would ask Benny Thau or Eddie Mannix, the studio's general manager, if she had to return them or whether she could add them to her own closet of clothes. She once kept a dress I had worn in an early film.

"M-G-M indulged us. For instance, if you had to fly someplace, they booked the flight, reserved the hotel room, and made plans for ground transportation. If you needed an escort, they volunteered one. If you gave a party, they hired the band, contacted the caterers, even invited the guests.

"In other words, they organized your daily affairs. M-G-M was a very busy, active world, with the longest contract lists and biggest stars in town. The young stars took drama lessons with Lillian Burns Sydney, diction lessons with Gertrude Fogler, singing lessons with Arthur Rosenstein, fencing lessons, ballet lessons—every kind of lesson imaginable.

"I found Elizabeth Taylor highly competitive, rather spoiled, very insecure. She didn't seem to like many of the younger actresses at Metro, with the exception of Judy Garland, who experienced several of the same problems—alcohol and drug addiction—that Elizabeth would encounter at a later stage.

"Elizabeth, like Judy Garland, always manifested a domineering personality. Both stars rebelled against the prevailing system of control utilized by M-G-M. The studio would not tolerate unladylike behavior: no alcohol, no cigarettes, no cleavage—those were Papa Mayer's golden rules for the public comportment of his actresses. To enforce the principle, Mayer thought nothing of personally removing a cocktail or cigarette directly from an actress's mouth or hand."

Metro considered any number of properties for Elizabeth Taylor's first motion picture following *National Velvet* before opting for another animal story, this one concerning a young girl's devotion to a collie named Bill. The misnomered film, *Courage of Lassie* (1946), contained no mention of her former canine costar, and the ensuing confusion did not help matters at the box office.

Although Elizabeth Taylor demonstrated an uncanny ability to memorize lines—she has often boasted of possessing a photographic memory—the actress failed to fulfill the promise she had first shown in *National Velvet.* Among other acting defects, she insisted on exclaiming her lines rather than merely saying them. Moreover, her accent shifted without reason from British to American, then back, a fault line that plagued her throughout her career.

During the making of *Courage of Lassie,* Elizabeth found a chipmunk on the set. Adopting the tiny animal, she named it Nibbles and proceeded to acquire from pet shops a dozen other chipmunks to add to her already burgeoning menagerie of frogs, snails, dogs, cats, mice, and horses. Her other collectibles included oversized rag dolls and miniature porcelain animals as well as a valuable assortment of gold and silver animal charms she exhibited on a gold bracelet. By incongruous measure, Elizabeth received only a twenty-five-cent weekly allowance—her father's notion of a stern upbringing—until she turned fifteen, at which point it was raised to a whopping five dollars per week.

"Liz the Whiz," as her brother liked to call her, named all her chipmunks Nibbles. She brought them with her everywhere, including Hedda Hopper's house, where one of the furry creatures had the temerity to crawl up the columnist's arm and down the front of her dress.

In 1946, Elizabeth penned *Nibbles and Me,* a seventy-seven-page book about one of her pet chipmunks, which featured a text and sketches (supposedly by the aspiring actress) as well as a dedication ("To Mummie, Daddy, and Howard, who love Nibbles almost as much as I do"). The book was published the same year by Duell, Sloan and Pearce, a New York–based firm specializing in children's books. Several reviewers accused the author of receiving help on the project from M-G-M's art and editorial staff, a charge neither the publisher nor the actress ever denied.

It was the same year that Debbie Reynolds joined M-G-M. Elizabeth became an early acquaintance. "It was perpetual girl talk with Elizabeth, flippant, light, casual," Debbie wrote in her 1988 autobiography. "She was fun and outgoing and not at all conceited. She wanted to know what it was like to go to a basketball game or to go on a date to a drive-in; simple events that would never happen to her."

Daria Hood, an attractive young M-G-M starlet and classmate of Elizabeth's, found enchanting her friend's penchant for movielike solutions to complex problems, a simplistic outlook bearing sparse relation to reality. If Daria told Elizabeth a story which did not end happily, Elizabeth would invariably interrupt and say, "Oh, don't end it that way. I want it to end *happily.*"

There was frequent talk at M-G-M of changing Elizabeth's name to Virginia and at the same time lightening her hair a shade. It was so dark, it tended to appear on film as blue. The studio also hoped to change the shape of her mouth with makeup and to trim her eyebrows. Finally, they wanted to remove the mole on her right cheek, a feature which would become one of Taylor's trademarks. Elizabeth's father refused the alterations, insisting that the studio take his daughter in her natural state or not at all.

Actress Anne Francis, two years older than Liz, signed with M-G-M in 1946–47 and enrolled in the Little Red Schoolhouse, "along with the other captives, including Jane Powell, Dean and Guy Stockwell, Natalie Wood, Claude Jarman Jr., and, of course, Elizabeth Taylor.

"Elizabeth exuded 'star' quality. There was not an ounce of teenage awkwardness in this remarkable young woman. At the time, she was much impressed by Jennifer Jones's Gypsy looks in *Duel in the Sun;* she wore peasant blouses and full skirts with a cinched waist, accentuating her magnificent femininity, which she flaunted, much to the consternation of studio authorities, who were concerned that her utter abandon would only lead to a dangerous liaison of some sort. My opinion is that Elizabeth thoroughly enjoyed their squirming concern.

"In reality, she was a romantic. I remember her breathless and starry-eyed arrival one morning as she recounted her date of the evening before with actor Marshall Thompson. The rest of us were spellbound as she told how he had held her hand ever so gently, looked profoundly into her eyes, and sung 'A Small Café, Mam'selle' or was it 'Golden Earrings'? It was definitely one of Frankie Lane's hits of the period, and Elizabeth wore golden hoop earrings in imitation of Jennifer Jones."

Elizabeth had evidently been awakened during this sensitive period to the allure of older men, and they in turn could hardly help but notice that the fifteen-year-old had developed into a full-blown woman. She later admitted that she felt frustrated because she possessed a child's mind and an adult's body. She lay awake nights practicing the art of "making out" by embracing and French-kissing her satin-encased pillows.

Her first serious date took place with nineteen-year-old Marshall Thompson, a tall, reedy, WASPish character actor at M-G-M who played the guitar and enjoyed serenading his girlfriends, among whom he soon counted Elizabeth Taylor.

Elizabeth's mother played a hand in guiding her daughter's initial outing with Thompson. Sara enlisted Thompson's mother to accompany her in chaperoning the twosome to the premiere of *The Yearling,* then to a postpremiere party at Romanoff's.

Marshall at last took matters into his own hands, escorting Elizabeth to a Christmas dance, where, "beneath the mistletoe," as he put it, he planted a hot kiss on her cool lips.

"What surprised me," Thompson said years later, "was that when I attended her father's funeral in 1968, Elizabeth's then husband Richard Burton and I became embroiled in a kind of confrontation over that fateful first kiss.

"I had seen Dick and Liz at the funeral, and when I joined them, Richard looked up to say, 'Hello,' and he added, 'Oh, I know you—you're the chap who gave Liz her first screen kiss. . . .'

"Elizabeth interrupted and remarked, 'No, darling, Marshall gave me my first *real* offscreen kiss. . . ."

"Burton's facial expression soured. 'Well, that makes it even worse,' he said. He seemed somehow offended by the entire notion.

"Elizabeth had obviously changed a great deal over the years. When I dated her, she seemed shy and quiet. She had already starred in *National Velvet,* so she had developed a following. I happened to be a character actor, and people didn't often recognize me.

"There was the feeling at M-G-M that although I was four years older than Elizabeth, I wasn't mature enough to play opposite her. She had a fully developed female body, and the studio talked about such virile, masculine costars as Robert Taylor and Clark Gable.

"Our relationship wasn't serious; we were basically friends, with a little kissy-face thrown in for good measure. We would go to dinner together at Trocadero or dancing at the Coconut Grove. On Sunday afternoons, we often dropped in for brunch at Roddy McDowall's home. There was always a large group, and Roddy's mother made the best creamed spinach in the world. Another time, *Photoplay,* one of Hollywood's leading fan magazines, organized a party for Liz, which I attended. They ran a seven-page spread on the evening, with numerous photographs featuring Liz in a pink-and-silver gown, with an orchid corsage pinned near her right shoulder."

"The boys were smooth," read *Photoplay*'s text, "the girls were SDB [strictly dreamboat]." There was a band, and the article—"Elizabeth

Taylor's First Formal Party"—provided Metro with a surfeit of advantageous publicity, save for one momentous oversight: Elizabeth Taylor's dress boasted an immoderate décolletage, revealing far too much cleavage. When her mother viewed the photographs, she marched into Ann Straus's office and blamed the publicist for the faux pas. Ann's response to Mrs. Taylor: "What did I have to do with it? I didn't dress the child; you did."

L. B. Mayer grew livid when he first saw the Taylor spread in *Photoplay* and let his feelings be known. A memo to Howard Strickling, eventually dug out of the M-G-M archives, read: "She looks like a little tart. Can't something be done to rectify her attire for future shoots?"

Mayer's reaction reflects a bit of a double standard. June Petersen, a Hollywood producer, found Mayer's attitude toward women at best patronizing. "He wasn't exactly a womanizer," she proclaimed, "but he did have an eye for the ladies and pursued young, aspiring actresses whose favors he hoped to gain. Apparently, he had a long tunnel built under the studio foundation that allowed him immediate access to several select dressing rooms.

"Many of Metro's dressing rooms were set on soundstages topped by unusually high ceilings. In some instances, the dressing rooms had no ceilings at all; on one occasion, Mayer followed a starlet to just such a dressing room.

"One event led to another, and soon Mayer managed to lower his pants. The starlet was on her knees and was busy ministering to the mogul when Mayer heard an unusual noise, looked up, and saw a set designer perched high in the rafters with his brown lunch bag. The designer had a perfect bird's-eye view of the proceedings below.

"Considered too venerable a figure to be caught in such a compromising position, Mayer jumped to his feet, pulled up and hitched his trousers. Feigning innocence, Mayer said, 'Young lady, you ought to be ashamed of yourself.'"

Elizabeth Taylor's offscreen kiss by Marshall Thompson took place only weeks before she received her first on-screen kiss. The vehicle was *Cynthia,* a motion picture derived from *The Rich Full Life,* Vina Delmar's short-run Broadway play about a sickly fifteen-year-old girl whose physical frailties are exacerbated by her overprotective parents. The child eventually breaks loose from her parental bondage, gains a boyfriend, and attends her high school prom, proving herself capable of a normal lifestyle.

The cinema boyfriend, played by James Lydon, recalled the film kiss as taking place "about a century ago. The publicity department made too much of the so-called milestone—it felt more like a handshake than a kiss. Elizabeth also sang a song in the picture, but her voice was reedy and shrill in those days."

George Murphy, an actor and future U.S. senator, who played Elizabeth's screen father in *Cynthia,* found her "a wonderful little gal," although Mary Astor, her screen mother, described her in a personal memoir as "cool and more than slightly superior. There was a look in those violet eyes that was somewhat calculating, as though she knew exactly what she wanted and remained convinced of getting it."

In a subsequent interview Astor expanded upon her earlier comments: "I had the impression Elizabeth had already begun using sedatives, however mild, to calm her nerves. She appeared high-strung and brittle, frequently complained, and required more sick leave than any other performer in the film. It could be she took her role too seriously, or perhaps she saw herself as preparing for the melodramatic lifestyle she would lead in later years."

A likely reason for Elizabeth's troubled outward demeanor may well have been the increasingly hostile domestic relationship that existed between her parents. According to Jackie Park, a longtime mistress and confidante of Jack Warner's, Francis Taylor had begun what would become a lengthy and caring sexual relationship with still another man: M-G-M fashion designer Adrian, then married to actress Janet Gaynor.

Doris Lilly, a young Hearst reporter formerly based in Hollywood, became a friend and client of Adrian's: "Adrian designed very mannishly tailored suits for women like Greta Garbo, Jean Harlow, and

Marlene Dietrich. He began designing clothes for me as well and soon had a long list of private patrons.

"I once encountered Adrian in New York, and he invited me to a very 'in' gay bar on Madison Avenue called Cerutti's, which is where he informed me of his affair with Francis Taylor. Apparently, both men wanted to leave their respective wives to live together, but Francis felt that the inevitable hint of scandal might ruin his daughter's acting career."

To add to the intrigue, Sara Taylor commenced a romance with the noted Hungarian-born Hollywood director Michael Curtiz, whom she met when he directed her daughter in Warner Brothers' 1947 film version of *Life With Father.* (Though completed first, the film was released a month after *Cynthia.* For the loan-out of Elizabeth Taylor to Warner Brothers, Metro received a minimum guarantee of $3,500 per week for a period of eighteen weeks, five times Elizabeth's base salary.)

Irene Dunne, who starred in *Life With Father,* found Elizabeth "extremely agitated during the shooting of the film. She had continual sinus problems and constantly frequented the set medic. Everybody seemed to know of the affair between Curtiz and Sara Taylor; it's difficult to imagine Elizabeth also wasn't aware."

James Lydon, who also appeared in the film, was more outspoken about it and, particularly, its director, Michael Curtiz. "Curtiz was a very talented but extremely excitable Hungarian who stood six feet two inches, emerged bald as a billiard ball, and assumed the mien of 'the Swedish Angel,' a well-known professional wrestler. Curtiz was a big, powerful, ugly man who fractured the king's English. When he tried to explain something to Elizabeth Taylor, he couldn't make himself understood and would get violently angry.

"He hated to waste time. He didn't even want us to take lunch breaks. He himself never did, and when you returned from the commissary, he would be pacing back and forth on the soundstage. He would be muttering to himself, 'Damn no good actor, you feed your face . . . you yawn for two hours. You no damn good to me. I take no lunch—why you eat lunch?' We could all hear him.

"One day he caught me leaning against a ladder after lunch, and he kicked me in the butt so hard he nearly broke my spine.

"When Elizabeth Taylor and I were doing our boy-girl scene—this one didn't include a kiss—he grew infuriated at her for some reason and started shouting. She began to cry and without a word raced from the set into her dressing room. Curtiz pursued her. The poor man was soon seen striding the corridor outside her door. You could hear his booming voice halfway across the lot.

"'Goddamn, Elizabeth, don't cry for chris' sake. Son of a bitch, you break my heart—don't cry.'

"His attempted apology merely succeeded in distressing her further."

Whether Elizabeth's tears were caused by the director's caustic words and abrasive manner or by the covetous attention he paid the wistful child's mother is anyone's conjecture. A photograph of Curtiz and Sara arm in arm at the beach began to circulate among the film trade publications, along with speculative items hinting at the impending dissolution of the Taylor marriage.

An article in the French newspaper *Tele-Loisirs* reported that Elizabeth had been so traumatized by her situation that she agreed, after completing *Life With Father,* to consult with an M-G-M-recommended psychiatrist.

"The true tragedy of Elizabeth's early life," surmised James Lydon, "had nothing to do with her parents' sexual endeavors. The real problem is that she had to continue working in the industry. She was earning far too much to simply quit. She couldn't stop because by this point she had become the family breadwinner. They depended upon her, and she had nothing else to sustain her hopes and visions."

Chapter 6

On July 15, 1947, Elizabeth Taylor appeared on a local Hollywood radio interview program hosted by Louella Parsons. Asked about the rumor that Marshall Thompson had been the first male to kiss her offscreen, she replied: "If a young man ever tried to kiss me, I would probably slap him." A moment later, she altered her course by admitting she wanted "to do crazy, silly things with *men* of nineteen and twenty. Boys my own age bore me." The statement made little sense, since Marshall Thompson was four years older than Elizabeth; it insinuated that she considered him something more than a friend but less than a potential lover.

One of Elizabeth's childhood girlfriends, Ann Cole, the daughter of Fred Cole, founder of Cole of California Swimwear, reminisced about this youthful period in their lives: "Elizabeth had two early major crushes—Vic Damone, the singer, and Peter Lawford, the M-G-M actor born in England.

"She would play Vic Damone records day and night, and she would try to learn from Damone's press agent where Vic and his latest paramour could be found on any given evening. Usually we would track him down at Ciro's or Mocambo's. We would then drive to one or the other in an effort to catch a glimpse of the singer.

"By this time, Elizabeth had begun to pay more attention to her appearance and started purchasing her clothes at the fashionable Amelia

Gray Boutique on Rodeo Drive. She had reached nearly her full height and had a bustline that even 'sweater queen' Lana Turner found impressive. Her legs were her most noticeable shortcoming—they were flabby, especially below the knees. She would go to the Will Rogers State Beach with Peter Lawford, and he would practically ignore her in favor of young blond starlets with hard bodies and perfect gams.

"Not even Sara Taylor could help her daughter with Peter. At Elizabeth's behest, her mother telephoned the actor and tried to convince him to go out with Elizabeth. 'We're friends, Mrs. Taylor, just friends,' he insisted. 'To be honest, she's not my physical type.'"

In an effort to firm her legs, which Lawford surreptitiously and cruelly referred to as Elizabeth's "pods," she embarked on a strict diet-and-exercise regimen. She had an insatiable craving for peppermint milk shakes and loved going to Will Wright's, a Hollywood-landmark ice-cream parlor, for hot-fudge sundaes. To shed extra pounds, she temporarily gave up sweets and started imbibing pitchers of mint-laced iced tea and bottles of club soda. Although her waistline subsequently dropped from twenty-two to eighteen inches, her legs unfortunately remained as stout as ever.

"Her parents had acquired a summer cottage on the beach at Malibu," said Ann Cole, "and Elizabeth attempted to reduce further via a strenuous daily swim routine. She exhausted herself so thoroughly one morning she nearly drowned. Her brother had to dive in to retrieve her."

During the late-1947 production of M-G-M's flimsy musical *A Date with Judy,* Jane Powell was privy to one of Elizabeth's lamentations about Peter Lawford: "I had the female lead in the film, but Elizabeth and I nevertheless shared a dressing room. She complained bitterly that the men she liked never seemed to like her, and vice versa. She meant Peter Lawford, of course. 'Elizabeth, darling,' I said, 'that holds true for nearly everyone. It's not only you.' Yet she remained inconsolable; she couldn't accept rejection."

As fate would have it, M-G-M cast Lawford in Elizabeth's next film, *Julia Misbehaves,* a mediocre romantic comedy about an insolvent music-hall actress (Greer Garson) who returns to the society spouse (Walter Pidgeon) she left years before because her daughter (played by Elizabeth Taylor) is to be married and has asked her mother to attend the ceremony.

On February 27, 1948, Taylor celebrated her sixteenth birthday during filming, and the cast gave her a chocolate-layer birthday cake, a pair of jade earrings, and a silver choker.* As a gesture of *their* appreciation, the studio presented her with a shiny new beige Ford convertible replete with twin exhaust pipes (a vehicle then popular with the young Hollywood set). Elizabeth, not yet in possession of a driver's license, kept the automobile in M-G-M's parking lot. "Do you want to hear my pipes?" she inquired of her costars, demonstrating the turbo-jet effect by flooring the accelerator while keeping the emergency brake engaged. On one notable occasion she drove her car into John Wayne's fire-red Thunderbird, eliciting Wayne's understated comment "Elizabeth would do well to enroll in a professional driving school."

It was her mother who finally taught her how to drive. A few months after Elizabeth's sixteenth birthday, her parents bought her a second automobile, a 1948 light blue Cadillac convertible, which she later returned to them as an anniversary present.

The usually uncommunicative John Wayne also noticed that Elizabeth was frequently ill as a teenager and that her mother and nanny turned housekeeper, Gladys Culverson, took turns reciting versions of Gentle Presence, a Christian Science prayer popular for its healing effect.

Another early friend of Elizabeth's visited her just as the actress developed a severe case of mumps. Despite her illness, Taylor discussed her crush on Peter Lawford, vowing she would conquer her beloved the moment she regained her health.

"Peter epitomizes the first and last word on sophistication," she

*Elizabeth's parents also threw a "sweet sixteen" party for their daughter. Terry Moore, a guest at the birthday celebration, remembered that Peter Lawford had been invited as Liz's date. "He arrived hours late," said Moore. "And by the time he got there, Elizabeth had passed out. She had become the victim of too many glasses of champagne."

said. "He's princely and refined, the kind of man you wouldn't mind introducing to your parents."

Lillian Burns Sydney, M-G-M's highly respected acting coach, recalled that "the entire cast and crew of *Julia Misbehaves* knew of Elizabeth's attraction to Peter. In the scene where he kisses her she was supposed to say, 'Oh, Richie, what are we going to do?' Instead, she gazed at him and murmured, 'Oh, Peter, what am I going to do?' The whole company howled with laughter.

"The word around the lot had it that anybody who so much as breathed on young Miss Taylor faced permanent banishment. She was considered one of M-G-M's invaluable properties. That's why Peter Lawford steered clear of her—he didn't want any trouble."

"The irony was," according to Lucille Ryman Carroll, "Elizabeth wanted to be loved by everybody. Because of her beauty every man on the lot stared at her, and she mistook their curiosity for emotion. She also happened to be the most amorously competitive of M-G-M's young cluster of stars. After Jane Powell announced her engagement to Geary Steffen Jr. (her first husband), Liz came running into my office. 'You have to make her call it off,' she wailed. 'Why?' I asked. 'Because I'm number one around here,' she responded, 'and I'm supposed to be married before anyone else.'"

In contrast to her recently hardened Hollywood persona ("I can't remember a day when I wasn't famous," she would remark years later), there was a tomboyish innocence about Elizabeth that was endearing.

Elizabeth Taylor experienced her first youthful romance with a graduate of West Point (class of 1947), a highly publicized all-American football player named Glenn Davis. As Davis recalled, "I met the sixteen-year-old actress through Hubie Kerns, a track star at USC [University of Southern California], who brought me to the Taylor house for dinner one evening.

"Kerns had won a bronze metal in the 400-meter event in the '48 Olympics. He also appeared as an extra in *The Spirit of West Point*, a film about Army's championship football team. His wife, Dorismae, worked both as a stand-in at M-G-M as well as with their publicity department. She had been appointed Elizabeth's publicity representative at M-G-M.

"The press greatly exaggerated my relationship with Elizabeth. In reality, we went out no more than six or seven times. I gave her a miniature gold football and my letter sweater, which she wore on several social occasions. It was all very childlike, a few pecks and kisses—nothing serious.

"I once took her to a Los Angeles Rams intrasquad game; afterward visited the Taylors at their summer home in Malibu and played touch football with her brother, Howard, and some of his friends. It became obvious her father had quite an alcohol problem and stayed in the background, while her mother did all the talking and organizing.

"Elizabeth and I saw each other mainly during her appearance in *Little Women;* after a few weeks she informed the press we 'were engaged to be engaged.' That wasn't at all the case. We were neither engaged nor 'engaged to be engaged'—we were just two kids trying to enjoy ourselves. There were card games, charades, barbecues, and at one point we double-dated with actress Janet Leigh and her boyfriend, Arthur Loew Jr., whose family owned the highly lucrative Loews movie theater chain as well as substantial stock in M-G-M."

Despite Davis's apparent dismissal of the importance of the relationship, Elizabeth appears to have taken their romance more seriously. When she learned Glenn's tour of service duty would take him to Korea, she implored Howard Young to intervene. In an effort to keep Davis at home, Young contacted his friend and frequent houseguest Dwight D. Eisenhower, who explained that a West Point cadet was first and foremost a soldier and only then a football player.

Davis shipped out for active duty in Korea, while Elizabeth, barely disguised in a fluffy blond wig, continued her role as Amy March in M-G-M's film adaptation of Louisa May Alcott's classic novel *Little Women.*

Janet Leigh, cast in the same picture, observed that "Mervyn LeRoy did a masterful job of direction. He understood the problems of working with four young ladies—you know, they giggle a lot and talk endlessly of their boyfriends. Elizabeth loved to jabber about Glenn Davis, even to the extent of reading aloud excerpts from his love letters. Believing in happy endings, Elizabeth had such high hopes that she magnified the importance of the romance."

June Allyson, playing the lead character of Jo March, was then married to Dick Powell and expecting their first child. After a day's shooting, all the girls, including Elizabeth, would congregate in her dressing room.

"Elizabeth wanted to know how I enjoyed being married," recalled Allyson. "Marriage seemed to be her favorite topic of conversation. In her desire to escape her parents' influence, she insisted that she and Glenn Davis intended to wed the minute he completed his tour of duty in Korea.

"I remember one day we were at the studio sitting around and talking, and Elizabeth glanced over at me and said, 'June, I would give anything to look like you.' Can you imagine? The most beautiful young woman in the world saying that to me?"

Mary Astor, who portrayed Mother March in *Little Women,* offered a much more critical appraisal of her young colleague: "In one scene of the film there was a snowstorm. In those days they used cornflakes to simulate the effect of snow. The studio would dispense eye drops to anesthetize the eye; if a cornflake hit your eye, you wouldn't flinch or blink—doing so at the wrong moment meant the entire scene had to be reshot. Elizabeth complained vehemently about the eyedrops, practically comparing her lot in life to that of Oliver Twist.

"In addition, she spoke constantly on the telephone with her boyfriend in Korea while the production clock mercilessly ticked away the company's money. I had never before encountered such a brazen attitude on the part of a child actor. Nobody in the company dared utter a word about it to Elizabeth despite her holding up the shooting schedule for weeks."

According to Hubie Kerns, "Elizabeth fell in love with Glenn Davis. When he left for Korea, she attempted to occupy herself by taking up oil painting and sculpture. She made a bust of herself and called it *Mona Lizzie.* She also bought a dog, Butch, a black shaggy miniature French poodle who soon outgrew the *mini* stage and began to resemble a Doberman pinscher.

"Elizabeth had a keen sense of humor. I once visited her at her summer place in Malibu. She took me to a nearby house, which had what looked like a chicken coop in the backyard. We entered the pen, and I suddenly found myself confronted by a wild cheetah. Elizabeth was nowhere in sight, but I could hear her laughing in the background. The cheetah let out a roar, and I became nearly hysterical. Elizabeth reappeared and began to pet the animal, which turned out to be quite tame. It, in fact, belonged to an M-G-M director. That's the sort of practical joke Elizabeth loved to pull.

"I fixed her up with several other pals besides Glenn Davis, including George Murphy, USC's quarterback, whom she subsequently invited to a party given by her parents at their Beverly Hills home. I then offered to introduce her to Bill Bayliss, a fellow member of the track team. 'Oh, I like him.' she said. 'He's handsome. What's he like?' So the four of us—my wife and I included—went out for Sunday brunch, then to Laguna Beach.

"After brunch, Bill and I went into the men's room together. Bill seemed ill at ease. 'She's beautiful, Hubie,' he pointed out, 'but I don't know what to say to her. She's not laughing at any of my jokes.'

"He proceeded to act like a deadhead that whole day at the beach, couldn't think of anything to say. The next morning, Elizabeth telephoned and said, 'Don't you ever stick me with a dud like that again.'

"I introduced her to another friend, Tommy Breen, whose father held the post of chief Hollywood film censor. Tommy only had one leg—the other had been shot off at Iwo Jima, and he endured a wooden leg in its place.

"One weekend, a group of us, accompanied by Elizabeth and Tommy, rented a cabin overlooking Lake Arrowhead, not far from San Bernardino. The cabin contained two bedrooms and a living room. Two of the couples occupied the bedrooms. Dorismae and I spent the night in sleeping bags in the living room with Tommy and Elizabeth.

"I'd forgotten about Tommy's war injury until it came time to go to bed. He stuck out his wooden leg—kind of an embarrassing moment—and he announced, 'I don't care how cold it gets in here tonight, don't you dare put this baby in the fireplace.'

"Elizabeth howled. She and Tommy grew close. She didn't seem bothered by his handicap, though their relationship remained platonic."

Among Elizabeth's other escorts during Glenn Davis's army stint was Ralph Kiner, the present-day baseball announcer and former home-run king of the Pittsburgh Pirates.

"Bing Crosby owned the Pirates at the time," said Kiner. "It was off-season, and I then lived in California. Bing called and asked if I wanted a date with Elizabeth Taylor. 'Who wouldn't?' I responded.

"I arrived at what struck me as a rather modest house. We were going to the film premiere of *Twelve O'Clock High,* and I wore a tuxedo. She was late, so I had to spend an hour chatting with her parents.

"Her father turned out to be an affable soul, but her mother behaved in an abrupt, almost rude manner. Mrs. Taylor treated her husband as if he were an incidental person in the household. Elizabeth finally emerged in an evening dress and proved to be a lovely young lady, not yet spoiled by her success.

"After the premiere, we attended a party at Romanoff's. Hedda Hopper asked Elizabeth about me, and since the Pittsburgh Steelers were in town to play the Los Angeles Rams in a football game that weekend, Liz erroneously identified me as the Steeler quarterback. I didn't bother to correct her."

Elizabeth Taylor in her mid-to-late teens was unquestionably a Hollywood anomaly, a fish out of water. For much of her life she had been overprotected by a cautionary, watchful mother and jealously guarded by an alcoholic, homosexual father whose income largely depended on his daughter's continuing cinematic appeal.

Hollywood producer Joe Naar remembered a birthday party for Arthur Loew Jr. at Arthur's house. The guest list featured such Hollywood celebrities as Dean Martin, Jerry Lewis, Peter Lawford, Gene Kelly, and Sammy Davis Jr. "It consisted predominantly of the Rat Pack and their spouses—thirty to forty people—sans Frank Sinatra, who was out of town at the time.

"Draped head to toe in yellow chiffon and looking like a delectable lemon meringue pie, Elizabeth Taylor suddenly walked through the door. She appeared sixteen going on thirty. For most of the evening she sat in a chair in the corner, smiling rather wistfully and saying nothing, nor did anybody say anything to her. The men wouldn't address her because they didn't know where to begin and because their wives or lovers would have stared at them in a way that would have made speech impossible.

"I tried conversing with her, but the problem was, Elizabeth didn't have much to say at that stage, although she liked to listen. She was one of those people who, if she hadn't been so attractive, you might never have noticed.

"Next on the agenda came dinner, after which the men remained in the dining room while the women gathered in the den. Elizabeth remained with the men because the 'birthday boy,' Arthur Loew Jr., asked her to stay.

"The *boys* had been drinking a bit, and they started prodding Elizabeth. They wanted her to say the word 'fuck,' but she refused. People attempted to coax her into saying it; they would say, 'Say sexual intercourse, Elizabeth,' and she would articulate, 'Sexual intercourse.' 'Now say copulation,' and she would utter, 'Copulation.' 'And now say make love,' and she repeated, 'Make love.' She went through a list of synonyms and euphemisms, but nobody could cajole her to say the word 'fuck.' She stood up to the group, and it amazed me in a way, because she was so damn young."

Amazement must also have been the reaction of Howard Hughes in the course of his brief exposure to Elizabeth. At age forty-four, with more than $150 million in the bank and a well-earned reputation as a womanizer, Hughes began chasing Taylor with the same insistence that had marked his pursuit of Lana Turner, Ava Gardner, Ginger

Rogers, Yvonne De Carlo, and other leading female film stars. Having purchased several costly paintings from Francis Taylor's art gallery, Hughes asked the family to join him for a week in Reno. "And bring along your daughter" were the words he used in extending his invitation.

According to the late Earl Wilson, former entertainment columnist for the *New York Post,* "Elizabeth couldn't tolerate Hughes. He invited her entire family to stay in one of his hotels and arranged a series of dinner parties for them. He spent the better part of one evening ignoring Elizabeth and talking to her parents about money, promising to pay a million-dollar dowry and buy Elizabeth her own film studio if they would allow him to marry her. He wasn't disturbed in the least that Elizabeth already considered herself semiengaged to Glenn Davis."

The next day, Hughes decided to prove his noble intentions by filling an attaché case with jewelry—diamonds, rubies, emeralds. Elizabeth, clad in a bikini, reclined in a chaise lounge next to the hotel swimming pool. Hughes approached her from behind, unclasped the case, and spilled its priceless contents across the actress's bare tummy. "Get dressed," he yelled, "we're getting married."

Elizabeth wanted nothing further to do with Hughes. A day later, after he dispatched an aide, Johnny Meyers, to the actress's room to offer an apology, Liz exploded: "Tell that madman to stay away from me. He bores me with all his talk about money. He reminds me of L. B. Mayer."

Meyers conveyed Elizabeth's message to his boss. A difficult man to discourage, Hughes met with Mr. Taylor and renewed his million-dollar offer. Although Francis Taylor assured the tycoon that his daughter "wasn't for sale," he later informed his friend Adrian that he had been sorely tempted to accept the proposition.

By October 1948, Elizabeth, her mother, and Melinda Anderson, a private tutor provided by the Little Red Schoolhouse, sailed for England so that Elizabeth could appear in *Conspirator,* a maudlin drama about a young woman's marriage to a British army major who is also a Communist agent and informer.

Playing the young spouse opposite thirty-eight-year-old Hollywood heartthrob Robert Taylor, Elizabeth termed her part "my first adult role" and proclaimed in a newspaper interview: "To be kissed on the screen by Robert Taylor means I will never again be considered a little girl."

Jane Ellen Wayne, Robert Taylor's biographer, noted that the grand embrace and kiss in *Conspirator* took place "in the bedroom and that Elizabeth wore only a black negligee on the set.

"I did a good deal of research into that movie. According to the press agents on the set, Robert Taylor developed a 'hard-on' during the shooting—yes, he did—and it proved a total embarrassment. Here was this sweet, highly attractive nymphet he had first seen in *National Velvet* emerging as a femme fatale. Robert Taylor had appeared in films with Greta Garbo, Lana Turner, Katharine Hepburn, and Myrna Loy—you name it. He had enjoyed an affair with Ava Gardner, among others, and was currently married to Barbara Stanwyck. It wasn't as though he hadn't been exposed to the crème de la crème; yet there he stood with an enormous erection in the presence of the young Elizabeth Taylor, and he didn't know what to do. He tried talking to the cameraman to rectify the situation. 'You're going to have to shoot me from the waist up,' he urged.

"After Robert Taylor's kiss, Elizabeth's tutor approached her on the set and told her, 'You have to complete your algebra lesson.' Elizabeth retorted, 'I've just been kissed by Robert Taylor, and I have no intention of doing math homework.' M-G-M built up the kiss scene into an event approximating a major earthquake. Robert Taylor finally telephoned the studio from London and shouted at their publicity chief, 'Enough already—stop exploiting the poor child, will you? Knock it off.'"

But during the last three months of her stay in London, she became friendly with the veteran British actor Michael Wilding, who was making a film with Anna Neagle at M-G-M in London. He would come to the commissary for lunch and often sit at the same table as Elizabeth and her mother. I noticed that whenever he appeared, Elizabeth's eyes brightened. It didn't seem to bother her that Wilding was twenty years her senior or that he had been estranged from his first wife, actress Kay Young, for years and was presently dating Marlene Dietrich. And Wilding, I must say, seemed equally enthralled by his new teenage admirer. He enjoyed her bravado and energy."

More than a hundred guests turned out for Elizabeth's seventeenth birthday party, held at still another of Howard Young's palatial retreats, this one located on Star Island, not far from Miami Beach, Florida. At the party, Elizabeth met William Pawley Jr., an ambitious twenty-eight-year-old business executive and radio-station owner, whose father, an oil magnate, had once been the U.S. ambassador to Brazil. The family had money. What's more, Bill stood six feet tall, with jet black hair and bright blue eyes. Elizabeth spoke to almost nobody else at the party.

One week after Elizabeth's birthday, Glenn Davis, on a forty-five-day military leave, flew into Miami International Airport. Liz met his plane. She planted a moist kiss on his lips and answered questions posed by a bevy of newspaper reporters:

"Are you serious about Glenn Davis?" asked one.

"As serious as I've ever been."

"Will the two of you marry?"

"If we do, you'll be the first to know."

She had grown adept at sidestepping journalists and had become less the ingenue. Two weeks after Glenn's return, he and Elizabeth attended the Academy Award presentations in Los Angeles. "It marked our swan song," revealed Davis. "I never saw Liz again. She returned my West Point letter sweater and the miniature gold football I'd given her. Reporters asked me what I thought of Bill Pawley Jr. 'Who's he?' I questioned. I honestly had no idea." Only later would Glenn Davis discover the identity of his successor and learn of Elizabeth's deceitful manner; she had been dating William Pawley Jr. on a regular basis throughout her Florida sojourn.

After Davis's dismissal by Liz, Bill Pawley arrived in California and presented her with a 3.5-carat diamond engagement ring valued at $16,000. Elizabeth's mother, never very enthusiastic about Glenn Davis, proclaimed her daughter's latest suitor "brilliant, understanding, strong, poised . . . and full of fun."

On June 5, 1949, Sara Taylor officially announced her daughter's engagement to Pawley. By summer's end, the engagement had mysteriously been terminated. According to M-G-M sources as well as Elizabeth's parents, the romance ended because Pawley insisted that his fiancée give up her acting career to become a homemaker; Elizabeth refused.

"The true story had quite a different ring," began Jackie Park. "I had been dating Claude Karin, a wealthy partner and associate in the Pawley family oil business. According to Claude, the family wanted nothing to do with Elizabeth Taylor. They wanted Bill to marry a debutante, not an actress. They didn't care whether she continued acting or not. The family wielded considerable political power, and they didn't feel Elizabeth would fit into their circle. Her low-cut dresses, her avaricious parents, her link to Hollywood—Elizabeth Taylor wasn't good enough for their son.

"She was most upset about the Pawley family's judgment of her. They threw a big bash aboard a yacht in Miami while Elizabeth and Bill were still together, and you could feel the undercurrent. All the well-connected members of southern society showed up and viewed Elizabeth in one of her patented Hollywood gowns. Her breasts were hanging out. The Pawleys wanted somebody more demure and subtle for Billy, and they eventually forced him to end the relationship. From what I understand, Elizabeth never bothered to return the engagement ring—or so claimed the *Hollywood Reporter* and other periodicals of the day."*

*Liz's well-chronicled lust for jewelry had evidently begun. In the spring of 1949 she became princess of the Diamond Jubilee of the Jewelry Industry Council. Crowned with a $22,000 diamond tiara, she promptly asked, "Can I keep it?"

Chapter 7

In 1949, prior to appearing in *The Big Hangover,* a flat, often forced comedy in which Elizabeth Taylor costarred opposite Van Johnson, the fledgling actress flew to New York to have her picture taken for *Life* magazine by master portrait photographer Philippe Halsman. Yvonne Halsman, Philippe's wife, attended the session in the studio of their apartment on Manhattan's Upper West Side.

"Elizabeth arrived alone," Yvonne recalled. "At first she appeared reticent, but once the shoot began, she came alive. She reacted to the camera in the manner of a true actress. Although she embodied the kind of beauty one associates with goddesses, I was struck by the sight of her arms; they were covered with what my husband called 'dark eyelashes'—an abundance of unsightly black hair.

"On a purely technical level, Philippe pointed out to her that her face photographed differently depending on the angle—one side looked younger, the other more mature. He favored the younger side, but she preferred her womanly aspect."

Elizabeth herself perceived the sitting as something of a breakthrough. "I became intensely aware of my body," she wrote in her 1965 autobiography. "Whatever the discussions over my face, [Halsman] had no interest in making my figure appear childish. 'You have bosoms,' he would shout, so stick them out. . . . ' Halsman saw I had a woman's body and insisted I exploit it for the camera. In one day I learned how to look sultry and pose provocatively. In short, I developed sex appeal, even though I knew that, somewhere inside, the child had still not completely grown up. The most important result of the shoot, though, was that it gave me increased confidence in my camera image."

A touching postscript to the photographic encounter transpired after the session, when the subject revealed to Halsman that she had nothing to do, no place to go. "It's so strange," she said. "Everybody takes for granted that I have a date every night, and nobody thinks of inviting me. Tonight I'm again facing a lonely evening."

The Big Hangover presented little opportunity for Elizabeth to exhibit her newly realized sensuality. Playing the overly concerned daughter of Van Johnson's boss, she makes it her mission to save Johnson from an alcohol problem he originally developed while stuck in the wine cellar of a monastery after a wartime accident.

Eve Abbot Johnson, at the time Van Johnson's wife and one of Hollywood's most popular hostesses, thought the picture "so blatantly silly I had to wonder why anybody had bothered to make it. Its sole benefit was it brought me in contact with Elizabeth Taylor, for whom I discovered I had a great deal of empathy.

"I shared her disdain for the 'system,' her inherent distrust of Hollywood studio bosses such as L. B. Mayer. For my money, Mayer was the worst of the lot, a dictator with the ethics and morals of a cockroach.

"I had my own problems with Mayer. I had been happily married to Keenan Wynn, an M-G-M character actor, whose best friend was Van Johnson, a Metro matinee idol with far greater box-office appeal than Keenan but about whom there were nasty rumors afloat regarding his sexuality. Mayer decided that unless I married Van Johnson to quell hearsay about his being bisexual, he wouldn't renew Keenan's contract. I was young and stupid enough to let Mayer manipulate me; I divorced Keenan, married Van Johnson, and thus became another of L.B.'s little victims."

Ned Wynn, the son of Eve Abbot Johnson and Keenan Wynn, visited Elizabeth in Malibu during the production of *The Big Hangover.* "She was about seventeen, and I was maybe eight," he ventured. "She smiled radiantly as we threw rocks in the ocean and watched them skip along the waves. There had never been a seventeen-year-old girl like her before on earth.

"I never understood why people claimed her eyes were violet. They were the color of the skin of an eggplant. Aubergine. Garnet. But then only women and gays discussed the color of her eyes. It was her breasts. Oh, Jesus, the breasts. Those breasts fueled my fantasies for decades to come."

Although Elizabeth hadn't yet starred in an internationally acclaimed adult film, her salary at M-G-M had escalated to a highly respectable $2,000 per week; her mother's weekly custodial fee had risen to $250. But M-G-M's reluctance to recognize Elizabeth's acting talents and cast her appropriately caused no end to her grief.

She complained to everyone, including her most recent escort, Arthur Loew Jr., who took it upon himself to contact George Stevens. Stevens had just signed with Paramount to direct and produce *A Place in the Sun,* based on Theodore Dreiser's 1925 novel *An American Tragedy.* He agreed to meet with Elizabeth and shortly after offered her the role of Angela Vickers, a spoiled society girl deeply attracted to an ambitious social climber from an uncertain midwestern background who yearns for the finer things in life and is swept off his feet when he comes into contact with wealth and class. His love for the beautiful debutante is threatened by the plain and plump factory girl he has already impregnated. The latter (played by Shelley Winters) wants marriage, but her lover wants Angela Vickers.

In the story, based on an actual criminal case, the aspiring beau takes the factory girl boating on a lonely mountain lake. The boat capsizes, and the lover swims off, leaving his pregnant and unwanted companion to her watery grave. Ultimately, the social climber is apprehended, tried for murder, convicted, and executed.

The male lead in the film went to the talented twenty-nine-year-old Montgomery Clift. Elizabeth's initial reaction to her handsome costar was one of awe and trepidation. "I was absolutely terrified," she admitted, "because Monty, first of all, was a New York Method-trained actor and I felt very much the inadequate teenage Hollywood sort of puppet that had just worn pretty clothes and hadn't really acted except with horses and dogs. . . ."

The poor-boy, rich-girl, poor-girl triangle sizzled on the screen. Equally notable were the offscreen relationships. Shelley Winters and Elizabeth Taylor became immediate adversaries. Winters described Elizabeth as "a Hollywood baby who never had the experience of living on her own. What with the coddling and conditioning she had from the studio, she was afraid of the real world and longed for it at the same time."

Elizabeth and Monty, on the other hand, grew so close and fond of each other that Elizabeth became convinced she had fallen in love with the actor. He dubbed her "Bessie Mae" because of her earthy personality. She responded by writing him torrid love letters, which she later learned he had given to one of his male lovers. Monty was gay, but Elizabeth failed to recognize his sexual preference. She solicited him with such vigor that the day before the movie's heartrending final scene was shot, headlines trumpeted "CLIFT AND TAYLOR TO WED."

Studio publicists, with the apparent approval of George Stevens, had leaked the story to draw attention to the film and goad its stars into an emotional finish. "Monty will think I've done this," Taylor wept. "I can never face him."

Mira Rostova, Montgomery Clift's personal drama coach and confidante, had accompanied the actor to Hollywood and observed firsthand the film's progression as well as the burgeoning friendship between Monty and Elizabeth. "I was on the set," said Rostova. "George Stevens clearly didn't necessarily like having me around, but he didn't say much. He had even less to say to the actors. Essentially, he communicated with them through body language and facial expressions. At other times, he would play recordings on a phonograph to help the cast get into a certain mood or frame of mind. Stevens had the reputation of being a kind of fearsome fellow—very severe. There were times he played his role to the hilt.

"It turned out Monty coached Elizabeth more than the director did. They rehearsed their scenes for hours; Monty would take copious notes on Liz's performance and then review them with her. Their camaraderie not only helped her acting; it forged a lasting tie between them.

"On the other hand, perhaps too much has been made of their friendship. It was primarily Elizabeth who wanted a romantic involvement. Monty would go to bed at night, and she would invariably find some excuse to visit him. She would make him a cup of tea and then maintain she needed to rehearse the following day's scene. Elizabeth always used an aggressive approach concerning men."

Luigi Luraschi, a vice president with Paramount International, first encountered Elizabeth on the set of *A Place in the Sun* and recalled her practicing her lines with Montgomery Clift: "They looked almost like twins—the dark hair and blue eyes, the incredible facial features. They both possessed an animal magnetism which reverberated off the large screen and filled the darkened movie theater.

"I remember going to lunch with Elizabeth; it was pouring and she drove—she couldn't stop talking about Montgomery Clift. I had the distinct and unmistakable impression that she had fallen in love."

William "Billy" LeMassena, an actor who had grown up with Clift, found that "Monty had the facility of making anybody—male or female—fall in love with him. I thought Elizabeth Taylor, like Marilyn Monroe during a later period, truly adored him. He encouraged Elizabeth, mainly, I imagine, because he was a bit ashamed of being homosexual. I'm not suggesting he didn't care for Elizabeth—he did. But, from his viewpoint, he saw their relationship as essentially platonic."

At first, Elizabeth seemed to ignore Monty's sexual leanings. She later admitted that during the filming of *A Place in the Sun* her costar continually played the ardent male; although just as it appeared to her that he had overcome his inhibitions about making love to a woman, he would turn up with "some obvious young man he had evidently picked up."

On more than one occasion Elizabeth proposed marriage to Clift, only to have her proposal ignored or brushed aside. One of her letters to Monty read: "I love you! I love you! I can't live without you, my dear, dear, darling Monty." Like her other notes to the actor, this one also wound up in the hands of one of his boyfriends.

A pal of Monty's from the Actor's Studio in New York, Ashton Greathouse, recalled, "Whenever he drank too much, he tended to relate Liz tales. While working on *A Place in the Sun,* she would take three baths a day, and he would keep her company in the bathroom; the baths supposedly calmed her nerves. One day, Monty, who had always been a walking pharmacy, told her, 'Take a benny [Benzedrine]. It'll relieve your tension after a hard day at the studio. You'll forget your worries.' Liz downed the pill with a glass of scotch and soon perked up. Within weeks she became dependent on a variety of habit-forming medications.

"I never witnessed the two together, so I can't corroborate the veracity of Monty's sexual claims concerning Elizabeth. I know he found her physically and psychologically attractive—and that's all he required to be interested in somebody. He once told me, while making *A Place in the Sun* with her, they attempted but failed at having sex. He couldn't, in his words, 'rise to the occasion.' In later years they tried again, and I understand their endeavors were more successful.

"I had heard Elizabeth's father was homosexual, which may explain her attraction to and interest in gay men—Monty, Rock Hudson, James Dean, and others. Her father's sexual bent may also shed light on her overriding concern for the present-day AIDS movement, her great desire to raise funds for the cause and help those afflicted with the disease."

One scene in *A Place in the Sun* stood out in Elizabeth Taylor's memory as a profound moment during her formative years. The scene in question focused on Elizabeth and Montgomery Clift at Lake Tahoe in late autumn, when it had already begun to snow. The film crew had washed down the snow on a sandy stretch of beach and off the tops of trees that were to appear in close-up in order to re-create a balmy summer day when the ardent lovers supposedly sunbathed and then went swimming.

As Elizabeth recounted the episode, "Lake Tahoe is a [glacially] cold lake, and it was just miserable that day. Monty and I stood on a wooden float in the middle of the lake. George [Stevens] sat in a boat with his big boots on and his earmuffs and gloves and made us do take after take after take. I wanted to kill him."

According to Montgomery Clift biographer Robert LaGuardia, Stevens treated Taylor cruelly, ignoring her pleas and complaints, demanding that Monty drop her repeatedly from a full standing position into the ice-cold water.

Sara Taylor finally intervened, insisting that her daughter had menstrual cramps and could continue no longer. Stevens reacted by issuing his final order for the day: "Throw the garbage into the lake!" Gazing apologetically at Elizabeth, Montgomery Clift plunged her into the frosty depths.

In an interview with *Look* magazine, George Stevens etched a succinct but apt portrait of Elizabeth Taylor: "She has been kept in a cocoon by her mother, by her studio, by the fact that she's the adored child who has been given everything she ever wanted since the age of eight. What most people don't realize is there has been a smoldering spirit of revolt in Elizabeth for a long time."

That "smoldering spirit of revolt" emerged partially and painfully as a result of the sobering treatment she suffered in working with George Stevens as well as from an ongoing sense of futility over her mother's omnipotent presence. It surprised few that by the time of Elizabeth's high school graduation in February 1950, the actress had once more become engaged.

Her latest fiancé, Conrad Nicholson (Nicky) Hilton Jr., heir to his father's vast international hotel chain, had first set eyes on Elizabeth during a bridal shower for Jane Powell at the Mocambo. The following day he burst into his father's office; he announced he had seen the most fabulous-looking girl in the world and insisted he had to meet her.

Nicky called upon his friend Peter Lawford to effect an introduction. Lawford arranged a discreet luncheon for the couple. Nicky apparently made a favorable impression, and Elizabeth soon invited him home to dinner with her parents. Despite his considerable wealth and physical attractiveness (he stood over six feet, had broad shoulders, an athlete's waist, brown hair and eyes),* the twenty-three-year-old playboy harbored a plethora of personal problems that were not at all evident at the outset. Unstable and volatile, Nicky had an acute addiction to heroin, among other substances, as well as an uncontrollable craving for both alcohol and gambling.

Curt Strand, former director of Hilton Hotels International, testified to Nicky Hilton's general dearth of ambition: "It drove his father, Conrad Hilton Sr., crazy that Nick didn't show the least interest in the family business. He was the eldest of three brothers, but it was the middle brother, Barron Hilton, who would become his father's successor. Nick's shortcomings as a potential hotel magnate were early demonstrated when his father enrolled him as a student at a hotel school in Lausanne, Switzerland; they suspended him after six months, and he never returned.

"His father seemed closer to Nicky than to either of his other two sons, which is the main reason he became so discouraged by the boy's lack of drive. Not only did Nick fail to take part in the management of the firm; he continually embarrassed the family by his involvement in a series of scandals. We shuddered each time we opened the newspaper for fear of discovering still another Nicky Hilton misadventure.

"The man with 100,000 beds," as the newspapers dubbed Conrad Hilton, had a sharp eye for beautiful women, as did his son Nicky Hilton. At one time married to Zsa Zsa Gabor, Conrad Sr. also became involved with socialites Kay Spreckles and Hope Hampton, Gladys Zender (a onetime Peruvian Miss Universe), actresses Jeanne Crain,

*Actress Terry Moore, who became Nicky Hilton's girlfriend after his divorce from Elizabeth Taylor, attested to one of his physical endowments: "He had absolutely the largest penis—wider than a beer can and much longer—I have ever seen. To make love to him was akin to fornicating with a horse."

Ann Miller, Denise Darcel, and dozens of other minor and major celebutantes.

Zsa Zsa Gabor remembered her 1944 marriage to Conrad Hilton with mixed emotions. "He could be a great charmer," she observed, "but he also possessed the capacity for tremendous cruelty. He pretended to be a devout Catholic, but was instead self-righteous, pushy, and dictatorial. He always had to have his own way.

"He managed to spoil Nicky by letting him have whatever he desired. If he wanted a car, his father bought him one. If he asked for an airplane, he got it. One result of his father's magnanimity was that Nicky developed an inferiority complex. He realized he could never surpass his father's accomplishments; he would always be second best. He thus drew the logical conclusion: Why compete when you can't win?

"Nicky and I were roughly the same age. I know he liked me—more than liked me, he had a crush. I once kissed his father in his presence, and Nicky said, 'What does one have to do to get a kiss like that from Zsa Zsa?' Conrad gave the boy such a backhand to his face that it sent him reeling across the room.

"Later, while still married to his father, I had a love affair with Nicky. It lasted through my divorce from his father, into my marriage to actor George Sanders, and beyond Nicky's betrothal to Elizabeth Taylor."

Francesca Hilton, Zsa Zsa's only child, became aware of her mother's liaison with Nicky: "I always adored Nicky. He remained the only fun-loving, warmhearted member of the family. Nicky and Mother enjoyed a mutual attraction; when the marriage between my parents began to erode, Nicky and my mother embarked on a loving and long-lasting relationship."

Carole Doheny, the widow of Larry Doheny and a close friend of Nicky Hilton's and a former M-G-M starlet who performed under the name Carole Wells, remained on extremely friendly terms with Nicky: "I recall a party we all attended at Dean Martin's place before Nicky married Elizabeth. She wasn't present at the party, but Nicky cornered me and inquired about Elizabeth. 'I think she has the saddest eyes,' I ventured. 'You can't tell what lurks behind that unhappy gaze.'

"Nicky paused for a moment and suddenly began to laugh. He said he had never thought of the world's fastest-rising star as particularly malcontent.

"I knew Elizabeth well enough to share her sense of indignation at M-G-M. The studio maintained a deplorable attitude toward its contract players, treating us more like indentured servants than professionals. You had to do exactly what they wished—be photographed with your hair up, your hair down, in two-piece swimming suits, whatever. Elizabeth said once she couldn't even pee without somebody standing over her in the ladies' room. But she couldn't give up acting, because it was all she knew or had been trained to do.

"'I had to escape,' she told me, 'and I had only two options—go to college or get married. I chose the latter. I was barely eighteen. I really did think being married would be like living in a little white cottage with a picket fence and red roses.'

"Personally, I always considered Nicky Hilton a prototypical Cain-and-Abel figure, an idiosyncratic combination of good and evil. He and Elizabeth Taylor were never especially well suited. He was spoiled silly, while she exuded the air of a pampered prima donna. He resented her fame, and she envied his wealth. His money made her so nervous, she used to bite her nails to the quick and began to wear fake fingernails."

Asked by Louella Parsons about her relationship with Nicky Hilton, Elizabeth responded: "Nothing comes off until the ring goes on."

One visit through the ornate iron gates up the long driveway to Conrad Hilton's columned, forty-seven-room Bel Air mansion, Casa Encantada, convinced Elizabeth's mother that her daughter had made a sage choice in selecting Nicky Hilton, even if his father did dominate him completely.

Elizabeth remained more wary. Dining with Nicky at Chasen's, she discovered his weakness for alcohol and his ensuing metamorphosis. While gulping drink after drink, he gradually changed from a shy, withdrawn young man into a feisty, aggressive tyro.

He gave the impression of being more at ease several weeks later when Elizabeth arrived alone for supper at Casa Encantada. After strolling the grounds, they joined Conrad Hilton Sr. in the formal dining room. The meal was served on gold plates by a team of impeccably attired servants. Nicky and his father sat at opposite ends of a twenty-five-foot mahogany table, with Elizabeth between them. Nobody said a word. The only sound was an occasional jarring belch on the part of Conrad Sr. Elizabeth, in a state of disbelief, stared at her future father-in-law, while Nicky continued to eat as if he had heard nothing.

When the meal was nearly completed, the old man stared at his son and proclaimed, "What you need, Nicky, is a family—a wife and children. Barron did it. It's the only way to succeed."

The servants cleared the table and brought glasses of port. Conrad Sr. lifted slightly from his chair, raised his glass to Elizabeth, proposed a toast, then let forth a hollow, rumbling passage of gas that echoed through the cheerless room. Elizabeth rolled her eyes; Nicky nonchalantly lit an expensive Havana cigar and poured his father another glass of port.

Nicky Hilton and Elizabeth Taylor were engaged on February 20, 1950, during her making of *Father of the Bride.* Joan Bennett, Elizabeth's harried mother in the Vincente Minnelli–directed comedy, saw her the morning after her engagement party wearing a pair of diamond-and-emerald teardrop earrings and a matching knuckle-to-knuckle square-cut diamond ring, both items bought at George Headley's, the Beverly Hills jeweler.

"They're my engagement presents from Nicky," said Elizabeth, holding the sparkling ring to the light.

"Strangely," remarked Joan Bennett, "she didn't seem overly pleased, almost as though she understood the impending marriage might not be easy for her.

"She and Spencer Tracy, who played the role of her father in the film, huddled for hours in his dressing room. He confided to me later that she had certain misgivings about Nicky Hilton. Spence delivered a rousing pep talk in an effort to convince her that young Hilton effused boyish charm and would make an excellent husband; I'm not so sure he himself believed any of this. I think Spence thought they were both too immature and unformed to walk down the aisle."

Actor Tom Irish, who had a small role in *Father of the Bride,* remembered Nicky Hilton's visiting the set on several occasions: "He never looked overly interested in being there. Elizabeth even offered to introduce him to Spencer Tracy and Joan Bennett; he declined.

"Liz owned a black Cadillac convertible at the time, which she told me she replaced with a new model every year. 'It's my only mode of escape,' she explained. 'But now I also have Nicky Hilton.'

"She always struck me as unique. The entire universe kowtows and bows to her, which has been happening since childhood. There have been adequate reasons for her becoming spoiled over the years; she has been, for example, insulated from the general population and has had to formulate a kind of imaginary universe—'the World According to Elizabeth Taylor.'"

If Elizabeth found herself on the verge of marrying a man she couldn't quite trust, she didn't always reveal her true feelings. Doris Lilly encountered the actress approximately a week before the wedding ceremony: "We were at a party in Hollywood. I had accompanied William Randolph Hearst and his wife. Elizabeth attended the event by herself. She was a star, but had not reached the heights she would in later years. In fact, she wasn't such a big banana in those days and for that matter seemed more thrilled to meet me than vice versa.

"My first impression of her bordered on mild shock. First of all, she looked much smaller in person than I imagined she would. I also thought she looked rather hairy. Her hairline wasn't clearly defined. . . . There was more hair coming down than there should have been. I peered at her eyebrows and knew she often plucked them; if she hadn't, they would have grown together. There was hair on her cheeks, like fuzz on a peach. She had marvelous eyes, naturally, and a pretty little nose. Large bosoms weren't in fashion in those days, so she tried to hide them while accentuating her tiny waist.

"She was marrying Nicky Hilton; they were like the prince and princess of Wales, a touch of American aristocracy—only Nicky wasn't such a respectable blue blood.

"I had a girlfriend, Jessica Saunders, a high-fashion model for the Ford Agency, who dated Nicky before Elizabeth. I used to hear hair-raising tales from Jessica about Nicky's violent nature—how he would drink too much and then beat her up; how he kept a loaded .38 revolver by the side of his bed and would shoot out the lights while high on drugs.

"Liz and I were having a nice little chat at this Hollywood affair: She seemed fond of me until I casually interjected, 'Elizabeth, I don't think you should marry Nicky Hilton.'

"She stared at me. 'What do you mean?' I explained I had heard he liked beating up girls whenever he got drunk. 'How can you say such a thing about Nicky?' she responded. 'I've never heard anything so terrible.' At this juncture, William Hearst took my arm and pulled me out of the room. To say the very least, Elizabeth Taylor never spoke to me again."

Elizabeth's marriage to Nicky Hilton had been timed to coincide with the release of *Father of the Bride.* The result was additional publicity for the movie and, thus, increased revenue at the box office. The wedding also gained Elizabeth more personal press coverage than she might ordinarily have wanted. The media reported, for example, that she had recently cofounded a group called S.L.O.B., a sorority of young unmarried Hollywood actresses, or as Liz dubbed them, "Single, Lonely, Obliging Babes."

Reflecting on the group, Carole Doheny found "the idea revolting—it suggested if you were young, intelligent, and female and you were not married, you were undesirable, an oddity. Something had to be wrong with you. It set the wrong tone; it spoke against independence and feminism. Elizabeth Taylor always defined herself by the latest man in her life. The danger was, actresses were considered role models for millions of young women around the world."

Ann Cole spoke of the "usual round of showers with gifts and ribbons that we threw for Elizabeth. Then, maybe four weeks before the wedding, she and I drove out to the Palm Springs Racquet Club for lunch. We were followed the entire route by three busloads of gaping newspaper photographers. The entire adventure wearied Elizabeth, to a point where she wished the wedding were already behind her.

"She still seemed very pure. Occasionally, a man would tell her an obscene story to which she would react with outright embarrassment. How could men be like that? Her marriage to Nicky Hilton ultimately became her initiation to life. She would never again feel the same way about men."

Betty Sullivan Precht,* daughter of the late television personality Ed Sullivan, met Elizabeth when both were bridesmaids at the wedding ceremony of Jane Powell and Geary Steffen Jr. "Later, Elizabeth asked me to be a bridesmaid at her wedding to Nicky Hilton," remarked Betty. "I obliged, although I didn't know her very well. She just didn't seem to have many girlfriends. She lacked the necessary free time to develop normal associations with other women her age. Her entire existence appeared to revolve around 'the business.'

"Frankly, I found myself developing negative feelings towards Nicky Hilton soon after meeting him. He could be personable, I admit, but he drank too much. Elizabeth tended to romanticize the relationship because she loved him. I wish I could say the same held true for Nicky."

One illustration of Elizabeth's affection for Nicky manifested itself in a letter she wrote to Olive Wakeman, Conrad Hilton Sr.'s administrative assistant. Elizabeth communicated her love for her fiancé while imploring Olive, whom she had met on several occasions, for advice on how to make the marriage work.

*By chance, Bob Precht, Betty's husband since 1952, "won" a date with Elizabeth Taylor in December 1949 during his junior year at UCLA. The date, a promotional gimmick arranged by Paramount in connection with Bob Hope's latest film, *The Great Lover,* actually resulted in a meeting between Bob Precht and Betty. "Elizabeth asked me to check him out before she met him," recalled Betty. "She wanted to be certain he would be presentable to the press so as not to defeat the purpose of the date. She went out with him, but I married him."

Olive responded by sending Elizabeth a selection of international cookbooks—American, Italian, French, Spanish, and German (Nicky's favorite cuisine), along with a note which included the age-old cliché "The way to a man's heart is through his stomach." To which she added: "Don't forget his ego. And men tend to have fragile egos, much more than women."

Elizabeth telephoned Montgomery Clift: "Will you come and visit me after I'm married?" she asked him.

Monty's reply did not please her: "Bessie Mae, I don't think dear Nicky is my kind of guy."

Elizabeth didn't communicate with Clift again for several months. His condemnation kindled her own doubts. She wanted to wed. The opportunity offered not only an escape from home, it also gave her the hope of achieving a necessary rite of passage into womanhood. (Elizabeth was still a virgin, and she didn't intend to remain one forever.)

Elizabeth herself wrote tellingly later: "I had always had a strict and proper upbringing, and that was absolutely necessary, living the existence I did. The irony is that the morality I learned at home required marriage, I couldn't just have an affair. . . . I guess I never gave myself the time to find out whether it was love or infatuation. I always chose to think I was in love . . . but I didn't have my own yardstick."

In preparation for "the wedding of weddings," Elizabeth and her mother spent three days at Marshall Field in Chicago acquiring Wallace sterling-silver flatware, powder-blue Limoges china, Swedish crystal, and monogrammed Italian lace-trimmed sheets. These and a slew of other household items were charged to Nicky Hilton's account.

Mother and daughter next journeyed to New York and stayed as complimentary guests at the Waldorf-Astoria, a Hilton-owned hotel. The manager of the Waldorf presented Elizabeth with a block of one hundred shares of Hilton stock, a wedding gift from her future father-in-law. Connie also threw in an all-expenses-paid three-month European honeymoon.

New York couturiere Ceil Chapman, an acquaintance of Sara Taylor's, prepared Elizabeth's trousseau, which included dozens of slinky negligees and the usual array of accessories. Edith Head, costume designer for *A Place in the Sun,* contributed evening gowns based on patterns worn in the film. The wedding dress, created by Helen Rose, came courtesy of M-G-M. Fifteen seamstresses had worked for two months to complete the gown—a billowy creation in white satin embroidered with beige beads and seed pearls. It was topped by a cream-tinted tiara with ten yards of misty veiling; she wore a simple pair of satin slippers on her feet.

A week prior to the ceremony, the Taylor residence began filling up with presents, mainly from members of the Hollywood cinema set. Liz's favorite gifts were, however, from members of her immediate family: a painting by Frans Hals and a mink coat from her father, a white mink stole from her mother, and a $65,000 diamond and platinum ring from Howard Young.

On May 5, Elizabeth and Nicky and their entourage of bridesmaids and ushers held a rehearsal at the Church of the Good Shepherd in Beverly Hills. M-G-M supplied a platoon of security guards to keep gawkers at bay. During rehearsal, Elizabeth began to run a fever and develop a sore throat. A physician administered penicillin injections and sent the bride-to-be home to rest.

Early the following day, the Los Angeles Police Department cordoned off Elizabeth's street, permitting entry to an occasional delivery van transporting a last-minute load of wedding gifts. Enough crystal and silverware had arrived to outfit a Hilton hotel.

Directly across the street from the Taylor residence, at the home of Anne Westmore's parents, the bridesmaids had arrived to change into their saffron-yellow dresses. Jane Powell, Betty Sullivan Precht, Marjorie Dillon (Elizabeth's part-time movie stand-in), Marilyn Hilton (married to Barron Hilton), Barbara Long Thompson (Marshall Thompson's wife), Mara Regan (the future wife of Elizabeth's brother, Howard), and Anne herself were preparing for the milestone.

At noon, an unexpected visitor appeared at Elizabeth's house in the person of a grim-faced Bill Pawley Jr. He had come to warn his former fiancée about Nicky Hilton's violent mood swings and erratic behavior. For fifteen minutes, he engaged Elizabeth in solemn conversation and departed as mysteriously as he had arrived.

Sidney Guilaroff, M-G-M's chief hairstylist, arrived next, followed by the studio's head fitter, Susan Ryan, who spent several hours squeezing Elizabeth into her wedding garb. Liz and her mother had a last-minute tiff when the bride refused to wear stockings.

M-G-M had stage-managed a dream bride. At 4:45 P.M., she emerged from her home and entered a waiting limousine. Her father sat beside her and held her hand. The bridesmaids followed in a second limousine, the small procession headed by a half-dozen motorcycle policemen, their sirens wailing.

Despite the local police and M-G-M's security force, the streets filled with throngs of spectators; men, women, and children perched in trees, clambered atop automobiles, and sat on the roofs of homes that lined the church route. Another ten thousand onlookers had gathered in front of the Church of the Good Shepherd. When Elizabeth's limousine arrived—only five minutes late—a huge cheer rose from the crowd.

There was a small mishap when Elizabeth attempted to step out of the car. The hem of her dress caught on a door handle and nearly ripped as the chauffeur struggled to assist her. She sat back in her seat, and then descended from the automobile without incident.

The pews were filled with dozens of M-G-M executives as well as the managers and officers of nearly every important Hilton hotel in the world. Other major film studios had also sent their top brass. Prominent pews had been assigned to the William Powells, the Phil Harrises (wife, Alice Faye), the Gene Kellys, the Bing Crosbys, the Walter Pidgeons, the Dick Powells (wife, June Allyson), the Red Skeltons, the Van Johnsons, to say nothing of Peter Lawford, Margaret O'Brien, Ginger Rogers, Fred Astaire, Ann Miller, Janet Leigh, Mickey Rooney, Spencer Tracy, Joan Bennett, and, of course, Roddy McDowall. M-G-M had sent out many of the six hundred guest invitations with little consideration to anything but the publicity inherent in such an event. Even Louis B. Mayer occupied a pew, dabbing the sporadic tear from his eyes with a white silk handkerchief as Elizabeth, on the arm of her father, made her way down the aisle in time to Wagner's "Wedding March."

Geoff Miller, current publisher of *Los Angeles* magazine, was one of four altar boys at the Taylor-Hilton wedding. He remembered the day—May 6, 1950—as "among the hottest of the year . . . over one hundred degrees. It was a somber nuptial mass laden with all the ecclesiastical trimmings, except for the news photographers clambering about the altar and taking pictures of the wedding.

"Nicky Hilton wore lily of the valley in the lapel of his cutaway coat and looked like a young boy dressed for Sunday school. Otherwise, the twenty-minute ceremony, conducted by Msgr. Patrick J. Concannon, came off as unadulterated Hollywood.

"When they were done, Nicky asked, 'Monsignor, may I now kiss the bride?' A kiss was simply not bestowed in those days, particularly not in a strict Roman Catholic ceremony. But the monsignor, apparently swept up in the glamour of the moment, assented to Nicky's desire.

"Nick drew his new wife to his chest, pressed his lips to hers, and dipped her practically to the ground. They embraced until monsignor emitted a loud cough, something akin to a director yelling, 'Cut!' The couple then turned and walked down the aisle, pausing on the steps of the church to repeat their censored performance, with Nicky dramatically sweeping the bride into his arms."

Chapter 8

Following their wedding, Nicky and Elizabeth Hilton were given a reception by Conrad Hilton at the Spanish-style Bel Air Country Club. It took nearly six hours for their more than seven hundred guests to wind through the reception line, wolf down a slice of vanilla-frosted, five-tier wedding cake, and quaff the requisite glass or two of chilled Dom Perignon champagne.

Elizabeth then changed into an Edith Head ensemble for her send-off—a blue silk suit with dyed-to-match leather pumps and pocket-book, complemented by a white-on-white embroidered blouse and linen gloves.

Embracing her father and kissing her mother and brother, the bride, and her beaming husband, struggled through a storm of rice and confetti to Nicky's silver-and-gold Mercedes-Benz convertible. So anxious were they to get under way that they neglected to tip the staff at the Bel Air Country Club, just as they had earlier departed the Church of the Good Shepherd without leaving the customary donation for the altar boys.

The newlyweds drove to Carmel and passed the first part of their honeymoon at the Carmel Country Club in a luxurious three-bedroom villa overlooking the Pacific. Best known for its golfing, gambling, and entertainment facilities, the club had long been a favorite Nicky Hilton bastion, a spot he had frequented with former girlfriends on previous outings.

Humorist Art Buchwald happened to be at the same resort at the time of the couple's stay. "It amazed me to find Nicky Hilton seated by himself in the bar on his nuptial night when any other man would have been in bed with his wife, particularly when the wife's initials were 'E.T.'

"I congratulated Hilton's good fortune in marrying one of the most beautiful women in the world. 'I'll drink to that,' he chortled. He'd evidently been drinking most of the evening, because he could barely stand or even sit up straight.

"'Why don't you join Elizabeth?' I prodded him. 'She must be lonely without you. It's your wedding night.'

"I suspected Elizabeth had retired after waiting hours in vain for her husband's return. Hilton spent an entire night at the bar, drinking himself into an absolute stupor. He hadn't budged even when they closed the place at four in the morning. I found him glued to the same bar stool the next day. Rumor had it he didn't consummate his marriage to Elizabeth until their third night together—and then she practically had to drag him to bed. I had the impression she found him extremely physically appealing, but I'm not at all certain he found her so totally irresistible."

Elizabeth spoke for countless hours on the telephone with her mother, complaining about Nicky and wondering what she could do to improve the situation. One morning, Nicky and Liz contented themselves by walking the first nine holes of the resort's golf course. At the ninth hole, a golf ball sailed out of the rough and ricocheted off Nicky's forehead; he carried around an ice pack the rest of the day to reduce the swelling.

They were two spoiled children with too much time on their hands and not enough in common. Elizabeth perused fan magazines, while Nicky barely read. Elizabeth joined him at the bar one night and drank herself sick. While she spent the remainder of the evening vomiting into a toilet bowl, her husband lingered at the bar and picked up other women, taking their names and telephone numbers for future reference.

Jake Holmes, a reporter for *Variety,* managed to sneak into the club the following afternoon and corner Elizabeth by the outdoor swimming pool. What did she anticipate doing about her film career? the reporter queried. "Give it up," she retorted. "I'd rather be a housewife than an actress." Holmes recorded her reply but had difficulty believing it. He said as much to Elizabeth, who merely smiled in response.

Ten days after departing on her honeymoon, Elizabeth, with Nicky in tow, returned to her parents' Elm Street residence to celebrate Mother's Day. She and Nicky turned up in public next at the Empire Room of Chicago's Palmer House. Seated at a banquet table in the hotel dining room with a dozen guests, including Barron and Marilyn Hilton, were a number of Hilton family friends. Garnett I. Sherman, a Chicago homemaker, sat in the same room and observed events.

"Every eye seemed focused on Elizabeth. I thought how difficult it must be for her to go through life being a constant magnet to every voyeur.

"The finale to their dinner party consisted of a large, lovely torte rolled out on a silver serving cart by three or four waiters. The cake replicated the ship *Queen Mary;* it had tiny portholes illuminated by miniature electrical lights. The newlyweds had booked passage aboard the vessel for Europe and were presently en route to New York to board the ocean liner."

On the eve of their departure, they dined at New York's Stork Club with Nicky's father and Martha Reed, a socialite and frequent companion of Conrad Sr. "Nicky had all the makings of a playboy," observed Reed. "He had acquired too much too soon and didn't know how to handle it. He was a naughty fellow, very irresponsible and after a point no longer the apple of his father's eye. Connie gradually became disillusioned with Nick and turned his attention to the more serious, hardworking Barron Hilton.

"Elizabeth seemed an attractive young girl but had not yet attained mature beauty. For one thing, she didn't know how to dress. Unless the studio outfitted her, she invariably wound up a fashion disaster, a contender for the annual 'Worst-Dressed List.'

"I heard from Connie that once they reached Europe, Nick and Liz engaged in a series of dramatic fights and altercations. They were obviously incompatible. At some point I crossed paths with them in Paris, and Elizabeth looked rather pained."

Actually, their fights and altercations began long before they disembarked in Europe. They boarded the *Queen Mary* on May 23, bringing along a vast array of trunks and suitcases. Nicky repeated his nuptial-night antics by spending his first night aboard ship drinking and socializing in the grand sitting room, leaving Elizabeth to her own devices. She was periodically spied on deck throughout the ocean voyage looking forlorn. Also aboard were the duke and duchess of Windsor; Elizabeth spent her second night in their company, while Nicky managed to lose in excess of $100,000 in the ship's gambling casino.

Whether it was the sudden and considerable loss of funds or a subsequent drinking bout which drove Hilton into a fury is anybody's guess. In any case, he returned to his stateroom violently drunk. He found his wife not in bed but in the shower, recovering from her late night out with the Windsors. Without a word, Nick suddenly slammed his fist into Elizabeth's midsection; she fell to her knees, clutching her stomach while trying to catch her breath. Nick turned off the shower and collapsed into bed.

In recounting the episode for the benefit of director Larry Peerce, Elizabeth Taylor would say of Nicky Hilton: "We had a very prim and proper courtship, a very fiftyish type of courtship where a woman didn't go to bed with a man prior to marriage. During the courtship, except on one or two occasions, Nicky was able to control what I later determined to be his violent nature. Once I discovered his problem, it was too late to do much about it. We were already married, and I was too ashamed to admit I had committed such a grievous error."

The Hiltons made Paris their first port of call, staying at the Hotel George V and attending several parties, including a dinner dance given by Elizabeth's shipboard companions, the duke and duchess of Windsor. Line Renaud, a young French singer, performed that evening for the duke and duchess. "I played the piano and sang in their salon," the soprano reminisced. "Elizabeth sat on the floor in front of me while the duke of Windsor leaned against the piano, looking at both of us, staring fixedly at our blue eyes. He said, 'I have the most wonderful view from here of two pairs of eyes the color of *blue lavender,'* which happened to be the title of one of his favorite songs."

Another guest that evening, Elsa Maxwell, later feted Nicky and Elizabeth at Maxim's, inviting Maurice Chevalier, Orson Welles, the maharajah of Kapurthala, a gaggle of barons, baronesses, earls, and duchesses, as well as Jimmy Donahue, the obstreperous gay cousin of five-and-dime heiress Barbara Hutton. Maxwell's most salient memory of the evening had to be the thick wad of chewing gum Nicky Hilton took from his mouth prior to dinner, which he meticulously wrapped in a napkin and placed in his trouser pocket. At the end of the meal, after dessert, he resumed chewing.

"As a couple, they seemed frankly unimpressive save for their natural good looks. They were reserved to the point of indolence. I seated Elizabeth next to Baron Alexis de Rede, who, while affable and loquacious, failed to engage the actress in a great deal of conversation. She answered questions but posed none of her own. She refused to initiate verbal exchange. It seemed odd, but I attributed it to her being on foreign soil.

"Nicky Hilton, on the other hand, appeared inattentive to his wife's needs, as if he didn't care a whit about her. The French press ran a profusion of articles romanticizing their marriage, but in actuality they didn't seem to be the least bit in love. It had all the trappings of what the French call 'a marriage of convenience.' There was a tradeoff—her beauty and cinematic celebrity in exchange for the Hiltons' family wealth.

"When I knew her, she was a charming, polite, well-brought-up young lady, but lacking in character; she hadn't yet cultivated a personality. She would have been of little interest to the public had she not been so stunning. I saw Elizabeth Taylor once or twice, years later, at soirees given by the Rothschilds. By then she had clearly emerged as a creature of considerable temperament. She had developed into one of those *sacred American monsters,* like Jackie Onassis and Katharine Hepburn."

From Paris the twosome traveled to Berlin for the opening of the Berlin Hilton, then to Rome, where Nicky recommenced drinking and manifesting violent behavior toward Elizabeth. To escape her husband, Taylor contacted Mervyn LeRoy, who was also in Rome directing M-G-M's epic *Quo Vadis.*

"Can you hide me, Mervyn?" she asked. "I don't want him to find me."

"Sure," agreed LeRoy. "What better place to hide than in a crowd? Come on over to the set."

When she arrived, he sent her down to wardrobe. They dressed her in a toga, like all the other extras, and for a few days Elizabeth played the part of a Christian martyr in a Colosseum mob scene, preempting the role of British starlet Claire Davids. "The part meant nothing to her," said Davids, "but it meant everything to me. I was pregnant at the time, and I told Elizabeth if I lost the part, I wouldn't qualify for health insurance. She scoffed at the notion: 'Oh, I'm certain Mervyn can fit you in somewhere.' He couldn't, and eventually I forfeited my health insurance. I blamed it on Elizabeth and felt she behaved in a heartless manner to satisfy her own needs. She had no regard for my feelings."

Elizabeth's fleeting appearance in the film prompted Nicky's latest outbreak of violence. When his wife failed to return to their rented Roman villa, Hilton proceeded to demolish an entire room of museum-quality sixteenth-century furniture, incurring a sizable bill from the owners.

The honeymoon couple moved on to the south of France, where they reserved the largest suite at the Carlton Hotel in Cannes. There they encountered Betty Sullivan Precht and her parents, who were vacationing on the Riviera.

"At this period," recounted Betty, "Nicky and Elizabeth's marriage had begun to rapidly deteriorate. He gambled and drank with complete abandon, entirely neglecting his wife. Elizabeth subsequently spent more time with my family in Cannes than she did with her husband.

"Whenever anybody asked Elizabeth for her autograph, Nicky would stomp off in a frenzy and wouldn't be heard from for the rest of the day. He loathed the idea that she was the more recognizable of the two. Don't forget, he was an heir to a fortune, and his family had clout. But Hollywood gave Elizabeth a magic appeal with which Nicky could not compete.

"Three friends of mine from Princeton University came to visit me in Cannes. One afternoon we went waterskiing and asked Elizabeth and Nicky to join us. Nicky wanted nothing to do with the venture and left us to go drinking. Elizabeth came along and enjoyed herself immensely. That evening, Nicky beat Elizabeth so badly that a physician had to attend to her."

Taylor later admitted to Larry Peerce that she desperately wanted to leave her husband. "She desired to return to the United States without him," averred Peerce, "but in those days, couples traveled on one passport. She tried approaching an immigration official at the U.S. embassy in Nice; he couldn't issue her an individual passport, and she couldn't use the joint one because it contained Nicky Hilton's photograph. In other words, they had to leave the country together."

After Betty Sullivan Precht and her family departed from Cannes, Elizabeth found herself alone again. Several days later, however, she made a new acquaintance at the Carlton. Sondra Ritter Voluck, a young woman Elizabeth's age, who attended Fieldston, an expensive private school in New York, was also vacationing in Europe with her parents.

"Elizabeth and I spent two weeks swimming, bicycling, and shopping together while Nicky Hilton gambled, drank, and womanized. They argued incessantly. One of their major conflicts arose over Elizabeth's extravagant shopping sprees. She would purchase an overabundance of clothes and jewelry, mainly, I felt, out of boredom and disgust with her husband. Nicky Hilton in turn had terrible temper tantrums, reprimanding and cursing Liz in public. His only noble gesture was to buy her a French poodle named Banco, which she later brought back with her to the States."

After twelve weeks abroad, the Hiltons returned to New York aboard the *Queen Elizabeth.* The Volucks, their summer vacation similarly at an end, were also on the ship. Sondra Voluck recalled the return voyage as a "sad and terrifying interlude for Elizabeth. Behaving more outrageously than ever, Nicky would slap her around for no reason whatsoever.

"One evening he hit her, and she came running into my stateroom. She was crying. I said, 'You'll stay the night.' She slept in my room and reluctantly returned to Nicky the next day.

"By the time we reached New York, she'd had enough. Nicky returned by himself to California, and Liz stayed with my family in our Manhattan apartment at 927 Fifth Avenue. I became the envy of my senior classmates at Fieldston, all of whom hoped to be invited to meet Elizabeth. My boyfriends also went gaga over her. They always insisted on taking her along whenever we went out so she wouldn't 'be left by herself.'

"One problem we soon encountered related to her celebrity. We were literally mobbed wherever we went. Going to a restaurant or nightclub with her became an ordeal. We began hiding out at my parents' country club in Westchester, where she felt safe from prying eyes and troublemakers.

"During the weeks she spent with us, she and I grew close. We engaged in long talks late at night. She expressed disdain for several actress friends, particularly Jane Powell, about whom she would confide, 'She's so cheap, she makes her own clothes.'

"At a certain point Elizabeth's mother telephoned my mother. 'I've never met you folks,' she said, 'and I would like to know with whom my daughter is staying. Do you mind if I send my fashion designer friend Ceil Chapman to your apartment?' It was a peculiar request, an indication of just how protective Sara Taylor had always been of her daughter. Nevertheless, we assented; Ceil Chapman came over for a visit, and Mrs. Taylor felt reassured.

"She then sent my mother a letter expressing gratitude for looking after Elizabeth during those difficult days: 'You don't know what it meant . . . to know that she was there with you and that you were taking care of her and advising her just as we would have done. God is indeed good and ever-present to supply our needs, and I do thank *him* for having you there.'

"The same letter summarized Sara's reaction to her daughter's failing marriage: 'She is still such a baby, as you well know. Being in pictures has made her seem older, but at heart she is still a very *little* girl. She wanted to experience life in all its fullness and completeness, and we could not make her see that it would be better to wait a little to get to know each other better, to learn how to overlook or accept each other's faults. . . . The only thing that has ever worried us was her refusal to wait a little to know Nicky better and to mature a little more before marrying, but she felt so mature, and everything we said had the opposite effect. The whole thing has been such [an] emotional experience for her after the sheltered family life she has lived.'

"An intriguing aside to Sara's note is the one my father received from Nicky Hilton, who, like Mrs. Taylor, expressed appreciation for our concern for Elizabeth. He asked that we forward any bills or expenses Elizabeth incurred, even down to the film she bought for her camera.

"After several weeks of telephone conversations with her husband, Elizabeth agreed to join him again. My father accompanied her to Chicago, and Nicky drove out from Los Angeles to meet her. The couple returned to the Coast together by car."

Once there, they moved into a five-room suite (including a kitchen) at the Bel Air Hotel. By September 1950, Elizabeth had gone back to work, appearing in *Father's Little Dividend,* a sequel to the financially successful *Father of the Bride* starring the same cast as the earlier picture. According to Joan Bennett, who again played Elizabeth's screen mother, "Spencer Tracy's favorite expression pertaining to the production of the sequel was 'boring . . . boring . . . boring.' We both felt one family film had been enough; I imagine Elizabeth shared our sentiment."

Taylor appeared, albeit briefly, in *Callaway Went Thataway,* a sophomoric spoof featuring Dorothy McGuire and Fred MacMurray as a pair of advertising promoters intent on the resurrection of a movie cowboy's career. Elizabeth Taylor plays herself in a nightclub sequence in the film. She is introduced to the *real* cowboy (Howard Keel), who has been hired to impersonate screen-cowboy Callaway, whose penchant for women and alcohol have led to his temporary disappearance.

By mid-October, Elizabeth had begun to suffer from high blood pressure, the result of ongoing tension in her marriage, too much work, and too many parties. "All both of us are doing is working and of course going to parties almost every night," she wrote Sondra Voluck from Palm Springs, where she claimed she had gone on a weeklong doctor-prescribed rest cure with her film stand-in Marjorie Dillon. She needed to recuperate physically and mentally from what had become an abortive attempt at reconciliation with Nicky.

Robert Quain, a Hilton Hotel Corporation executive who worked closely with Nicky Hilton, placed the burden of blame for the failure of the marriage essentially on Elizabeth:

"It's true Nicky drank and his drinking exacerbated his manic-depressive nature. When inebriated, he often displayed racist tendencies, ranting and raving about 'kikes' and 'niggers.' What ultimately destroyed their union was Elizabeth's career."

On December 1, 1950, Nicky and Elizabeth officially separated. She had already embarked upon *Love Is Better Than Ever,* an insipid comedy about a dancing school directed by twenty-seven-year-old Stanley Donen, who had launched his career by appearing as a chorus boy on the Broadway stage before relocating to Hollywood. Although still married when he met Elizabeth, he began to pursue her almost at once. Donen was Jewish, a fact that disturbed Elizabeth's mother. "Sara Taylor never actually asked me about my religion," Donen reports. She did, however, upbraid the director in Elizabeth's presence.

Taylor had vacated the Bel Air suite and moved in with her parents, transporting the multitude of wedding presents she and Nicky had received. During her brief return, she and her mother argued incessantly.

Their most frequent topics of discourse ranged from Stanley Donen to Nicky Hilton.

To add to her disappointment over the apparent dissolution of her marriage, Liz was daily exposed to newspaper reports of her husband's latest female conquests. Hilton's dates included a number of Hollywood's more attractive actresses, among them Natalie Wood, Mamie Van Doren, Terry Moore, Betsy von Furstenberg, and British newcomer Joan Collins, who blithely announced that Nicky was not just "a sexual athlete," but between his brother Barron, his father, and himself, "the boys possessed a yard of cock."

When life under her parents' roof proved unbearable, Elizabeth fled. For weeks, she camped like a Gypsy in one friend's house after another, often telephoning late at night to ask, sobbing, if she could come over. She stayed with Marjorie Dillon, with designer Helen Rose, and at the home of her agent, Jules Goldstone, and his wife.

The strain of her separation from Hilton wore on Elizabeth. Unable to eat, she was pale, thin, and quivering with nerves. She would often burst into hysterical weeping on the set of *Love Is Better Than Ever,* necessitating undue delays and scheduling difficulties.*

She was a guest of the Goldstones when she finally decided to terminate her marriage. Meanwhile, Hilton had undergone a change of heart and was frantically trying to work out a reconciliation. Locating his estranged wife at whatever friend's house she happened to be staying, he sent her two dozen roses a day and bombarded her with telephone calls. Having made her decision, Elizabeth felt she must tell Nicky face-to-face that she wanted a divorce. Upon his arrival, the two withdrew into the Goldstones' den for almost an hour. Then Hilton's raised voice, hurling furious insults, penetrated the closed door so strongly that Goldstone raced in and demanded he leave.

*In the end, *Love Is Better Than Ever* was not released by M-G-M until 1952. Larry Parks, Elizabeth's costar in the film, had been called to Washington to testify before the House Un-American Activities Committee, where he admitted past membership in the American Communist party. The confession cost Parks his career; it also convinced M-G-M executives to push back the release date of the Parks-Taylor film.

Soon after, Elizabeth Taylor spent a week in Cedars-Sinai Hospital in Los Angeles to recover from what her studio termed a "serious viral infection." Her associates knew better. She had suffered a nervous collapse and a second attack of high blood pressure.

After her release from the hospital, she traveled briefly to New York to visit Montgomery Clift. She stayed at the Plaza Hotel, compliments (she assumed) of the management. At the time, the hotel belonged to Conrad Hilton. While checking out, she was presented with a $2,500 bill and informed she was "no longer considered a member of the hotel family."

Elizabeth became infuriated and telephoned Clift. She asked him to come over and help her pack. Accompanied by Roddy McDowall, Monty turned up within the hour. The three of them ordered a pitcher of martinis and proceeded to ransack Elizabeth's hotel suite, upending pictures, stuffing pillows down the toilet, cutting up sheets and draperies, dueling with the giant chrysanthemums Elizabeth had been sent by a fan, and littering the carpet with hundreds of yellow petals and broken stems. As the coup de grâce, Monty filled Elizabeth's suitcases with the hotel's monogrammed towels, for which the management of the Plaza later sent her an invoice.

She returned to Los Angeles, and on January 30, 1951, still eighteen years of age, she marched into Los Angeles Superior Court, Judge Thurmond Clarke presiding, to obtain a divorce decree. Her attorney, William Berger, placed her on the witness stand. For the next twenty minutes she presented a detailed chronology of the abuse she had endured in less than nine months of marriage. She referred to the experience as "a disaster, a nightmare," citing Hilton's drinking, gambling, and violent outbursts as the root cause of her unhappiness. Her plea was mental cruelty; she asked for no alimony, although she retained the Hilton Hotel Corporation stock, the jewelry, the wedding presents, and other gifts received from Nicky during their brief marriage. In today's equivalent, she reaped altogether more than $500,000 for her misery.

Following the divorce, Nicky issued only the briefest of public statements: "I have never seen such beauty in my life. But God, she can be difficult."

Nicky Hilton died of heart failure on February 5, 1969, at age forty-two. He and his second wife were separated at the time of his death. Elizabeth Taylor offered nothing by way of public comment.

Chapter 9

Announcing its annual cinema awards for 1951, Harvard University's *Lampoon* magazine named Elizabeth Taylor "one of the . . . most objectionable movie *children* of the year, the actress who gave [in *Conspirator*] the worst performance of the decade, the most objectionable ingenue," with a special mention for "so gallantly persisting in her career despite a total inability to act." The periodical made Elizabeth its first recipient of the Roscoe ("Oscar spelled sideways"), a newly established trophy "for total ineptitude in the acting profession." Taylor accepted the award with good grace when it was presented to her by fifteen Harvard students at Boston's Logan Airport as she prepared to board an airliner for New York. She subsequently disposed of the trophy in one of the plane's lavatories.

In New York, she stayed with Monty Clift at a town house he had recently bought and renovated in Manhattan's East Sixties. They spent their nights frequenting the city's pubs, such as Gregory's at Lexington Avenue and Fifty-fourth Street. Penny Arum, an actress-friend of Monty's, remembered Gregory's as a "dark, dingy hole-in-the-wall with a dynamite jukebox. It contained wooden tables and chairs and served as a kind of unofficial hangout for gays and working-class stiffs. Elizabeth never cared much for the place; it was a bit too shabby for her cultivated taste. Actor Kevin McCarthy and Blaine Waller, a nineteen-year-old photographer, used to hang out there as well. Another spot

Monty took Liz to was Camillo's, his favorite Italian restaurant, likewise a dive. "Monty also visited posh eateries—the Colony, Le Pavillon, Voisin—but he preferred the down-and-out, particularly because he knew it annoyed Elizabeth. He could be on the contentious side at times.

"Elizabeth drank heavily during the days following her divorce from Nicky Hilton. As such, she grew quite dependent on Monty, who unfortunately encouraged her along these lines. They had something else in common: both had pushy, controlling mothers as well as retiring, diffident fathers. Liz hoped to marry Monty and mentioned the subject at every opportunity. Clift discouraged her by changing the course of conversation."

Despite the improbability of marriage, it was obvious Monty and Elizabeth had enjoyed a loving, however short-lived, liaison. Marge Stengel, Clift's steadfast private secretary, often found the two lying in bed in the morning "looking like a pair of sleepy Siamese kittens." They shared an intimacy that transcended, but which also appeared to include, sexuality.

While in New York, Elizabeth went dancing with Merv Griffin and ice-skating with Roddy McDowall. Frank Farrell, a newspaper columnist, took her out on several occasions. She returned to Los Angeles and again stayed with her agent, Jules Goldstone, while hunting for an apartment of her own. She found one at 10600 Wilshire Boulevard, a two-bedroom arrangement which she occupied with Peggy Rutledge, a secretary and close-mouthed companion who prepared breakfast and sometimes dinner for her roommate. She likewise tidied up after her, an assignment one Taylor friend described as "a full-time job." Downstairs, in the same five-story, pink stucco apartment building surrounded by palm trees, lived newlyweds Janet Leigh and Tony Curtis, frequent hosts of dinner parties to which Elizabeth alternately invited Arthur Loew Jr. or Stanley Donen, depending on her mood. Loew doted on practical jokes and nonstop amusement, while Donen displayed an earnest, contemplative nature.

Defying her mother's objections, Elizabeth continued to date Stanley

Donen. Her rift with Nicky Hilton had brought on a case of colitis and another stay in hospital with round-the-clock nursing care. For the benefit of the press, the studio described her ailment as "a severe flu." Several M-G-M executives, however, including Benny Thau, privately expressed concern over Liz's health. "I've known her for years, and I've never seen her quite so downhearted," read one of Thau's in-house memos.

As usual, Elizabeth rebounded quickly. According to Janet Leigh, "A novel form of socializing began about the time Elizabeth left the hospital. A group of us started meeting for Sunday-morning brunch. We called ourselves 'the Fox and Lox Club.' Among the regulars were Naomi and Dick Carroll (the Beverly Hills haberdashers), Tony Curtis and myself, producer Stanley Roberts, writer Stewart Stern, Stanley Donen, and Elizabeth Taylor. Others gradually joined.

"We took turns hosting the brunch and preparing the meal. When it came time for Elizabeth to host, she made french toast—or attempted to. She somehow managed to set her kitchen ablaze, and the Los Angeles Fire Department had to be called. We wound up at the local delicatessen."

Stewart Stern recalled Elizabeth's wit and foul language. (She had evidently adopted at least one of Nicky Hilton's traits.) "She knew some fabulously erotic limericks, one so risqué I can only bring myself to quote the first and last lines," claimed Stern. "It begins: 'When I was only seventeen . . . , ' and it ends with 'half me bloody arm!' You can fill in the rest.

"It's an experience, I tell you, to hear those lyrics pour forth from the planet's most beautiful lips and to have those wide purple eyes shining at you!"

By mid-June 1951, Elizabeth Taylor journeyed to London to appear in M-G-M's version of *Ivanhoe*, with Robert Taylor (as Ivanhoe), Joan Fontaine, and George Sanders. Elizabeth had been offered the role of Rebecca the Jewess in *Ivanhoe.* She protested, insisting it was the heroine Rowena she wanted to play in the film. Joan Fontaine had locked up the role of the heroine, and Elizabeth had little choice but to accept her assigned part.

Liz did gain one concession from M-G-M. She asked that Peggy Rutledge be placed on the studio payroll instead of her mother and that Peggy, rather than Sara, accompany her to London. The altercations she had endured with her mother over her seeing Stanley Donen had inevitably turned Elizabeth against her parents.

As for Stanley Donen, Elizabeth gradually came to understand the futility of their long-distance affair. The letters and telephone calls between London and Los Angeles slowed until they ceased altogether. Once she was established in London, Taylor's romantic attention shifted in the direction of an old friend—Michael Wilding.

After the Sturm und Drang of her marriage to volatile Nicky Hilton, the more mature, urbane, and composed Michael Wilding must have come as a welcome relief. Wilding shared, however, at least one quality with Hilton. Both men agonized over their uncontrollable mood swings, which ranged from immense joy to unaccountable depression. Such a temperament evidently appealed to Elizabeth, who possessed a similarly fluctuating makeup.

Zsa Zsa Gabor, married to George Sanders after her divorce from Conrad Hilton Sr., heard numerous stories from George about Elizabeth's comportment on the *Ivanhoe* set. "Although he didn't appear in the film," averred Zsa Zsa, "Michael Wilding had by now completely fallen for Liz and took every opportunity to hang around the set. Years later he commented on her: 'The real tragedy concerning Liz is that there is not a man in the world she cannot have at the snap of her fingers.'

"In any case," continued Zsa Zsa, "most of the leading cast members had been put up at the Savoy Hotel in London. Following an arduous shooting schedule, they would gather for an evening of poker, Wilding included. At night, Elizabeth would emerge from her bedroom in a translucent nightgown and say, 'So which of you boys is going to spend the night with me?' She meant it as a joke of course, but still . . ."

Although Richard Thorpe, the director of *Ivanhoe*, found Elizabeth's work on the film "intelligent and on the mark," producer Pandro Berman appeared far less impressed. Viewing a batch of rushes, Berman complained to Thorpe that Elizabeth "is practically inaudible, and when you do hear her, you wish you didn't. She still has that whiny, shrill voice."

Berman insisted that Elizabeth completely redub her part. In an effort to win over the director, Elizabeth gave Richard Thorpe an engraved miniature gold heart. To no avail: Berman placed Elizabeth under the auspices of drama coach Lillian Burns Sidney, whom Thorpe happened to dislike. Lillian dragged Liz "kicking and screaming" through her dialogue until it sounded letter-perfect.

While all this was going on, Elizabeth, with Jules Goldstone working as her agent, became embroiled in an argument with M-G-M's contract department. Goldstone wanted Elizabeth to form her own production company. By doing so, he pointed out, she would be able to acquire more interesting scripts. In addition, she would have more of a say in the production. Moreover, not only would she receive heftier paychecks, she could also demand a percentage of the gross receipts.

Goldstone and Taylor were on the verge of forming their own company and establishing a series of independent picture deals when one night, as they were about to take action, Liz telephoned her agent in the States: "Jules, do you know I have been thinking about all this? You and Metro are my only ties to the past. I need that sense of security that has come with this relationship since I was a child. And in spite of all the heaps of money and other advantages I would reap from an independent deal, I think I ought to stay with Metro."

Michael Wilding, to whom she now turned increasingly for moral support, seconded Elizabeth's decision. Although she would eventually live to regret it, she signed a new seven-year contract with M-G-M. The terms of the contract called for her to receive $5,500 per week, which made her one of the highest-paid and youngest adult stars on Metro's illustrious roster.

Elizabeth had concluded her stint in *Ivanhoe* by September 14, 1951, but stayed on with Michael Wilding in London for an additional three weeks. At twice her age, he could have easily passed for her father, though he demonstrated a light, playful side and a shy youthfulness which made him seem far younger than his thirty-eight years. His lively gait, bright blue eyes, height (six feet one), and lean image added to the veneer of boyishness.

He and Elizabeth made the requisite rounds. In addition to their usual haunts, they were spotted at the Mirabelle, the Ivy, and the Caprice—three of London's leading nightspots. Wilding made Elizabeth laugh by recounting amusing tales of his father's misadventures as a pre-Revolutionary intelligence officer in the czar's army.

In the process of legalizing his divorce from Kay Young, Wilding had continued his involvement with Marlene Dietrich and several other actresses, including Margaret Leighton. Elizabeth, not to be denied in her pursuit of a new heartthrob, said to Wilding. "You'd marry me if I were older, wouldn't you?" She informed a reporter from the Associated Press that whereas she intended to marry again, she had chosen neither the time nor the person. In an effort to elicit a marriage proposal from Wilding, she twice dated the American actor Tab Hunter, whose latest film project, *Island of Desire,* had likewise brought him to England. Wilding wasn't the least bit impressed.

Wilding and Hunter both escorted Liz to the airport when she boarded her New York–bound flight on October 6. She lightly embraced Hunter, but she kissed Wilding twice on the lips before takeoff. "Goodbye, Mr. Shilly-Shally," she added. "Let's forget we ever met."

Wilding's friends knew of his burgeoning interest in Elizabeth and his intention to follow her to America. Herbert Wilcox, a former British producer and man of the theater, warned against it, suggesting that Michael's sophisticated humor and British sensibility would never "go over" in Hollywood. He cited David Niven as an example of a top British wit who had simply failed to conquer the American cinematic imagination.

Wilding convinced himself that Elizabeth Taylor's celebrity would rub off and boost his own reputation, which was limited in scope to Great Britain and a smattering of countries abroad. Moreover, he enjoyed Elizabeth and admired her strong will, an attribute that actually reminded him of Marlene Dietrich. He also desired to start a family, and in this regard Elizabeth seemed the ideal candidate.

On October 8, one day after her return to the United States, Elizabeth, as a member of a representative group from the motion-picture industry, resurfaced at the Truman White House for a tea held in connection with the celebration of the Golden Jubilee of the American Cinema. Michael Wilding read about the event in the British press and sent Elizabeth a telegram: "Well done, darling. Harry ought to appoint you his V.P., or at the very least Secretary of State."

Early in December, armed with his long-awaited divorce papers, Wilding turned up in California at the Beverly Hills home of fellow countryman and actor Stewart Granger, whose best man he had been when Granger married British actress Jean Simmons the year before in Texas. Granger was then under contract to M-G-M, while Simmons had recently signed with Twentieth Century-Fox.

Shortly after Wilding's arrival, he heard from Taylor. She had just purchased an expensive sapphire ring from Cartier on Rodeo Drive and wanted him to pick it up with her. On the verge of bankruptcy after his divorce, Wilding feared that he might have to foot the bill. Nevertheless, he accompanied her to the shop. No doubt with a sigh of relief, he watched her pay for the ring. When he offered to slip the ring on her finger, she hesitated, stretched out the fourth finger on her left hand, and said: "I think that's the finger it should go on, Michael, the engagement-ring one."

Elizabeth wasted no time in announcing their engagement. On February 1, 1952, she called a press conference and made her plans official. "It's a leap year, isn't it? Well, I leaped," she told reporters. Then she added: "Seriously, I just want to be with Michael, to be his wife. He enjoys sitting home, smoking his pipe, reading, painting. And that's what I intend doing—all except smoking a pipe."

"LUSCIOUS LIZ TO WED BRITISH FILM STAR MICHAEL WILDING!" read the following day's headline in the New York *Daily News.* The media had developed a bevy of sobriquets for Elizabeth—"Lovely Liz," "Lustful Liz," "Lissome Liz"—stressing both her physical beauty and sensuality. She had barely turned twenty and was already on the brink of her second well-publicized marriage. In addition to her renown as an actress, she had established herself, perhaps unintentionally, as a brunette counterpart to the bleached-blond film version of lasciviousness epitomized by bombshells Marilyn Monroe and Jayne Mansfield. The image may have had its drawbacks. Immediately after the announcement of Liz's engagement to Wilding, she began receiving a succession of anonymous telephone calls of explicit and menacing content.

The hoarse, whispery-voiced male at the other end of the line threatened to dynamite Taylor's flat unless she agreed to a rendezvous. Jack Owens, an FBI agent assigned to the case, encouraged Elizabeth to "engage the caller in conversation so we can try to trace the call."

"And how do I manage that?" Elizabeth inquired. "Do I discuss explosives with him?"

"Improvise," said Owens. "You're an actress. Convince the fellow you're passionately in love with him."

Elizabeth apparently managed an "Oscar-winning" performance. The caller, when finally apprehended, turned out to be an unemployed twenty-nine-year-old elevator operator who had been placed in a mental hospital years earlier for intimidating Kathryn Grayson in the same manner. He was remanded to the same institution.

Elizabeth had been exposed to a similar but equally harrowing experience sometime earlier. In November 1949, three letters arrived (each bearing a Brooklyn, New York, postmark), all obscene in nature and threatening in tone. The correspondence had been turned over to the FBI's Los Angeles bureau. Several months later the culprit was captured while climbing over a rear wall onto the grounds of Francis and Sara Taylor's home in Beverly Hills. A British subject, the man received a six-month jail sentence and was eventually deported to England. The matter did not end there.

In the summer of 1951, having completed *Ivanhoe* in London, Elizabeth received another note from her British harasser. Aware of her presence in England, he wrote:

> Dear Miss Taylor,
>
> Quite clearly you do not remember me; I am the man you had thrown in jail for six months and deported from the United States of America. I think you owe me something and I intend to collect.

On this occasion Scotland Yard got involved in the affair, and they, too, apprehended their man. The terror of the two events alarmed Elizabeth to the extent that she quietly moved out of the apartment previously shared with Peggy Rutledge and swiftly took up residence with Michael Wilding, then still living with friends Stuart Granger and Jean Simmons.

Recalling the period, Granger remarked that "Liz was always brighter than Jean. In fact, she's a very bright girl, in a way I'm not mad about, but she is and has always been very intelligent. The problem is she perpetually has to be at the center of attention. She loves spending two hours every day making herself up and getting ready and choosing what dress she's going to put on, what jewelry she's going to wear.

"Oh, my God, it became an endless process with her—searching for publicity, searching to be at the center of everything. The pattern had already been established with Elizabeth early on in her career, and it never changed. She claims to loathe Hollywood, but she's such a typical product of that town. Like Mae West and Bob Hope, she scrambled for the spotlight, for the brightest glow of neon. She was always late, regardless of the occasion, no matter what the event. She was so self-centered. And she treated Michael so badly. That was a terrible thing. She treated him shabbily from the beginning.

"After Michael and Elizabeth moved in with us, living in sin as it were, she took him to meet Hedda Hopper. Perhaps she thought the mention of Michael's name in Hopper's column would create welcome publicity and afford him the possibility of being offered better American movie roles. Hedda had her own ideas about Michael Wilding and expressed openly in her column and later in a book that he was homosexual. She hadn't amassed the slightest bit of evidence or corroboration to support her inflammatory charge, but that didn't trouble her in the least.

"After the Hopper meeting, they returned home, and Michael related the incident. They were seated in Hedda's living room, and Hopper says to Elizabeth—and this is just before they're planning to be married—'Did you know Mike Wilding's homosexual, Elizabeth?' And Mike's perched there in a chair, of course, saying nothing while Hedda's prattling on about him. What can you say? What can you do?

"Elizabeth sits there and says nothing. She doesn't defend Mike. . . . As he tells me the story, Elizabeth says in a sickening sweet voice, 'Oh, Mikey, don't worry about it.' I can still hear her now. I said, 'Look, you silly bitch, what the fuck are you talking about? Why didn't you say anything?' Elizabeth gaped at me with those vacant violet eyes and the same numb expression I've seen a hundred times in her films.

"I became infuriated. I picked up the telephone and dialed Hedda Hopper. I told that frigging bitch exactly what I thought of her. She never forgave me for it. Next thing I know she dragged me into her Wilding story. We had shared a room during the early days of the London air blitz, so naturally she assumed we were lovers.

"Years later Michael hit her with a three-million-dollar libel suit. I also sued, but I lacked the necessary finances to keep it going. I had also run out of time—statute of limitations, that sort of thing. Michael collected some money, and the scandal didn't help Hopper's reputation. In the end, it worked to Mike's advantage, but it also caused damage. After he moved to Hollywood, Michael's career came to a virtual halt. Part of it had to do with the fact that Michael had epilepsy. The medication he took for his seizures made him slur his speech; nobody understood him when he spoke, and everybody attributed it to his thick British accent, which had nothing to do with it in reality."

While Elizabeth and Wilding were living together in Los Angeles, Marlene Dietrich met Michael's friend Herbert Wilcox for lunch in New York and asked him, "What's Taylor got that I don't?" "Youth," said Wilcox as gently as possible. Marlene turned beet red. Referring to Taylor as "that English tart," Dietrich later told her daughter, Maria Rivas. "It must be those huge breasts of hers—Mike likes them to dangle in his face." It would not be the last time she would lose a suitor to Taylor. Mike Todd, Elizabeth's next husband, dropped Dietrich (and others) for Elizabeth. "That terrible woman again," said Dietrich. "She ruined Michael Wilding's life, and now she's going after Todd. She's positively evil."

Dietrich became only one of many Taylor detractors. "She made enemies easily because she always insisted on being the focus of attention," said Ava Gardner. Irene Mayer Selznick, daughter of L. B. Mayer and the elder sister of Edie Goetz (with whom Taylor always remained amicable), invited Wilding and Elizabeth to a party.

"I didn't admire her as an actress," said Irene Selznick. "I liked her in *National Velvet, Butterfield 8,* and *Who's Afraid of Virginia Woolf?* But that's about it. Notably, in all three, she plays a prototype of herself.

"When I encountered her with Wilding, I sensed the relationship would never last. He seemed too mild and staid for her. Her attraction to Michael could only have been in reaction to Nicky Hilton's recklessness. In a very protective manner Michael would hover around Elizabeth at parties, or, by contrast, she would cleave to him like a puppy dog. I recall seeing them at one Hollywood gala; Liz was shadowing Michael to a point where she practically escorted him to the men's room. Humphrey Bogart took Elizabeth aside and told her how ludicrous she looked chasing after Mike. 'You ought to be more independent,' he chided. 'You're one of the major stars in this town, and you're not even aware of it.'

"Thereafter I saw her only occasionally, once at publisher Bennett Cerf's house in New York after Michael Todd's death. She always seemed rather ordinary to me, cheap-looking in a way, a person who preferred attention and publicity above all. She didn't strike me as an interesting person. She had small, pudgy hands and always wore a garish shade of nail polish—bright red or purple—and her nails appeared embedded somehow in her flesh."

Doris Lilly found herself seated near Elizabeth and Wilding at El Morocco in New York. The two were still in the courting stage. "They had a corner table, and I was seated at a table facing them," said Doris. "I couldn't help but observe them; they were holding hands and rubbing their legs together. Their feet were entwined beneath the table. The waiter brought them a bottle of champagne, and they never uttered a word to each other the entire time they sat there. Instead, they wrote notes back and forth; he would jot something down on a piece of paper and pass it to her; then she would write something in response and pass it to him. This went on for hours, and neither showed any sign of fatigue or boredom.

"I believe Elizabeth was a totally sensuous being. I think she had wildly romantic notions about life, which included her approach to love and her desire to do things differently."

Chapter 10

Because both had remained British subjects, Elizabeth Taylor and Michael Wilding elected to be married in the country of their birth. On February 17, 1952, they flew to London on British Airways and checked into the honeymoon suite at the Berkeley Hotel. On arrival Liz found she had forgotten to bring along the necessary divorce documents from her marriage to Nicky Hilton. Copies had to be wired to London by her attorney.

On the evening of the nuptials, the couple and a handful of friends feasted on broiled lobster, roast duck, and poached salmon at an intimate supper party in the Wilding hotel suite. Then, in a fifteen-minute civil ceremony in the registry of London's Caxton Hall, on February 21, Elizabeth married her second husband, Michael Wilding. Herbert Wilcox and his wife, Anna Neagle, were official witnesses. Elizabeth wore a gray wool suit with a rolled collar and cuffs of white organdy, designed for the occasion by Helen Rose.

Outside Caxton Hall, five thousand nearly hysterical fans had gathered. As the Wildings emerged arm in arm, trailed by a stampeding herd of photographers, somebody in the crowd reached up and ripped the bride's pillbox hat from her head. Two policemen rushed forward and lifted Elizabeth bodily above the crowd and into the limousine that would transport the newlyweds to the reception at Claridge's. "I'm glad I'm still alive," Liz remarked.

Eager to be perceived as a model of English sobriety, Elizabeth demurred when photographers at the reception begged, then cajoled, her to kiss the groom. "I'm too shy," she ventured. The press settled for a light embrace. A second, smaller reception took place at Mike Wilding's maisonette, 2 Bruton Street, Mayfair. The couple finally retired alone to their suite at the Berkeley and dined at midnight on split pea soup, bacon, and eggs, chocolate mousse, and champagne. Four years later, to the day, they celebrated their wedding anniversary by ordering the same meal at Romanoff's in Hollywood.

They took an eight-day honeymoon at a ski chalet high in the Swiss Alps before returning to Wilding's Bruton Street home so he could appear in a film called *Trent's Last Case.* Elizabeth set up housekeeping and for a few weeks, at least, seemed content reading books and writing letters to family and friends. She gave one in-depth interview during this period to David Lewin of the London *Daily Express.* "I never put my career first," she said, adding that she and Michael were eager to have children.

Lewin's initial reaction to Elizabeth was on the whole negative: "She seemed steel-willed and overly dramatic. Mike Wilding, whom I'd known for some years, seemed weak-hearted by comparison. Given the prevailing Hollywood standards of the day, I couldn't imagine Wilding lasting any longer than Nicky Hilton."

By mid-March the Wildings had arrived in Los Angeles in search of a permanent address. While house hunting, they stayed at the Beverly Hills home of Elizabeth's parents, who were vacationing with Howard Young in Westport, Connecticut. One of Michael Wilding's current problems was the considerable tax debt he had accrued over the years in England. To oblige Elizabeth, M-G-M offered Wilding a three-year contract at $3,000 a week (forty weeks per annum guaranteed) with an option of two additional years at $5,000 weekly. The studio further agreed to grant the Wildings a $50,000 loan, repayable over three years, to purchase a new home. The loan couldn't have come at a more propitious time: In April 1952, Elizabeth announced that she and Mike were expecting a baby.

After scrutinizing countless houses in the area, the Wildings settled on a contemporary three-bedroom at 1771 Summitridge Drive, Beverly Hills, high on a bluff overlooking greater Los Angeles. They purchased the dwelling and ordered the exterior painted yellow and white and the interior (including the nursery) gray and periwinkle blue.

They moved into the house in June, the same month Elizabeth began filming *The Girl Who Had Everything.* Directed by Richard Thorpe and produced by Armand Deutsch, the movie was a modernization of the 1931 film *A Free Soul,* which had catapulted Clark Gable to stardom. The story concerned a lawyer's spoiled daughter (played by Elizabeth Taylor in the contemporary version) who falls in love with a slick gangster. (Fernando Lamas costarred opposite Taylor.)

Armand Deutsch's recollection of that time demonstrated his own reservations concerning the picture: "As producers at Metro, we were instructed to look through the studio's voluminous film archives and see if we could find anything suitable for a remake. Under Dore Schary, M-G-M in the early 1950s had established a minimal production quota of as many as forty films a year—thus, the necessity of occasionally recasting and reshooting old films.

"We all hated the process of dusting off tired scripts and ancient scraps of film, but we were under the gun to come up with fiscally workable packages. I was given whatever credit came to me for culling out from the files, which had been scrutinized and pored over countless times, that which could be molded into a conceivably lucrative vehicle.

"The selection process became a boring, arduous task, but the film fell within M-G-M's agenda. Art Cohn, who became a great friend of Mike Todd's and eventually died with him in that terrible airplane crash, had written a passable but not very inspiring screenplay of *The Girl Who Had Everything.* I sent it to Benny Thau, who, with a nod of the head, agreed to read it.

"A few weeks hence he telephoned and said, 'We're sending the script to Elizabeth Taylor.' I responded, 'You're sending *it* to Elizabeth Taylor? Are you out of your mind? She's one of the studio's most valuable assets.' I mean, this particular film bordered on the dismal. I thought they'd get somebody like Gloria DeHaven. When Thau reiterated they were sending the script to Liz Taylor, I again protested. 'Benny, for Christ's sakes, this is insanity. Elizabeth is a great star, and *The Girl Who Had Everything* is a waste of her time and talent.'

"Thau said, 'Well, Elizabeth's pregnant, we think, and we want to get one more picture out of her while she can still work.'

"'Benny,' I observed, 'this is a criminal thing to do. I'm going to tell her not to do the film.' Thau said, 'You do that, Armand, and we'll either put you on suspension or fire you so fast you won't know what hit you. She's not paying you—we are. You're on our side. You work for us.' 'Benny,' I responded, 'you're absolutely right. I work for you. I won't say a word, but I hope she turns you down. It's very poor judgment to waste Elizabeth Taylor like that.' And he said, 'We're not asking your opinion. Giving advice is not your job, anyway.'

"I can't say he was unpleasant during the discussion—just firm. The studio had made a decision, and they stuck to it. To my horror, Elizabeth agreed to make the film. She didn't want to be placed on immediate suspension, which the studio automatically did whenever an actress became pregnant. Liz couldn't have been thrilled by the film. . . . The critics panned the picture, and it failed to draw an audience.

"Years after the fact, I approached Liz at some big do in New York, and I said, 'Elizabeth, have you got the compassion to greet the producer of your worst film, *The Girl Who Had Everything*?' She recognized me and laughed. 'That wasn't my worst film,' she said. 'Metro forced me to do a lot of that kind of crap.' I told her I had aspired to do better films myself, and she suddenly became earnest. 'I needed the dough,' she admitted. 'I had recently married Michael Wilding, and we were flat broke.'"

On August 1, 1952, Elizabeth Taylor, having completed work on *The Girl Who Had Everything,* was placed on studio suspension and given a reduced salary until after the birth of her first child. During Elizabeth's pregnancy, Michael Wilding would amuse himself by painting faces on Liz's distended stomach. At parties she would often shock guests by lifting her maternity blouse to reveal her husband's latest artwork.

The baby was due on January sixteenth, but on January sixth, after a routine checkup, Liz's physician, M. E. Anberg, took X-rays and determined that the umbilical cord had changed position and now threatened to become wrapped around the baby's neck. The doctor informed Elizabeth that a cesarean section had to be performed at once. The operation ensued shortly before midnight at Santa Monica Hospital. At birth, Michael Howard Wilding weighed seven pounds and three ounces; he had a thick crop of black hair and dark blue eyes. "Fortunately," quipped the boy's father, "our son resembles his mother."

By mid-March, Taylor had been restored to full pay and loaned out to Paramount as Vivien Leigh's replacement in *Elephant Walk.* The film's producer, Irving Asher, had intended at first to use Elizabeth in his adaptation of the Robert Standish novel about a love triangle at a Ceylonese tea plantation. When Elizabeth's pregnancy intervened, Asher decided *Elephant Walk* would be a promising showcase for the talents of Laurence Olivier and his then wife, Vivien Leigh. Olivier was still occupied with *The Beggar's Opera,* being filmed in London, but his wife accepted Asher's proposition and immediately flew to Ceylon for a month of work on location. By the time cast and crew reached Paramount Studios in California, Leigh had suffered what her physicians described as "a nervous breakdown."

Asher revived the prospect of hiring his original choice to play the Vivien Leigh role. Elizabeth Taylor and Vivien were proportioned similarly; from afar their height and build bore a distinct resemblance. This meant that much of the costly Ceylon footage could be salvaged; Taylor needed only to perform for the close-ups and dialogue segments.

But not even the pulchritude of Elizabeth Taylor could compensate for *Elephant Walk*'s weak and disjointed script. Nor could the acting of Elizabeth and costars Peter Finch and Dana Andrews (the former plays her screen husband; the latter, her lover) bring this static melodrama to life. Moreover, production problems on the set mounted with Taylor's advent. While posing for postproduction publicity stills, Liz nearly lost sight in her right eye when a minuscule splinter of steel from an overhead wind machine pierced her cornea. Following surgery to remove the shard, baby Michael accidentally poked Liz in the eye; another operation ensued, landing Elizabeth in the hospital for two weeks, during which time she lay blindfolded, immersed in total darkness. Michael Wilding stood guard by her bedside and read poetry to her until the day of her discharge.

Elizabeth's next screen endeavor, *Rhapsody,* another tedious romantic drama, proved equally frustrating. Liz portrayed Louise Durant, a beautiful rich girl in love with a temperamental violinist (played by Vittorio Gassman) and an earnest young pianist (John Ericson). A film critic for the *New York Herald Tribune* wrote: "There is beauty in the picture all right, with Miss Taylor glowing into the camera from every angle . . . but the dramatic pretenses are weak, despite the lofty sentences and handsome manikin poses."

Because of editing difficulties, the release of *Elephant Walk* was delayed, and *Rhapsody* entered the movie theaters first. Film buffs still debate which of the two is the more hackneyed production. But Elizabeth Taylor may not have been carefully considering the merits of the projects. Her willingness, even eagerness, to appear in such dim and paltry films may well have been dictated by financial necessity. Her husband had been offered a slew of third-rate roles by M-G-M, and when he refused to sign a contract to appear in *Latin Lover,* starring Ricardo Montalban, he was placed on suspension.

His disappointment over the situation was augmented by further annoyances, such as his rapidly receding hairline. In public he took to wearing sailor caps and toupees, sometimes both, while lamenting a fact of life. "I look twice Elizabeth's age," he complained to his friend Stewart Granger, to which he added, "And I *feel* four times her age." Another of his grievances related to Elizabeth's unusual attachment to a vast menagerie of pets; Wilding complained she spent "almost as much time with the dogs and cats as she does with me. One of our two Siamese cats even spends nights in our bed."

As their relationship began to deteriorate, the financial situation took an even greater turn for the worse. Elizabeth withdrew increasing sums of money from her bank account, taking out a total of $47,000, which represented 15 percent of the childhood earnings her parents had invested in U.S. savings bonds on her behalf. The money came in handy. During a stopover in New York en route to a European vacation, Elizabeth had more than $17,000 in only partially insured jewelry stolen from her hotel suite. Straightaway she ordered replacements from Bulgari on Fifth Avenue. She wore one of her new acquisitions, a double-strand pearl necklace, to Lindy's, where she sampled three slices of the restaurant's famous cheesecake. She and Wilding attended a small party given in their honor by Merv Griffin, whose guests included Montgomery Clift, Roddy McDowall, Jane Powell, and Eddie Fisher, whom Liz would one day marry.

The Wildings then departed for Europe. Arriving in Copenhagen, Elizabeth contracted influenza, complicated by pericarditis, an inflammation of the outer heart muscle. She recuperated in North Zeeland, encouraged by the domestic efforts of her spouse. Mike Wilding passed his time preparing chicken soup for Elizabeth and spoon-feeding her at night.

When her condition improved, the Wildings journeyed to Madrid, where Elizabeth walked out on a bullfight because it was too bloody. She posed for *Vogue* on the island of Capri in Italy and engaged in her first series of altercations with Wilding because of what she considered his heavy drinking. As he eventually confessed in his autobiography: "I had nothing else to do."

Taylor's next film assignment took her, without Wilding, to M-G-M's studio in London. As the elaborately costumed Lady Patricia in the epic *Beau Brummell,* Liz personified the perfect screen prop—a ravishing beauty whose sole purpose was to lend romantic support to the film's title star, Stewart Granger.

"I remember our first day on the set," said Granger. "There I am, and here comes Elizabeth Taylor. She looked splendid in her usual voluptuous way—big tits, big ass, big violet eyes, and her tiny rosebud mouth. I took one look at those bosoms and said, 'Whoooa!' The camera crew cracked up.

"In the course of making the film, I learned something about Liz. She had this 'I don't give a shit' attitude which I found rather endearing. We had a very pompous Austrian director—naturalized American, of course—named Curtis Bernhardt. Neither Elizabeth nor I, nor anybody else, cared very much for Mr. Bernhardt. Elizabeth showed her disdain by yawning in his face whenever he gave her detailed instructions on how to play a certain scene. She seemed fed up with the whole enterprise, as she, like most of us, had been forced by Metro to perform her role."

Oswald Morris, chief cinematographer for *Beau Brummell,* confirmed Granger's assertions. "Elizabeth Taylor was a very spoiled young lady in those days," he acknowledged. "For years she had been showered with praise regarding her beauty—and, indeed, she bore extremely attractive features. But she let it go to her head. She became difficult to work with. She would roll her eyes or let them wander around the set whenever Curtis Bernhardt gave her instructions. She realized if it came to a showdown between the director and herself, the director would have to go. Bernhardt never had a contract with Metro; rather, he worked on a freelance basis. Sam Zimbalist, the producer of the film, had always been under contract to M-G-M. Elizabeth knew she and the producer could make the director do whatever they wanted.

Her next cinematic endeavor, a movie called *The Last Time I Saw Paris,* turned out only slightly better, although Elizabeth appeared to appreciate the results a bit more. In a 1964 *New York Times* interview, she remarked:

> A rather curiously not-so-good picture, *The Last Time I Saw Paris,* first convinced me I wanted to be an actress instead of yawning my way through parts. [My character] was offbeat with mercurial flashes of instability—more than just glib dialogue.

The film, adapted from F. Scott Fitzgerald's short story "Babylon Revisited," was loosely based on the life of the author, played by Van Johnson, and his wife, Zelda, portrayed by Elizabeth Taylor. Directed by Richard Brooks, the movie also marked the acting debut of Eva Gabor.

"I'll never forget my first scene with Elizabeth," said Gabor. "She wore the most glamorous red chiffon gown. Her hair had been cut shorter than usual, and she looked young and beautiful. Van Johnson and I were driven to the studio together in the same vehicle. I had on the same yellow coat I would wear in my scene with Elizabeth. It happened to be pouring that day; by the time we stepped out of the car and reached the set, both my hair and coat were completely drenched. This could only happen to me—to have my opening scene with the most ravishing girl in the world and to begin by looking like a little wet rabbit."

Dorismae Kerns, handling publicity on the film, described how Elizabeth's hair turned out "shorter than usual" in the film. "I had a short haircut at the time, and Elizabeth wanted me to cut hers the same way. I refused at first. She then picked up a pair of scissors and simply sheared off half her hair. I finished the job. L. B. Mayer became inflamed because the film was half completed and the director had to invent a haircutting scene to explain her new hairstyle."

In early May 1954, shooting came to a close on *The Last Time I Saw Paris.* Later in the month Taylor announced what the Metro brass already knew: She was again pregnant. In lieu of automatic suspension and a pay cut, she agreed to add an extra year to her M-G-M contract.

Elizabeth's decision to extend her contract would eventually have dire results, but for the moment it seemed to be a sage tactical maneuver. The Wildings were now able to embark on a search for a new and larger home to accommodate their growing family. They found what they wanted at 1375 Beverly Estate Drive, the last house along a spiraling road in Benedict Canyon. Actress Kathryn Grayson, likewise house hunting at the time, had seen the place shortly before the Wildings acquired it.

The couple were still decorating their modern dwelling on the date of Elizabeth's twenty-third birthday, February 27, 1955, the same day she gave birth to her second child, Christopher Edward Wilding. Like his brother, Christopher was delivered by cesarean section at Santa Monica Hospital. He had blue eyes and blond hair that soon turned brown.

Visitors who arrived at the Wilding residence not long after the baby's birth were struck by the casual atmosphere. Joan Bennett spent an afternoon and recalled a luncheon served on "mismatched and chipped china. A British nanny tried desperately to put both of Elizabeth's infants to sleep, but neither would stop wailing long enough to doze off. The house smelled like an animal shelter, dog and cat odors permeating every room. They seemingly defecated where- and whenever it suited them. A pet duck had free run of the place and routinely used a dark green living room rug to relieve itself. The cats had scratched up much of the furniture and gnawed through every sheet and blanket in the house.

"Michael Wilding and I sat outside by the swimming pool most of the afternoon. Elizabeth, supposedly resting upstairs, intermittently barked orders at her husband over the intercom: 'Michael, bring me a gin and tonic! Michael, the babies are crying—please check on them, won't you! Bring me this, bring me that!' He obliged, leaping out of his seat whenever she called on him. Finally, I couldn't take it any longer. 'Why don't you just tell her to go fuck herself?' I said. He smiled sheepishly. 'I wish I could,' he responded in a pathetic tone. 'I wish I could.'"

After Christopher Wilding was born, Elizabeth commenced a crash diet to shed the more than thirty-five pounds she had gained during pregnancy. She became so compulsive about her food intake that for several weeks she gave up solids altogether, restricting herself to ice water and fruit juice. The primary reason for this sudden reduction, aside from health and beauty benefits, was Elizabeth's desire to be cast opposite Rock Hudson and James Dean in *Giant,* an epic production that George Stevens had been preparing for Warner Brothers.

Based on the sprawling novel by Edna Ferber (who had been secretly hired to help rewrite the screenplay), the film offered Elizabeth a choice role in the person of Leslie Benedict, a young lady from bluegrass country who marries, relocates to a huge cattle spread in oil-rich Texas, and founds a family dynasty. The part, which covers three decades in a woman's life, had first been promised to Grace Kelly. As Kelly's plans included marriage to Prince Rainier of Monaco (and retirement from the industry), the role remained unfilled. Audrey Hepburn, another notable candidate, was thought "too sophisticated" for the role. "I want somebody with guts," George Stevens, the director and coproducer wrote to fellow coproducer Henry Ginsberg. The latter recommended Marlene Dietrich for the role. "Too Teutonic," Stevens responded.

Rock Hudson, assigned to play Bick Benedict, Elizabeth's husband in the film, became particularly instrumental in casting the part. Taken to lunch by George Stevens, the director posed the question "What do you think of Elizabeth Taylor for the role?" "She sounds fine to me," said Hudson. "I have no objections at all." M-G-M received $175,000 from Warner Brothers for the loan-out of Taylor. Hudson's personal endorsement meant a great deal to Elizabeth. She was determined to become his friend.

On location in Marfa, Texas, a drought-stricken whistle-stop of thirty-six hundred inhabitants, Rock Hudson and Elizabeth Taylor became more than mere friends. In spite of Rock's overriding homosexual tendencies, Phyllis Gates, Hudson's private secretary and wife (a marriage arranged by studio moguls to dispel rumors about Hudson's homosexuality), thought that Rock and Elizabeth had an affair. Although their marriage was short-lived, Gates on occasion visited Rock on the *Giant* set.

In her detailed memoir, *My Husband, Rock Hudson,* Gates comments on the amorous nature of the relationship between Hudson and Taylor and reveals the major source of her information:

> Before I left Hollywood, someone had whispered to me that Rock and Elizabeth were having an affair. Elizabeth's husband, Michael Wilding, had stayed in California, and she

> found herself on a faraway location with two extremely attractive leading men. She seemed intrigued by the quirky charm of James Dean, but his remoteness precluded romance. What about Rock? He devoted much attention to Elizabeth. They were almost childish with each other, talking a kind of baby talk and playing pranks like throwing water at each other. . . . It wouldn't have surprised me if Rock had made a play for Elizabeth, hoping to maintain his balance of power in the *Giant* company.

The opportunity for a sexual encounter between Rock and Liz presented itself partially because of the proximity of their living quarters. Most of the cast and crew had been relegated to in-town living. (Marfa consisted of a twenty-five-room hotel, two small motels, three cafes, two beer halls, one grocery store, a used-car dealership, and an old movie theater, the Palace, which had been boarded up for two years and which George Stevens now used as a screening room for the daily rushes.) The stars—Rock Hudson, James Dean, and Elizabeth Taylor—were accorded modern but humble cottages with cooking facilities. One of Rock and Liz's more inventive cooperative projects had to be what Elizabeth dubbed "the chocolate martini" (vodka mixed with chocolate liqueur). The two companions frequently became inebriated together, on one occasion so drunk Elizabeth kept racing to the *honey wagon* between takes to vomit into the toilet bowl.

Within days word of the purported romance between Taylor and Hudson reached Hollywood. Michael Wilding, at home with the nanny and his two sons, reacted at once to the story. Joseph C. Hamilton, a young desk clerk at the hotel in Marfa, was working the evening shift when a tall gentleman in a bowler and a dark, single-breasted suit came storming through the front entrance of the hotel and up to the marble check-in counter. He had no luggage, but instead carried a French poodle under each arm.

"My name is Michael Wilding," he said. "I've just flown into this place on an army transport from the air corps base in El Paso."

Hamilton regarded the Englishman and said nothing.

"I am Michael Wilding," he reiterated. "I am Elizabeth Taylor's husband, and I would like very much to see her. Do you know where she can be found?"

"Oh, yes, sir," stammered the desk clerk. "I believe she's having dinner with Mr. Hudson in the hotel dining room."

Hamilton pointed, and Wilding stalked off through a lounge leading into a dining room crowded with actors and crew members. Ten minutes later, Wilding reemerged, still clutching the two French poodles, and stomped out of the hotel without another word.

"Shortly after Wilding's departure," said Hamilton, "Chill Wills and Monte Hale, two of the actors, drifted into the main lobby and sat down on a sofa near the front desk. Hale began strumming a guitar, softly singing some folk tunes and western ballads. In Chill's southern drawl, he observed: 'Well, I guess all ain't perfect in Paradise.' Monte Hale giggled just as Liz Taylor and Rock Hudson, who towered above her, emerged from the dining room, laughing heartily. I knew then Taylor and Wilding were headed for a divorce."

Michael Wilding returned to Hollywood and immediately became embroiled in a scandal of his own. Lonely and dispirited, he visited a burlesque house one night, and when the show ended at four in the morning, he invited two of the strippers to his living quarters. The children and their nanny were spending the week in Beverly Hills with Francis and Sara Taylor. Wilding and the strippers partied until dawn, at which point he tipped them each $250 and sent the women on their way. Both made more than twice as much by selling their story to *Confidential.* Elizabeth's response to the published piece became public: "Whether it's true or not, you can't let an article like that break up your marriage." She then telephoned her husband and, according to Alexander Walker, told him: "I can't help it, but I always seem to fall a little in love with my leading man. And I guess I always will."

Wilding's pain could hardly have been assuaged by his wife's explanation. The press, for its part, had cooked up an even more unlikely romance between Elizabeth Taylor and her other leading man, James

Dean, whose performance as the sensitive young lead in *East of Eden* earned him a considerable and faithful following. Fate and talent conspired to mark him as the fastest-rising star among a new generation of actors. Like Rock Hudson, Dean had strong homosexual proclivities but occasionally found himself attracted to and involved with women.

Jeffrey Tanby, an acquaintance of Dean's and a periodic visitor on the *Giant* set, remembered that Rock and Jimmy "weren't exactly on the best of terms. They roomed together for a brief period in the early stages of shooting. According to Jimmy, Rock tried to 'queer' him, and when he resisted, Hudson became embittered and asked him to leave. That's when Hudson took up with Elizabeth Taylor. Rock couldn't make enough negative comments about Dean. He constantly complained to George Stevens that Dean had been given the best lines and close-ups in the film. Stevens abhorred Jimmy, considered him irresponsible and disrespectful, but recognized his undeniable acting ability. As Jett Rink, the impoverished dirt farmer who strikes it rich on oil, Jimmy had the perfect role to upstage Hudson. And that's precisely what he did."

Although Elizabeth Taylor similarly resented Dean's shameless scene-stealing efforts and disregard for other actors' feelings, a strong rapport soon developed between them. Jimmy demonstrated not only a bewildering recklessness but also an unorthodox, at times crude, sense of humor. While crew members, spectators, and fellow actors looked on, Dean once interrupted an outdoor shoot by yelling, "Cut," and then proceeded to unzip his jeans and urinate in full view of the crowd. Elizabeth found such audacious behavior amusing rather than insulting.

As *Giant* continued shooting in Marfa in June 1955, Elizabeth and Jimmy drew closer. Carroll Baker, who played Elizabeth's daughter in the film, observed in her autobiography, *Baby Doll:* "Elizabeth went off mysteriously with Jimmy each evening, and none of us could figure out where they went. They would arrive for dinner together. She would sit in the balcony next to him during the rushes and then they would slip away for what seemed like most of the night."

Years later, on March 11, 1993, when Elizabeth was given the American Film Institute Award for Lifetime Achievement, she informed a live audience of fifteen hundred at the Beverly Hills Hotel that she had "loved" James Dean—whether in the physical or platonic sense, she did not specify. But in Liz's own words in her autobiography, she described the bond as one of friendship: "We had an extraordinary friendship. We would sometimes sit up until three in the morning, and he would tell me about his past, his mother, minister, his loves, and the next day he would just look straight through me as if he'd given away or revealed too much of himself. It would take, after one of these sessions, maybe a couple of days before we'd be back on friendship terms. He was very afraid to give of himself."

Another factor uniting Taylor and Dean was the difficulty they both experienced with the director. At one juncture George Stevens admonished Taylor in public for looking too glamorous. "Until you tone down your veneer, you'll never be an actress," he told her. To compound the problems, Dean remained constantly "high" on drugs, predominantly marijuana and hashish, while Elizabeth had a variety of health problems, including a leg infection, heat exhaustion, and laryngitis, necessitating repeated delays in the shooting schedule. Stevens suspected the female star's ailments were either imagined or contrived.

Before the completion of *Giant,* Elizabeth presented Dean with a kitten; he named it Marcus, after an uncle in Fairmount, Indiana. Taylor later stated: "I think he loved that kitten and was as close to that kitten as anything else in life."

Then disaster struck. On September 30, 1955, several days after wrapping up his role in *Giant,* James Dean was killed in an automobile accident while speeding to a road race in Salinas, California, in his newly purchased Porsche 550 Spyder. He had just turned twenty-four.

Elizabeth Taylor, Rock Hudson, Carroll Baker, George Stevens, and a small group were viewing rushes at Warner Brothers in Burbank when the telephone started to ring. Stevens picked up the receiver and listened. When he finally spoke, he could be heard saying, "No, my God. Are you sure? When?" He hung up the phone and ordered the film stopped and the lights turned on. He grimly regarded those present and spoke: "I've just been given the news that Jimmy Dean has been killed." There was one unified inhalation of breath, and then everybody in the room fell silent.

The set remained closed for the rest of the day. Taylor encountered Stevens in the studio parking lot. "He had it coming to him," Stevens lectured. "He drove like a maniac. He had an obvious death wish."

The twenty-three-year-old actress's eyebrows arched as she stared at the seasoned director. "Go to hell, George," she hissed, turning away and heading for her car.

The day after James Dean's death, a Saturday, Stevens ordered work to recommence on the film. Elizabeth Taylor balked. James P. Knox, a stuntman in *Giant,* recollected that "Stevens seemed unnecessarily harsh on Elizabeth. She appeared highly upset and 'left' her breakfast in her dressing room. Once on the set—they were shooting interiors—she broke down and sobbed. She couldn't stop crying. She became semihysterical. Stevens became infuriated and forced her to complete the scene."

Elizabeth finished the scene but remained in a state of near collapse for three days. She was subsequently hospitalized (October 1–10, 1955) at St. John's for a variety of ailments—infected bladder, intestinal obstruction, lung congestion, leg pains, migraine headaches. Stevens remained convinced that the major cause of Elizabeth's health problems was her reaction to the death of James Dean and that what followed was purely psychosomatic. He tried to conclude the picture by using a double, but when he failed to obtain the desired results, he had to delay the completion of the picture an additional two weeks.

Lester Persky, an associate producer of the 1968 Elizabeth Taylor film *Boom!,* recalled a conversation he once had with Richard Gulley, who handled public relations for *Giant:* "Gulley confirmed that George Stevens nearly went berserk working with Liz on the film. By this stage in her career, she had become a holy terror—spoiled, difficult, completely self-absorbed. No doubt the death of James Dean genuinely affected her—she had related to him in a very motherly fashion. But this represented only one of many events during production that Liz used to her own benefit."

Elizabeth Taylor had begun calling M-G-M "the iron lung—a place where they won't let you breathe." The studio had come up with the score and script for a hackneyed musical version of *Cinderella,* retitling it *The Glass Slipper.* Donning white tights and ballet slippers, Michael Wilding played Prince Charming. He followed this production with an appearance in *The Scarlet Coat,* a military story set in the days of the American Revolution. Not unexpectedly, both pictures flopped at the box office. In January 1956, M-G-M chose not to renew Wilding's contract. By age forty-three, the former British matinee idol had acquired a reputation as a colossal has-been.

On the day Metro terminated Wilding's contract, his wife was in New York with their two sons. They were staying at Montgomery Clift's apartment. Diapers and baby bottles filled the rooms. Liz anguished over the possibility of another divorce and cried, as she had in the past, in Monty's arms. At night he would massage her back for hours and feed her warm milk to calm her brittle nerves.

Bill LeMassena, Monty's friend, claimed Clift "had grown close to Mike Wilding. He admired his casual British charm and gentleness. Elizabeth, however, resented having to support Wilding both financially and psychologically. She told Monty, 'I yearn for a big strong guy to look after me, to buy me lots of jewelry and to pay my bills.'"

In February 1956, Columbia Pictures offered Wilding a supporting role opposite Victor Mature and Anita Ekberg in *Zarak Khan,* an adventure film to be shot in Spain and Morocco. Elizabeth felt the picture might help restore her husband's self-confidence. She encouraged him to accept the part and offered to accompany him on location.

The moment they arrived in Morocco, she began to complain. She found the living conditions unbearable, the heat unrelenting, the food abominable. Wilding had his own set of complaints, beginning with Liz. He accused her of spending a veritable fortune on semiprecious stones and silk caftans, none of which she wore. Instead, he pointed out, she donned only tight sweaters and short skirts without stockings, giving the impression of a "woman on the make," particularly in a country where females habitually draped themselves from head to toe.

Elizabeth perceived Wilding's ongoing commentary as endlessly paternal. "Stop treating me like your daughter and start regarding me as a wife," she railed. Liz's criticism went unheard, and the couple's lack of communication led to public feuds.

By mid-production most of the cast had moved from the original site, an inn in the mountain village of Xavien, into the more capacious and comfortable Dersa Hotel, located forty miles away in the city of Tétouan. The Wildings occupied suite 106. Husky and handsome Victor Mature took a room two doors away. One afternoon, Wilding returned early from the set, entered his suite, and found Mature in bed with Elizabeth. Wilding spent the remainder of the shoot by himself at the inn in Xavien, while Mature and Liz carried on their affair, forever dispelling her oft-repeated avowal that she would never betray a husband.

At the completion of *Zarak,* Wilding turned up in London; Elizabeth returned to the States with her children.

Mike Wilding later rejoined his wife in California, only to discover in the interim she had taken up with none other than Frank Sinatra. The romance, if it can be called that, ended almost before it began. According to the late Jilly Rizzo, one of Sinatra's closest confidants, "Frank and Liz were together only two or three times. He dropped her the moment she brought up marriage, and she apparently brought it up right away. She wanted to be the next Mrs. Frank Sinatra."

Even after the termination of her fling with Sinatra, Elizabeth continued to torture Wilding by constantly playing Frank Sinatra recordings on the hi-fi. When Wilding finally admonished her for "being unbearably indiscreet," she retorted, "Why don't you give me a spanking, Michael? That's what my father would do."

Wilding did nothing. Elizabeth reacted by becoming involved in another affair, this time with an Irish screenwriter-cinematographer, Kevin McClory, who of late had been working as unit director and chief cameraman for Mike Todd's most recent production, *Around the World in 80 Days.*

With his dark hair and blue eyes, McClory cut a dashing figure. A military hero during World War II, he befriended John Huston after the war and joined Huston's film company a few years later. He later signed on with Mike Todd, who, McClory complained, vastly underpaid his employees. McClory also had continual arguments with Todd on how best to produce a film. Both men had powerful personalities.

Recapitulating the details of his liaison with Elizabeth Taylor, McClory would tell Mike Todd Jr., the producer's son, for the latter's 1983 biography of his father (*A Valuable Property*), that they had been seeing quite "a bit of each other. Very, very quietly. The only people who really knew were Shirley MacLaine and Steve Parker, Shirley's husband, because we used to go out to their place in Malibu. . . . We were planning to get married."

When Mike Todd inevitably learned of the courtship, he confronted McClory. "I don't think it's right that you're going out with a married woman," he said angrily. Within weeks, Todd, too, had begun to crave Elizabeth Taylor.

Chapter 11

"I'd like to meet Elizabeth Taylor," Mike Todd informed Kevin McClory. "Why don't you bring her around sometime?" McClory suspected his boss wanted to use Elizabeth's fame to help promote *Around the World in 80 Days,* and he wasn't wrong. Todd, the former carnival barker and street hawker (born Avrom Hirsh Goldenbogen, in 1907, to an indigent immigrant family in Minneapolis), made it a business to seek out supercelebrities to help "boost" his properties, in this instance a production he deemed "the film of the century." (McClory later learned that Todd had in fact already attempted to coax M-G-M into allowing Elizabeth to appear in *Around the World in 80 Days.* As salary, he offered to buy her a new Cadillac limousine. The studio, which demanded cash for its star, declined.)

McClory agreed to make the introductions but pointed out that Taylor was currently working on a new film, *Raintree County,* which he described as "a Yankee rendition of *Gone With the Wind.*" As Todd chomped on one of the twenty Cuban cigars he smoked each day, McClory explained that Liz and her costar, Montgomery Clift, were flying to Kentucky in a few weeks to shoot on location. "I'll invite Elizabeth before she leaves," he promised.

McClory had continued to spend romantic weekends with Taylor at their borrowed Malibu beach house. They spoke freely about the prospect of marriage and made no secret of their affair despite McClory's claims to the contrary. They were spotted together at the film premiere of *Moby Dick* and at almost all of Hollywood's "in" nightspots.

"He's campy," Taylor said of her devoted companion, implying Kevin could be as frank about sex and as libidinous as she.

To his credit, Michael Wilding tried to close his eyes and ears against the din and clatter of Liz's latest extramarital relationship. He confided primarily in Montgomery Clift, who had leased an apartment on Dawn Ridge Road, in the Hollywood Hills, twenty minutes from the Wilding home in Benedict Canyon. After Elizabeth fell asleep at night, Wilding would drive to Clift's apartment to tell his side of the story; Elizabeth presented Monty with hers during their filming at M-G-M of interior scenes for *Raintree County*.

On weekends, in Elizabeth's absence, Clift became surrogate "mother" to her young boys, feeding, bathing, changing, and entertaining them. He would spend his spare hours attempting to console an often inebriated Mike Wilding, who had begun mixing alcohol with habit-forming antidepressants.

When not playing baby-sitter or peacemaker in the Wilding ménage, Monty found himself beset by a deluge of his own problems. His finest cinematic effort to date, *From Here to Eternity,* had done little to bolster his self-confidence. He remained enslaved to the twin curses of drugs and alcohol despite an endless series of sessions with psychiatrists and psychoanalysts.

On May 12, 1956, Elizabeth and Michael Wilding invited Monty to a small dinner party at their home. The other guests that evening were Rock Hudson, Phyllis Gates, and Kevin McCarthy. Clift had passed the afternoon in his apartment, resting and drinking. Wary of becoming more deeply entrenched in Elizabeth's domestic situation, he told her he didn't know whether he could attend. Taylor, as grinding and stubborn as her mother, repeatedly telephoned Monty that afternoon, begging and cajoling him to come. She forced her husband to do likewise. "We need you," Wilding told Monty. "You're an interpreter to two people who no longer speak the same language." At the last moment, having fortified himself with a handful of Seconal, Clift agreed to go.

He passed much of the evening discussing *Raintree County* with Elizabeth; the other guests wandered about making inane conversation. Frank Sinatra records played on the hi-fi, and after supper, Mike Wilding experienced lower back spasms and stretched out on the couch. Monty also felt ill and lay down on the floor.

Kevin McCarthy, who had come to Hollywood to complete a segment for a television series, detailed the remainder of the evening: "I'd rented an automobile, a four-door brown-and-white Chevrolet, and I took myself to Beverly Estates Drive. In those days, Monty and I thought we knew it all, so we both wound up leasing the same-model-and-year car.

"I'd finished my work and had booked an early-morning flight for New York. I didn't want to make a late evening of it. I also happened to be on the wagon and didn't have anything to drink. Monty didn't drink much either that night. He had recently contracted a case of amoebic dysentery while in Mexico, and I know he'd been taking medication for it—and maybe a few other pills on the side. He had a doctor in New Orleans, a tropical-disease specialist, who had been treating him for the amoebic dysentery. On the whole, he appeared in decent shape, although nobody knew for sure because he mainly kept to himself. Later, I heard he had been drinking all afternoon.

"When I first met him in New York, he would mix vodka freely with all sorts of drugs. You would go to his apartment and find countless unmarked bottles of pills scattered everywhere. He became friendly with the fellows at his local drugstore. They would let him wander behind the counter and take whatever pharmaceuticals he wanted. That can happen when you're a star; everyone just looks the other way.

"Anyway, I'd seen him in far worse shape. When I decided to leave the dinner party, Monty drew himself up and announced, 'I'm going, too.' We walked out to the parking lot. Monty expressed concern over Edward Dmytryk, the director of *Raintree County.* One way Monty built a role is that he would continually invent certain gestures, some quirky body movement or facial expression that lent credence to the character he was portraying. But while shooting *Raintree County,* he discovered Dmytryk had been editing out Monty's additions. The director's actions both preoccupied and agitated Monty.

"As we were climbing into our respective vehicles, I asked him which way he was heading. He told me he wanted to go home, and I said I knew a shortcut. I'd become fairly familiar with the canyon roads by this time. I told him to follow me and I would show him how to get there. He started down the hill after me. It was a dangerous road with a lot of hairpin turns. I became somewhat leery—Monty had always been a daredevil, and I thought he might try to bump my fender when I slowed down at a curve. As a result, I accelerated. I kept looking for him in my rearview mirror. At one of the turns, I looked back and saw only a cloud of dust and his headlights shining all over the place.

"I stopped, backed up, and stepped out of the car. There were no occupied homes in the area—they were all under construction. Nor were there any lights on the road. After looking around, I finally spotted Monty's car. It had careened down a hill and wrapped itself around a tree. I descended the hill. The car engine hadn't stopped running, but I knew how to shut off the motor under the hood. I didn't see Monty anywhere.

"I ran back to my car and maneuvered it so the headlights would illuminate the wreck. I started toward Monty's car again. Now I could see his inert form beneath the dashboard. His face—all pulp and gore—had seemingly been crushed by the steering wheel. I couldn't get to him—the car doors had jammed upon impact.

"I didn't know what to do. There were no public telephones from which to place an emergency call. So I retraced my steps and drove back to the Wilding house. I rang the doorbell, and Michael opened the door.

"'Monty's been in a horrible accident,' I yelled. 'We need an ambulance and a doctor.'

"By now, Liz had appeared at the front door. She hadn't missed a word and went off to call both an ambulance and Dr. Rex Kennamer, Monty's West Coast physician, well known in Hollywood as a 'doctor to the stars.' Wilding suggested his wife stay behind, but Liz insisted on coming and raced to my car, while Rock and Phyllis drove off with Mike.

"Elizabeth and I arrived first. She immediately jumped out and made her way toward Monty. By sheer force of will, she somehow managed to open one of the back doors a crack. Slithering in, she crawled over the front seat and positioned herself next to Monty. Cradling his mangled head in her lap, she removed a pink silk scarf from around her neck and used it to stanch the flow of blood. Still alive but unable to breathe adequately, Monty pointed to his throat. His nose had been broken in two or three places and his upper two front teeth had cracked off and become lodged in his windpipe. Knowing instinctively what to do, Liz reached between his blood-splattered lips, placed two fingers down his throat, and yanked out the teeth. [Monty later had one of the teeth mounted on a silver strand, which he gave Elizabeth as a token of his appreciation. She occasionally wore it as a necklace.]

"She behaved very maternally, holding Monty's hand, stroking his brow, whispering soothingly into his ear. Then the press appeared. Like a den of hungry wolves, a pack of photographers swept down the slope, snapping pictures as they approached.

"Liz saw them coming. 'Get those goddamn cameras out of here,' she snarled, blocking Monty's face with her scarf and hands. When the photographers failed to relent, Liz let loose another roar: 'Get the hell away or I'll make certain none of you ever works in Hollywood again!' This time they retreated en masse."

Thirty minutes had elapsed since Elizabeth's arrival on the scene, and still there was no ambulance. Lost amid a labyrinth of canyon roads, the ambulance driver sped aimlessly through the night, his siren echoing off the barren hillsides. Better acquainted with the surroundings, Dr. Rex Kennamer had less difficulty locating the site, and he pulled up first.

"It looked to be a major, serious accident," he recalled. "The car had been totally demolished. Monty had suffered a serious head trauma. He was barely conscious when I arrived. As I peered in at him through the shattered door window, something quite astonishing took place. Monty regained not only his senses but also his good humor. He opened his eyes and recognized me. 'Doctor,' he gasped, 'I'd like you to meet Elizabeth Taylor. Elizabeth, this is Dr. Kennamer.'

"We had never met, but as a result of the accident we gradually grew close. I became Elizabeth Taylor's personal physician for years to come.

"Next the ambulance arrived. The paramedics managed to disentangle Monty from the wreck and strap him onto a stretcher before lifting him up the hill. Phyllis Gates stationed herself in the front of the ambulance, while Elizabeth rode in the rear, clutching Monty's hand all the way to Cedars of Lebanon Hospital."

Taylor stood by at the hospital while a team of surgeons performed a lengthy operation to try and restore the contours and features of Clift's face. According to medical reports, the actor suffered a crushed jaw and sinus cavity, split lip, broken nose, severe concussion, broken teeth, perforated eardrum, four fractured ribs, and acute facial lacerations.

Phyllis Gates subsequently wrote: "Elizabeth [remained] composed until Monty was taken into the operating room. Then she became hysterical, and I comforted her as best I could."

She grew more frantic several days later when the bawdy torch singer Libby Holman flew in from New York. She and Libby, having long vied for Monty's friendship and affection, distrusted one another.

Betsy Wolfe, a registered nurse at Cedars Sinai Hospital in Los Angeles, noted that the ladies began squabbling the moment Holman entered Clift's hospital room.

"What the fuck is *she* doing here?" said Holman, motioning with her head in Taylor's direction.

"Screw off," Taylor rejoined.

According to Betsy Wolfe, "the two nearly came to blows while poor Monty, his face swaddled in bandages, lay helplessly in bed."

Holman blamed Elizabeth for Monty's accident, insisting the actress should not have permitted Clift to drive by himself that night, according to Patricia Bosworth, Monty's biographer. Holman accused Elizabeth of being "sensual and silly—rather like a heifer in heat. There's no telling," said Libby, "where her lust will lead her next."

Aware of Montgomery Clift's erratic behavior and problems with pills, M-G-M production chief Dore Schary had insured the actor for $500,000, an amount far beyond the usual fee for such possibilities, to cover his role in *Raintree County.* A nine-week suspension of the shooting schedule—barely enough time for Monty to heal properly—cost the studio more than twice that sum. The hiatus also put an end to the Wilding-Taylor marriage and gave Mike Todd an opportunity to meet Elizabeth Taylor.

Although Todd had previously seen her at several Hollywood bashes, they had never spoken. Now, with a break in the filming of *Raintree County* and with production of *Around the World* nearing an end, the chance for an encounter arose. It occurred on June 30, 1956, approximately six weeks after Montgomery Clift's crack-up. Mike Todd had chartered a 117-foot motor launch for a weekend cruise to Santa Barbara and had asked some friends to join him, including Hollywood agent Kurt Frings and his wife, Ketti, as well as Kevin McClory, who kept his pledge by bringing along Michael Wilding and Elizabeth Taylor. Also aboard was Todd's then fiancée Evelyn Keyes, a character actress best known for her role as Scarlett O'Hara's younger sister in *Gone With the Wind.* Keyes, a petite blonde with wide blue eyes, had been married three times before, to Barton Bainbridge and to directors King Vidor and John Huston.

"I'm lucky to have known a few interesting men during my lifetime, but Mike Todd existed in a class by himself," claimed Keyes. "He had built-in energy, great drive, and vivacity. He was a dynamo, always running. He required only four hours' sleep a night, and he could sleep anywhere—in a car, on an airplane, in his office. He would remove his shoes, shut his eyes, and he would be asleep. In addition, he enjoyed excellent health. I never knew him to be sick, for even a day. Like a turbine, the man kept going and going. You have to admire men like that—they bowl you over with their power and energy. They steamroll you, and you succumb.

"As with most wheeler-dealer types, Mike Todd possessed an abundance of charm. He never had a formal education, but he did have more savvy and chutzpa than anyone I've ever known—which is one reason he attained success both as a Broadway and motion-picture producer. He remained a total workaholic; he couldn't relax. If he took a vacation, his mind would constantly revolve around business."

Once out on the high seas with Elizabeth Taylor, Todd developed a clever scheme. Kurt Frings, who in time became one of Elizabeth's agents, described the two-day ocean voyage as "a campaign on Mike Todd's part to conquer Miss Taylor. He accomplished his mission by totally ignoring her and by doting on Evelyn Keyes. Elizabeth, who had the entire world at her feet, had to be intrigued by the treatment she received that weekend. Todd hardly looked at her, but then he planned it that way."

Todd showed more interest at several subsequent meetings with Taylor, but never so much that she felt he might be pursuing her. Short and muscular, with deep-set eyes and a protruding chin, Todd had never banked on physical appearance but rather on his drive and charisma to draw women. One evening not long after the boat trip, he hosted a cocktail party at his Beverly Hills home. He and Elizabeth sat back-to-back on a love seat, carrying on conversations with other people. Each time their backs and shoulders touched, Liz felt a mild current of sexual energy run between them. "I was attracted to him, but not overly," she would one day admit to his son.

In mid-July, Todd gave still another party—a poolside barbecue—again inviting the Wildings, who attended. While Elizabeth may not originally have found Todd "overly attractive," she gradually warmed to him. After the barbecue she and Wilding drove home. In the car Elizabeth proclaimed boldly that Todd reminded her of a character out of the *Arabian Nights.* "I admire men who can get anything they want so long as they set their hearts on it," she added.

The next afternoon, Wilding dropped in on Stewart Granger to discuss the previous day's events. He had hoped to receive some sound marital advice from his confrere. They were deeply engaged in conversation when the telephone rang. Granger picked up the receiver. "It's for you," he said, handing it to Wilding. "It's Elizabeth."

Elizabeth Taylor addressed her husband in a somber, businesslike tone. She said she had something to read him, something she wanted him to hear from her rather than see in the press. She then read a formal announcement of their legal separation, at the end of which Wilding said: "Thanks, but I would rather have read it in the newspapers. Then I could have pretended it had to do with two other people."

"The telephone call sent Michael into an even deeper depression," testified Granger. "Here he had given up career and country, only to have Liz drop him like a lead weight. He further realized he would lose his two sons—at that point, he couldn't afford the cost of a drawn-out legal battle. She had the money; therefore, she controlled the terms of the separation and divorce. Consequently, he saw little of his children as the years passed.

"He did a bit of writing after the separation and became an agent at one point. He even did some agenting for Elizabeth—her notion of helping him. After their divorce, he remarried twice, first Susan Nell, formerly a dairy owner's wife, and then one of his old flames, actress Margaret Leighton, with whom he seemed relatively content but not terribly happy. No, Liz cut off his balls. She's a ballbreaker.

"He had been a dear man. Liz never understood him. She gave a recent interview, one of those lengthy accounts of her myriad marriages, in which she said: 'Well, unfortunately, Michael was a weak man.' He wasn't a weak man, you silly ass, he was a gentleman.

"You've got to be a street-tough brute like Michael Todd for her to appreciate that you're a *man*—that's bullshit! I'm cross with her because Michael Wilding was a darling, darling fellow, and he went through hell for her."

On July 19, an M-G-M spokesperson released the formal separation announcement to the press. Mike Wilding had already packed his suitcases and moved into a small, dingy West Hollywood hotel with a ground-floor bar in which he spent most of his waking hours.

While preparing a day later to fly to Kentucky to resume work on *Raintree County,* Elizabeth received a telephone call from Mike Todd. He had something pressing to tell her and urged they meet as soon as possible.

They made an appointment for that afternoon at M-G-M. Todd found her, as she recounted the episode,

> sitting [in Benny Thau's office] with my feet on the table, and came in and picked me up by the arm and without a word dragged me out of the room, down the corridor, shoved me into an elevator, still not speaking, just marching along breaking my arm, and took me into a deserted office. He sort of plunked me on the couch, and he pulled a chair around and started in on a spiel that lasted about half an hour without a stop, saying he loved me and that there was no question about it, we were going to be married. I looked at him the [. . .] way I imagine a rabbit looks at a mongoose. All kinds of things went through my mind. I thought, Oh, well, he's stark raving mad. I've got to get away from this man!

Not knowing what to say, Elizabeth began to talk about her present relationship with Kevin McClory, insisting she and Kevin were "madly in love" and had planned on being wed.

Absorbing these words, said Liz, caused Mike to go "absolutely berserk." He shouted at her, "You are never going to see me again." He rose and vacated the room, slamming the door behind him. Left alone, Taylor broke into tears. Todd's rejection hit her like a fist. It occurred to her that she had lost a potential friend.

Kevin McClory visited Liz at home that evening and listened patiently while she told him of Mike Todd's impetuous marriage proposal. She appeared to Kevin to be unusually shaken. "I've lost a friend," she kept saying. "I've lost a friend."

"You've only just met him," insisted McClory. "He's not a friend; you don't know him. He's just someone I work for. That's who he is. . . . You've not lost a friend."

McClory felt Liz was being unnecessarily dramatic. He urged her to "forget Todd." He, Kevin, loved her, and they would marry the instant her divorce from Wilding became official.

As soon as Elizabeth arrived in Danville, Kentucky, to resume her *Raintree County* role as Susanna Drake (a semideranged New Orleans belle), she received a telegram from Mike Todd. The wire—which read simply: "I love you"—came with two presents, an emerald bracelet from Cartier and a magnificent bouquet of exotic flowers. Todd, she soon realized, was as taken with her as she with him.

"Mike's courtship was like being hit by a tornado," Liz avowed.

> It swept you up and carried you away. I was on location in Kentucky, making *Raintree County*, and somehow he found out where I'd be almost every minute of the day. He'd [call] at all hours, and at night we had long conversations. Then presents would arrive, and huge bundles of flowers. I like presents. I like pleasant surprises—we have our share of unpleasant surprises. But with Mike it was one pleasant surprise after another. His tenderness, his consideration, his enormous sensitivity—that came as a surprise. . . . He was full of energy and vitality and at the same time was a gentleman.

How sensitive and gentlemanly Mike Todd might have been depended largely on the other person involved. The first Mrs. Todd, the former Bertha Freshman, the mother of Mike Jr., died in 1947 as the result of a self-inflicted stab wound incurred while chasing her husband around the house with a steak knife. According to Earl Wilson, their nearly twenty-year marriage teemed with violence, but no less so than Todd's second marriage, a three-year alliance with actress Joan Blondell. Wilson claimed Todd borrowed $3 million from Blondell and never repaid her, driving the actress into personal bankruptcy.

"Todd and Blondell were staying at the Waldorf-Astoria during a trip to New York," said Wilson. "I met them there to do an interview for a magazine article. During our meeting, they became embroiled in a loud altercation. Without warning, Mike grabbed her by the scruff of the neck and forced her toward an open window. He began pushing her out the window, sixteen floors above street level. He let her dangle out the window, holding her upside down by the ankles for a minute or two before pulling her back into the room. He then turned on me. 'Write one word about this,' he warned, 'and I'll break every bone in your body.' I had every reason to believe him."

Although she tended to admire Todd, Evelyn Keyes similarly had cause for complaint and ultimately came to regard him in a more critical vein:

"When Elizabeth Taylor arrived on the scene, Mike tried to get me out of the way. He didn't say anything. Instead, he asked me to go to Mexico with Kevin McClory to scout additional shooting sites for *Around the World in 80 Days.* In this manner he managed to usher us both out of the picture. From Mexico he sent me to South America. In the interim, he courted Elizabeth.

"When I grasped what had developed, I was disappointed—not because he dropped me but because he'd been dishonest. He could have been more forthcoming.

"I think his evasiveness regarding Elizabeth resulted from his not wanting to hurt me. In the long run, his cowardice injured me much more. He behaved like a shit despite the fact I had provided some of my own savings to fund *Around the World,* for which Mike rewarded me with five percent of the company. He put it all in writing. Although the film became a huge success, nobody wanted to make good on the debt after Mike's death. I sued his estate and won.

"People sometimes ask whether I think Mike Todd or Richard Burton became the love of Elizabeth's life. Most of us know that Elizabeth Taylor is the love of Elizabeth Taylor's life."

Kevin McClory—summarily dumped by Elizabeth the moment Todd started seeing her—would probably concur with Evelyn Keyes.

Being caught up in the Hollywood rat race, McClory realized that in the love lives of movie stars the notion of romance was more germane than that of marriage. In Tinseltown, nobody stayed married. There were exceptions, such as Gregory and Veronique Peck, but permanent couplings of this sort were indeed rare.

Elizabeth Taylor loved romance, just as Mike Todd adored excitement. His nonstop telephone calls to her on the set of *Raintree County* intrigued her. Meanwhile, Elizabeth toiled diligently to keep up Monty Clift's spirits. The doctors had mended his visage but not his psyche; Monty's dependence on drugs and alcohol increased. "When he wasn't drunk or under the influence of dope and drugs, he could be a wonderful actor and person," said director Edward Dmytryk. "But whenever he turned to alcohol and pharmaceuticals, he tended to go out of control."

One evening the local police arrested the actor for "indecent exposure." Monty had removed his clothes and strolled nude down the streets of Danville. A search of his hotel room turned up more than 250 vials of assorted drugs and medications. "He suffered a great deal of physical pain after the accident," Dmytryk pointed out. "His jaw had been wired in three places and became a major source of irritation. He couldn't eat properly; he lost weight and continued to shed pounds during the entire making of the film. His increasing discomfort prompted his drug abuse and drinking; the alcohol made his eyes and face grow puffy. The same phenomenon happened to Richard Burton, Elizabeth Taylor's future husband. You could always tell by looking into Burton's eyes whether he had embarked on another bender.

"As for Elizabeth Taylor, she helped to keep Monty on track. On occasion, when drugged or inebriated, he would forget his lines; we would turn to Dore Schary for advice. Schary would fly out to meet with Clift. Dore understood that Liz was the only member of the cast who could adequately control Monty, and he implored her to keep an eye on Clift."

✦ ✦ ✦

The effect of having constantly to look after Montgomery Clift eventually took its toll on Elizabeth Taylor. Toward completion of *Raintree County,* the entire company flew from Kentucky to Natchez, Mississippi, to shoot several climactic scenes. Gwin Tate, an acquaintance of Elizabeth's and a native of Natchez, recalled two strange events that took place in his hometown:

"A friend of mine, the widow of a district judge from Natchez, drove to the airport to meet Elizabeth's plane. Hundreds of spectators went to greet the celluloid princess. My friend revealed that Elizabeth apparently had so much to drink aboard the flight that she had to be carried off the airliner into a waiting limousine. Her feet never touched the ground.

"People were still buzzing about the airport episode when a second story began to circulate. Elizabeth had again become drunk and had been seen running barefoot with Montgomery Clift, equally intoxicated, through downtown Natchez." The pair were said to have ended their adventure with a leap into a public fountain.

Having arrived in Danville, Elizabeth discovered two new presents from Mike Todd—a bouquet of two hundred long-stemmed roses and a $30,000 black pearl ring—with an attached note assuring her that she would soon receive her engagement ring.* Two days later, Todd arrived in a private twin-engine aircraft and whisked Liz off to Chicago for lunch and a whirlwind tour of the town he had known as a young boy whose family had moved there from Minneapolis.

During their brief stay in the Windy City, Todd spent thousands of dollars on gifts, and Liz squealed with delight at each acquisition. She howled with laughter when, because of her jet-black hair, he referred to her as "Lizzie Schwarzkopf" in front of reporters and gave her an irreverent slap on her well-padded rump.

Edward Dmytryk observed that Mike Todd's name cropped up

*Despite Taylor's growing attraction to Todd, she had developed a strong sexual interest in Lee Marvin, who had been given a minor supporting role in *Raintree County.* According to Terry Moore, a good friend of Lee's, Elizabeth approached the actor on the set one day and said, "I hope you don't consider me too forward, but I'd like to go to bed with you." Marvin thanked her for the offer but promptly declined.

increasingly in conversation with Taylor. "She had obviously fallen for him," reminisced the director. Montgomery Clift became the only member in Liz's intimate circle of friends who expressed misgivings about Todd. Monty attempted to convince her that the producer was "utilizing" her for publicity purposes, just as he had used other actresses before. He accused her of suffering from "a father complex"—the men she chose as lovers were usually two decades her senior. Monty's bluntness offended her and resulted in a temporary rift. In the course of her marriage to Todd, Elizabeth would see little of Monty (just as she had seen little of him during her marriage to Nicky Hilton).

In early October, Todd spent a weekend with Liz in Atlantic City. A week later, they checked into the Hotel Pierre in New York. He slipped the 29.4-carat diamond engagement ring (worn previously by Evelyn Keyes) on her finger. An impromptu press conference in the hotel lobby netted several quotable statements, including Todd's claim that the bauble, measuring an inch across, had cost "in excess of $200,000." When first given to Evelyn Keyes, the same ring had been appraised by an insurance company and said to be worth "in the neighborhood of $50,000."

Although the press practically camped out in front of the Pierre, they were allotted few interview opportunities. Mike and Liz rarely left their suite. They ordered food and beverages from room service, magnums of champagne at all hours of the day and night. They snuck out one afternoon for a stroll through Central Park, visiting the zoo and the Metropolitan Museum of Art, but when crowds began to gather, they returned to their hotel. Their first bona fide "public appearance" took place in mid-October, when Elizabeth accompanied Todd to the New York opening of *Around the World in 80 Days,* which won the Academy Award for Best Picture of the Year.

There remained little question as to Taylor's future plans. She issued the same announcement she had made on two similar occasions, merely substituting the name of the future husband in the by-now-familiar declaration "I am far more interested in being Mrs. Michael Todd than in being an actress."

On November 14, Elizabeth filed divorce papers against Michael Wilding in Santa Monica Superior Court, waiving alimony but demanding $250 a month for partial support of their two sons. She also requested—and received—full custody of the children.

To escape a barrage of media coverage, Michael Wilding departed on a well-deserved vacation to his native England. When news broke of Liz's impending marriage to Todd, a British journalist located Wilding at a small inn outside London. Refusing commentary at first, the English actor shortly blurted out a terse summation, the last resentful swipe he would ever take at Taylor: "I wish them well. I hope Elizabeth finds in Todd a certain peace and happiness she never found with me. She should—they're two of a kind."

Chapter 12

Michael Todd was far more than a producer of plays and films. He had been a showman, an impresario, a promoter, a public relations expert, and an inventor. He had earned millions of dollars and lost his fortune as quickly as he had made it. Whether solvent or not, Todd had grown accustomed to a lifestyle that invariably exceeded his funds, sustaining himself and his multitude of ventures by virtue of credit, bank loans, and promissory notes. In addition, he had been a ladies' man with a considerable assemblage of followers. His conquests included Marlene Dietrich, Gypsy Rose Lee, and Marilyn Monroe, whom he had persuaded to ride seminude atop a jumbo elephant around Madison Square Garden to promote the Ringling Brothers circus—the circus owners were so piqued by the exhibition that they threatened to sue. Lawsuits, civil litigation, and bankruptcy court peppered Todd's career. The consummate con man, he survived (even thrived) by skirting the edge. As Elizabeth Taylor once concluded, "Nothing frightened Mike, not even fear."

Todd had come of age in an Orthodox Jewish household, so impoverished that the family had been forced on occasion to forage garbage cans in search of food. Todd vowed during adolescence he would one day be both rich and famous; he would also endeavor to associate predominantly with people of similar accomplishment.

At the beginning of November 1956, Lord Beaverbrook, the British industrialist and press magnate, asked Mike Todd and Elizabeth Taylor to join him at his newly acquired home in the Bahamas. Todd gratefully accepted. Beaverbrook possessed the kind of credentials the producer admired. As a housewarming gift, Mike and Elizabeth presented their host with a tape recorder. Todd also provided a tape, which Beaverbrook played while alone in his bedroom that evening. It turned out to be a recording of Mike and Liz making love, thirty minutes of fervid moaning and groaning. The next morning, Beaverbrook complained to his private secretary, Josephine Rosenberg, that the couple had deliberately planned the tape: "They did it to heat me up for the night." (Unbeknownst to Elizabeth, Todd made an entire series of tape recordings of their lovemaking sessions and frequently presented the tapes as mementos to friends and business associates.)

Todd and Taylor returned to Miami aboard Lord Beaverbrook's yacht. En route they encountered stormy weather and rough seas. Elizabeth lost her footing while on deck one morning and landed flat on her back. At first unable to move, she had to be carried to her stateroom and helped into bed. It was this unfortunate fall—and not the fictitious stumble during the filming of *National Velvet*—which brought on Liz's chronic back problems.

From a Miami hospital Taylor had to be transferred by private aircraft to the Harkness Pavilion at Columbia-Presbyterian Hospital in New York. Tests revealed that Elizabeth had ruptured two spinal discs and impacted a third; all three had to be removed and replaced with human discs supplied by the hospital's bone bank, reinforced with connective tissue taken from the patient's hip and pelvis. The complex surgical procedure proved only partially successful. Experiencing severe pain, Elizabeth spent weeks convalescing. Her body had to be rotated by nurses every twenty minutes to ensure proper blood circulation.

Todd did his utmost to keep Elizabeth preoccupied. He had her meals imported from New York's finest restaurants. He transformed her antiseptic hospital room into a miniature art museum by acquiring a Pissarro, a Renoir, and a Monet from Elizabeth's relation Howard

Young.* In typical Todd fashion, he neglected to pay Young for the paintings, and the art dealer subsequently threatened to sue Todd's estate for the money. Todd also bought Liz a customized Rolls-Royce Silver Cloud, to be delivered to Hollywood from a showroom in London. The automobile cost him nearly $100,000.

Following her release from the Harkness Pavilion, Elizabeth flew to Los Angeles, stopping briefly in Reno, where Todd joined her. Screenwriter-director Phillip Dunne, who had first been introduced to Elizabeth during her marriage to Michael Wilding, saw Todd and Taylor gambling at Harrah's.

"They had stationed themselves at the roulette wheel," said Dunne, "and Todd dispensed thousand-dollar chips as if they were quarters. A host of thug types in the casino kept their eyes glued on Todd. Elizabeth Taylor was by far the best-looking woman there. Her husband exhibited her like a showpiece.

"I can't say her conversation ever impressed me; she never demonstrated a sparkling wit or soaring intelligence. Yet she didn't give the impression of being cheap or second-rate. Ultimately, aside from her appearance, she seemed rather ordinary."

Following the couple's return to California, Liz and her two sons vacated their Benedict Canyon home and moved in with Todd. She placed the Canyon residence on the market. Actress Ingrid Bergman and her teenage daughter, Pia Lindstrom, made an appointment with Taylor to view the house.

"Elizabeth gave us the royal tour but behaved strangely," noted Pia. " 'This is the living room,' Liz began. When we entered the living room, our guide vanished. She had already entered the next room. 'And this is the master bedroom,' she announced. By the time we reached it, she had moved on. 'Now where did she go?' my mother puzzled. The three of us were never in the same place at the same time. It became a game of hide-and-seek. I had the impression Elizabeth felt intimidated by my mother, who had long established herself as an esteemed actress."

*The paintings became part of Elizabeth Taylor's private collection, today one of the more valuable personal holdings of Impressionists in the United States.

Another parent-child team, Michael Anderson (director of *Around the World in 80 Days*) and his son David, dined with Mike and Liz at Chasen's. "We had gathered," confirmed David Anderson, "to discuss Todd's latest film idea, *Don Quixote,* for which a script remained to be written. Todd indulged in his usual loquaciousness, recounting youthful days when he would sit in the back of a truck with a machine gun running whiskey across the border from Canada to Chicago during Prohibition. He related dozens of anecdotes spotlighting himself, then tossed in several of his favorite axioms, such as, 'Anyone who says it can't be done is lying.'

"Mike Todd was as narcissistic and demanding as Elizabeth, maybe more so. He was an absolute control freak and tyrant who felt women enjoyed being mistreated. He had a volatile temper; I heard he used to manhandle Elizabeth, and on one occasion he knocked her unconscious."

The Taylor-Todd brawls became the talk of Hollywood. Eddie Fisher, Todd's friend and protégé, recalled a dinner he and his then wife Debbie Reynolds gave for Mike and Liz. They had finished eating and were sitting in the den when Mike and Liz began to argue. "All of a sudden," said Fisher, "Mike leaned toward Elizabeth and whacked her, knocking her to the floor. He really belted her! Elizabeth screamed, walloped him right back, and from there they flew into a ferocious battle. Mike dragged her by the hair, while she was kicking and scratching him, across the dining-room floor into the foyer. Debbie became alarmed and went running after them; she jumped on Mike's back to try and pull him off Elizabeth. Suddenly, Mike and Liz turned on Debbie.

"'Hey, goddammit, knock it off, will you?' Mike screamed at her.

"'Oh, Debbie,' Elizabeth added, getting to her feet, her hair wild and her dress rumpled. 'Don't be such a Girl Scout. Really, Debbie, you're so square.'

"What Debbie didn't realize was that not only did Mike and Elizabeth have a volatile relationship, but also they regarded the fighting as foreplay; they loved having a huge fracas as prelude to a heavenly roll in the hay."

According to Debbie Reynolds, whose autobiography, *Debbie Reynolds,* also details the fight, "Mike Todd was the kind of guy who would say anything—and I mean anything. It wasn't unlike him to look across the dinner table and say to Elizabeth, 'I'd like to fuck you as soon as I finish this.'"

For the benefit of the press, Mike Todd, by his own account "a hardened critic," described his famous future wife as a person who has "a bit of the pioneer spirit to her. I have often seen her pour her own champagne for breakfast."

The more Todd derided her in public, the more devoted she seemed to become. Given the nature of her previous romances, an assumption can be made: Elizabeth Taylor enjoyed a sadomasochistic relationship with Mike Todd; Todd fulfilled the role of sadist. Their partnership reversed for Elizabeth her former pattern with Wilding; with him she had occupied the dominant spot.

Todd's skill in manipulating Taylor had much to do with his innate ability to gauge the latest turn in her ever-changing mood swings. "She's like a child," he confided to intimates, "a beautiful child who has never known happiness—not in her two earlier, unsuccessful marriages—and has been afflicted with all kinds of medical problems. I'm going to make that dame happy if it kills me."

The opportunity represented Mike's fairy tale come true: A lonely, ravishing, doleful princess would fall into the arms of a brilliant, powerful prince. As Todd put it, "The casting was right. So was the timing."

The Todd-Taylor nuptials took place on February 2, 1957, in Acapulco, Mexico, following by only two days Elizabeth and Michael Wilding's divorce. Having become pregnant by Todd two months earlier, Elizabeth had wanted a quick Mexican divorce from Wilding. By appealing to his sense of dignity, Todd had been able to convince the actor. After all, how would it look for Elizabeth to give birth to Todd's child while married to another man? The effect on her career could have been devastating. To help Wilding with his decision, according to Stewart Granger, Todd offered him $200,000, and Elizabeth agreed to give him the total proceeds from the sale of their home in Benedict Canyon.

Two hundred thousand dollars was more appealing to the impoverished Michael Wilding than the prospect of trying to resuscitate a dead marriage. Wilding flew to Acapulco to facilitate the divorce and departed Mexico the day before the wedding. A last-minute guest list included Elizabeth's parents, Mike Todd's son and older brother (a Los Angeles cabdriver), Eddie Fisher and Debbie Reynolds (who, respectively, served as best man and matron of honor), Helen Rose (who designed a deep blue cocktail-length wedding dress for the bride), and Cantinflas (Mexico's popular screen comic who had appeared as David Niven's valet in *Around the World in 80 Days*).

Hedda Hopper, in a column that ran the day of the wedding, advised caution. Miss Taylor, she wrote, should take stock of her life before embarking on another marriage—her third in five years—which could once again end unhappily. Liz's multitude of fans, the columnist continued, were concerned with her state of mind and well-being.

In response, Elizabeth told Hollywood scribe Joe Hyams: "I don't care what people think about me as long as I have my children, my new husband, and my friends. I can't worry about fifty million other people. I don't subscribe to that 'You owe it to your public' jazz. What do I owe to my public? Do I owe my life to them? No. I owe exactly what they see on the screen, and if they don't like it, they don't have to pay to watch me act."

Considering Todd's penchant for "extravagant productions," the wedding ceremony seemed relatively simple, though not without its accordant charms. Held at the hillside villa of former Mexican president Miguel Alemán, the civil rites were conducted in Spanish by the mayor of Acapulco and were followed by an outdoor reception. Illuminated by dozens of flaming kerosene torches, a local Mexican Indian tribe performed festive dances while guests quaffed champagne and feasted on caviar, oversized prawns, lobster tails, and spit-roasted pig. A group of wandering musicians in traditional Mexican costumes played and sang. A fireworks display (Cantinflas's wedding gift) represented the blazing finale: An amalgam of red, yellow, and orange rockets spelled out the initials "MT" (Mike Todd) and "ETT" (Elizabeth Taylor Todd) in the heavens.

When the embers fizzled and plummeted to earth, Elizabeth became suddenly terrified. "Mike . . . Mike . . . don't leave me," she sobbed. Todd rushed to embrace her. Several years after Todd's death, she explained the outcry. The sight of the initials plunging to the ground had aroused in her "a fleeting premonition of tragedy."

Prior to their marriage, Elizabeth had expressed a desire to convert to Judaism, Todd's religion. "She's the original Jewish mother of all time," her husband had said of her. A conversion, with all the publicity (not necessarily positive) it would engender, didn't appeal to him. "Forget it," he told her. "You're Jewish enough for me." Liz acquiesced, but when she later married Eddie Fisher, she made her conversion—in memory of Mike Todd.

In his lifetime, Todd appeared more intent on indoctrinating his wife to a life of wanton acquisition. "Mike Todd could never hold on to money," Evelyn Keyes had said of him. "It burned holes in his pockets."

Before leaving on their honeymoon, he gave Elizabeth a smorgasbord of presents, ranging from a $350,000 pair of double-tier pendant ruby-and-diamond earrings and matching bracelet to her own movie theater in downtown Chicago, which added considerably to her annual income.

The day after their wedding, Todd hired the entire troupe of the Ballets Africains from an Acapulco nightclub and had them perform in the privacy of their borrowed hillside villa.

Two days after their wedding, Hedda Hopper again featured the newlyweds in her column, this time admonishing Todd "not to spoil Liz. She's impossible enough already." But Todd had early intuited that the way to Elizabeth's heart was—in Eddie Fisher's words—"through her vanity." He continued to pamper her privately with gifts and compliments while treating her with shocking disdain and savagery in public.

Ernesto Baer, a New York City businessman, sat opposite the Todds at a luncheon in Manhattan given by one of Todd's more generous financial backers. "The Todds had recently been married," recollected Baer, "and were obviously in love, so much so that at one point during the meal, Todd simply reached over and plunged his hand down the front of Liz's dress. She didn't bat an eye as he began to fondle first one ample breast and then the other."

Todd's bravado and lust for life soon rubbed off on Elizabeth. He took her to Pratesi in Beverly Hills, and she invested thousands of her own dollars in custom-made towels and sheets. According to Brian Sullivan, manager of the store, she ordered bedding to match her lingerie, the shades and material of which varied with each new husband. Todd purportedly preferred Elizabeth in sheer black silk.

Mike's perpetual motion led to Elizabeth's conclusion that she had married "a roulette wheel." Her assessment was shared. Henry Woodbridge, former vice president of the American Optics Company in Rochester, New York, became acquainted with Todd in 1955 when the film producer visited the firm to discuss a wide-screen cinematic technique he wanted them to help him develop.

"Todd had phrased his request rather oddly," remarked Woodbridge. "He said, 'I want to get Cinerama out of one hole, one projector. The present wide-screen systems are far too costly and complex. They'll put the studios out of business.'

"At first we were reluctant to work with him because he had a bad track record. An investigation revealed he'd been involved in several criminal bankruptcy proceedings. But his enthusiasm and self-confidence convinced us to support the project, which became known as Todd A-O, a precursor to many of the wide-screen systems in use today. We were encouraged to form a partnership by virtue of the fact he'd brought along a cashier's check for $100,000, which he promptly removed from his wallet and handed over to us. 'Here's my first contribution,' he chimed. It was difficult to resist such flamboyance.

"I became president of Todd A-O and consequently saw a good deal of Mike Todd, who struck me in many ways as a most remarkable man. Whether you liked him personally or not, you had to be impressed with his imagination and guts. On the other hand, there was something amoral about him and more than a trifle crass. He drove an awesome white Cadillac convertible with a black leather interior, wore gold rings and loud Hawaiian shirts. Conversely, he knew, too, the leading tailors and couturiers of Europe, the choice four-star restaurants of France, the greatest hotels in the world. The man had many sides to his character, many facets, many shadings.

"He and Elizabeth were forever surrounded by an entourage, including people like Eddie Fisher and Sidney Guilaroff, the celebrated M-G-M hairstylist, who became an Elizabeth Taylor confidant. There were Howard Taylor [Liz's brother] and his wife, Mara Regan Taylor, both of whom depended financially on Liz. Dick Hanley, at one time an assistant to Louis B. Mayer, now worked for Mike Todd; after Mike's death Dick stayed on as Elizabeth's personal assistant. He and Liz constantly entertained each other by recounting unflattering stories about Mayer, for whom they shared a common aversion. Todd also maintained in his employment Midori Tsuji, an attractive, young Japanese woman who had spent several years in an American internment center during World War II.

"During the months I knew Mike Todd, I only met Elizabeth once. The encounter took place at the Hotel Westbury, where I used to stay in New York when visiting Todd. Their apartment at 715 Park Avenue happened to be nearby.

"Todd came to my hotel one morning to talk to me over breakfast. His wife accompanied him. She wore no makeup and looked like she'd just crawled out of bed. I had never previously understood the great fuss people made about her physical beauty. But without being glamorous that morning, she managed to look splendid. I couldn't take my eyes off her. I realized her value to Todd as an attention getter and as an invaluable commercial asset.

"Marrying Elizabeth Taylor could only have elevated Todd's Dun and Bradstreet rating. Remember, Liz remained far better known to the general public than Mike. It had to buoy his ego considerably to be her husband.

"I never actually knew her, but from everything I'd read and heard she would appear to be somebody who enjoyed making love. I have a hunch that Mike particularly pleased her. I'm convinced they enjoyed a strong mutual attraction."

About to embark on a European honeymoon and publicity tour for *Around the World in 80 Days,* the Todds dropped in on Bill Paley at his Long Island estate. Paley, founder and president of CBS, had previously invested company assets in *Around the World,* funds that enabled Todd to complete production of the picture. He and Paley ultimately developed a close working relationship, visiting each other on frequent occasions.

In attendance at the Paley residence that day was Jeanne Murray Vanderbilt, who had known Todd since her previous marriage to Alfred Gwynn Vanderbilt. "Mike seemed like a guy on the make," said Jeanne. "He went after women, money, status, anything that would enhance either his bankroll or his social standing.

"I was staying at Bill's for the weekend, and Elizabeth and Mike drove out for lunch. I can remember Elizabeth playing backgammon with Bill at a table in the corner of the room. It was just before lunch, and they were engaged in the game when Bill spotted the twenty-nine-carat diamond ring Todd had given her. It was the biggest stone either of us had ever seen, and Bill couldn't resist saying something like 'It's so big and vulgar.' He put it in a jocular tone so as not to offend. Elizabeth threw her head back and let out a raucous laugh."

Late in March 1957, M-G-M announced that Elizabeth Taylor had become pregnant with her third child. The due date fell at the end of the year. Meanwhile, she and Todd were honeymooning abroad, attending the Cannes Film Festival for the European premier of *Around the World.* Todd continued to deride Elizabeth in public, intentionally trying to embarrass her. "Come on, fatty—move that big ass!" he jeered at her as they exited their limousine in front of the motion-picture exposition center in Cannes.

They turned up in Barcelona, Spain, and spent a day at the beach surrounded by a throng of onlookers. José María Bayona, a popular

Spanish journalist, interviewed them. "I recall thinking Elizabeth quite attractive," he remarked, "although she looked poorly in her bathing suit. Mike Todd, an utterly unattractive character, was short, stout, with homely features. He didn't come off as being particularly nice to Elizabeth, yet she seemed to take pleasure in the torment. I suppose most of the men in her life tended to fawn over her."

The couple flew to Athens, Greece, then back to the French Riviera and on to Paris, where they had reserved the honeymoon suite at the Hotel Ritz, overlooking the Place Vendôme. As with every other country they visited, Todd had timed their arrival to coincide with the inaugural screening of his big-budget film.

Among the couturiers Elizabeth frequented during their Paris stopover were Balenciaga, Yves St. Laurent, Givenchy, and Marc Bohan of Christian Dior, who became her favorite and with whom she remained associated for decades.

"Elizabeth never had the ideal mannequin figure," declared Bohan, "but she possessed a fabulous face and shattering eyes. She was animated, attractive, seductive. She came to Dior the first time with Mike Todd to acquire a gown for the Paris opening of *Around the World.* We gave her our top dresser, Simone Noir, and we fashioned an elaborate ruby-colored chiffon dress for Elizabeth, which she wore with ruby earrings and matching diadem. Liz preferred solids—violet shades and pastels—because they best brought out the color of her eyes. She similarly favored décolleté dresses, with tightly cinched belts around the waist, as well as short dresses. She knew the effect she wanted to create.

"I often went to London or Rome for a fitting, or we would dispatch Simone Noir and a fitter named Monique, who had a great affinity for Elizabeth. We would go to her hotel suite, or occasionally, when in Paris, Elizabeth would see me in my office at Dior on Avenue Montaigne. Unlike other affluent clients, Liz rarely pulled rank on us. To the contrary, she was cordial, polite, easy to please. She never insisted, for example, that we reserve a particular model exclusively for her. On the other hand, she refused to attend the fashion shows at Dior, preferring to deal with us privately.

"If she demonstrated one negative quality, it had to be her acquisitiveness; she adored receiving presents. Over the years, she purchased a hundred separate outfits from Dior, but whenever she bought anything, she expected an accompanying gift. When she entered my office, she always looked over the accessories and would exclaim how much she adored a certain belt, scarf, or chapeau. I would then offer her the items, and she would beam like a little girl who had just received a new doll. 'I love presents,' she exclaimed every time I extended a gift. Our tacit understanding became that each time she purchased an outfit at Dior, she would acquire the accessories without charge."

Elizabeth's taste in clothes didn't appeal to everyone. Hebe Dorsey, a fashion writer living in London, thought "Elizabeth Taylor looked dreadful in Christian Dior. She resembled a call girl attempting to impersonate a princess. Nothing seemed to fit her right." Diana Vreeland, the American fashion arbiter, found Taylor "the worst-dressed American actress since Mae West, whose career had been constructed around skin-tight sweaters and see-through nightgowns. ET lacks taste, which you either have or you don't."

James Galanos, a Los Angeles-based fashion designer whose clothes Elizabeth wore in later years, described Elizabeth's propensity for *la mode:* "Elizabeth has always looked spectacular in her jewelry and in the types of outfits she selected. But, let's face it, she doesn't have the traditional model figure; she compensates for her inadequacies by exaggerating her assets. I've seen her on-screen looking lovely and slim. Her avoirdupois is a problem and has been since her marriage to Mike Todd."

Art Buchwald, who in 1958 had become a columnist for the European edition of the *Herald Tribune* and part owner of a Chinese restaurant, named Chinatown, in Paris, saw Todd and Taylor during their sojourn in France.

"Prior to their coming to Paris," said Buchwald, "they had rented a Palladian villa, the Fiorentina, at Saint-Jean-Cap-Ferrat in the south of France. I spent a few days swimming, eating, and lounging around with them. Elizabeth and I have always gotten along beautifully because I never wanted anything from her and never wrote negatively about her in my column.

"We used to stroll, just the two of us, around Cap-Ferrat; everyone recognized Elizabeth. People went crazy when they passed her on the street. I never saw a public get so excited about anyone; not even Jacqueline Kennedy Onassis drew such attention.

"Mike Todd rented the Chinese restaurant I co-owned in Paris for a reception following the French premiere of *Around the World.* We seated approximately one hundred, but he invited three times as many guests. The resultant bedlam drove away our chef, who insisted he couldn't prepare food under such conditions. So Todd decided an open bar and fifty pizza pies would do the trick. The pies were ordered from a nearby pizzeria.

"At evening's end, Todd came over to tell me to be in his hotel lobby at noon the next day so he could give me a check to cover the restaurant's expenses. Elizabeth whispered in my ear, however, that they were checking out at seven in the morning. I turned up in the lobby of the Ritz at 6:45 A.M. Todd seemed surprised to see me but maintained a straight face. He scribbled a check for fifteen hundred dollars and handed it to me while Elizabeth winked in complicity."

Their final port of call before returning to the States was London, where Todd promoted the opening night of his epic film by taking over Battersea Gardens, an amusement park on the Thames. He transported two thousand guests, half of them members of the British aristocracy, by ferry and double-decker bus. When it began to rain, he distributed two thousand black plastic raincoats he had purchased in case of inclement weather.

Elizabeth wore a Dior creation as well as $500,000 worth of jewelry. Visibly pregnant, she shrugged when asked by the duchess of Kent if she wanted to have a girl or boy. Overhearing the query, Liz's husband spoke up.

"A girl," he asserted. "The world's not ready for another Mike Todd."

Chapter 13

The day the Todds planned to leave London for the United States, Elizabeth arrived two hours late at Heathrow Airport. Their scheduled flight had left long before, and Mike Todd became incensed at his wife. He and Elizabeth argued so vociferously and ardently that airport security had to be summoned. Photographs of the feuding duo appeared in newspapers and magazines throughout Europe and the United States. Mike Todd finally chartered a private airliner to transport them across the Atlantic on the homeward leg of their extended honeymoon journey.

In New York, they settled into their Park Avenue apartment and awaited the birth of their child. Margaret Lambkin, a British friend of Elizabeth's, introduced her to a Spanish-born fashion designer, Miguel Ferreras, whose studio was located at 785 Fifth Avenue, near the Sherry-Netherland Hotel. Elizabeth commissioned Ferreras to create a maternity wardrobe for the final months of her pregnancy.

"I remember seeing Elizabeth for the first time," the couturier began. "She sat before a large plate-glass window which looked out on Fifth Avenue. She had a striking face, exquisitely beautiful—and those eyes! I thought her most cordial, unusually polite, the consummate geisha, a term which amply describes her temperament and principal social role in life. She was and is and will always be a geisha whose primary interest is to please a man—and thereby herself.

"She employed her eyes to attract men; her eyes had a spirit of their own. She spoke with her eyes, communicated through them, utilized them, when necessary, as weapons. Otherwise, Elizabeth appeared to have nothing of interest or import to convey. She had the attention span of a flea. Her character paled in comparison to the obvious attractiveness of her face.

"Perhaps because she was small in stature, Liz gave the impression of spilling over: she had gargantuan breasts, a mammoth ass, and lumpy, shapeless legs. Her former beau, Kevin McClory, had attested to her consummate skill between the bedsheets. He insisted she manipulated his penis with tremendous dexterity. She was wonderful in bed, 'totally pornographic,' claimed McClory, a reference to her sensuousness. She enjoyed sex for the sake of sex, without being overtly sexual.

"As to the maternity wardrobe I designed for her, the bill came to thirty-eight thousand dollars," Ferreras continued. "The collection ranged from lounging apparel to evening wear. My only problem with Elizabeth—and I'm certain everyone complained about it—was her habitual tardiness, her absolute inability to be *anywhere* on time. I would say, 'Let's meet at eleven in the morning for a fitting,' and she would arrive at four-thirty in the afternoon, without a word of explanation or apology. She took it for granted that you understood she wasn't going to appear at the appointed hour. Because of her status as one of America's most illustrious and sought after personalities, you had to make allowances. After all, she aided my career. By becoming a client, she increased my visibility."

In contrast to Taylor, Todd struck Ferreras as "more than a little on the vulgar side. Whenever I visited him at his office, I found him dressed in a pair of jockey shorts, his bare feet on the desk, a cigar in his mouth, and four or five telephone wires wound round his barrel chest. He would carry on any number of telephone conversations at once, at the same time yakking with his office staff—personal secretaries, mail clerks, administrative assistants. The place had the feel of a three-ring circus, with Todd as ringmaster. Elizabeth was left substantially to her own devices. With the exception of their lovemaking, I had the impression she had grown generally bored with him."

On August 6, 1957, Elizabeth ("Liza") Frances Todd was born by cesarean section at New York's Harkness Pavilion. Weighing four pounds, fourteen ounces, the daughter of Mike and Elizabeth Todd was somewhat less than full-term but not quite as premature as M-G-M's public relations staff led their star actress's fans and followers to believe. That Taylor had been impregnated by Todd prior to her divorce from Wilding became an acceptable morsel of popular gossip.

Less than a month after Liza's birth, the Todds moved into a large house at 1330 Schuyler Drive in Beverly Hills. On October 17, 1957, they flew to New York to host a first-anniversary gala for *Around the World in 80 Days* at Madison Square Garden before eighteen thousand spectators paying $15 a head to attend the ceremony. In addition, CBS-TV gave Todd $250,000 for broadcast rights to the extravaganza. The printed invitations and advertisements billed the event as "a little party for a few chums," including celebrities by the dozen, circus acts from around the world, and performances by the casts of numerous Broadway musicals. The impresario also promised those who attended free champagne, coffee, pizza, hot dogs, egg rolls, and hundreds of house prizes—from neckties to a Cessna airplane and a Chris-Craft power boat. In exchange for television plugs to manufacturers, Todd procured most—if not all—the prizes gratis, thus ensuring that the party would turn a tidy profit.

The results of the celebration were not, however, quite what Todd expected. Earl Wilson, present at the Garden, reported that waiters

> were hawking champagne for $10 a bottle, rather than giving it away. The guests, many in tuxedo and formal evening gowns, staged a furious scramble into the arena to seize food parcels that were being confiscated and consumed by security guards. Instead of stars and dignitaries, the party attracted hundreds of looters and freeloaders. Elizabeth made a stab at cutting a huge layer cake in honor of Todd's epic film. The

six-foot-high creation had been tinted blue so it would photograph better for TV, but the cake proved inedible. Long before the soiree reached its sad and tedious end, Mike led Liz out of the Garden by way of a side exit.

"Going so soon?" Wilson inquired, seeing them duck out.

"It's a total depression," moaned Mike. "I'd rather be at home with our newborn daughter."

The Todds soon returned to Los Angeles and were greeted at the airport by Jack Smith, film critic for the *Los Angeles Times.* "A week had passed since the Madison Square Garden fiasco," noted Smith. "My photographer and I arrived at the airport just after Mike and Liz had deplaned. Quite a few reporters were milling about, but no Mike or Liz. Word came that they were climbing into a limousine at the curb outside the gate. We rushed after them. They were on the verge of pulling away when I poked my head through an open window of the car and addressed Mike Todd. 'If we don't get a picture of you and Liz,' I said, 'our ass is grass.'

"He understood our plight. 'Come on, honey,' he cajoled her, 'step out of the car. These fellows want to take a picture.' She seemed both reluctant and annoyed. She didn't give a damn whether or not we got our shot. Todd practically had to shove her out of the car for the photograph.

"'I'm growing old climbing in and out of this automobile,' she complained. 'Let's just give them their shot,' said Mike. Feigning profound uninterest, Elizabeth, dressed in a tight-fitting, slit-leg Chinese dress, finally emerged. Todd placed an arm around her shoulder. 'Let's go,' he said, 'show the boys your leg.'"

While in California, the couple attended what promised to be a sedate dinner at Beachcombers, hosted by songwriter-composer Jule Styne. Present were Eddie Fisher, Debbie Reynolds, Frank Sinatra, and Lauren Bacall (whose husband, Humphrey Bogart, had recently died). Sinatra and Bacall were dating, and Bacall hoped to marry Sinatra, although Frank hardly shared her desires. At a certain point during the evening, Sinatra and Bacall began to exchange insults. Fisher and Reynolds, their marriage on the rocks, also engaged in a verbal dispute. Mike Todd, thrust into the unfamiliar role of peacemaker, attempted to pacify both couples. While staving off Elizabeth, who had become annoyed because she felt ignored, Todd suddenly turned to Styne and exclaimed: "Dinner was a fabulous idea, Jule. We ought to do this more often."

On November 1, 1957, the Todds again traveled to New York to prepare for yet another series of international showings of *Around the World in 80 Days.* Their latest grand tour featured France, Sweden, Norway, the Soviet Union, Australia, Hong Kong, then back to France. The evening before their departure, Elizabeth slipped on a bar of soap and reinjured her back.

Wayne C. Brockman, station manager for Air France at New York's LaGuardia Airport, had to carry a "weak and incapacitated" Taylor to her seat. "She arrived at the Air France desk in a wheelchair," said Brockman. "When it came time to board, we wheeled her to the loading ramp. I had to carry her the rest of the way. Fortunately, I could lift her because in those days she wasn't as heavy as she later became. She and Todd were very much a couple. He was aptly concerned with her comfort and well-being. They had reserved the Sky Room, a deluxe suite on the plane with sleeping quarters and a sitting room.

"Once abroad, Elizabeth asked the stewardess for a Parliament cigarette. The attendant could offer her every other brand *except* Parliament.

"'Why must it be a Parliament?' Todd queried.

"Because that's what I want,' insisted Liz.

"Todd yanked a twenty-dollar bill from his pocket and dispatched one of the attendants to the terminal to purchase a carton of Parliaments. Apparently satisfied, Elizabeth sat back and began to relax."

Elizabeth's back condition showed marked improvement in Europe, and she seemed to be fully recuperated by the time she and Mike reached the Soviet Union. Nevertheless, Marina Tal, one of the couple's Russian interpreters, thought the actress as "spoiled as an invalid.

We had to wait on her hand and foot. On one occasion, she sent me to buy toys for her children, who had been left behind with a governess in the U.S. When I asked what kind of toys her children liked, she shrugged. 'Anything expensive will do,' she responded. 'The sky's the limit.'

"Elizabeth Taylor and Mike Todd were both rather gaudy. Elizabeth wore deep crimson lipstick, matching nail polish, and an overabundance of eyeshadow. She dressed in a full-length mink coat and fur-trimmed, red-leather designer boots. She became vexed because Russians tended to regard her as an oddity rather than a cinema star. The only genuine 'stars' in the Soviet Union were our prima ballerinas. Elizabeth Taylor had short legs and a large bosom, making it impossible to mistake her for a classical dancer. People didn't know what to make of her.

"She consistently issued rude and insensitive comments. She complained about the food, the long lines in shops, the weather. Taylor kept reiterating that her visit to the U.S.S.R. had taught her to appreciate the lifestyle she enjoyed in the U.S.—an acceptable statement to make among friends, perhaps, but not before a group of high-ranking Soviet government officials.

Once back in Europe, Mike and Liz met up with Eddie Fisher and Debbie Reynolds. "We were vacationing together in the south of France," reminisced Eddie Fisher. "Debbie and I were our usual incompatible selves. Mike and Elizabeth were as cozy and contented as a pair of lovebirds. Their closeness put our paltry marriage to shame. Those who later criticized me for marrying Elizabeth after Mike's death had no idea of the discordance Debbie and I experienced. If they ever made a movie of our relationship, it would have to be entitled *The Razor's Edge.*

"Following our rendezvous with the Todds, I took off by myself for Israel, while Debbie traveled to Spain in the company of a female gym teacher who happened to have a mustache. They went to the bullfights. I guess Debbie liked to fight with bulls, or at least enjoyed watching them."

✦ ✦ ✦

By mid-December 1957, the Todds had returned to the States for the New York premiere of *Raintree County.* They had given up their Manhattan apartment in favor of a leased seven-bedroom estate in Westport, Connecticut, not far from the newly purchased farm of Paul Newman and Joanne Woodward.

Newman had recently signed with M-G-M to perform in the film version of *Cat on a Hot Tin Roof,* based on the play by Tennessee Williams, to be directed by Richard Brooks. Elizabeth got hold of the screenplay, read it, and contacted both Brooks and Lawrence Weingarten, producer of the film. The role she desired, Maggie the Cat (Newman's screen wife), had not yet been filled. Intrigued by Liz's interest in the picture and the potential for a box-office bonanza, Brooks and Weingarten conferred with M-G-M, then offered her the part. When the press asked Liz the reason behind the resumption of her career, she responded: "The opportunity to appear in a production based on a work by our greatest living playwright, Tennessee Williams, precludes the possibility of refusal."

Shooting was scheduled to begin in early March 1958. Meanwhile, the Todds enjoyed their Westport home, periodically visiting New York for dinner parties and shopping sprees. At one dinner party, Elizabeth encountered author Truman Capote, whose name had continually cropped up during her past conversations with Montgomery Clift. She invited Capote for a weekend in Connecticut.

"Considering the season, I recall the weather as having been unusually warm," reminisced Capote. "I drove to their home and found Mike and Liz standing on a long, sloping lawn surrounded by a dozen golden retriever puppies. It was one of those scenes you never forget. It was perfect. They both started rolling around on the ground with the dogs on top of them. As a couple, they were evidently at the height of their happiness.

"I must admit I admire Liz. She's one of the most misunderstood and underestimated people of our time. Judging from her publicity, one would never have any idea of the real character of this incredible, multifaceted woman. She has an unusual sense of humor and is extremely loyal; she loves to clown around; she is unusually bright, a voracious reader of little-known novels despite the rumor that as a teenager she read nothing but comic books; and, most interestingly, she fears nothing. She will risk everything, yet at the same time worries about some of the most trivial matters; she has the utmost courage, yet the merest trifle can throw her for a complete loss.

"There are other contradictions. She adores children, is gentle to animals, but loves to curse. She once referred to a certain M-G-M executive as a 'Shitassedmotherfuckingfaggotcocksucker,' a word not to be found in the Oxford English Dictionary.

"There exists a myth in Hollywood that Mike Todd taught her everything she knows concerning the business end of filmmaking. I don't subscribe to that theory. If anything, Liz taught Mike how to raise money, how to bargain for a fatter contract. He only infected her with his bravado, while she, in fact, possessed the practical know-how. Mike was a dreamer; Liz remained a doer. In the course of their too brief marriage, she lent him tens of thousands of dollars."

From the start, Todd opposed his wife's desire to appear in *Cat on a Hot Tin Roof.* Shortly before her scheduled appearance in front of the cameras, he took her to London to see a new production of the play, with Kim Stanley starring as Maggie the Cat. When the play ended, he accompanied her backstage to Miss Stanley's dressing room.

According to Stanley, Todd lauded her performance, then gave her what amounted to a backhanded insult. "You have to help me convince Elizabeth that Maggie the Cat isn't the part for her," he pleaded. "She mustn't play the role. No one's going to believe that anybody wouldn't want to go to bed with her."

Referring to the role of Brick Pollitt, Maggie's stage husband, Kim Stanley responded: "But if you're gay, the identity Williams assigned to the husband, you wouldn't want to sleep with a woman, no matter how beautiful she was—that's the whole point of the story."

In retrospect, Kim Stanley concluded that Todd's true reservation stemmed from his desire to keep Elizabeth at home: "He wanted a housewife, not an actress, as a mate."

Elizabeth reported for work on March 2, 1958. Her fellow actors viewed her appearance and performance from a variety of perspectives. Burl Ives, Big Daddy in the film version, found Elizabeth "entrancing."

"I felt she did a wonderful job in *Cat,*" he remarked. "I had recently come off the Broadway production with Barbara Bel Geddes as Maggie. Barbara is tops, but Elizabeth played the part just as well, maybe even better. She has a quality that can neither be denied nor easily described. Gazing at her, I was immediately reminded of the words to that famous jazz number: 'You ain't got a thing if you ain't got that swing.' Well, Elizabeth's got it."

Dame Judith Anderson, portraying the role of Big Mama, felt Elizabeth "had a tendency to 'dog it' during rehearsals. Paul Newman became so exercised by her seeming lack of enthusiasm that he raised the issue with director Richard Brooks. 'She's not giving me anything to work with,' railed Paul. 'Don't worry,' responded Brooks. 'Once the camera begins to roll, she comes alive.' And that's exactly what happened. The minute we started filming, she began to emote.

"The only weakness I detected in her performance involved her inability to sustain a true southern drawl. Although that failing would have marred almost any other actor's performance, it became insignificant in her case. People thronged to the movie theaters to witness Elizabeth Taylor enacting the role of Elizabeth Taylor. She was so magnetic, so beautiful, nobody gave a damn about her ability to act.

"I hasten to add, however, that certain members of both cast and crew found her performance incompatible with Paul Newman's. As actors, they simply didn't bring out the best in one another—they didn't click. Moreover, although I perceived her as a charming creature, others found her to be an out-and-out spoiled brat."

The film's most vocal critic was Tennessee Williams. Meade Roberts, a screenwriter and confidant of Williams, visited the playwright at home in Key West, Florida, not long after Williams had seen the first rushes of *Cat on a Hot Tin Roof:* "Tennessee felt that Elizabeth performed her role admirably, but the rest of the actors had been miscast. And Richard Brooks's efforts were the most appalling; he had botched the play by erasing from the film any suggestion of homosexuality, thereby destroying the spirit, if not the letter, of Williams's frank work." Williams was so displeased with the film version of *Cat on a Hot Tin Roof* that once it appeared in movie theaters, he frequently confronted ticket buyers and told them the picture wasn't worth viewing. "He advised strangers against seeing the film," said Roberts, "even though his contract with M-G-M called for him to receive a percentage of the film's profits."

Richard Brooks defended his direction and coscripting of the movie (in tandem with James Poe), pointing out that the 1958 film production code "prohibited us from exploiting the homosexual content of the original play."

Brooks's commentary on Elizabeth Taylor: "First, she's a beauty. Then, she's a combination of child and bitch. Third, she wants to love passionately and to be loved. She found and lost a great love in the person of Mike Todd, who died suddenly in an airplane crash during the filming of *Cat.* The tragedy nearly crushed all hope for completing the picture."

Three weeks into the production of *Cat on a Hot Tin Roof,* Elizabeth Taylor contracted a bothersome head cold. Reluctantly, Richard Brooks placed her on three-day sick leave, during which time she took to bed. Ironically, the illness would save her life.

She later told friends that she wished she had been with her husband the night he died. He had recently given a small birthday party for her at their Beverly Hills home, attended by Eddie Fisher, David Niven and his wife, Hjordis Niven, and Art Cohn, who had just completed his book *The Nine Lives of Mike Todd.* Todd spent much of the evening analyzing his wife's role in *Cat,* in addition to discussing his own ideas for his prospective film rendition of *Don Quixote.* He then mentioned the upcoming Friars Club International Dinner for twelve hundred guests at the Waldorf-Astoria in New York. Mike had been named Showman of the Year, and the award would be presented to him at the hotel banquet. He and Elizabeth had planned to fly to New

York aboard the *Liz,* a twelve-seat, twin-engine Lockheed Lodestar, which Todd had recently leased for one year. He had refurbished the plane's interior, installing a violet-tinted boudoir with a king-sized bed for his wife and himself.

Elizabeth's head cold, coupled with a high fever and a bronchial infection, necessitated a last-minute change of plans. Overriding his wife's objections, Mike opted to make the trip without her. He began calling friends he hoped might accompany him in Liz's stead. He telephoned Kurt Frings, Kirk Douglas, Eddie Fisher, comedian Joe E. Lewis, director Joseph Mankiewicz—they all had made other arrangements. He finally turned to his old standby, Art Cohn, who jumped at the opportunity.

At 10:11 P.M., the night of March 21, 1958, Mike Todd's plane took off from Burbank Airport, California, bound for New York. Todd telephoned his wife shortly before departure and assured her he would call again when they landed in Tulsa, Oklahoma, for refueling. Because heavy thunderstorms and strong winds had been predicted, Elizabeth had pleaded with her husband all day to delay his trip until the following morning.

"Don't worry, sweetie," responded Todd. "I can fly above any storm."

The aircraft accident report of the Civil Aeronautics Board (CAB), issued on April 17, 1959, more than a year after the fatal crash of the *Liz,* reported that due to ice-formation conditions the plane's two pilots, William S. Verner and Thomas Barclay, requested an air-traffic controller at Winslow, Arizona, to grant them clearance to climb from eleven thousand feet to an altitude of thirteen thousand feet. The aircraft's next radio communication was heard by air control at Zuni, New Mexico. The pilots, having climbed to thirteen thousand feet, now reported not only an increase of icing but also the advent of an intense storm front. The transmission marked the plane's final air-to-ground communication.

Thirteen minutes later, a CAB agent at the Grants Airport control tower in New Mexico saw a blaze of light illuminate the winter sky. He mistook the flash for lightning. But the pilot of an air force B-36 flying in the vicinity contacted the control tower and reported seeing a plane go down in the same general area. The recorded time was 2:40 A.M.

According to the CAB's report, "The right master engine rod had failed in flight and the right propeller was feathered. Complete loss of control of the aircraft followed and the plane then struck the ground in a steep angle of descent." The site of the accident was a small, snow-encrusted valley between two mountains at an elevation of approximately seventy-two hundred feet, twelve miles southwest of Grants.

At daybreak a search party located the sparse remnants of the *Liz*—a scattering of smoldering wreckage that had become Mike Todd's funeral pyre. Only two objects remained intact—a copy of *The World's Great Religions* (a book Art Cohn had been reading) and a red cloth napkin embroidered in gold: *The Liz.* There were no survivors.

The final cause of the disaster, as determined by the CAB, was "the loss of control of an overloaded aircraft, following the failure of an engine at a cruising altitude which proved critical for single-engine operation. The loss of control was aggravated by surface ice accretion. . . ." (Although Todd invested some $25,000 in his and Taylor's new boudoir aboard the *Liz,* he spent only $2,000 to improve the aircraft's anti-icing system.) The maximum certified takeoff weight for Todd's Lockheed, as revealed by aircraft documents and corroborated by other sources, was 18,605 pounds; the plane had carried 20,757 pounds at takeoff. The extra ton made a vital difference. Mike Todd died at age forty-nine.

Chapter 14

As she lay in bed the night of Mike Todd's fatal flight, Elizabeth Taylor became increasingly worried. She had expected to hear from her husband by telephone, but the call never came. She subsequently began ringing up friends, including her agent, Kurt Frings. "I ought never to have let him fly without me," she said. "After our marriage, we formulated a golden rule: 'Whither thou goest, I will go, too.' I should have gone with him."

"Stop fretting," Kurt responded. "Mike can take care of himself."

"I'm not so sure," said Elizabeth.*

Unable to sleep, the twenty-six-year-old actress spent the remainder of the night shuffling back and forth between the master bedroom and her children's nursery. By early morning, her worst fears had been confirmed.

An M-G-M switchboard operator, Eva Guest, became one of the first to hear of the airplane crash. "I arrived at M-G-M shortly before eight A.M.," she began. "A few minutes later, an urgent telephone call came in for Metro security from a liaison officer with the Los Angeles Police Department. Mike Todd's body had been burned beyond rec-

*Mike Todd, like Elizabeth, seemed to have had a premonition of his impending death. The day before he flew, he gave a full-length interview to Bob Levin, an editor of *McCall's* magazine, in which he spoke directly to Elizabeth. "If I'm not around," he said, "don't be competitive with the children's nanny." The night he left, he returned five times to Elizabeth's bed to kiss her goodbye.

ognition; the coroner's office in New Mexico needed his dental records for identification purposes."

M-G-M contacted Dick Hanley, who had once been employed at Metro but lately worked as Mike Todd's assistant. Upon hearing the shattering news, Hanley telephoned the Todd residence and ascertained from the children's governess that Elizabeth hadn't yet been informed. Hanley next phoned Rex Kennamer, Elizabeth's personal physician, and asked the doctor to accompany him to Todd's house. He also called Sidney Guilaroff and Eddie Fisher. Guilaroff offered to drive directly to Elizabeth's home. Eddie Fisher had already flown to New York to attend the Friars Club banquet, but Debbie Reynolds agreed to pick up Elizabeth's children.

Debbie arrived first, followed by Guilaroff. Both were seated in the living room when Hanley and Kennamer turned up. Hanley climbed the stairs to Elizabeth's room. The moment she saw him, Liz bolted out of bed. "It can't be, it just can't be!" she screamed. Hanley hadn't said a word to Elizabeth; his silent, sullen face expressed it all.

In her autobiography, Debbie Reynolds recounted the "look of terror and anguish" that distorted Elizabeth's features as she came tearing down the stairs. In a state of "hysteria," she emitted a "piercing scream of agony" from someplace deep in her throat. "In a sheer white nightgown," Elizabeth raced through the living room, past Sid and Debbie, crying out Mike's name. Her violet eyes appeared desperately sad, thought Debbie, the light suddenly gone out of them.

"I stepped back as she ran past me and headed for the front door," Debbie noted. "Rex and Dick Hanley got to the door just in time to stop her. Elizabeth collapsed in their arms, sobbing. 'Why Mike? Why did it have to happen?' Elizabeth wailed as the two men led her back up to her bedroom."

Once in Liz's room, both men tried to pacify her. When their approach failed, Kennamer proceeded to inject Elizabeth with morphine and phenobarbitol. The shots only seemed to stimulate her. Unable to rest, she paced the floor, endlessly calling out Mike's name, intermittently talking about him as though he were still alive, as if he had merely stepped out to the corner store for a few minutes to pick up a morning newspaper. Then, without warning, she would break into tears, quietly at first, followed by loud, gulping sobs. Hanley and Kennamer remained by her side for hours.

Others had joined the crowd downstairs, including Edith Head, Helen Rose, and Irene Sharaff, three of Hollywood's top designers, all of them close to Elizabeth. Sharaff remembered the experience: "It had become a house of bedlam. Metro had sent over three or four of their public relations people to answer the telephones and handle the press. Reporters were crawling out of the woodwork. A columnist for the *Los Angeles Times* gained access to the house through an unlocked basement window and was subsequently arrested for trespassing.

"Press photographers and onlookers could be found everywhere—in trees, on top of cars, even on the roof of the house. The surrounding streets were clogged with pedestrians who had appeared after hearing of the tragedy. Looters had broken into the garage, where Todd kept his liquor inventory, and were walking off with cases of scotch and champagne. Elizabeth watched in horror from her bedroom window, finally asking members of the household staff to move the alcohol from the garage into the house."

Eddie Fisher returned to Los Angeles aboard the first available flight and arrived at Liz's home that night. He was, as Debbie Reynolds wrote, "perfect for her. He had been Mike Todd's best friend. He had slowly begun to pattern himself after Mike. He was almost as grief-stricken as she was. They could share that grief like no two other people. He was her only link to Mike. I knew that, and I was glad my husband could be of comfort to her."

In days to come, Dr. Kennamer kept Elizabeth so sedated that to many of her friends she appeared almost incoherent at times. Drifting in and out of sleep, she admitted dreaming of Mike and often woke up screaming. Benny Thau visited the day after Todd's death and was shown to Elizabeth's bedroom. "Mike and I were married for only 413 days," Liz wept. "Nobody will ever know how much I loved him."

The funeral had been arranged by relatives of Mike Todd for

March 25 at the Jewish Waldheim Cemetery in Forest Park, Illinois, outside Chicago. Todd's remains would be laid to rest at the foot of his father's grave in the Goldenbogen family plot. The day before the funeral, Howard Hughes called to inform Elizabeth he was making available a TWA Constellation to take her to Chicago. They left that evening, a travel party that included Elizabeth; her brother, Howard; Dr. Rex Kennamer; Helen Rose; Sid Guilaroff; Eddie Fisher, and M-G-M publicist Bill Lyon. They were met at the airport in Chicago by Mike Todd's son, Michael Jr., and his wife, Sarah. Following a tearful embrace, Michael Jr. attempted to make light conversation with Elizabeth. Still in shock, she could only stare at him.

The group spent the night at the Drake Hotel and set out for the funeral the following morning. Eddie Fisher described the event as "an agonizing ordeal, a repeat of the situation that had prevailed outside Elizabeth's home in Beverly Hills." Thousands of fans lined the sidewalks and streets of Forest Park. At the site of the cemetery, cars were double- and triple-parked. A mob of teenagers and housewives scampered across tombstones for a better view of the aggrieved widow.

"We somehow managed to reach the tent that had been stretched over Mike's open grave," said Fisher. "Elizabeth saw the bronze casket, tried to embrace it, and said over and over, 'I love you, Mike. I love you, Mike.' Rabbi Abraham Rose of Chicago conducted the Orthodox service. Rabbi Rose's prayers were continually interrupted by the shouts of fans outside the tent; all one could hear were chants of 'Liz! Liz! Liz!'

"As we left the tent, the throng surged forward with a roar. Somebody ripped away Elizabeth's black veil; others attempted to tear off her hat and coat. The ground was littered with crumpled potato-chip bags and empty Coca-Cola bottles. The police helped us get back to our limousine, but we were instantly set upon by a mob intent on catching a final glimpse of Elizabeth's tear-stained face. They surrounded the car and began pounding on the windows."

An afternoon reception for Todd's friends and relatives, at the Chicago Hilton, found Elizabeth in better spirits. "She was unbelievable," observed Fisher. "She wandered around the room, consoling everybody. She had—and still has—an uncanny ability to 'rise to the occasion.' It wasn't until we boarded the Constellation to return to California that she broke down again."

The next two weeks proved difficult for Elizabeth. At best she slept fitfully, or not at all. Eddie Fisher spent countless hours with her, reading aloud from the thousands of letters and telegrams that poured in. Having joined them on the return flight to Hollywood, Michael Todd Jr. also attempted to aid her recovery. But it was Fisher whose attentions meant most to Elizabeth.

"After Mike died I went crazy, but Liz went crazier," Eddie insisted. "I tried to boost her morale by recounting humorous experiences Mike and I had shared. I told her something Mike had said to me shortly before his death. 'Some young boys,' he remarked, 'want to grow up and become president of the United States; myself, I just wanted to grow up and marry Elizabeth Taylor. And I did.'"

The Academy Award presentations were held three days after Mike Todd's funeral. Although nominated for Best Actress for her performance in *Raintree County,* Elizabeth had lost all interest in the outcome. "I only care what Mike would have thought had I won," she told Eddie Fisher. The Oscar went to Joanne Woodward for *The Three Faces of Eve.* After the ceremony, which Elizabeth watched on television, she sent Woodward a bouquet with an appended note: "I am so happy for you. [signed] Elizabeth Taylor Todd, and Mike, too."

Eddie Fisher recalled that Elizabeth received a telephone call from Nicky Hilton a few days after the Academy Award presentations. "He wanted to see Elizabeth," said Eddie. "Now that Mike was dead, Hilton hoped to effect a reconciliation with Elizabeth. She wanted nothing to do with him. After they hung up, she spent hours rehashing horror stories of her aborted marriage to Hilton. Then she started talking about Mike again. 'Without him,' she moaned, 'I feel like half a pair of scissors.'"

Richard Brooks visited Elizabeth. Metro, the director informed her, feared she might never resume work on *Cat.* Brooks, for his part, retained complete confidence in Liz. He maintained that her performance in the film could provide a therapy of sorts.

"At the same time," he said, "I realized that finishing the film would be something of an ordeal. Liz had always been a high-strung individual; she remained under Dr. Kennamer's care and confined to bed. I had to wonder if she had the strength to complete the picture."

Brooks filed a pessimistic report with Metro's insurance department concerning the ongoing production of *Cat on a Hot Tin Roof.* On the basis of the report, Benny Thau paid a return visit to Elizabeth, bringing along a second M-G-M executive. After they departed, Taylor voiced her opinion. "My God," she said, "Mike's barely cold in his grave, and all they're worried about is their goddamn movie."

Sid Guilaroff, who frequently dropped in on Elizabeth, began dragging along his friends. One afternoon he asked Eva Marie Saint to accompany him. "Elizabeth was very ill at the time because of the death of Mike Todd," she said. "Not many people saw her, but she wanted me to come over. I was then pregnant, and my husband became a bit concerned—it was such an emotional period for Liz, and he felt the environment might not be healthy for me. I went, anyway.

"I joined a number of guests in the living room. Her children, who had been staying with Eddie Fisher and Debbie Reynolds, were home at this point. Christopher and Michael Wilding were three and five years old, respectively, and Liza Todd was only six months.

"The downstairs contingent appeared to be holding a wake of sorts, which consisted of a good deal of drinking and reminiscing. Sid Guilaroff retreated to Elizabeth's room to do her hair. Dressed up for the occasion, she had promised to visit her guests. I'll never forget what happened next. It's one of the most vivid, saddest memories I have of Liz. She had started down the staircase on Sid's arm. Her two little boys were standing at the foot of the stairs. As their mother came into view, they started vocalizing in a singsong fashion: 'Mike Todd is dead . . . Mike Todd is dead. . . . '

"Elizabeth just sort of went limp on Sydney's shoulder, and they both turned back upstairs. We just didn't see them that day."

Following the incident, Elizabeth's children, including Liza, were sent to Arthur Loew Jr.'s home in Bel Air. He offered to look after them until Elizabeth felt better. In the wake of their departure, another bizarre episode transpired. Elizabeth was standing among a bevy of guests in her den when into their midst walked none other than Greta Garbo. Looking neither to the right nor to the left, the legendary Swedish actress walked straight toward Elizabeth, placed a hand on Liz's arm, then whispered into her ear: "Be brave!" She then turned on her heels and left.

The encounter with Garbo encouraged Elizabeth only to the extent that she decided to vacate the Todd residence, which to her mind contained too many painful memories, and move into a suite at the Beverly Hills Hotel. Hedda Hopper visited her there and found Taylor living as she had during her earliest bachelorette days, with her clothes scattered across tables, chairs, and sofas. The large diamond ring given her by Mike Todd had been left by an open window on the bathroom windowsill; Hedda returned it to Taylor, who absentmindedly slipped it back on her finger.

That evening, Elizabeth and Hedda attended a party at Romanoff's hosted by Arthur Loew Jr. The soiree marked Liz's first night out after the death of Mike Todd.

"We rolled down to Romanoff's in her Rolls an hour and a half late," wrote Hedda Hopper. "Everybody clustered around her as though she were a queen. I am sure she believed she was."

Next morning, Elizabeth took Hopper to see Liza, asleep in a crib in a room of Arthur Loew's house "no bigger than a closet, with its only ventilation provided by a skylight that could be pulled open by a thin chain. The room was stifling."

"Good Lord, Liz," Hedda cried. "She can't get enough air in here."

"Oh, she's all right," her mother said, flicking on the light switch and waking the baby.

Hopper became convinced that Elizabeth had lost touch with reality.

Taylor, her children, and her entourage—consisting of Dick Hanley,

Michael Todd Jr., and Midori Tsuji (Mike Todd's aide)—spent a week as Arthur Loew Jr.'s guests at a horse farm he owned in Arizona. In the course of their visit, it became evident to Michael Todd Jr. that "Arthur was more than just fond" of Elizabeth. "On a couple of occasions, in an effort to get Elizabeth to relax," wrote Michael Jr., "Arthur massaged her feet. Although she made no comment, I felt Elizabeth interpreted the foot massages as subtle sexual advances, and she became rather uneasy about our stay in Arizona." The group returned to California.

In Michael Todd Jr.'s words, "It was a step backwards. Elizabeth relapsed into a state of near hysteria. Several times every night she called out to me. When I appeared in her room, she would be crying and fighting against the fact of [my father's] death." After a point, no longer able to cope with Elizabeth's apparent nervous collapse, Michael Jr. returned to the East Coast. Only Eddie Fisher remained steadfast in his devotion to his best friend's widow.

When Elizabeth came down with a painful throat infection, Dr. Rex Kennamer called in a specialist, who examined the patient and recommended the immediate removal of her tonsils. "Her physicians were always pushing her into one operation or another," said Eddie Fisher. "They would wheel her into the operating room, open her up, then stitch her closed. It was a good way to make money."

The tonsillectomy was performed at Cedars Sinai Hospital in Los Angeles and lasted less than an hour.

Liz returned to the Beverly Hills Hotel and took to bed again. For once taking a more drastic approach, Eddie Fisher arrived at her suite and reprimanded her for failing "to get on with it." Mike Todd, he argued, would have never "sanctioned such behavior. You have a commitment to complete *Cat on a Hot Tin Roof.* You must finish it and stop feeling sorry for yourself."

One month and three days after Todd's untimely death, Elizabeth's limousine pulled through the M-G-M gates. Midori Tsuji, who had accompanied Elizabeth to the studio, went off to locate Richard Brooks. She found the director poring over the script and informed him that Elizabeth wanted to see him.

"I followed her outside to the limousine," noted Brooks. "The curtains were drawn across the car windows, so I opened the back door. There sat Elizabeth. She looked pale and haggard, the whites of her lilac eyes reddened by too many tears. I thought for sure she had stopped by to announce her withdrawal from the film. She smiled wanly, then said, 'Richard, I want to come back to work.'

"'Swell,' I responded. 'Get your ass over to makeup.'"

Burl Ives had visited Elizabeth Taylor on several occasions during her recuperation from Mike Todd's death. "When she felt up to it," he said, "she would relate stories about Mike. For instance, she told me he had taught her how to write a check and balance her bank book at the end of each month. It amazed me that somebody as worldly as Elizabeth Taylor didn't know how to write a personal check.

"Back on the set of *Cat on a Hot Tin Roof,* Elizabeth appeared ready to throw herself once again into her role. Her most telling problem seemed to be a severe weight loss. The white satin slip and silk dress she wore in a number of scenes had to be taken in more than once. She didn't exactly look emaciated, but she needed to gain weight. So Richard Brooks and I concocted a plan to induce her to eat again.

"In the film there's a scene in which Big Daddy is welcomed home from the hospital with a sumptuous dinner, consisting of baked Virginia ham, southern fried chicken, mashed potatoes drowned in butter, corn on the cob, and a lot of other luscious treats. The scene would begin, and Richard would shout through his megaphone: 'Eat, Elizabeth, eat the food on the table.' She would begin nibbling at the food, and Richard would yell, 'Cut! Then he'd find some excuse for reshooting the scene. This went on for two full days, and over that period Elizabeth devoured the equivalent of a half-dozen solid meals. More important, having to eat in this fashion restored her appetite. She quickly gained back all the weight she had lost."

Elizabeth's performance in *Cat*—though rough-hewn and often uneven—won her the plaudits of film critics and a second Oscar nomination. The completion of the film also set in motion her next real-life drama—an illicit but not unexpected love affair with Eddie Fisher.

Fisher, born in South Philadelphia in 1928 (he was thus four years Liz's senior), came from a family nearly as indigent as Mike Todd's. Of Russian-Jewish descent, Eddie's father made and repaired trunks and suitcases for a living, supplementing his small income by peddling fruits and vegetables from a sidewalk pushcart. Eddie used his sonorous, youthful voice mainly to shout his father's wares.

Discovered as a teenager by comedian Eddie Cantor at the Catskill Mountain borscht-belt resort of Grossinger's, Fisher went on to win first place on *Arthur Godfrey's Talent Scouts,* a popular early 1950s radio show. Pushed to further heights by his agent and friend Milton Blackstone, Eddie swiftly became a television idol as the star of NBC's *Coke Time.* He cut a string of number-one hits that brought him fame and fortune, along with the favors of dozens of ambitious and attentive Hollywood starlets.

One such starlet, Debbie Reynolds, struck him as sweet and unspoiled. "I had found a really nice girl—in Hollywood, of all places," he wrote in his autobiography. He invited her to his next opening show at the Coconut Grove. They began dating, and to Eddie's amazement he discovered she was still a virgin. Louella Parsons soon dubbed them "America's Sweethearts." They were married at Grossinger's but spent their honeymoon at a Coca-Cola bottlers' convention in Atlanta, Georgia, where outspoken, health-conscious Debbie informed a conclave of Fisher's sponsors, "I don't drink Coke. It's bad for your teeth."

Later in the marriage, she became stingy with her own money. Eddie complained that she hoarded her personal earnings while freely spending his. They made a third-rate movie together, *Bundle of Joy,* during Debbie's pregnancy with daughter Carrie, born in 1956. They were already talking divorce when Debbie announced she was again pregnant. Their son, Todd, was born in February 1958, a month before the death of his namesake. Nevertheless, Elizabeth Taylor prompted Eddie to sever his ties with Debbie. He pronounced his marriage a failure and evidently needed little cajoling to terminate it. Fisher claimed that their marriage could be accurately summed up by a portrait Debbie once commissioned. "In the oil painting," said Eddie, "Debbie, dressed as a clown, dominates the picture; I appear in a gray outline behind her. That's how she liked to conceive of our relationship."

In his autobiography, Eddie Fisher goes to great lengths to delineate some of the differences between his two wives: "Elizabeth with her flashy dresses and even flashier jewelry, Debbie in clothes that made her look like everybody's high school sweetheart, Elizabeth with a cigarette in her mouth and a drink in her hand, Debbie giving us all prim lectures on the evils of smoking and drinking. She thought her virtue was her one superiority over Elizabeth, so she played her Girl Scout role to the hilt."

Eddie Fisher resented the outrageous flow of gossip that "broke once my affair with Elizabeth became public. The press ran a series of excoriating articles insinuating that she and I had made love on the plane to Mike Todd's funeral in Forest Park. Nothing could have been further from the truth."

Not since 1949, when Ingrid Bergman and Roberto Rossellini divorced their spouses in order to marry, had Hollywood been privy to a more salacious romantic drama than that of Debbie Reynolds, Eddie Fisher, and Elizabeth Taylor. Elizabeth had vacated her suite at the Beverly Hills Hotel and moved back into her and Todd's former residence when she and Eddie realized the inevitability of their relationship.

"The turning point occurred the summer of 1958," said Fisher. "In June, I began a six-week run at the Tropicana Hotel in Las Vegas. To Debbie's credit, she had invited Elizabeth to join us, knowing how much we both missed Mike and needed each other's consolation. In mid-August, my wife threw a surprise thirtieth birthday party for me at Romanoff's. Elizabeth didn't show, which disappointed me. She telephoned during the middle of the party to explain, 'Oh, Eddie, I feel sick. I have my period.' I said, 'You've just got a hangover.' She laughed and asked me to visit her the following day. And I did.

"She wore a flesh-colored bathing suit and sat by the swimming pool, her feet dangling in the water, while little Liza perched in her lap. I stared at Elizabeth, and she stared at me—our eyes locked in an embrace, and I knew I had fallen in love. She went inside the house and returned with Mike's gold money clip. 'Mike would have wanted you to have this,' she remarked softly.

"We arranged to see each other again the next day. We drove to the beach, way up the coast past Malibu, holding hands in the car. 'Elizabeth, I want to marry you,' I said. 'When?' she asked. 'I don't know,' I said, 'but I *am* going to marry you.' When we reached the beach, we kissed—with Liza playing near us—and that sealed the promise."

Elizabeth and Eddie were inseparable after that. "We would take long drives and eat at out-of-the-way restaurants," he remarked. "We then realized there was nothing unusual about our being seen together—Elizabeth was Mike Todd's young widow and I his closest companion. We were soon frequenting spots such as La Scala and the Polo Lounge. More often than not, we would bring Debbie, and Elizabeth and I would hold hands under the table. Initially, no one seemed to notice we were in love, not even Debbie. I knew we couldn't hide our feelings for long and felt wary about what people would say when they found out."

Toward the end of August, Elizabeth announced her intention to take a prolonged European holiday, with Midori Tsuji as traveling companion. Eddie Fisher talked about having business to look after in New York. The pair actually planned to rendezvous in Manhattan for a weeklong vacation. The mistake they made in hatching their grand scheme was to drag Hedda Hopper into it. Hopper penned an initial column based on individual interviews with Liz and Eddie in which she detailed their respective alibis. When it became clear that Hedda had been intentionally misled by the couple, she vowed to seek revenge and did so by revealing the truth.

Eddie had reserved a room for himself at the Essex House on Central Park South, while Elizabeth took a suite at the Plaza. "I stayed at the Essex House long enough to shower and shave," said Fisher. "I then walked to the Plaza and spent the night with Elizabeth. The moment I saw her, she said, 'When are we going to make love?' Before that night, we'd only kissed and held hands."

From Fisher's perspective, the prospect of a night with Elizabeth Taylor had been well worth the wait. "How would I describe Elizabeth?" he mused aloud years later. "She's all woman, the most sensuous female I've ever known."

Eddie told an acquaintance, Ken McKnight, how "hot" Elizabeth became when making love, how she would crawl around the floor on hands and knees purring like a sex kitten, how he would mount her from the rear—and the hotter she became, the louder she purred.

Author and film historian Jane Ellen Wayne, who worked in public relations at NBC-TV during the years Fisher had his Coca-Cola show on the air, said that Fisher's sexual prowess "may well have been one of the main reasons Elizabeth married him. Eddie dated a couple of girls on the staff as well as a few starlets," Wayne said. "They would talk about how well endowed he happened to be and how adept at lovemaking, supposedly among the best in show business—in a class with Frank Sinatra and Gary Cooper. If anyone had an interest in good sex—and Elizabeth Taylor is said to have been ardent about it—Eddie Fisher was somebody who would have impressed her."

Angela R. Sweeney, a voice coach who dated Fisher briefly following his divorce from Elizabeth Taylor, spoke not only of his impressive organ but also "his ability to have sex as often as a dozen times a night. It was unreal. He would reach climax and immediately he would have another erection. I attributed his sexual prowess to his amphetamine ['speed'] addiction. I'd been with other speed addicts, and they all manifested a voracious sexual appetite. Eddie had been for years seeing a New York physician named Max Jacobson—the original 'Dr. Feelgood.'" In addition to giving Fisher amphetamine shots several times a week, Jacobson taught him how to inject himself.

Elizabeth's personality, however, proved problematic for Fisher. The singer described her psychological need and desire for sexual roughhousing: "Elizabeth loved to fight. I'd give her my shoulder, tease her, then I'd give her my other shoulder and let her punch away. Next I'd get on top of her and pin her to the ground, and she'd burst out laughing. Finally, we'd make love. But she still wanted to brawl and unlike Mike Todd I was never much of a fighter.

"Elizabeth's tough and I'm a softie. I served as a stabilizing force in her life, but I don't think Mike Todd would have approved of our relationship."

While staying in New York, Elizabeth and Eddie were anything but discreet. They had temporarily deserted Hollywood in order to be "less visible," but they almost seemed to gloat over the impending scandal. The morning after their encounter in the Plaza, they took a ride around Central Park in a horse-drawn hansom and visited the Central Park Zoo, which had been one of Elizabeth and Mike Todd's stops during their courting period.

In the evening she and Eddie attended a cocktail party given by Nicky Hilton at which Hilton became inebriated and tried unsuccessfully to goad Fisher into a fistfight. The couple left to dine at Quo Vadis. When a reporter spotted them and asked about their future plans, Liz barked, "I have nothing to say."

After dinner they went nightclubbing and wound up at the Blue Angel, where Mike Nichols and Elaine May were performing. The club wasn't crowded, and as they entered, Elizabeth noticed Eva Marie Saint and M-G-M publicist Rick Ingersoll sitting at a table. "Liz came over and asked us to join them," said Ingersoll. "We sat together and watched the show. Later in the evening, we were warned that a number of reporters had gathered outside the club. My first reaction was 'So what?' I had no idea there was anything going on between Liz and Eddie and assumed they were just good friends. I offered to step outside and handle the situation.

"When I went outside to speak to the crowd, I was immediately besieged with questions about the rumored affair. I assured the press they were simply buddies and returned to the table to tell the couple what had happened. Eddie responded by saying, 'Uh-oh!' and buried his head in his hands. It became obvious at this moment that the rumor had validity. Eva Marie Saint was as shocked as I had been. But she told me the next day she felt happy for Elizabeth. 'She has finally found some peace of mind.'"

Back in their Plaza suite that night, Eddie and Liz began discussing their relationship. "We agreed we had to tell Debbie," said Fisher. "She'd been trying for two days to reach me at the Essex House. It was three in the morning, so I decided to call her in California the next day. Elizabeth and I had gone to bed when suddenly the telephone rang. I answered. It was Debbie. She had traced me to Elizabeth's suite. I had no alternative but to admit everything. 'Elizabeth and I are here together, and we're in love,' I said.

"We felt certain Debbie had already heard about us, but for a few moments she seemed utterly shocked. She didn't make a sound. After she regained her composure, she said, 'Well, we can't discuss this over the phone. We'll talk when you come home.'"

Debbie's seemingly nonchalant reaction puzzled Fisher and Taylor, but feeling liberated by their confession, the couple accepted an invitation from Jennie Grossinger, proprietress and founder of Grossinger's, to join her at the resort for Labor Day weekend.

"By now the whole world seemed aware of our romance," remarked Eddie. "I told reporters that I had come to Grossinger's to celebrate the opening of the resort's new swimming pool. Elizabeth claimed she had shown up for the same purpose. We stayed at Joy Cottage, Jennie Grossinger's private home on the property, in the same room I had shared years earlier with Debbie Reynolds."

Tania Grossinger, a younger member of the family, happened to be staying at the resort over Labor Day weekend. "One afternoon," she said, "I encountered Eddie Fisher on one of the athletic fields at the hotel. He was alone and didn't appear overly pleased. 'You don't look very happy for a guy who's about to become betrothed,' I said. 'I'm not,' he responded. 'This is Milton Blackstone's idea, not mine,' a reference to Eddie's agent and a public relations representative for Grossinger's. I never learned whether Eddie felt upset about the prospect of marrying Elizabeth or of having brought her to Grossinger's."

New York Post scribe Earl Wilson, covering the ribbon-cutting ceremony of the new swimming pool at Grossinger's, wound up writing about Eddie Fisher and Elizabeth Taylor. "I realized they were having an affair," he said, "and I told Milt Blackstone that all hell would break loose once word got out. Debbie Reynolds was tough, despite her image, and wasn't going to take it lightly. Moreover, I didn't think Elizabeth could ever really love a guy like Eddie Fisher. He was sweet, but naïve; and she was a tyrant."

Elizabeth and Eddie ended their East Coast sojourn by returning to Los Angeles in separate airplanes. Fisher rejoined his wife and two children, while Liz evaded a pack of frenzied reporters by hiding out in the home of Kurt Frings. Only Hedda Hopper, in her avid pursuit of the story, intuited Elizabeth's whereabouts; she reached Taylor by telephone.

"Elizabeth," she said, "this is Hedda. Level with me, because I shall find out anyhow. What's happening with Eddie Fisher? Are the two of you going to marry?"

"Last time I looked," retorted Liz, "Eddie was still married to Debbie Reynolds."

"Obviously," said Hopper. "But it's been reported that they're breaking up and that you're the cause."

"That's a lot of bull," snapped Elizabeth, her voice bristling with anger. "I don't go around breaking up marriages. Besides, you can't break up a happy marriage. Debbie's and Eddie's never has been."

"You even went to Grossinger's with him?"

"Sure. We had a divine time."

"And what about Arthur Loew Jr.? He's been in love with you forever, and your kids are still living in his house."

"I can't help how he feels about me."

"Well, you can't hurt Debbie like this without hurting yourself more—she's in love with Eddie."

"But he's not in love with her and never has been."

"What do you think Mike would say to this?" inquired Hedda.

"Well," Elizabeth said calmly, "Mike's dead and I'm alive. . . . What do you expect me to do—sleep alone?"

The last line became the centerpiece around which Hedda Hopper composed her newspaper portrait of Elizabeth Taylor. When it ran in the next day's press, it created a furor. Elizabeth contacted Hedda.

"You've depicted me as absolutely cruel and heartless," she railed. "And you're the one person in Hollywood I trusted and respected."

"I wrote only what you told me," said Hopper. "The words are your own."

"But I didn't think you'd print them," Elizabeth wailed. "You betrayed me."

Chapter 15

Debbie Reynolds eventually admitted she'd been "floored" by her husband's admission of a love affair with Elizabeth Taylor. Her mind, she said, had gone "numb, blank. I felt as if I were floating in space." She reserved the brunt of her anger for Eddie, whom she described as "a needy, dependent person. I don't know what to compare him to—he's like an elevator that can't find the floor. I don't think Eddie ever knew who he was. Perhaps the drugs totally put him away."

Debbie's sentiments were shared by a number of her friends, including Lillian Burns Sidney. "Eddie's boyish appeal," noted Sidney, "his shy, self-effacing presence, had little or nothing to do with the man behind the mask. He had neither talent nor personality. His taste in women ran from bimbos to showgirls."

Lillian Burns Sidney did credit Eddie with a degree of honesty in his public admission that he and Debbie had never exactly been "the perfect Hollywood couple." According to Sidney, the marriage had long before "run out of gas." Debbie, she suggested, had gotten Eddie drunk and had then seduced him in order to become pregnant a second time "because she didn't want Carrie to be an only child."

Despite her seething embitterment, Debbie somehow hoped to preserve the marriage, and after Eddie's return from New York, she insisted they consult a marriage counselor. They saw a psychologist associated with UCLA, in whose presence Eddie revealed once more how deeply attached he felt to Elizabeth Taylor.

"What about your children?" inquired the marriage counselor.

"Oh, they'll be fine," countered Eddie.

The Fishers promptly announced their legal separation. Eddie vacated the Holmby Hills residence he had shared with Debbie and rented a room at the Bel Air Hotel. He spent most of his time with Elizabeth, who had reclaimed her children from Arthur Loew Jr. and leased a house belonging to actress Linda Christian on Copa de Oro Road, only minutes from Fisher's hotel. In fear of an onslaught of newspaper, tabloid, fan magazine, and radio and television coverage, Eddie and Liz resumed their initial low-profile approach. They made few public appearances. On Sunday mornings, Eddie would drive to Nate 'n' Al's delicatessen and bring back a brunch of bagels, lox, and cream cheese, which he and Elizabeth usually washed down with a bottle or two of champagne. Three decades later, Eddie confessed they both had been heavily addicted to drugs, Liz to painkillers for her chronic back pain, Eddie to amphetamines and whatever other substances Dr. Jacobson saw fit to inject into his veins.

"On more than one occasion, Fisher suggested that Elizabeth consult with Jacobson," said Ken McKnight. "Jacobson, he felt, could relieve her back pains. But Elizabeth wouldn't hear of it. In his baggy trousers and bloodstained lab coat, Jacobson reminded Elizabeth more of a kosher butcher than a medical doctor. Conversely, Jacobson wanted nothing to do with Taylor. He habitually refused to treat patients who had any kind of drinking problem, and in his opinion Elizabeth had been hooked on booze for years."

Debbie Reynolds chose to tackle the situation in her own inimitable manner. She stepped outside her house and faced reporters camped on her front lawn. In her best "Girl Scout" mode—no makeup, her hair in pigtails, and a row of safety pins fastened to her white lace blouse—she informed the press she still loved her husband. She had been trying in vain to arrange a "face-to-face" meeting with Elizabeth Taylor to discuss the matter; Taylor, she added, had never bothered returning her calls.

From a public relations standpoint, Debbie could do no wrong. In the eyes of the media, she came to personify the perfect young wife and mother, free of personal vanity and wholly dedicated to her mate's happiness. Elizabeth Taylor had reemerged in the course of the fracas as a spoiled, materialistic, callous woman—a home wrecker whose selfish needs and hedonistic sex drive knew few limitations. Movie fans and film critics alike hastened to note that a subtheme of *Cat on a Hot Tin Roof* had been Maggie's lustful seduction of somebody else's husband, namely, her screen spouse's best friend. The similarity between the real-life Liz and her movie counterpart drew vast audiences to *Cat.* If religious and civic groups lambasted her, if the *New Yorker* published outrageous cartoons lampooning her predicament, if the Academy of Motion Picture Arts and Sciences passed her over for an Oscar, she nevertheless appeared to profit from that which the press had dubbed the "Debbie-Eddie-Liz biz." By November 1958, she had signed to make two new movies, *Two for the Seesaw,* from which she later bowed out, and *Suddenly, Last Summer.* Both contracts called for her to receive $500,000 against 10 percent of the gross. Elizabeth Taylor had emerged as the world's highest-paid, most-sought-after actress.

Earl Wilson observed that Elizabeth Taylor's "bad" behavior "brought her rewards rather than punishment. It seemed the thing to do in the motion picture industry was to create such an outlandish personality for yourself that the public had to grant your every exigency. Eventually you would get away with holy hell. Everybody said, 'Oh, Elizabeth Taylor is so naughty'—but then they forgave her.

"As for Debbie Reynolds, she wasn't quite the 'little darling' she appeared to be. To put it bluntly, Debbie has more balls than any five guys I've ever known. She pretends to be sweet and demure, but at heart she's hard as nails."

Adding to the complexity of Elizabeth's current predicament, she made a decision that would add her to a list of show-business names that included Marilyn Monroe, Sammy Davis Jr., Carroll Baker, Diana Dors, and Polly Bergen. These and other figures had in recent years converted to the Jewish faith. It was Elizabeth's intention to do the same.

The emotions she felt for Mike Todd after his death only partially fueled her decision to convert to Judaism. A secondary influence may well have been the result of a defiant attitude she had always demonstrated in regard to her family. She hadn't yet forgotten her mother's unkind treatment of Jewish director Stanley Donen. More recently, another family disagreement occurred when she and Eddie Fisher stayed with Howard Young in Connecticut. According to Fran Holland, one of Young's neighbors, Uncle Howard took "an instant dislike to Fisher. He couldn't understand why Elizabeth would become involved with *so many* Jewish men. 'First,' he complained, 'she marries Mike Todd, and now she's dating Todd's best friend. What the hell does she see in all these Jewish guys?'"

Howard Young's attitude toward Fisher no doubt encouraged Elizabeth's desire to rebel against the middle-class conventions of her family background. What better way to revolt than to commit an act of spectacular nonconformity? Ironically, Eddie Fisher staunchly opposed the idea of Taylor's conversion to Judaism. "I didn't see the need for it," he explained, "nor had Mike Todd. It only resulted in a fresh torrent of unwanted publicity, a flood of accusations among enemies who believed the ploy was simply one more grandstand play on the part of a spoiled child. In terms of my own marriage to Elizabeth, her religious convictions made no difference to me. Debbie Reynolds, don't forget, wasn't a Jew and never became one."

Dr. Max Nussbaum of Temple Israel in Hollywood, a former associate of Mike Todd's, offered to serve as Elizabeth's spiritual adviser. Known in Tinseltown as "the Rabbi to the Stars," Nussbaum provided Elizabeth not only with encouragement but also with a long reading list—books on philosophy and Judaism; excerpts from the Old Testament; histories of the Jewish people; even a bestselling novel, *Exodus,* by Leon Uris. "The only problem," noted Eddie Fisher, "is that Elizabeth never bothered reading the books herself. I read them to her."

Fisher's candid admission may account for at least one erroneous statement subsequently issued by his future wife. In an interview with author Bill Davidson for a *Look* magazine profile, Elizabeth commented that there was "comfort and dignity and hope for me in this ancient religion that [has] survived for four thousand years." That Judaism has been around for more than fifty-seven hundred years seems completely to have eluded its newest devotee.

More to the point was Taylor's assertion that "today I perform all the rituals and go to a Reform Jewish temple, and I feel as if I have been a Jew all . . . my life." Elizabeth Taylor converted to Judaism in Temple Israel on March 27, 1959, but with this single exception (as well as her Las Vegas synagogue wedding to Fisher), Eddie could recall not one occasion on which she attended formal services at a temple. She did, however, pledge to invest $100,000 in Israeli bonds. Whether she ever met her obligation is not a matter of record.

Not even Ruth Nussbaum, the widow of Rabbi Max Nussbaum, could fully comprehend the motivation behind Taylor's religious conversion. "Neither Mike Todd nor Eddie Fisher cared," she pointed out. "Eddie would have married her without it, and Mike *did* marry her without it. Thus, it must have been an inner emotional urge that drove her to it. Elizabeth seemed young for her age; she seemed young in more ways than one."

Ann Straus, one of the first of Metro's public-relations staff to arrive at Elizabeth Taylor's house after Mike Todd's death, felt "amazed and shocked" when she learned about the Eddie Fisher–Elizabeth Taylor nuptials. "I'd known both Debbie Reynolds and Elizabeth Taylor since their formative days at M-G-M, and it stunned me to watch Elizabeth take away Debbie's husband just because she felt lonely. Debbie had a tough veneer, but it must have been an extremely difficult period for her."

In marrying her fourth husband, Elizabeth Taylor had emerged as the temptress, the seductress of her generation. While dining at Chasen's with Liz one evening, Eddie Fisher noticed Nicky Hilton and Mike Wilding seated at separate tables in the same restaurant. It must have seemed odd, even for Hollywood, to be able to glance around and find within one room a triad of "Taylor-made" spouses.

Eddie Fisher had left his Los Angeles hotel and rented an apartment on Sunset Boulevard, though he continued to be a frequent guest at Elizabeth's leased Spanish-style stucco house in Bel Air. Officially, they maintained separate addresses, she told her friend Dorismae Kerns of Metro's publicity department, "out of concern" for "all the children involved—mine and Eddie's." Her "concern" didn't prevent her from jumping into her Rolls-Royce Silver Cloud with Eddie and her children and passing the day at Disneyland. The junket prompted *Photoplay* to write that Eddie and Liz's affair "should be marked in silence and sorrow, not in public revels." The same periodical reproduced a photograph of a van from I. Magnin arriving with a rack of evening gowns at Liz's home; she would choose a half dozen for herself in the comfort of her bedroom. Van Cleef & Arpels on Rodeo Drive utilized a similar methodology, dispensing a sales representative and a security guard with sample cases of their finest jewelry. Elizabeth examined the merchandise and made her selection. Although journalists continued to dog her and Eddie, Liz had ceased defending herself in the press. Eddie and Elizabeth's stay in Los Angeles culminated one evening in a drive down Hollywood Boulevard in an open convertible: They couldn't have made themselves more conspicuous.

L'affaire Liz had caused the termination of Fisher's *Coke Time* television series and thus a good portion of his income. In addition, the high cost of divorce lawyers and the steep settlement he anticipated having to make with Debbie Reynolds threatened to devour the bulk of his savings. So, on April 2, 1959, Eddie Fisher began a new six-week engagement at the Tropicana in Las Vegas. The stint provided much-needed income.

Other problems soon arose. Hate mail (including voodoo dolls with pins stuck in them) and death threats (among them notes from the Ku Klux Klan) arrived for Eddie and Liz in such volume that Fisher began carrying a loaded gun—"not that I knew how to use it," he ventured. When Elizabeth appeared at the Tropicana for Eddie's opening night, she was greeted by dozens of pickets waving placards that read Liz Leave Town! and Liz Go Home! She stayed, but she insisted on hiring a team of bodyguards to protect her and her children.

Elizabeth and her brood stayed at the Hidden Well Ranch in Pleasant Valley, five miles from Las Vegas. While at the ranch she gave but one brief interview in which she declared her expectation to be married to Fisher for no less than "a century." To this she added, "But first Eddie has to get divorced."

On the morning of May 12, 1959, having fulfilled Nevada's residential requirement and having cleared the way with Debbie Reynolds, Fisher spent twelve minutes before Nevada district judge David Zenoff in order to dissolve his existing matrimonial ties. He requested that the divorce papers be permanently sealed; Judge Zenoff complied.

At noon of the same day, Elizabeth Taylor joined him at the marriage-license bureau in Las Vegas's two-story town hall. Eddie jokingly offered to pay for the license in gambling chips. When the clerk declared he could only accept cash, Liz reached into her pocketbook and plucked out a crisp ten-dollar bill.

Patricia Newcomb, a press agent with the Los Angeles public relations firm of Rogers and Cowan, had been chosen to orchestrate the Fisher-Taylor nuptials. As a spokesperson for Marilyn Monroe and a close friend of the powerful Kennedy family of Massachusetts, Newcomb possessed the credentials for the job.

It had been Newcomb's idea to hold the wedding the day of Eddie's divorce and to limit the guest list as much as possible. The ceremony took place at Las Vegas's one-year-old Temple Beth Shalom, Rabbi Max Nussbaum (Elizabeth's religious mentor) officiating (assisted by Rabbi Bernard Cohen). Michael Todd Jr. served as best man, while Mara Taylor, Elizabeth's sister-in-law, was appointed maid of honor. Others in attendance included Liz's children, her brother, her parents, Eddie's parents (recently divorced), Dick Hanley, Sid Guilaroff, Ketti and Kurt Frings, Milton Blackstone, Mr. and Mrs. Eddie Cantor, Philip and Gloria Luchenbill (friends of Eddie Fisher), Dr. Rex Kennamer, Benny Thau, Eddie's lawyer, and several of Eddie's representatives from the William Morris Agency.

Eddie wore a white yarmulke and a blue business suit, while Elizabeth (whose Hebrew name was Elisheba Rachel) had on a Jean Louis green chiffon dress with a loosely draped hood, high neckline, and long sleeves. Bride and groom stood beneath a *chuppah* adorned with carnations and gardenias. They recited their marital vows in Hebrew and English, sipped sacramental wine, broke the wineglass, and signed the marriage contract. They then kissed. Elizabeth finally turned to her guests and announced: "I've never been happier in my life. We will be on our honeymoon for thirty or forty years."

The only photographer permitted to take pictures of the ceremony and reception was Bob Willoughby, who had been the still photographer on *Raintree County.* "A few days before the wedding," he said, "I received a telephone call in New York from Pat Newcomb. 'Elizabeth Taylor wants you to photograph her wedding,' she said. The request surprised me because I hadn't known Elizabeth very long. I'd danced with her at the cast party following *Raintree County,* but that was the extent of our friendship.

"I offered my services gratis, asking only that I be provided a round-trip airplane ticket. Pat Newcomb met me at the airport in a Rolls-Royce and drove me to Beth Shalom, a synagogue so new they hadn't yet landscaped the property. There were hordes of tourists, reporters, photographers, and police outside the temple. They whisked me in via a back entrance, and I took my shots. They then drove me to the Hidden Well Ranch, where they had set up tables and chairs for a reception, after which the couple spent several minutes with the press."

While answering questions, Elizabeth spotted Vernon Scott of UPI. Several weeks earlier, Scott had written a negative story on Eddie and Liz. As usual, Elizabeth was intent on having the last word. "Why don't you screw off, Vernon!" she said, her eyes boring holes through his.

Later that night, the newlyweds flew to New York for what they hoped would be the beginning of a restful European honeymoon. Surrounded by children (Elizabeth's), pets, aides, employees, and luggage, Eddie shortly cast himself in the twin roles of concierge and nursemaid. One of his tasks, as assigned by his demanding wife, was to keep a running inventory of their more than sixty pieces of combined luggage. Hearing of the singer's travails, Truman Capote began calling him "the Busboy." When Richard Burton met Fisher during the making of *Cleopatra*, he referred to him as "the Waiter," whereas the press now knew him as "Mr. Elizabeth Taylor," a sobriquet they had formerly bestowed on both Nicky Hilton and Michael Wilding. Regarding Taylor, Eddie registered his own early note of frustration: "Elizabeth fought over anything and everything. I couldn't deal with it, so I tried to appease her, but she would become even more ferocious.

"She did try to help me with my drug problem, and she was beautiful, of course. But to keep her happy you had to give her a diamond before breakfast every morning."*

Elizabeth likewise acquired gifts for Eddie—a Cartier watch inscribed "When time began . . ." and a Piaget platinum timepiece engraved "You ain't seen nothin' yet." "Except for a green Rolls-Royce, which she gave me for my birthday, Elizabeth enjoyed purchasing gifts in pairs," remarked Fisher. "I recall a set of diamond-and-emerald cuff links for formal wear and cabochon emerald-and-gold links for business meetings. She wasn't chintzy."

Elizabeth's generosity notwithstanding, Eddie Fisher very quickly understood that their marriage would be a trying endeavor. The least setback in her life—in health or otherwise—led to a major crisis. An idle cough or sneeze by Elizabeth occasioned a dozen telephone consultations with Dr. Rex Kennamer, often resulting in an office visit with some other highly recommended and costly medical specialist. Fisher realized Liz's ailments were not just psychosomatic in nature but an urgent call for love and attention. He must have also seen that his own career would forever play second fiddle to hers.

*Among the more valuable gifts Elizabeth Taylor received from Eddie Fisher were a $270,000 diamond bracelet, a $150,000 evening bag studded with diamonds, and a $500,000 emerald necklace from Bulgari.

Sam Spiegel, producer of Liz's next scheduled film, *Suddenly, Last Summer,* had lent Liz and Eddie his 120-foot yacht, the *Orinoco*, for a honeymoon cruise in the Mediterranean. The boat featured a full crew and a service staff comprised of French maids and a Belgian chef. Stormy weather cut short their journey. The newlyweds disembarked at Cannes and spent several days on the Riviera as guests of Prince Aly Khan, taking day trips to visit the yachts of Gianni Agnelli and Aristotle Onassis. They then flew to London, where in two weeks Elizabeth would begin shooting *Suddenly, Last Summer.*

For their comfort and privacy, Sam Spiegel gave them the keys to a fifteen-room estate next door to Windsor Castle. The property, surrounded by high walls topped by barbed wire, was made further secure by the presence of a private security team. Elizabeth rested and gave occasional newspaper interviews, but only to members of the press she knew and thought she could trust.

One reporter, an acquaintance of the late Mike Todd, gained access and asked her about her future ambition. "To be a good wife and mother," she responded in the saccharine-sweet but impatient tone she had reserved for such occasions. When the reporter reminded her she had presented a nearly identical response to the same query after marrying Mike Todd, the interview abruptly ended.

A British publication called *Weekend* printed a fabricated interview with Elizabeth Taylor. After Fisher and Taylor sued the periodical for damages, the tabloid printed an apology and donated a moderate sum to charity in Elizabeth Taylor's name.

If Taylor expected to be invited to parties and dinners by Britain's aristocracy, she must have been sorely disappointed. "Elizabeth couldn't bring herself to admit it," remarked Eddie Fisher, "but we were royally snubbed. Nobody in British high society would either invite us to their homes or visit us in ours."

Unaccustomed to being so thoroughly rebuffed, Elizabeth insisted on leaving the country estate and moving instead into the Dorchester Hotel in London proper. " 'The Dorch,' said Eddie Fisher, "had the only suites in town large enough to accommodate us, the children, the pets, the employees, and all the rest, including Elizabeth's ego, which had been somewhat reduced by her lack of popularity among the British."

Having performed at least proficiently as the voluptuous beauty in *Cat on a Hot Tin Roof,* Taylor seemed adequately suited for the latest Tennessee Williams adaptation. The problem with *Suddenly, Last Summer,* once again, was the difficulty of transmogrifying a Williams stage piece into a workable screenplay. In addition, Sam Spiegel had to contend with the complex lives of those involved in the making of the picture.

Directed by Joseph L. Mankiewicz and scripted by Gore Vidal (from "Tenn's evil and vicious tale," noted Vidal), the film starred Taylor as the emotionally traumatized cousin of the poet Sebastian, whose violent death on a beach in Spain at the hands of a pack of lecherous cannibals she had been forced to witness. Sebastian's mother (brilliantly played by Katharine Hepburn) is anxious to persuade Dr. Cukrowicz, a young neurosurgeon (Montgomery Clift), that her alluring niece is mentally deranged and in drastic need of a lobotomy. The action advances to Elizabeth's climactic monologue, which she accomplishes almost miraculously without overacting (she received her third successive Oscar nomination for the role) and in which we learn that Sebastian was a homosexual.

The film received decidedly mixed reviews. *Variety* called it "possibly the most bizarre film ever made by a major American company." Bosley Crowther of the *New York Times* began his critique: "Mr. Williams and Gore Vidal have indulged in sheer verbal melodramatics which have small effect on the screen and are barely elevated from tedium by some incidental scenes of inmates of a mental institution." The *New York Herald Tribune* cited it as a film of "poetic strength," whereas *Film Daily* noted that "Tennessee Williams' brooding, probing study of a set of introverted people and how they use each other in a devouring way is here brought to the screen with striking theatrical flair."

Cinematographer Jack Hildyard revealed some of the problems that occurred in the course of the movie's production. "First of all," he remarked, "Elizabeth Taylor arrived on the set at Shepperton Studio appearing a trifle soft around the edges. Joe Mankiewicz, whom she'd known through Mike Todd, took one look and said, 'Are you planning to lose any weight?' Elizabeth responded that she hadn't actually thought about it. Joe then lifted her arm and said, 'I think maybe you should do a little toning up, because this (he indicated her upper arm) looks like a bag of dead mice.'

"As brutal as the criticism sounded, Joe and Elizabeth hit it off in the end. Neither Joe nor Liz, however, got along with Katharine Hepburn, who had personal problems; her lover, Spencer Tracy, had fallen ill in New York and couldn't join her in London. The consummate professional, Hepburn always arrived on the set on time, whereas Elizabeth Taylor was invariably late. She kept us waiting, and *nobody* kept Katharine Hepburn waiting. What Hepburn didn't know was that Liz had been experiencing a great deal of pain from an impacted wisdom tooth and had to apply ice packs every morning to keep down the swelling. Mankiewicz tried explaining the situation to Kate, but she refused to listen. Liz finally had the tooth extracted, by which point Kate, out of exasperation, had taken to directing portions of the film. Joe became so infuriated that on one occasion he threatened to close down the production. 'We will resume shooting, Miss Hepburn,' he screamed, 'when the Directors Guild card which I ordered for you arrives from Hollywood.' Kate stormed into her dressing room and refused to return that day.

"By the termination of the film, Hepburn and Mankiewicz were mortal enemies. Everyone knows the story of how on the final day of shooting she went to see Joe and said, 'Are you finished with me?' The director indicated he was. 'You're quite sure you don't need me for retakes or dubbing or additional close-ups?' Hepburn inquired. 'I've got it all, Kate,' said Joe, 'and it's great. *You're* great.' Hepburn persisted. 'You're absolutely certain that I'm through with this picture?' Joe grinned and nodded. 'Absolutely.' On that note, Hepburn remarked, 'I just want to leave you with this.' She threw back her head and spat in his face. She never worked with Mankiewicz again."

If the director's greatest personal problems on the set were with Katharine Hepburn, he had more than his share of professional difficulties with Montgomery Clift. According to Hildyard, "By the late 1950s, Monty's health had degenerated so completely that he could barely make it onto the set, no less perform. Overcome by the effects of his addictions to drugs and alcohol (he carried around a bottle at all times and would tip it up and drink from it directly), he had become a bog of tics and tremors. Nor could he remember lines. I don't recall a single scene he did which didn't have to be reshot a dozen times." In a moment of rare humor, Sam Spiegel said to Hildyard: "We would have been better off casting Monty as one of the mental patients in the film rather than a doctor."

"It reached the stage where Sam Spiegel expressed the need to replace Monty with another actor," said Hildyard. "They were talking about Peter O'Toole. Elizabeth Taylor got wind of this and said to Spiegel: 'Over my dead body. If Monty goes, I go.' What's more, she meant it. She eventually had Spiegel banned from the set. Now that's power for you. Even Joe Mankiewicz had to admire the manner in which Liz pushed Spiegel around."

There were several people close to Joe Mankiewicz who believed that the director, an avid ladies' man,* had more than mere "admiration" for Taylor. Christopher Mankiewicz, eldest of Joe's two sons, insisted that his brother Tom Mankiewicz, who had been closer to his father than Chris, "felt that following the completion of *Suddenly, Last Summer,* it was possible they had been involved."

However, Joe Mankiewicz's companion in London during the production of the film, Jeanne Murray Vanderbilt, thought a romance between them seemed highly unlikely: "I surmised Elizabeth and Eddie Fisher weren't too happy together, but I saw no evidence of anything unusual between Joe and Liz. Then again, I wasn't around all the time, so anything's conceivable. Joe was a son of a bitch, and I wouldn't

*Among Joe Mankiewicz's former lovers were Joan Crawford, Gene Tierney, and Linda Darnell. "He had a habit," said his son Chris Mankiewicz, "of bedding down with his leading ladies."

have put anything past him. A fine director, he was also completely self-absorbed, extremely jealous, forever complaining and grumbling about this and that. But in his defense, I never saw him put a move on Elizabeth."

The final scenes of *Suddenly, Last Summer* were shot at Begur, a small fishing village on Spain's Costa Brava. Actress Evelyn Keyes, who had married bandleader and clarinet player Artie Shaw, was living in a nearby hillside villa. She bumped into Fisher and Taylor in town one morning and invited them to dinner.

"I tried to be hospitable," said Evelyn. "I knew Fisher from my days with Mike Todd. It didn't surprise me when he and Liz got married. She needed a man by her side, and Eddie had been in the right place at the right time.

"He arrived first with Elizabeth's children. At one point he accidentally shattered a nearly invisible sliding-glass panel, suffering a few minor cuts and bruises in the process. Elizabeth appeared a few minutes later but didn't seem the least bit concerned by Eddie's mishap.

"The children were sent back to the hotel in a studio car, while Eddie and Liz stayed for supper. But the evening didn't go well. The couple began arguing the moment they were served, and with each succeeding course their voices grew louder. The origin of their disagreement had to do with a French newspaper, which had run a story suggesting that Elizabeth and Eddie had been involved *before* Mike Todd's death. She wanted to sue. Eddie, having already endured a similar process with the British press, opposed the notion. 'Don't make waves with the press,' he advised Elizabeth. 'They'll only say worse things about us.'"

Evelyn Keyes further observed that the "underlying hostility accompanying their disagreement gave off the acrid odor of disenchantment. I couldn't help but notice that Elizabeth wore Eddie's wedding ring on her left hand and Mike Todd's on her right—or so she pointed out after Artie took Eddie into his study. She told me that thinking about Mike's death had enabled her to muster the psychological force she had needed to realize her climactic nonstop monologue in *Sud-*

denly, Last Summer. But after shooting the scene, she had been unable to stop crying."

Mary Jane Picard, a British socialite vacationing with her husband in Begur at the time Taylor and Fisher were there, recounted her reaction to the couple: "Whenever they appeared in public together, Elizabeth behaved rather indifferently toward Fisher. He, on the other hand, seemed very much in love. He was always trying to touch Elizabeth, to hold on to her, to put his arms around her and give her a kiss. While she didn't shrink from his touch, she certainly didn't encourage him. She was cool toward him.

"I hasten to add she seemed just as unresponsive with respect to her children, whereas Fisher, though he wasn't their natural father, appeared much more connected to them. He would hold their hands, make certain their coats were properly buttoned, and play little games with them.

"One heard all sorts of stories about Eddie and Liz. I was told they attended a dinner party at the home of some Spanish aristocrat. The other guests were all titled Spaniards. Elizabeth arrived an hour or two late, decked out like a Christmas tree, with necklaces, bracelets, rings, earrings—everything in diamonds. The real aristocrats were understated in their choices of jewelry. The world of European royalty went beyond Elizabeth's understanding. She and Fisher came off like a pair of flashing neon signs—a couple of uncouth Americans. It immediately became clear that they were out of place. They left promptly after dinner. In England, people like Noël Coward and Cecil Beaton had complete disdain for Elizabeth Taylor. They considered her unsophisticated and "low-brow.""

While still in Spain, Elizabeth Taylor became involved in what surely must rate as one of the great screen follies of the century. Utilizing a technique (or gimmick) he called Smell-O-Vision, Michael Todd Jr. had opted to follow in his father's footsteps and produce a film, *The Scent of Mystery* (*Holiday in Spain*), calculated to make him equally rich and famous. To increase the chances of both, he asked his father's widow not only to invest in the project but also to appear in it (albeit in a cameo role). Elizabeth agreed, and the results were laughable.

An artless, loose-jointed chase picture starring Peter Lorre and set against the picturesque backdrop of Spain, the film centers on a vacationing Englishman who happens upon a plot to kill a young American female tourist. The girl disappears, and her trail becomes tangled with odd occurrences and characters. A complicated projection setup in select American movie theaters called for the periodic emission during the screening of the film of certain odors and scents related to the plot, including the perfume of the missing girl, tobacco, shoe polish, port wine, baked bread, coffee, lavender, and peppermint.

Reviewing *The Scent of Mystery* for the *Saturday Review*, Hollis Alpert observed: "Some odors come early, some late and some not at all, and the whole business made me confused, especially since I was trying to equate the evidence of my eyes with the evidence of my nose." The film proved a box-office disaster and resulted in several lawsuits, including one by Elizabeth Taylor and Michael Todd Jr. against the film's distributor.

Having departed Spain for Paris, Elizabeth Taylor received a telephone call from Hollywood producer Walter Wanger.* Several years earlier, Wanger had signed a tentative agreement with Buddy Adler, then the president of Twentieth Century-Fox, to produce an epic motion picture based on the life and loves of Cleopatra. Not long after approving the deal, Adler died. He was succeeded by Spyros P. Skouras, who had once headed the studio.

Walter Wanger had first approached Taylor about the title role during her marriage to Mike Todd, at which time she showed little interest. Todd had died by the time Wanger contacted her again, in November 1958, to inquire whether she might have undergone a change of heart.

*Wanger had received a great deal of unwanted publicity in the early 1950s when he was convicted of shooting and injuring the agent of his second wife, actress Joan Bennett. The episode took place after Wanger, in a fit of jealous rage, discovered the two were involved in an illicit romance. Wanger served a brief jail sentence, after which he returned to Miss Bennett. They divorced in 1962.

On the latter occasion, she demonstrated more enthusiasm for the project. She would consider it, she said, provided Wanger came up with a workable script; she didn't want a simpleminded, low-budget rewrite of the silent-screen version of *Cleopatra* which Twentieth Century-Fox had made starring Theda Bara in 1917.

Wanger's next conversation with Taylor, the telephone call he placed to her in Paris on September 1, 1959, changed not only the course of Elizabeth's private life but also the financial future of the entire film industry.

"I'll do it for a million dollars," she told him, "against ten percent of the box-office gross."

"I'll have to get back to you," replied Wanger. He called again within the hour. "We've got a deal," he said.

The record-smashing seven-figure fee surpassed even Elizabeth Taylor's boldest expectation. She and Eddie Fisher, in an exuberant mood, celebrated by dining at Maxim's. Their joy was short-lived. Having carefully monitored the progression of the Fox deal, the lions at M-G-M soon began to roar in defiance.

According to her latest contract with Metro, Elizabeth owed the studio one last film performance, and M-G-M meant to enforce her contractual obligation. Before she could sign with Wanger to appear in *Cleopatra,* she would have to agree to a single film contract with the studio that had weaned her since childhood.

To make matters more difficult, M-G-M wanted Elizabeth to play the female lead in the film *Butterfield 8,* which was based on a John O'Hara novel, itself inspired by the intriguing saga of Starr Faithful, a notorious call girl of the 1940s and 1950s. In the screen version, scripted by Charles Schnee and John Michael Hayes, the Starr Faithful character is renamed Gloria Wandrous (as in the novel). In order to satisfy the strict regulations of the Morals Production Code then operative in the motion-picture industry, certain details concerning the story and its main character had to be toned down.

The changes ultimately satisfied Geoffrey M. Shurlock, the Production Code administrator, but Elizabeth Taylor remained highly skeptical. "The leading lady is nearly a prostitute," she moaned. "The whole thing is so unpalatable, I wouldn't do it for anything—under any conditions."

What Elizabeth found particularly unpalatable was having to take only $125,000 for *Butterfield 8* and possibly jeopardizing a million-dollar payday with Fox. She telephoned M-G-M production supervisor Sol C. Siegel and asked if she could do *Cleopatra* first. "The answer is the shorter of the two possibilities," he responded. "In fact, Elizabeth, if you don't comply with the conditions of your current contract with us, we'll have no choice but to place you on suspension. You won't be allowed to appear in anything for the next two years."

"Is this any way to end an eighteen-year relationship?" Elizabeth asked.

"Fortunately or unfortunately, Elizabeth," Siegel countered, "sentiment went out of this business a long time ago."

On September 9, Taylor (along with her children) and Fisher returned to Los Angeles and rented two bungalows at the Beverly Hills Hotel. One evening they entertained Liz's former husband Michael Wilding and his current wife, Susan. On another occasion, Eddie's two young children, Carrie and Todd, were brought over for dinner. It marked one of the few times Eddie would have direct contact with them during his marriage to Taylor.

Ten days after their arrival, the Fishers joined more than four hundred of Hollywood's heralded stars, including Frank Sinatra, Marilyn Monroe, Cary Grant, Gregory Peck, Rita Hayworth, David Niven, and Bob Hope, at a Twentieth Century-Fox luncheon honoring Soviet premier Nikita Khrushchev. Following lunch, Khrushchev debated Skouras on the respective merits of communism and capitalism. Richard Burton, also present at the affair, had to be restrained from jumping out of his chair and yelling at Khrushchev for what he later defined as the Soviet premier's malicious comments. Elizabeth Taylor, seated toward the rear of the room, stood atop her table for a better view of the proceedings. She saw Burton moving about and whispered to Eddie Fisher that the Welsh actor "seems to be foaming at the mouth."

Elizabeth shortly went to see Pandro Berman, producer of four of her earlier M-G-M films, including *National Velvet.* Berman had volunteered to produce *Butterfield 8.*

"What she said and what she did is beyond belief," revealed Berman in a subsequent newspaper interview. "She was furious. She said to me, 'You'll be sorry. You can make me do it, but you can't make me act in it. I won't show up! I'll be late!'

"I said, 'I'll take that chance.'

"'I'm going to give you all kinds of grief,' she added.

"Then I became angry. 'Now look, I'm going to tell you something. There'll be a lot of good people working on this film with you. You'll screw things up for them, as well as for yourself, if you don't cooperate. I think you're too professional to do that. Furthermore, in my opinion, you're going to win the Academy Award with this picture.'

"Elizabeth roared with laughter. She informed me she thought it the worst script ever written. Anyway, she finally signed the contract. She made several demands, and for the benefit of all, we complied. She wanted the film to be made in New York, not in Los Angeles, where people were still castigating her for having married Eddie Fisher. She insisted that Helen Rose design her outfits and Sidney Guilaroff style her hair. She also wanted Eddie Fisher to be given a supporting role in the picture. The part she wanted for him, originally slated for David Janssen, was that of Steve Carpenter, a young composer and best friend of Gloria Wandrous, whose true purpose in the film is to serve as Gloria's conscience. Fisher had little desire to play the role but did so to satisfy Elizabeth."

The couple departed for New York on October 19, 1959. They traveled by train (the *Super Chief*), accompanied by Robert Wagner and his wife, Natalie Wood. Six years Liz's junior, Natalie, about to costar with Warren Beatty in *Splendor in the Grass,* looked up to Taylor as she might to an older sister. For the three days of their cross-country railroad journey, the two actresses chatted amicably about their difficult childhoods. Both were the products of domineering mothers and docile fathers, and both had broken the shackles of parental control by marrying at a young age—too young, they each concluded.

Eddie and Elizabeth checked into a suite at the Park Lane Hotel in New York, placed a Do Not Disturb sign on their door, and spent the next three days in bed. "Elizabeth began taking three and four baths a day," noted Eddie, "to relieve pains in her back and a series of acute headaches which she continued to suffer for the remainder of our marriage. One of her doctors diagnosed her migraines as psychosomatic, the result of her feelings of guilt for not having perished in the airplane crash with Mike Todd.

"I soon began joining her in the bathtub. She loved to be pampered, to have me wash her hair and scrub her back. She also liked to make love in the tub; it alleviated her aches and pains, at least temporarily.

"We didn't dwell on comparisons, but Elizabeth told me I was her greatest lover. She claimed she loved me more than she had ever loved anyone before, even more than she loved her children. I soon realized Elizabeth tended to *romanticize* romance. The man she loved at the moment was always her greatest love and her best lover.

"She would tell the managers of the hotels we frequented not to let the maids into our rooms until the afternoon. 'Eddie's favorite time to fuck is the morning,' Liz would say. She wouldn't bat an eye when she said it."

Eddie Fisher began a nightly engagement in the Empire Room of the Waldorf-Astoria. During the day he would meet with Monty Clift, and Clift would attempt to help him master his forthcoming role in *Butterfield 8.* "I would be flying on amphetamines administered by Max Jacobson," recalled Fisher, "and Monty would be floating in an alcohol-induced haze. He usually passed out in the middle of the session."

Elizabeth, meanwhile, raced around town in search of a screenwriter who could possibly improve the "ghastly" *Butterfield 8* script. Joe Mankiewicz read it, told her, "It sucks," but declined to make changes. She received a similar response from Tennessee Williams. She next sought out Paddy Chayefsky and Daniel Taradash and asked them if they could at least build up Eddie Fisher's part.

Pandro Berman received a telephone call from Elizabeth. Could he come over to their hotel? He went, and they handed him a new version of the script.

"Now this is something we *would* like to do," said Elizabeth.

"Well, I wouldn't," responded Berman as he walked across the room and dropped the batch of papers in a wastebasket.

Elizabeth flew at Berman with her nails ready to scratch his eyes out. She was spitting and hissing.

"I won't read it," insisted Berman. "I'm not interested in any re-writes. I have a writer on this picture, and he has done a fine job. We're going to make the script we've got!"

Shortly after they began shooting, Elizabeth came down with what doctors diagnosed as double pneumonia. "She had been so heavily sedated at the hotel," said Fisher, "that she was out cold in the ambulance that rushed her, lights flashing and siren wailing, to the Harkness Pavilion. As we approached the emergency entrance, Elizabeth suddenly regained consciousness, sat up on the stretcher, removed a compact from her pocketbook, and started powdering her face. 'Get my lip gloss,' she said, handing me the bag. I found it, and she applied it to her lips before being wheeled away.

"As usual, she felt she was about to die. But considering the serious nature of her ailment, she made an amazingly speedy recovery. Almost too speedy. I began to doubt the accuracy of the diagnosis."

Once Elizabeth left the hospital, work on the film resumed. Daniel Mann, director of the movie, depicted the production as a "short, painful operation, particularly for Elizabeth, because she made it that way for herself and for everybody else. She hated nearly everyone who worked with her to help make it a better film. Even an old comrade like Helen Rose suffered at Elizabeth's hands. Liz griped constantly about her costumes. For that matter, so did M-G-M. They had sent me a wire: 'Too much cleavage. The censors won't go for it.' We had put a stagehand on a ladder; his only job was to peer down the front of Taylor's dress to see if the camera might be recording an excess of bosom. One day I blew my stack and sent a memo to M-G-M: 'She's supposed to be a hooker for chris' sake, not a Mother Superior.'

"Almost everybody connected with the film despised her, including costar Laurence Harvey, who nicknamed her 'the Bitch' and at other times called her 'Fat Ass.' But as the movie progressed, he began to gain respect for her. He alone came to defend her. My opinion never changed. I thought she behaved indecently.

"We would schedule an eight A.M. shoot, and she would show up at two in the afternoon. Most of us were driven to and from the Gold Medal Studios, located in the Bronx, in Cadillac town cars provided by the Carey Transportation Company. Elizabeth insisted they provide her with a Rolls-Royce. 'Every bartender in America drives a Cadillac,' she said. She criticized the size and color of her dressing room, the low temperature on the soundstage, even the food. She had to have hers sent daily from Lindy's in midtown Manhattan."

What mostly distressed Daniel Mann was the manner in which Elizabeth Taylor dealt with producer Pandro Berman. "One evening," Mann recalled, "Pandro and I went to see Elizabeth about some of the problems she'd been creating with respect to the picture. We arrived just as she and Eddie Fisher had sat down to supper in their hotel suite. They were having turkey, mashed potatoes with gravy, hot rolls, and wine—a bona fide southern feast. We walked in, and Elizabeth looked over at Berman and said: 'Look, fuckface, get the hell out of here!' Then she looked at me and winked while Berman turned to leave.

"I considered her caustic and overindulged by all the years of stardom she'd enjoyed. We made a mistake in trying to pamper her. M-G-M demonstrated a willingness to do almost anything to appease her so as not to jeopardize the film. I imagine these were difficult times for her. She seemed a little rearranged in the head, probably because of the circumstance of Mike Todd's dying and her becoming immediately involved with Eddie Fisher. When she first arrived in New York, she appeared unattractive. She was overweight and had dark circles under her eyes. The reason she looked great in the film was because she received a great deal of assistance. The clothes she wore in *Butterfield 8* had to be constantly refitted. Special undergarments and corsets were employed to hold her body in shape. She had lost the firmness of youth and looked matronly before her time. I also determined that she couldn't see a thing without contact lenses; she was myopic."

Elizabeth's mood didn't improve even after she signed a contract in November 1959 to make *Cleopatra* her next film. During the same period, Daniel Mann remembered an episode on the *Butterfield 8* set when, true to form, Liz arrived hours late "accompanied by her usual entourage of secretaries, publicists, hairdressers, and lackeys, whose only responsibility involved carrying Taylor's daily supply of wine to her dressing room.

"I finally couldn't bear it any longer. On this particular day, I followed the parade into Elizabeth's dressing room and let loose with more than five thousand years of Jewish persecution. I gave her hell. I told her she was part of a collaborative effort, and out of respect for her coworkers she owed it to herself—and to us—to comport herself professionally.

"She seemed flabbergasted that anybody would have the temerity to enter her dressing room and talk to her that way, using a succession of four-letter words that even she found shocking.

"We had a second confrontation a few days later. I had been setting up a scene with my assistant director, and I could hear Elizabeth jabbering away on the soundstage, telling one and all how *she* would shoot the scene. I walked out from behind the camera and again made it abundantly clear that she was interfering with my work. I informed her that what I had to say to the actor and the way I chose to communicate were part of my function as director. I didn't need her advice on how to make a movie."

To complicate Daniel Mann's problems with Elizabeth, he had to contend with Eddie Fisher, whose $100,000 salary for one week of work rankled the director. "He couldn't act," said Mann. "One scene required that he give Gloria Wandrous an extremely disgusted look. 'What's the matter, Eddie?' I asked. 'I can't do it,' he said. 'I'm in love with her.' I tried to explain that in the film she wasn't his wife; she was only a character. I took him outside to the street and pointed to a pile of dog shit in the gutter. 'Do you see that?' I said. 'I want you to look at Elizabeth as though she were that mass of excrement.' The directive elicited one of Taylor's few humorous quips during the picture. The next time she saw me, she ventured: 'Don't you think that "the Method" is a bit too sophisticated for Eddie?'"

Mann, labeled by some film critics as "pure Actors Studio," attempted to utilize the same stratagem with Elizabeth. One day when they were about to shoot a bathtub scene, he approached her and said, "Imagine you're fucking the faucet; that's the expression I want." Elizabeth responded by giving Mann the finger and stomping off the set.

Elizabeth's hostility toward the entire *Butterfield 8* experience continued beyond the conclusion of filming. Following a studio presentation of the rough-cut version, she hurled a drink at the screen and used her lipstick to scrawl the words "No Sale!" on the producer's office door, thereby re-creating a variation on the movie's memorable opening scene in which Gloria Wandrous, after spending a night with her lover (Laurence Harvey), splashes the same message across his bathroom mirror.

Daniel Mann's displeasure was heightened by events surrounding the company's final cast party. "When the picture came to a close," he recalled, "Eddie Fisher approached me and said he and Elizabeth hoped to give everybody involved with the film a souvenir. They wanted to buy pewter mugs inscribed 'From Elizabeth, Eddie and Daniel.' Would I be willing to contribute? 'Of course,' I responded. They had only an out-of-state account, so I wrote out a check for the entire amount. 'We'll settle up later,' said Eddie. Needless to say, I never heard from either of them again. And I never made a claim for the difference. I didn't want to give them the satisfaction."

Chapter 16

During their stay in New York, Eddie Fisher and Elizabeth Taylor stopped in a Lexington Avenue pet shop and purchased Matilda, a small and mischievous woolly monkey with an endearing look in her eyes and a voracious appetite for hotel furniture. Her annoying eating habits became obvious when one of the room maids accidentally let the animal escape and a desk clerk found Matilda nonchalantly chomping on an upholstered couch in the hotel lobby. Elizabeth offered the monkey to her longtime friend Roddy McDowall, then sharing a ten-room apartment with fellow actor John Valva in the El Dorado, a grand art deco building at 300 Central Park West on Manhattan's Upper West Side.

"My recollection," said Valva, "is that Liz asked us to board the beast for only a few months. I transformed one of our bathrooms into a holding pen for Matilda. Once they completed *Butterfield 8,* Roddy gave Eddie and Elizabeth a bon voyage dinner party at which she gleefully announced she was placing the pet in our permanent care. After dinner Elizabeth and I lingered in the dining room. The other guests had retired to the den for coffee and cognac. Liz and I were chatting when she suddenly grasped my arm. 'You know,' she said, 'everybody thinks I married Eddie because of his connection to Mike Todd. Well, that's not true. Actually, I love Eddie Fisher.'"

In March 1960 the Fishers returned to the West Coast, again taking up residence at the Beverly Hills Hotel in the same adjoining bungalows they had previously occupied. Their next-door neighbors at the hotel were Yul and Doris Brynner. Yul Brynner, like Eddie Fisher, had been a devoted patient of Max Jacobson, but he had managed to break his amphetamine habit and no longer consulted with the controversial New York physician. Eddie Fisher, however, had grown increasingly dependent on Max's brand of medication. Not long after Eddie's return to Hollywood, Jacobson sent a substantial shipment of drugs and accompanying paraphernalia, personally delivered by Ken McKnight.

"I brought a large amount of injectable material to Fisher's bungalow at the Beverly Hills Hotel," remarked McKnight. "Elizabeth Taylor opened the door and explained that Eddie had left for the day. Did I want to come in and have a drink? She had on a see-through peignoir, with nothing but her birthday suit underneath. She had an imposing body, and I imagine I must have stood in the doorway gawking like a fool.

"Looking back on the experience, I probably should have accepted the invitation and joined her for a drink. She seemed quite eager for company. Under the circumstances, I felt shy. I simply handed her the package and left."

Had Ken McKnight entered the bungalow, he would have beheld a spectacle not unlike the one witnessed by the desk clerk at New York's Park Lane Hotel. In her descriptive history of the Beverly Hills Hotel, *The Pink Palace,* author Sandra Lee Stuart recounts how each day the hotel maids in charge of the Fisher-Taylor bungalow found "a trail of clothes . . . starting at the front door, going through the living room and into the bedroom." The bathroom contained "all of Taylor's numerous makeup bottles, wands and brushes" scattered about "as if a cyclone had hit a Bloomingdale's cosmetics counter." Sometimes there would be smudges of lipstick on the ceiling, although nobody could figure out how they got there. The dining-room table was covered with dozens of "half-empty bottles of liquor, jars of vitamin pills, and diamond bracelets, earrings and rings, all of which Liz had flung higgledy-piggledy."

A more immediate problem involved Elizabeth's assemblage of pets, particularly her canines. One of them, an ill-mannered collie, caused a flap when it mistook a hotel guest's trouser leg for a fire hydrant. None of her dogs had been housebroken. Frequently, they wet the bed on which Eddie and Liz slept. The smell became so offensive that the mattress had to be thrown out. The hotel added the cost of a replacement to Taylor's bill.

Two months after arriving in Los Angeles, the Fishers decided to vacation in Jamaica. Along the way, they stopped in Philadelphia to visit Eddie Fisher's mother. Elizabeth took one of her patented spills on the sidewalk in front of her mother-in-law's home and sprained an ankle. She soon began limping around on crutches. "As time passed," noted Eddie, "I came to suspect she enjoyed playing the invalid. It was a way of testing the devotion of those around her."

They spent a week at the newly constructed Marrakesh Hotel in Ocho Rios, Jamaica, before moving in with an acquaintance, Ernie Smatt, a wealthy businessman who owned a breathtaking oceanfront estate, a house that had been featured in *Playboy* magazine. To make them feel at home, Ernie gave his guests the master-bedroom suite, a sacrifice which upset his girlfriend. Possessing a sense of humor, Ernie told her: "The master bedroom is where the master sleeps. But if he sleeps in the guest bedroom, then *that* becomes the master bedroom."

"Elizabeth and I fell in love with Jamaica," Eddie remembered. When a real-estate agent showed us some property overlooking Mammee Bay, we purchased it. We financed the acquisition with funds from a copartnership we were in the process of establishing, MCL Films S.A., appropriately named after Elizabeth's three children (Michael, Christopher, and Liza). We commissioned an architect to draw up blueprints for a house which, like so many other of our ventures, remained only in the planning stage."

They returned to the States to attend a dinner dance at the Cavalier Hotel in Virginia Beach. Bandleader Lester Lanin, who had known Elizabeth since her early days at M-G-M, led the orchestra that evening.

"We shared a running joke," Lanin explained. "Whenever I saw her, I'd say, 'My, but you're ugly.' It made her laugh, because she was so weary of being told the opposite."

Eddie and Elizabeth headed for New York, where, on June 20, 1960, they joined a capacity crowd of fifty thousand at the old Polo Grounds for a heavyweight championship bout between Floyd Patterson and Swedish-born Ingemar Johansson. Johansson, an acquaintance of Taylor's, had provided her with a pair of ringside seats.

Another boxing fan at the Polo Grounds that night, Tania Grossinger, hadn't seen the Fishers since their premarital visit to Grossinger's. Her titillating account of the fight appeared in her book *Growing Up at Grossinger's:*

> Crazy things happened. We were seated a few rows behind Elizabeth Taylor and Eddie Fisher, she in a revealing low-cut blouse that left nothing to the imagination. Suddenly out of nowhere a gentleman walked over, plucked a breast out of her top, held it up for all to see, and shouted: "Ladies and gentlemen, I ask you. Isn't this a beautiful sight?" All agreed it was that, and Elizabeth, completely nonplussed, majestically put it back where it belonged. . . .

Floyd Patterson, the victor with a fifth-round knockout of Johansson, recalled hearing that after the fight, as Elizabeth was preparing to leave, people were "booing and hissing" her. "Hitting one arm across the other, she pushed up a clenched fist and made a sign to them, which meant 'Fuck you!' She didn't mouth the words, but she made the gesture."

In August 1960, Eddie and Elizabeth sailed to Europe with her children on the maiden voyage of the *Leonardo da Vinci,* arriving in Rome in time to attend the opening ceremony of the Olympic Games. Accompanied by Eddie Fisher, Dr. Rex Kennamer, Art Buchwald, and former New York State Lieutenant Governor Charles Poletti, Elizabeth entered the stadium late and drew the same general crowd reaction she had encountered at the Polo Grounds.

Art Buchwald, who attended several additional Olympic events with Liz, noted that "the crowds instantly recognized her and surged forward. They began pinching whatever part of her anatomy they could reach. The four men in the party, myself included, formed a phalanx around her to ward off the multitude of wandering hands. The situation grew increasingly bizarre. At the water-polo semifinals, not only the spectators but also the officials and even the athletes were reaching for Elizabeth's rump and breasts."

By early fall, Elizabeth and family were ensconced in two penthouse suites atop the Dorchester Hotel in London. Preproduction work on *Cleopatra* had been initiated at Pinewood Studios, with Peter Finch as Julius Caesar and Stephen Boyd as Mark Antony. It had been decided to use 70-mm film and the Todd A-O process, thus guaranteeing even more revenue for Elizabeth Taylor. Screenwriter Dale Wasserman was hired to improve and smooth over a script that had already undergone endless revision.

"Walter Wanger instructed me to write only for Elizabeth Taylor," said Wasserman. "I wasn't to think of anybody else. 'Elizabeth is the entire film,' Wanger told me.

"Remarkably, I never encountered the woman. Instead, I ran some of her old film footage to better acquaint myself with her acting style. I didn't want to meet her because I don't consider actors a particularly interesting group of people. I generally think of them as personalities in search of an identity. I find them curiously empty."

Although preliminary plans for *Cleopatra* advanced steadily, London's cold, damp climate eventually brought the venture to a halt. Rouben Mamoulian, the director of the film, received countless complaints from the Taylor camp. She was suffering her usual onslaught of headaches, toothaches, eyestrain, back spasms, coughing spells, and fevers of indeterminate origin. In the course of an average week, she often consulted with as many as a half dozen of London's leading physicians. Not one could produce a specific diagnosis.

"Elizabeth's problems in 1960 were basically the same as they were in 1990," said Eddie Fisher. "She had become addicted to every pill on the market—pills to help her sleep, pills to keep her awake, pills to dull her pain, pills and more pills."

Fisher had troubles of his own. According to Shelley Winters, who stayed at the Dorchester during her appearance in the London production of *Lolita,* Eddie spent hours drinking heavily at the hotel bar. "He was in a very depressed and despairing mood," she wrote. "He looked as if he was evaluating what he had done to his career and his life by divorcing. . . . Debbie Reynolds."

More likely than not, Fisher concerned himself not only with his own tribulations but also with the constant presence of Elizabeth's co-star, Peter Finch. Every evening, like clockwork, Finch appeared in Eddie and Liz's suite with news of the day's activities at Pinewood. Peter and Elizabeth would drown themselves in scotch and play marathon games of poker. One evening, Finch became so intoxicated that he passed out. Hotel personnel had to carry him from Taylor's bedroom to the chauffeur-driven limousine waiting for him in the Dorchester driveway.

Shelley Winters* recalled attending a dinner party for thirty-five guests, including Taylor and Fisher, Albert Finney, Michael Caine, Sarah Miles, Stanley Kubrick, Françoise Sagan, Sean Connery, and Peter Finch, during which Finch and Taylor huddled in a corner quietly conversing while Eddie Fisher morosely consumed a pitcher of martinis. "That night, when we all trooped out onto Abbey Road to get in our cars, I had the feeling that Eddie Fisher was trying to run over Peter Finch with his Rolls-Royce."

Fed up with London and the endless delays that had impeded the continuation of *Cleopatra,* Fisher hoped to try his hand at producing. Leaving Elizabeth behind, he flew to Hollywood and met with Harold Mirisch of United Artists. They discussed the possibility of striking up several movie deals for Elizabeth. *Irma La Douce* was mentioned, but

*Shelley Winters had little respect for Elizabeth Taylor's supposed intelligence and often made cracks about her "empty-headedness." One example: "While I was making *Lolita* in London, I was writing a letter and asked her: 'What's today's date?' Liz looked at a newspaper and replied: 'I can't tell you. This is yesterday's paper.'"

the lead eventually (and deservedly) went to Shirley MacLaine. Eddie next saw Jack Warner of Warner Brothers and proposed a package deal involving four motion pictures, two of them to star Elizabeth Taylor. Among the ideas considered and rejected were a remake of *Anna Karenina* and the story of modern dancer Isadora Duncan. Jack Warner later confided to his mistress, Jackie Park, that Taylor was eminently bankable but lacked true acting talent. "She can play herself," Warner persisted, "and that's about it. She's at her best when the plot revolves around sex."

Fisher rejoined Elizabeth in London. During his absence, she had remained bedridden with a low-grade fever. She had passed her days eating junk food, listening to records, trying on new French designs sent by Dior, and playing her nocturnal games of five-card stud with Peter Finch. She had appeared on the set only twice, each time complaining to cinematographer Jack Hildyard about backaches and headaches. Joanna Casson, Elizabeth's wig maker on the film, suggested she wear a pair of low, comfortable shoes, even tennis sneakers, during rehearsals to help alleviate the strain on her spine. Elizabeth, self-conscious about her height, continued to put on high heels.

On the night of November 13, 1960, Taylor was struck with such a piercing headache that Lord Evans, physician to Queen Elizabeth II, was summoned to the Dorchester. Alarmed by what he saw, he called a private ambulance service and had the patient removed to the exclusive London Clinic, where she was examined by Dr. Carl Goldman. Rex Kennamer, Elizabeth's personal physician, flew to London from Los Angeles; by the time he arrived, it had been determined that the patient was suffering from meningitis, an inflammation of the outer layer of brain and spinal-cord membrane.

Elizabeth remained in the hospital for a week, after which she embarked for Palm Springs on an enforced rest cure with her husband. Fisher's role in his wife's life remained unchanged. He answered her telephone calls, attended to all her whims (including lovemaking at any hour of the day or night), walked her dogs, supervised her meals, called for the car, spoke to her friends when she was either too busy or lazy, arranged travel schedules, and looked after her children. "The only way I could ever have hoped to resume my own career," he conjectured, "would have been to leave Elizabeth, but she could never have managed without me."

Following Liz's attack of meningitis, Twentieth Century-Fox temporarily shut down the eight-acre outdoor lot constructed at Pinewood for *Cleopatra.* The project had already cost Fox nearly $6 million without a single frame of usable film to show for the gargantuan effort. Spyros Skouras blamed the fiasco on director Rouben Mamoulian. According to Jack Hildyard, "Rouben made the mistake of turning to Elizabeth Taylor for help. She advised him to resign, with the understanding that she would refuse to appear in the film unless they rehired him. He resigned, and she in turn insisted they hire Joe Mankiewicz to direct what became known in the industry as *Cleopatra II.* When Rouben gave me the full story, I resigned as well."

Eddie and Elizabeth welcomed Joe Mankiewicz into the fold by leaving Palm Springs and returning to London to be present at a New Year's Eve dinner party hosted by Walter Wanger at Caprice, a British nightclub best known for its French cuisine. Also there that evening, among others, were Wanger's two teenage daughters, Stephanie and Shelley.

"There were eleven of us around the table," said Shelley Wanger. "Elizabeth wore a lavender off-the-shoulder dress by Christian Dior which had been flown in for the occasion. Liz's breasts stood out wildly that night, so much so that a distracted waiter managed to spill coffee all over the front of her dress. Elizabeth said nothing, but my father made such a fuss that the manager agreed to replace the garment."

The following day, Joe Mankiewicz set to work on a completely new rendition of the *Cleopatra* script. "I wanted to make an epic," said the new director. "I had in mind two separate but closely linked Elizabeth Taylor films—*Caesar and Cleopatra* and *Anthony and Cleopatra*—each to run three hours, both segments to receive simultaneous theatrical release. Moreover, I felt compelled to undertake the writing of both halves myself, a measure of my total dissatisfaction with the material that had been produced to date."

Presented with the outline of Mankiewicz's ambitious undertaking, Twentieth Century-Fox announced that work on interior scenes would commence at Pinewood no later than April 4, 1961; exteriors were to be shot afterward in Egypt and possibly Italy. Eddie Fisher remained dubious: "I didn't see how Mankiewicz could possibly rewrite an entire script in ninety days. I also wondered how Elizabeth, who had become more dependent than ever on painkillers, would be able to complete such a grueling assignment."

In February 1961, Eddie and Liz took the Orient Express from Paris to Munich to attend the annual winter carnival. Two days into their stay, they argued. "I was tired and needed some rest," said Fisher. "Elizabeth wanted to go to a nightclub. I told her I'd had enough. 'I'm going to leave in the morning,' I yelled.

"'You're leaving in the morning,' she echoed. 'Well, I'm leaving now.' Impulsively, she grabbed a bottle of Seconal, opened it, and began pouring the tablets down her throat. I tried to wrestle the bottle away from her. She ran into the bathroom, where she stumbled and fell. A physician had to be hastily summoned and paid off to revive her in the privacy of our hotel room, thereby avoiding the embarrassment of facing an inquisitive hospital staff and possibly the press."

Elizabeth's health continued to deteriorate. On returning to London, she came down with the Asiatic flu. Eddie Fisher added a fulltime nurse to the already overcrowded Taylor entourage. "Following the Munich incident, I understood that Elizabeth was capable of almost anything," he explained.

A few minutes after midnight on March 4, 1961, the newly hired nurse discovered that her charge was gasping for breath. She picked up the hotel telephone and asked the operator at the Dorchester front desk for a doctor. The employee knew that a few floors away a stag party was being given for a young medical student soon to be married. By chance, one of those present was a lung specialist. The man, dressed in tails, rushed to Elizabeth's room. Examining her, he lifted Taylor by the heels and shook her vigorously in an effort to dislodge the congestion that had suddenly blocked her lungs. When she failed to respond, he jammed two fingers down her throat to make her gag and spit up. He then tried to break up the congestion by pounding on her chest. When all failed, he took his thumb and began gouging first at one eye and then the other. The sharp pain forced her finally to take a deep breath. An ambulance arrived, and she was transported, yet again, to the London Clinic.

Semiconscious when she reached the hospital, Elizabeth Taylor (with Eddie Fisher in tears) was wheeled into the operating room. A team of surgeons performed a tracheotomy, a relatively elementary procedure which entails making an opening in the windpipe. A tube is then inserted through the incision and connected to an electronic breathing device which pumps premeasured amounts of air into the lungs. According to the hospital's medical experts, the twenty-nine-year-old actress was suffering from staphylococcus pneumonia, with severe lung congestion. Per Eddie Fisher's assessment, Liz's respiratory collapse resulted from her overuse of sedatives, including Seconal, and a heavy intake of alcohol.

For the next three days, the world press made much of Taylor's sinking health, leading readers to the inevitable conclusion that the actress had little chance of survival. Several newspapers went so far as to run front-page obituaries of the star. Others printed "exclusive" interviews with Elizabeth's parents. Notified of the situation by Eddie Fisher, Francis and Sara Taylor had crossed the Atlantic to be by their "dying" daughter's side.

Months later, as the guest of honor at a fund-raiser for Cedars of Lebanon Hospital in Los Angeles, Elizabeth gave a rousing speech describing her "miraculous recovery" and detailing her close brush with death:

"And still, even in the terrible darkness, there remained within me that stubborn insistence on living, on seeing that light again. But now I could no longer move legs or arms or eyes or any part of me or make any kind of sound. The blackness grew blacker and deeper. I knew then that by myself, physically, I could no longer fight alone for my life. And suddenly it seemed as if I were filled with a thousand voices, deep within me, calling out desperately for help, with cries that could not conceivably be heard. . . ."

Rambling on for an additional thirty minutes, Elizabeth Taylor delivered her speech with all the melodrama she reserved for most of her film roles. What her enraptured audience didn't and couldn't know was that although she presented the address as her own, she hadn't written a word of it herself. As a personal favor, Joe Mankiewicz created the entire oration; Elizabeth merely recited it.

Samuel Leve, a stage designer who at one time worked with Mike Todd, summarized Taylor's 1961 attack of pneumonia as "little more than publicity mongering. She may have been ill, but she wasn't dying. My knowledge of the situation emerged as a result of my friendship with Eddie Fisher's agent, Milton Blackstone. The day Liz entered the London Clinic, Blackstone dropped by my studio. He had brought along some twenty vials of a clear liquid medication (identified in the press as staphylococcal bacteriophage lysate, commonly used in the 1960s as an antigen to pneumonia) which he planned to deliver to Elizabeth Taylor's doctors in London. 'Is it true she's dying?' I asked. 'Like a swan,' he shot back. 'Actually, she's in better shape than Eddie Fisher seems to be.'

"The next time I saw Blackstone, he had a big smirk on his face. 'That miracle serum did the trick, all right,' he ventured. 'Elizabeth Taylor is alive and well—she'll no doubt win an Oscar for her performance in the London Clinic. I can see the headlines now: "TRACHEOTOMY WOWS ACADEMY!" '

"I said, 'Look, there's only one Elizabeth Taylor, and she takes advantage of it. If there were another Elizabeth Taylor, they wouldn't make such a fuss over her.' "

Truman Capote entertained a similarly dubious view of the severity of Elizabeth's ailment. Residing at the Dorchester Hotel during the same period as Fisher and Taylor, he had been one of the first to visit her at the clinic. "It was a major media event," Capote began. "The streets around the hospital were clogged not only with newspaper reporters and television crews but with thousands of tourists and fans waiting and praying for Elizabeth's recovery. I had the impression she must be desperately ill. But when I saw her, I realized she wasn't quite as sickly as she might have wanted people to believe.

"She seemed pale and a trifle thin, but she looked wonderful and gave me a big hello. 'I'm so glad you came,' she gurgled. She was alone, no Eddie Fisher in sight. She had just had her tracheotomy, but they'd removed the breathing tube. She had what looked like a silver dollar in her throat, some circular metal device. It was simply stuck in there. I couldn't figure out what held it in place, and it surprised me she wasn't bleeding or oozing.

"I had brought her a few books to read and a magnum of Dom Perignon, which she wasn't supposed to have; we split the champagne and hid the empty bottle under the hospital bed. I repeated the exercise on my next visit.*

"A few days later, I went out to dinner with Eddie Fisher. The following morning, Elizabeth said to me, 'You won't believe it, darling, but my husband thought you were making a pass at him!' At that moment she played a trick on me and yanked the plug out of her throat, spurting champagne all over the room. I thought I was going to pass out. I probably turned a few shades of green as I burrowed into my coat."

During one of her last days in hospital, Liz received a visit from Walter Wanger. She informed him she needed a long rest before she could resume work on *Cleopatra.* She added that he would have to find a sunny locale; she had no intention of returning to the dank climate of England.

Taylor vacated the London Clinic on March 27, and that evening she, her parents, Dr. Rex Kennamer, and Eddie Fisher jetted to Hollywood. Holding a bouquet of spring flowers and wearing a black dress under a white sable coat, Elizabeth was helped aboard the TWA air-

*Van and Edie Johnson also visited Taylor in the hospital. Edie reported that "ET produced a bottle of champagne for us but drank most of it herself. I wondered how she could drink alcohol in the wake of what she purported had been a 'life-threatening condition.'"

liner by a pair of airport security guards. A square patch concealed the incision at the base of her neck, and an ankle-to-knee bandage hid the black-and-blue bruises on her left leg, the limb through which she had been intravenously fed while hospitalized. In the end, her illness cost Lloyd's of London, the insurer of *Cleopatra,* some $2 million to cover the costs of Taylor's unavailability.

The publicity resulting from Taylor's "moment of truth," as Eddie Fisher labeled her purported life-and-death struggle, had one benefit: It enabled the actress to regain much of the public sympathy lost when she married Fisher. It set the stage for her hushed acceptance of the Oscar on April 17, 1961, for her appearance in *Butterfield 8.* Her reaction to winning the Best Actress Award became known at a later date:

"The reason I got the Oscar was that I had come within a breath of dying of pneumonia only a few months before. Nevertheless, I was filled with gratitude when I got it, for it meant being considered an actress and not a movie star. My eyes were wet and my throat awfully tight. But it was the wrong picture. Any of my three previous nominations was more deserving. I knew it was a sympathy award, but I was still proud to get it."

An addendum to the prize was issued by Debbie Reynolds. "Hell," she told a reporter, "even I voted for her."

Back in California, Elizabeth made an uneasy pact with Hedda Hopper, inviting the columnist she felt had betrayed her to the Beverly Hills Hotel for a midday meal of chili and beer. The Fishers entertained more frequently than they had in the past, socializing with Hollywood's most illustrious couples: Kirk and Ann Douglas, Desi Arnaz and Lucille Ball, Cary Grant and Dyan Cannon, Mel Ferrer and Audrey Hepburn, Dean and Jeanne Martin. The Martins and the Fishers, accompanied by Marilyn Monroe, attended a performance by Frank Sinatra at the Sands Hotel, Las Vegas. Marilyn, who was having an affair with Sinatra (at the same time she and President John F. Kennedy were seeing each other), swayed back and forth to the music and pounded both hands on the stage.

"Marilyn was beautiful but drunk," reported Eddie Fisher. "She was jealous of Elizabeth, whose million-dollar *Cleopatra* fee exceeded tenfold the $100,000 Marilyn received from Fox to do *Something's Got to Give.* After Liz became ill, Lloyd's of London suggested to Fox that Marilyn replace Elizabeth in *Cleopatra,* if only to reduce the film's budget. Walter Wanger retorted: 'No Liz, no Cleo!'"

While in Vegas, Elizabeth agreed to do an in-depth interview with *Look* magazine. The *Look* writer had brought along a neophyte photographer, Douglas Kirkland, but Elizabeth refused to have her picture taken. The tracheotomy scar on her neck remained all too visible. "You can use old photographs," she advised the writer. The photographer, recently hired by the magazine, registered disappointment. "I didn't know what to do," he reminisced. "I sat in on the interview, and at the end of it, I looked her in the eye and said, 'Elizabeth, do you know what it would mean to me if you would give me an opportunity to photograph you?' She seemed startled by my directness, but at the same time she appreciated it. 'All right,' she agreed, 'come tomorrow at eight-thirty.' When I arrived the following evening, she said, *'I don't have to do this, you know.'* She didn't, but she did, and she gave me my first cover on a mass-circulation magazine. The photographs I took of her launched my career."

Back in Los Angeles, the Fishers gave several parties for the visiting Moiseyev Dance Company. Their guests' informal invitation to visit their native Russia became official when the U.S. State Department asked Taylor and Fisher to represent the United States at the first Moscow Film Festival.

The couple departed for the Soviet Union on July 11, 1961. In Moscow, they stayed at the Sovietskaya Hotel. On July 14, a reception for all foreign representatives to the festival took place at the Kremlin. Elizabeth made her grand entrance an hour late, bedecked in a Dior original, a white chiffon cocktail dress with a boat neckline and a wide, bell-shaped skirt. As she gazed about the room, her eyes began to widen. There stood Gina Lollobrigida in an identical outfit. Moreover, both women had the same hairdo, a version of Alexandre's fashionable artichoke cut. (Alexandre was part of Elizabeth Taylor's retinue in

Moscow, as were Kurt and Ketti Frings and the omnipresent Dr. Rex Kennamer.)

Marc Bohan, Elizabeth's designer at Christian Dior, theorized that "somehow Gina Lollobrigida learned which dress Liz had selected and then, as a publicity stunt, had a copy made. As compensation, we gave Liz a free dress the next season. She chose a very expensive embroidered gown."

While in Moscow, Elizabeth went to the various festival screenings and events, visited Lenin's tomb, and had a private meeting with Premier Nikita Khrushchev and Yekatarina Furtseva, the minister of culture, who was rumored to be his mistress.

Eddie and Liz subsequently returned to Los Angeles, where she underwent plastic surgery at Cedars of Lebanon to remove her tracheotomy scar, and Eddie began an engagement at his old stomping ground, the Coconut Grove.

Donald Sanderson, a Boston travel agent, attended Fisher's opening night. He remarked: "There were many movieland figures on hand, including John Wayne, Yul Brynner, Danny Thomas, and Henry Fonda. Frank Sinatra, Dean Martin, Sammy Davis Jr., and Joey Bishop, collectively known as 'the Clan,' were also present. Eddie Fisher appeared nervous, forgetting the words to two or three songs. Dean Martin yelled out, 'Come on, Eddie. Let's get it together.' The comment rattled him further. He finally managed the words to 'That Face!' and he sang the lyrics to Liz. 'If I were you, I wouldn't be singing. I'd be home with my wife,' screamed Martin. This ignited the Clan to the extent that they, all four of them, clambered onstage, drinks in hand, and started harassing Fisher, doing imitations of him, mocking him, cracking jokes. Sammy Davis Jr. must have been totally smashed. He kept sloshing whiskey all over the place and became excessively abusive toward Eddie. After about twenty minutes, the four musketeers left the stage, and Eddie completed the set.

"To be candid, I didn't take the Coconut Grove episode too seriously," reflected the singer. "I had other concerns, such as the well-being of my wife. I never stopped worrying about Elizabeth. Within days of her tracheotomy, she was back on pills and alcohol. Once, after doing both, she simply passed out in the middle of a sentence. On another occasion, when she had far too much to drink, I caught her in my arms just as she was about to tumble down a flight of stairs. I began to feel rather foolish trying to help her when she did so little to help herself."

Elizabeth's self-destructive behavior may in large measure have been dictated by her growing dissatisfaction with Eddie Fisher. Even Truman Capote, who found Fisher "dull and dreary," felt sorry for him. "Elizabeth demonstrated greater compassion for her cats and dogs than she showed to Eddie Fisher," maintained Capote. "She treated him like an errand boy."

Among other cruelties, Liz made little secret of the fact that during their marriage she had engaged in an on-again, off-again romance with another man. The man, Max Lerner, thirty years her senior, was a syndicated political columnist and a professor of American civilization at Brandeis University. With a B.A. from Yale and a Ph.D. from the Robert Brookings Graduate School of Economics and Government, Lerner had written more than a dozen books and had recently completed a year in India as a Ford Foundation professor at the School of International Studies. He had been twice wed—married to his second wife, Edna, since 1941—and had fathered five children.

Although his academic credentials surpassed those of anyone she'd ever dated, he seemed, with his long, curly white hair and potbelly (he bore a passing resemblance to Albert Einstein), an inappropriate candidate for Liz's affection.

Patricia Seaton, the widow of Peter Lawford, was once also involved with Lerner. "I knew Max when he would hang out at the *Playboy* mansion in Los Angeles. He had his own room there and would lure the young *Playboy* bunnies into his web by promising to read poetry to them. He pulled the same routine on me, and to my amazement it worked.

"He possessed a romantic nature and a seductive manner, even though he had larger boobs than most of the *Playboy* centerfolds. He was old and saggy; the majority of girls who stayed at the mansion thought of him as 'a dirty old man.' 'Poor old Max!' they would exclaim. I found him very dear. He would sit downstairs in the Mediterranean Room, where Hugh Hefner kept the pinball machines, endeavoring to pick up all those 'nubile young things,' as he referred to the Bunnies and Playmates who lived there. And sometimes he even succeeded."

He succeeded in charming Elizabeth Taylor. They met in London in 1959, during the filming of *Suddenly, Last Summer.* What brought them together was a favorable column Lerner wrote about Mike Todd's death and the beating Elizabeth and Eddie took from the press when they married. At the end of the day's shooting, Max and Liz would occasionally rendezvous in London's smoke-filled pubs. She spoke of her new but already shaky marriage. "I thought I could keep Mike's memory alive . . . ," she said. "But I have only his ghost."

Elizabeth called Lerner "My Little Professor" and compared their strange liaison to the alliance between Sophia Loren and Carlo Ponti—"the perfect complement of brain and beauty." He described her in print as an "extraordinary, enchanting, passionate, exasperating, impossible woman." He admitted falling in love with her. She teased him with tales of her former lovers and husbands, including current husband Eddie Fisher. "Eddie made love to me four times last night," Taylor bragged of her potent "boy-husband." Lerner considered asking her to marry him but soon changed his mind. "In the end," he offered, "I realized . . . she would use me the way a beautiful woman uses an older man—as a front while she goes on fucking everything in sight."

Max Lerner and Elizabeth Taylor spent a weekend together in Paris. They went dancing with writer Françoise Sagan and director Michelangelo Antonioni at the Epi-Club, after which Max took Liz to Les Deux Magots, the historic sidewalk cafe made famous by Jean-Paul Sartre and the existentialists. "Such a crowd gathered round us," Lerner said, "that we had to be rescued by the gendarmes."

The "Little Professor" saw Elizabeth again during her recuperation at the Beverly Hills Hotel, following her tracheotomy: "When I arrived, I found a wan Elizabeth seated on a chaise longue and wrapped in a shawl. She was drinking beer by the gallon in an effort to regain the weight she had lost during her medical crisis.

"We spent untold hours together over the next month or two. I have no idea what Eddie Fisher made of my presence. Perhaps he felt relieved, because looking after Elizabeth could be construed as a full-time occupation.

"During this phase, Elizabeth suggested we collaborate on a book, the working title to be *Elizabeth Taylor: Between Life and Death.* "I'll do the recalling, you can do the *heavy thinking,*" she suggested. "The book, had it come to pass, would have been a personal rumination into the heart and soul of Elizabeth Taylor. As it happened, we abandoned the opus."

In delving into his own heart and soul, Max Lerner revealed that he had once been as close to Marilyn Monroe as to Liz: "When Marilyn died in 1962, I penned an article comparing the two actresses, terming Elizabeth a legend and Marilyn a myth. Elizabeth read the piece and gave me a call. She sounded perturbed. She wanted to know 'how in hell' I could refer to Marilyn Monroe as a myth while she had to settle for being placed in the legend category.

"'But Marilyn's dead,' I pointed out. 'That makes her a myth.'

"'I don't give a damn,' retorted Elizabeth. 'She couldn't hold a candle to me while she was alive.'

"I considered her rebuttal for several moments before offering a rejoinder. 'Very well,' I said. 'If it'll make you happy, Liz. Marilyn can be the legend and you the myth.'

"'Never mind,' she countered. 'The damage has already been done.'"

Chapter 17

Eddie Fisher's agent, Milton Blackstone, harbored great animosity toward Elizabeth Taylor. "Whenever the lady recounts her near-death experience, it makes me want to retch," he informed his friend Sam Leve. To Fisher he said: "Why don't you get out before it's too late. Your entire existence with Elizabeth has been transacted in hotel and hospital rooms. Two years into your marriage and the two of you still don't have a legitimate home."

"I heard what Milt had to say, but I didn't listen," remarked Fisher. "Besides, there wasn't time to sit around and evaluate the situation. Between Elizabeth's frequent hospital stays, we were always on the move."

By late summer 1961, Taylor and Fisher were en route to Rome, where shooting on *Cleopatra* had been scheduled to resume. Walter Wanger had chosen the Italian capital because of its generally warm climate and historic landscape. Before arriving, Eddie and Liz cruised the Greek islands in a yacht belonging to the son of Spyros Skouras. The vessel came with a captain and a crew of twenty. "The trip became our second honeymoon," Fisher crooned, "the most wonderful time we spent together.

"We sunbathed on deck, and I dove for stones, which we used as chips in our nightly games of gin rummy. We ate shrimp and lobster tails and washed them down with delicious Greek wines. I later put this self-contained period into proper perspective—it represented the calm before the storm."

An indication of events to come took place in Athens. Despite her teetering marriage, Elizabeth decided she wanted to adopt a new baby. After visiting several orphanages, the actress came across one little boy who particularly appealed to her. At age one, he was affectionate and outgoing. She was ecstatic when the nuns informed her she could have him. "Return tomorrow to fill out the papers," they ordained, "and you can take him with you."

That evening, Elizabeth came up with the name Alexander for her new son, and the next morning, she and Eddie went back to the orphanage. The mother superior greeted them with several key questions. "Have either of you been divorced?"

"Yes, we've both been divorced," Fisher admitted.

"And what is your faith?"

"We're Jewish," he responded, immediately sensing that the adoption process would be stymied.

"I'm very sorry," the mother superior said, "but it will be impossible to let you adopt the child."

"I don't understand," remarked Taylor. "They told us we could have him. They said he was ours." She began to cry, softly at first and then with great vehemence.

"I attempted to console her," said Fisher, "but I had mixed feelings about it. She already had three children and couldn't find enough hours in the day to be with them. Why add another, I wondered. But if that was what she wanted, I had no intention of thwarting her desire."

By September 1, 1961, Elizabeth, Eddie, and their retinue had settled into a leased fourteen-room walled villa—complete with four-car garage, heated outdoor swimming pool, sweeping lawns, and formal gardens—set in eight pine-studded acres on the ancient Appian Way, seven miles from Rome and only a fifteen-minute drive from Cinecitta Studios, where shooting on *Cleopatra* would soon commence. Management of the Villa Papa, as it was called, had been assigned to Dick Hanley, who headed a staff of ten. Likewise housed at the estate were a dozen of Elizabeth's pets, including two rabbits, a pair of Persian kittens (whose main nocturnal activity was trapping rats in the kitchen), and a Saint Bernard named Rocky Marciano; the latter had been a present from Elizabeth to her sons, Michael and Chris, who were currently enrolled in the fourth and second grades of the American Day School in Rome. Liza, three years of age, remained in the care of her governess.

Among the first guests to see the Fishers in Rome were Mel Ferrer and Audrey Hepburn. The foursome ate lunch in the garden by the swimming pool. Midway through the meal, an immense fellow appeared with what looked like a police nightstick in hand and began fanning the bushes with it. Elizabeth reassured her astonished guests that "Lucky," one of the Fishers' security guards, was just beating the hedges to chase away the paparazzi.

Two weeks later, the Ferrers visited the Fishers again. Audrey Hepburn had just landed the coveted role of Eliza Doolittle in the film version of *My Fair Lady.* She was ecstatic about it, and Elizabeth seemed to share her enthusiasm. But that evening, after Liz and Eddie went to bed, Taylor suddenly blurted out, "I want *My Fair Lady.* Get it for me, Eddie."

Fisher was puzzled. "Elizabeth," he said. "Audrey has the part. You saw how excited she was today."

Elizabeth repeated the order: "Get me *My Fair Lady,* Eddie!"

"You know I can't do that," he said.

Elizabeth's voice grew even more demanding. "I want *My Fair Lady!* I want the role of Hilda [*sic*] Doolittle!"

"I refused to argue with her," recalled Fisher, "and by the next morning, she had shifted gears. Maria Schell, another actress-client of Kurt Frings (as was Audrey Hepburn), had heard about Elizabeth's pressing desire to adopt a child. Estranged from her current husband, German director Horst Haechler, Maria was living outside Munich, next door to a nurse who worked in an orphanage. Maria sent us pictures of three infants, all of whom were available for adoption. Scanning the photographs, Elizabeth selected a nine-month-old baby girl with abundant curls and huge, saucer-shaped eyes. Her birth parents had placed her for adoption because they already had three children and couldn't afford to raise another."

Dr. Rex Kennamer, who had been staying with the Fishers in Rome, accompanied them to Munich.* "I was present when the orphanage brought the baby to Maria Schell's home," said Kennamer. "Her skin was covered with festers, and she looked a bit undernourished, but Elizabeth took to her at once. The Fishers named her Maria in honor of their benefactress. The following day, a local pediatrician examined the child and pronounced her in good health. All she needed, he suggested, was a little fattening up."

The German pediatrician evidently failed to detect what readily became apparent to doctors in Rome. Elizabeth and Eddie's legally adopted daughter had a serious birth defect—a malformation of the pelvis; if not surgically corrected, the condition could leave her permanently crippled. The operation was performed in England. The child, spending two agonizing years in a full-length body cast, made a slow, painful, but full recovery.

Beyond the dual resignations of the original director and cinematographer of *Cleopatra,* the production's shift to Rome brought with it additional changes. The most significant of these involved the replacement of the two male leads, Stephen Boyd and Peter Finch, both of whom had made previous professional commitments. While Rex Harrison, whose presence in the film Elizabeth Taylor had desired from the start, took over as Caesar, Richard Burton, despite initial resistance on the part of Spyros Skouras, left the Broadway cast of *Camelot* and signed on to play Antony. Another *Camelot* defector, Roddy McDowall, agreed to fill the role of Octavian. As an accommodation to McDowall, Joe Mankiewicz created a minor part for Roddy's live-

*Because of Elizabeth Taylor's ongoing health problems, Twentieth Century-Fox offered Dr. Kennamer a $25,000 retainer plus expenses to temporarily give up his private Beverly Hills practice and look after Elizabeth Taylor in Rome. Kennamer accepted the offer.

in companion; accordingly, the director cast John Valva as a Roman soldier named Valvus.

While Elizabeth Taylor felt ecstatic about having Roddy McDowall with her in Rome, she appeared more uncertain when it came to Richard Burton. Born Richard Walter Jenkins Jr., on November 10, 1925, in Pontrhydfen, South Wales, he was the twelfth of thirteen children in a family fathered by a hardworking, hard-drinking coal miner. Ebullient and bright, Richard won a scholarship to Oxford, thanks to the tutelage of his schoolmaster, Philip Burton, from whom he later acquired his professional name.* Shortly before entering the university, he made his stage debut in *Druid's Rest* in 1943 in Liverpool. The following year, he quit Oxford and went with the play to London. From 1944 to 1947 he served with the Royal Air Force as a navigator. He returned to the stage in 1948 and in the same year made his British film debut in *The Last Days of Dolwyn.* It was on the set of this picture that he met his first wife, eighteen-year-old Sybil Williams.

She was blond and perky, new to acting, and like Richard, from a mining village in Wales. They married in 1951. Later, when they performed together at Stratford, some of her reviews were superior to his. "That's when," confided his friend, theater-and-film critic David Lewin, "he ordered her to 'pack it in.'" She gave up her career, had two daughters, Kate and Jessica, and stood by Burton through his interminable boozing and flamboyant womanizing.

The philandering became as addictive as the alcohol. Claire Bloom, who costarred with him in such films as *Alexander the Great* and *Look Back in Anger,* became "the great love of Burton's life," that is, until he met Elizabeth Taylor. Actress Tammy Grimes claimed to be in love with him "for at least a week," the most he accorded the majority of his sidebar girlfriends. Susan Strasberg, the twenty-year-old daughter of Lee Strasberg, director of the famed Actors Studio in New York, ap-

*Philip Burton, a prepatory-school drama couch and Shakespearean authority, eventually became Richard's foster father. As a teenager, Richard lived with Philip, thereby developing tastes and talents he could never have cultivated had he remained in poverty-ridden Pontrhydfen.

peared in a Broadway play with Burton. As usual, he made little effort to camouflage his indiscretions, making love to Susan with such ardor in her dressing room that fellow actors complained about the noise level to the stage manager.

Zsa Zsa Gabor became another pre–Elizabeth Taylor conquest, and although Burton never had an affair with her sister, Eva, they knew each other well. "I found him an absolute charmer, irresistible," exclaimed Eva. "He had pockmarks all over his face and back—very bad skin—and stood no more than five feet six. But he had a powerful torso, rugged features, hypnotic blue eyes, and a compelling voice. I'm one of the few ladies he didn't try to take to bed."

One of Burton's most gossiped about escapades involved Jean Simmons. The episode took place in 1952 during Richard's first visit to Hollywood. He and his wife, Sybil, initially stayed with James and Pamela Mason. "Then," as Stewart Granger picked up the thread, "I invited them to move in with my wife, Jean, and myself. The four of us went back a number of years, and Richard and Jean were rehearsing together to appear in *The Robe.* I was headed for Jamaica to be in a film, but first I had to go to England to help liberate my alcoholic first wife from some goddamned awful sanatorium in which she had been placed. So I asked Rich and Sybil to look after Jean in my absence.

"When I returned, there were all sorts of rumors afloat concerning Rich and Jean. As soon as I saw him, I said, 'Look, for Christ's sake, why do you fuck the wife of one of your best friends?' He offered some lame excuse about having been drunk at the time. It was a pity, because it spoiled a decent friendship. Let's face it, Burton was a prick. He was a clever actor but a shit, an absolute shit."

Before Stewart Granger left for England, he and Jean Simmons gave a Sunday brunch–cocktail party. Richard and Sybil attended, as did a very youthful Elizabeth, married at that time to Michael Wilding and pregnant with their first child. In those days, as Liz later attested, "I used to watch, observe, overhear conversations, and make my own comments to myself, often cynical." She sat on a deck chair by the swimming pool, her nose buried in a book, catching glimpses of Burton while he put on a one-man show, quoting lines from Shakespeare, reciting verse by Dylan Thomas, performing burlesques of Laurence Olivier and John Gielgud. Elizabeth admitted thinking that Burton seemed "rather full of himself." He, in turn, considered her "the Mona Lisa type, beautiful but very somber." When a friend asked his reaction to her, he replied: "Dark. Dark. Dark. Dark. She probably shaves."

Their paths crossed five years later in a London restaurant. This time Liz sat with her third husband, Mike Todd, and waved across the room to Burton. A few months afterward, Richard saw the Todds at a New Year's Eve party given by Tyrone Power in his Manhattan penthouse apartment. Before a soaring fireplace Liz had removed her shoes and lay curled up in her spouse's lap, while Burton carried on in his usual manner, singing bawdy songs and suggestively approaching every woman in sight—with the exception of Elizabeth Taylor.

Their final and briefest encounter prior to *Cleopatra* took place at the Nikita Khrushchev–Spyros Skouras luncheon debate in Hollywood, which Elizabeth attended with husband number four, Eddie Fisher. It is doubtful Burton spotted Elizabeth at the overcrowded gathering, though she noticed him. In her most recent memoir, *Elizabeth Takes Off,* she wrote: "Since I was a little girl, I believed I was a child of destiny, and if that's true, Richard Burton was surely my fate."

Richard and Sybil Burton and their two young daughters arrived in Rome in mid-September, accompanied by Roddy McDowall and John Valva. The entire group moved into a villa one and a half miles from the Taylor-Fisher residence. The other film principal, Rex Harrison, had taken a suite in the Excelsior Hotel with his bride-to-be, Rachel Roberts, a British-born actress whose best-known film had been *Saturday Night and Sunday Morning.*

John Valva described the relationship between Rex and Rachel as "bordering on mayhem." Rex had a short fuse, while Rachel tended to be highly emotional. Harrison registered endless complaints about *Cleopatra.* His chief lament was that neither he nor Richard Burton reaped nearly as much publicity as Elizabeth Taylor. On one occasion he told Walter Wanger, "Just because Elizabeth's tits are bigger than mine doesn't entitle her to be driven around in a mile-long limo, while you restrict me to the backseat of a two-bit Fiat sedan."

"Rex had nothing per se against Elizabeth," observed John Valva, "but he did feel slighted by her enormous star power. He held Rachel Roberts to blame for his troubles and began bouncing her around. As a former pal of Sybil Burton's, Rachel would seek shelter with her during periods when Rex became abusive. Her frequent visits deprived Richard of his wife's company. Having become Elizabeth Taylor's earpiece, Roddy McDowall also spent hours away, listening to Liz discourse ad infinitum on life with Fisher.

"Burton resorted to taking Italian lessons, playing with one-year-old Jessica, attending the garden tea parties four-year-old Kate gave each afternoon for her collection of Raggedy Ann dolls."

"The highlight of my first three months in Rome," maintained Richard Burton, "turned out to be an electrical fire that swept through our rented villa late one night. In an effort to reach the source of the blaze, a malfunctioning space heater, I broke down a door and wrenched my back. Once the smoke cleared, we moved back into the house and resumed our humdrum lives."

Day-to-day existence in the Taylor-Fisher abode became the subject of public scrutiny when a trusted member of their household staff gave *Photoplay* an extensive interview. Fred Oates, Elizabeth's butler, characterized his employer as "a dictatorial empress, a true-to-life Queen of the Nile who treated her husband like a virtual slave, rejected telephone calls from her parents, invited guests for supper and then refused to dine with them." Oates went on in the same article to depict Eddie Fisher as a "good, generous, discreet, tolerant, unselfish and . . . submissive man."

Just as Elizabeth Taylor had found it impossible to tolerate former husband Michael Wilding's passive gentility, her current husband's submissive nature heightened her indignation and amplified her inner rage. Max Lerner put it more bluntly when he remarked: "Elizabeth Taylor devoured men like Eddie Fisher for breakfast and spat them out at lunch. She couldn't stomach weakness in a male. Vulnerability, yes; sappiness, no."

Taylor's demeanor during much of the production process of *Cleopatra* added substantially to the film's massive failure in both fiscal and critical terms. More than three decades after its overpublicized release, it remains one of the longest and by far most expensive motion pictures ever made. Although various estimates exist concerning *Cleopatra's* final cost, the figure most commonly cited is nearly $42 million, which, in today's currency, would equal approximately $125 million. Yet Elizabeth Taylor, notwithstanding her constant shenanigans and obstructive activities, bore only partial responsibility for the film's downfall; there were other people and problems involved.

One element included Twentieth Century-Fox's demand that the producer and director adhere to a shooting schedule which even under the best of circumstances could never have been met. In order to satisfy the money-minded bosses at Fox, Walter Wanger intentionally falsified his weekly production reports, claiming they had shot far more footage than they actually had.

Joe Mankiewicz, having recently married his production assistant, Rosemary Matthews, became the first to realize the futility of his self-appointed herculean task. Still hoping to create two films rather than one lengthy epic (a plan that Fox later abrogated), Mankiewicz directed by day and wrote by night. He lived at the Grand Hotel and took his meals around the corner at the Taverna Flavia, a small bistro that caught on with the cast and crew members of *Cleopatra* and consequently became one of Rome's most popular eateries. He took amphetamine injections to ward off sleep and wore special protective gloves because of a serious case of eczema he had contracted on both hands. Ultimately, Mankiewicz proved an unwise choice to direct and script *Cleopatra.* A peerless creator of dialogue, he nonetheless demonstrated little skill in choreographing crowd scenes of the Cecil B. De Mille variety. Pronouncing judgment on his own methodology, Mankiewicz declared: "If you want a textbook on how *not* to make a film, this is it!"

Christopher Mankiewicz, the director's son, spent six months in Rome working for his father. "I was second assistant director, a title as meaningless as the film," noted Chris. "I did a little of everything and as a result witnessed the lowest point of my father's otherwise formidable career: *Cleopatra* became his Waterloo. The only benefit he derived from the experience was that in addition to paying him an exorbitant salary, Fox purchased a small production company he'd recently founded for a fee of $1.5 million, making him the highest-paid motion picture director of his day.

"One of my assignments was to keep tabs on Elizabeth Taylor. I would fetch her every day and drive her to Cinecitta. This thankless task put me in direct contact with Dick Hanley, her personal secretary. He was an angry, embittered, shrill 'fagola,' the most important nobody in the universe because his job consisted of picking up and examining Elizabeth Taylor's underpants. He would call up in the early morning and in a high-pitched voice inform me that 'Elizabeth's got the rag on.' Her contract stipulated that whenever she had her period, she didn't have to appear on the set. After a while, the calls came with such frequency that my father mounted a chart on his office wall to track Taylor's menstrual cycle. He soon determined that Liz was a candidate for *The Guinness Book of World Records*—her period appeared to be an almost weekly event.

"It surprised me that my father never rebuked Elizabeth for her recurrent delays and absences. Even when she appeared at the studio, she invariably arrived several hours late. Yet my father, under normal circumstances a very tough director and a dominating force, accepted her behavior and sat around with a thousand extras, smoking his pipe and waiting for her to show up. Occasionally, he would set up another scene and try to shoot without her. The trouble with this approach was that, on any given day, nobody knew whether or not they might be needed—the entire cast had to remain on call, adding needless expense to the already overburdened budget.

"It became impossible to control Elizabeth; she basically had everyone connected with the production in a stranglehold. As producer,

Walter Wanger might have taken the initiative with Elizabeth, but he, too, proved useless. A ludicrous old fop, he would invariably show up on the set at noon, crack a few jokes, then disappear for the remainder of the day. Dressed like a dandy, the old man would spend his afternoons on the Via Veneto, chasing after bimbos.

"It was through Wanger that Elizabeth Taylor tried to get me fired. Costume designer Irene Sharaff told me over lunch one day that dressing Elizabeth was extremely difficult because she tended to gain weight with every meal. She had recently put on almost fifteen pounds. Her previously engorged breasts now looked like twin icebergs, large enough to sink the *Titanic.*

"At a party Liz gave at her villa a few nights later, I walked up to her and blurted out, 'I don't know why Irene Sharaff thinks you're overweight—you look fabulous to me.' The next morning, I received a telephone call from Walter Wanger. 'You're off the picture,' he announced. 'Elizabeth doesn't want you around any longer.' Perhaps I'd been injudicious in making the comment, but it had never been ill intentioned. I couldn't understand Elizabeth's reaction. I told my father the story, and he intervened in my behalf. Wanger allowed me to stay, while Irene Sharaff, who evidently also received hell from Elizabeth, never spoke to me again."

The financial reports emanating from Rome alarmed the executive chiefs at Twentieth Century-Fox to such a degree that Spyros Skouras himself appeared on the set, trailed by a small army of accountants and advisers. Skouras insisted on viewing the early rushes of *Cleopatra* and in the course of running them, dozed off, snoring so vociferously that he drowned out the sound track.

While poring over Walter Wanger's monetary statements, Fox's accountants uncovered a "serious" discrepancy—"the mysterious disappearance," read an interoffice memo, "of more than 1,500 paper drinking cups." When Peter Levathes and Sid Rogell, two of the Fox executives who had accompanied Skouras, asked Wanger to explain, the producer found it difficult to restrain his laughter. Joe Mankiewicz, witness to the Levathes-Rogell-Wanger exchange, found it equally amusing: "Here we had a pair of Fox's top honchos lamenting the disappearance of a few paper cups but who had nothing to say about any of the other irregularities. Also unaccounted for were some twenty thousand shields and spears, a herd of African elephants, a dozen Bengal tigers, a two-hundred-foot yacht, and a half-dozen studio-owned vehicles."

With the financial losses at Twentieth Century-Fox soaring to unprecedented heights, the board of directors replaced Spyros Skouras with former Fox head Darryl F. Zanuck. One of Zanuck's first steps involved the sale to Realtors of vast chunks of Fox-controlled land and properties, including much of the Los Angeles-based movie lot itself. He next cut the studio's workforce in half. Those employees he couldn't fire because of contractual obligations he merely placed on *Cleopatra*'s payroll. Hairdressers, set designers, private secretaries, and other hired hands soon became the recipients of IRS income tax forms for salaries they had supposedly earned while residing in Rome. The majority of these workers had never so much as visited Italy, no less been involved with the production of the film.

"Zanuck gave up on both *Cleopatra* and *Something's Got to Give*, starring Marilyn Monroe," noted Joe Mankiewicz. "The latter never got off the ground, and the former became Zanuck's prime excuse for the studio's final decline."

While Elizabeth Taylor continued her role opposite Rex Harrison, Eddie Fisher acquired motion-picture rights to *The Gouffé Case*, a novel by German author Joachim Maass. Set in turn-of-the-century Paris and based on the true case of a highly seductive but seemingly angelic woman who commits a series of brutal murders, Fisher planned to cast Elizabeth as the murderess and hoped to coax Charlie Chaplin out of retirement to play the aging police inspector who pursues and eventually identifies the criminal. Having corresponded with Chaplin, Eddie received an invitation to visit the seventy-two-year-old comic genius at his home in Vevey, Switzerland.

Said John Valva: "Chaplin clearly had no intention of accepting Eddie's film offer. 'I'm retired,' he kept saying. After lunch, Fisher lit a huge cigar in imitation of Mike Todd; he then leaned back in his chair and remarked, 'No actor in America is like you—you're one of a kind. The only person who comes close is Jackie Gleason.' Chaplin stared at Fisher and asked, 'Who?' He'd never heard of Jackie Gleason. 'Sorry to disappoint you,' he said, 'but I no longer follow the world of show business. However, I am aware of Elizabeth Taylor and would be interested in meeting her.' On this note, he rose and again did his little dance number."

From Vevey, Valva, assistant director Hank Moonjean, actor Joe Destefano, and Eddie Fisher drove to Gstaad. For tax purposes, Elizabeth and Eddie had been advised to establish residence in Switzerland. The fashionable ski resort of Gstaad, with its many foreign stars and dignitaries, seemed as good a place as any to buy a house.

"We checked into the Olden Hotel," said Valva. "The owner of the Olden, Hedi Donizetti-Mullener, a longtime resident of the village, knew of a chalet for sale. Located on the side of a ski slope, it had been built by a Texas oil millionaire for his bride, a ballerina; their marriage had dissolved and the house, Chalet Ariel, presently remained vacant.

"We took a look at it the following morning. It was perfect. Eddie consulted by telephone with Elizabeth and then bought it for $285,000, the money apparently belonging to Elizabeth. She later invested an additional $100,000 for renovations and remodeling.

"During our week on the road, Eddie must have gone through at least $450,000, including the purchase price of the chalet. Like Mike Todd, he prided himself on being a big spender, even if the money wasn't always his own. He thought nothing of spending fifty dollars for four dishes of ice cream at Gstaad's five-star Palace Hotel. He bought brandy, cigars, chocolates, gifts for Elizabeth, presents for her children. He picked up all of our tabs. The act of treating everyone, of paying all the bills, made him feel important."

On their return to Italy, the group stopped first in Geneva to do more shopping. From a jewelry store called Vacheron Constantin, Fisher purchased a $50,000 diamond necklace for Elizabeth. When they reached Rome, John Valva told Eddie: "I'd like to be there when you give her the necklace. It's magnificent. I want to see the expression on her face."

Valva drove to the villa with Fisher. He watched as Eddie presented her with the necklace. Elizabeth examined it and said, "How much did you pay for this, Eddie?"

"Fifty thousand," he said with a smug smile.

Her eyes took him in. "Eddie," she remarked, "there's not a decent stone here. You've been taken."

For his birthday, Elizabeth gave her husband an olive-green Rolls-Royce sports coupe, the second Rolls she had bought him during their marriage. Fisher attempted to return the favor by buying Liz a white Maserati for Christmas 1961. She took the car on a trial spin, returned to the villa fifteen minutes later, and once more humiliated Eddie by announcing that she "hated" the automobile. He eventually sold it to actor Anthony Quinn.

The cast of *Cleopatra* celebrated Christmas with a late-night dinner party at Bricktop's, an underground jazz club in Rome owned by an ageless black woman from Harlem whose unusual professional name was Bricktop. As the evening wound down, Richard Burton and Elizabeth Taylor danced. When the dance ended, Burton whisked Liz back to her seat, kissed her on the cheek, and wished her a happy holiday.

Several days later, at their first face-to-face rehearsal, Richard Burton turned up drunk. He could barely walk. His hands shook as he tried to sip hot coffee from a cup. Seeing his difficulty, Elizabeth helped by holding the cup to his lips. She ultimately claimed that with this one simple gesture, a bond was forged; Liz took notice of Burton and found in him many of the traits she had formerly identified in Mike Todd: power, strength, intellect, and vulnerability.

He also had, she soon learned, a tendency to be extremely remote, particularly when drunk. He became so distant at these times that not even Sybil could reach him, and she understood him better than anyone. He likewise became exceedingly insulting when inebriated, berating and cutting down everyone in sight.

"He once excoriated me for no reason," said John Valva, "and a day later I received a handwritten letter of apology in which he referred to his 'black Welsh moods.' Such epistles, often accompanied by a single flower, usually a rose, were commonplace with Burton.

"Richard reminded me of a combination troubadour and modern-day gunslinger. The notches on his proverbial gun belt stood for the numerous women he'd conquered. He took pride and pleasure in regurgitating the details of his frequent trysts. Sybil knew about them as well. On occasion she even kidded him about 'breaking the heart of some young actress.' I recall once when she returned from the beach and said to her husband, 'There are two of them down there, Rich, both your type. You'd better go before they leave.'"

John Valva and Sybil threw a New Year's Eve party at the Burton villa. Valva made chili, and the guests imbibed a large quantity of liquor. Stewart Granger and Eli Wallach were both visiting, and afterward the revelers headed for Bricktop's.

"This was the night," said Valva, "when it first became evident that something was going on—or about to go on—between Burton and Taylor. They were off on their own, laughing and smooching, and Eddie Fisher tried to induce Elizabeth to leave early—she became very offensive toward Eddie in front of everyone."

It reminded Stewart Granger of the abysmal end of Taylor's marriage to Michael Wilding. "It had been the same with Michael Wilding versus Mike Todd," he said. "What I never understood was her incessant need to emasculate the old lover while making the transition to someone new."

Richard Burton's first amorous opportunity came during the third week of January 1962, after he and Elizabeth had started to shoot their initial scenes together. Christopher Mankiewicz remembered Burton briskly striding onto the set one morning and informing a few dozen actors and crew members that he had *"nailed"* Elizabeth Taylor the night before in the backseat of his Cadillac. "I was amused by his use of the word *nailed,*" said Chris. "I hadn't heard it used that way since my earliest days in high school."

Joe Mankiewicz overheard Burton's indiscreet admission as well and reported the news to Walter Wanger, who rationalized that the ensuing publicity could help sell *Cleopatra* at the box office.

The film's director envisioned quite another advantage to the relationship: "I felt that Burton, being a professional actor, might have a positive influence on Elizabeth. I even told him, 'Perhaps you can convince her to arrive at the studio on time.' It didn't happen. If anything, she became more unmanageable, more intransigent. She went crazy when she didn't get her own way. If the refrigerator in her dressing room wasn't stocked with her favorite goodies when she arrived for work, all hell broke loose. The slightest mishap sent her into a frenzy. On one occasion when she locked herself in her dressing room, I sent Richard Burton in there to bring her out. An hour elapsed and still no sign of the actress. Finally, they emerged, looking very happy indeed. Quite obviously, they had done more than converse."

Eddie Fisher heard the rumors and observed the strange expressions he elicited during his rare appearances at Cinecitta. He attributed most of the talk to tabloid journalists and Twentieth Century-Fox public relations specialists who wished to exploit all the gossip purely to draw attention to the film.

Looking back, Fisher admitted having placed too much faith in his wife and too little in himself. "The husband is always the last to know," he complained. "I blocked out every suspicion until the night Bob Abrams, a friend who had come to visit me in Rome, gave me a telephone call. Elizabeth and I were in bed going over her lines for the following day, and the phone rang just as we had turned out the lights. 'Eddie,' Bob said, 'I think there's something you ought to know. People are talking about Elizabeth and Richard Burton.'

"'What're they saying?'

"Bob told me everything. After I hung up, I lay in the dark next to Elizabeth. 'Is it true that you and Richard Burton are seeing each other?' I asked.

"Elizabeth hesitated before responding. 'Yes,' she answered softly."

Fisher spent the night in downtown Rome in a small apartment with Bob Abrams. In the morning, he drove to the studio to see Joe

Mankiewicz. The director denied all knowledge of an existing intimacy between Taylor and Burton.

"I lacked the heart to go into it with him," acknowledged Mankiewicz. "The only advice I gave him was to stay put in the villa or he could be charged with desertion."

When Fisher returned, he received a shabby reception from Elizabeth, who took undue pleasure in chiding and torturing him. "She seemed to delight in teasing me, trying to make me jealous," Fisher wrote in his autobiography. "A little tipsy when she got back from the studio, just to get a reaction from me, she said: 'Guess what I did? I had a fitting with Irene [Sharaff] and then I had a drink with Richard.'"

Fisher, a little tipsy himself, "sipping vodka while waiting for her to come home," asked her: "What else did you do, Elizabeth?" Elizabeth added nothing; they ate dinner in silence. Fisher didn't tell her that he had acquired a gun, courtesy of a friend. "The friend told me to use it on Burton—'no judge in the world will convict you, especially in Italy. Why, they'll stand up and cheer—a gentleman defending his honor. They'll make a national hero of you.' I stored the gun in the glove department of my car, realizing that I could never use it, although occasionally I would hold and stroke it.

"I told Elizabeth I would gladly spend time at our new home in Gstaad, thereby permitting her the opportunity to straighten out her priorities. She didn't want me to go—'Don't leave me, Eddie,' she pleaded. 'You must stay and help me exorcise this cancer.'" The statement suggested to Fisher that he still had an outside chance, that his wife considered Burton—with his wife and children—as something of a dangerous illness from which she hoped to be purged. Fisher stayed. "He was grasping for straws," said John Valva. "He hoped that Burton's familial conscience would emerge or that Elizabeth might realize the error of her ways.

"What spoke against the second possibility was Liz's sobering admission to me in Rome that she now realized she had married Eddie Fisher only because she had hoped to resurrect the ghost of Mike Todd.

This was quite different from her earlier comments in New York. She had shifted allegiance to accommodate the situation."

Once Richard Burton's family—his brothers and sisters—were made aware of his involvement with Elizabeth, they were protective of Sybil, who remained largely unaware of her husband's latest conquest. On a train ride from Rome to Naples, Richard's brother Ifor Jenkins became so incensed over Burton's licentious behavior that he punched Richard in the nose.

David Jenkins, another of Richard's brothers, confirmed that Ifor had always been "the ruling force in the family, the guiding influence. Our father paid scant attention to the children, and our mother died at a relatively young age. That left Ifor and Cis, the eldest sister, to look after the youngest members of the family. Cis became Richard's surrogate mother. He stayed with her whenever he returned to Wales. When she was still in her twenties and thirties, Cis, with her raven hair and intense blue eyes, bore an uncanny resemblance to Liz Taylor—and that may account for Richard's strong attraction to Elizabeth."

Despite Burton's already complicated personal life, his overactive libido continued to lead him astray. Dale Wasserman, one of the original screenwriters of *Cleopatra,* traveled to Rome to discuss "a new film project with Richard. We had a few of those four-martini luncheons and each time wound up talking about women. It had become common knowledge by this point that he and Elizabeth Taylor were heavily involved. He began speaking about Liz, adding that he had no intention of marrying her. 'Marry that girl,' he said. 'Never!' I had the impression he meant it.

"I also had the feeling he preferred women en masse; I'm not implying he took more than one woman to bed at a time, only that he enjoyed variety. Whenever we met for lunch, he asked the names of the newest Hollywood starlets. What did they look like, which studios had signed them, and so forth. What were their sexual proclivities? He would record names and notes on a paper napkin, which he then stuffed in his billfold for future reference.

"Burton's two favorite activities were drinking and womanizing, not that the two were necessarily compatible. He often drank past the point where sex was desirable or even possible. He loved to enjoy life to its fullest, even though he seemed a bit on the lazy side. There was a kind of laziness of morale. It extended to his profession. He stuck with acting because it came easily to him, but he conveyed a sense of shame about being an actor in the first place. He would have preferred being a minister, a college professor, or an author, not necessarily in that order."

Unable to choose between his retiring wife and a gregarious Elizabeth Taylor, Richard Burton asked former girlfriend Pat Tunder, a twenty-five-year-old Columbia University graduate student he had met during his appearance in *Camelot,* to visit him in Rome, sweetening the invitation by promising her a small role in *Cleopatra.* When Taylor saw the leggy blonde waiting around the set for Burton, she offered Walter Wanger an ultimatum: "Either she goes, or I go." Pat Tunder returned to the States on the next available flight.

Normalcy—or what passed for normalcy on the set of *Cleopatra*—resumed the following day with the arrival of scriptwriter Phillip Dunne. Dunne joined Taylor and Burton for lunch at Cinecitta. "I wanted to convince Burton to play Michelangelo in *The Agony and the Ecstasy,* with Spencer Tracy to play the pope. The luncheon didn't succeed because Burton and Taylor remained hung over from the evening before and were both still drinking. They spent most of the meal exchanging insults. Burton would say, 'You were quite a mess on the set this morning, old girl.' 'You were a bit of a mess yourself, old boy,' she responded. As the meal proceeded, the exchange became increasingly provocative. It had all the makings of a scene from *Who's Afraid of Virginia Woolf?* The altercation lasted the entire meal, and the subject of Burton's assuming the role of Michelangelo never arose. The part finally went to Charlton Heston."

According to John Valva, Richard Burton swung back and forth like a pendulum between his wife and Elizabeth Taylor. "One day Richard would say, 'I'm leaving Sybil and going off with Elizabeth.' And then he would say, 'I can't leave Sybil. I'm not going to see Elizabeth anymore.'

"The greatest cruelty of this endless Ping-Pong match was that while Sybil sensed what was happening, she couldn't entirely admit it to herself. A few of us, including Roddy McDowall, Walter Wanger, Joe Mankiewicz, and myself, reached the conclusion that somebody had to tell Sybil before she read about it in the press. Because he had known her the longest, Roddy volunteered his services. Such is the fate of the bearer of sorrowful tidings that when he did inform her, she reacted by slapping him across the face."

A day or so later, Richard Burton—suffering one of his "black Welsh moods"—interrupted a dinner party at Villa Papa by pounding on the front door. Elizabeth's butler opened the door, and there stood Burton, spouting Shakespeare. "He had clearly guzzled several drinks too many," ventured one of Elizabeth's dinner guests. "What took place next has to rate as one of the weirdest scenes I have ever witnessed.

"Burton entered the house and demanded to see Elizabeth. She appeared while Eddie Fisher, who had been resting in an upstairs bedroom, emerged to investigate the commotion. He stood at the top of the stairs, dressed in a blue terry-cloth robe with matching terry-cloth slippers; both robe and slippers had Fisher's initials embroidered on them. 'What are you doing here?' he inquired of Burton. 'I'm in love with that girl over there,' growled the actor as he pointed to Elizabeth Taylor. Fisher responded: 'But you have your own girl; you have Sybil. Why are you trying to ruin my marriage? Go away; go home.'

"Determined to assert his masculinity, Burton turned the confrontation into a total drama. 'Sybil and Elizabeth are both my girls,' he ventured. Gazing at Taylor, he said: 'You are my girl, aren't you?' Before replying, a terrified Elizabeth Taylor looked first at Fisher and then at Burton. 'Yes,' she answered.

"Burton wasn't done. 'If you're my girl,' he said, 'come over here and stick your tongue down my throat.' In front of Fisher and her dozen dinner guests, Taylor went to Burton and gave him a long passionate kiss. Fisher turned around and walked slowly back to his room."

The same source noted that the following day on the set, "Elizabeth behaved like a little puppy, trailing Burton and playing up to him, while he ignored her completely. In other words, he played her like a maestro would a violin. He played her to perfection."

By mid-February 1962, the scandal had reached its pinnacle. Eddie Fisher had dishonored himself in everyone's eyes by telephoning Sybil Burton and telling her what she already knew: "Your husband and my wife appear to be deeply involved." That evening, Sybil reproached Richard for the first time. Fisher escaped Rome for several days. Calling his wife from Florence, Eddie was startled to hear Burton's voice on the other end of the line. "What're you doing in my home?" asked Fisher. "What do you think I'm doing?" Burton responded. "I'm fucking your wife."

During Eddie Fisher's absence, John Valva had spent a weekend trying to look after Elizabeth Taylor at her Roman villa. "She was inconsolable," said Valva. "Richard Burton had pulled another of his guilt-trip departures, romancing Elizabeth and then returning to Sybil. Liz and I were sitting on her bed discussing the situation when, without a word, she rose and ran toward a plate-glass window overlooking the garden below. The plate glass was hidden behind drapes, and Elizabeth smashed into the center divider and bounced back, sustaining a number of cuts and bruises.

"I cleaned up her wounds and put her into bed, then fell asleep next to her. I awoke in the middle of the night and saw she wasn't there. Alarmed, I searched the house and found her downstairs in the kitchen. The first thing I noticed was this big knife in her hand; my immediate impression was that she might attempt to kill herself. When I saw she was only making a Swiss cheese sandwich, I felt a great surge of relief.

"A few weeks later, while on a weekend trip with Burton, she did try to commit suicide by swallowing some thirty sleeping pills. She had to be taken to the hospital to have her stomach pumped. Twentieth Century-Fox tried to cover up the incident by announcing that Taylor had endured a severe case of food poisoning. During her two-day hospital stay, Eddie Fisher again reappeared, looking more in need of health care than Elizabeth."

One of the last functions Eddie and Liz hosted was a big party for Kirk Douglas in the ballroom of the Grand Hotel. Richard Burton sat to Taylor's left; Fisher, to her right. She and Burton were so enamored of each other, they could barely restrain touching. They clasped hands and played footsie under the table. Fisher couldn't help but notice.

By March 19, Fisher finally gathered his personal belongings and returned to New York, where he checked into the Pierre Hotel. "His friends saw to it that he wasn't left alone," said Ken McKnight, who stayed with him at the Pierre. "The most difficult job was to hold the press at bay. Like ants at a picnic, they were everywhere. As for Eddie, he couldn't stop exalting Elizabeth Taylor, recounting her skills as a lover, her sensuousness and beauty. 'Why don't you give it a rest?' I admonished him. 'You're torturing yourself for no reason. After all, you're the guy from South Philadelphia who wound up marrying Elizabeth Taylor. That's like winning the lottery ten times in a row.'"

At the same time Eddie Fisher departed for the States, Sybil Burton took her two young daughters and left for London. Dick and Liz were together at last. "The bottom line," said Stephanie Wanger, Walter's daughter and a regular weekend visitor on the set, "is they were deeply in love. It was the real thing, and everybody knew it. As a couple, they fit well together. They had a rapport, and all Rome seemed to be caught up in the romance. It became what Camelot ought to have been for Jack and Jackie Kennedy."

With the approach of summer, the romance between Burton and Taylor had received worldwide coverage. Photographer Bert Stern, hired by Walter Wanger to take stills on and off the *Cleopatra* set, had been one of the first to realize that Richard and Liz were not just *playing* Antony and Cleopatra.

"At first the romance struck some people as too campy, too Hollywood to be true," observed Stern. I remember telling my editor at *Life* about Liz and Burton. 'There's a love story here,' I said. 'What're you talking about—they're merely having an affair,' he countered. 'No,' I said. 'It's a real relationship.' 'Don't be absurd,' he told me.

"I used to hang out with Burton and Taylor, and frankly they didn't go to extremes to keep their liaison a secret. I took that notorious photographic series of them in their bathing suits while they smooched on the deck of a boat. Elizabeth wore the briefest of bikinis and looked very sultry and bosomy, but not in the same trashy way as somebody like Jayne Mansfield."

The publication of Stern's revealing photographs of Dick and Liz initiated a wave of public speculation, culminating in the Vatican's denunciation of Elizabeth Taylor as "a woman of loose morals." Just as the pope issued his censorious edict against Elizabeth, playwright Meade Roberts arrived in Rome, a guest of Richard Burton's.

"Elizabeth couldn't have cared less what the Vatican said about her," asserted Roberts. "It wasn't Taylor but rather Burton who lacked total commitment to the relationship. Whatever feelings Richard had for Liz, he remained confused and guilt-laden. He was in awe of fame and impressed by money, but he similarly understood the enormity of the decision he presently faced. He was almost schizophrenic about the entire episode and didn't know what to do.

"Of the two, Elizabeth seemed the assertive one. She was the pursuer; Burton, the pursued. In addition, Twentieth Century-Fox wanted to hold her personally responsible for the company's financial losses. Initially, they had been delighted by the scandal; then they began to worry. Elizabeth had recently received a telephone call from Kurt Frings, who had just gotten a call from Peter Levathes at Fox. Levathes had dictated a letter intended for Elizabeth Taylor, but before sending it to her, he wanted to read it to her agent.

"In substance what the letter said was: 'Suggest Elizabeth desist involvement with Richard Burton, or Fox will sue on the basis of a violation of the morals clause in her contract.'"*

"Her response to Frings: 'You tell Mr. Levathes to save himself a stamp. If that letter gets shoved under my door, I walk. If I walk, I'll

*When the picture ended, Fox sued both Taylor and Burton for violating the morals clause in their respective contracts. Pretrial depositions were given by many of the key personnel and players in *Cleopatra*. In the end, Taylor and Burton won the case and were permitted to retain their earnings from the film. Burton gave his share plus other earnings to Sybil Burton in settlement of their divorce.

never work again. I'm not going to starve if I never work again. I'll be sued, but Mr. Levathes will lose his empire, and Twentieth Century-Fox will crumble. *Cleopatra* is three-quarters done, and it's too late for them to replace me, and if I walk out of here, Fox is as good as dead.' Then she added: 'Nobody tells me who to love or not to love, who to be seen with and not to be seen with.'"

Meade Roberts spent ten days in Rome with Burton and Taylor and came away with a cache of memories. "Elizabeth bought Burton a replica of the Rolls-Royce she had given Fisher," he said. "Richard gave her a $67,000 emerald brooch from Bulgari.

"She was wearing the brooch one day as we drove around Rome. Richard sat behind the wheel, and Elizabeth sat next to him. I was in the backseat with a British actor named John Wood. It was lunch hour, and the top of the car was down. The streets were packed with construction workers eating their midday meal. As we drove past them, they could see Dick and Liz. They started screaming lewd obscenities at Liz and even making suggestive hand gestures. Elizabeth practically stood up in the front seat and began gesticulating and yelling, 'Fuck you!' She gave back exactly what she received."

At the beginning of June 1962, shortly before the cast and crew of *Cleopatra* moved to Ischia for the climactic barge scene, Dick and Liz decided to take a weekend away together. Now that the film was winding down, they wanted to consider future developments. German actor Curt Jurgens owned a beach house near Nice and offered it to them for their getaway. To avoid the press and paparazzi, Elizabeth devised elaborate travel plans. Burton would be driven to the destination at night, while she would travel by train.

"Amazingly, they pulled it off," said Meade Roberts. "Nobody discovered their whereabouts. Richard Burton almost seemed disappointed; he secretly longed for the press coverage. 'How else am I going to become a Hollywood star?' he said to me. He wasn't joking. The evening after their arrival in Nice, he accompanied Elizabeth to the Monte Carlo casino. The whole world now knew they were in town."

Chapter 18

On August 4, 1962, Roddy McDowall and John Valva arrived at Chalet Ariel, Elizabeth Taylor's new residence in Gstaad. They had just celebrated the long-overdue completion of *Cleopatra* by visiting Sybil Burton in Céligny, a Swiss village sixty miles to the east. Richard and Sybil, Céligny's best-known denizens, had purchased their old-fashioned alpine cottage in the mid-1950s.

At Elizabeth's home, McDowall and Valva were greeted by an ill-at-ease Richard Burton. "Our presence unnerved him," said Valva. "He felt embarrassed, especially because we'd all lived together in Rome before Elizabeth entered the picture. The day we appeared in Gstaad, Burton returned to Sybil. His departure upset Elizabeth. She became extremely tense and started drinking a great deal. Her tension had to do with the worrisome prospect of losing Richard; it was also related to the situation as a whole. Once again, she had cast herself in the antagonistic role of 'the other woman.' In the present instance, though, she happened to respect her rival. Elizabeth admired Sybil Burton and felt genuine concern, whereas Debbie Reynolds had primarily incurred her disdain."

Elizabeth spent hours conferring with McDowall and Valva about Richard Burton. "She knew what she was up against," said Valva. "She realized that Richard's family and closest friends were all urging him to stick with Sybil. Philip Burton told him that if he left his wife, he would never speak to him again. The Welsh actor and playwright Emlyn Williams, one of Dick's most intimate friends, disliked Taylor and everything she represented. He labeled her 'a hopped-up chorus girl,' before remembering that he had met his own wife in the chorus.

"Burton himself could also be deprecating when it came to Elizabeth. He constantly uttered negative remarks about her. She had an oversized bust (he referred to her as 'Miss Tits'), wasn't pretty, couldn't act, didn't speak the king's English, had surgical scars on her back, terrible legs, etc., etc. He often made such comments in front of her, but in reality the insults had an affectionate undertone. Elizabeth's physical appearance tended to intimidate people, and having Burton put her down in this manner only turned her on. Mike Todd had utilized a similar tactic."

While alone with Dick Hanley and her children in Gstaad, Elizabeth attempted once more to steel herself against the ongoing attacks that filled the press. The British magazines and newspapers were particularly hostile toward her. A London tabloid, *Tempo,* called Liz "an avaricious vamp who destroys families and devours husbands." The *Daily Mirror* described her in equally unflattering terms: "The lady is one long eruption of matrimonial agitation." In the United States, *Life* magazine ran a feature story containing photographs of Liz's children under the cruel heading "Please . . . Who's My Daddy Now?"

According to John Valva, "Pouches of hate mail arrived daily at the Gstaad chalet. In addition, Liz received hundreds of 'Queen for a Day' letters, e.g., 'I need $10,000—my husband's dying of a brain tumor,' and, 'Please send me $50,000 because I have eight children and I can't afford to feed them.'

"Liz informed me that on one occasion she received a letter from a woman in London who didn't possess the money to pay for her daughter's ballet school, although the child had proven talent. Elizabeth investigated the story, found it to be true, and sent the woman a sizable check."

During the summer of 1962, Elizabeth Taylor's lawyers dissolved MCL Films (Taylor purportedly paid Eddie Fisher $1 million to cover his share of their film company); in its stead her attorneys created Taylor Productions Inc., a Bermuda-registered corporation. In time, Liz also established multi-million-dollar trust funds for each of her four children.

As Elizabeth passed her days at Chalet Ariel waiting to hear from Richard Burton, Twentieth Century-Fox fired Joe Mankiewicz and hired director Elmo Williams to supervise the completion and final editing of *Cleopatra.* Elizabeth Taylor rushed to Mankiewicz's defense, telling *Newsweek,* "What has happened to Mr. Mankiewicz is disgraceful, degrading, particularly humiliating."

Elmo Williams worked three consecutive sixteen-hour days at Fox's New York film laboratory and cut a total of thirty-three minutes from the original version of *Cleopatra,* which ran in excess of four hours. "Joe Mankiewicz," ventured Williams, "had worked so long and ardently on the project, he had lost all perspective. He convinced himself he'd created a masterpiece. When he first saw my version, he began ranting and raving and carrying on. He had finally given up the idea of releasing the picture as two separate films, but he hadn't counted on the released version being reduced in length.

"Besides Joe Mankiewicz, I had problems with Elizabeth Taylor. We had been trying for weeks to convince her to do retakes of close-ups that hadn't turned out well. We both wanted her to reread some dialogue. Liz was reluctant to cooperate. She was difficult to handle at the time, possibly because I had been asked to replace Joe Mankiewicz and she didn't appreciate my presence. I finally said to her, 'Elizabeth, this is your performance. You're on the screen; I'm not. You're the one who looks bad; I don't.' Following my pep talk, she agreed to come from Gstaad to Pinewood Studios in England to complete the work. On three separate occasions I called in a crew; each time Elizabeth stood us up.

"I decided to schedule another meeting on a Sunday, which meant the crew would be paid overtime. I telephoned Liz and said, 'Look, you failed to show up three times over the last month. I've called the crew in on Sunday, so they'll all be on golden time [overtime]. It's costing the company a lot of money, and we're trying to help your performance.' 'All right,' she agreed, 'I'll be there.' She arrived the following Sunday, holding a tray with a bottle of brandy and a couple of glasses on it. The first words out of her mouth were 'I understand everybody's on golden time.' 'That's correct,' I acknowledged. 'Well, I want golden time, too,' she remarked. I knew the studio wouldn't stand for it, because she was currently earning roughly $10,000 a week, and they weren't about to shell out twice that sum to appease her. I told her I'd have to contact Darryl Zanuck to obtain his authorization. 'Oh, forget it. Let's do it and get it over with,' she said. So we did, and when we were done, she turned to me and quipped, 'Well, I hope you're satisfied.'

"I'm afraid my memories of Liz aren't as fond as they should be. She has never lived the life of a normal human being. She has been a movie star since childhood. She has never had any notion, I don't think, about the average man or woman. I doubt she realized the troubles we were experiencing with *Cleopatra.* She was too busy playing the role of the big, temperamental star."

As John Valva recollected, "Liz flew from London to Gstaad and was joined there by her mother. Soon thereafter, she heard from Burton. He wanted to see her, ostensibly to discuss the possibility of their appearing in another film together. While in Ischia, they had been approached by producer Anatole de Grunwald and screenwriter Terence Rattigan, who had penned *The V.I.P.s,* a motion picture in the *Grand Hotel* tradition, dealing with the troubled lives of a group of airline passengers stranded at Heathrow Airport in London during a heavy fog. Burton and Taylor had both hedged at first. Now Burton claimed to be interested."

Elizabeth drove down with her mother, while Richard arrived by himself in the green Rolls-Royce Liz had given him. After Sara Taylor returned to Gstaad in her daughter's automobile, the lovers ordered lunch in the hotel dining room. They spoke little at first. Finally, Elizabeth began to communicate; she said she had given the situation much thought and had decided if they couldn't marry she could at least become his mistress. Describing the moment in her personal memoir, Taylor would comment: "By making myself so readily available, I lowered my stature in everybody's eyes but mine—and, as it turned out . . . [in] Richard's."

Burton, in his own fashion as deeply in love with Elizabeth as she with him, returned with her to Gstaad. Ascertaining that he had made a final decision to stay with Liz, Roddy McDowall and John Valva departed at once to be with Sybil in Céligny. Within days, they accompanied her and the children to another Burton family home, this one in the Hampstead section of London.

"One afternoon Sybil asked me to take little Kate to the movies," said Valva. "At the end of the picture, as we emerged from the theater, Kate said to me: 'My daddy isn't coming home, is he?' I had no idea what to say, so I said nothing. Sybil showed great strength during these difficult hours. She never lost her composure, at least not in front of others. Several weeks after Roddy and I returned to New York, we encountered Mike Nichols, who had just seen Sybil in England. 'How is she?' asked Roddy. 'Not bad,' said Nichols, 'except for the two red razor-blade scars on her left wrist.'"

It appeared as though Sybil couldn't escape the Burton-Taylor saga. Every newspaper and magazine contained photo features on what they hailed as "the romance of the century," more newsworthy than the marriage of King Edward VIII and Wallis Simpson. Only the future 1968 nuptials of Aristotle Onassis and Jacqueline Kennedy would create the same degree of public excitement. *Time* discussed the Dick-Liz adventure in an August 1962 article: "If he should ever marry her, he will be the Oxford boy who became the fifth husband of the Wife of Bath. If she loses him, she loses her reputation as a fatal beauty, an all-consuming man-eater, the Cleopatra of the twentieth century."

Elizabeth had no intention of letting him go. They had both signed contracts to appear in *The V.I.P.s,* and during the first week of December 1962 they arrived at the Dorchester in London to begin rehearsals. When they didn't work, they played. Richard took Elizabeth on an "insider's" tour of the city in which she was born. They attended several rugby matches and made nightly rounds of his favorite pubs. She led him to a high-priced jeweler and watched as he bought her $150,000 worth of trinkets, including a gold-and-ruby necklace.

On two occasions he visited Sybil and his girls in Hampstead, each time returning drunk and in tears to the Dorchester. Following the second visit, Elizabeth pressured him to telephone Sybil and announce his intention to divorce. His friend, Welsh actor Stanley Baker, supported the decision; another confederate, actor Robert Hardy, needed to be persuaded. "Don't hate me," Elizabeth said to him when introduced.

Other pals of Burton had mixed feelings regarding Elizabeth. Welsh journalist John Morgan wrote of her: "Sober, she can be a boring woman. The tedium of her conversation is noticeable. She talks mainly about her children. But when she's got a few drinks in her, she becomes very lively and flirtatious. Sexually attractive? I'll say."

At first, Richard's family continued to resist their "favorite son's" desire to replace Sybil with Elizabeth. His brother David Jenkins reflected on the matter: "Divorce from Sybil seemed almost inconceivable. Being Welsh and from our background, she was considered a member of the clan; she was one of us. We looked on Elizabeth Taylor as an interloper, an outsider. Then, during a break in the shooting of *The V.I.P.s,* Richard had the good sense to bring Liz back to Wales with him. Without much fuss, she succeeded in winning us over. It helped that Richard presented her not as his mistress but as his future wife."

Graham Jenkins, who physically resembled Richard and even doubled for him in *The V.I.P.s,* compared Liz's brief stopover to an election campaign. "She had come to garner votes," he pointed out. "And essentially, she succeeded." A keen judge of character and wily as a fox, Elizabeth knew how to manipulate people. Cramped with Richard into his sister Hilda's minuscule guest room, the actress demonstrated her down-to-earth charm. When the moment demanded, she could be the most natural of women. She soon had both Richard and his siblings under her spell. Beautiful and entertaining, she commanded attention and usually received it.

Compared to *Cleopatra, The V.I.P.s* encountered relatively few production problems. Slated to be shot over a six-week span, the picture actually took eight. Elizabeth was accorded one week to recuperate from torn cartilage in her knee, while Burton spent another week recovering from a bar scuffle in which he suffered a black eye and facial lacerations. Between them, Dick and Liz earned $3.2 million for appearing in the film (much of it from gross-profit participation).

"I earned my share," Elizabeth later told Meade Roberts. "For one thing, the film was made by the British division of M-G-M—I can never seem to escape that studio. Secondly, the press propagated a rumor suggesting that Louis Jourdan [Liz's screen lover in the film] and I were having an affair. The truth of the matter is, I didn't even like Jourdan. In fact, I hated shooting love scenes with him. The man had a terrible case of halitosis—bad breath."

Dick and Liz remained in London through the summer and early fall of 1963. Burton starred opposite Peter O'Toole in *Becket* (filmed at Shepperton Studios in Middlesex), while Taylor received a $500,000 paycheck to narrate and appear in a CBS-TV special called *Elizabeth Taylor's London.* S. J. Perelman, scriptwriter of the glorified television travelogue, wrote a friend denouncing Taylor's participation in the project: "Elizabeth . . . gave it all the histrionic fervor of a broom handle and managed to effectively louse up the airwaves."

For his thirty-eighth birthday, Liz bought Burton the complete Everyman Library of classics—five hundred volumes—and had each tome bound in calfskin. Burton celebrated Elizabeth's thirty-first birthday by bestowing on her a $200,000 diamond necklace. Her father's gift consisted of a "small" Utrillo. Francis Taylor also represented his daughter at a Sotheby's auction; for $250,000 he acquired for her Van Gogh's *Lunatic Asylum, St. Remy.* Thirty years later Elizabeth attempted but failed to sell the same oil painting at an auction price of $20 million.

One of Richard Burton's biographers employed the term "sinful splendor" to define the actor's new lifestyle. The Faustian pact he had struck by opting for Taylor brought him renown and riches—at an unspeakably high price. With the exception of an abbreviated telephone conversation five years after their divorce, Sybil Burton never again communicated with her former husband. At age three, Jessica Burton had been diagnosed as catatonic by child psychiatrists and other experts in the health field. The only word she uttered—then and subsequently—was "Rich," her father's nickname. When Burton visited her in the institution near Philadelphia where her mother had placed her (and where "Jessie," as the family called her, still resides today), she greeted him with a barrage of unintelligible squawks, followed by the more familiar "Rich! Rich! Rich! Rich!" The sound of his name echoed down the institution's dark corridors and pursued the actor throughout his remaining years.

Before departing London, Dick and Liz arranged a fund-raiser for the Bolshoi Ballet. To aid the cause, the couple agreed to screen the completed version of *Cleopatra.* It marked the first time Elizabeth had seen the finished film. After viewing the first twenty minutes, she leaped out of her seat and ran to the ladies' room, where she proceeded to vomit into a toilet bowl. Relating the incident to Meade Roberts, she said that the movie seemed like such a waste of time. "I spent more than two years shooting that horror; it turned out to be such a lousy film."

A vaguely similar scene took place several days later. Michael Mindlin, head of a public relations firm, had arranged for Richard Burton and Peter O'Toole to plug *Becket* on the *Ed Sullivan Show.* Sullivan was flying to London to tape the duo. Burton, however, had reservations about doing the interview. He, Elizabeth Taylor, and Mindlin met at the bar in the lobby of the Dorchester to discuss the situation.

"As we sat there talking, Dick was bolting down one drink after another," said Mindlin. "Elizabeth was drinking, as I recall, champagne. All of a sudden, without warning, Dick threw up. It was humiliating for him. Elizabeth jumped out of her seat and went to him and touched his forehead. 'Oh, I think you must be very sick,' she said. She was covering up for him.

"I rushed off and found a waiter with a wet towel. We cleaned him up as best we could. At that moment, director Otto Preminger entered the lobby of the Dorchester, saw us sitting at the bar, and walked over. He was about to say hello when Richard looked up and interjected, 'Will you please fuck off!'"

Richard agreed to do the Sullivan show, and the following day we met with Ed Sullivan at Shepperton. The first words out of Sullivan's mouth were: 'I understand this is the first time you two have worked together?' Burton responded: 'Yeah, and it's liable to be the last.' Peter O'Toole realized that his partner was thoroughly bombed and said nothing. But the entire interview went like that, and Sullivan finally flew back empty-handed."

In October 1963, Elizabeth and her daughter Liza accompanied Richard Burton to Puerto Vallarta, Mexico, where he would appear in Tennessee Williams's *Night of the Iguana,* a film about the trials and tribulations of a down-on-his-luck man of the cloth, the Reverend T. Lawrence Shannon, who has been defrocked for dallying with an underage parishioner. Burton had signed to play the role of the reverend.

Meade Roberts, who had returned to New York to complete a screenplay, received a telephone call from Richard Burton in Mexico.

"Why don't you come down here and keep Elizabeth company?" he suggested. "She's bored to tears."

"Fine," responded Roberts. "Do you need anything?" "Elizabeth says to bring some Hershey's chocolate bars, the kind with almonds. We can't get anything like that in Puerto Vallarta."

After Roberts hung up, he started racing up and down Broadway, cleaning out every drugstore and candy store in sight. "I bought enough chocolate bars to fill a large suitcase," he ventured. "What I failed to realize was that in those days you couldn't fly to Puerto Vallarta without first clearing customs in Mexico City. The customs officials in Mexico City asked me to unlock my luggage. When I opened the suitcase with the Hershey's bars, I immediately saw that they had melted into one molten mass. The agent took one look and ordered me to step out of the line. For the next three hours, a team of drug inspectors interrogated me in a locked room no larger than a broom closet. 'Why would anyone come to Mexico with a thousand bars of melted chocolate?' one of them asked. When they finally released me, they insisted on retaining the suitcase. Suffice it to say, I never saw it again."

Roberts boarded a small plane in Mexico City and flew to Guadalajara, where he transferred to an even smaller plane bound for Puerto Vallarta. He disembarked wearing only a swimsuit and sandals. "It had to be 110 degrees in the shade," he noted. Puerto Vallarta was nothing but a tranquil fishing village on Mexico's west coast, three hundred miles north of Acapulco. The town boasted one thoroughfare lined on both sides by run-down cafes and taverns, a hotel, a post office, a bus depot, and two or three boarded-up restaurants. Thanks to Dick and Liz's presence, Puerto Vallarta grew into a thriving resort, with a profusion of hotels, spas, apartment buildings, nightclubs, movie theaters, and a marina filled with dozens of yachts.

"The idea to shoot the picture in the surrounding area originated with John Huston, the film's director and coproducer [together with Ray Stark]. Huston owned a hacienda ten miles outside the village and visualized the potential profits he could reap by investing in local real estate. And that's precisely what he did.

"As for Liz, she wanted to be there to keep an eye on Burton. Sue (*Lolita*) Lyons, Deborah Kerr, and Ava Gardner were Richard's co-stars, and Elizabeth had no intention of following in Sybil Burton's footsteps. Far more possessive and outwardly emotional than her predecessor, Taylor attempted to maintain a tight hold on Richard, though not always with complete success."*

After Meade Roberts arrived in Puerto Vallarta, he found Dick and Liz ensconced in Casa Kimberley, a capacious seven-bedroom, seven-bath white stucco villa they had leased for two thousand dollars per month. Burton gave Meade the "royal tour" and informed him that he and Elizabeth planned to buy the dwelling. "What's more," said

*Just before shooting began on *The Night of the Iguana,* John Huston called the major cast members together (including Elizabeth Taylor, a non-cast member) and solemnly presented to each of them a gold-plated derringer pistol with gold-plated bullets inscribed with their names. "If he competition gets too fierce," he said, "you can always use the guns."

Roberts, "they wanted to build another house across the cobbled alleyway, linking the two by a construction modeled after the Bridge of Sighs in Venice. Burton led me to a window and indicated the other lot, which to my amazement contained a wire enclosure occupied by a family of pigs. They were oinking and rolling about in the mud. 'It's a pigpen!' I exclaimed. 'Brilliant, Watson,' said Dick. 'But it will soon be a mansion.' Frankly, I couldn't see it. In fact, I never quite understood what attraction Puerto Vallarta held for the couple. Presumably it represented a place where they could be themselves without being mobbed by outsiders.

"Elizabeth, as I'm sure many can attest, had a very down to earth side. I recall walking along the beach with her when she announced a poignant need to relieve herself. We soon passed a rickety outhouse, rotten with the odor of human waste.

"'I'll be back in a jiffy,' purred Elizabeth.

"'You're not going in there?' I asked.

"'When you gotta go, you gotta go,' she said.

"Upon her return, she added: 'If you don't have the luxury of Los Angeles and Hollywood, you make do with what you have. If I had to, I could probably pitch a tent in the desert and live there, at least for a while. You do what you have to do.'

"The natural, laid-back lifestyle of the region obviously suited Elizabeth. One afternoon she invited me to lunch at Casa Kimberley. It was cook's day off, so Liz said, 'I'm going to fry some chicken.' 'Where did you learn to cook?' I inquired. She said, 'I didn't. But what's so difficult about frying chicken? You simply take a pan, pour some oil into it, place the chicken parts in the pan, and turn on the heat. I don't understand the big deal all these people make about cooking.'"

If Elizabeth sought refuge from the world by indulging herself in medical problems, Burton found solace in the bottle. For the next ten years, he drank practically nonstop. Sue Lyons observed that "Burton imbibed so much at night, by the next morning the alcohol literally oozed out his pores. He gave off a terrible odor; playing a scene opposite him could be most unpleasant.

"I wasn't impressed by the relationship between Dick and Liz. Richard was very domineering. Elizabeth seemed almost meek around him; she would do whatever he wanted her to do. But what I liked least was his tendency to drink and then to be rude to her. At times, he used to ride her until she broke down in tears."

Meade Roberts attended a dinner party at a restaurant in Puerto Vallarta to which Dick and Liz invited several friends and cast members. "Burton was plastered," said Roberts. "Elizabeth and I were discussing a recent Hollywood rumor concerning a possible takeover of Warner Brothers by Frank Sinatra. I said, 'Why would Sinatra or any performer want the headaches associated with running a large film studio?' A few minutes into the discussion, Burton blew up at us and started shouting. 'The two of you are just jealous of Sinatra. You should only have his power. You're hypocrites and opportunists.'

"'Richard,' said Elizabeth, 'I can think of somebody else who has been accused of opportunism.'

"The implication couldn't have been more clear. Dick had hooked up with Elizabeth because of her stardom and the money he stood to make. In response to the accusation, he released a torrent of the most demeaning language I've ever heard. He didn't use four-letter words. Instead, it was Shakespearean and antiquated, at points incredibly withering. 'You scurrilous low creature, you,' he said. Elizabeth began to sob. Oblivious, Burton continued his tirade. When he finally stopped, it was obvious he had become nauseated from all the alcohol he had downed. He rose and headed for the bathroom. I offered to accompany him, but he didn't want my help. 'His pride won't allow it,' said Liz. Several minutes later, he returned and apologized. For the rest of the evening, he and Elizabeth acted very lovely-dovey. In a sense, he'd spewed out all the bile that had built up as a result of Taylor's barb."

With her addictive personality, it didn't take Liz long to increase her already prodigious drinking habit. Ramón Castro, former bartender at the Oceana Hotel, corroborated a number of the stories that circulated in Puerto Vallarta regarding Elizabeth's alcoholism.

"She would come in almost every day at ten o'clock in the morning and order a vodka collins or vodka martini. She would then switch to tequila. She appeared to have a hollow leg; she spent hours drinking at the bar but apparently experienced no discernible side effects. Burton would stumble in by midafternoon and order tumbler upon tumbler of straight scotch. Occasionally, he had an *amigo* in tow, and the two would compete in a scotch-swigging contest. The first man to hit the floor was declared the loser and footed the bill.

"Whenever Dick and Liz would throw a party at Casa Kimberley, they asked me to tend bar. These private galas were held around the property's swimming pool. The couple feted Tennessee Williams one night, and everyone, including Williams, drank themselves sick. To be honest, there wasn't much to do in Puerto Vallarta except drink."

Besides the Oceana, Dick and Liz enjoyed the Casablanca, an informal bar-restaurant named after the popular Humphrey Bogart film. Pico Pardo, manager of the establishment, noted that the couple usually dropped in during happy hour. Five minutes before happy hour ended, Liz would bang on the table and demand a last round of drinks at happy-hour prices.

"Elizabeth drank too much, perhaps in an effort to keep up with Richard Burton. She could be exceedingly competitive, particularly with the men in her life. Because of Richard's highly trained stage voice, she returned to the same king's English she had known as a child living in London.

"At heart, Elizabeth's tough; she's a true fighter. The heavy drinking may have adversely affected her personality, but in many respects she remained the stronger of the two. One of her greatest strengths was her ability to make Richard feel as if he wielded all the power. It's fair to say they were both puissant in different ways. Elizabeth had better control of her emotions. Richard could be sullen, morose, and introspective. Conversely, he seemed less dependent on Elizabeth than she on him. He would go drinking with Ava Gardner, with visiting newsmen, with writers, with other members of the cast, with anyone he could coerce into bending elbows with him. When Liz wanted to be near him, she had to go to a tavern.

"Once, as Richard sat around drinking with a group of reporters, Elizabeth came in and joined the table. After an hour she excused herself and drove home in her jeep. She soon began calling Burton every five minutes. 'My sexual presence is herewith summoned,' he announced. Two hours and many phone calls later, he got up and headed for the door. 'Duty calls!' he roared, disappearing into the night."

Author Stephen Birmingham, an intimate of Ava Gardner's, spent several months in Puerto Vallarta during the filming of *The Night of the Iguana.* In his opinion, "Elizabeth went so far as to encourage Richard to drink, and nobody could figure out the reason. He'd perch on a bar stool and comment, 'I'm not going to have anything to drink tonight because I'm supposed to do close-ups in the morning.' 'Oh, Richard, have a little bourbon, have a little wine,' Liz would coax him. She'd implore him to drink something, and after an initial pause, he'd say, 'All right,' and twenty-seven drinks later they'd carry him home and put him to bed.

"I couldn't figure out what made Elizabeth Taylor tick. She once said to me, 'Richard and I had the most wonderful time last night.' I expected to hear a scintillating sex tale; instead, she remarked, 'We sat up all night and read Shakespeare.'

Genuinely impressed by Elizabeth Taylor's parenting skills, Meade Roberts couldn't help but notice her close bond to Liza Todd. He and Stephen Birmingham considered Liza a strange, almost wistful child. At age six she spoke fluent French but didn't yet know the alphabet in her native tongue, for she had never attended school.

Meade Roberts described an incident involving Liza Todd which took place at Casa Kimberley: "Richard had a raging hangover and had been taunting Liza all morning. Elizabeth suddenly wheeled around and faced Burton. 'Don't you ever speak to my daughter like that or I'll leave,' she warned. Richard immediately toned down and later took

Liza for a walk, stopping along the way to buy her as many presents as they could carry home."

Author-screenwriter Budd Schulberg, then living in Mexico City, drove to Puerto Vallarta and witnessed still another example of Elizabeth in action. "Liz and I were sauntering along the beach with Elizabeth's daughter," he recounted. "We were discussing childhood film stars like Jackie Coogan and how difficult and unnatural their lives had been. 'Whatever else I do for Liza,' Elizabeth said, 'I will never expose her to the kind of experiences my parents forced me to endure.'

"At that moment a speedboat approached the shore. I barely glanced at it, but Elizabeth had her antennae raised. She spotted the photographer aiming his camera at Liza. This self-composed woman, who a moment earlier had been talking to me in a quiet voice, turned into a banshee. 'Get away! Get away! You son of a bitch! Get out of here! Stop following us! I'll break your goddamn camera!' She waded out into the ocean, in the direction of the boat, throwing sand and pebbles and shouting at the photographer. She continued advancing until the crew turned the boat around and sped off."

When Budd Schulberg recounted the event to Richard Burton, the actor surprised him with his candor. "Why shouldn't the press and photo corps have a go at us? We make an absolutely enormous amount of money for an absurd bit of work."

Elizabeth adhered to her own code of right and wrong. When a penniless ten-year-old native boy who shined shoes in Puerto Vallarta developed an advanced cataract in one eye, Taylor paid an eye surgeon in Guadalajara to treat the child. She constantly bought food and clothes for other indigent families in town.

When an apartment building collapsed that had been constructed to house some 250 of *Iguana*'s crew members, one worker suffered a broken back and a fractured skull. While others looked the other way, Elizabeth reenacted the nurturing role she had adopted during Montgomery Clift's near-fatal automobile accident. She cradled the worker's head in her arms until a helicopter arrived to fly him to the nearest metropolitan hospital.

1934, England. Elizabeth Rosemond Taylor, at the age of 2½, with her mother, the former Sara Sothern, a well-known former stage actress, and her brother, Howard. (Bettmann/CORBIS)

1943, Hollywood. Lassie, the ten-dollar collie runt that became a high-priced star in the movie *Lassie Come Home,* stamps an inky paw on a five-year contract with M-G-M, aided by eleven-year-old Elizabeth, who made her film debut in the same picture. (Bettmann/CORBIS)

Elizabeth, playing with her beloved dogs. (Bettmann/CORBIS)

Liz with her then fiancé, Conrad Nicholson "Nicky" Hilton Jr., ready for a night out in 1949. (Underwood & Underwood/ CORBIS)

Elizabeth Taylor and Michael Wilding with their first child, Michael Howard Jr., in 1953. (mptvimages.com)

Liz goes head over heels as actor James Dean helps on the set of the movie *Giant*. Dean would die in an auto accident only days after completing his last scenes. (Frank Worth/Getty Images)

Elizabeth and Montgomery Clift had already formed an intense friendship by the time they appeared together in *Raintree County*. (© 1978 Bob Willoughby/mptvimages.com)

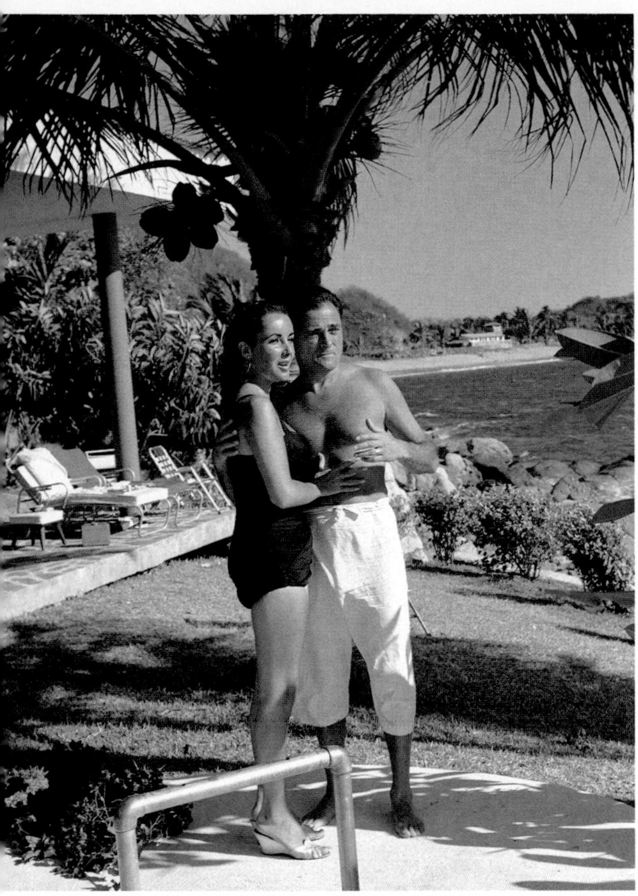

Elizabeth's Acapulco honeymoon with husband number three, impresario Mike Todd, seemed like the beginning of a marriage that would last forever. (Bettmann/CORBIS)

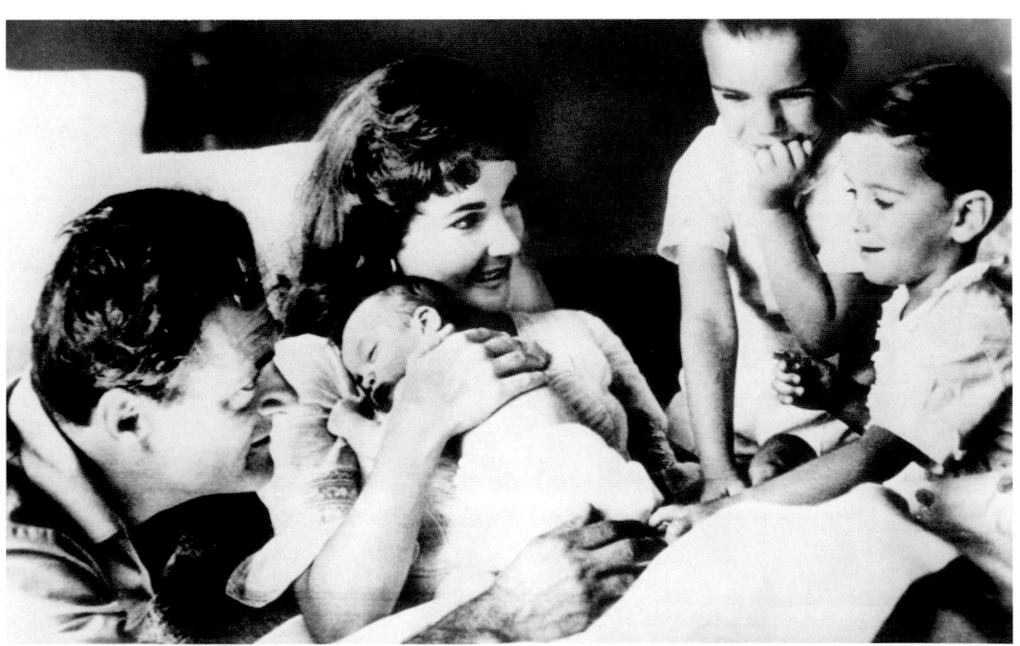

Mike, Liz, and baby Liza, with sons Michael and Christopher Wilding looking on. (Shooting Star)

Triangle Number One: Liz, Eddie Fisher, and Debbie Reynolds in 1958. (Bettmann/CORBIS)

Accompanied by her mother and father, Elizabeth watches Eddie perform during his opening night at the Las Vegas Tropicana in April 1959. The couple had announced they would marry in six weeks if Debbie gave her consent for a quickie Nevada divorce. (Bettmann/CORBIS)

Liz shows off her 1960 Oscar for *Butterfield 8*. Burt Lancaster won for *Elmer Gantry*. (The Kobal Collection)

Triangle Number Two: Elizabeth sits in Eddie Fisher's lap on the set of *Cleopatra,* while Richard Burton looks on. Taylor would soon leave Fisher for Burton. (Bettmann/CORBIS)

Elizabeth hugs son Michael Wilding Jr. at the Rome studio where she and Richard Burton, in his Marc Antony costume, are filming *Cleopatra*. Her daughter, Liza, has her back to the camera; younger son Christopher is in the right foreground. (Associated Press)

Behind-the-scenes sensuality on the set of *Cleopatra*. (mptvimages.com)

Burtons and brood. (Bob Penn/Camera Press/Retna)

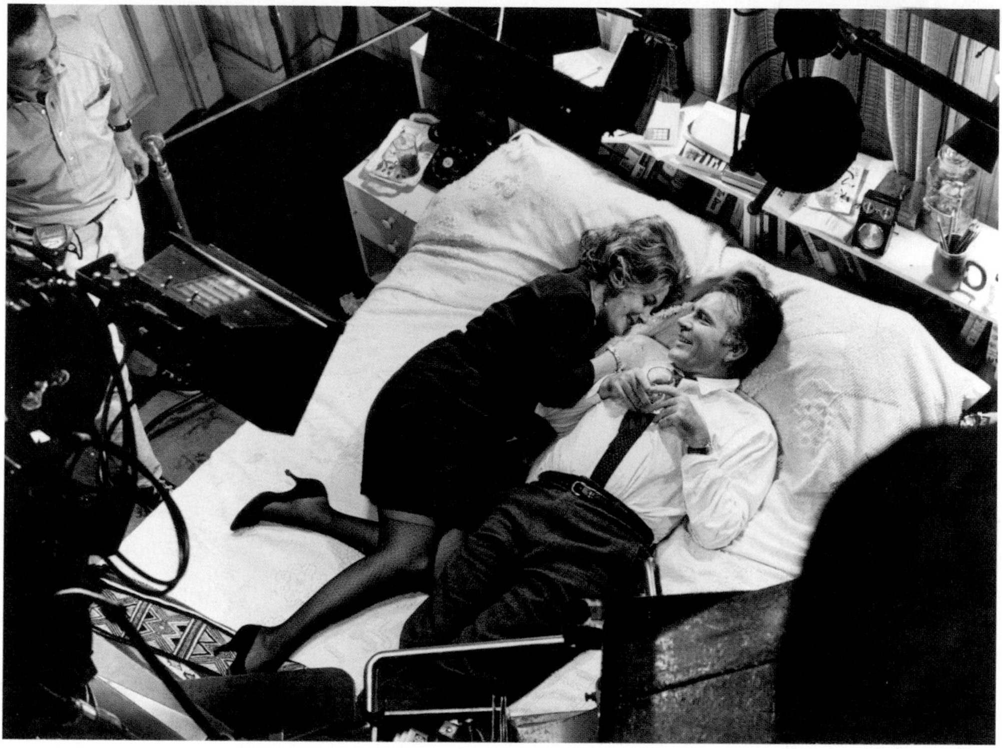

Liz won her second Oscar for her performance as Martha opposite Richard Burton as George in the film of Edward Albee's *Who's Afraid of Virginia Woolf?* Many believed the movie mirrored the couple's own tumultuous relationship. (Photo by Mel Traxel/mptvimages.com)

Elizabeth Taylor meets with her son Michael Wilding Jr. for the first time in six years, at Ffynonwen Farm, Michael's home in Wales, in 1975. (Keystone/Getty Images)

Having temporarily abandoned Hollywood glamour, Elizabeth presided with husband number seven, Senator John Warner, at an annual country-style barbecue at Warner's Virginia estate. (Bettmann/CORBIS)

Liza Minnelli, Rock Hudson, and Liz at the Golden Globe Awards in 1985. Hudson's death from AIDS later that year galvanized Taylor's commitment to fighting the disease. (Bettmann/CORBIS)

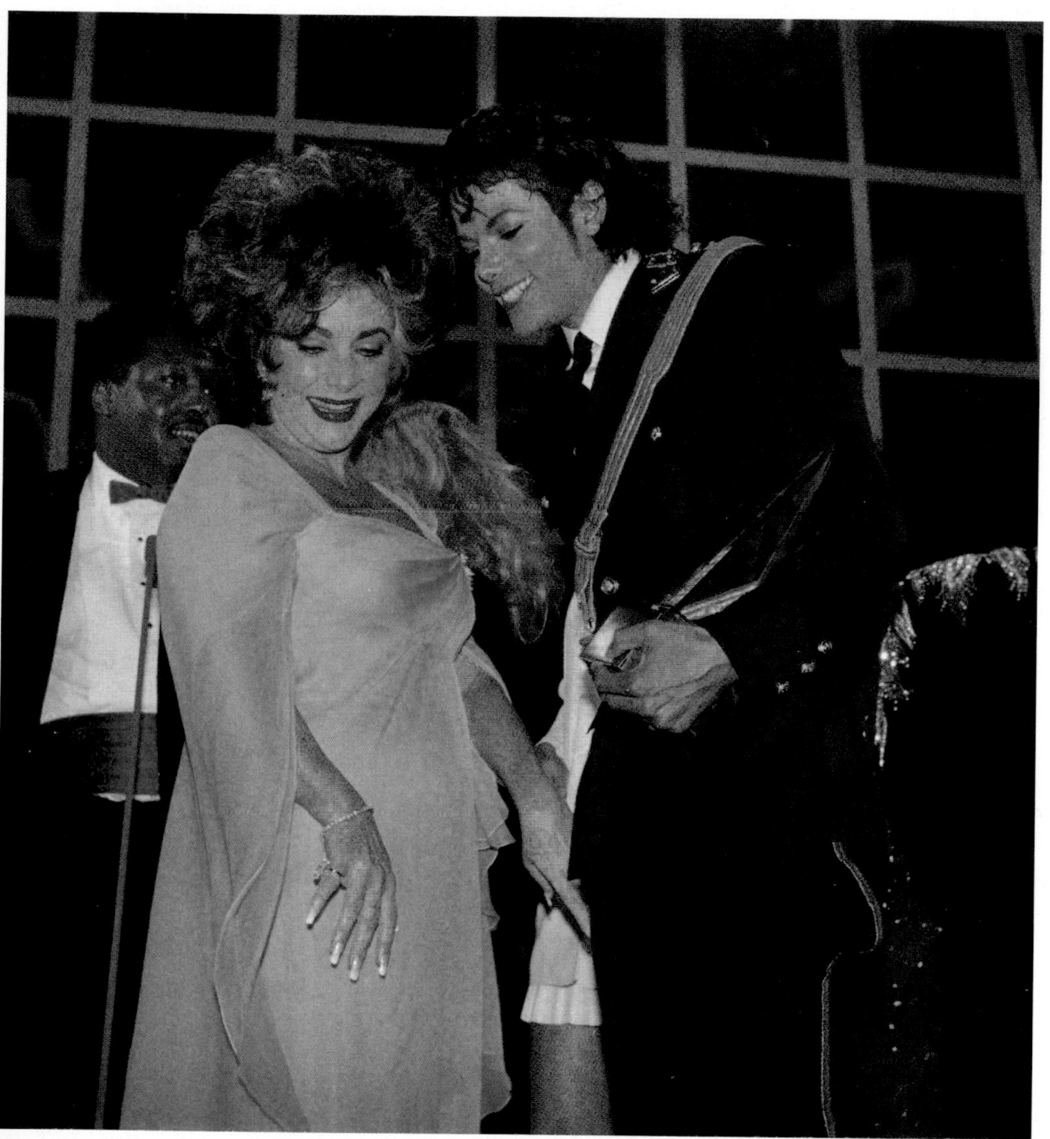

Elizabeth and Michael Jackson relax after singing "We Are the World" at the close of the American Music Awards in 1986. (Associated Press)

A tanned Liz and her date, George Hamilton, arrive at the Cannes Film Festival in 1987. (Eric Gaillard/CORBIS)

Liz and husband number eight, Larry Fortensky, arrive at an AIDS charity dinner during Art Basel, Switzerland, in 1991. (Walter Bieri/EPA/CORBIS)

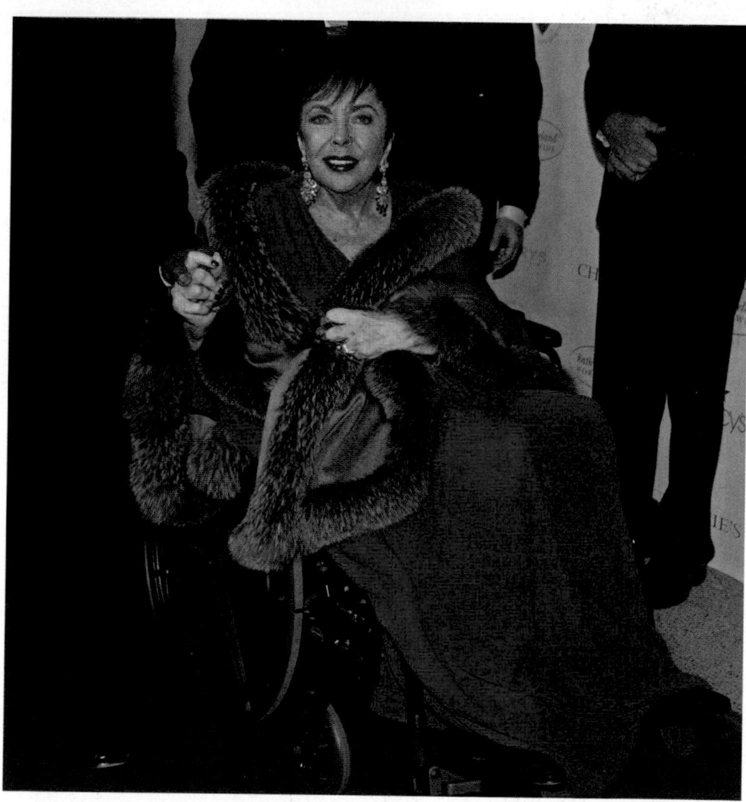

Elizabeth arrives at Paramount Studios to give a benefit performance of A. R. Gurney's play *Love Letters,* with James Earl Jones, for the Elizabeth Taylor HIV/AIDS Foundation, in 2007. (Associated Press/Stefano Paltera)

Dame Elizabeth Taylor speaks during the 26th annual Macy's Passport Gala in 2008.
(Associated Press/Matt Sayles)

The collapse of the dwelling resulted in a serious rift between Ray Stark and Guillermo Wulff, the architect-builder in Puerto Vallarta responsible for the construction of the structure.

"I built everything in Mismaloya," claimed Wulff. "I constructed the film sets, the roadways, the water system, the sewage system, and the crew accommodations. With the collapse of the crew's quarters, I wound up losing a fortune on the project. Richard asked me to build a second home adjacent to Casa Kimberley. I submitted an estimate for $45,000, and he changed the figure to $55,000. 'Why did you do that?' I asked. 'Because you're in financial trouble and you're a friend,' he answered."

Nelly Barquet, Wulff's former wife, designed clothes for Richard and Elizabeth. "I made shirts and jackets for Richard," said Nelly. "He purchased twenty-five of each and wore them when he performed his Broadway 'street-clothes' version of *Hamlet.*

"I fashioned many gaily colored dresses for Elizabeth. They were loose fitting, with wide arms and a low, round neckline. It was called a *gazela* dress and was always made in cotton or wool voile. Elizabeth didn't have good taste in clothes, but she at least followed the advice of those who did. I can't say I envied Elizabeth's way of life. Because of the demands of their acting careers, she and Richard were forever on the run. They loved Puerto Vallarta, with its lush papaya, lemon, and banana trees, but they rarely stayed for more than a few weeks at a time."

Chapter 19

In December 1963, as work on *The Night of the Iguana* ended, Sybil Burton terminated her fifteen-year marriage to Richard Burton in a Mexican divorce court on the grounds that the burly Welsh actor had been seen repeatedly in the company of "another woman." Burton and John Huston celebrated the divorce at the Oceana by drinking *raicilla,* a blend of cactus brandy more potent than tequilla.

Although the Richard and Sybil Burton divorce case went smoothly, Elizabeth Taylor and an embittered Eddie Fisher encountered problems. Earl Wilson interviewed Fisher in mid-December 1963. "Eddie had hired the preeminent Louis Nizer, Esq., to handle his divorce claim," noted Wilson. "Fisher referred to Dick Burton as 'Richard the Lion-Hearted.' When I asked him what Elizabeth wanted from the divorce, he said, 'I don't think she knows what she wants, or ever has. Whenever she or Burton want something, everybody has to hop to it. They stomp their feet, and if they don't get what they want, the world must stop. Elizabeth deserves the Oscar for sheer gall.'"

Elizabeth's divorce attorney, Mickey Rudin, journeyed to Puerto Vallarta to confer with his client. Richard Burton greeted him by proclaiming, "The sooner we resolve this bloody battle, the better." From Las Vegas, where Fisher had gone to rehearse his latest nightclub act, he fired another volley at Dick and Liz: "They've been acting like a couple of kids in a playpen. . . . Well, they can wait a few more days."

Following additional exchanges of insults, Taylor and Fisher finally filed their respective divorce petitions in Puerto Vallarta, clearing a path for the dissolution of their marriage.

In early January 1964, Burton and Taylor, accompanied by Richard's newly hired bodyguard, Bob LaSalle, flew into Los Angeles for a visit with Elizabeth's parents. Tom Snyder, the future radio-television talk-show host and news anchor, was then a young reporter with KTLA, Channel 5, and had been assigned to cover their arrival.

"Their return to the U.S. constituted big news," said Snyder. "Their plane landed at eleven P.M., and the entire L.A. press corps had gathered. The couple had resolved not to do any interviews, but we were allowed to place our cameras on a line and could photograph them stepping off the plane. In jockeying for position, everybody kept moving closer and closer to the airliner. As the couple disembarked, we found ourselves practically on top of them. My crew had the videotape and the wind-up [sound] going. As the pair approached, we could hear them arguing. They were going at it rather intensely. 'Fuck you!' screamed Burton. 'Go fuck yourself!' Elizabeth responded. I couldn't tell you what they were bickering about, but the profanities were such that we had to kill the sound."

Shades of Todd-Taylor became apparent, although Dick and Liz ceased quarreling the moment they climbed into their limousine. *Los Angeles Times* film critic Jack Smith and a hundred other print-media reporters in a long caravan of cars trailed the duo from the airport. "We followed Burton and Taylor into Inglewood," said Smith. "They were on their way to Beverly Hills. But then they stopped, climbed out of the limo, and sauntered into a roadside bar. They sat in a booth, and the rest of us crowded around, and we chatted with them. Burton held court. He was charming, and the more he drank, the more charming he became.

"Burton gulped down eight or nine drinks. A member of the press told the waiter, 'I'll have a glass of cold, dry white wine.' Burton looked at the reporter and said, 'A glass of cold, dry white wine is *not* a drink.'"

Burton's biting wit continued to find expression after he and his intended left Los Angeles for Toronto, where Richard was about to rehearse for the title role in a modern-dress stage production of *Hamlet,* under the direction of John Gielgud. "Elizabeth wants me to play Hamlet," Richard told the cast, "and I want to earn two million dollars a picture." Over lunch with Liz in a Toronto pub, Burton lightheartedly informed a reporter: "I introduced Elizabeth to beer; she introduced me to Bulgari's."

On March 6, 1964, Elizabeth's attorney notified her that the Eddie Fisher divorce decree had at last cleared. Because Toronto (province of Ontario, Canada) didn't recognize the validity of a Mexican divorce, Taylor and Burton's wedding ceremony took place on March 15 in a hotel suite at the Ritz-Carlton in Montreal (province of Quebec). Of the eleven guests gathered for the Unitarian service, more than half were employees of either the bride or groom. Irene Sharaff designed a replica of the yellow gown Elizabeth wore in the first scene she and Burton shot together in *Cleopatra.* White hyacinths adorned her hair, and she boasted a pair of diamond-and-emerald teardrop earrings which Burton had given her for her thirty-second birthday. Her wedding present included a matching brooch and necklace.

Days before taking the play to Boston, the producers learned that U.S. representative Michael Feigham, Democrat of Ohio and head of the House Subcommittee on Immigration and Naturalization, had demanded that the State Department investigate the validity of Richard Burton's visa. The reason for the inquiry, according to Feigham, was his intention to spare the American public "all this discussion of morals."

Within a week's time the State Department concluded that the investigation had produced no grounds for the revocation of Burton's visa. The newlyweds joined the Shakespearean troupe at the Ritz-Carlton in Boston. In anticipation of their arrival, a crowd of over a thousand filled the hotel lobby. Squeezing through and around the mob with the help of police, private guards, and hotel employees, Elizabeth sprained a shoulder. One desperate onlooker went so far as to yank out a handful of hair from Taylor's scalp. The following morning, Richard

Burton went to a gun shop in Roxbury, a run-down section of Boston, to purchase a .22-caliber pistol and a supply of ammunition.

The Boston crowds were benign compared to what awaited the Burtons in New York. The play's appearance at the Lunt-Fontanne Theatre on West Forty-sixth Street created major traffic jams. Streets and avenues had to be sealed off, and dozens of cops in full riot gear, many on horseback, were deployed to control the swarms of humanity that greeted the star couple each evening as they left the theater. The half-mile ride from the Lunt-Fontanne to the Regency Hotel, where they were staying, often took up to an hour. Burton reveled in the attention; Elizabeth claimed she could do without it.

"Liz feigned general disinterest in her public," reported Earl Wilson, "but in truth she keened on the attention. She imported Alexandre de Paris to do her hair. She wore the latest American and European fashions. She stood in the wings, sipping champagne during almost every performance of *Hamlet.* Sammy Davis Jr. came to a matinee with his tailor, Cy Devore, whose clientele included Frank Sinatra, Dean Martin, and Peter Lawford. Sammy convinced Liz that Richard's wardrobe needed revamping; it wasn't 'mod' enough. Dick and Liz commissioned Devore to invent a whole new look for Burton."

Meade Roberts appeared backstage after a performance and found Burton trying on a Cy Devore suit. "He had three or four gold chains and medallions hanging around his neck, and in my eyes he looked ridiculous," said Roberts. "Sammy Davis Jr. and Elizabeth Taylor were crawling about the floor, adjusting his cuffs. Burton peered into a full-length mirror and evidently liked what he saw, an opinion shared by Elizabeth Taylor, who assured him that in his new apparel he would soon become 'the Frank Sinatra of Shakespeare.'"

Richard Burton wasn't always quite so pleased with himself. The astute theater critic Harold Clurman walked out on *Hamlet,* saying of Burton: ". . . this is an actor who has lost interest in his profession."

The comment set Burton off on a drinking binge. A heckler in the audience one evening had a similar effect. Elizabeth had the flu and couldn't attend the show. Richard returned to the hotel suite totally inebriated, complaining that he had been *booed.*

"Oh, darling," said Elizabeth, lying in bed watching a Peter Sellers movie. "It's probably just some idiot. Don't pay any attention to that."

"Turn off that motherfucking television," ordered Burton.

"Oh, but I'm watching the most marvelous movie," protested Taylor.

Burton ran barefoot over to the TV and gave it a kick. The set grazed the wall, and one of the knobs fell off. Stepping back to deliver a second boot, Burton knocked the set to the floor and cut his foot in the process. It took Elizabeth nearly an hour to stem the flow of blood.

Philip Burton, Richard's early mentor, had originally supported Sybil Burton over Elizabeth Taylor but had gradually been won over by Liz. Currently a faculty member at the American Musical & Dramatic Academy of New York, Philip had agreed to Richard's suggestion that they stage a literary evening at the Lunt-Fontanne Theatre to raise funds for the academy.

The program, called "World Enough and Time," was thankfully a once-only affair, with Dick and Liz alternately reading a mélange of excerpts from such wordsmiths as Shakespeare, D. H. Lawrence, Edwin Markham, and John Lennon of the Beatles.

Whereas Burton "winged" his way through the presentation, Taylor rehearsed for more than two weeks, largely in vain. "Elizabeth Taylor Fluffs Lines in Stage Debut," read the *New York Herald Tribune,* describing Liz's attempts to giggle her way through a series of bungled lines.

"I'll begin again," she gaily remarked while doing a somber elegy about pestilential death in the seventeenth century. "I got it all screwed up," she added, taking a sip from a glass of water.

As members of the audience shifted nervously in their seats, Richard Burton said drily: "This is getting funnier than *Hamlet.*"

More disconcerting to her avid public (as well as to the Internal Revenue Service) was Elizabeth's ever-changing citizenship. In an effort to avoid paying the preponderance of her income toward taxes in England, Taylor had in the past given up her British allegiance to become an American citizen; now she became English again, providing the press with a cute but lame excuse: "It is not true that I love America less, but I love my husband more." Guided by a staff of lawyers, agents, and moneymen, the Burtons also set up independent corporations. Richard's became Atlantic Programmes; Elizabeth's was dubbed Interplanet Productions.

While still at the Regency, Elizabeth received a telephone call from Truman Capote. Their mutual friend, Montgomery Clift, was being held a virtual prisoner in his apartment by a male lover who had moved in and refused to leave.

"Pack Monty's bags and send him over here," said Taylor.

Monty arrived at the Regency the next day. He looked unkempt and sickly and remained with the Burtons for only three nights before returning home. Eddie Fisher next visited the Regency. He had seen Richard Burton in a restaurant, and Richard invited him up for a drink.

"I arrived in the middle of an argument," Fisher ventured, recalling Elizabeth's makeup being "smeared, her voice loud and shrill. [She] was furious about something and I thought, I was married to that woman, that wild thing. Burton was trying to soothe her, and as I watched him walk around their suite, apologizing, straightening up, retrieving things she had dropped, I saw myself. . . ."

Chaos reigned. Altercations between the Burtons were commonplace. Richard charted the arguments and outbursts of violence in a series of leather-bound notebooks—a daily diary—portions of which formed the framework for a biography of the actor by Melvyn Bragg. "He would flip into black moods, viciousness, sarcasm with anyone and most of all with Elizabeth," noted Bragg. "He flayed her. . . . She, though grand and large enough to absorb the shocks of his battering ram of an ego, would fly back at him, often physically 'beating him,' and he had the greatest trouble in not returning the blows. He did once 'and I didn't hear very well for a month,' she said."

Dick and Liz both published books in 1964. Burton wrote a

modern-day fable entitled *A Christmas Story* as well as a thinly disguised version of his romantic entanglement with Taylor, which he published as fiction under the title *Meeting Mrs. Jenkins.* Elizabeth, who had once contemplated a personal memoir under the aegis of Max Lerner, chose to work on *Elizabeth Taylor* with *Life* magazine staff writer Richard Meryman. Harper & Row paid Taylor $250,000 for the project, a superficial "autobiography" of 177 pages, including fifty-six black-and-white photographs of the actress by Roddy McDowall.

"I don't think she was terribly pleased with it," said Richard Meryman. "She didn't promote it. She didn't put much of herself into it. There was virtually no gossip. *Elizabeth Taylor* didn't sell well; it disappeared without making a ripple."

At the end of 1964, the Burtons starred together in *The Sandpiper,* a movie in which Elizabeth plays a free-spirited single mother who lives in a beach house at Big Sur amid a close-knit community of Bohemian artists. Burton's role in the picture is that of an Episcopalian minister (the third clergyman he had portrayed since uniting with Elizabeth Taylor). The minister and his wife (a role filled by Eva Marie Saint) operate a private school for boys. The characters performed by Burton and Taylor become involved in a tumultuous affair. When his devoted wife discovers the misdeed, the reverend separates from her and embarks on an uncertain future.

Martin Ransohoff, producer of *The Sandpiper,* had hoped to shoot the film sooner. "Elizabeth wouldn't agree," said Ransohoff, "because she wanted to be in Mexico while Burton made *Night of the Iguana.* I told her we'd hire Marlon Brando in place of Burton and fly her down to Puerto Vallarta by private jet every weekend. 'No, no, no,' she responded. So we delayed our picture to accommodate her. I'd originally wanted William Wyler to direct, but the revised schedule created a conflict for Wyler. Elizabeth chose his replacement, Vincente Minnelli, with whom she had worked before.

"I went along with Minnelli, but then Elizabeth wanted Sammy Davis Jr. to play the role of her Big Sur Bohemian boyfriend. That was a pretty radical idea. She had befriended Sammy in New York and insisted I cast him in the picture. I'm a liberal—I had hired Dalton Trumbo, one of the original 'Hollywood Ten,' as coscreenwriter on *The Sandpiper*—but Sammy Davis Jr. as one of Elizabeth Taylor's love interests in a 1964 movie would have caused all kinds of grief. We ultimately gave the role to Charles Bronson.

"We took three weeks to shoot exteriors at Big Sur, but because of tax considerations on the part of Richard Burton, we decided to complete the shoot in Paris."

An intriguing sidelight to the film involved an actual Big Sur artist, Edmund Kara, who had been commissioned by the production company to complete a life-size nude sculpture of Elizabeth Taylor. "The script called for the artist in the picture [Charles Bronson] to sculpt Elizabeth au naturel," said Kara. "I did the artwork. I carved the sculpture out of a solid piece of redwood, and it took three months. They couldn't get Elizabeth to pose in the nude for me. She had refused, so I used a model who possessed similar proportions. I also had a life mask of Elizabeth's face which gave me a clue to her physiognomy and her character. When the piece was finished, Elizabeth Taylor and Richard Burton came around to have a look. 'Bravo, you've done masterfully,' said Burton. 'You even captured the dimples in her ass.'

"After that the crew tied a sheet around the sculpture, trucked it to New York, and placed it in a stateroom aboard the *Ile de France,* this apparently being the most economic way to transport it to the film studio in Paris. They used it in the picture, even had a mock unveiling for the sake of publicity, then shipped it back to the States. It sat in a storeroom at M-G-M, which owned the rights to the movie and therefore to the sculpture. I believe they leased out the sculpture once or twice for use in showrooms. They toyed with the idea of trying to make miniature ornamental replicas of it in bronze to put on people's desks.

"One day I telephoned the producer, Martin Ransohoff, and asked if perhaps M-G-M wouldn't mind returning the sculpture to me. He said he thought it could be arranged. And he did arrange it; the studio lawyers sent me a contract stipulating in the event I sold the piece,

M-G-M would receive half the proceeds. I signed, although I had no intention of selling it. I liked Elizabeth's head; I wanted to rework it a bit and keep it. The rest of the wood I would eventually use for new work.

"As soon as they delivered it, I called a friend and asked him to come over with a chain saw. He arrived, and I told him to decapitate the sculpture. He took off the head straight across the shoulders and then cut away the arms, leaving the torso. He was holding the chain saw rather suggestively in front of his crotch. The blade protruded like a giant phallus. So I said to him, 'Go ahead, give it to her.' He plunged the blade deep into the vagina and ripped the log in half down to the floor. And when he had completed the cut, thousands of Big Sur army ants came marching out. They had been living inside the wooden goddess's uterus for months. In some strange way the episode had a mystical, almost legendary quality to it."

While finishing *The Sandpiper* in Paris, the Burtons stayed at the fashionable Hotel Lancaster and attended several dinner parties at the home of Baron Guy de Rothschild. They hired a chauffeur, Gaston Sanz, and at one point were joined by all four of Elizabeth's children. Maria, the adopted child, now had her own nurse and governess. Elizabeth's sons had a private tutor, twenty-two-year-old Paul Neshamkin, whose major task was disciplining rather than teaching the boys. As a joke, Richard Burton gave Paul a wooden paddle and instructed him to "use it if and when necessary."

The Sandpiper completed, Dick and Liz vacationed at the Hotel Santa Caterina in Amalfi. There, according to the *New York Post,* the couple engaged in one of their epic battles. Scores of guests were seated on the hotel terrace (perched on a cliff hundreds of feet above the Italian Riviera) when Richard's entire wardrobe—still on hangers—came flying out a window of the Burton suite and landed in the sea.

In February 1965, Elizabeth accompanied her fifth husband to Dublin, where he appeared as an old and worn-down foreign agent in John le Carré's *Spy Who Came In From the Cold.* Cast as Richard's lover in the espionage thriller was his old flame Claire Bloom, who complained that Burton cold-shouldered her throughout the filming. He apparently had little choice in the matter: Elizabeth kept him under constant surveillance.

While in Dublin, Richard drank as much as ever. His personal assistant, Bob Lee, whom he once referred to as "my version of Elizabeth's Dick Hanley," was frequently dispatched to buy and bring back bottles of scotch and Irish whiskey. Burton later claimed that he had valid reasons for drinking during this period. He and Elizabeth were beset by a series of misfortunes. First, Taylor's father suffered a stroke and spent months recuperating. Next, a burglar gained access to their Dublin hotel suite and made off with $50,000 of Elizabeth's jewelry, including the wedding band worn by Mike Todd which had been recovered after his demise in the airplane crash. Then their French chauffeur, Gaston Sanz, had a road accident while at the wheel of Burton's Rolls-Royce; a crazed pedestrian ran headfirst into the side of the automobile and died several days later.

Rock Brynner, the son of Yul Brynner, recounted another tragic occurrence involving Gaston Sanz. "I had transferred from Yale University to Trinity College in Dublin," reflected Rock. "As a result of my family's friendship with Elizabeth Taylor, I spent a considerable amount of time with her and Richard Burton during their stay in Ireland. I recall a most unfortunate event which transpired not long after their arrival: The nineteen-year-old son of Gaston Sanz perished in a shooting accident at an arcade rifle range in Saint-Jean-de-Luz, France. Rumor had it that the young man committed suicide, but that simply wasn't the case.

"Elizabeth, who had developed a serious and painful intestinal ailment, nevertheless accompanied Gaston to the funeral. They flew to Paris and then on to Saint-Jean-de-Luz. Gaston couldn't bear to see his son's body; the bullet had torn away half his skull. Elizabeth went to the mortuary to identify the corpse and determine whether the head was intact enough to be viewed at an open-casket ceremony. I believe she recommended that the coffin remain closed. She further made certain the police report indicated the death had been accidental and not a suicide. She organized and paid for the funeral."

In April 1965, the Burtons spent two weeks at Elizabeth's chalet in Gstaad. While there, they enrolled the Wilding boys in a year-round Swiss boarding school. As had become her custom, Taylor experienced one more accident by bumping into a kitchen cabinet and blackening both eyes. Richard Burton told her: "You're not accident-prone, you're incident-prone."

They continued their vacation by secluding themselves in a cozy villa at Cap d'Antibes, where they received a script by screenwriter and producer Ernest Lehman for a forthcoming film adaptation of Edward Albee's play *Who's Afraid of Virginia Woolf?* While weighing the advantages and disadvantages of the script, the couple heard that Sybil Burton had remarried.

Sybil had begun to flourish once she settled into the mainstream of New York, becoming involved as casting director and coproducer of the Establishment Theater Company, a British troupe whose productions included *The Ginger Man* and *The Knack.* When the group disbanded, Sybil and a contingent of financial backers took over the Establishment's studio on East Fifty-fourth Street and turned it into a restaurant-discotheque called Arthur (after a type of Beatle haircut). "Arthur," as film critic Hollis Alpert put it, "quickly became the most famous, the most 'in,' the hardest to get into night spot in the City."

Although she proclaimed she would never remarry, thirty-six-year-old Sybil found herself deeply attracted to Jordan Christopher, the slim, twenty-four-year-old, dark-haired leader of the Wild Ones, a five-man rock band she had hired away from the Peppermint Lounge to play each night at Arthur. Regarding her feelings for Jordan Christopher, Sybil told a reporter: "I couldn't believe it, wouldn't even let myself think about it." But she could think of nothing else, and in June 1965 she and Jordan Christopher were married. Richard Burton sent them a congratulatory telegram; he received no answer.

At first, eight-year-old Kate Burton also had reservations. A newspaper article reported that she had once run away from home and tried to join her father and Elizabeth Taylor in Hollywood. Over a span of time, she began to accept her "second father" and spoke favorably of him, acknowledging that the environment at her mother's house seemed tranquil by comparison to the ever-present turbulence she experienced whenever she visited Dick and Liz. Kate's later summation of her real father's marital difficulties had more to do with his own problems than with those created by Elizabeth. "Dadda," said Kate Burton in the *Daily Mail,* "could not live with himself." If upheaval and turmoil beget art—and they often do—then Richard Burton and Elizabeth Taylor were likely choices for the lead roles in Edward Albee's *Who's Afraid of Virginia Woolf?* As the slatternly, provocative Martha in Mike Nichols's directing debut, Liz brays, curses, coos, mocks, screams, scolds, and howls so hard we expect her to implode. Dragging around in thick spectacles and a baggy cardigan, Richard Burton captures the meekly professorial, but only superficially weak, George. As their young guests, Sandy Dennis and George Segal seem highly confused once the boozing and bloodletting begin. "Fat and forty!" crowed (inaccurately) the headlines over Liz's appearance in this drama about middle-age rebellion and self-denial.

Albee had at first questioned Taylor's appearance in the film. Although eventually pleased with her performance, he nevertheless felt she was too young for the role.

Haskell Wexler, cinematographer for the picture, observed that Taylor, in an effort to embrace the personality of Martha, had gained considerable weight. "She didn't mind looking puffy and haggard, nor did she want to resemble the Fat Lady in the circus. Extremely conscious of her screen appearance, she constantly reminded me that she wasn't supposed to look good. Then she whispered, 'Well, I'm not supposed to look awful, either.'"

In adhering to their roles, the couple did their fair share of offscreen drinking, especially Richard. "After lunch," recalled Haskell Wexler, who won an Oscar for his work on the film, "it became difficult to get Burton to concentrate. By contrast, I found Elizabeth to be a dedicated performer. In terms of her career, she sensed the importance of

Virginia Woolf; it became the first film in which she depended more on ability than good looks. She tended to 'pooh-pooh' her range as an actress, but from my perspective she did a good job. She took her craft seriously. In later years, she often cited *Virginia Woolf* as one of her two favorite film performances, the other being *National Velvet.*

"To relax between takes, Elizabeth, Sandy Dennis, and I held belching contests. Sandy invariably won. She could belch on cue and louder than anybody. I should add that although she'd acted in a number of Broadway productions, *Virginia Woolf* marked Sandy's beginning in film."

In the past, Richard Burton had referred to his wife as "Lazybones," suggesting she had been "taking it easy" on previous projects. Mike Nichols, however, had managed to reverse the syndrome. He'd gotten Elizabeth to lower her voice for the role, to carry herself differently, to gain twenty unwieldy pounds. Sidney Guilaroff designed several wigs to make her appear older than her thirty-two years. During one sequence Taylor broke a tooth, which delayed the production by nearly a week. In another incident she injured an eye and took several days off. But in general the Warner Brothers work log indicates she was responsible and punctual.

Richard Burton, on the other hand, had his own set of problems. Costume designer Irene Sharaff thought it overly simplistic to suggest that in their private lives the Burtons carried on like George and Martha of *Who's Afraid of Virginia Woolf?* Nevertheless, there were elements of similarity between the real and the screen couple. Not unlike Martha, Elizabeth could be excruciatingly difficult—she could grind on people, wear them down. The same could have been said for Richard Burton, who, like many brilliant men, happened to be a highly complex and unpredictable individual.

Richard Burton had reached the apex of his drinking and pill-popping phase. His daughter Kate Burton, in a 1985 television documentary (*Richard Burton: In From the Cold*), voiced the sentiment that her father and Elizabeth were mutually codependent: "Of course, Elizabeth had a drinking problem . . . and pills. Dad never did the pills to that extent, although I know he was used to having painkillers all the time when his back was so awful."

Speaking in the same documentary, Mike Nichols offered a consistent point of view: "Things began to slip for [Burton]. . . . He prided himself enormously, that sort of Welsh pride, in being able to do a whole performance . . . completely sloshed. Once he took the leap into movie-magazine immortality with Elizabeth, I think he left behind any core of being. . . .

"Burton got tired of the limelight. Taylor never [grew] tired of it. She couldn't get enough of it."

Chapter 20

Location shooting for *Who's Afraid of Virginia Woolf?* took place on the Northampton, Massachusetts, campus of Smith College; interiors were shot at Warner Brothers studio in California. Elizabeth Taylor garnered her second Oscar as Best Actress for her performance in the film. In addition, for her fine work, Mike Nichols presented her with a male Lhasa apso puppy, George, named after Richard Burton's character in the film.

Following completion of *Who's Afraid of Virginia Woolf?* the Burtons went to San Diego to visit Liz's brother, Howard, and his family, which now consisted of his wife, Mara, and their five children. Howard, employed as a marine artist with an oceanic institute in San Diego, had his own forty-six-foot sailboat on which he took Dick and Liz for an overnight cruise. According to an entry made later in Richard Burton's diaries, Burton felt that over the years his wife had exceeded the bounds of duty in helping finance her brother, particularly as Mara earned a good living by working in the executive ranks of several posh resorts. Despite his criticism of Elizabeth's liberal spending on her brother's family, Burton behaved similarly, often sending his brothers and sisters exorbitant sums of money and gracing them with expensive gifts.

British film critic David Lewin confirmed that Burton had little passion for acting: "He did it for the money, especially after he and

Taylor paired off. Accordingly, Burton chose some terrible but highly lucrative roles. Like Elizabeth, he remained particularly generous with members of his own family, giving large sums to his siblings and their children."

The essential difference between their respective generosity had to do with political affiliation. Elizabeth's contributions to the Zionist cause were common knowledge; less well known were Burton's donations to radical political enclaves, such as the Black Panthers. His contributions to the Panthers eventually caught the attention of the Federal Bureau of Investigation (FBI), which saw fit to place Burton's name on a list of "suspect subversives" along with the names of Leonard Bernstein and Lillian Hellman.*

In the mid-1960s, Burton made an effort to attain intellectual respectability by agreeing to appear as the lead in an Oxford University Dramatic Society stage production of Christopher Marlowe's *Doctor Faustus.* The idea for the project had originated with Professor Nevill Coghill, one of Burton's former instructors at the university. Coghill's long-range plan called not only for a stage version but also a motion picture of the same play, the roles to be filled primarily by Oxford students (as in the play) and to be shot at the Dino De Laurentiis Studios in Rome. To add luster to the project, an enthusiastic Elizabeth Taylor agreed to fill the silent role of Helen of Troy in both the stage production and the film. The two stars agreed to donate their time, in addition to any profits the production might earn, for the purpose of building a new Oxford University theater complex as well as to help establish a Richard Burton chair in the theater arts division, which Richard would presumably occupy for a year or two. Burton hoped that this, in turn, would lead to knighthood, an honor he sought even more than the elusive Oscar. To his disappointment, Burton missed out on all three—Oxford chair, knighthood, Academy Award.

While in Rome completing the filming of *Doctor Faustus* and

*Following their investigation into Burton's political connections, the FBI concluded that he had "acted independently and appears to have no specific contacts with individual members of the Black Panther movement."

costarring in a classic movie production of Shakespeare's *Taming of the Shrew,* the Burtons, during the early-morning hours of July 23, received word of the death of Montgomery Clift. New York's chief medical examiner, Dr. Michael Baden, determined that Clift's death, after years of deteriorating health and drug and alcohol abuse, had been the result of a heart attack. "In his last years," said Truman Capote, "nobody—not even Elizabeth Taylor—could have helped him." For weeks Elizabeth was despondent, but she mourned privately and issued no public comments about Clift.

Among Liz and Dick's visitors in Rome were Gisella Orkin and her theatrical agent husband, Harvey. "Elizabeth and Richard were living in a huge palazzo," said Gisella. "Alexandre had flown in from Paris to fashion her hair. She was showing off several exquisite mink coats Richard had recently lavished upon her. One particularly magnificent mink had an attached hood. She asked me if I would care to have one, too. She further offered the services of Alexandre. I ought to have accepted both, but I was too bourgeois at the time.

"I remember eating lunch with the Burtons on the terrazzo of their palace. It was a gorgeous dwelling surrounded by fragrant fruit trees. Elizabeth wore a purple caftan—she adored caftans—no makeup, and looked extraordinarily gorgeous. Her two sons were there, the Wilding boys, and my small son Anthony, age two, was also present.

"The children were playing while we sat down to lunch. There were servants wherever you looked—waiters, busboys, maids, a chef. The houseboy came out carrying this beautiful antique silver platter and very ceremoniously lifted the top of the platter, and underneath were these pork sausages. They were apparently Richard's favorite. They were these little English pork sausages, and that's what we had for lunch."

Prior to appearing in *The Taming of the Shrew,* Elizabeth underwent minor back surgery at a medical clinic in Rome. The film's director, Franco Zeffirelli, feared that the shooting schedule would be delayed.

It wasn't. Elizabeth—cast in the role of the shrew—showed up punctually and adhered to a rigorous timetable.

The years 1965–67 were highly productive for the Burtons. Not only did *Doctor Faustus* and *The Taming of the Shrew* make it to the big screen; so, too, did *Reflections in a Golden Eye,* produced by Ray Stark and directed by John Huston, as well as *The Comedians,* a film based on Graham Greene's tempestuous novel about political turmoil amid the Haitian dictatorship of "Papa Doc" Duvalier. In all four films, Elizabeth came across not as a British-born actress but rather as a bona fide Hollywoodian.

According to film buff and socialite Robert Gardiner, Elizabeth Taylor "might have been born in England, but she had been raised in Hollywood. In *The Taming of the Shrew,* Burton's lines were spoken in the proper king's English, whereas Elizabeth sounded like a Brooklyn fishwife. Yet somehow the combination of accents worked." The critics awarded the film consistently high marks, especially the performance of Elizabeth Taylor, who had lost the twenty-five-odd pounds she had gained to play Martha in *Who's Afraid of Virginia Woolf?* She also endured more pratfalls in *Shrew* than in any other picture to date. Whereas she and Burton had wrestled and argued in *Virginia Woolf,* their antics were wilder in *Shrew.* At one point, Dick and Liz tumbled onto a tile roof which gave way and plunged them twenty feet onto a pile of wood remains.

Elizabeth Taylor's next film, *Reflections in a Golden Eye,* based on a sultry novella by Carson McCullers, withstood a difficult beginning. Elizabeth had found the story line dealing with a 1940s southern army post intriguing, especially as a vehicle that would have reunited her with Montgomery Clift. Clift's death prior to the production of the film, however, caused a host of problems. The role he was to have filled, that of a repressed homosexual army major married to a contemptuous, adulterous wife (played by Taylor), had seemed ideal for him. Richard Burton declined the part, as did Lee Marvin. Elizabeth then sought out Marlon Brando at a time when Marlon proved available and willing. Brando accepted the offer, flew to Rome, where much of the film was to be shot, and signed the contract. John Huston, meanwhile, shot some scenes at Long Island's Mitchell Air Field.

During this particular film production, it was Richard Burton who kept a close eye on his wife rather than the other way around. Marlon Brando, although remote and often withdrawn, had a long-standing reputation for seducing his leading ladies.

Burton needn't have worried. As Brando confessed in his 1994 autobiography *Brando,* he and director John Huston were perpetually stoned: "John did a lot of heavy pot smoking on that picture, and before he filmed one scene, he gave me some marijuana, which I smoked. Before long, I had no idea who or where I was or what I was supposed to be doing. The only thing I know was that the world was very funny and that John thought so, too. I could barely stand up, and if somebody asked me a question, I'd say, 'What?' about five minutes later."

Julie Harris, cast in the movie as the neurotic wife of the army post's commanding officer, found Elizabeth "luscious and energetic. She and Brando were the superstars on the film. I, for example, just wasn't in their country club, so to speak. I was sort of the Cinderella on the scene. Some days I'd be called in to do a scene, and I'd arrive in the morning, and late in the afternoon I would say to John Huston, 'Are you going to get to me next?' 'Oh, I didn't realize you were here,' he would say. And that happened over and over again. It was very weird."

Of the films in which Taylor and Burton appeared together during these years, *The Comedians* proved to be the one with the most realistic setting. Since filming in Haiti would have been impossible due to political conditions there, British director Peter Grenville chose Dahomey, West Africa, with some exteriors shot in the south of France and interiors in Paris.

Set designer Robert Christedes recalled Dick and Liz arriving in Dahomey in an airplane packed with trunks. "We watched as three trucks were filled with about eighty suitcases. We later learned that most of the suitcases were stocked with food products. The local food supply carried a variety of diseases, so it became necessary to import our edibles."

Elizabeth arrived in Africa some thirty pounds overweight. Within eight or nine days, prior to shooting, she lost most of the weight. "It wasn't difficult to lose weight in Dahomey," Christedes noted. "The climate was unbearably hot and humid. You could sweat off five pounds a day."

Film editor Françoise Javet confirmed the tropical conditions, pointing out that the heat led to a lot of after-hours drinking. "Elizabeth and Richard drank very heavily. I had the impression it was a trying time for them. But the drinking didn't seem to affect their acting. They were punctual. They knew their lines. They rarely had to do a second take."

While still in Dahomey, West Africa, Elizabeth began to think of adopting still another child. The sight of so many young lives wasted by poverty in this Third World region often brought tears to her eyes. She visited several orphanages, but Burton vehemently opposed the idea on the grounds that they traveled too much. From moviemaking to vacations in Gstaad, Hollywood, and Puerto Vallarta, there was hardly time to devote to another new baby. Elizabeth gave in, but not without an argument.

Burton and Taylor, meanwhile, had begun discussions with director Joseph Losey over the possibility of their appearing in a film called *Boom!,* a combination of two works by Tennessee Williams—a Broadway play starring Tallulah Bankhead, *The Milk Train Doesn't Stop Here Anymore,* and a short story, *Man Bring This Up the Road.*

The film project, originally conceived by producer Lester Persky, had undergone a number of changes. The first director envisioned for the film had been Tony Richardson. The main leads had been James Fox and Simone Signoret. When Fox declined because of another commitment, Persky selected Sean Connery for the part. Finally, Persky's option ran out, and John Heyman and Norman Priggen took over. Heyman, whose wife, Norma, had been Elizabeth's friend, suggested Burton and Taylor for the leads.

Elizabeth played the role of Flora ("Sissy") Goforth, a flamboyant, much-married, now-widowed millionaires whose last exotic summer is spent on the same Mediterranean island that she has visited annually for much of her life. Burton plays the role of a young, handsome poet who is known to the islanders as a gigolo.

Filmed on Sardinia, *Boom!* was poorly received by the critics. Almost unanimous was the opinion that Elizabeth Taylor seemed too young to play her role, while Burton appeared too old for his.

Shortly before opening in *Boom!* the Burtons first rented and then bought a beautiful twenty-year-old, 147-foot yacht (originally a steamboat) finished in mahogany and other fine woods. They paid roughly $200,000 for the luxuriously appointed craft, renamed it *Kalizma,* and filled it with books and rare paintings. They acquired a British captain, a large, well-uniformed crew, and several security guards. As soon as they took possession of the boat, Burton began talking about the prospect of buying or leasing a Learjet. He and Liz discussed yachts and jets as if they were mere toys. Elizabeth allowed how she preferred a set of emeralds to the jet. When Burton pointed out that the aircraft would fly them anywhere in the world within hours, Taylor countered, "But you can't wear a Lear jet."

In February 1968 the *Kalizma* arrived in London, docking on the River Thames. Aboard the yacht were a half dozen of Elizabeth Taylor's dogs. A new scandal immediately broke in the press to the effect that Dick and Liz were using their boat as "a floating dog kennel." England had established a six-month quarantine restriction against the importation of canines into the country. To circumvent the situation, the Burtons kept their pooches with a caretaker aboard the *Kalizma,* while they themselves encamped in their usual quarters at the Dorchester, returning to the yacht each day to check on the dogs.

The Burtons had arrived in England to appear in separate films—Elizabeth in *Secret Ceremony,* Richard in *Where Eagles Dare.* Again, Elizabeth Taylor had teamed up with Heyman-Priggen, coproducers, and director Joseph Losey. Besides Taylor's box-office draw the producers looked to Mia Farrow and Robert Mitchum to help give the film a boost.

Secret Ceremony's plot revolves around a fading, middle-aged prostitute who is befriended by a wistful young girl who resembles the older woman's young child. The prostitute, played by Taylor, visits the girl's home, where she is persuaded to remain and play "mother" to this love-starved child, who passes her guest off as her mother's sister. The film's final scenes suggest incest, sexual depravity, and violence.

In November, Mia Farrow, her then husband, Frank Sinatra, Dick, and Liz had dined together and had decided the film would be an exciting vehicle for Farrow. In the interim, the Sinatra-Farrow marriage had fallen on bad times. Thirty years Mia's senior, Sinatra had announced, on a nightclub stage, in her presence, "I finally found a broad I can cheat on."

Appearing in *Secret Ceremony* became an almost unendurable assignment for Mia. She turned to Elizabeth Taylor for moral support and help and received both. "I was fortunate to have spent time with her during a difficult period in my life," wrote Farrow.

Elizabeth had her own problems in the film, mostly with Joseph Losey. Although *Boom!* had been a disappointment from a fiscal standpoint—it was one of the few Burton-Taylor ventures to lose a substantial sum of money—relations between Losey and Elizabeth had been solid. But with *Secret Ceremony* their bond began to fray.

Losey told Michael Ciment in *Conversations with Losey:*

> I had a big struggle with her before we ever began, because she's got very little taste about clothing. [Elizabeth] has exquisite eyes, exquisite skin, and in many ways she is still, and was then particularly, a most beautiful woman. But she's got a bad figure, she doesn't take care of it, she has chubby hands, she is short, and she's got a common accent. I knew that the first problem was going to be clothes because she always wears clothes that accentuate the fact that she's short and fat, instead of the opposite. And I got Marc Bohan of Dior, who was mar-

> velous and knew the problem. I got Alexandre . . . who did the wigs, though I had tried my best to persuade her to do without them because they are a kind of mask for her and distort her. In order to avoid her making herself more frumpy than usual, I decided with Bohan that she never wear more than one color and that she mostly wear white, as a bride, and sometimes wear black as death, and once we let her wear purple.

By project's end, Elizabeth and Losey had reached a tentative peace. Elizabeth's mood was temporarily heightened when she and Burton invested in several commercial ventures, among them the Harlech television network in Bristol, England. For Harlech's May 18, 1968, ceremonial opening, Burton presented his wife with the $305,000 Krupp diamond, which he had won in a bidding war with none other than Harry Winston several days earlier at the Parke-Bernet Galleries in New York. Named for its previous owner, Vera Krupp, the widow of the German steel magnate, the 33.19-carat emerald-cut diamond was (and is still) considered one of the world's most perfect specimens.

To this day, the Krupp diamond appears on Elizabeth Taylor's hand almost daily. The ring's size and brilliance gave rise to a now-historic exchange of views at a wedding when Princess Margaret asked Taylor if she could model it. Once it was on her finger, the princess noted, "How very vulgar!"

Taylor responded, "Yeah, ain't it great!"

Chapter 21

If one had to date the beginning of the end of the Burton-Taylor marriage, it would have to be the summer of 1968. In July of that year a number of events placed the relationship in considerable jeopardy. Early in July, Richard Burton reported for work on a new British film, *Laughter in the Dark,* and immediately became involved in a row with Tony Richardson, the film's director. Richardson sacked him, and Burton went on a serious drinking binge.

While the binge continued, Elizabeth Taylor, badly hemorrhaging, underwent a partial hysterectomy in a London hospital. While Elizabeth remained in the hospital recuperating from surgery, Richard visited frequently, doubling back and forth between his wife and their brood. In fact, between drinks, Burton took over the management of Elizabeth's children and *"l'Entourage,"* as the French press currently referred to their circle of attendants.

Dick experienced myriad problems trying to discipline Liz's sons, Michael and Christopher Wilding, who were inhabiting a suite at the Dorchester, having spent terms at boarding schools in Switzerland and England. According to Melvin Bragg's biography of Burton, Dick "squared up" to the boys regarding their behavior—"loud records at two-thirty A.M., cigarette burns in the sheets and curtains, booze all over the place." The booze, it later turned out, belonged to Burton.

In the midst of Richard's difficulties with Christopher and Michael, he received a telephone call from Roger and Janine Fillistorf, proprietors of the Café de la Gare, the bistro not far from Burton's Swiss chalet at Céligny. André Besancon, for many years Burton's gardener at Céligny, had committed suicide by hanging himself. The bad news came at a time when Burton's daughter Kate was visiting with him. Burton decided to fly to Switzerland to attend the funeral and took with him Kate and Liza, his brother Ifor, and a friend, Brook Williams.

While the group waited at the Café de la Gare, Ifor set off in the dark to open his brother's house. When after an hour Ifor failed to return, as he said he would, the group went to look for him. As Bragg had it: "Ifor had caught his foot in a newly installed grille (he didn't know it was there), tripped, fallen awkwardly, and broken his neck on the window ledge. He was paralyzed from the neck down."

Burton was, as Bragg put it, "inconsolable." He blamed himself for the accident. Not even alcohol could assuage his feelings of guilt. Ifor was now "confined to a wheelchair . . . waiting to die."

In August the Burtons, still deeply in love but now frequently at loggerheads with each other, returned, exhausted, for a well-deserved rest in Los Angeles. They flew to Paris in September to begin new films for Twentieth Century-Fox.

Elizabeth costarred with Warren Beatty in *The Only Game in Town,* based on Frank D. Gilroy's Broadway play about a Las Vegas love affair between a stranded chorus girl and a piano player with a compulsion for gambling. Gilroy wrote the screenplay; George Stevens directed but failed to recapture the quality of performances he had elicited from Taylor in *A Place in the Sun* and *Giant.* One difficulty Stevens (and producer Fred Kohlmar) faced was that they were forced to construct the Las Vegas settings in a Paris studio, while second-unit cinematographers tried to enhance the film by shooting backdrop scenes in the States. The results were decidedly mixed, and the film's reception suggested that Elizabeth Taylor was no longer the box-office queen of the celluloid screen.

While Liz played opposite Warren Beatty in *The Only Game in Town,* Richard Burton costarred with Rex Harrison in another production shot in Paris, the film *Staircase,* directed by Liz's former flame Stanley Donen. A story about two homosexual barbers, *Staircase* netted Burton $1.25 million in advance plus percentages. Regarding his own actual homosexual experiences, Burton admitted, "I tried it once," but would elucidate no further. Meade Roberts, in an interview with the current author, named Sir Laurence Olivier as the likely partner.

While in Paris the Burtons were feted by the Rothschilds, the duke and duchess of Windsor, and Baron Alexis de Rédé and other members of the French aristocracy. They also dined with opera diva Maria Callas, who had been recently abandoned by Aristotle Onassis in his long-planned, successful campaign to win the hand of former first lady Jacqueline Kennedy. More often than not, Burton arrived drunk at these affairs and departed even more intoxicated and out of control. He and Elizabeth argued incessantly but invariably made up before going to bed. In this respect, their marriage resembled millions of others of far less renown.

On November 22, 1968, at age seventy, Francis Taylor, Elizabeth's father, died of complications from his earlier stroke. The Burtons returned to Beverly Hills to attend the funeral. The death of her father led to deep depression that was exacerbated by complications resulting from her recent hysterectomy. Less than three months later, on February 5, 1969, Liz was notified of the death of her first husband, Nicky Hilton.

To cheer up his wife, Burton went on a spending spree, acquiring an assortment of expensive baubles for Liz, including "La Peregrina," a historic pearl that cost him $37,000; a diamond-and-ruby necklace for $100,000; a sapphire-and-diamond brooch, $65,000; a heart-shaped diamond, $105,000; and an array of rubies, diamonds, and emeralds for $60,000. Burton and Taylor also bought each other matching mink coats—his and hers.

The couple returned to Europe in April 1969 and sailed the Mediterranean aboard the *Kalizma.* Kevin McCarthy, who hadn't seen Elizabeth Taylor since the night of Montgomery Clift's near-fatal automobile accident years earlier, happened to be in the south of France that spring. "I was in Saint-Jean-Cap Ferrat making *Flamingo Road* for ABC-TV with Lana Turner and George Hamilton," said McCarthy. "We were all staying at the most gorgeous hotel, Le Val d'Or, and one morning a crowd gathered on the beach in front of the hotel to watch the arrival of Richard and Elizabeth on their yacht.

"The next morning, there was no boat in the harbor. It had pulled further out to sea and had anchored where no one could get to it. I would go for a long swim every morning, and on a whim, I swam out to the boat. It was a hell of a good swim, and as I approached the yacht, several crew members appeared. Then Richard Burton came out on deck and yelled, 'Hello, who is that?' And I shouted, 'Kevin McCarthy,' and his reply was 'Good heavens, man. What're you doing out here?'

"They lowered a rope ladder and helped me aboard. They were drinking salty dogs—gin and grapefruit juice—and having a mid-morning repast. Burton was writing in his diary. Elizabeth Taylor and I spoke about Monty Clift. Before I swam back to the shore, they invited me to an upcoming Sunday afternoon brunch aboard the *Kalizma.* So I returned. ABC executive Grant Tinker attended, as did Eli Wallach and George Hamilton. It was just an incredible setting in the water on this yacht with Richard Burton and Elizabeth Taylor, an impressionistic oil painting in the dining room and exquisite decoration everywhere.

"A few weeks later, I was in Paris staying at the Georges V, and we—I was there with a Swedish girlfriend—met Richard Burton in the hotel lobby. He asked us to have a drink with him at the bar. After several drinks, he suggested that we go up to his suite and see Liz. So we went to their rooms for a while, but it got a bit tense. Burton had apparently been doing a good deal of drinking and became very rude to Elizabeth. She tried to make the best of the situation, but soon they began to squabble. It was embarrassing to see them act in that fashion."

The altercations between Burton and Taylor ran the gamut from ferocious to hilarious. Hedi Donizetti-Mullener, owner of the Hotel

Olden in Gstaad, observed that "later on in their relationship, unfortunately, they often fought. Most often it was the result of too much alcohol on Richard's part. He could be extremely difficult.

"On one occasion they were having lunch at the Olden with the children. Elizabeth was seated at one end of the table, and Richard sat at the other end. He had arrived late for the meal, and Elizabeth had evidently said something. When he finally sat down, he became furious. He picked up the table and drove it into her midsection. She let out a scream."

On the lighter side was Richard and Elizabeth's luncheon at the White Elephant Club in London. Seated at one adjacent table were Irish novelist Edna O'Brien and her husband. As they and others watched the Burtons, Elizabeth devoured an enormous portion of pasta saturated with butter sauce. As she downed the last strand of spaghetti, she reached for the bread basket and grabbed a large roll with which to soak up the remaining sauce. Richard Burton leaned forward and slapped her hand, berating her in a brash voice: "Aren't you fat enough already?" A crimson-faced Taylor refused to speak for the rest of the meal.

The arguments persisted during a brief respite in Puerto Vallarta and into May when the Burtons arrived in London aboard the *Kalizma* so that Burton could begin the role of King Henry VIII in *Anne of the Thousand Days.* Elizabeth had wanted to play Anne Boleyn but was advised that she was too old. The part went to the French-Canadian actress Genevieve Bujold, who was a decade younger than Taylor. Elizabeth eventually played a cameo role in the film. She kept a vigilant eye on Bujold, for whom Burton appeared to demonstrate more than a passing interest. According to Kitty Kelley, the fact that he had given her a nickname—"Gin"—indicated that they were more than friends. Bujold herself has never confirmed or denied the allegation. More important, perhaps, is that Elizabeth suspected the worst and as a result spent hours on the set.

Charles Jarrott, director of *Anne of the Thousand Days,* acknowledged that Genevieve and Richard "were having a little flirtation. Elizabeth was extremely uptight about this. I don't know that anything particularly startling happened, but nevertheless they had a little flirtation. I think that's probably why Elizabeth felt some pressure.

"There wasn't much to do about Taylor being on the set because Richard's contract stipulated she could be present whenever she pleased. There was even a chair with the initials ETB on it, which stood for Elizabeth Taylor Burton. One day when we were about to do one of Genevieve's most important scenes, Elizabeth came and sat in the chair facing the set. Bujold took me aside and asked, 'Is she going to stay there?' 'Yes,' I responded, 'she is. And there's nothing we can do about it. It's part of the deal. I shouldn't worry about it. Let's just get on with the scene.' And she said, 'Right. I'll teach that bitch what acting's all about.' Bujold had backbone. She was as feisty as Elizabeth. And she pulled off a beautiful acting job that day."

Ron Galella, the aggressive New York paparazzo who attained fame by his single-minded pursuit of Jacqueline Kennedy Onassis, soon set his sights on Dick and Liz. "They were still using the *Kalizma* as a hideaway for their dogs," said Galella. "The couple would spend weekdays in the Dorchester and visit the dogs on weekends. This was during the production of *Anne of the Thousand Days.* I don't know if anything went down between Burton and Bujold, but I do know the demand for candid shots of Dick and Liz was greater than ever.

"As a photographer, I found Burton and Taylor almost better as a team than they were individually. They were certainly the most important celebrity couple I have ever photographed. Let's face it, they were the couple of the century. They were the duo who counted. They were the pair that everybody in the U.S., if not the world, looked to and chased after. They were bigger than life. Their love story, as played out in the pages of every newspaper and magazine from Australia to Zanzibar, made them instantly and forever famous. None of that 'Andy Warhol fifteen minutes in the sun' business. They were international celebrities in a class with Jackie Onassis and Aristotle Onassis, Queen Elizabeth and Prince Philip, Prince Rainier and Grace Kelly. Even bigger. Their relationship encompassed all the facets of love. They were loving, volatile, intense, tremendously drawn to each other, repelled, everything that a romantic relationship should be."

In order to take photographs of the Burtons aboard their yacht, Ron Galella spent a weekend in a coffee-bean warehouse on the London waterfront. "I bought a sleeping bag in an army-navy supply store and tipped the warehouse watchman to let me in and set up shop. It was the longest stakeout of my career; also the most uncomfortable. The floors were damp and the rats rampant. There were rats everywhere, so I slept on the roof of the warehouse. I liked the aroma of the coffee beans; it soothed me. I spent much of my preliminary time putting gauze in the windows so that neither I nor the cameras could be seen. The *Kalizma* sat directly adjacent to the warehouse: I could see and hear everything. Also across from the warehouse were the headquarters of the harbor patrol; I had to be careful not to be detected by them.

"By early Saturday afternoon, people commenced boarding the boat, including Dick and Liz, a number of their children, Aaron Frosch (Elizabeth's and Richard's newest New York lawyer), Richard's brother Ifor (in his wheelchair), and Richard's assistant Bob Wilson (whose wedding they were celebrating). They were flying two flags—the American and the British—and a host of sightseeing boats would approach very closely, and all these tourists would immediately grab their cameras and start taking pictures. Elizabeth would dash either behind something or disappear below deck. The following day, Dick took the children out on a speedboat that had been moored to the yacht. When he returned, he and Elizabeth had one of their frequent altercations. I could hear and see them cursing and screaming at each other.

"Elizabeth's high level of energy surprised me because she was still recuperating from illness [her hysterectomy and continued bleeding]. But of course when you get down to it, she was always recuperating from something or other. Her whole life has been a recuperation of sorts."

Following his weekend in the warehouse, Galella began stalking the Burtons at the Dorchester. "On one occasion," he quipped, "Elizabeth came out of the hotel with her son Michael Wilding Jr. They walked over to Trader Vic's, located in the then London Hilton. A few minutes later, a white Oldsmobile Toronado pulled up in front of the Hilton, disgorging Richard Burton. A chauffeur sat behind the wheel. Burton had arrived to join Elizabeth and Michael for lunch during his break from *Anne of the Thousand Days.*

"I waited in front of the London Hilton," recalled Galella. "After lunch, Dick and Liz disappeared out the back door but then reappeared in front of the hotel. It was immediately obvious that Burton was staggering drunk. I knew he was a bad drunk who tended to become violent when smashed. It was obviously when drunk that he would strike Elizabeth. Of course, it was his nature to be drunk. He pictured himself as the reincarnation of Dylan Thomas, who was always out on his feet. When Liz and Dick appeared after lunch, she was practically holding him up. His car was nowhere in sight, so they began walking back to the studio. Richard was wearing a beard for his role as Henry VIII. The moment I spotted them, I began snapping pictures. Burton became enraged and started yelling at me. 'Get the fuck away from us, you fucking bastard!' he screamed. Finally, he came running toward me, red-faced, with fists raised. He never made it all the way. He was staggering toward me, shouting, 'You've had enough, you motherfucker!' Then he suddenly stopped and pitched forward onto his face. It was embarrassing, really, just how plastered he had become, and I wondered how in God's name he planned to continue to shoot that day.

"The chauffeur appeared, and he ultimately chased me off, while Burton continued to sputter invective. It was both funny and a little sad."

Elizabeth Taylor never ascertained the truth about her husband's purported fling with Genevieve Bujold. Nor, for that matter, did she realize he had been to bed with another candidate—Rachel Roberts, the then wife of Rex Harrison. The liaison with Roberts had begun earlier, during a 1968 Mediterranean cruise aboard the *Kalizma.*

"It had been long in the making," noted John Valva. "When we were filming *Cleopatra* in Rome, it became evident that Rachel, who eventually committed suicide, was quite mad. I recall a party during which Rachel walked around from man to man unzipping everyone's fly."

Meade Roberts learned from Burton of Rachel's antics aboard the *Kalizma.* "Richard told me she would sunbathe in the nude," recounted Roberts. "Other times, she would run around without any panties while continually hiking up her skirts. She had a dancer's body—long legs and tight muscles. Finally, Dick could no longer resist the temptation. He took her to bed."

Elizabeth may not have known the facts, but she suspected the worst. She had an acute sense of what moved men's souls, Richard Burton's in particular. A number of her friends and acquaintances credited her with the possession of a highly developed sensibility. She herself once described a dream she had in 1961 prognosticating the death of Gary Cooper. Cooper died the following day at the exact hour Elizabeth had conjured in her reveries. A believer in the powers of extrasensory perception (ESP), Taylor consulted on several occasions, through the intervention of a friend, with Rose Stoler, the well-known Parisian clairvoyant whose clientele included Sophia Loren and Charles de Gaulle. In later years Liz had her horoscope read by J. Z. Knight, who had more than once done the same for Nancy Reagan.

Whether out of guilt or altruism, Richard Burton decided in the fall of 1969 to buy Liz the largest, most valuable diamond in the world. Owned by Mrs. Paul A. Ames (sister of billionaire Walter Annenberg, then the U.S. ambassador to the Court of St. James's), the 69.42-carat pear-shaped diamond was about to be auctioned by the Parke-Bernet Galleries on Madison Avenue in New York. Aristotle Onassis had dropped by the gallery to examine the stone, creating speculation that he intended to buy it for Jacqueline Kennedy Onassis. When Dick and Liz heard of Ari's interest in the diamond, they asked that it be sent to Gstaad for their inspection as well.

Bidding from England, Burton gave Aaron Frosch, his attorney, a ceiling price of a million dollars. The bid fell short; Cartier carried off the prize for $1,050,000, the highest amount ever paid for a diamond to that date. The Burtons were both disappointed. Dick telephoned Frosch and instructed him to buy the stone directly from Cartier, regardless of the final price. A deal was struck at $1.1 million. On October 25, 1969, the date of the transaction, the *New York Times* quoted Richard Burton: "It's just a present for Liz."

The Taylor-Burton diamond, as it became known, was by mutual agreement placed on exhibit at Cartier's New York and Chicago stores, where, the press reported, in excess of six thousand people a day came to view it. Originally worn as a ring by Elizabeth Taylor, she later commissioned Cartier to design a necklace for it. When the job was completed, Cartier dispatched three men, each bearing an identical carrying case, to the *Kalizma,* which was anchored in Monaco. Only one of the men carried the actual piece of jewelry. The security measure worked to perfection. Even Elizabeth gasped when the priceless necklace was unveiled and clasped around her neck. She wore the jewel to Princess Grace's fortieth birthday party at the Hotel Hermitage in Monte Carlo, escorted by her husband as well as a pair of security guards armed with machine guns, as stipulated by her million-dollar insurance policy with Lloyd's of London.

At the start of 1970, Richard Burton made an honest effort to curtail his drinking. While Burton managed to remain sober during the early part of the year, Elizabeth remained exceptionally active. She posed for photographer Lord Snowden, the husband of Princess Margaret, for the cover of *Vogue.* In Rome she joined Aristotle Onassis (sans Richard and Jackie) for dinner at the Osteria Dell'Orso, igniting rumors that she and Ari were engaged in an affair. Back in New York, she attended the funeral of Carson McCullers at St. James Episcopal Church. She visited her son Michael, then staying with "Uncle Howard" in Hawaii; to her surprise, Michael passed much of his time residing in a tree house which Howard Taylor had constructed for him atop a palm tree. She and Burton spent three days at Rancho Mirage, California, visiting with Frank Sinatra. According to Burton's diaries, "Elizabeth made sheep's eyes at him the whole time, and sometimes he at her. I've never seen her behave like that before, and apart from making me jealous—an emotion which I despise—I was furious that he didn't respond!"

When Bob LaSalle, the Burton's personal bodyguard, chose to leave his job, his place was taken by a new employee, Bobby Hall, whose responsibilities included procuring women for Dick and filling prescriptions for Elizabeth. Ted H. Jordan, a character actor who had played a stable boy in *National Velvet,* knew Hall and heard numerous stories from him about his employers. "Hall always called them Burton and Taylor," remarked Jordan. "He constantly spoke about having to run out and fill prescriptions for Taylor, especially Seconal."

Elizabeth had become so heavily addicted to Seconal and similar pharmaceuticals by this time that when she entered Cedars-Sinai in Los Angeles for a hemorrhoid operation in May 1970, her doctors made an effort to withdraw her from the drugs. Burton wrote that they gave her tranquilizers and told her they were painkillers. As usual with Taylor, there were complications. Recuperating in a borrowed house after the operation, she began to bleed heavily and had to go back to the hospital, where it was determined that one of her stitches had come undone. Burton fretted that giving Liz narcotics once more would "mean another period of withdrawal."

Despite Liz's medical problems, she and Dick agreed to appear as themselves in an episode of Lucille Ball's television show *The Lucy Show.* In July 1970, back on the bottle, Burton made *Raid on Rommel* in Mexico, followed that September by *Villain,* which was shot in England. Elizabeth accompanied him on both ventures.

They remained in England while Taylor appeared opposite Michael Caine in *Zee & Co.,* which was released in the States early in 1972 as *X, Y and Zee.* A poor man's version of *Who's Afraid of Virginia Woolf?,* the film featured Elizabeth once again playing one-half of a volatile marital relationship, replete with earsplitting verbal boxing, physical violence, nudity (Taylor again used a stand-in), adultery, and lesbianism. Interviewed by the British press while appearing in her role, Elizabeth maintained: "I enjoy acting, but I'm slothful. I'm so bloody lazy. I think I should retire. I should quit and raise cats."

Produced at Shepperton Studios outside London, *Zee & Co.* additionally featured stage and screen veteran Margaret Leighton and Susannah York (who portrays "the other woman" for both Michael Caine *and* Elizabeth Taylor). Despite the renown of the other players, Taylor's magical name eclipsed the film itself. Michael Caine, who hadn't previously met Taylor, described their initial encounter in his autobiography:

> As we worked for the first ninety minutes that morning, the tension mounted as various messengers came scurrying in to report the imminent arrival of my costar. "She has left the hotel," was the first one, followed at intervals by, "She's in the studio . . . in makeup . . . out of makeup and into hair. She's out of hair and is getting dressed. She's dressed and on her way."
>
> I was reminded of a royal film premiere as well all stood there in line waiting to be presented to the Queen. Like the Queen, Elizabeth was preceded by various minions—in fact, quite a large entourage was finally lined up. The joke on the film quickly became that if the entourage alone went to see the film we would be in profit. Finally Elizabeth arrived and behind her, as I had been warned, was Richard [who wasn't in the film but accompanied her nonetheless]. . . . I had never seen her in the flesh before and she was much smaller than I had expected. The next surprise was that she was holding a huge jug of Bloody Marys, and at some hidden signal a new minion came forth bearing two glasses and handed one of these to me and one to Elizabeth. She filled both of them, kissed me on the cheek, clinked her glass with mine and said, "Hello, Michael. Good luck!" and we both downed a healthy swig.

As to Richard Burton, Caine noted that the actor spent his nights drinking, then sleeping off his hangover the following day on the sofa in Elizabeth's dressing room.

Brian Hutton, director of the film, told the current author that

"Elizabeth meant no more to me than a charlady." In a certain respect he treated her like one, although Elizabeth didn't seem to care. To make her height more consistent with Caine's, Hutton insisted that in their scenes together she stand on a wooden box. In her presence, the director once referred to Taylor as "a pain in the arse." On another occasion, when Elizabeth interrupted a scene she was shooting and announced her need of a bathroom, Hutton remarked, "You mean to tell me that Elizabeth Taylor goes to the toilet just like the rest of us! I thought that in your case, fairies came and took it away in toothpaste tubes."

Although some critics credited Taylor with giving a riveting performance in *X, Y and Zee,* the major film reviewers, among them Vincent Canby of the *New York Times,* gave her poor marks. "Miss Taylor is not a very interesting actress, but she need not seem as bad as she does here," wrote Canby. "Mr. Hutton allows her to play Zee as if she were the ghost of whores past, present and future, clanking her jewelry, her headbands, her earrings and her feelings behind her like someone out to haunt a funhouse. It is an unfortunately ridiculous performance."

In March 1970 the Burtons appeared on CBS-TV's *60 Minutes.* Asked about her children by interviewer Charles Collingwood, Elizabeth concentrated primarily on Michael Jr. "My eldest son is seventeen, has hair that is [repellent] to the oldsters, the clothes that appall squares. He's been hippie-hunted down. He's not—Well, I don't know what the word hippie means; I really don't understand the word. He has long hair. . . . [People] insult him; they say, 'Hey, girlie,' tug on his scarf, or something."

The characterization of Michael Wilding Jr. as "hippie-hunted" should have been emended to "hippie-haunted." On October 6, 1970, wearing long hair and maroon velvet, young Wilding married Beth Clutter, the nineteen-year-old daughter of a Portland, Oregon, oceanographer. The ceremony took place at London's Caxton Hall, where Elizabeth had married Michael's father in 1952. Hundreds of spectators gathered to goggle at the bridegroom's mother (in white wool pants and a rock-sized diamond ring) as well as Richard Burton (in a plain business suit). Suffering from heart disease, Michael Wilding Sr. did not appear.

The Burtons were generous in their selection of wedding gifts. Elizabeth treated the penniless couple to the Dorchester's honeymoon suite and later gave them a Jaguar and a large check. When she learned several months later that Beth was pregnant, she showered her daughter-in-law with jewelry and designer fashions. Richard bought them a $70,000 town house in London.

Following the ceremony, Dick and Liz wasted little time before resuming their respective projects, though not entirely to their mutual benefit. Elizabeth completed *X, Y and Zee* and then flew to Wales to do a bit role in the erudite film version of a Dylan Thomas play, *Under Milk Wood,* which featured Richard Burton and Peter O'Toole. Elizabeth's walk-on cameo as Rosie Probert, the prostitute, enthralled neither critics (who increasingly found her acting abilities wanting) nor audiences. *Newsweek* tersely (and not very kindly) dismissed her: "Fortunately, Elizabeth Taylor, as Welsh as Cleopatra, plays only a small part, her harsh, yawling cadence a bit of intrusive tourism."

From Wales, Dick and Liz, having stopped over in California, went on to Cuernavaca, Mexico, to appear in *Hammersmith Is Out,* a comic but jumbled rendition of the Faust legend. The Burtons had signed a joint contract calling for them to receive expenses plus a prohibitively generous 15 percent of gross box-office receipts. As a result, they were guaranteed a hefty return whether or not the film itself earned a profit. The entire project was financed by California mobile-home manufacturer J. Cornelius Crean in what was to be his first and last motion picture venture.

"Given the high income-tax rates of that era, the film seemed like a solid financial proposition," contended Crean. "It also promised to be a great deal of fun. Richard Burton had been cast as Hammersmith, a fanatical gangster and the modern-day counterpart of Mephistopheles, whereas Elizabeth played the role of Jimmie Jean Jackson, a curvaceous blond waitress who slings hash in a run-down diner. Peter Ustinov directed the picture and in so doing wrote a sizable part for himself as the German physician in whose asylum Hammersmith resides.

"Despite these elements, the production wasn't fun at all. First of all, given the terms of the contract with the Burtons, they were the only ones who stood to make money on the film. At the end, I sold them the rights to *Hammersmith,* and they in turn sold the movie to Cinerama. Then there was producer Alex Lucas—he and I couldn't agree on a single aspect of the project; we argued incessantly. Peter Ustinov likewise presented problems. We previewed the film in several different locations, and I sat next to Peter in sundry movie theaters. Each time his own character appeared on screen, he would just laugh himself silly. Unfortunately, the rest of the audience remained stone silent. Finally, the sound track of the finished film contained all sorts of background noise and had to be completely looped and relooped, a costly and time-consuming process."

Regarding Crean's relationship to Elizabeth Taylor, public relations maven Jerry Pam had been told by Michael Caine that at a preproduction meeting at the Beverly Hills Hotel, the trailer manufacturer had begun deprecating the acting profession. "Elizabeth was about to throw a glass of ice water in Crean's face and had to be restrained by Richard," said Pam. Crean's impression of Taylor was expressed at a later date: "She got herself straightened out pretty well to make the picture and did a good job as far as I was concerned. After that she was back into whatever it is she does to make herself crazy."

A separate incident, this one again involving photographer Ron Galella, further complicated the making of the movie. An Australian newspaper, the *Sydney Morning Herald,* hired Galella to take exclusive photos of the Burtons during the production of *Hammersmith.* "I arrived in Cuernavaca and checked into a small hotel," reported Galella. "At this point in my career I had an assistant, Jean, working with me. She was quite attractive and very voluptuous, and she came with me to Mexico. We soon discovered that they were filming *Hammersmith* around the swimming pool of another resort hotel in town. Jean succeeded in gaining access to the set and shortly befriended a good-looking fellow named Ron Berkeley, Elizabeth Taylor's makeup artist and a member of the couple's entourage. From Berkeley, with whom she began an affair, Jean learned the shooting schedule."

Meanwhile, Galella made the acquaintance of the resort owner whose hotel had become the site of the *Hammersmith* production. "His name for Liz and Richard was *Monstruos Sagrados,* or Sacred Monsters," recounted Galella. "He was publicity crazed and welcomed my taking photographs. I disguised myself as a Mexican gardener with a fake mustache, a sombrero, and a wheelbarrow in which I kept my camera equipment. I hid in a small corridor just off the swimming-pool area.

"This went on for about a week, until one day they discovered me. Before I knew it, three or four Neanderthals, who had been working on the film, attacked me and beat me up. I sustained a broken tooth, bloody nose and lip, black eye, lacerations of my face and scalp. Then the Mexican police hauled me off to jail. On Richard Burton's orders, another cast member broke into my hotel room and confiscated fifteen rolls of film, the lot containing hundreds of photographs of Richard and Liz. I eventually sued the Burtons but received nothing for my trouble. It occurred to me that I could just as easily have been killed and little would have been done. Burton and Taylor were invincible."

On August 25, 1970, Beth Clutter Wilding gave birth to a daughter, Leyla, while the Burtons were staying in Monte Carlo. They immediately set out for London, Elizabeth arriving at the airport wearing a pair of "white lace hot pants, a low-cut white lace top, and white boots with white lace eyelet decorations sewn up to the knee."

When asked by a reporter how it felt to be a thirty-nine-year-old grandmother, Liz responded: "You know, everybody assumes that this whole thing would upset me. That's silly. In fact, I feared turning thirty more than I fear being called Grandma."

Taylor followed this with another thought: "I can't get over it—this is the baby Richard and I could never have."

Richard Burton appeared in two additional films that year. In September, accompanied by Elizabeth, he traveled to Yugoslavia to play Marshal Tito in *The Battle of Satjeska.* While in Yugoslavia, he and Taylor met frequently with President Tito. According to Burton's diaries, he found the Communist leader a bit on the "tedious" side.

A month later, the couple arrived in Paris, where Burton starred in *The Assassination of Trotsky,* opposite Alain Delon and Romy Schneider. The film was directed by Joseph Losey, who claimed that Richard couldn't remain sober "for more than an hour at a time." Losey, also having difficulty with alcohol, could do little to help his leading man. And Elizabeth Taylor had long before lost her ability to curtail her husband's drinking.

Chapter 22

While the cinematic appeal of Richard Burton and Elizabeth Taylor continued to plummet, their glamour quotient both in America and abroad remained on the rise. On December 2, 1971, the Burtons were among a select group of aristocrats and global celebrities invited to an event predictably called "the Ball of the Century," which was thrown by the Rothschilds at their palatial estate in Ferrières, outside Paris. So grand was the occasion that anyone *not* on the guest list was all but forced to flee Paris in shame.

One of the guests that evening, Andy Warhol, had been seated at the same table as Richard Burton. "Burton appeared to be on the wagon that evening," recounted Warhol, "and was therefore far less entertaining than he'd been rumored to be. Elizabeth, her hair having been tailored that evening by Alexandre, sat at another table next to Princess Grace and opposite the duchess of Windsor, who wore a huge ostrich feather affixed to a headband. Guy de Rothschild, seated beside the duchess, kept having a duck the feather whenever the duchess moved her head."

Although Warhol had long before completed one of his best-known lithograph-paintings, of "superstar" Elizabeth Taylor, he retained a balanced viewpoint of the person behind the mask. He understood, as he put it, "how some people detested her. She's too conscious of being the cat's meow, the star of stars. She has the makings of an empress, but there's also something tawdry and a bit cheap about her. She can act but isn't a first-rate actress. She has energy, and her money shot is the close-up, the camera in her face. Her coloring—the violet eyes, dark hair, and flawless skin—is what made her. That's what people pay to see when they attend her films. She's also the last in a line of great Hollywood stellars—not in her profession, necessarily, but at playing herself.

"In truth, you never know what to expect of her. She has an unpredictable nature. You can never tell how outsiders will react to her. One of my friends said, 'She represents everything that's bad about America.' Another friend said, 'She's great, immense, larger than life.'

"One of the best stories I heard about Richard and Elizabeth took place in Puerto Vallarta. They went to the circus with some friends. They were watching the knife thrower when the fellow asked Elizabeth if she would stand against a backdrop and let him throw knives at her. She agreed, and everybody held their breath. Then he turned to Richard and said, 'Your turn, *señor.*' Richard didn't want to go through with it, but he had no choice because Elizabeth had done it. He looked scared to death as he took her place. Nothing scared Elizabeth; she was much stronger than Richard."

In early February 1972, Dick and Liz checked into the Duma-Intercontinental Hotel in Budapest, Hungary, where Richard was to play the title role of Baron Kurt von Sepper in the film version of *Bluebeard.* Among the supporting cast members were four of the most attractive actresses in the world: Raquel Welch, Nathalie Delon, Virna Lisi, and Joey Heatherton.

Not long after arriving in Budapest, just after Burton had begun shooting, Dick and Liz agreed to do a taped television interview with David Frost. Elizabeth came to regret the decision. Edward Dmytryk, the director of *Bluebeard,* recalled that "before they began taping, Liz fortified herself with several shots of Jack Daniels. During the interview, which ran for nearly two hours, she kept drinking sour-mash whiskey from a tumbler which one of her minions refilled at regular intervals. It soon became obvious that Elizabeth was drunk."

On February 27, Richard Burton threw a gala fortieth birthday celebration for his wife which, in terms of pure luxury, competed favorably with the recent Rothschild bash. Leasing the entire Duma-Intercontinental for their more than two hundred guests, the Burtons also chartered a British Airways Trident to bring many of their friends and relatives to Budapest, a contingent that included Michael Caine, David Niven, Ringo Starr, Alexandre, Gianni Bulgari, the Cartiers, Princess Grace, Susannah York, Michael Wilding Sr. (his heart condition apparently improved), a dozen international statesmen, a number of Richard Burton's brothers and sisters, Elizabeth's mother and brother, Christopher Wilding, and Liza Todd (currently enrolled at Heathfield, a British boarding school). Also invited were the *Bluebeard* "girls," until Taylor decided to uninvite them.

Burton's birthday gift to Liz, which she wore for the occasion in tandem with the Krupp diamond, was the $900,000 Shah Jahan yellow diamond, a seventeenth-century gem from India designed by the Mogul emperor responsible for the building of the Taj Mahal.

Not everyone reacted favorably to the birthday celebration. Alan Williams, son of Emlyn and brother of Brook, took exception to the event. A novelist and student of the Hungarian Revolution, Alan angrily criticized Dick and Liz on their choice of Budapest as a location for their two-day event. When he persisted, he was shown the door. He later described the "forty-year-old birthday child" in something less than glowing terms, calling Taylor "a beautiful doughnut covered in diamonds and paste."

The point hit home: A day after the Alan Williams imbroglio, Burton pledged to give an amount equal to the price of the party to a leading charity. But his promise was only partially fulfilled. The festivities had cost well in excess of a million dollars; later in the year, he presented UNICEF with a check for $45,000.

March and April of 1972 represented the most trying marital period the Burtons had as yet faced. The first catastrophe came with the report of the death of Richard's brother, Ifor, whom he had always regarded as a father figure. "Ifor had been a paraplegic since breaking his neck in an accident at Richard's home in Céligny," said Edward Dmytryk. "His death occurred while we were still filming *Bluebeard.* Richard was profoundly affected. He took off a few days to attend the funeral in Wales. When he returned to Budapest, he had become a different person.

"For a short while he kept himself in check. Then, one night, the British ambassador invited a small group for dinner. When I arrived, Richard and Elizabeth were already there, and Richard was reciting poetry by Dylan Thomas. He had clearly been drinking, and when they served dinner, he continued to drink while declining all offers of food.

"The intimate gathering included the Swiss ambassador and his wife and a young American attaché, accompanied by his wife. About midway through the main course, Richard interrupted his recitation and directed his attention to the Swiss ambassador.

"'You remind me quite distinctly of a hungry vulture,' he railed.

"When the ambassador from Switzerland failed to react, Richard let fly another insult. 'You Swiss are an extremely bad lot,' he added.

"'*Richard!*'

"It was Elizabeth's voice. Richard looked over at her, caught her steely-eyed gaze, and excused himself from the table.

"'I had better go home,' he ventured.

"And he did. The rest of the evening passed in relative calm."

The following evening, a semipolluted Richard Burton left the set arm in arm with Nathalie Delon (she was blond, French, and the former wife of Alain Delon), shoved her into his Rolls-Royce, and spent most of the rest of the night with her.

"That was the beginning of a difficult time for everybody concerned," noted Dmytryk. "Burton was often inebriated when he arrived at the studio in the morning and always inebriated when he left in the afternoon. We were lucky if we could squeeze three or four hours' work out of him. His acting was nowhere near his usual standard. He himself admitted as much. One day he said to me: 'I used to think I could perform just as well when I was drunk as when I was sober. I've discovered I can't.'"

Besides alcohol and cigarettes (as many as three packs per day), the Welsh actor had begun to sniff cocaine. In a state of helplessness, Elizabeth departed Hungary and went to Rome, where she sought counsel with, among others, Aristotle Onassis.

Dmytryk confirmed that following Liz's departure in May, "the *Bluebeard* 'broads' (Miss Lisi excepted) devoured Richard. They were falling all over him, and he was reciprocating their affections. One morning during this phase, while we were conversing in his dressing room, he shook his head.

"'Elizabeth telephoned me from Rome at five o'clock this morning,' he remarked. 'All she said was, "I want you to get that woman out of my bed!" He shook his head again. 'I can't figure out how she knew.'

"'Richard,' I told him. 'Don't you realize you're surrounded by her entourage? They tell her everything. You can't pick your nose without her finding out.'"

By June 1972 the Burtons has settled some of their differences and were together again in London. Elizabeth Taylor had signed to star in a new film, *Night Watch,* an adaptation of a Lucille Fletcher thriller which Alfred Hitchcock had declined for reasons of ill health. With Taylor on the set all day, Richard Burton agreed to present several lectures to graduate students at Oxford.

Despite the couple's reconciliation, a new dilemma loomed on the horizon. Having thoroughly trashed the Hampstead house given them as a wedding present by Burton, Michael Wilding Jr. and his wife, Beth Clutter, moved to a commune in Wales, not far from Richard's birthplace. They took their young daughter, Leyla, with them. After a few weeks in this rustic setting, Beth left with Leyla and arrived at Elizabeth Taylor's suite at the Dorchester. Agreeing with her daughter-in-law that a commune was no place to raise a child, Elizabeth immediately took them in. She even went a step further, offering to look after Leyla as though she were her own. An argument ensued. Beth finally departed the Dorchester and with her daughter returned to Oregon.

Although depressed when she began rehearsals for *Night Watch,*

Taylor rapidly perked up. Financed by George Barrie, director of Fabergé, and Joseph E. Levine, the film also starred Laurence Harvey, who had remained on good terms with Liz since *Butterfield 8,* twelve years earlier. The director of the film was Brian Hutton, whose deprecating and humorous banter during his direction of *X, Y and Zee* had amused Elizabeth.

Following his Oxford lectures, Richard Burton flew to Yugoslavia to reshoot select scenes from *The Battle of Sutjeska.* During his absence, Elizabeth had one of her usual mishaps, falling from a set platform and fracturing her left index finger. Two days later, Brian Hutton contracted bronchitis, and the set had to be shut down for a week. It was closed for a month when Laurence Harvey underwent emergency abdominal surgery. (It turned out that Harvey was suffering from terminal cancer.) Taylor spent part of the month in Yugoslavia with Burton, during which time she slipped on the steps of a hotel swimming pool and severed an artery in her left forearm. She flew to Switzerland for treatment before returning to London and the *Night Watch* set.

Although George Barrie and producer Marton Poll praised Elizabeth for maintaining a professional attitude throughout the production process ("As far as I can recall, she was never late on the set," said Barrie), others had reason to complain. Stanley Eichelbaum, a columnist for the *San Francisco Examiner,* had gone to considerable lengths to arrange a simultaneous interview with Elizabeth Taylor and Laurence Harvey. "We were supposed to meet at the Mr. Charles Restaurant," said Eichelbaum. "Harvey arrived, and so did Cary Grant, who was then working for Brut, a subsidiary of Fabergé. But Elizabeth never showed.

"I eventually interviewed her, but this ensued several years later at the Beverly Hills Hotel. I found her friendly, bright, and articulate. But she looked quite fat, had a double chin, and wore something gaudy and shimmering. Her appearance disappointed me."

Although Laurence Harvey lauded Taylor's performance in *Night Watch* ("She's the most talented screen actress in the world today," he assured Tom Toper of the *New York Post*), the critics once again found her less than impressive. Even worse than her performance, however, was the quality of the picture itself. Alexander Stuart of *Films and Filming* summed up the general reaction when he wrote: "What's so amazing about this film is that it's so *bad.* In fact it almost defies description."

In the spring of 1972, their relationship floundering, the Burtons agreed to star in an ill-fated drama entitled *Divorce His—Divorce Hers,* with John Heyman as executive producer and young Waris Hussein in the director's seat. The film would be shot in Rome and Munich at the close of 1972 in the form of two ninety-minute acts to be broadcast the following February on consecutive evenings as a special feature of ABC-TV's *Movie of the Week.* As suggested by the title, the twin dramas were supposed to probe the disintegration of a lengthy marriage, the first segment of which would examine the breakup from the husband's vantage point; the second, from the wife's. Riddled by tedium, separations, quarrels, and adultery, the collapsing television marriage bore an uncanny resemblance to the true-life misadventures of the Burtons.

Technical and personality problems marred the production from the first. The Burtons themselves engaged in endless rows throughout the making of the film. Waris Hussein started shooting exteriors with Richard Burton in Rome that November. "Richard had been off the bottle of late, and everything progressed on schedule," recalled Hussein. "Suddenly, in the middle of a scene, there was an uproar in the distance—hooting horns, flashing lights, a caravan of cars. Elizabeth had just arrived in Rome surrounded by police and paparazzi. She stepped out of a slick black limousine wearing a full-length black mink. 'Waris, I'll just stand in the corner and watch,' she whispered. Burton had taken off for parts unknown, although I could well imagine his whereabouts. When he returned after half an hour, he could no longer walk a straight line. With Liz in attendance, he just couldn't curb his drinking."

One of the gravest problems the producer and the network faced was that the Burtons weren't accustomed to the modest budgets and limited scheduling associated with television drama and weren't willing to adapt. Nobody knew what to expect next; they were virtually out of control. During her single camera appearance in Rome, Elizabeth arrived on the set two hours late. "It's all right, baby," she assured Hussein. "I've read the script."

Later that day, when the director requested that Taylor blow her nose on camera to set the mood for a flashback, she refused.

"Blow my nose?" she snorted. "I've never blown my nose on the screen, and I'm not going to start now."

Luncheons were a major enterprise, often two or three hours in length, served by waiters wearing white gloves. "I attended one such affair," said Hussein, "and made the error of asking Burton about his early acting days at the Old Vic, where I'd once seen him perform as Hamlet. He started telling a story about how he'd been drunk one night and took a leak in his armor. Elizabeth had obviously heard the tale a thousand times and gave him an indignant scowl. He paused and looked across the table at her. She said, 'Come on, Richard, finish the story.' And he said, 'That's all right, darling, we won't go on.' 'Oh, no, Richard,' she answered. 'I'm always fascinated to know what a wonderful stage actor you were.' For the next hour they tore into each other like savages."

What Waris Hussein saw during the period it took to complete *Divorce* "was the tension of two people now experiencing the souring of a very passionate beginning. I discovered quickly that Liz and Dick each had a separate camp of loyalists. There were no crossovers. This added to the tension. I also perceived that Elizabeth resented the congenial relationship I had been able to establish with Richard before she arrived in Rome. And I was too young and inexperienced as a director to know what it meant or how to deal with it.

"There are two sides to Elizabeth. She can be extremely warm and generous, yet incredibly cruel and indifferent. She's as complicated as they come, but she doesn't know how to deal with the complexity of her nature because, to be frank, she lacks the education. When you're nine years old and supervised by an M-G-M teacher, you don't get to know what the outside world is all about. You get into a Rolls-Royce that takes you to the studio, and from the moment you arrive, you belong to them. She has been supervised since childhood. She doesn't know how to go out and buy an apple at a fruit stand. In a sense, life has passed her by.

"Of course, it's truly not her fault. An incident occurred during our shoot in Munich which convinced me how difficult it must have been for Elizabeth Taylor. One weekend I drove around Munich and its environs visiting all of Prince Ludwig's castles. They were full of exquisite decorations. On Monday I told Elizabeth I had thought of her while touring the castles because both she and Ludwig shared an appreciation and awareness for beautiful objects. I suggested she visit the castles as well. She said, 'You know, I'd love to be able to go, but I can't. They'd have to shut down the place before I could go in.'"

The critical bashing accorded *Divorce His—Divorce Hers* surprised none of the television executives associated with the project. *Variety* led the attack: "This two-part soupbone makes it official: Liz and Dick Burton are the corniest act in show business since the Cherry sisters. . . . Miss Taylor wallowed in suds to a point where the many closeups between her ample bazooms failed even in distracting from the nonsense."

Divorce was the last film project Burton and Taylor would appear in together. This by no means meant that either of them had any serious intention of curtailing their career. It now seemed that work was the only means by which the warring twosome could assuage their guilt and sorrow. A line scripted for Elizabeth in *Divorce* and which she had recited with appropriate feeling seemed to sum up her current emotions concerning Burton: "Beat me black and blue, but just don't leave me."

They were still together in February 1973 when Elizabeth embarked, without Burton, on a new film entitled *Ash Wednesday,* to be shot in and around Rome. Larry Peerce, the son of opera singer Jan Peerce, had been chosen to direct the movie for Paramount. Dominick Dunne, a producer at that time, accompanied Peerce to Rome for an initial meeting with Taylor.

"I had never previously met Taylor or Burton," Larry Peerce explained. "So Dominick Dunne and I went to the Grand Hotel in Rome, where they had ten or eleven connecting rooms full of luggage, retainers, attendants, pets, etc. When we arrived, I knocked at the door, and Richard Burton, in his booming Welsh brogue, said, 'Enter!' We entered and found Burton on his hands and knees scraping dog shit off the rug. He looked up and said, 'I suppose you'll now tell everyone this is how we met.'

"He poured us each a glass of champagne and himself a scotch on the rocks, which he downed as if it were club soda. Within minutes, he polished off three more glasses.

"Elizabeth came into the room soon afterward looking very regal, bedecked in lavish jewelry. She joined us for drinks. She told me at some point that she drank mostly when Richard drank. It soon became obvious that she could tolerate alcohol much better than he could. She drank champagne by the magnum, but she had the constitution of a horse. This pertained to drugs as well. When we made *Ash Wednesday,* she was taking all manner of drugs and medications. What distinguished her from other substance abusers is that she ate so much. The food tended to absorb the alcohol and chemicals in her body. She would vary in weight from week to week, but she rarely became inebriated. She continued to drink vast quantities throughout the making of the film—champagne and vodka mostly—and although I encouraged her to cut down, she never did.

"The first night in Rome we went to La Toula, one of the city's poshest restaurants. When we left the hotel, I was told to get in the Burton's limousine. It was the largest Rolls-Royce I'd ever seen. You didn't have to bend over to get in; you could just step into it. In any case, Dominick Dunne was told by the Burtons to take a taxicab and meet us at the restaurant. I don't know why they snubbed Dunne. I do know he didn't get along very well with either cast or crew on this film, even less so with screenwriter Jean Claude Tramont, the husband of Hollywood superagent Sue Mengers."

In *Ash Wednesday,* Taylor portrays an overweight, prematurely wrinkled, affluent American matron who goes to Europe for plastic surgery with the hope of rekindling her relationship with her husband of thirty years, who is now in the clutches of a younger, more beautiful woman. While the operation, which restores her own good looks, enables the woman to attract the attention of a young gigolo, she fails to win back the affection of her husband, who is played by Henry Fonda.

On Burton's recommendation, Paramount hired Dr. Rodolphe Troques, an experienced French plastic surgeon who the year before had performed a partial face-lift on the actor. Troques became a technical adviser on the film and did an actual face-lift in his clinic on an aging Elizabeth Taylor look-alike, footage of which was used in the picture.

"Elizabeth did wonderfully in the film," said Troques. "It took her makeup artist, Alberto De Rossi, two hours every morning to prepare her face so that she looked like an older woman.* Every afternoon she had to go through the reverse ordeal of having the makeup removed. 'I don't mind looking like an old hag,' she always insisted.

"I got to know the Burtons fairly well," stressed Troques. "My sense of Richard is that he possessed incredible presence. Women were drawn to him. They fell completely under his spell. Elizabeth didn't seem to like women. She had some women friends, but in general she was reserved when it came to women. She appeared far more comfortable with men, and men couldn't keep away from her. She was even more beautiful in person, as you can imagine, than on the screen.

"As for the dynamics between Dick and Liz, he appeared in command. He made all the decisions concerning Elizabeth. He told her what she should and shouldn't do. Or so it seemed to me."

Maurice Teynac, an actor who appeared in the film, noted that shooting began in the Italian ski resort of Cortina d'Ampezzo and continued in Treviso, a village thirty miles north of Venice. "On certain days Elizabeth looked weary on the set," remarked Teynac. "At the time, she had her share of problems with Richard Burton. They had

*Elizabeth's face was insured for $1 million during *Ash Wednesday* should any damage occur as a result of the extensive makeup requirements.

once enjoyed a great love affair, but because each was so strong and independent they began to have troubles."

Actress Monique Van Vooren, also cast in the film, had known Elizabeth Taylor since her days with Mike Todd. "I was living in Rome when she and Richard were staying at the Grand Hotel prior to *Ash Wednesday*," recalled Van Vooren. "Since I was also in the film—and an old acquaintance of Liz's—we saw a lot of each other. She was having difficulties with Richard, so we became close. She was in pain. She would call me at all hours of the night, and I would go to her hotel. She was very generous. She used to give me bundles of clothes that she had never worn. They would never fit me because we weren't the same size, but she was so kind, and I enjoyed her. I liked her immensely. I still do. As a matter of fact, when we were in Rome, we used to go out together—Richard, Elizabeth, myself, and a friend of mine. We would go to restaurants and clubs, and the paparazzi would take photographs of the four of us and then crop Elizabeth and my friend out of the picture to make it appear as if Richard and I were having an affair."

Another intimate observer during this troubled period was Raymond Vignale, Elizabeth's butler from 1968 to 1975, who had bit parts in several of his employer's films, including *Ash Wednesday*. "I became equally attached to both Richard and Elizabeth," stipulated Vignale. "I would have done anything to keep them together. I was there; I was aware of the dilemma. Richard perpetually drank too much. At this point, he could no longer control himself or hold his liquor. I used to have to clean up after him all the time. In an effort to keep them sexually interested in each other, I would buy them pornographic magazines. It wasn't part of my job; they didn't tell me to do it. I did it because I wanted to help in any way I could.

"I did practically everything for Elizabeth. I went shopping for her. I would hang up her clothes at the end of the day. I felt a need to protect her, and as a result, I would read the daily papers and cut out unflattering remarks that journalists might have made about her. I did my utmost to get Liz to her appointments on time. She would say, 'I kept the queen of England waiting for twenty minutes, Princess Margaret, thirty minutes, and President Tito an hour. They can damn well wait for me a few minutes at a meaningless dinner party.'

"Another of my jobs was to keep Elizabeth's mother at bay. She would call on a daily basis. 'Can I speak to my baby angel girl?' she would ask. Elizabeth loved her mother, but she loathed the way Sara tried to coddle her, as if she were still six years old. So I would have to invent excuses as to Liz's whereabouts."

The height of Elizabeth's dissatisfaction with Richard came during the production of *Ash Wednesday.* Their arguments, their boozing and drug consumption, and his womanizing placed more strain on their fragile bond than it could bear. *"Ray-baby,"* as Elizabeth called the Swiss-born Vignale, spent hours holding Liz and rocking her to sleep while she cried and intermittently drank—usually bourbon. She would often spike her alcohol with Seconal or other, even more potent medications.

One of Dick and Liz's major points of departure, according to Vignale, was her "lack of taste." Richard would accuse her of dressing improperly for certain occasions. He would implore Vignale to make certain Elizabeth didn't leave the house attired like "a Jewish mom."

"In better times," Vignale confided, "the couple would play a little game. They would attend a party, and Richard would pretend to flirt madly with some woman, while Elizabeth feigned jealousy." Later, apparently, he flirted for real, and she no longer *feigned* jealousy.

Monique Van Vooren attested to Burton's lustful appetite for other women. "When we reached Treviso with *Ash Wednesday,* Richard and Elizabeth bought an abundance of Venetian glass objects—plates, glasses, decorative items. Richard kept insisting that I come up to his suite and have a look at the collection. His invitation began to sound like that age-old come-on 'You must come see my etchings.' Out of respect for Elizabeth, I never went."

Elizabeth Taylor's behavior during the filming of *Ash Wednesday* became more erratic with each passing day. Director Larry Peerce had an altercation with her the day she kept the esteemed Henry Fonda waiting on the set. "She was almost always late," said Peerce, "but when she kept Henry Fonda waiting for two and a half hours, I became irate. I cleared the set and spoke with her alone, and she said something like 'Now what?' She used an ironic tone, knowing that I was going to berate her. And berate her I did. 'How could you be two and a half hours late when you knew you had a scene to shoot with Henry Fonda?' I fumed. 'It's a blatant insult to a man of his stature, and it's unforgivable.' She never apologized. She didn't apologize to Fonda; she never apologized to me. We didn't talk for about a week, but then we finally made up."

There were days, according to the director, when Taylor failed to show up on the set at all. "Part of it," said Peerce, "I attributed to the sad fact that she and Burton were breaking up. We were behind schedule, and the budget had gone out the window weeks before. We were becoming another *Cleopatra.* I was convinced I would never work again. The chiefs at Paramount would scream at me to 'tell that bitch to get her ass over to the set and start working.' I said, 'You tell that bitch to get her ass over to the set. I'm doing everything I can possibly do.' And they insisted, 'No, you tell her.' Everybody was shouting at everyone else.

"Elizabeth had a well-founded reputation as a hypochondriac. The slightest sniffle was enough to keep her away from the set. I had difficulty believing that she was ever really sick. But one morning Richard Burton called up and said, 'Well, love, it looks as if my beloved is ill.' 'What else is new?' I responded. So Richard said, 'You'd better come over here and have a look for yourself.' I gathered up Dominick Dunne, and off we went to the hotel where Richard and Elizabeth were staying. We walked into their suite, and Richard greeted us with the words 'I think she has the German measles.' I took one look at Liz propped up in bed and started to laugh. 'What's so funny?' she screamed. The humor in the situation was that every kid in America has the German measles by age ten, but here's Elizabeth Taylor with this childhood illness at age forty-one and we have to put off production for another week.

"Moments of humor were few and far between. I recall an episode when I'd told Elizabeth she didn't need to wear makeup for some scenes in the film. She had truly flawless skin and a beautiful complexion. But she insisted on makeup, and as I entered her dressing room, she had her mouth open and was even dabbing powder on the roof of her mouth. 'What are you doing?' I asked, and she replied, 'Well, they'll see inside my mouth when I speak my lines. I want to look perfect.'

"I also remember a very humorous Richard Burton comment. The two of us were sitting around one evening having drinks and talking about women. Suddenly, Richard said, 'If I'm called upon, I can sometimes summon up a good eleven and a half inches,' which was obviously a reference to his penis. 'But of course I'm only joking,' he added."

Ash Wednesday premiered in New York on November 21, 1973. Possibly the briefest and saddest commentary on its quality was offered by its producer. Said Dominick Dunne: "It's a minor film. It's not like *A Place in the Sun.* It's a [nothing] movie, the end of [Elizabeth Taylor's screen] career. There's nothing riveting about *Ash Wednesday.*"

The motion picture, however, was not Taylor's last. By June 1973, Dick and Liz were in Rome again, engaged in preproduction preparation on separate films. Burton was to star in Carlo Ponti's *Massacre in Rome;* Elizabeth had contracted to appear in *Identikit* (or *The Driver's Seat,* as it was titled in English-speaking countries), a picture based on a 1970 novella by Muriel Spark.

With preproduction arrangements completed, the couple returned to the States, arriving in New York in late June. Richard chose to stay on Long Island at the home of lawyer Aaron Frosch; Elizabeth flew on to Los Angeles and the Coldwater Canyon home of Edith Head, with whom she often stayed. The press was informed that Taylor had gone to California to visit her ailing mother. Soon reports began to circulate that Liz was living it up in Hollywood, escorted by new friends and old acquaintances. Following a series of angry telephone calls between her and Richard, they agreed to meet in New York on July Fourth, Independence Day.

Burton picked up his wife at JFK Airport. Besotted and embittered, he sternly lectured her as they drove out to Aaron Frosch's house. When they arrived, Liz ordered the driver to turn around and take her and the limousine back to New York City. The following day, while still in New York, she released a handwritten note to the press:

> I am convinced it would be a good and constructive idea if Richard and I were separated for a while. Maybe we loved each other too much. I never believed such a thing was possible. But we have been in each other's pockets constantly, never being apart but for matters of life and death. . . . I believe with all my heart that the separation will ultimately bring us back to where we should be—and that's together! . . . Wish us well during this difficult time. Pray for us.

Befuddled as to why his wife should make public such an intensely private letter, Richard Burton was nevertheless determined to have the last public word. His published response: "I told her to go—and she's gone."

Chapter 23

Accompanied by her adopted daughter, Maria, Elizabeth Taylor arrived in Los Angeles aboard George Barrie's corporate-owned jet. Staying with Edith Head at her home, Elizabeth refrained from making further statements to the press and instead saved her choice comments on Richard Burton for the confidence of close friends. The main reason she had left him, she admitted, was his alcoholism. Among other limitations, Burton's drinking had rendered him temporarily impotent.

On the other hand, Taylor seemed to be indulging herself not just with alcohol but with recreational drugs. According to James Spada, a biographer of Peter Lawford's, Elizabeth saw a good deal of Peter during her stay in Los Angeles. Lawford would turn her on with marijuana, a charge reiterated by Peter's widow, Patricia Seaton.

In his Lawford biography, Spada relates an episode he had heard about from Dominick Dunne. Dunne, who had recently returned to Hollywood after producing *Ash Wednesday,* accompanied Taylor—and others—on an afternoon's frolic to Disneyland. Also in the group were Dunne's daughter, Dominique; Elizabeth's daughters, Liza and Maria; Peter Lawford; Christopher, Peter's son; George Cukor; and Roddy McDowall.

"This huge helicopter picked us all up at the top of Coldwater Canyon and Mulholland Drive and took us to Disneyland," reported

Dunne. "It was the first helicopter allowed to land *inside* Disneyland." A huge crowd gathered around the group for a gander at Taylor. To escape the mob, Elizabeth and her coterie took the Pirates of the Caribbean ride "through the buccaneers' nighttime world."

Dunne recalled what happened once their boat disappeared into the darkness: "Elizabeth had a bottle of Jack Daniels, and Peter had something, and everybody got the bottles going. Then a bit of coke was going around, and you'd hear sniffing. Everybody was . . . screaming with laughter. It was one of the maddest moments I ever saw in my life."

To Peter Lawford's distress, Elizabeth had formed an attachment of sorts to Christopher, his eighteen-year-old son, a nephew of the late John F. Kennedy. Tall and lanky, the young man was living with his father while trying to break into the film business. Whenever Liz and Christopher were seen in public together, the middle-aged actress seemed to be flirting with him. She took Chris along when Roddy McDowall arranged a meeting for her with Mae West. McDowall opened the door and showed them into the living room, where West was standing in a skintight silver gown, flanked by two muscular bodyguards. After a few minutes of idle conversation, Taylor leaned over and whispered, "Christopher, let's get the hell out of here." They rose and left. The following day, he escorted her to a barbecue at the home of Edith Goetz, the widowed daughter of Louis B. Mayer. They also spent time together at the Candy Store, a trendy Hollywood discotheque.

When reporters approached Peter Lawford and inquired whether his son and Elizabeth Taylor were having an affair, he vehemently denied it. "Yet the possibility that this might actually be the case distressed him," said Patricia Seaton. "Peter had enough of his own problems—from cash-flow troubles to a serious drug dependency. He had no intention of being party to a romance between Christopher and Elizabeth."

To remedy the situation, Lawford decided to find an older and more appropriate squire for Elizabeth. The name that first came to mind was that of his friend Henry Wynberg, an automobile wholesaler who had gained a certain notoriety by keeping company with a bevy of beautiful women. It seemed fitting that Lawford should bring the two together, as it had been Wynberg who had introduced Peter to Patricia Seaton.

Seaton, one of Wynberg's many former girlfriends, could attest to his prowess as a lover. "Henry, two years younger than Elizabeth, emoted pure sexuality," she noted. "Dark-haired, slim, at five feet nine slightly taller than Richard Burton [who augmented his stature by wearing two-inch lifts in all his shoes], Henry spoke with a charming Dutch accent he hadn't lost since arriving in the U.S. from Holland. His outstanding feature, however, was an organ of almost equine proportions—long and thick and hard. And he possessed the kind of anatomical control and amorous appetite once attributed to vintage playboys such as Porfirio Rubirosa and the Aga Khan. Henry had been with hundreds, perhaps thousands, of women, many of them well known in the entertainment world or international social circles, such as Tina Turner and Dewi Sukarno, the ravishing widow of the late Indonesian president. To use a contemporary term, Henry was an awesome lover."

Unfortunately, there was also a negative side to Henry Wynberg. Indicted on grand-theft charges for turning back the odometers on four used cars he sold between July 1972 and May 1973, when he operated a car-sales firm, the defendant subsequently entered no-contest pleas to all four counts. The case was resolved when the presiding judge reduced the charges to a misdemeanor and ordered Wynberg to pay the negligible fine of $250. More than twenty years after the fact, Wynberg still harbored resentment over the case, assuring the current author, "There's not a used-car dealer in America that doesn't turn back the odometer before attempting to sell a vehicle. But I'm the one who got caught."

The incident didn't deter Peter Lawford from proceeding with his plan. Wynberg reconstructed the flow of events: "Peter called me one evening from the Candy Store. 'Henry,' he said, 'I'm here with my son Christopher and Elizabeth Taylor. Why don't you come down and join us?' So I drove to the Candy Store, and when I got there, I saw that Peter and Elizabeth were seated in the corner and were engaged in an intense conversation. All these customers in the place kept staring at Taylor, but nobody approached or bothered her. She simply ignored everyone and focused on Peter. I spent about thirty minutes conversing with Chris Lawford. Then I said to him, 'Your father asked me to come down to meet Elizabeth Taylor, and I've been here for half an hour and I haven't even said hello yet. I'll see you later; I'm going home.' Peter called again and said, 'Henry, I'm terribly sorry about what happened at the Candy Store. Would you have any objections if I brought Elizabeth and Christopher to your house for a cocktail?' I said I had no problem with that, so they arrived at my house on Beverly Estates Drive, and Elizabeth and I were properly introduced.

"In those days I had a great tropical-fish collection from Hawaii. I had several tanks, including a huge one facing the couch. Elizabeth sat down on the couch, and we had a drink and talked. Richard Burton's name never came up in the conversation. Mostly we talked about the fish. I think she found them more interesting than she found me. In the tanks were gorgeous sea anemones and other beautifully colored creatures.

"At two in the morning, Peter Lawford decided he wanted to go home. He asked Elizabeth if she wanted him to drop her off. She stepped outside with him for a minute and then returned. 'Would you mind if I stayed?' she asked me. 'Not at all,' I said. So while Peter and Christopher went home, Elizabeth and I continued our conversation. We became a bit more personal. I told her I'd been divorced and had one young son. She spoke a little about her past. Needless to say, I found her interesting. At six in the morning I drove her back to Edith Head's house.

"Several days later she telephoned and invited me to a small dinner party at the home of Ginger Rogers. Elizabeth's mom had also been invited. It turned out to be a cordial evening. We dated a few more times while she remained in town. She returned to my house and again sat and watched the fish. After about two weeks she said she had to go to Italy to make a film. I should add that nothing of a sexual nature had as yet transpired between us. Nor did I realize, until I read it in the press, that she and Richard Burton were going to attempt to patch up their marriage."

To satisfy his own contractual obligations (on the film *Massacre in Rome*), Richard Burton had departed for Italy ten days before Elizabeth. Prior to boarding his flight, he had given reporters a brief interview. Referring to Taylor as "Ocean" (his original nickname for her), he had asked a rhetorical question: "How can I attend to her endless array of needs and problems, yet at the same time get on with my own life?"

While appearing in *Massacre in Rome,* Burton stayed with Carlo Ponti and Sophia Loren in their fifty-room, sixteenth-century villa in the Alban Hills, thirty minutes outside Rome. During his first days there, he received an offer from Ponti to play the male lead in *The Voyage,* a film based on a short story by Luigi Pirandello. Ponti would produce; Vittorio De Sica would direct; Sophia Loren would play the female lead. Without hesitation, Richard accepted the offer. He further agreed to star opposite Sophia in a television production of Noël Coward's *Brief Encounter.*

Burton's career plans in this instance indicate an avid desire on his part to distance himself from Elizabeth. In addition, he felt a strong attraction for Sophia, who in many respects reminded him of his wife. Like her, the Italian actress had the characteristics of a devoted earth mother. She was strong-minded and independent, yet attracted to flawed, needy men. Given her dark hair and curvaceous figure, she even bore a certain physical resemblance to Liz.

When he wasn't drinking, working, or speaking to his wife by long-distance telephone (a daily chore), Burton could usually be found in the company of Sophia. They took long walks and drives in the country, played Scrabble, and went swimming. He spent one weekend alone with her on the Ponti yacht. For public consumption, Burton once wrote (in a magazine profile he did of her) that he adored Sophia

Loren, although platonically. In private, he hinted that the relationship may not have been limited to friendship. Certainly Elizabeth had her suspicions. When she appeared in Rome, there was a noticeable iciness between the two actresses.

Elizabeth arrived in Rome on July 20, maneuvered her way (with the help of police) through a maze of fans and photographers into the backseat of Burton's limousine, embraced Richard, then returned with him to the Ponti estate. They lived together in the Ponti guesthouse, exchanging barbs and insults. Burton's name for Henry Wynberg was "Wine-stein," whereas Elizabeth shot mental daggers at her hostess whenever Sophia Loren wandered into sight. By the end of July, Dick and Liz had again separated. Elizabeth moved into Rome's Grand Hotel and began making *The Driver's Seat,* a morbid and depressing film about a psychotic German housewife who goes to Rome in search of the perfect lover and instead finds the perfect murderer. Richard stayed on at the Ponti villa with Sophia Loren, adding to his own "hit list" a band of Burton groupies.

It was from the Grand Hotel that Elizabeth telephoned Henry Wynberg, inviting him to join her in Rome. She reserved a separate bedroom for him, adjacent to her own $40,000-per-month, seven-room suite. It wasn't long, however, before Henry found his way into the mistress's master bedroom. "We first became intimate at the Grand Hotel in Rome," commented Wynberg. "Was she an accomplished lover? Let's just say she put her heart into it."

Franco Rossellini, the producer of *The Driver's Seat,* had asked his friend Andy Warhol to make a guest appearance in the film. Although allotted only a few lines of dialogue, Andy repeatedly fluffed them. "He looked absolutely petrified," observed Wynberg, who spent several days on the set. "He simply couldn't remember his lines. After ten or more takes I walked up to the director, a fellow named Giuseppe Patroni Griffi, and I said, 'I'm not a moviemaker or even an actor, and I don't want to interfere, but may I offer a suggestion? Print up some cue cards and let Andy Warhol read his lines.' 'That's a wonderful idea,' responded the director. 'Why didn't I think of it?'"

Elizabeth's customary tardiness on the set drove Franco Rossellini absolutely wild. "That woman will be the death of me," he repeatedly declared. For once there appeared to be good cause for her delinquent behavior. Although in the same city as Elizabeth, Richard Burton declined to take her calls. She felt both angry and anguished; she wanted him back, but she didn't want to give in, didn't want to compromise. Her stake in sorrow and remorse increased her own tendency to drink, and his increased drinking only enhanced her sorrow. They were both wounded.

Andy Warhol's assistant, Bob Colacello, had accompanied Andy to Rome. In his biography of Warhol, Colacello recounts another Rossellini outburst provoked by Elizabeth. Comparing her to Maria Callas, the director said, "People think that Callas was a prima donna, very difficult and insecure and demanding, but she was nothing, nothing at all, compared to Elizabeth Taylor." Rossellini then told his auditors, "Whatever you do, don't call her Liz. She hates to be called Liz. It's always Elizabeth and only Elizabeth. Like the queen."

Like the queen, Elizabeth surrounded herself with her omnipresent troupe of attendants, including secretary, hairdresser, and wardrobe mistress. Unlike the queen, she frequently downed what she called a "Debauched Mary," a drink consisting (in her words) of "five parts vodka and one part blood." She launched into a lengthy diatribe about a female friend of Warhol's, a member of an aristocratic Italian family, referring to her as "a fucking dyke." She showed Andy her scars, and he showed her his. Invited by Warhol for lunch, she arrived two hours late, refused to eat, drank Jack Daniels after Jack Daniels, stated that her secret ambition was one day to direct films, ridiculed Sophia Loren, accused another guest—an associate producer who had worked with Richard Burton on *The Night of the Iguana*—of attempting to seduce her, and finally locked herself in a bathroom and refused to come out until a doctor was called.

Reflecting on Elizabeth Taylor, Andy Warhol asked the inevitable question: "She has everything: magic, money, beauty, intelligence. Why can't she be happy?"

✦ ✦ ✦

In early November 1972, Elizabeth Taylor, having completed *The Driver's Seat,* and Henry Wynberg flew to London and stayed with John Heyman. At age forty-five, Laurence Harvey was dying of cancer, and Elizabeth wanted to see him one last time.

"We went to his house, and Larry was in bed upstairs," said Wynberg. We sat downstairs and had cocktails with his wife, Pauline. Then, while Pauline remained in the living room, we both went up to Larry's bedroom. He was in bed, with two doctors and a nurse attending to him. They left us alone with him. The poor guy looked like he was in great pain. As we sat by the side of his bed, Elizabeth leaned over, put her arms around him, and said, 'I'm so sorry you're not feeling well.' He tried to lift his head but couldn't. We were with him for no more than three minutes.

"I was amazed to read reports after his death to the effect that Elizabeth had actually climbed into bed with him. That simply wasn't the case. It was merely indicative of the kind of rumors that people tended to spread about her. I know what occurred because, aside from Larry, I was the only person in the room with her. I thought it an extremely moving gesture on her part, and I'm certain that Larry appreciated the visit."

After Laurence Harvey's death Taylor organized a memorial service for him at St. Alban's Episcopal Church in Westwood, California. The ceremony confused most of Harvey's friends; the deceased actor was a Lithuanian Jew.

A medical checkup revealed the possibility that Elizabeth might be suffering from the same disease that had ended Laurence Harvey's life. Doctors suspected the presence of a malignant tumor. On November 27, 1973, Liz entered the UCLA Medical Center to undergo exploratory surgery. Henry Wynberg occupied a hospital suite next to hers.

Richard Burton was in Palermo, Italy, still filming *The Voyage,* when he received (and took) his wife's telephone call. "Can I come home?" she is supposed to have asked. Burton flew to Los Angeles. The growth, an ovarian cyst, proved to be benign. "Hello, Lumpy," Burton said to

Elizabeth upon entering her hospital room. "Hello, Pockmark," she retorted. Wynberg knew enough to step aside. "I always understood that one day he would return," noted Henry, "and that she would go back to him. In my opinion, he was the most important man in her life. But I didn't think it would work, and I told her so." Burton took Elizabeth to Italy with him, then went with her to Puerto Vallarta for Christmas. "I believe in Santa Claus," Taylor announced. NBC-TV news anchor John Chancellor apprised his viewers: "Elizabeth Taylor and Richard Burton are reconciled permanently . . . as opposed to temporarily."

By March 1974 the Burtons were in Oroville, California, where Richard was starring with Lee Marvin in *The Klansman,* based on the Pulitzer Prize–winning novel by William Bradford Huie about racial violence in the South. "That's a picture," Burton later attested, "I hardly remember making." And little wonder. He drank vodka on the rocks from a coffee cup by day and double martinis most of the night, reported newspaper scribe Jim Bacon. Burton had fallen back on old and self-destructive habits.

Prevalent among his faults, besides drinking, had to be Richard's incessant womanizing, which began anew on the first day of shooting. Spotting a young black model-actress standing on the sidelines, Burton walked over and introduced himself. Jean Bell had been *Playboy* magazine's first African-American centerfold (October 1969) and dreamed of appearing on the big screen. Burton arranged a small part for her in *The Klansman* and promised more lucrative pickings in the future. He later had an affair with her.

Other carnal opportunities also presented themselves to the craggy-faced, sex-driven actor. His marriage floundering, Richard took up with Kim Dinucci, a nineteen-year-old blond beauty queen who dumped her boyfriend to be with Richard. He wined and dined her, then presented her with a $450 diamond friendship ring. Next, Richard's roving eye fell on vivacious Anne DeAngelo, a married thirty-three-year-old motel receptionist, whose former husband, bartender Tony DeAngelo, eventually told the press what had transpired:

"Burton promised Anne he'd take her to Switzerland once he finished filming. It was just a line, but Anne fell for it—she was walking on air for weeks thinking Burton really loved her. Then he left without her, and I watched her fall utterly apart.

"Anne couldn't take the humiliation. So she divorced me, left Oroville, and moved to Monterey."

Elizabeth Taylor similarly fled Oroville and returned to Los Angeles, where she contacted Henry Wynberg and asked to see him again. "You were right about Richard," she added. "It didn't work. He couldn't give up the booze or the other women." Raymond Vignale, Elizabeth's butler, tried to dissuade her from returning to Wynberg. "I didn't like him," said Vignale. "I thought he was using her. I told her if Dick Hanley were still around—he had died several years earlier—he would have told her the same thing. But Elizabeth was headstrong. She did what she felt like doing."

While Richard Burton spent six weeks drying out in a hospital in Santa Monica, California, Liz began reconstructing her life. She attended the Academy Award presentations; appeared as one of eleven narrators in Jack Haley Jr.'s *That's Entertainment!** (a two-hour documentary tribute to M-G-M musicals); joined Prince Rainier and Princess Grace for the premiere of *The Driver's Seat* at a Red Cross benefit in Monaco; and vacationed at Portofino, Italy, with Henry Wynberg.

On June 26, 1974, Richard and Elizabeth were divorced by a village judge in Saarinen, Switzerland. Wearing a pair of sunglasses and a brown silk suit, Liz attended the thirty-minute proceeding; Dick did not. The judge asked Taylor only one key question: "Is it true that to live with your husband was intolerable?"

"Yes," she responded. "Life with Richard became intolerable."

In his biography of Elizabeth Taylor, Alexander Walker pointed out that "together [the couple] had gone through ten years of marriage, eleven movies and thirty million dollars."

Following the divorce, Taylor and Wynberg took a brief cruise to-

*When *That's Entertainment, Part 2* came out in 1976, Taylor refused to participate in publicity for the film, complaining that the producers had used only a few brief clips from her Metro performances.

gether aboard the *Kalizma.* They next showed up in Munich for the World Cup soccer final between Germany and Holland. By September, Elizabeth had leased an Italian-style mansion in Bel Air, California. Novelist Gwen Davis, whose fictional work *Motherland* Elizabeth hoped to acquire for a possible film project, became one of the first visitors.

"Elizabeth and Henry were ensconced in a house with Greek statues in the living room," said Davis. "Enormous tanks filled with exquisite tropical fish were everywhere. There were ornate outdoor fountains, a swimming pool, patios covered with bird-of-paradise flowers, a bedroom whose walls were papered with silver butterflies." The wallpaper, which was garish to say the least, had already been there when Elizabeth rented the home.

In late 1974 word reached Taylor from London that Richard Burton had become engaged to Elizabeth, princess of Yugoslavia, whose family ties extended to the British royal family and whose present marriage to British banker Neil Balfour was about to be dissolved. Princess Elizabeth, a beauty at thirty-eight, had been linked romantically with the late president John F. Kennedy. She also counted herself a longtime friend of Burton and Taylor's, which made the engagement announcement all the more difficult for Liz to accept.

Within days of the announcement Elizabeth's back gave out. A hospital bed was installed in the butterfly-papered bedroom, and she was put in traction, trussed in place like a goat, a twenty-pound weight tugging at her spine.

Gwen Davis continued to visit. "Elizabeth never bought the film rights to my book," recalled the novelist, "but I saw a lot of her during these days." Max Lerner also showed up, once more renewing their friendship. But when he speculated that there might be a connection between her condition and Richard's finding a new partner, Elizabeth scolded him. "I have disintegrating vertebrae," she howled. "Do you want to see the X-rays?"

Despite Liz's insistence that her pain wasn't psychosomatic or precipitated by Richard Burton's latest affair, she persisted in discussing Burton. "I love Richard Burton with every fiber of my soul," she told Gwen Davis. "But we can't be together. We're too mutually self-destructive."

In true Burton fashion, he gradually wearied of the princess. Having completed a television drama in which he portrayed Winston Churchill (*Walk With Destiny*), he flew to Nice on the French Riviera to make *Jackpot,* a film which, for lack of funds, was never completed. Also in the movie was Jean Bell. According to Melvyn Bragg, Burton and Bell were photographed by the press strolling "arm in arm along the Promenade." The photograph was widely published. Burton hastened back to London to appease his fiancée. When a second picture of Dick and Jean appeared in the tabloids several weeks later, the princess made an appointment to see Richard at the Dorchester. She arrived two hours late. He had waited for her at the bar and was drunk when she finally appeared. On breaking off their engagement, she issued a cutting epitaph: "I didn't realize that it takes more than a woman to make a man sober."

In early January 1975, Elizabeth threw her own party to celebrate her "full recovery" and her forthcoming trip to Russia to appear in the first major Soviet-American coproduction in film history, a screen rendition of *The Blue Bird,* Maurice Maeterlinck's 1908 children's classic. "Elizabeth entered her own party nearly an hour late," wrote Gwen Davis. "She was wearing brilliant green flowing chiffon, and her hair was strung with what seemed to be beads of light." The color-coordinated decorations consisted of purple orchids in the dining room, violet orchids for the centerpiece, five-foot-tall lavender orchids all around the swimming pool, and lilac orchids in the living room. The tablecloths were lavender, the matches purple, the napkins violet. White candles sparkled everywhere. The fare was Japanese, as were the waiters. Special security police had been hired for the safety of the guests.

At the end of January, Elizabeth and Henry were off, headed first for a brief vacation in Gstaad. They traveled in the style to which Taylor had grown accustomed, with twenty-two pieces of luggage; Liz's usual troupe of retainers, including a secretary, maid, and hairdresser (her latest hairdresser was Arthur Bruckel); a pair of Shih Tzu dogs; one Siamese cat; and a rack of fur coats. (Truman Capote could never comprehend how somebody who loved animals as much as Elizabeth did could own and wear so many furs.) While staying in Gstaad, Taylor busied herself by painting a series of humorous pictures. "She used to paint between takes on the set of her films as well," said photographer Phil Stern, who covered her on special newspaper assignments during several of her movies, including *The Blue Bird.* "I remember one painting she did called *Happiness Is a Bloody Mary.* It consisted of a wineglass in a heart."

Phil Stern was on the set in Leningrad when Taylor appeared to begin work on *The Blue Bird,* which seventy-six-year-old George Cukor was directing. "Cukor," said Stern, "had been the first to arrive in Leningrad. He immediately fell in love with a young Hungarian boy and remained distracted by him for the remainder of production.

"I'll never forget the first day of shooting," continued Stern. "Elizabeth's costars were all present, among them Jane Fonda, Ava Gardner, Cicely Tyson, and James Coco, who'd brought along his boyfriend, an aging queen whose grotesque efforts to hide his femininity were more than a little bizarre. The Russians were particularly anxious to see that great world beauty Elizabeth Taylor. A 9:00 A.M. set call had been arranged, which meant that she would be with the makeup artist no later than 7:00 A.M. By 9:00 A.M. she still hadn't arrived at the studio. Everyone stood around and waited. She finally waltzed in around ten in the morning, without makeup or wardrobe. But what made the moment truly memorable was her appearance. Elizabeth Taylor was a fat, frumpy, potbellied dame with a big head and short legs. One of the Russians turned to me and said, 'This is your Catherine the Great?' She looked terrible. I'd seen aging store clerks at Woolworth's who looked more attractive. Her entire wardrobe for *Blue Bird* had been designed to play down the weight problem. Her hair was curled down around her neck so her double chin wouldn't show. Elizabeth Taylor is a classic example of a Hollywood fabrication."

Elizabeth Taylor, in the quadruple role of Mother/Light/Maternal Love/Witch, had agreed to perform in *The Blue Bird* for a percentage of the box-office gross. She hadn't, however, counted on any of the other circumstances that arose during the film's seven-month production schedule. She wound up spending $8,000 of her own money to have some of her costumes redesigned. She had a small dressing room and had to use Ava Gardner's bathroom. Liz caught colds, the flu, and a severe case of amoebic dysentery. Her accommodations at the Leningrad Hotel (which she shared with Henry Wynberg, who had been hired as American set photographer on the film) were only mediocre. The Russian food was unpalatable. Elizabeth was used to the best and arranged to have Fortnum & Mason airfreight her victuals from London. That worked until Russian officials discovered several English-language books stowed among the foodstuffs and put a halt to the shipments.

Ava Gardner noted that James Coco ended up cooking for everyone. "He was a marvelous cook," she said, "and was appointed chef for George Cukor and all the American and British actors. When he grew weary of the chore, we agreed to take turns with the cooking. We all had hot plates in our hotel suites, courtesy of the management. When it came time for Elizabeth to prepare the meal, we showed up at the appointed hour, only to find her standing over a bubbling can of boned chicken on her little hot plate. The can was about to explode; we made other dinner plans for the evening.

"Another memory springs to mind. *People* magazine sent a photographer to Russia to take pictures of Elizabeth wearing one of her elaborate costumes. They decided to photograph her seated in Catherine the Great's throne at the Hermitage. Without making prior arrangements, they went to the museum, marched up to the throne, took down the velvet ropes surrounding it, and proceeded to take their shots. The Hermitage guards and officials became so incensed they nearly used physical force in getting rid of the group. Once outside, they were faced with a raging snowstorm. Elizabeth had to walk quite a distance through the driving snow. There she was, her hair drenched, her makeup running, her gown soaked through and through. She was in an absolute fury."

In July 1975, Elizabeth Taylor and Henry Wynberg prepared to leave Leningrad and fly to Helsinki, Finland. "We arrived at the airport," recalled Wynberg, "and were told there were two Finnair flights to Helsinki that afternoon. An official with the airline said, 'What we're going to do for you, Mr. Wynberg, is put everyone in one plane and put you and Miss Taylor on the other—you'll have the entire airplane and a full flight crew at your disposal.' And that's exactly what took place—it was just the two of us on a jumbo jet."

At the start of August, Liz and Henry were staying in Geneva. Richard Burton and Jean Bell were at Richard's chalet in Céligny. Jean had seen Burton through some of his heaviest drinking bouts. He had spent six weeks drying out at St. John's Hospital in Santa Monica, California. His hands now shook uncontrollably, and he suffered severe arthritic pains in his back and legs. With Jean Bell's encouragement, he had again sworn off alcohol and felt better, he said, than he had in years. He and Elizabeth, both now in Switzerland, were in regular telephone contact.

"Elizabeth had always been very frank and straightforward," attested Henry Wynberg. "She didn't attempt to hide the telephone calls to Burton. She said to me, 'Henry, I've got to give Richard another shot in life because I really love this man.' There wasn't much I could do or say to stave off the inevitable.

"They had scheduled a meeting to see if, one way or another, they could work out their differences. We were still in Geneva. I awoke one morning and went out and bought Elizabeth a black dress and little black hat and veil, as well as a large sunflower, and I returned to the hotel room and said to her, 'Here's what you are—you are my sunshine, and you're making a wrong decision, you're going to a funeral. So here's your black dress and black hat. You're going to a funeral, and you're going to lose both of us.'

"She ate breakfast in the room, after which she tossed the dress into a trash barrel, though she kept the hat. I don't know why she kept it, but she did.

"I accepted the situation," continued Wynberg, "but I had given up my automobile business to be with Elizabeth, and I needed a new professional outlet to fill the void. For months she and I had been discussing the possibility of Elizabeth entering the cosmetics-and-perfume business. Because she owned a fabulous collection of jewels and knew the market, we also discussed the diamond business in some detail. But perfume was at the top of the list. I dreamt up the idea and said to her, 'Darling, eventually your film career will end—I don't know when and neither do you—so let's develop a business scheme of some sort that will yield enough income to support your children and yourself. You're an internationally acclaimed actress, and you could "create" a superb perfume, with superb packaging, advertising, etc. Then you can start to merchandise all the by-products that go with the perfume, and that will make you very comfortable for years to come.'"

Elizabeth wanted to give the proposition some thought. She flew to London, checked into the Dorchester, and from a jeweler ordered a gold wristwatch for Henry. She also spent several days in a London hospital undergoing medical tests. In mid-August she arrived at the Hotel Beau Rivage in Lausanne, Switzerland. Richard Burton joined her there.

Several days later, on August 18, Elizabeth, Richard Burton, and Henry Wynberg had a three-way meeting at Taylor's home in Gstaad. She had decided to enter the perfume business with Henry but at the same time to break off her affair with him and to return to Richard. She gave Henry the gold watch and sat down to go over the terms of their business agreement.

Devised by Aaron Frosch and addressed to "Mr. Henry Wynberg, Los Angeles," the one-page contract stipulated:

> For $100 and other consideration, receipt of which I acknowledge, I grant you the exclusive irrevocable worldwide and perpetual right to use my name and likeness (including photographs) or both, in and in connection with the creation, manufacturing, distribution, marketing and sale of any and all kinds of Cosmetics, perfumes, colognes and any other related items, including the right to advertise and publish these items and give licenses to others to permit them to do any of the above.

> The benefits of this agreement will belong to you, your licensees and assignees and would be binding on your Heirs and Executors. It is contemplated that any cosmetic line using my name or likeness will be of top quality. I will have the right to approve any, and all photographs or likenesses of me.
>
> Which approval I will not unreasonably withhold.
>
> A corporation will be formed immediately on which Henry Wynberg will own 60% of the stock and Elizabeth Taylor will have 40% of the stock. Before profits are divided Henry Wynberg is to receive 30% of the net profits first. All other profits to be divided 60% to Henry Wynberg—40% to Elizabeth Taylor.

The document, which clearly favored Henry Wynberg—who would presumably be doing the greatest share of the work—concludes with: "Elizabeth Taylor, Chalet Ariel, 3780 Gstaad, Switzerland," and her signature. It was witnessed by Richard Burton, and his signature is likewise appended.

Their business dealings complete, Wynberg took off for London with a personal check from Elizabeth for $50,000 to help cover initial expenses. A week hence, Richard Burton and Elizabeth Taylor boarded an Israeli-bound jetliner in Geneva to attend a benefit concert at which the actress would read the story of Ruth, and Burton the Twenty-third Psalm.

Burton and Taylor spent a week at the King David Hotel in Jerusalem. During their stay, their presence at the Wailing Wall in the Old City caused such a mob scene that one American tourist was heard to proclaim: "The Messiah has come."

September found them once more in Gstaad, then on to Johannesburg, South Africa, for still another charity event. Elizabeth, obsessively, compulsively, in love with Burton, wanted to marry him again; he had reservations. She cajoled, pushed, bullied, and wrote letters which somehow found their way into the public eye. "I know we will be together forever in the biblical sense," she scribbled, "so why are we afraid of that legal piece of paper which the missionaries made necessary?" They went to Botswana, accompanied by, among others, Marguerite Glatz, Richard Burton's housekeeper in Céligny for more than two decades. According to Glatz, the twosome courted and argued almost simultaneously. "It wasn't always harmonious between them," she said. "It was difficult for Mr. Burton because Liz loved whiskey and always had a bottle with her and he wasn't supposed to drink. It created tension.

"Liz was very beautiful and very moody. One minute she could be nice, the next . . . you didn't know what had happened to her. She was a star and perhaps thought everyone should accommodate her."

In one of her more exuberant moments, Elizabeth placed another note under Richard's pillow: ". . . Maybe I'll carry you off on a white charger, but I'd prefer it to be the other way round. . . ."

Her courtly challenge appears to have hit a nerve. Burton proposed (supposedly on one knee); she immediately accepted. As she put it, they would marry in the bush, "amongst our own kind." A day after reaching their decision, Richard Burton contracted malaria. The local Belgian doctor, then the only Western-trained physician in Botswana, wasn't around; his office suggested they contact Chen Sam, a pharmacologist in Johannesburg. Sam, an attractive thirty-seven-year-old woman with knee-length brown hair and a bulging medical bag, arrived by helicopter the following day. She nursed the actor, though he kept ripping out his saline drip.

The Burton-Taylor nuptials, act 2, took place on October 10, 1975, in Botswana on the edge of a riverbank in the Chobe Game Reserve before an African district commissioner from the Tswana tribe. The couple was informally attired, Elizabeth in a long green robe decorated with exotic birds, Richard in white slacks and a red turtleneck shirt. Hippos, monkeys, and a rhinoceros looked on as the newlyweds toasted each other with champagne. Burton added to Elizabeth's $15 million jewelry collection by giving her another extravagant diamond. She announced they would be together "always." It seemed as if nothing had changed. In reality, everything had changed.

Chapter 24

Before leaving Botswana, Burton and Taylor toured several of the country's outmoded medical clinics. Aware of the need for larger and more modern facilities, Elizabeth pledged to sell the costly diamond she had just received from Richard and to donate the proceeds to Botswana's struggling hospital system. According to Alex Yalaia, ambassador from Botswana to the United States, the offer "dissipated into thin air." A onetime donation of $25,000 was apparently contributed by the Taylor camp, but neither Yalaia nor anybody else could confirm receiving any further funds from the actress.

Elizabeth demonstrated far more generosity when she threw a fiftieth birthday party for Richard Burton in mid-November 1975 at London's Dorchester Hotel. Cases of champagne were brought in to accommodate the more than 250 guests. Burton sipped mineral water during the nightlong celebration and looked sullen except when surrounded by members of his own family.

When Elizabeth took to a London hospital several weeks later for pains in her back and neck, Burton refused to stay with her. She railed at him, but Burton's pals sympathized with him. Her demands on his time and what little independence he still had knew no boundaries. In mid-December, he wheeled her out of the hospital, up an airplane ramp, and they flew on to Gstaad. Everyone they encountered there predicted a quick end to their second marriage.

Hedi Donizetti-Mullener related the story of a post–New Year 1976 visit she received from the Burtons at the Olden. "Elizabeth came into the hotel wearing a new and very stunning red leather coat and hat," revealed Hedi. "The coat was lined with long white sheep fur. Elizabeth asked Richard, 'Why haven't you said anything about my new coat?' He responded, 'Well, my dear, of course I noticed it. You look just like Santa Claus.' Elizabeth was furious. She could be extremely bad-tempered. Their relationship always teetered between blissfulness and imminent collapse. In January 1976, it approached the latter."

J. S. Bach, the caretaker of Elizabeth's chalet, confirmed Hedi's statements by informing a newspaper reporter that the Burtons were sleeping in separate bedrooms. On Liz's instructions, Bach arranged to have intercom units installed that connected her bedroom to her secretary's room and to the kitchen. There was no internal phone to Burton's room, located at the other end of the house.

"There were ominous signs everywhere," noted Peter Lawford, who passed through Gstaad and spent an afternoon barhopping with Burton. "Richard put away an enormous amount of booze in a relatively short space of time," said Lawford. "He couldn't stop drinking. He suggested that remarrying Elizabeth had been an act of pure folly. 'Nothing has changed,' he told me. 'She would do better with a full-time personal attendant than a perpetually semicrocked husband.'" Then, according to Lawford, Burton compared Elizabeth to Norma Desmond, the central character in the film *Sunset Boulevard,* a faded actress whose dreams of stardom are kept alive by an obsequious band of admirers and servants.

Another visitor to Chalet Ariel was Brook Williams. One morning, Burton and Williams were riding in a cable car when, as Richard recalled, "I turned around, and there was this beautiful creature about nine feet tall. She could stop a stampede. I kept wondering when she was going to turn up again. Brook knew her a little, and my luck was in. She started coming to the house—two, three, and then four times a week."

A former model, twenty-seven-year-old Susan ("Suzy") Hunt was the estranged wife of British racing-car driver James Hunt. A willowy blonde with the effervescent beauty of an English country girl, she immediately became the focus of Elizabeth Taylor's rage. When Richard asked Suzy to join him in New York while he took over the lead in the Broadway play *Equus,* Elizabeth angrily told her young rival, "You'll only last six months with Richard." Hunt replied, "Perhaps, but those six months will be very worthwhile." Burton credited his new companion with literally saving his life, getting him (for a time) off the bottle, and rejuvenating him "with her enthusiasm."

Soon after Richard's departure, Elizabeth found temporary solace in the arms of another man. Whiling away the lonely hours at her daughter Maria's birthday party at the Olden Hotel bar, she spotted a stranger, Peter Darmanin, thirty-seven, a handsome advertising executive from Malta. "I felt a pair of devastating eyes staring at me as I turned around," Darmanin told *People* magazine. "It was Elizabeth Taylor. She told me she was happy . . . to see me. I bowed, kissed her hand, and told her how happy I was to see her." Twenty minutes later, they were dancing, and that evening Peter moved into Elizabeth's chalet. He remained for five days, returned briefly to Malta to borrow money from a friend, then spent four additional weeks in Gstaad as Liz's consort. They even exchanged gifts. He gave her a filigreed Maltese cross brooch; she gave him a gold trinket with the words "I need you" engraved on it in Italian.

Need him she apparently did. She also used him, the impetus for the fling—at least on Elizabeth's part—being her jealousy over Burton's relationship with Suzy Hunt. Darmanin told Alexander Walker: "She'd call me over the intercom and order me into the bedroom." On another occasion, he quipped: "We were with each other every moment. She needs that kind of loving." To make certain they were seen, Elizabeth took Peter everywhere, including the exclusive Eagle Ski Club. She belonged, although she didn't ski—her back doctors wouldn't permit it.

Then, during a party at her house, tempers flared, and Liz cracked Peter with her famous 33.19-carat diamond ring, leaving a nasty gash in his left eyebrow. Feeling rejected by Liz, Peter slipped back to Malta to nurse his wounds. (He was also suffering from a bruised right hand, the result, he claimed, of a bite from one of Liz's dogs.) Taylor and Darmanin met again briefly in London in April 1982.

The latest separation between Burton and Taylor became official in January 1976. In February, Liz ditched Darmanin and flew to New York at Burton's request. She thought at first he might be ill and wanted to help. He was staying at the Lombardy Hotel, where Elizabeth also checked in. That evening, Burton told her he wanted an immediate divorce; he and Suzy Hunt had decided to marry. "You mean you called me all this way to tell me that," screeched Taylor. A row broke out. The next day, Elizabeth asked Burton's stage producer in *Equus,* Alexander Cohen, to cancel the party he had arranged to celebrate her forty-fourth birthday. She contacted Aaron Frosch and asked him to prepare two sets of divorce papers—one for herself, one for Richard. The second and final divorce took place on August 1, 1976, in Haiti.

On February 27, 1976, while Richard Burton and Suzy Hunt toasted his triumphant reviews in *Equus,* Elizabeth was back in Los Angeles with, of all people, Henry Wynberg. He had leased a four-bedroom house at 400 Truesdale Place. "It was a super house," he said, "one of the best I've ever had. Elizabeth called me and said, 'Let's get together.' Then she simply moved in, clothes and all."

Henry arranged a small, impromptu birthday party. Elizabeth's mother, Sara Taylor, came up from Palm Springs, where Liz had bought her a condominium. They dined on squab and wild rice. The cake, with a single candle, was inscribed: "Happy Birthday from all of us who love you." During the day, her four children—Michael and Christopher Wilding, twenty-three and twenty-one; Liza Todd, eighteen; and Maria Burton, fifteen—telephoned from various parts of the globe to wish their mother a happy birthday.

Wynberg was pleased to have Elizabeth back in his life, though there had been no shortage of women during her absence. Patricia Seaton testified that Henry enjoyed the favors of many new women every month. Wynberg dismissed the claim as "an exaggeration" but admitted that being linked with Elizabeth Taylor "definitely changed my life, because suddenly all these women were very interested in me and, the fact is, I wasn't so interested in them. One of them came back to my house and kissed me on the lips. 'Darling, do I kiss as well as Elizabeth?' she wanted to know. It was the most outrageous question I'd ever been asked."

One day after Elizabeth moved into 400 Truesdale Place, Henry Wynberg, who saw she was still suffering over Burton, said to her, "How about a couple of weeks in Mexico? Not Puerto Vallarta—somewhere else. I have a place in mind I love very much, and I'm sure you'll love it, too."

She agreed, and they flew to Palmilla, a small resort hotel outside Cabo San Lucas at the tip of Baja, California, where they walked along the beach, sunbathed, swam, watched the sun set, dined out, and made love. They drank Jack Daniels and smoked marijuana, rolling the joints in their bedroom. One afternoon they went deep-sea fishing, and Elizabeth reeled in a 150-pound marlin. On another afternoon Wynberg took intimate photographs of a voluptuous Elizabeth sporting a sheer aquamarine beach robe while splashing in the surf.

Summarizing what was to be his final fling with the goddess, Henry later told a tabloid: "Sex was one of Elizabeth's great discoveries—and she has indulged in it relentlessly."

Following their return from Mexico, Taylor took Wynberg by surprise, telling him, "I want to be your friend and live with you; but I don't think you and I are meant to be married to each other. But I'd like to stay here with you and you do what you want to do and I'll do what I want to do."

"That doesn't sound too hot to me," responded Wynberg. "Let me give it some thought."

Wynberg thought it over and decided the thing to do was terminate their relationship but maintain their business association. "I didn't appreciate it particularly when she brought around her latest boyfriend, Harvey Herman, a screenwriter and director of television advertisements. They ended up going out and dating every few nights, and then I figured out at some point that they were spending nights in Bungalow eight at the Beverly Hills Hotel.

"'I think, Henry, you've had enough,' I finally told myself. I called the Beverly Hills Cab Company, and I said, 'Come up to 400 Truesdale Place.' I tied Elizabeth's two dogs to a suitcase—with a long rope, of course—and I filled her suitcases with her clothes, and I told the cabdriver, 'Do me a favor. Drop this off with Elizabeth Taylor at the Beverly Hills Hotel.' And that was the end of our affair, period. That was it."

Elizabeth's first meeting with Harvey Herman, forty-seven and tall and stocky, took place in Gstaad during the winter of 1976, presumably during the short span of Peter Darmanin's return to Malta. Recalling his encounter with Elizabeth, Harvey Herman detailed the circumstances:

"A friend, John Allen, and I had written a film script together, my first, called *The 42nd Year,* and on a long shot we sent it to Elizabeth Taylor in Gstaad. The script dealt with a forty-two-year-old woman torn between her husband, a business executive, to whom she had always been very loyal, and a new man in her life, a wonderful lover who wanted her to himself. We felt Elizabeth might be just right for the role.

"It turned out she loved it and wanted to do it. She invited me to Gstaad. I stayed in Geneva the night before, and I went to see her the next day. Something quite peculiar occurred. I got dressed sort of like a junior Hamlet—a woolen black top, black socks, black shoes, the white collar of my shirt just peeking out. When I arrived at her chalet and she descended the stairs, she wore the exact same black outfit I had on, down to the little white-collared shirt. She walked up and looked me straight in the eye and said, 'Which one of us is going to change?'

"We met again after Elizabeth arrived in California. We spoke purely business at first. I was married and had a family in New York, so that an affair with Taylor wasn't the first thing on my mind. Moreover, it seemed a difficult period in her life. She loved Richard Burton, and he had given her the boot. She didn't strike me as a very happy woman.

"Anyway, we were smitten with each other when we first met. We became close very quickly. I tried very hard not to get involved with her, but it was impossible. It was business at first, but then it became more than business. I think we knew immediately we were going to become lovers. She's a very exciting woman to be around, a terrific, dynamic lady, absorbing and all that. We were in love with each other for a short while. We talked about getting married, but it just didn't work out.

"My sense is that it was difficult to be with Elizabeth Taylor. She couldn't walk down the street of any city in the country without being instantly noticed. While she probably enjoyed that instant-recognition factor, there's something eerie about not being able to go to a drugstore and buy a comb without being surrounded by a mob.

"On one occasion, I suggested, 'Let's go to the movies.' 'I can't,' she answered. 'I'll be besieged.' I insisted that she accompany me to *One Flew Over the Cuckoo's Nest.* We were on line, and of course the management came out and offered us free tickets and immediate admission, but we stood our ground, bought our own tickets and even two giant boxes of buttered popcorn. She said she'd attended the movies only once or twice before 'like a normal person.'

"As I soon discovered, Elizabeth is very childlike. In her eyes, you're either committed to her or not; you're friend or foe. I had a lot of my own projects going on the Coast, but I found myself putting them aside to be with Elizabeth. I had no desire to become either her factotum or another Mr. Elizabeth Taylor.

"Our affair lasted about six months and took place predominantly in Los Angeles and New York. Several times in New York we went to dinner with Richard Burton and Suzy Hunt. When they were together, it felt like something out of a Noël Coward play. Liz and Dick were always very catty with each other—reverberations of *Who's Afraid of Virginia Woolf?* They loved each other, but they had a volatile relationship. And Burton added to the volatility with his drinking.

"Elizabeth had something of a cash-flow problem at this time.

The movie offers weren't rolling in the way they once did. I seconded Henry Wynberg's idea that she package her sensuality and go into the fragrance business.

"We dated for about six months, and then it ended. It terminated because it was my wife's birthday and we were having a party for her. I warned Elizabeth not to call me at home. She did, anyway, and I told her not to telephone me anymore. That did it."

In April 1976, Taylor ventured to Washington, D.C., for several bicentennial events as the guest of Henry Kissinger, whom she first met in Israel in 1975. One event was a fund-raiser for the American Ballet Theatre at the John F. Kennedy Center for the Performing Arts. Performers included ballet stars Mikhail Baryshnikov and Natalia Makarova, among others.

To prepare for her ascent in the capital, Liz contacted New York fashion designer Halston, whose client list featured the likes of Jacqueline Onassis, Doris Duke, Liza Minnelli, and Anne Ford.

"When she originally telephoned me," reminisced Halston, "it was in connection with an Academy Award gown she needed. Her first question was: 'Is this really Halston?' I said, 'Is this really Elizabeth Taylor?' I made the Academy Award ensemble, and it had been a success. Now she wanted me to fly to L.A. for a multiple fitting for her round of festivities in Washington. 'I hate to travel,' I told her, but she seduced me by the telephone."

For her Washington expedition Liz had Halston design something yellow to match "my yellow diamonds." She already owned a blue gown for the sapphires, a red number for the rubies, a green one for the emeralds. He also made Elizabeth the same offer he extended another leading client—a 40 percent discount if she allowed him to handle her entire wardrobe needs. "This is a woman who orders a hundred new outfits a year," he speculated. "She refuses to be seen in public more than once in the same design. We both stand to gain."

Bedecked in her finest jewelry and attired in her new Halston gown, Elizabeth attended first the ballet gala at the Kennedy Center, followed by a sumptuous reception hosted by Ambassador Ardeshir Zahedi at the Iranian embassy. The ambassador's soirees, sponsored by the fabulously wealthy shah of Iran, to whose daughter the ambassador had once been married, left few unfulfilled. Guests were afforded their every desire, from champagne and caviar to sexual favors and recreational drugs.

Doris Lilly, a frequent guest at these functions, had seen the Iranian ambassador in action many times. She depicted Zahedi as "middle-aged, a terrific charmer, intelligent, well-spoken, sophisticated, wealthy, influential, and powerful. He had haunting black eyes and a shiny black head of hair, and he flirted outrageously with everyone—everyone, that is, of importance on Washington's power circuit."

That evening, Zahedi trained his dark piercing eyes on a non-Washingtonian—Elizabeth Taylor—and by the end of the evening both had their date books out and were planning their future. She insisted he escort her to the May fourth Washington premiere of *The Blue Bird.* Zahedi not only consented but offered to have the embassy's private jet meet her at the airport in New York so she could travel to Washington in style.

They attended the premiere and then danced and smooched at the Pisces Club. The next day, Zahedi gave a caviar luncheon in Liz's honor and that evening took her to the Bicentennial committee's star-spangled gala. Seated in a VIP box, they likewise attended the trotters at a horse track in Maryland, feeding each other delicacies, with Liz perched much of the time in the ambassador's lap. Journalist Barbara Howar anointed Zahedi and Liz the town's "hottest couple." Not only had Taylor moved into the Royal Suite at the Iranian embassy (ordinarily reserved for Empress Farah Diba during her stateside visits), there was prattle in the press about a possible betrothal between ambassador and actress, particularly as Elizabeth was soon to be free of her second marriage to Richard Burton. Elizabeth—and other celebrities, such as Cloris Leachman, Connie Stevens, Page Lee Hufty (a Washington socialite), and Francesca Hilton—were invited by the shah to take an all-expense paid vacation in Iran. Elizabeth's personal escorts on the sojourn were photographer Firhooz Zahedi (a nephew of the ambassador) and Dr. Louis Scarrone, a New York physician attempting to fund and establish a world nutritional organization. Ardeshir Zahedi was dissuaded by the shah from making the trip with Elizabeth Taylor because of their religious differences—Muslim versus converted Jew. The ambassador promised Elizabeth he would try to join her in Tehran, a promise never kept.

In preparation for the journey, Firhooz Zahedi went to Saks-Jandel, a chic boutique in Chevy Chase, Maryland, and chose a dozen ensembles for Elizabeth. Ronnie Stewart, the store's buyer, noted that "they wanted to take the clothes on approval. We called the Iranian embassy and were able to complete the transaction, since one of the ladies in the store had known Ambassador's Zahedi's daughter. They charged the purchase and had it sent to the Iranian embassy, where presumably Miss Taylor was staying."

Another member of the Iran-bound group was Boston journalist Marian Christy, who recalled the May 15 departure from JFK Airport. "There stood the celluloid queen Elizabeth Taylor in an all-wrong bosom-revealing striped dress making seductive glances at her man of the hour. Ambassador Zahedi had come to the airport to see her off and throw a bon voyage champagne party for her."

At Mehrabad Airport in Tehran a phalanx of bodyguards and secret police drove Liz away in an air-conditioned Mercedes-Benz, reported Christy, "while the rest of us boarded overheated buses. After a stopover in our hotel, we were transported to the Nalvaran Palace, the royal summer residence, for a private reception with the empress in the palace gardens, a sprawling mass of pools, pavilions, and man-made forests. Liz, decked out in gold and diamonds, couldn't take her eyes off the empress, Farah Diba, a real-life star. Farah, lean and elegant, towered over the short, stocky figure of Liz Taylor."

Assuming she would be received first, Taylor positioned herself at the head of the receiving line; purposely snubbing Elizabeth, the empress started at the end of the line, saving Taylor for last. Another American journalist, Frances Leighton, noted that she and other women in the group were "horrified and disgusted" by Taylor's garish dress and gaudy jewels. "We nevertheless felt sorry for Elizabeth," said Leighton. "She'd gone to Iran to meet the royal couple in the event Zahedi decided to marry her. Contrary to expectations, she was being badly mistreated."

When the leading Iranian magazine, *Zan E Rus,* described Elizabeth in its pages as "a short, fattish, big-busted woman with poor makeup and totally out of fashion," Firhooz Zahedi advised her to return to her hotel room and "dress down." "Make yourself look like Elizabeth Taylor," he preached.

The Iranian fiasco and her inability to entice Ambassador Zahedi into marriage only briefly detoured Taylor. In June 1976, when Arab terrorists hijacked an El Al airliner, which was then used as a bargaining chip between the Israelis and the Palestinians, Elizabeth jumped into the fray, offering to substitute herself for the predominantly Jewish hostages being held by Idi Amin at Entebbe Airport in Uganda. On July 4, Israeli soldiers raided the airport and rescued the hostages. Later, Taylor appeared in an ABC television movie, which aired January 13, 1977, called *Victory at Entebbe.* The all-star cast featured Kirk Douglas, Burt Lancaster, Anthony Hopkins, Helen Hayes, and Linda Blair.

Artist Claudia del Monte, who once dated Firhooz Zahedi, recalled several days she spent during the early summer of 1976 at Andy Warhol's summer home in Montauk, Long Island. "Andy called and said, 'Elizabeth Taylor is coming out for the weekend. Everybody change rooms.' Elizabeth wanted the room with the bathtub and shower in it. So we all switched rooms to accommodate her, and I expected some kind of terrible divalike, demanding creature. But to the contrary, she seemed quite nice. We played softball and had a picnic. We met again a few weeks later during the Bicentennial celebrations, which seemed to go on for months. Anyway, she was staying at the Sherry Netherland Hotel, and various friends had sent her hundreds of roses. In the middle of the afternoon she began tossing the roses one at a time out the window. How bizarre, I thought. If only the people on the street knew that it was Elizabeth Taylor pelting them with flowers."

With the visit to Warhol's summer retreat, Elizabeth began what Halston called her "flirtation" with New York café society. She made Studio 54 her home base and socialized with co-owners Steve Rubell and Ian Schrager as well as regulars Andy Warhol, Truman Capote, Bianca Jagger, Liza Minnelli, Paloma Picasso, and, of course, Halston. She still felt a sense of rejection from the offhanded manner in which Ardeshir Zahedi had dispensed with her. At a party held at the Waldorf Towers in Manhattan, Elizabeth cried on Andy Warhol's shoulder about Zahedi; Warhol secretly taped her talking not only about the ambassador but the majority of her other lovers as well. "Elizabeth often spoke in depth and detail about her former husbands and partners," confided Harvey Herman.

The late Broadway choreographer Michael Bennett, another Studio 54 regular, invited Elizabeth to spend the weekend with him at fashion designer Calvin Klein's oceanfront house in the Pines section of Fire Island. Bennett, who was openly gay, had met Elizabeth through Halston and Warhol. As Edward Caracchi, a friend of Klein's, related the story, "Elizabeth absolutely trashed the place. Every towel in the house was covered with makeup and lipstick. When Calvin returned at the end of the weekend, he was horrified, as were the maids." A few weeks after the incident, Michael Bennett appeared at Calvin's beach house with Cher. Klein was beside himself. "No more Hollywood stars," he told Bennett, banishing Cher from his home.

A few days later Taylor attended a party at the Manhattan home of Halston, where she was seen all curled up on a long ottoman, posing for snapshots with Kevin Farley, a tall, handsome Manhattan art dealer. Fat marijuana joints were passed around the room. Liz adjourned to a powder room for an extended stay with Farley. Their hearty laughs and giggles permeated the party. Later, at a discotheque, Elizabeth danced and drank with abandon.

On July 8, 1976, Elizabeth attended a Bicentennial ball in honor of the queen of England at the British embassy in Washington. Liz's escort for the evening was former secretary of the navy John Warner, recently appointed chairman of the Bicentennial Year Committee.

Lady Frances Ramsbotham, the wife of the British ambassador, had arranged the date. "John reminded me," she said, "of a physical cross between Mike Todd and Richard Burton. Though taller than both, he was thick and muscular, with strong facial features. I only thought he might be a little politically conservative for Elizabeth."

Warner had called for Liz at the Madison Hotel that evening, looking rugged yet stately in his white tie and tails. In anticipation, Liz had dispatched Chen Sam to the hotel lobby to have a first look. "Pretty dishy" came back Chen's report. "All I saw," said Liz, "was this marvelous silver hair. Then he turned around and said, 'Ah, Miss Taylor,' and I thought, Wow!"

Heads swirled at the British embassy at Elizabeth Taylor, shining star of the cinema, entered on the arm of fifty-year-old John Warner, up-and-coming national politician. Columnist Teddy Vaughn, having interviewed Elizabeth, wrote that she "perceived Warner as an extraordinarily handsome, powerful and wealthy man" whose millions had accrued as a result of his marriage to Catherine Mellon, the daughter of billionaire entrepreneur and philanthropist Paul Mellon. John and Catherine disagreed on almost every political issue of the day. Paul Mellon, a staunch Republican, supported Warner rather than his "radical chic" daughter, with the result that Warner received a hefty postdivorce settlement.

Full of ambition, Warner, whose father had been a prominent gynecologist, attended Washington and Lee University in Virginia, where he unabashedly selected dates and debutantes out of the Social Register and Washington, D.C., Green Book, copies of which he kept on his desk at all times. He subsequently attended the University of Virginia Law School, dropping out after a year to serve as a commissioned officer in the Korean War. He completed his legal studies in 1953, joining the elite Washington law firm of Hogan and Hartson. After his divorce from Catherine Mellon in the early 1970s, he continued to date some of the nation's most desirable and popular women, even asking Barbara Walters, host of ABC's news-magazine show *20/20,* to marry him. "A woman like you could probably get me elected senator," he told her. She declined his proposal.

In Elizabeth Taylor he found a similar, if not greater, driving force. Following the British embassy reception for Queen Elizabeth, he and Taylor danced the night away at Washington's Pisces Club. Dropping Liz off at her hotel for a few hours of rest, he retrieved her later that morning to take her on a tour of his 2,700-acre Middleburg ranch, called Atoka, which was adjacent to the vast Mellon estate. They also visited Warner's elegant town house in Georgetown (with its outdoor swimming pool), another Mellon memento.

Paul Mellon, a major contributor to the Republican party, saw to it that his son-in-law received the full benefit of his largesse. In 1969, President Richard Nixon repaid Warner for working in his campaign by appointing him undersecretary of the navy. (He was later elevated to secretary.) In his book *Witness to Power,* John Ehrlichman accused Nixon of rewarding Warner with influential positions as a result of contributions by Mellon that could be measured in the millions. "Warner was extraordinarily pompous as a young man," observed Ehrlichman. He had married into the very wealthy and influential Mellon family. No doubt his style went with that social territory, but it wasn't winning the hearts and minds of the . . . politicians he encountered. In one of his less serious moments, Richard Nixon declared that being secretary of the navy was "such an easy job" even John Warner could handle it.

Washington insiders, from Nixon down, considered Warner a political lightweight. Television producer and journalist Gregg Risch said, "I covered John Warner . . . he was one of the most uninformed politicians I ever interviewed. I mean he was really unaware." Washington-based journalist Rudy Maxa said, "Warner is everything they say he is—dull, trite, unenlightened. I once ate lunch with him, and it turned into the longest lunch I ever had." Veteran *Washington Post* reporter Chuck Conconi said, "John Warner is one of the worst senators this country has ever suffered." Former secretary of state Alexander Haig recalled that when he first spoke to Warner about becoming chief administrator of the Bicentennial, Warner retorted, "Al, I can't even spell it."

Elizabeth regarded Warner's remark as a joke and saw it as an indication of his political style and genial manner. He may not have been a great intellect, but he could captivate Liz with talk of a world that was far from Hollywood and largely unfamiliar to her. Above all, from Elizabeth's perspective, John Warner represented the possibility of future happiness.

Chapter 25

Elizabeth Taylor fell fast for John Warner and his pastoral life in Virginia. Although he often referred to himself as "just an old country farmer," Warner's modest claims belied the opulence of Atoka, his immense estate. In fact, when he used the country-farmer line on seasoned local people, they would say, "You're the only farmer in the state with a swimming pool in your barn." Liz was suitably impressed when she got the full tour of his "farm" that first day, including its twenty-room 1816 fieldstone house replete with a wine cellar, custom kitchen designed by Warner himself, and a den reminiscent of the Oval Office—bedecked with a U.S. flag, navy flag, navy chair, marine flag, and various Bicentennial mementos. Outdoors she was shown numerous barns that sheltered Warner's six hundred head of Hereford cattle and small band of horses, an outdoor pool and bathhouse, several ponds, vegetable and flower gardens, springhouse, smokehouse, tennis courts, and a five-hundred-acre wildlife preserve. "Elizabeth just loved the Virginia countryside," Warner remarked. "She said it reminded her of England, of the region where she grew up." They took long walks with the dogs, Liz sharing John's fondness for animals. Although John would later claim he didn't fall in love with Elizabeth at once, their initial weekend together stretched into the better part of a week. For the first time in his career, John Warner called in sick for two days.

The following weekend, Warner and Taylor returned to Atoka,

where they confided to each other their desire to marry. "We both decided at the same time," Liz told the press. "We had taken a picnic and gone into the jeep to watch the sunset high on a hill. There was a rainstorm all around us, and we just lay back in the grass, hugged each other, soaked by the rain but in love. It was a magic moment." "Instead of screaming and complaining that she wanted to go home," said Warner, "Elizabeth wanted to sit up there and watch the lightning, I thought she was special after that."

From that day forward, Taylor and Warner became a devoted couple. Liz, combination Hollywood legend and "earth mother," set out to foster John's political career while living as a "country farmer's wife." "I feel at home here," she told the press. "It's been a long time since I felt that way. I have indeed found my roots, and they are firmly planted. We've even chosen our burial site. When I love somebody, I love them 100 percent. I like to feel cozy; I like the idea of the family being together, growing up together, growing old together, and dying together." She even tried to conform to Warner's view that "all those days of big jewelry are . . . over. It's not my bag."

But Elizabeth hadn't changed. Stephen Bauer, former White House military social aide and author of his memoir *At Ease in the White House* (written with Frances Spatz Leighton), saw John and Liz at a Bicentennial ball that summer, an extravagant affair attended by President and Mrs. Gerald Ford, legions of Washington diplomats, and four hundred assorted guests who were entertained in the Rose Garden by Ella Fitzgerald, Tammy Wynette, and Roger Miller. "Liz's behavior," suggested Bauer, "lacked good taste, given the occasion. She had burned her right leg while riding a motorcycle out at Atoka that day and whined so loudly people could hear her fifteen feet away."

From the start of their very public relationship, the question of whether or not Elizabeth Taylor would help or hinder Warner's political career was hotly debated in Washington. Everyone knew of Warner's plans to run as the Republican senatorial candidate in 1978, when the Virginia seat became vacant. Influential Republicans doubted his chances if he married this multidivorced "Jewish" movie queen whose exploits regularly appeared on the covers of the supermarket tabloids. But Warner was undeterred. Journalist Garry Clifford, chief of *People* magazine's Washington bureau, suggested that while Catherine Mellon had been Warner's greatest mentor—her family's money and power providing him entrée into Washington's higher echelon—now it was Taylor's chance to help him out. "There was an old expression around the Time & Life bureau here," Clifford recalled. "It was called 'fucking upward.' And Elizabeth Taylor was responsible for netting him the Senate seat."

Despite Liz's devotion to Warner, she would never would be a lockstep Republican and, when it suited her fancy, even campaigned for Democratic candidates. On July 30, 1976, she and Shirley MacLaine cosponsored a gala fifty-sixth birthday party and fund-raiser for Democratic Senate hopeful Bella Abzug at the swank Privee restaurant in Manhattan. Liz, said Abzug supporter Harriett Wasserman, drew thousands of contributors and herself donated a considerable sum of money. "Although Bella didn't win," recalled Wasserman, "she had Liz on her side." Taylor participated, in fact, in several events on Abzug's behalf. She also attended a campaign fund-raiser in New York for presidential candidate Jimmy Carter and, wearing a golden peanut necklace, posed for photographers with her arms around him.

In July she also showed up for the New York debut of the Austrian Ballet at Lincoln Center with public relations executive James Mitchell and Trumbell "Tug" Barton, a friend since the early days of her marriage to Burton. "This was just before Liz was set to go to Vienna to film *A Little Night Music,*" said Mitchell. "She had just learned the song 'Send in the Clowns' for the movie and sang it to us over dinner and drinks at Jim McMullen's after the ballet. She didn't have a great voice, but she could carry a tune." (When writer/director Mike Nichols heard of Liz's new film, he suggested voice lessons, but she refused, saying she had never taken lessons before and wasn't about to start now.) During the intermission of the ballet that night, Liz, Mitchell, and Barton encountered Jacqueline Kennedy Onassis, with her escort, art critic Henry Geldzahler, in the VIP reception lounge. "The ladies stared at each other," said Mitchell, "so I introduced them. Taylor seemed curious, but neither of them said anything. Superstars rarely do."

John Warner had encouraged Elizabeth to do *A Little Night Music,* an adaptation of the musical Harold Prince and Stephen Sondheim had successfully mounted on Broadway in 1973, itself based on Ingmar Bergman's 1955 film *Smiles of a Summer Night.* The film of *Night Music* was being produced by Sascha Wien and Elliott Kastner, with Heinz Lazek as executive producer, and directed by Harold Prince. Liz would play Desiree Armfeldt, the role originated on stage by Glynis Johns, whose rendition of "Send in the Clowns" had made it the show's hit number. Over Sondheim's objections, Kastner insisted on casting Liz as the ardent, middle-aged actress because she was the film's only bankable star. Heinz Lazek also held out for Elizabeth. "Before we hired her," he noted, "everybody said, 'Don't take her. She's crazy, and you will only have problems with her.' But we didn't experience many problems with Liz. She was a model of cooperation. Even the Austrian actors who played in the film were impressed with her professionalism."

Elizabeth charmed everyone who worked with her on the movie despite a bumpy start when the cast discovered the star's special perks: a suite at the Imperial Hotel and a seven-passenger white Cadillac, the largest car in Austria, for driving around with her visitors. The quarters for other cast members at the Vienna Hilton were spartan by comparison. Nevertheless, Liz managed to captivate them, hanging out in the studio cafeteria, where they ran lines and joked together. "I like her," said Hermione Gingold. "She may be a little late, but she knows her lines." Harold Prince praised her, too, saying once the picture got under way, "She seems to have no vanity."

Other cast members included Diana Rigg, Len Cariou, and Lesley-Anne Down, whom Liz "adopted" as a protégée. The male lead had first been offered to Peter Finch, who declined, telling screenwriter Hugh Wheeler that he had worked with Liz on the film *Elephant Walk* and, as he put it, "once is enough." Next, British actor Robert Stevens was cast, but it was rumored that he "behaved rudely" toward Taylor.

She would say only that "the chemistry was not right," to which Stevens replied, "Chemistry? Chemistry? We're actors, not bloody pharmacists!" The male lead finally went to Len Cariou.

Bette Davis was briefly considered for Hermione Gingold's part and was thrilled at the prospect. When matters didn't go as she had hoped, Davis said, "I was asked to costar, but Elizabeth Taylor declined to costar with me. She's such a fool. I thought to myself, after all these years in the business you'd think she would want to perform with a professional, not a deadbeat." Several reports stipulated that Taylor had specifically requested Davis but that Stephen Sondheim had insisted on Gingold.

Tension between Davis and Taylor dated back to *Who's Afraid of Virginia Woolf?* Davis had implored Edward Albee, the playwright, to give her the part of Martha and quipped, "I wasn't thrilled when I didn't get the role, but I was amazed to hear that it went to Elizabeth Taylor. I mean, I thought they were making another picture altogether with the same title. I wasn't impressed with her performance, though everyone else seemed to be. Too much huffing and puffing. . . . The real problem with Liz is that she bought the *little lost princess image* invented for her at M-G-M."

Elizabeth arrived in Austria still in discomfort from the injury sustained while motorcycling with John Warner in Virginia. The damage was compounded the second week of rehearsals when, while running across the stage, she stubbed her toe on a loose floorboard and broke a small bone in her right foot, prompting a delay in the shooting schedule. Next, Liz contracted severe bronchitis after filming an outdoor dance scene on a cold, damp night. Dressed in a sumptuous red velvet ball gown, her bountiful bosom exposed to the elements, Liz had been soldiering on despite chilling temperatures, but she ended up being hospitalized for a week.

During the nearly seven weeks of shooting, ensconced in the grand Imperial Hotel with her entourage, including Chen Sam; her latest hairdresser, Zak Taylor; makeup artists; wardrobe assistants; and whichever of her friends or family dropped in for a visit, Elizabeth was happily working and in love. Zak Taylor, a longtime intimate of Liz's, said, "She told me the hardest thing she ever had to do was sing 'Send in the Clowns.' I know she worked hard on the production. She even wrote letters to independent German and Austrian producers to help raise funds for the film."

On September 1, Elizabeth Taylor, still in production with *Night Music,* ran into Ina Ginsburg, a Washington friend, at the season opening of the Vienna Opera. Ginsburg asked her to join her for lunch at the Sacher Hotel the next day. "We met on the terrace, and everyone was staring at Elizabeth. At one point she said to me, 'Ina, what do you think of John Warner?' I said I'd known him for a long time and thought him a nice man, very attractive. I said only positive things, and Elizabeth smiled and said, 'Well, he's coming tomorrow.' Until then I didn't realize how serious it was between them."

Florence Klotz, commissioned to design costumes for *A Little Night Music,* met John Warner his first day on the set, an old Bavarian *schloss* thirty miles northeast of Vienna. "I thought him nice, though square and very stuffy, but Elizabeth was crazy about him. Her nickname for him was 'Stuffed Shirt.' "

On October 10, 1976, in her Viennese hotel suite Elizabeth Taylor and John Warner formalized their engagement with a ring. It featured red, white, and blue jewels—a ruby, diamonds, and a sapphire to symbolize their meeting in the Bicentennial year. "My engagement ring doesn't weigh 210 carats," Liz told the press. "John designed it, and it means a lot more to me than any ring I've ever had. . . . It's really very simple and unostentatious. It's very lovely."

The engagement between Taylor and Warner took place just six weeks after the Haitian divorce of Taylor and Burton and three weeks prior to the marriage of Burton and Suzy Hunt. Both Warner and Burton were fifty years of age; their mates were, respectively, forty-four and twenty-eight. The Burton-Hunt nuptials took no more than five minutes. "Stuck again," Burton quipped at the ceremony. Reading about it, Liz commented, "I suppose when men reach a certain age they are afraid to grow up. It seems the older men get, the younger they want their new wives to be, so perhaps I was just getting too old for him. Of course, I am very fond of Richard. You can't have loved somebody for so many years and just completely throw them out of your life. But you can get over the agony of love. Richard is a bridegroom with a bride. I have John. I have a whole world ahead of me."

To Liz's disappointment, when *A Little Night Music* opened in 1978, the reviews were poor. One critic referred to Elizabeth's "corpulent proportions"; another called her "fat and faded." Stephen Sondheim wasn't the least bit surprised. Writing to the present author, he said: "The fact is that I was opposed to making the movie in any city at any time. I simply thought it would not adapt well to the screen. Unfortunately, I was right. . . ."

After Elizabeth's return to Washington, D.C., she was pulled back into the political maelstrom. Quietly, but generously, she supported Democrat Jimmy Carter's bid for the presidency with occasional testimonials and financial contributions. In typical Taylor style, she did the same for Republican presidential incumbent Gerald Ford, flying by small plane to Martinsville, Virginia, for the Cardinal 500 auto race, where Liz smiled and signed autographs, violating her long-standing taboo against this practice. She mixed, too, with the "good ol' boys," swilling beer and screaming, "I belong in Virginia like fried chicken."

Taylor soon became part of the tactical team that hoped to make possible Warner's eventual victory as Republican senator from Virginia. Although she had shown only a superficial interest in politics until this point in her life, Elizabeth nevertheless was fervent about John's candidacy and envisioned the campaign as a project that could be willed, and willfully won. Warner saw Taylor as a high-profile asset, a person adored by the masses, even in Virginia, who could help him negotiate his way through the political labyrinth. Did it matter that she lacked true party affiliations, that she considered herself a Republican one day, a Democrat the next? These inconsistencies didn't seem to concern the politically ambitious John Warner, and if they did, he made no mention of it.

On December 4, 1976, John Warner, accompanied by his son and several personal friends, marched to the top of Engagement Hill, as he and Elizabeth had named the slope where he had asked her to marry him—or she, perhaps, had asked him to marry her. According to Philip Smith, Warner's press secretary, Elizabeth arrived late, long after Warner's herd of Herefords had come and gone, leaving behind their day's offerings. By the time Taylor trudged up the hill at sunset, hours late, the area was covered by cow paddies and smelled like a dairy farm. Elizabeth wore a dress of lavender gray, with gray suede boots and a matching coat of silver fox. She had on a lavender turban and carried a bouquet of heather. The Episcopal ceremony was performed by Rev. S. Nagle Morgan of Middleburg, Virginia. "Because of the cows," he said, "the guests had to step carefully to avoid their droppings." The couple honeymooned in Israel and then England.

In mid-March 1977, Taylor and Warner granted an interview with Barbara Walters for an ABC television special. They were seated, at Walter's request, in the kitchen of Atoka's main house. When asked to name Liz's greatest fault, after he has named her greatest asset, Warner said, "She burns up a lot of food now and then. I wish she'd take better care of herself." His nicknames for her, he confessed, were "Chicken Fat" and "My Little Heifer." Liz attributed her weight gain to cortisone injections she required after falling from a horse. "I know," said Warner, "but you ought to eat a few more vegetables and drink orange juice for breakfast." Liz confessed to eating potatoes with her morning coffee. Walters asked Liz if she minded the extra weight. "I am fat," she retorted. "God, yeah. I can hardly get into any of my clothes, but I eat out of enjoyment. I think eating is one of the great pleasures in life." When asked her opinion of the proposed Equal Rights amendment, Taylor expressed total support, but Warner interrupted: "We're not here to discuss political issues." "Do you ever want her to shut up?" Walters asked as he shook his head in agreement.

Jackie Park, onetime companion of movie mogul Jack Warner, remarked, "On the Barbara Walters show he was a wimp she could control. She told him, 'Will you please let me talk?' She was already bored with it all. I think she's slumming with him. She's old enough to feel perhaps that's all she can get."

To break the tedium of playing the "country farmer's wife," Elizabeth amused herself with friends. Following her appearance at the tenth anniversary gala of the American Film Institute, she went on a wild midnight romp with pal Halston. Donning a mink coat and wearing only a nightgown underneath, Liz drove, with the designer, in a tuxedo, to the foot of the Lincoln Memorial, where the actress delivered a moving rendition of the Gettysburg Address while several homeless men and women looked on in awe. Afterward, she and Halston still in their formal attire, visited a White Castle hamburger stand and told the counter girl, who had confused their order, that they wanted ketchup with their burgers. "Excuse me," she said to the actress, "aren't you Liz Taylor?" "Yes!" boomed Elizabeth. "Now where's the goddamned ketchup?"

Comedienne Joan Rivers, appearing on NBC's *Tonight* show, debuted Elizabeth Taylor fat jokes, which soon became a regular part of her act. Among the most popular were: "I took her to Sea World, and it was so embarrassing. Shamu the Whale jumped up out of the water, and Liz asked if he came with vegetables." "I won't say she's fat, but she had a face-lift, and there was enough skin left over to make another person." "She has more chins than the Chinese phone book and loves to eat so much she stands in front of the microwave and yells, 'Hurry.'" Rivers later claimed she felt guilty about hurting Liz's feelings, especially when Taylor sent an elaborate floral bouquet after the suicide of Rivers's husband, Edgar Rosenberg, but couldn't omit the jokes from her routine because her fans yell out, "What about Liz?"

Supermarket tabloids also thrived on picture-filled stories about Liz's battle with the bulge. A popular format was to print dated photographs showing Elizabeth's progression from girlhood slimness to middle-aged heft. Later, in her book *Elizabeth Takes Off,* the actress traced her weight gain to indolence in Washington, D.C. "I was almost fifty when for the first time in my life I lost my sense of self-worth," she wrote. "I lost it because my husband, John Warner, was elected to the

U.S. Senate and I felt I'd become redundant like so many Washington wives and other women at different times in their lives. I had nothing to do. . . ."

Later in June 1977, ABC's *Good Morning America* sent former New York mayor John Lindsay to interview Liz in Wisconsin, where she and Warner had gone to dedicate a hospital unit in memory of her uncle Howard Young, who had bequeathed $20 million for that purpose when he died in 1972. "She and John had just come by private plane to Minocqua from Chicago, where they had visited Mike Todd's grave," said Joyce Laabs of the hospital committee. Elizabeth and John also spent time fishing in the rain with Ed Behrend, who taught Liz how to fish as a child. "During her stay," added Laabs, "Liz heard about a girl in the hospital who had just had her leg amputated, so she brought her some flowers." At the conclusion of Lindsay's interview, he asked the couple how they remained so happy. "The secret of our happiness," said Warner, "is total giving. This woman is world-renowned for her beauty, but few realize she's far more beautiful inside than she is outside."

By September, Liz and Warner were in the full swing of political life, attending frequent Republican fund-raisers as well as hosting several at Atoka. On most occasions, she showed herself to be a first-rate campaign companion. Liz had been in and out of the hospital at summer's end with bursitis but managed to make appearances in a wheelchair. The evening before John Warner's political ally, John Dalton, was elected governor of Virginia, Liz checked out of the hospital and flew down to Richmond. "I broke my hand. I broke my hip and I busted my ear and my ass for Dalton," she said. "I'll be damned if I'm going to miss the victory party." On occasion, however, she showed signs of stress, openly teasing her husband, losing her temper in public, and drinking large amounts of liquor.

In the midst of their Washington obligations, Taylor and Warner flew off to Los Angeles to discuss her making the movie *Winter Kills,* a black comedy modeled in part on the presidency of John F. Kennedy.

Director William Richert hoped Liz would play a presidential madam to Warner's silent role as president. "I told Elizabeth her character in the film didn't speak but that her presence on-screen would be powerful enough to make it work. She said, 'It would be a giggle to do the part.' Warner agreed. 'If you want to do it, we'll do it.' They seemed to enjoy themselves." The cast included John Huston, Jeff Bridges, Anthony Perkins, Sterling Hayden, Eli Wallach, and Richard Boone. Richert was finally convinced to let Liz keep a lynx coat she wore in her role. "At first I told her she couldn't have it," said Richert, "because it was rented. And she raised her voice a little so that people around us could hear. She spoke a little louder then: 'Now, what do you mean I can't have it? John, this man won't give me the coat.' Then, at one point, she was supposed to write a note during a close-up. She did such a convincing job, the entire crew applauded. After the take, she walked up to me and handed me what she'd actually written during the scene. The note said: "If Bill Richert doesn't give me that fur coat, I won't give him any more close-ups.' And, of course, I gave her the coat. We had a great time with her."

On January 6, 1978, John Warner announced his candidacy for Republican senator from Virginia and launched a fund-raising drive. Elizabeth offered to sell some of her priceless jewels to help the campaign, but didn't. Overall, Warner spent $561,000 on the campaign, $471,415 of it his own money. His Middleburg neighbors were piqued when Warner considered selling off all twenty-seven hundred acres of his land, to be divided into twenty-five-acre lots. According to Joel Broyhill, chairman of Warner's Senate campaign committee, "His neighbors nevertheless turned out in droves at every fund-raiser that Elizabeth attended. And she attended most of them."

On Elizabeth's forty-sixth birthday in February, Halston threw her a party at the legendary New York City discotheque Studio 54, with Andy Warhol and other friends in attendance. John Warner stood on the sidelines as thirty Radio City Rockettes danced into the disco carrying a five-hundred-pound chocolate cake in the shape of Elizabeth Taylor's body. Liz blew out the candles and lopped off her own right chocolate breast for Halston, who gobbled it down while "stuffing her like a goose with her own birthday cake," recalled photographer Felice Quinto. Warner headed for the exit and was not seen for the remainder of the night. Elizabeth Taylor remained. In his book *Simply Halston,* Steven Gaines wrote of that period, "The nights at Studio 54 began to meld into one snowy blitz of cocaine and scotch and Quaaludes. Every night there held some new, small titillation, a fat Elizabeth Taylor in a silly flowered hat with Halston in the disc jockey's booth playing with the lights all night, Mick Jagger falling asleep on Baryshnikov's shoulder . . ." Studio 54 co-owner Steve Rubell claimed that the lurid stories that appeared in the papers were mild. "The stuff that happened was much worse," he said. "You couldn't believe it."

According to Sara Lithgow, mother of actor John Lithgow, who was starring in a production of *Anna Christie* at the John F. Kennedy Center in Washington that spring, Elizabeth arrived to see the play in the middle of the second act with Halston and others, disrupting the whole theater as they noisily clambered to their seats. At another time, Taylor and Warner arrived midway through the Young People's Drama Festival at the Kennedy Center, both of them drunk and rowdy.

Despite Elizabeth's participation in her husband's campaign, on June 3, 1978, she watched helplessly at the Richmond Arena as Warner's incumbent opponent, Dick Obenshain, won the nomination by a narrow margin. Warner was still nursing his loss when, ten days later, Obenshain's small plane crashed near his home in Chesterfield, Virginia, killing the nominee. Promising to assume Obenshain's campaign debt, Warner was nominated as his party's senatorial candidate.

Before summer ended, Elizabeth went back to California to tape "Return Engagement," her first appearance on TV's *Hallmark Hall of Fame,* starring in a role screenwriter James Prideaux had originally conceived for Jean Stapleton. Thrilled to have her for the movie, he and director Joseph Hardy gave Elizabeth the full star treatment, readying her hotel room with flowers and champagne. "I found a great big bath towel for her that said 'Stolen from M-G-M Props Department,'" recounted Prideaux, "and I had it sent to Miss Taylor at the Beverly Hills Hotel. When I met her, she said, 'Oh, I loved the towel. It's really great.'"

John Warner visited his wife several times during the shooting, and Prideaux thought him to be "nothing special." "I'm told she took drugs to get up in the morning," he said. "I would arrive at seven A.M., and her limo would be there, and I'd think, Thank God she's here. She'd be in the dressing room putting on her right eyebrow in the mirror . . . and I'd go back about an hour later, and she'd be doing the other eyebrow. It would take her about three hours to get down onto the set, and the first couple of days we almost went mad. But once on the set, she was the total pro."

John Warner returned to Virginia and the campaign trail wearing an Oray new-wave haircut. Oray, who for some time had styled Elizabeth's hair, recalled Warner as "wanting to be a political star, another John F. Kennedy. I think he assumed that with Elizabeth Taylor's help, that's what he would become. But he lacked the brains, the finesse, the charisma. In turn, Elizabeth hoped against hope to become another Jackie Kennedy."

While in Los Angeles, Warner attempted one favor for Elizabeth. He met with Henry Wynberg in an effort to induce Henry to nullify the perfume-and-cosmetics contract he and Elizabeth had signed. Obviously, Warner, like Henry, understood the potential monetary value of such a deal. In order to make the abnegation of the contract more palatable, Warner offered to cancel several years' worth of IOUs that Henry had accrued in Elizabeth's favor. No fool when it came to business, Henry Wynberg let loose a loud chuckle and promised to take the offer "under advisement."

Wynberg, for that matter, had already instigated the complicated search for a proper fragrance and matching packaging for such a commercial undertaking, and the final results he attained, after conferring with a number of chemists and public relations firms, were startlingly similar to Elizabeth's eventual product, "Elizabeth Taylor's Passion."

(Since another "Passion" perfume was already on the market, Taylor's name had to be included in her fragrance.)

After Warner's return to Washington, Elizabeth attended a dinner party with director George Cukor. The party, which was catered by Ma Maison, was for approximately eighty guests, George Cukor being the guest of honor. Those at his table included Lillian Hellman, Fred DeCordova and his wife, Mr. and Mrs. Sam Jaffe and their daughter Ann Carroll, and Elizabeth, who arrived about forty-five minutes late. Richard Stanley, Cukor's friend, recalled that "the first course was an avocado half-topped with pink and yellow caviar. There she was in this gorgeous Nolan Miller–type evening gown. She started to eat the caviar and just screeched, 'This is atrooooocious,' and started pulling it out of her mouth with her hands and spitting it out on the table. Needless to say, everyone was in shock."

After rejoining Warner, Elizabeth swallowed a chicken bone at a campaign stop in Stone Gap, Virginia, and was rushed to a local hospital, where the fragment was removed by a surgeon. Subsequently, Taylor was burlesqued in a now notorious *Saturday Night Live* sketch by comedian John Belushi in which he, dressed as an obese Elizabeth Taylor, chokes on a half-eaten chicken leg. The clownish image of a former film beauty now twice her original size embedded itself in the American consciousness. Dinner guests reported seeing her eat mounds of mashed potatoes drowned in gravy at one sitting, followed by five desserts and several bottles of champagne.

Elizabeth herself blamed the weight transformation (at one point she weighed over 180 pounds) on having to attend "all those campaign luncheons, dinners, and barbecues for John." The stress of these functions also played a role. It became impossible for Taylor to go to a public bathroom without strangers following in her wake. Women would clutter around the bathroom mirror and watch the star freshen herself, or they would stand outside her private stall and listen and make comments, occasionally sneaking glances or even a camera underneath the stall door for a candid snapshot. The countless fat jokes and silent stares did little for Liz's disposition. She finally plastered a ghastly photograph of herself on the side of her refrigerator as a reminder of her extra weight.

Taylor's public behavior also reflected a growing insecurity about her appearance. Producer Lester Persky, recalling a benefit he attended in New York at about this time, said, "I sat next to actress Maureen Stapleton at a dinner, and Liz Taylor sat at another table, perhaps twenty feet away. Maureen and I were in deep conversation when suddenly a security guard appeared before us and said to Maureen: 'Miss Taylor would appreciate it if you would not look at her during dinner.' The statement was all the more absurd in that neither of us had so much as glanced over in Liz's direction.

"Elizabeth had some peculiar ways of doing things. When it was first announced that I would produce the screen version of *Equus,* she cornered me in a restaurant and told me what a great choice Richard Burton would be for the film, since he had been performing in the Broadway version. I needed little encouragement. I was aware of Burton's thespian skills. Several months later I ran into Liz again. By this time Burton had married Suzy Hunt. Liz wasn't pleased. She excoriated me for even considering Burton for the role in the *Equus* film. 'He's a very bad boy,' she said in a patronizing tone. 'You mustn't give him the part, Lester.' I gave him the role. She never spoke to me again."

In much the same way she had made legendary the chemistry between her and Richard Burton, Elizabeth Taylor made no secret of her lust for John Warner, whose sexual prowess had been much discussed among the women of the Washington–New York circuit. Jim Boyd, creator of a dating service for women, verified Liz's preference for well-endowed males. "John Warner was big," he said, "but so were Eddie Fisher and Henry Wynberg. We found this out from Liz's hairdressers. She would always confide in them. She also complained that Warner, after their first year of marriage, didn't give her enough sex. Once, shopping in Beverly Hills at an early stage in their relationship, Liz asked the owner of a Rodeo Drive men's boutique to help her locate some briefs with an extra large pouch for her well-hung husband."

Elizabeth rejoined John Warner on the political trail by giving a drama seminar at Emory and Henry College in Marion, Virginia. Introduced to the class by her husband, Elizabeth spoke about her adventures in Hollywood and then, like a veteran wife, said: "My job is now with my husband." She informed a reporter from *People:* "I just love my life in Virginia. I'm making myself right at home. Besides, John's the only man I've ever let call me Liz. We've got the most gorgeous thing going between us. I don't think of him as husband number seven. He's number one all the way. He has an honesty and integrity I've never seen in any man I've ever known before." After a pause she added, "And he's the best lover I've ever had."

Back in Richmond, Virginia, Elizabeth accompanied Warner to a luncheon meeting of the Richmond Bar Association, winning over even the stuffiest, most conservative lawyers. After John gave his formal speech, she mixed with the crowd, drank Bloody Marys, and planted a kiss on the cheek of one retired judge as she presented him with an award, causing a ballroom filled with Republican stalwarts to whoop and holler like fraternity brothers at a strip joint.

A few days later, at the Charlottesville Dogwood Festival, she and John rode in the parade on the back of a white Cadillac convertible. People on the sidelines waved placards that read Liz, We Love You! But at the University of Virginia, in that same city, where she had agreed to give another drama seminar, Professor Arthur Green, chairman of the theater department, openly criticized her husband, accusing him of using Elizabeth. "I think he used that woman miserably," Green told the current author. What Arthur Green overlooked was that Elizabeth was "used" by men only when it suited her. As Pia Lindstrom put it, "In person Elizabeth covers her rage. She becomes shy, quiet, unsure of herself, the lost little girl. At least that's the role she embodies. She's markedly changeable. Every time we met, she was different: fat, thin, sober, drunk, chaste, or in love. Her public pose is loud, spontaneous, pushy. I can't see many men—or women—getting the better of her. She was skimpily educated but very adept at handling people."

By this time, Chen Sam had leased an apartment in a high-rise building in Washington, D.C., to be near her employer. Harriet Meth, subsequently a talent coordinator with *Entertainment Tonight,* suggested that within the public relations circuit Chen Sam was referred to as "Genghis Khan." She's "a real barracuda," said Meth. "She definitely has Liz's ear."

In Washington, Elizabeth and Chen often lunched and dined out together, partied together, and frequently spent quiet evenings in each other's home. Liz's circle of professional handlers and colleagues knew that Chen was the one and only person who knew all of the star's most closely guarded secrets.

John Warner's senate campaign manager, Joel Broyhill, worked with Chen during 1976 and 1977, and, in fact, Warner and Taylor occasionally double-dated with Broyhill and Sam. "Chen and Elizabeth were very close," he said, "and they still are. Elizabeth needs someone close. She doesn't have many people she trusts. But she had complete faith in Chen. Chen eventually resigned as personal secretary and became more of a special assistant to Liz. She moved into the public relations arena. Elizabeth and John and Chen and I traveled together."

Meanwhile, Warner and Taylor continued to traverse Virginia on the campaign trail. At the Virginia Military Institute (VMI), where Warner gave the Founder's Day speech, he told his audience: "I think it would be wrong for any individual to accept an invitation here and then use his presence on these hallowed and venerable grounds to foster any political self-interest." Yet halfway through the speech, Elizabeth joined him at the podium. "And my wife is here to salute the corps of cadets," he announced. The crowd went wild, cheering and whirring their hats into the air. Liz sparkled and Warner beamed.

Gossip columnist Cindy Adams spotted Elizabeth not in Washington but in New York, walking down the aisle of a Broadway theater. "It was some kind of opening," recalled Cindy. "I was walking right behind her and then right alongside, and I made some conversation, and she, knowing who I was, gave me small answers—the answers weren't rude, nor polite, nor helpful, nor evasive, just out of it. . . . I knew, walking up the aisle, there was something very wrong with her—she was spacey—and some years down the line, when we read that she was jumped up, she was boozed up, and stuff like that, it made sense.

"I have to say that Elizabeth Taylor, largely because of her addictions, has lived a life that is very much out of control. Her weight and her drinking and her use of drugs appear to be out of control. Her career is out of control. Her emotions are out of control. I think she realized from her marriage to John Warner that she had to do something to check her excesses. Many people have compared Jacqueline Onassis with Elizabeth Taylor. I think Jackie was cold-blooded in the way she went after the men in her life; Elizabeth is less cunning, more emotional. She's hot-blooded, whereas Onassis was cold-blooded all the way, a glacier without a heart.

"About the same period as the theater debut, I saw Elizabeth at a benefit. My husband, Joey Adams, was emceeing the event, at which Elizabeth was guest speaker. He introduced her by saying, 'And here is Elizabeth Taylor Hilton Wilding Todd Fisher Burton Burton Warner.' She didn't appreciate it. She stood and told the audience, 'I am Mrs. John Warner.' And everybody applauded."

On November 7, 1978, John Warner won the senate seat by less than one percentage point (thirty-five hundred votes) over Democrat Andrew Miller. Elizabeth, still a British subject, couldn't vote for her husband. On January 16, 1979, she attended Warner's swearing-in ceremony as U.S. senator. "Just when she thought the fun would begin," said Phil Smith, "things got tough. Senator Warner worked his rump off and barely had time for Elizabeth. She insisted they move into his S Street town house in Georgetown and visit Atoka only on weekends, but it still didn't help. She had to practically beg him to go out for dinner at night. He preferred burning the midnight oil, an indication of his devotion to the job. He wasn't overly intellectual, but he busted his rump to make up for it."

On her forty-seventh birthday, Elizabeth ended up alone when John called to say he had too much work at the Senate to take her out for dinner at her favorite restaurant, Dominique's. Intent on celebrating, Liz called the owner, Dominique D'Ermo, whom she had known since Paris in the 1960s, and place an elaborate order: stone crabs, yellowtail tuna, chocolate cake, and the appropriate wines, including Dom Perignon. After preparing the food, Dominique took the birthday dinner over himself and kept Liz company while she dined.

In an effort to control her weight problem, Elizabeth spent a week at the Palm-Aire Spa in Pompano Beach, Florida. She evidently enjoyed the break from Washington, because she returned to the spa on several occasions. On July 16, 1979, she flew to England with her sons to attend the funeral of Michael Wilding, her second husband. The wreath from Elizabeth read: "Dearest Michael, God Bless You. I Love You. Elizabeth."

Back in D.C., she resumed her gluttony. "There was nothing for her to do but eat," observed Phil Smith. A Washington hairdresser, a friend of John Warner's son, described Elizabeth as sitting around the swimming pool in Georgetown, "tanning herself and imbibing calories." She became so bored she finally began partying with groups of young men, using her limousine, with its own bar, as home base. "Warner and Taylor were never in the limousine at the same time, but the senator heard accounts of her exploits with his son, including being driven around to Washington's disco and gay clubs by the black chauffeur, often visiting one notorious establishment called the Fraternity House on 22nd and P Street. She even would lend Warner's son her limo, and there would be about ten of us in the back."

The entire Washington experience had begun to sour for Taylor. Hank Lampey, a member of the inner circle of a group known as Friends of John Warner, was selected to advise Elizabeth that her attire was inappropriate to her position as a senator's wife. "It's too Hollywood," he told her. "You ought to dress down." Elizabeth's idea of dressing down was to start wearing cowgirl gear. Ronnie Stewart, of Saks-Jandel, remembered the day "Elizabeth came into the store with Chen Sam, both of them in jeans and fancy cowboy boots. Chen is rather tall and slender, with large breasts, and looked great in jeans, but Elizabeth just didn't have the figure to carry it off."

In May 1980, Elizabeth went to England to appear in a cameo role in *The Mirror Crack'd,* a film of an Agatha Christie mystery directed by Guy Hamilton. Although Liz, staying at the Savoy, showed up late the first three days of shooting, Hamilton said nothing. "She'd heard it all before," he said. "She had been berated for tardiness for years. When I did nothing, she began showing up on time."

In July, she and John Warner appeared with Ronald and Nancy Reagan at the Republican National Convention for Reagan's presidential nomination in Detroit. She and Mrs. Reagan—former Hollywood actress Nancy Davis—reminisced about M-G-M. Elizabeth and Warner had been seated alone in a VIP box, and that evening the crowds surged around them as if they—and not the Reagans—were the couple of the hour.

Elizabeth followed up with a visit to New York, where, according to Andy Warhol's *Diaries,* she saw Andy at Studio 54 and snorted cocaine with Halston in the privacy of the designer's town house. She told Halston that John Warner was no longer sleeping with her. Although she publicly denied reports of a rift in the marriage, the press suggested otherwise.

Chapter 26

By 1980, Elizabeth Taylor's unhappiness with her life as a political spouse was so evident that John Warner, his goal of a Senate job secured, agreed that she should resume a full-scale acting career. Up to that point, she had appeared in fifty-four films, but she was now close to fifty and severely overweight—not standard Hollywood material. Elizabeth was further handicapped by the lack of good roles for women in general in films of the 1980s. Most starring roles were suited to young actresses. Middle-aged actresses were at a tremendous disadvantage, and Elizabeth did not want to be limited to playing aging divas attempting comebacks, as she had in her cameo in *The Mirror Crack'd.*

Moreover, Elizabeth was used to making a great deal of money, and she intended to do so again. At parties in Washington and Los Angeles, Burt Reynolds had told her about the dinner theater he had bought in Jupiter, Florida. Like Elizabeth, he could no longer count on decent film roles, and he wanted her to appear onstage opposite him in *Who's Afraid of Virginia Woolf?* Elizabeth listened to Reynolds; she had an idea that had been brewing at least since February 1966, when she had made her one stage appearance at Oxford University with Richard Burton, who had the title role in Christopher Marlowe's classic *Dr. Faustus.* During the one-week run, Elizabeth had made a brief, silent appearance as Faustus' vision of the most beautiful woman in the world, Helen of Troy.

Burton's diaries record that by 1970, Elizabeth had been anxious to make more stage appearances. Burton had never encouraged her; he did not think she had the right voice, movements, or training. Elizabeth herself had had misgivings that her famously high, squeaky voice might not reach the back of a theater. In her 1965 autobiography, *Elizabeth Taylor: An Informal Memoir,* she wrote, "Someday I would love to do a play . . . on the stage. But I don't think I have the right voice. It's not big enough, though maybe I could train it."

Besides the possibility of reviving her stardom, Elizabeth had another reason to consider the theater. With her marriage to Warner ending, Elizabeth was also looking at the stage as a road to a reunion with her one true love, with whom she had stayed in touch. The stage was Richard Burton's territory, and it was probably no coincidence that she embarked on her new career just as Burton was planning to return to Broadway in a revival of *Camelot*—and as his marriage to Suzy Hunt was ending. (In December 1980, Elizabeth had been spotted in New Orleans at a performance of *Camelot.* The Warners' separation was made public in the fall of 1981.)

In May 1980, Elizabeth showed she was serious about resuming her career by losing forty pounds at her favorite Florida fat farm, the Spa at Palm-Aire in Pompano Beach. A constant supply of Jungle Gardenia perfume kept her spirits up. In October 1980 she attended the Washington opening of the revival of *Brigadoon.* Elizabeth arrived about fifteen minutes late, forcing her seatmate to make room for her. *Brigadoon*'s producer, Zev Bufman, had been told his seatmate would be "the wife of a senator who was working late." As the overture was ending, he heard the footsteps of someone running down the aisle, and then "someone slammed me on the shoulder very hard, like, 'Move over!'" The fifty-year old Bufman, born in Palestine, had started out as an actor and now owned eight theaters across the country, in New York, Los Angeles, New Orleans, and Miami. In 1967 he had brought to Broadway an American version of the Royal Shakespeare Company's sensational *Marat/Sade.*

Bufman invited Elizabeth to the *Brigadoon* opening-night cast party. There, according to director Austin Pendleton, Elizabeth said to Bufman, "God, I'd like to do a play."

"And Zev took her up on it," Pendleton said.

Bufman's attitude was: "If you're going [onstage], why not do it in New York?"

Later that October, Elizabeth announced that she planned to appear on the Broadway stage in a play coproduced by Taylor and Bufman. In strict secrecy, Bufman assembled a cast, including top actors like Derek Jacobi, to read various plays with Elizabeth in a New York rehearsal hall. The group considered Edward Albee's *Who's Afraid of Virginia Woolf?,* Tennessee Williams's *Sweet Bird of Youth,* James Goldman's *Lion in Winter,* and Noël Coward's *Hay Fever.* Elizabeth wanted a drama, but she was reluctant to repeat onstage her role in *Virginia Woolf:* "Martha is the most grueling part ever written. I wanted to do something meaty, but I didn't want to kill myself."

Elizabeth settled on what she thought was the right vehicle: *The Little Foxes,* Lillian Hellman's melodrama of a ruthless, grasping southern family at the turn of the century. Regina Giddens, the greediest, most treacherous fox in the family den, had already been immortalized by two formidable stars: Tallulah Bankhead onstage in 1939 and Bette Davis on-screen in 1941. The play had never been revived on Broadway after Bankhead's smash in 1939.

But Elizabeth decided that Regina, usually portrayed as a viper, had a feminist dimension that other actresses had left unexplored. With Hellman's blessing, Elizabeth prepared to play Regina as a kinswoman of her own fictional heroine, Scarlett O'Hara: a desperate woman, foiled by societal constraints, who uses the only means available to her to "never be hungry again." Her costumes, by Florence Klotz, who had designed her lavender-gray dress for her wedding to Warner and her costumes for *A Little Night Music,* reflected her highly personal view of Regina. In the first act, Elizabeth appeared in a dress that seemed to be sewn entirely of scarlet beads. By the second act, her dress had paled to lavender, Elizabeth's favorite shade. By the third act, when Regina has deliberately allowed her husband to die by refusing to fetch his heart medication and has blackmailed her brothers in order to escape her small southern town for Chicago, Elizabeth was dressed in pure white. All the period costumes that the play required were kind of Elizabeth's figure, still swollen at 125 pounds. "She wore the gowns I designed without any changes," Klotz enthused. "She is the kind of woman who is gracious to elevator operators, a mensch. She didn't care what kind of dress she wore so long as it had lavender in it."

Elizabeth had wanted her director to be either Mike Nichols, director of the film of *Virginia Woolf* and of a 1967 stage production of *The Little Foxes* at Lincoln Center, or her friend Joseph Hardy, who had worked with her on *A Little Night Music.* But since both were busy, Austin Pendleton took the job. He knew the play very well—he had had a character part in Nichols's production—but he was nervous about his first big directing job, about meeting Taylor for the first time, and about how she could play Regina. He met first with Lillian Hellman, who "sort of doped me out." Hellman had said, "When I wrote [the play], I was amused by Regina—I never thought of her as a villainous character—all I meant was a big, sexy woman." Reassured, Pendleton then met with Taylor and became a fan. "Elizabeth Taylor, more than any woman in America, symbolizes not greed to people but healthy appetite," Pendleton noted later. "What if *The Little Foxes* became about appetite—too healthy, in this case, but still appetite—that turned *into* greed, before our eyes, as a result of what happens in the play? What if Regina started out as a hearty, hedonistic lady, not unlike what we all think of Elizabeth Taylor as being. . . ." And after all, he noted, "all of her best work in film was in parts that had been conceived for the theater."

Bufman shrewdly cosseted his perennially tardy, frequently sickly star. "You want to please these people," he told a reporter. "Limos, aides, redecorated dressing rooms, flowers [delivered every night], and champagne go without saying. It pays off in the end." With Taylor, Bufman outdid himself, adding countless soothing phone calls to his customary coddling. He agreed to open *The Little Foxes* in February 1981 in Fort Lauderdale so that Elizabeth could spend weekends at the Spa at Palm-Aire to lose weight. He had a replica of the first ticket sold made up as a gold necklace for Taylor. He also took out $125,000 worth of insurance from Lloyd's of London against her canceling performances.

Rehearsals began in Florida. Elizabeth had said she wanted to assemble a topflight cast for *The Little Foxes.* But when she was told that Maureen Stapleton, who recently had been elected to the Theater Hall of Fame and had won an Oscar for her portrayal of Emma Goldman in *Reds,* had agreed to play Birdie, Regina's fluttery, put-upon sister-in-law, Elizabeth exclaimed, "I said I wanted good actors, but not that good." During one rehearsal, the rest of the cast looked aghast when Elizabeth, trying to follow Pendleton's direction, asked, "Stage right? Which is stage right?" Elizabeth cut short one rehearsal so that she, along with Irene Dunne, the Frank Sinatras, and the James Stewarts, could go to Washington for President Reagan's seventieth birthday party at the White House.

Hugh L. Hurd, one of the few black cast members, remembered director Pendleton as "the least intimidating person in the world." During one rehearsal "Austin was explaining to Elizabeth what was going to happen, and he said, 'Now, Elizabeth, in these next three lines this is what's happening . . . ' and he goes on and he elaborates the whole thing, and she started to giggle. He said, 'What's so funny?' and she said, 'All that in three lines?' "

Mike Nichols dropped in on rehearsals frequently. He had wanted Elizabeth to take voice lessons before filming *Virginia Woolf,* even though ultimately her voice could be enhanced by the sound track. "Baby," he now protested to Elizabeth, "you've never had any training. You won't be able to project." Once again, Elizabeth insisted that she would manage fine without lessons, just as she had in *Virginia Woolf.*

On opening night in Fort Lauderdale, the audience gasped when Elizabeth first appeared onstage. Perhaps on purpose, to help Elizabeth look better, three or four of the more experienced players flubbed their lines, so that Elizabeth, Pendleton said, had a chance to "rescue them." At the curtain call, Senator Warner leaped onto the stage and handed his wife a bouquet of roses dyed lavender. At the opening-night party at a Miami yacht club, Warner told reporters while lightbulbs flashed, "I'm the country boy who married the girl who's in this show." Agnes Ash, editor of *Palm Beach Life,* was not smitten with the visiting celebrity. When Elizabeth arrived at a post-performance party, Ash remembered "a great deal of fanfare—and you could just see that she demands a lot of attention and has this way of expecting it. She wasn't very outgoing that evening. She seemed very much under control and self-conscious about her weight. She still looked pretty fat. Her costumes were wonderful, but very stiff and formal. She looked great until you got a side view, and then you could really tell how heavy she was."

On Sundays and Mondays, the Fort Lauderdale theater was dark, and Elizabeth usually rented *Monkey Business,* the same yacht on which Senator Gary Hart's presidential aspirations foundered five years later, when he was caught sailing with girlfriend Donna Rice. (The yacht's owner, Don Soffer, has since renamed it *Miss Aventura.*) She invited Hugh L. Hurd and other cast members to join her. "Every weekend, we would be out in the Keys on a yacht," Hurd reminisced fondly, "and we were eating stone crabs and drinking champagne. She allowed me to take pictures of her any time I wanted to." At one Sunday yacht party Elizabeth and Warner threw, the guests were amazed that Elizabeth, who was drinking lots of champagne, was wearing the square-cut Krupp diamond shipboard. It was big enough to cover her ring finger, knuckle to joint, and Elizabeth referred to it as an "ice cube," played catch with it, and let everyone try it on.

In March 1981 the play moved to Washington for forty-seven performances. Reporters were so anxious to see the slimmed-down Elizabeth that Bufman had to hold a press conference. On opening night at the Kennedy Center, President and Mrs. Reagan and Senator Warner sat together in the same box and visited Elizabeth backstage. On March 30, when Reagan was wounded by would-be assassin John Hinckley, Nancy Reagan noted that "Elizabeth Taylor was in town with *Little Foxes,* and she canceled her show. . . ."

✦ ✦ ✦

When *The Little Foxes* moved to New York in April 1981, Elizabeth, for the trip up from Washington, hired a club car on the Amtrak Metroliner and threw a party on the train for cast and crew. There were fresh flowers, a French accordionist, and a meal catered by Dominique, Elizabeth's favorite Washington restaurateur. He provided champagne, pepper steak, spinach and ice cream—a seemingly unappetizing combination but one of Elizabeth's favorites.

For the next six weeks, Chen Sam booked Elizabeth into 1022 Lexington Avenue at East Seventy-third Street, an English country-style inn, now closed. The owner, Ed Safdie, described the lodgings as a place "for people who wanted to get away from photographers and the press."

When the cast and crew moved to New York's Martin Beck Theatre, on West Forty-fifth Street off Broadway, Bufman reportedly spent more than $20,000 redecorating Elizabeth's second-floor dressing room in her favorite lavender, adding floor-to-ceiling mirrors, ankle-deep white shag rugs, a handsome bar, and—because she had wanted a live pet in the dressing room—a $400 aquarium filled with lavender tropical fish. By then Elizabeth was snapping at anyone who referred to her weight loss: "Does it matter what Maureen Stapleton weighs? What does it matter what *I* weigh?"

In an article in *Film Comment* Pendleton remembered that during the New York rehearsals and previews the rest of the cast began to feel isolated from Taylor, and "things got strange for a while. During our week of previews, the audiences were so hysterical in their approval and excitement that it pulled [Elizabeth's] performance, or at least the comic parts of it, out of shape a little. We were unable to counterbalance this by rehearsing during the day because Elizabeth was sick with something her doctors were afraid might turn into the kind of pneumonia that had nearly killed her twenty years before."

Elizabeth was ill for a week during previews with fever and bronchitis. In mid-May, she fainted in her dressing room before a performance and was hospitalized for nine days with a respiratory infection and torn rib cartilage, caused by coughing. Also in mid-May, after the Tony nominees' party at Sardi's, she suffered a third bout of flu. In July, she bruised her hip in a fall in her hotel room. During *The Little Foxes'* ten-week run, she missed at least eleven performances, reportedly costing the insurance carrier $330,000 in claims. When she did appear, Pendleton thought her performances were uneven, and some "a little wild."

Things could be wild outside the theater as well. One day Elizabeth went into Bloomingdale's to pick up a lipstick. Word of her presence quickly spread, and soon she was surrounded by a mob. The police had to be called to get her safely out of the store. In August, firemen making a routine inspection at a West Forty-fifth Street restaurant had to rescue Elizabeth, Senator Warner, and a bodyguard from a crush of about a hundred autograph seekers outside the Martin Beck Theatre. "It looked like a riot scene," the fire company's lieutenant said. "I think my dog almost had cardiac arrest," Elizabeth commented.

Lillian Hellman's favorite Regina had been Tallulah Bankhead. Although Hellman was now seventy-three and badly needed a revival of her play to boost both her bank account and her reputation, she had mixed feelings about Taylor. She insisted on calling Elizabeth "Lizzie," even after Elizabeth asked her not to, and threw a public tantrum at a cast dinner at Jim McMullen's, a New York restaurant, because she thought Elizabeth wanted to bar her from rehearsals.

The Little Foxes opened in New York on May 7, 1981. On opening night, Bufman presented Elizabeth with a three-quarter carat diamond, reputedly "the world's smallest perfect diamond," and a six-inch, solid-gold star for her dressing-room door. She presented him with an 18-karat-gold Cartier watch, inscribed "To Zev, with love and thanks, from Your Fox, May 7, 1981." To every member of the company, she gave a gold fox-head pin with emerald eyes. Bufman's closing-night present to Elizabeth was a snow-white Norwegian fox cape, with two birds made of blue and purple bugle beads kissing on the back. Elizabeth gave Austin Pendleton and his wife a king-sized Craftmatic bed, which has a mattress that can be moved up or down by remote control.

Friends and family turned out for the opening and the party afterward at Xenon, the now-defunct fashionable discotheque. In the audience were Senator Warner, Elizabeth's mother, Maria Burton, Liza Todd, Michael Wilding, Liza Minnelli, Shirley MacLaine, Ann Miller, Joan Fontaine, Halston, and Bill Blass. Sara Taylor reminded reporters that she had opened on Broadway in a play called *The Fool* sixty years before. Pendleton recalled that Martha Graham and Joanne Woodward sent Elizabeth congratulatory letters. Halston called the Xenon party "uplifting, a tribute to Elizabeth's success, and also something of a drunken brawl."

After the performance, crowds, hoping for a glimpse of Taylor, thronged outside Sardi's, the watering hole where actors traditionally go on opening night to wait for the reviews. *New York* magazine's tart-tongued John Simon observed, "At forty-nine, Miss Taylor is not yet ready for the legitimate theatre." To audiences, however, Simon and other critics missed the point, which was seeing Elizabeth Taylor—live. The notices were also irrelevant to Elizabeth. During curtain calls, hand in hand with a mollified Hellman, she said, "I was overwhelmed by waves of love, which nourished me long after the curtain fell."

Besides the public adulation, Elizabeth also was nourished by a Tony nomination for Best Actress and by a box-office smash. She had made more than $1.5 million for only nine months' work. As *The Little Foxes* moved its successful run to Bufman's theaters in New Orleans and Los Angeles, she and Bufman formed the Elizabeth Taylor Repertory Company, their joint partnership. They talked of *The Little Foxes* moving to London, and even the Soviet Union. Meanwhile, Bufman was to sign other important stars to join Elizabeth in limited-run stage productions in New York, Washington, and Los Angeles. These would be filmed for cable and video. One ticket, priced at $99, would be good for the new company's first three productions, including *The Little Foxes.*

Bufman worked hard to satisfy Elizabeth's need for regular incentives to ensure that she kept showing up promptly at curtain time. During the New York run he presented Elizabeth with a handsome German Shepherd, and she gave his assistant a pedigreed Shih Tzu, which arrived with a lavender bow and leash. Since Senator Warner was able to join his wife only for weekends at the Carlyle Hotel, Bufman was her frequent escort after performances. Rumors of a Taylor-Bufman romance flourished in the tabloids, and were dismissed as "nonsense" by Chen Sam as well as by a Warner spokesman and Bufman himself. He became her escort, he said, because he "talked Elizabeth into doing the show" and because of "the demands the role places on her and the necessity she has to rest and relax." Richard Burton was convinced Elizabeth was sleeping with Bufman and felt sorry for him.

Felice Quinto, the backstage photographer for *The Little Foxes,* caught Taylor kissing prince Rainier of Monaco. According to Quinto, Rainier had come backstage with Princess Grace and somehow left Grace behind to have a conversation with Taylor. Suddenly, Rainier, who Quinto claimed was "worse than John F. Kennedy," dragged Elizabeth into a dark corner, and they kissed—"more than just kissing in a friendly manner"—for three or four minutes. "They were literally all over each other," Quinto said, "and they looked like very good friends."

Another of Elizabeth's visitors backstage was Natalie Wood, who dropped by shortly before she died. Quinto also saw Lauren Bacall arrive backstage and gape at Elizabeth's enormous diamond. "You've got to be kidding," Quinto heard Bacall say. When Elizabeth went onstage, she would take off her ring and hand it to her dresser, who would wear it backstage and return it to the star after the performance.

To writer Charlotte Chandler, Maureen Stapleton recounted one of the evenings the "two pistols" spent together in New York. During *The Little Foxes'* run, Elizabeth had given Maureen a diamond chain; in return, Maureen had given her a garnet pin that had belonged to her own mother. Still, Maureen felt stumped for a proper present: as she told Chandler, "I mean, what do you give to someone who has everything?" Maureen heard about a woman who made "the most beautiful portrait puppets." She ordered one for Elizabeth by phone: "I figured she would enjoy it."

When the doll was delivered, "I couldn't believe my eyes. I never saw anything so ugly. It was huge and deformed and . . . ugh!" Maureen didn't plan on showing it to Elizabeth, but some friends persuaded her that Elizabeth would laugh. Maureen brought the doll to the Helmsley Palace, where Elizabeth was staying on the fifty-third floor. Fearful of heights, Maureen drank a whole bottle of champagne "to get my courage up." When she arrived, Elizabeth had "a bottle of Dom Perignon waiting for me.

"Drinking it, I got up my courage to show her the puppet. . . . And Elizabeth said, 'Who is it?' I said, 'It's you.' It was really ugly. I'd forgotten how ugly it was. . . . [Elizabeth] wasn't laughing. She said, 'We'll burn it.' But first she looked at my dress and said, 'What's that you're wearing? You can't wear that thing,' and she brought out this great jeweled brown caftan and made me take off my dress and put it on. I didn't understand why what I was wearing wasn't good enough for burning a puppet.

"She said some other people were coming. Just then the phone rang announcing them, and they arrived at the door. It was a little surprise for me—Joel McCrea. Elizabeth had invited him and his wife, Frances Dee.

"We had some more of the champagne; then Elizabeth tried to burn the puppet, but it wouldn't burn. So she called and asked the hotel to send someone up to help us burn the puppet. Well, they sent a lot of [security] people and a special fireman and fire extinguisher. We all went up on the roof, and Elizabeth burned this ugly puppet of herself. It was really big.

"Then we went downstairs, and Joel McCrea and his wife said they had to leave. I guess they really did after all that. I'm sure he thought I was crazy."

In September 1981, *The Little Foxes* moved to Bufman's New Orleans theater, the Saenger, for a two-week run. Hugh L. Hurd noted that Elizabeth was struck by the way that "theater is like a family, not like the movies," where friends working on the same set may never meet. Elizabeth would hug and kiss everyone in the company: "She wants to be loved," Hurd said. "She really is a lonely woman." When the company traveled together, she would be checked in in first class but never sat there. "Most of the trip she sat behind me. One time the pilot came back and asked her what was wrong with first class. She said, 'My family is not sitting up there.' That's how she was. So we all sort of fell in love with this woman."

At a black-tie party in a big restaurant in New Orleans, Hurd and the three other black actors in the company found themselves seated in the kitchen "with the electricians," while the white actors sat in the main dining room. Furious, Hurd started to walk out. Chen Sam came up and asked him, "Where are you going?" Hurd said, "I'm leaving. Everyone [in the company] knows I'm here, and I'm not going to be sitting [with them]." Chen Sam told him, "Don't go anyplace," and she went to tell Elizabeth what was going on. Elizabeth made the reporters sitting around her move and had the black actors join her. She told Hurd, "I don't need them here. I don't even want to see them. I want to make damn sure that you don't go anyplace. Sit right there."

Rivet Hedderel, a local hairdresser, was doing Taylor's wigs during the run of *The Little Foxes.* Hedderel confirmed Patricia Seaton's observation that Elizabeth "hasn't got a lot of hair. Over the years, with all the hairstyling and dying and everything, it's very, very thin. She has to wear a wig."

By mid-September, *The Little Foxes* had arrived for a ten-week run in Los Angeles, where Elizabeth felt very much at home. At the opening-night party at Chasen's, Bufman said, "The opening-night party in New York was crazy. People do tend to get a bit rowdy around Liz." He said she picked Chasen's because "she wanted to spend a nice, quiet evening with her close buddies," including Roddy McDowall, the Sammy Davises, Governor Jerry Brown, and the Armand Hammers. Sara Taylor, who arrived from her Palm Springs home, talked of Elizabeth visiting her with the children and playing charades "until four in the morning." Maureen Stapleton added to the family atmosphere by announcing, "I have made my decision. *I* want to marry Elizabeth Taylor." Rock Hudson, a close friend of Elizabeth's since they had costarred in *Giant* in 1956, planned to throw a big party for Taylor and Stapleton, but by the time the two got to town, he was having major heart surgery, a triple bypass.

During the play's Los Angeles run, the Filmex Society of Los Angeles invited Elizabeth's old rival Bette Davis to present Elizabeth with an award. Onstage at the tribute, Davis paused meaningfully. "May one little fox present another little fox the Filmex Award?" Elizabeth, in diamonds and a violet gown, told the audience, "I was listening backstage, and you know, I kept thinking I was *dead.* I've never been so eulogized in my life. . . ."

While *The Little Foxes* was still in Los Angeles, top realtor Elaine Young, who had been Gig Young's second wife, got a call from Bufman, who said, "I have a client for you. Elizabeth Taylor needs [to rent] a house for three months." He and Young found Elizabeth a house on Stone Canyon in Bel Air. Then Young got another call, saying that now Elizabeth needed to buy a house. Taylor only had a single week to house-hunt, because she was separating from Senator Warner.

Young picked up Elizabeth and her companion, thirty-four-year-old actor Tony Geary, a regular on Elizabeth's favorite soap opera, *General Hospital.* The "one-woman soap opera" made a special guest appearance in five episodes of *General Hospital* in November 1981. Elizabeth was "all over" Geary, Young remembered, and "he was being really nice to her, but I don't see how he put up with it. There was something very fragile, almost sad, about her that day."

Young had three houses set to show Elizabeth. She was very surprised when, after looking at the first house, located at 700 Nimes Road in Bel Air, Elizabeth said, "This is it." In thirty-two years in business, Young had had only one other client, Sylvester Stallone, make a decision so quickly. Elizabeth "was frightened about [a killer like Charles] Manson," Young recalled. "She wanted to be sure she had total security. It was her dream house. It was moody and romantic," a spacious brick-and-shingle, California-rustic house built into a hillside, with many tall windows. Once owned by Nancy Sinatra Sr., the house cost Elizabeth $2 million. Young called it "ahead of its time. It was white and light and young, and [it had] the most romantic master bedroom and bathroom I have ever seen. The entire upstairs is master bedroom and bath, with cathedral ceilings." Young added that the house is "pretty simple, actually not that fancy. Not the type you would think a movie star like Elizabeth Taylor would like."

Elizabeth was photographed for *Life* in the elegant paneled bathtub of her new home, surrounded by greenery and her Lhasa apsos, Reggie and Elsa. From the bedroom windows, Elizabeth noted, "I can look out on the lovely garden, where one tree in particular inspires me if I am down. It has an exotic, magical quality, like the woods that come alive in *The Wizard of Oz.*"

On December 21, 1981, Elizabeth and John Warner formally announced that they had separated. On Christmas Eve in Los Angeles, she reportedly was hospitalized overnight with chest pains. She spent a great deal of time on the phone with Burton. "I can't live without her," he confessed. The previous April, he had had to withdraw from *Camelot* and had undergone marathon back surgery. He was in constant pain, and his health was rapidly deteriorating after years of heavy drinking. Elizabeth wanted to play Lady MacBeth, but Burton and other friends advised against it. In January 1982 she sparked rumors of a reconciliation with Warner by attending the gala Washington premiere of *Genocide,* a documentary about the Holocaust which she and Orson Welles narrated. Her escort was Simon Wiesenthal himself. For her contribution to the film, Elizabeth received the first Wiesenthal Humanitarian Award from the Simon Wiesenthal Center for Holocaust Studies in Los Angeles, where she was a member of the board of trustees.

In February 1982, Elizabeth arrived in London to appear in *The Little Foxes.* She told the press, "I will never marry again. Please don't ask me why. I'm a lady on the loose. I won't be seeing Richard Burton." Burton—now separated, like Elizabeth herself—was in London to read the part of the narrator in fellow Welshman Dylan Thomas's *Under Milk Wood.* Elizabeth had invited him to her fiftieth birthday party, which Bufman was throwing for her.

The Little Foxes' costs were soaring; grosses were down. Bufman had had to buy out Lillian Hellman, paying her a rumored $1 million for the rights to produce the play in London. And Bufman told journalist Sharon Churcher, Elizabeth's demands were a contributing factor: "What she wants is defined clearly in the contract when you make a deal with her, and she expects really big gifts." In London, Bufman was obliged to rent Elizabeth, her hairdresser, her dresser, her bodyguard, and Chen Sam a town house, at 22 Cheyne Walk in Chelsea, and to have it redecorated in lavender. Because her salary would be substantially less than in the United States, he bought her a $135,000 Rolls-Royce. He flew stone crabs to London for her from a Miami Beach restaurant. This time, her two dressing rooms and the marquee of the Victoria Palace, the ornate West End theater built like a Byzantine church, where *The Little Foxes* was staged, had been painted lavender in her honor.

"She is always saying that Richard never made it in the West End," Bufman said. "She really does desperately want to have a success here. She feels it is her first home."

On February 27, 1982, all of Elizabeth's children, Rudolf Nureyev, Tony Bennett, Ringo Starr, and other guests came to Elizabeth's birthday party at Legends, a trendy London restaurant. Baz Bamigboye, the entertainment editor of the *London Daily Mail,* remembered that everyone was very drunk and was speculating over whether Burton would turn up. Bamigboye was persuaded to dress up as a bellboy and deliver a "singing telegram." Elizabeth recognized him, and he sang "I Get a Kick Out of You." Bamigboye recalled that Burton arrived very late, looking "physically very run down. He looked quite emaciated," and he was "pretty drunk." For about four hours Burton talked of "his great love for Taylor. He said that they were linked, the way it is when a woman gives birth to a child. You're entwined. That's what he said: 'Elizabeth Taylor? Yeah, she came from my loins.' There were tears in his eyes, and I think he realized that he probably missed her a lot."

After dancing the last dance cheek to cheek with Elizabeth, Burton drove her home to Cheyne Walk in his Daimler and spent several hours alone with her, gossiping, talking about working together again, and, Burton implied, making love. Later, he described their intimacies to a reporter: "Then Elizabeth looked at me and said, 'Hey, buster—you're thin. Aren't you going to kiss me? I took her in my arms and kissed her. After we kissed, she said, 'I can't believe it all happened with us.' And I pulled her down on the couch—just like that. For old times' sake." Another press account said that at one point Elizabeth apparently kicked him and called him "a Welsh phony." At 7:00 A.M. the next morning, Burton returned to his hotel because he had "to rehearse early," and was intercepted by reporters. In a series of interviews, he confessed that he still loved Elizabeth, calling her "a kind of poem. . . . We're perfectly matched because we don't know what the other is talking about. But oh, yes, I love Elizabeth. I bred her in my bones." But Burton also admitted that he wanted to reconcile with his estranged wife, Suzy Hunt: "I love them both, dammit." And he added, "I still cannot firmly believe that [Elizabeth] can act in a play."

That night, Elizabeth tried another ploy to win him back. While Burton was reading onstage at the Duke of York Theatre, Elizabeth made a sudden surprise appearance behind him, wearing jeans and a sweater. She curtsied and threw a kiss to the packed house, then turned to Burton and said softly in Welsh, "I love you."

"Say it again, my petal!" Burton exclaimed. "Say it louder!"

She obliged. The crowd roared. Burton tried to kiss her as she passed him. But because he had lost the sight in his right eye, he missed her—and his place in his script.

He had to tell the audience, "I've got the wrong page. Excuse me—I'm distracted."

After his performance, Burton and Taylor were seen leaving the theater hand in hand. They drove off in her chocolate-colored Rolls. Reportedly, he gave her a portrait of Dylan Thomas, signed: "Love, Richard."

But Burton told the press, "The best way for Elizabeth and myself to keep each other together is to be apart." He even said she had begged him to remarry her; she denied it. "I'm involved with Elizabeth as an ex-wife, a mother, and as a legend," Burton tried to explain. "She is an erotic legend—a black-haired dwarf with a big stomach and overflowing breasts." Within a few weeks, however, he *was* talking marriage—to a new girlfriend, Sally Hay, a thirty-four-year old production assistant whom he had met while making a television film about composer Richard Wagner. Hay looked after him devotedly, as had his first wife, Sybil Burton Christopher. Some observers thought that Sally—slim, birdlike, and very silent—physically resembled Sybil. Screenwriter Jonathan Gems, who worked on Burton's last film, an adaptation of George Orwell's *1984,* remembered Sally as nice but dull, keeping Burton's appointments straight for him. "Jumble [secondhand] sales, that was the kind of thing she could get excited about."

The London opening of *The Little Foxes* seemed anticlimactic after the new Taylor-Burton drama. Elizabeth was putting on weight again, telling the press she was not worried about it because Warner (from whom she was separated) "likes me the way I am." Sarah Taylor came to opening night, reminding anyone who would listen that she had appeared on the London stage sixty-five years before. The critics were not kind: One said Elizabeth had made "an entrance worthy of Miss Piggy, trailing mauve lingerie." Another critic described her voice as "a needle screeching across an old 78 record." A third called her Regina no more threatening than "a pink blancmange." And another writer pointed out that the Victoria Palace's previous history as a vaudeville theater was entirely fitting.

But as in New York, Elizabeth was the public's darling. When she arrived at the London Palladium for a press conference, hundreds of fans cheered, and one presented her with an orchid. She met Princess Michael of Kent at a private supper and had dinner with Princess Margaret at Kensington Palace.

Because of Elizabeth's Christmas Eve hospitalization, Lloyd's of London issued a million-pound insurance policy against her not completing the sixteen-week run. Elizabeth sprained her ankle and played some performances from a wheelchair. Her backstage visitors included Princess Diana, heavily pregnant with her first child. Even Richard

Burton and Sally Hay came to *The Little Foxes* in July, its last month. Backstage later, Hay hovered, keeping an eye on Burton and Taylor. Elizabeth said to Burton, "What do you say to having some fun and making a pile of money on Broadway?" By September, she announced that Bufman would bring her and Burton to Broadway, Washington, and Los Angeles in *Private Lives,* Noël Coward's comedy about a long-divorced couple with a yen for each other.

Rehearsals for *Private Lives* were to start in March 1983. In the fall of 1982, Elizabeth went to Toronto to film *Between Friends,* a television movie with Carol Burnett about two middle-aged divorcées. In a spectacular example of miscasting, Burnett plays the man-eater; Taylor, the prude. The two actresses became close, called each other "CB" and "ET," and watched soaps together.

Actress Sharon Nobel was an extra on the *Between Friends* shoot for about four days. She found that she and one other actress were the only extras who were not "over sixty." To film a party scene, all the extras were told to wear black and "a neutral sort of flesh-colored lipstick." A makeup man applied red lipstick to the red-haired Nobel, only to be told, "Get it off her; nobody but Elizabeth wears red." As usual, Elizabeth did her own makeup.

On the set, Nobel said, "I suddenly discovered why everybody was dressed in black. Because Elizabeth was dressed in crimson, blood crimson. I think it was a Halston, a red chiffon. It was gorgeous, and she looked wonderful, even with the weight on. I have always liked her because she pays her own way, she drinks like a sailor and swears like a sailor. But the instant they called, 'Cut!' Elizabeth would turn her back, and there was no communication."

In October 1982, Taylor announced that she was suing the ABC television network. ABC was planning a miniseries, an unauthorized biography based on the life and times of Elizabeth Taylor. The visual biography was supposed to resemble recent "docudramas" about Jacqueline Kennedy Onassis, Princess Grace of Monaco, Gloria Vanderbilt, Prince Charles, Princess Diana, and other celebrities. Christina

Ferrare (former wife of automobile manufacturer John DeLorean) was supposed to play Elizabeth Taylor.

The ABC project distressed Taylor because she believed that although she was a celebrity, she owned all rights to both her public and private image. If a screenwriter working for ABC were to compose dialogue, for example, between Taylor and Burton, she believed that such dialogue would be not only potentially libelous but certainly an invasion of her privacy. The other, unspoken reason that Taylor wanted to stop the miniseries was that if she controlled the rights, she could make a considerable amount of money. Under the circumstances, she would make nothing.

Threatened by Taylor's lawsuit, ABC finally scrapped the project. Taylor held a press conference to proclaim her victory.

By November 1982, Elizabeth had been divorced from John Warner and had taken up with an unlikely consort, a wealthy, recently divorced, fifty-five-year-old Mexican lawyer and father of two young children. Politically well connected, quiet, and gentlemanly, he came from a distinguished and conservative family from Guadalajara who had no use for Elizabeth. His full name was Licenciado Victor Gonzalez Luna. The press had a field day with the fact that he was generally known as Victor Luna—the implication being that he was a Luna-tic to be involved with Elizabeth Taylor. They had met at a memorial for a mutual friend in Puerto Vallarta, where Luna had supervised the Burtons' real estate and oversaw his family's business. Hairdresser Zak Taylor and other members of Elizabeth's retinue were convinced that Luna was eager for the publicity of being seen with Elizabeth, much as John Warner had been.

Zak Taylor had had the idea to have Elizabeth go entirely blond ("she looked good blond because she was tan and she had freckles and her eyes are light") after she had begun bleaching it herself on the beach while visiting Luna in Mexico. At one point, "it all fell out. To her it was hysterical."

In December 1982, announcing that "I want to create peace between Israel and Jordan, Elizabeth set out for Israel on a ten-day peace mission with Victor Luna in tow. Her tour organizer, Phil Blazer, publisher of the Los Angeles–based newspaper *Israel Today,* had arranged similar trips for the Reverend Jesse Jackson, Jane Fonda, and Sammy Davis Jr. Elizabeth's trip had originally been planned for September so that she could attend Lebanese president Bashir Gemayel's inauguration. But on September 14, Gemayel was assassinated, and Princess Grace of Monaco was killed in a car accident. Elizabeth "was hysterical that day," said Blazer, "so we had to postpone the trip for a while." Taylor was supposed to meet Israeli prime minister Menachem Begin and possibly a high-level Lebanese official.

In Israel, Elizabeth did meet Begin, Israel defense minister Ariel Sharon, and the leader of the Christian militia in southern Lebanon, and went to the women's side of the Wailing Wall. She was photographed visiting an orphanage, bruised and bandaged, reportedly as the result of injuries, including torn ligaments in her left leg, sustained in a car accident. Blazer said that she had met Begin wearing a neck brace.

In May 1983, Elizabeth gave *New York* magazine her own voluble account of the accident:

> There we were, in torrential rains, crossing a deep ditch, when suddenly a car came up directly behind us and smacked into the stretch limo the five of us were riding in. I went hurling through the air, nothing to stop me, landing with all my weight against the dashboard, my calf swelling about five inches in front of me—I saw it just pop out! And a hematoma, an emormous hematoma, came out on my back, and there was blood spurting everywhere. Look at this leg of mine. It's still bruised, it still is so painful. And I couldn't think about anything but the sound of the metal screaming against the metal, and the terrible moaning. The first thing I heard when I found myself on the floor was all these excruciating moans and screams, and someone who was with us had a piece of metal miss his eye socket by a hair, and there we all were, stumbling

> and bloody—it was so awful, because we were in about five feet of water in the ditch. And we were on our way to Ariel Sharon's farm [in the Negev], just stuck there. Fortunately an Arab driver happened along and gave us a ride. He didn't know who we were or what we were doing there. But the *irony* of us dragging into Sharon's farm looking like these bloody refugees. And Sharon put ice packs on all of us and was terribly concerned, getting out blankets, calling the doctors, but what was amazing was that nobody was worried about themselves, everyone just kept saying to each other, "Are you all right?" One man with broken ribs started massaging my hematoma, and I just had to say to him, "Stop it. You'll hurt yourself." That's how much we cared.

In May, *Private Lives* sold out a limited run in Boston, where Burton and Taylor were photographed with Joan Kennedy, and then moved to New York's Lunt-Fontanne Theatre, where Burton had appeared in his 1964 *Hamlet.* This time in New York, Elizabeth stayed in her friend Rock Hudson's apartment on Central Park West. Since Hudson was very tall—six feet four inches—many of his furnishings and fixtures were apparently out of Elizabeth's reach. On a white bathroom stool she scrawled a joke in bright pink lipstick: "Elizabeth Taylor stood here. She had to because she couldn't reach the sink."

Bufman gave Taylor three gold-and-diamond bracelets and a 100-gallon aquarium for her lavender dressing room. The fish, changed daily for variety, cost as much as $100 apiece. The menagerie included two large horseshoe crabs, particular favorites of Elizabeth's. Bufman's decorator had had only eight days to overhaul Taylor and Burton's dressing rooms but did so well that the results were featured in *Architectural Digest.* One of Burton's red felt walls was hung with a Welsh flag. Taylor had shirred chintz panels, lavender towels, a purple mohair throw, and lavender and white silk flowers. A fan sent her a handmade lavender-fabric tissue box cover, shaped like a house.

During previews, crowds filled West Forty-sixth Street to cheer Taylor and Burton. Taylor often arrived with Alvin, a parrot she had bought in Los Angeles in 1980, perched on her shoulder. A local television station conducted a phone-in poll: Should Burton and Taylor marry a third time? Seventy-three percent of viewers answered yes.

Reviews, however, were devastating. Both Burton, fifty-seven, and Taylor, fifty-one, were too old for their parts, and comedy had never been Burton's forte. There was no chemistry between the two stars. But Taylor's performance and appearance—dressed in a low-backed, blue-beaded gown, she had "dorsal cleavage" in the first act—caught most of the blame. James Brady compared Taylor's acting to "the Hitler diaries—you don't believe it, but you gotta look!" Frank Rich remarked in the *New York Times* that both Taylor and Burton looked "whipped and depressed." Even in the second act, wrote Rich, when Burton tweaked Taylor's breast in a bit of horseplay, "she responds as if under anesthesia."

According to Ronald Munchnick, manager for director Milton Katselas, who left the show in Boston after a falling-out with Taylor: "Theoni Aldridge, as good a costume designer as she is, couldn't hide her weight, and Taylor refused to lose weight for the role." Taylor now weighed 167 pounds. One member of the audience said that in one scene Taylor sat with her legs spread. "She had sex appeal, no question."

After pretty much playing herself in *The Little Foxes,* "Taylor was not prepared to stretch," Ronald Munchnick said. "Playing high comedy is very difficult, and it was very hard for her to sustain high comedy eight times a week." Baz Bamigboye saw *Private Lives* in Boston and said that in one scene in the second act, Taylor hit Burton with a pillow. "Christ! I saw the feathers coming out of that pillow, she him so hard!" Audiences happily applauded Coward's lines that had become Taylor-Burton double entendres, like Taylor's Amanda saying, "Marriage scares me, really."

Bufman had taken out $3.25 million in coverage from Lloyd's of London against Taylor and Burton's absences—a record breaker.

Bufman told journalist Sharon Churcher that under Sally Hay's care—she was always backstage—Burton kept his promise to Bufman not to drink during *Private Lives.* But Burton's journals record that Taylor frequently arrived at rehearsals drunk. The refrigerator in her dressing room held a bottle of Jack Daniels. Taylor canceled twenty performances because of various ailments, including laryngitis, bronchitis, dizziness, fatigue, and conjunctivitis (pinkeye). An exasperated Lloyd's of London underwriter said she probably had become uninsurable. Bufman told Churcher, "It was all booze, huge amounts of it. That and the painkillers."

Taylor's public was losing patience. "I think she gets sick too often, on purpose," said one disappointed theatergoer. "Imagine if she had done this before one of her weddings," complained another. Demands for refunds and exchanges were so heavy that Bufman decided to shorten the New York engagement.

During the *Private Lives* run Taylor was asked to pose for one of Blackglama's ads, the series with the slogan "What becomes a legend most?" She apparently insisted on a free full-length coat—and then, according to Daphne Davis, author and former entertainment editor of *Cue,* the shoot took eight hours "because she sat in the dressing room doing nothing but taking drugs and drinking champagne."

In early July, during one of Taylor's absences from *Private Lives,* Burton and Sally Hay flew to Las Vegas and got married. Reporters clamored for Elizabeth's reaction. "I'm thrilled and delighted for both Richard and Sally," she said. "I've known all along they would be married and happy together." Soon thereafter she announced her own engagement to Victor Luna. But when she collapsed several days later with another respiratory infection, speculation raged as to whether she was prostrate with depression over Burton's new marriage.

Later, she told producer-director Patti Taylor that she had been very depressed and that doing the play with Burton was very difficult for her. Patti Taylor surmised that Elizabeth "was the one who pursued Richard Burton rather than vice versa, that she was a destructive force in his life."

Burton himself was depressed because he could not back out of his contractual obligations to *Private Lives* and Elizabeth to work with director John Huston. During the play's second month in New York, Huston had offered Burton the starring role in a film adaptation of Malcolm Lowry's *Under the Volcano.* The role eventually went to Albert Finney. Burton also lost what turned out to be his last opportunity to play Shakespeare again, in a production of *The Tempest,* directed by his old friend Anthony Quayle. Quayle was convinced that *Private Lives* finished Burton, robbing him of the little self-assurance he had left.

Elizabeth carried Alvin the parrot onstage during the last two performances in New York, possibly as a jibe at Burton. *Private Lives* limped on to Philadelphia, Washington, Chicago, and Los Angeles. In Philadelphia, Elizabeth threw an engagement party for herself and Luna and showed off an impressive diamond-and-sapphire ring from Cartier. But the party ended without her announcing a wedding date.

In Los Angeles, *Private Lives* was booked into the Wilshire Theatre, which had recently been redecorated in burgundy and lavender, including the dressing rooms. Elizabeth thought that the theater's color scheme had been chosen in her honor; it was, in fact, coincidental.

In L'Hermitage, a Los Angeles hotel, travel agent Didi Drew encountered Taylor, Burton, and singer Neil Diamond in the elevator. "By mistake she stepped on the dog," Drew recalled. "The dog was like the size of your handbag. [Burton] yelled at her, right in the elevator. He didn't care who was there. He said, 'Can't you watch where you're going, Fatty?'"

After each night's performance, Taylor and Burton went out with separate groups, seldom socializing together. Audiences lost interest, and the play finally closed in early November 1983.

Zak Taylor had been doing Elizabeth's wigs for the run of *Private Lives* in Los Angeles. Before and after the play closed, he had dinner frequently at her house with Rock Hudson and Carol Burnett. The foursome played Scrabble and other word games and laughed so hard that Zak "had to leave the table four times, crying." He and his friends also would raid Elizabeth's fur closet: "It's about ten, twelve feet. All furs. All the boys used to play dress-up, put on the furs and walk around in them. I used to wear her diamond ring a lot.

"She couldn't smoke grass. She makes the best marijuana brownies. The best."

But dinner was not usually served until 11:00 P.M. because of Elizabeth's drinking. Zak said she once decided to stop drinking "by not having a drink until 6:00 P.M. She would pass out after dinner and wake up at 3:00 A.M., stoned. No wonder she got fat." Zak would put her to bed and stay over to do her hair in the morning and "get her dressed right.

"I've always told her her biggest problem is people 'yes' her to death. Because she's Elizabeth Taylor. That's probably how she got into the terrible problem with the drugs and the drinking. If you're just sitting around with Elizabeth, she says, 'You know what? I've got to tell you. Pass me my tummy pills. Would you make me a Jack Daniels? With nine cubes of ice.' That was very good. 'With at least nine cubes of ice.' Five minutes later: 'You know, I've got a headache. I need a headache pill.' Well, who's gonna say no?" Zak Taylor said he had seen one of Elizabeth's doctors "handing her coke.

"She was living in a world without day or night. What does a woman like that do, especially if you're not working? How often do films come up? In between, what's a person supposed to do with her life?

"There were scary nights at her house when we thought she was dying, where she'd slip into these states from all the drugs. It would be like hyperventilating. The drugs would stop her breathing. We'd have to call the doctor."

At least one of Elizabeth's longtime doctors, Dr. Rex Kennamer, who was also Rock Hudson's physician, apparently refused to continue treating her. Kennamer told the present author that he had "never hesitated" to warn her about addictive medications. "Nobody questions that she has a terrible back. You compound that with the fact that obviously she's an addictive personality . . . I think there are times doctors just have to say, 'I have to walk away.'"

In December 1983, Elizabeth Taylor finally collapsed, emotionally and physically. After family and friends visited her in the hospital and pleaded with her, she entered the Betty Ford Clinic at Rancho Mirage, California, to recover from drug and alcohol abuse.

To give her support, Victor Luna checked into a nearby Marriott hotel. Photographer Russell Turiak and his partner, Philip Ramey, managed to photograph Elizabeth at Betty Ford, including one of her therapy sessions. (Taylor was the first celebrity to check into Betty Ford, and the clinic's no-photographs policy was not yet strictly enforced.) "It's amazing how [other patients] kissed her ass," Turiak observed. "Somebody was always running to get her a chair, a pillow to sit on," because of her bad back.

Stewart Granger, never a fan of Elizabeth's, ran into her at a Los Angeles reception for Great Britain's Princess Anne in January 1984, shortly after Elizabeth had emerged from Betty Ford. Granger had not seen her in years.

"I said, 'Liz! How are you?' She was sort of lobotomized. She was looking wonderful, but she wasn't the Elizabeth Taylor I knew. It wasn't the bubbling thing; it was very controlled.

"So I said, 'Darling, how are you? Haven't been in touch; I haven't got your number.'

"And she looked at me and said, 'Jimmy [Granger's nickname] . . . you've always had my number.'

"She was right. She didn't want to see me because I *did* have her number," Granger said, remembering how Elizabeth had treated so many men, especially his friend Michael Wilding. "She knew that I knew that she was a cunt."

Chapter 27

An early casualty of Elizabeth's disintegration during *Private Lives,* before she publicly admitted her problems with drugs and alcohol, was the Elizabeth Taylor Theater Company and her partnership with Zev Bufman. The company was already troubled: Elizabeth had promised Tennessee Williams that her next production with Bufman would be *Sweet Bird of Youth,* in which Taylor would appear as the heroine, an aging Hollywood star. Williams, who not only needed money but demanded great loyalty, had been enraged when Elizabeth had instead done *Private Lives* because Burton was available.

In November 1983, Bufman and Taylor announced that they were parting ways. By the spring of 1984, when Elizabeth, fresh from Betty Ford and another stay at the Spa at Palm-Aire, went on a trip to the Far East with Victor Luna, the only daily reminder of her theatrical career was the gold necklace she wore, with the gold ticket to *The Little Foxes* that Bufman had given her.

Photographers Russell Turiak and Philip Ramey, who had snapped Taylor at Betty Ford, were determined to follow Taylor and Luna throughout the trip. The two photographers clowned constantly, billing themselves in chorus as "the Exclusive Brothers." Taylor "laughed at everything we did after a while," Turiak recalled. Eventually, Elizabeth was so won over that she invited the pair to join her tour of Japan, China, Thailand, and India. Every day, as soon as she saw them, she would present her cheek so that they could kiss her good morning. Turiak described her as "quite a shutterbug," who often took pictures of the Brothers, and as a woman who enjoyed racy jokes and a great bargain. At the Taj Mahal, Turiak noted, Elizabeth knew her gems. "She did like shopping; she did like bargaining. Nobody took her. She bargained for every dollar that she could." Turiak was amazed at her technique in stores. "She'd buy something, and right away [the salespeople] would bring something else out, and they'd say, 'And this? What about this?' And she'd bat her eyes and say, 'Why don't you give that to me?' And they'd hand it right over! It was unbelievable—every time! . . . She was just playing the same game they were playing with her." Turiak said that Elizabeth would tell the patient Luna things like " 'Oh, Victor, I want that elephant,' and he would reply, 'No, Elizabeth, you can't take the elephant home'—in a tone that suggested he was very sorry indeed; he really wanted her to have it."

Turiak added, "[Ramey and I] were never supposed to photograph ET when she was eating or even contemplating food—that is, hitting the sweet shops, which she invariably did every day. She would lick her chops while looking into sweet shops and tell us to go away while she bought a bag of chocolates." Patricia Seaton recalled that when Elizabeth had been in Betty Ford the previous winter, she would have her maid send her Breyers vanilla bean ice cream, and melon balls—Spanish, honeydew, cantaloupe, watermelon—to put on top. Elizabeth had switched to Breyers because it was less fattening than Häagen-Dazs. While at Betty Ford, she also managed to dodge the strenuous water aerobics, even though she later recommended them as part of her weight-loss program in her 1987 book *Elizabeth Takes Off,* about her journey out of addiction and overindulgence to contentment and moderation.

Elizabeth and the long-suffering Luna finished their grand tour at a London pub, where they rendezvoused with Richard Burton and his new wife, Sally. That summer, Elizabeth divided her time between Bel Air and her home in Gstaad, Switzerland, not far from Burton and Hay, who had settled in Céligny to avoid British taxes. In July, Taylor broke off her engagement to Luna. Russell Turiak speculated that Luna simply did not have the financial resources to travel with her constantly and cater to her full-time. Also, he had been obliged to return to his family's business in Guadalajara. "Since we can't be together, we can't get married," Luna told the press, adding that he was disappointed.

Burton was working on his last film, *1984,* in which he played O'Brien, the inquisitor for the state. According to screenwriter Jonathan Gems, Burton would reminisce about Elizabeth "more like a lovesick adolescent than a grown man." Gems said that Sally Hay Burton commented, "He's always doing that." Another observer, the Baroness de Rothschild, told a French television interviewer, "I ran into Richard in the south of France; he was married to [Sally]. When he saw me, he asked me to sit down, and he spoke to me [about Elizabeth Taylor] for a half an hour straight . . . he never forgot Elizabeth." According to Burton's brother, sportscaster Graham Jenkins, who liked Taylor, Burton "was calling Sally, his wife, 'Elizabeth' all the time" in the months before he died. Jenkins said Burton told him that he and Elizabeth spoke on the phone every day.

While appearing in *Private Lives* with Taylor in 1983, Burton had predicted in an interview that he had only five years to live. He had been optimistic: On August 4, 1984, he suffered a cerebral hemorrhage at his home in Céligny and died the next day in hospital, at only fifty-eight years old. At home in Bel Air, Elizabeth fainted when she got the news.

Sally Hay Burton, who had been married to Richard for only thirteen months, asked Taylor not to come to the burial; she felt she could not cope with the attendant media crush that would trail the star. Undeterred, the paparazzi decided to lie in wait and watch around the clock for Taylor. On August 14, before dawn, Taylor, who is used to rising about noon, appeared at Burton's grave in one of Céligny's two small cemeteries. (She had arrived the night before, when she had gone first to the wrong graveyard.) The paparazzi were staked out and immediately began snapping. Taylor's four bodyguards held up multicolored umbrellas to shield her from their lenses. She knelt silently behind this screen for about ten minutes, then walked back to a waiting Mercedes, leaning on her daughter Liza Todd's arm.

On August 19, she went to Burton's home in Pontrhydyfen, Wales, wearing as her only jewelry the Krupp diamond, Burton's gift. (Hairdresser Zak Taylor said she used to tell him, "Imagine a Jewish girl ending up with the Krupp diamond.") Elizabeth had missed the family memorial in the local chapel, where mourners had sung Welsh hymns. Graham Jenkins maintained that while Sally had said that Burton's ex-wives were welcome at the Pontrhydyfen memorial, she had invited Elizabeth too late for her to arrive from Los Angeles in time. Burton's relatives welcomed Elizabeth warmly, putting her up for the night in the two-bed front room at the home of Burton's sister, Hilda, and her husband, Dai. (When Burton and Taylor were married, they had stayed at Hilda and Dai's home together.) Outside the house, a waiting crowd sang a Welsh song, "We'll Keep a Welcome in the Hillside." Elizabeth told Graham Jenkins, "If [Sally and I] had been together at Céligny, I would have been happy to have walked with her hand in hand."

On August 30, wearing a dignified black silk dress and turban, Elizabeth Taylor sat with Burton's family at his London memorial service at the Church of St. Martin's in the Fields on Trafalgar Square. Suzy Hunt, Burton's third wife, also came, as did Sally Hay. According to Baz Bamigboye of the *London Daily Mail,* Taylor was the last to arrive "so she could make the best entry—oh, it was wonderful!" Graham Jenkins said that Sally objected to Elizabeth's being seated with the family and to fellow Welsh actor Emlyn Williams's tribute, which mentioned Taylor several times, but not Sally. Later, Sally told an interviewer: "[Elizabeth] can't face up to the fact that when you've lost someone twice, you really have lost them—and she did."

The previous fall, Elizabeth's old friend Peter Lawford, increasingly ill, had joined her at the Betty Ford Center. But he continued to use drugs during most of his stay. After he left, he went back to drinking as well, and he vacuumed constantly between snorting lines of cocaine in the bathroom. Patricia Seaton Lawford called the clinic and complained that she had sent them Peter Lawford and they had sent her back "a fucking maid who gets high." Elizabeth thought Peter's discovery of housecleaning was hilarious. He thought her newfound sobriety was comic. "You used to have a personality," he teased her. "You used to be interesting."

Elizabeth remained loyal to her difficult friend. Although television movies represent a comedown for a star of Taylor's stature, she continued to make them. In November 1984, she appeared as her old nemesis, gossip columnist Louella Parsons, in *Malice in Wonderland.* Elizabeth tried to help Peter Lawford get back on his feet by securing him a small role in *Malice in Wonderland* as a Hollywood agent. Jane Alexander portrayed Parson's rival, Hedda Hopper. Asked if playing Parsons had changed her view of the press, Elizabeth answered, "No, they are just bitches." Former M-G-M publicist Esme Chandlee said that when the film was broadcast, "everyone in town just laughed. I mean it was so funny, it was a mess." The day Peter Lawford showed up on the set, Patricia Seaton recalled, he was jaundiced. "His eyes were bright yellow. Elizabeth was concerned. She followed him into the bathroom. 'He's not going to make it,' I said to her, meaning he couldn't play [his] role." Indeed, he left the set halfway through his first scene and did not appear in the version that was broadcast.

Roger Wall, then Taylor's secretary, arranged for his mother to visit the set from North Carolina. Taylor asked Frances Wall, who loved to cook, to make dinner for her. Mrs. Wall obliged with everything Taylor wanted—proper high-fat southern cooking: fried chicken, creamed potatoes, corn, green beans, coconut cake.

By this time, Elizabeth was seeing journalist Carl Bernstein, who, with Bob Woodward, had broken the Watergate story when both were with the *Washington Post.* Divorced from writer Nora Ephron, Bernstein was living in New York. Whenever Taylor was visiting New York, she saw Bernstein, who was about a dozen years younger than she.

Taylor was also dating New York entrepreneur Dennis Stein, a nonstop and frequently abrasive joker who was the diametrical opposite of the dignified Victor Luna. Still, Stein was an equally unlikely match for Taylor. Stein "looked like he should be wheeling a cart down the street," Patricia Seaton Lawford recalled. "He had that cheap look." Taylor said she liked Stein because he made her laugh—and he was attractive and unattached. Stein held a well-paid position with tycoon Ronald Perelman, whose holding company, MacAndrews & Forbes, owned Technicolor and later acquired Revlon.

Peter and his wife, Patricia Seaton, spent that Thanksgiving at Elizabeth Taylor's home in Bel Air with Elizabeth, her new beau, her mother, hairdresser José Eber, Roddy McDowall—one of Elizabeth's friends who had persuaded her to admit herself to Betty Ford—and comedian Jackie Gayle, who got along famously with Stein, both reminiscing about New York as they used to know it. Elizabeth was very informal, sporting blue jeans, a burgundy shirt, and cowboy boots. Throughout the dinner, McDowall teased Elizabeth mercilessly: "She's always been so vile." He made fun of her voice, saying she had a laugh "like a fishwife's." She feigned indignation at his comments.

At one point, Stein hit Taylor playfully on the rump. McDowall piped up: "Only Elizabeth Taylor would tolerate being smacked in the ass."

"Up yours," Elizabeth answered.

In the bathroom, Patricia Seaton Lawford found beautiful antique silver hairbrushes and two sets of towels, one with the initials "E.T.B." and the other with "E.T.W." In the bedroom, Patricia was amazed that the only thing Elizabeth pointed out to her was nothing extraordinary—something that looked like a child's rug on the floor, with a design that included two Siamese cats. Elizabeth told her visitor very proudly that she had made it from a kit she had bought. "Isn't it beautiful!" Elizabeth exclaimed. On the mantelpiece were an assortment of stuffed animals. Elizabeth pointed out gifts from Roddy McDowall, Carole Bayer Sager, and other friends.

On another occasion, Patricia Seaton was supposed to meet Elizabeth at her home. Taylor's assistant let Seaton in, and when Elizabeth didn't come down, Seaton went upstairs. There she walked in on Elizabeth and Stein making love. Stein, a hefty man, was on top of Taylor, who was not at her slimmest. Alvin the parrot, who had appeared with Elizabeth in *Private Lives,* was clinging to a window screen, intermittently screeching, "Help me! Help me!"

According to Patricia Seaton, Elizabeth had taught her pet bird this call. Once, when she was staying in a hotel with Alvin, hotel security heard someone in her room shrieking, "Help me! Help me!" Thinking that Elizabeth was being attacked, they entered the room.

To a newly sober Elizabeth, Dennis Stein may have been reassuring because he did not drink, smoke, or take drugs. A tall, heavyset man, Stein, like Elizabeth, had had trouble keeping his weight down. Stein's boss, Ronald Perelman, was then engaged to New York television gossip reporter Claudia Cohen, who, in December, was the first to announce Elizabeth and Stein's whirlwind engagement. Taylor sported another sapphire-and-diamond engagement ring, this one from Stein. Stein's sapphire was 20 carats to Victor Luna's 16.5. "Every time I fall in love, I get married," Elizabeth explained to the press. "My morality prevents me from having adventures. I was brought up in a very puritanical family." Stein also gave Taylor a pair of amethyst, yellow sapphire, and diamond earrings, a mink coat, and a white Pekingese puppy.

In January 1985, Elizabeth and the man who was going to be her eighth husband joined Frank and Barbara Sinatra at President Ronald Reagan's inauguration and were cheered by fans outside Washington's Madison Hotel. But by early February, Elizabeth had changed her mind, dissolving her second engagement in six months. She may have thought Stein was too fond of talking to the press. She gave Stein her customary parting present, a gold watch inscribed: "Forget me not." A year after breaking up with Stein, she told interviewer Dominick Dunne, "Let's just say I almost made a mistake. But I didn't." She added, "I will remarry once more, but *only* once more."

By December 1984, Peter Lawford had become terminally ill. Having missed Richard Burton's final hours, Elizabeth embarked on a new role as companion to the dying. She kept a vigil by Lawford's hospital bed. "I can't abide this hospital fare," he told her. "I would kill for a lobster." The next day, three of Taylor's staff entered Lawford's hospital room with trays, platters, a tablecloth and table setting, and several delectable courses. For the first time in weeks, Peter and Patricia sat at a table and ate a full meal. There was enough food for the hospital staff, and all the nurses on the floor joined them. At the end, the servers presented Peter with a pink box. Inside was a chocolate eclair, his favorite dessert. But by Christmas 1984, when Elizabeth had already left for Gstaad, Lawford was dead.

The morning of Peter's memorial service, Elizabeth called Patricia Seaton and asked if she knew where she could pick up a navy blue pillow case. She carried a pillow for her back, and she wanted to make sure the pillow case matched her outfit. Patricia Seaton was too busy to advise her, but Taylor did show up with a navy blue pillow, wearing a wide navy blue hat, and added her own flower to Peter's relatives' funeral wreath.

By 1985, Taylor was taking painkillers steadily again, and she spent a total of about five and a half months in bed, allegedly with back pain. In March, she began working on a forgettable TV miniseries, *North and South,* about the Civil War. She received $100,000 for one day's work in a role as a madam. Cameraman Don Fauntleroy recalled, "I've never seen producers so paranoid in my entire life. The day she came in was unbelievable. They were starstruck and afraid, and if she said 'Boo!' they would jump." Around this time, Taylor reportedly persuaded Liza Minnelli, another veteran of Betty Ford who had begun drinking again, to return to the clinic. In a Los Angeles nightclub, she allegedly told Minnelli, "I can't just stand by and let you destroy yourself. I owe it to you and to the memory of your mother." Later in the year, there were reports that Taylor herself was falling off the wagon, at least periodically.

Sometime in 1985, Bob Guccione, publisher of *Penthouse* magazine, mulled over Elizabeth Taylor's new health and image ("she was maybe ten pounds overweight, but that's nothing for her") and inquired through Chen Sam whether Taylor would pose in the nude. He offered her "any photographer in the world," including himself, the final choice of photos, and a million dollars for all rights to the photos. Guccione says he met three times with Chen Sam and was assured that Taylor was interested and wanted to meet with him herself. He invited her to come to his house the next time she was in New York. Instead, Taylor asked him to meet with her in "a little apartment with three tiny rooms above a restaurant . . . a very ordinary, dingy, little apartment"—presumably at the inn at 1022 Lexington Avenue.

"At the beginning, she was very affable," Guccione recalled. "I said to her, 'I really look forward to doing these photographs. Have you thought about the way you'd like them done and how you'd like them done—the parts where you would wear clothes. . . . '

"She said, 'The part where I wear clothes? I always wear clothes.'

"I said, 'You know what I mean. You're going to do some dressed pictures, some seminude pictures, and some nude pictures,' and I went into a whole philosophical discussion with her about the importance of her taking her clothes off. I said, 'There are lots of people out there who think you're over the hill. . . . People who have been making jokes about you and using you in their routines will drop dead once they see this.'"

Guccione thought that Taylor would look "a lot better than Joan Collins."

But according to Guccione, Elizabeth looked dumbfounded and told him, "I would never do nudes. . . . I might do a little décolleté, but I'm not taking anything off."

"I said, 'Surely this was explained to you by your manager. This is what we've been talking about. I was led to believe that you would do it.'

"She said, 'No, no.'"

After about a half-hour discussion, Guccione said, "I tell you what. Let's forget about the pictures. Let's just talk about doing an interview."

Elizabeth responded, "Well, that sounds more interesting. I don't have to take my clothes off for that. Of course, the price would be the same, wouldn't it?"

Guccione was flabbergasted: "I said, 'What? Are you saying that you want a million dollars to do an interview for *Penthouse*?' and she said, 'Yes, of course.'

"I said, 'I don't pay anyone for an interview. [We've interviewed] presidents of the United States, Castro, some of the biggest scientists and personalities in the world—no one expects money.'

"She said, 'In that case, forget it.'

"I looked at her for a long while and said, 'I'm terribly sorry, but I've been grossly misled about this, and I beg your pardon,' and I said goodbye to her, and I left. The minute I got outside I said to my bodyguard, 'Can you believe this?'"

In the summer of 1985, another dear friend of Elizabeth's was hospitalized and gravely ill: by August, just a year after Burton's death, Rock Hudson had been diagnosed with AIDS. Elizabeth's last appearance with him had been in *The Mirror Crack'd,* in 1980. She was among the first to visit him in the hospital. Although the medical establishment was not yet completely united about whether the virus could spread through casual contact, Elizabeth hugged and kissed Hudson, now thin and wasted. Meanwhile, Aileen Getty, Elizabeth's daughter-in-law, had been diagnosed as HIV-positive. Having left Christopher Wilding, Getty was staying with Elizabeth. She cried nightly, and Elizabeth held her and comforted her.

Galvanized by Hudson's illness, Elizabeth made her way back onstage, this time in a genuinely heroic role. In September 1985, a month before Hudson died on October 2, she announced the formation of a new organization championing those infected with AIDS. This organization eventually became the American Foundation for AIDS Research (AmFAR), which raises money to support AIDS research and the care of those with AIDS. Now both Taylor's celebrity and her characteristic bluntness had been harnessed to a useful cause—a cause that had often been associated with pariahs.

Some observers thought that Elizabeth was using AIDS in a quest for personal publicity. At an AIDS benefit Elizabeth helped organize two months before Hudson died, Burt Lancaster read a statement of support and appreciation supposedly written by Rock Hudson himself. But by then he was apparently too ill to be aware of the occasion, much less compose a greeting. The late Doris Lilly, an author and gossip columnist for the *New York Post,* could not take Elizabeth's activism seriously. "Elizabeth Taylor has always been part of a cause if it benefited her. Remember when she and Richard [Burton] were going to build a hospital in Africa? They never did it. The moment passed, and it was no longer amusing. . . . At the moment, it seems like a great idea but afterward she's got to have three dresses from Giorgio's. It's so far away, that hospital. She's romantic, Elizabeth." AIDS was still considered "a gay disease," and Doris Lilly thought that Taylor had a rapport with her many gay male friends because "Elizabeth Taylor doesn't have girlfriends, did you ever notice that? It's very unusual that a woman who's in the public eye as much as she has been doesn't have a girlfriend."

Others felt that even if she was involved with AIDS for personal publicity, it didn't matter. "She is a beautiful symbol that someone cared," said author and television talk-show hostess Virginia Graham. "I thank her." Author Steven Gaines concurred: "Elizabeth Taylor saw her boys dying, and I think this was her way of exercising her social conscience about an issue that had really touched her." Journalist Beverly Ecker, who had done volunteer work providing emotional support for people with AIDS, said that Taylor had paid all the bills and secured nurses around the clock for one of Ecker's clients, who was destitute. And Gloria Rodriguez, a public relations staffer at San Francisco General Hospital, watched Taylor visit the AIDS wing twice and boost patients' morale. "She walked around touching them and holding their hands like it was the most natural thing to do, and I couldn't help thinking, Who else is doing this kind of thing? She wore a chocolate-brown leather suit on one visit, and the guys teased her about wearing her best leathers to come see them."

Rock Hudson's memorial was held at his house, under a white tent with rows of chairs. Elizabeth, in navy blue and pearls, arrived fifteen minutes late. (Once, she airily explained her chronic lateness: "It's not that I'm *deliberately* rude or anything. I have no sense of time. I get distracted. I just stop and smell the roses on the way.") Anyone present could make a statement about Hudson. Taylor recalled working with him on *Giant* and laughed about the night they decided to invent a new drink—chocolate martinis or chocolate margaritas. The following spring, some of Hudson's possessions were auctioned at a New York gallery. They included the white bathroom stool with Taylor's inscription from her stay in his New York apartment during *Private Lives:* "E. T. stood here."

By March 1986, Elizabeth was seen frequently in and around Hollywood on the arm of her old friend George Hamilton. They had known each other for years but had never formally dated. The couple occasionally visited the Del Mar Race Track. Elizabeth bought a racehorse, Basic Image, and dressed her jockey in cerise with chartreuse diamonds—the colors she had worn in *National Velvet.* Elizabeth and George also went cruising on Hamilton's yacht, which he moored at Marina del Rey. A health faddist, Hamilton would clear his yacht of all alcohol and cigarettes before Elizabeth came aboard. He attempted to steer her into a healthful regimen. He told her about spas and holistic health centers, several of which she briefly visited. She took up transcendental meditation and spent several weekends at the Maharishi Ayur-Veda retreat in Lancaster, Pennsylvania. She investigated a cryogenics laboratory in California, where bodies are frozen just prior to death, to be prepared for resuscitation decades or even centuries later.

She apparently also underwent plastic surgery. Zsa Zsa Gabor happened to be seated one day in the waiting room of Dr. Frank Kamer, a favorite Hollywood plastic surgeon. "It was getting late," said Zsa Zsa. "The nurses told me the doctor was finishing up on Liz." Elizabeth herself has always vehemently denied having anything more than a chin tuck. In 1988, she told a reporter, "I have not had any suction. I have not had any surgery. The next time somebody asks me that question, I'm going to take all my clothes off. The answer is 'No!'"

Elizabeth certainly appeared more energetic than she had been in years. On May 9, 1986, she testified before a congressional subcommittee on behalf of the effort to release more funding for emergency AIDS care. Later in the month, she joined another old Hollywood friend, Robert Wagner, in another television movie, *There Must Be a Pony,* based on an impressionistic novel by James Kirkwood and co-produced by Wagner's own company. As in *The Mirror Crack'd,* Taylor played a faded movie star working on a comeback with help from a new love, played by Wagner. According to screenwriter Mart Crowley, "There was a dog in the story, and lo, all these many years after *Lassie,* Taylor was working with a dog again. It wasn't a collie, but the dog just wouldn't do what it was supposed to do. Finally, she said, 'This is without a doubt the last time I'll work with a dog!'"

Elizabeth ended 1986 in Gstaad with Hamilton. They denied a possible marriage but did say they planned to work together. They would both appear in *Poker Alice,* a TV movie filmed on location in Tucson, Arizona. Interviewed about her role as an ace poker player in this period western-comedy, Taylor said, "I have been a gambler all my life. That's not surprising, because I am rather compulsive about certain things. It's amazing, really, that I'm not a gambler." She also said, "Eating too much is like drinking too much. . . . I do allow myself to pig out once a week, but I always behave myself the next day."

Arthur Seidelman, director of *Poker Alice,* noted that the temperature in Tucson was unseasonably cold during filming. "In one scene," Seidelman recalled, "Elizabeth had to wear a low-cut, strapless gown outdoors. It was so cold we had to worry about goosebumps popping out on her neck and shoulders. But she was a trouper. In fact, she and I joked about her getting goosebumps on her breasts. She loved to giggle and had the ability to laugh at herself.

"I think it was our line producer who came up with the idea of giving ET a gift each morning. The gesture garnered a great deal of attention from the press, who assumed that Elizabeth had insisted on the presents, which wasn't the case. Besides, the gifts were usually very modest, even jokes [though they did include a Cartier stickpin and an Arpels travel clock]. For instance, one day we had a cowboy deliver her a gift on horseback. One of the Oak Ridge Boys [a country-and-western group] came by, sang her a song, and gave her a little present. It was a lot of fun. When Elizabeth accepts a gift, she becomes as excited as a little girl."

Actress Liz Torres, who also appeared in *Poker Alice,* recalled another gift that the entire cast bought for Taylor. "We went to Frederick's of Hollywood, the lingerie boutique, and bought her a G-string. When you kissed the G-string, it played 'Let Me Call You Sweetheart.' "

Early in 1987, Taylor became national chair of AmFAR. One of AmFAR's cofounders was Dr. Mathilde Krim, a pioneering research scientist married to millionaire producer Arthur Krim. Dr. Krim had been among the first researchers to investigate HIV, the virus that causes AIDS. It appeared that Krim felt that Taylor got too much attention for her work for AmFAR. Others involved in AmFAR had to be diplomatic around Dr. Krim. Trustee Beth Kummerfeld said, "But Elizabeth, as a glamorous and international movie star, is essential as a fund-raising symbol. . . . [Mathilde] feels slighted because the general public isn't aware. They associate Elizabeth Taylor with the organization."

Taylor frequently arrived late at AmFAR board meetings, but she did attend faithfully. (The organization's policy was that board members had to attend all four annual meetings, two in New York and two in Los Angeles, in order to remain on the board.) Abby van Buren, another board member, did not like smoking and banned it, even though the other members were smokers. Elizabeth showed up about two hours late for her first meeting, at the Beverly Wilshire Hotel, bringing along with her her hairdresser and her back pillow. Wayne Anderson, who was acquainted with a board member, described the scene: "So ET sits down and about five minutes later, out come her cigarettes. She lights one, and nobody's got the nerve to tell her to put it out. As soon as she [lights up], Mathilde Krim pulls out her cigarette holder and [someone else] takes out his cigarettes. I guess Abby wasn't too happy about it, but who's going to say no to Elizabeth?

"Remember the [Washington fund-raiser] where Reagan first used the AIDS word? I was there . . . The Foundation is against mandatory testing, and they weren't sure whether [the President] was going to recommend that. . . . He said something that didn't go over very well . . . people booed him, which was really kind of rude, considering that he was an invited speaker, and it was a big deal—so as soon as he got off the stage, Elizabeth went up and said, 'Of course, this is not AmFAR's position. It's President Reagan's position, and we want to thank him for coming to speak to us.' It could have been ugly, and she was very good; she's a professional."

One of Taylor's most successful public appearances on behalf of AIDS was a 1987 evening in and around Miami called An Extraordinary Evening with Elizabeth Taylor and Friends. Donors paid to dine with stars at any of a series of parties for fourteen to fifty people in private homes or on yachts. Elizabeth dined in Palm Beach with a donor who gave $1.2 million. Singer Julio Iglesias had the biggest party at his home. The evening's grand finale was champagne and dessert with Elizabeth and "a cavalcade of stars" at the Fontainebleau Hilton Hotel in Miami. According to Virginia Graham, who was in charge of Turnberry Island near Miami, the "conglomerate" raised "about eight or nine million" that night. Graham herself raised over $1.5 million. "Without Elizabeth," said Al Evans, president of the Community Alliance Against AIDS, which helped organize the evening and split the proceeds with AmFAR, "we wouldn't have raised that much money." Graham "admired the fact that Taylor has survived total self-destruction. She's almost like a building that they put a bomb in and it wouldn't go down." Nevertheless, when she saw Elizabeth in Miami, "she was acting very peculiarly. . . . I felt she was really oversedated."

Eve Abbott Johnson was invited to Celia Lipton Farris's reception under a tent in Palm Beach, which Johnson said cost $500 per person. Farris, a former actress who married the inventor of the milk carton, said that her party had raised $250,000. Johnson had known Taylor in the 1950s in Hollywood, where Johnson had been a prominent hostess during her marriages to Keenan Wynn and Van Johnson. "I tried to speak to [Elizabeth], but she was guarded as much as Hitler and Mussolini. I just yelled, 'Elizabeth, it's Evie!' She turned her head and gave me a smile, but they rushed her right through, and that was the end of it. I couldn't talk to her because she was being rushed everywhere." Al Evans noted that "[Elizabeth Taylor] surrounds herself with a whole retinue of people. Her security forces are enormous. When she walks into a room, sixteen people come in before she does and clear the way. I don't know whether she does that on purpose or if she needs all that. . . . It's part of the glamor and attraction of Elizabeth Taylor."

In Florida, Taylor's escort was James Stewart—not the actor but the industrialist and former CEO of Lone Star Cement. Despite her claims of crippling back pain, Elizabeth spent the night following the fund-raiser entertaining friends in her suite at the Fontainebleau. According to socialite Ronnie Britt, Elizabeth's painful back also didn't prevent her from making a play for the boyfriend of Jackie Stallone, Sylvester Stallone's mother. Britt saw Elizabeth look at Jackie and say, " 'Oh, I see you shopped at Giorgio's and got the dress from the mark-down rack.' And Jackie, who's clever, says, 'This dress belongs to Ronnie Britt and it isn't from the mark-down, and by the way, the next time Sylvester has a casting call for a lampshade or a rhino, he'll get in touch with you.' "

The next day, Elizabeth visited James Stewart at his nearby Indian Island estate. They made two or three trips on his yacht along southern Florida's waterways. According to Stewart's friend, lawyer Dan Paul, "James complained that Taylor constantly popped pills, never had any cash with her, and always used his credit cards. He tried his utmost to get rid of her."

Socialite Linda Ashmead confirmed that "Taylor pursued Stewart, because at the time he had a lot of money. Elizabeth was crazy about him, absolutely mad. She went on his yacht and brought along all her gaudy jewelry. I ask you—who brings $10 million worth of jewels on a short yacht trip? Stewart thought it was hilarious." Stewart ditched Elizabeth and eventually married Ava O'Neill, a close friend of Ivana Trump.

In May 1987, when *Poker Alice* had wrapped, Taylor was awarded the *Légion d'honneur,* France's highest civilian award, for her humanitarian efforts. She had participated in AIDS fund-raisers in Paris as well as in the United States. In fact, just a week before being presented with her award, she had paid nearly $750,000 for jewelry from the estate of the duchess of Windsor, including the diamond-and-gold crest of the Prince of Wales—a tribute to Richard Burton's heritage. The money raised by the auction went to the Institut Louis Pasteur in Paris, a leading center for AIDS research. On September 23, Elizabeth appeared before Congress again. This time, she told the committee members, "I'm a single woman and I think before embarking on a new relationship, I would have the AIDS test myself. And if I were serious—I would ask the other person to have the AIDS test."

Early in June 1987, Taylor and Hamilton turned up in Acapulco. News photographer Alec Byrne, who had been taking pictures of Taylor for several years, pursued the couple all over Acapulco. "They were staying in a villa in a very exclusive compound called Las Brisas," said Byrne. "I'd become very friendly with their maid, who assured me that they were hot and heavy throughout their stay. I'd always thought Hamilton was more of an escort, a pretty boy to have on her arm. But no, they were at it like cats and dogs, which really surprised me, because I'd thought he was just one of those convenient covers." But by the fall of 1987, Elizabeth's romance with Hamilton had begun to cool.

Beginning in June 1987, Elizabeth Taylor's AIDS activism began to coincide in a tangled way with her teaming up with Chesebrough-Pond's to launch a perfume line called Passion. That year, as part of a larger art-world effort for AmFAR called Art Against AIDS, Sotheby's hosted an auction and reception for nearly one thousand in New York. Dressed in beaded green silk and diamonds, Taylor arrived to receive a $400,000 check from gallery owner Leo Castelli. Art historian Robert Rosenblum said that Taylor was the lure at the Sotheby's auction: Guests could line up to be photographed with her. "She was so ravishing that I really felt as though Venus had come down from the skies, like I was some Greek meeting a god on earth. I was really scared, awed, like a teenager trying to get an autograph. I was trying to think of what I could say that was cool, witty.

"So I said, 'Miss Taylor, I just wanted to tell you that *Cleopatra* was one of the ten best movies I ever saw, and I didn't think it was long enough.' I got that out without stammering.

"And she said, 'You're the *only* one who didn't think it was long enough.'

"My photograph was taken [with her], and my wife put it in a leopard-skin frame, and so I am standing next to Elizabeth Taylor for eternity. She was cool, gracious, and Olympian, and I fell in love immediately. She was a superstar, and I for one feel blessed to be on the line of twenty or thirty who met her. It was one of those things that left a huge radiance in a grown-up's memory."

Sotheby's executive vice president, Robert Wooley, was her escort. For once Elizabeth Taylor was on time; she had to wait for New York mayor Ed Koch, who was late. She sat, continuously blotting her face with tissues. Trying to make conversation, Wooley leaned over her elaborate hairdo and complimented her: "You smell wonderful!" She told him it was Passion and smiled widely as she went on relentlessly about her new perfume.

Other people also managed to use Elizabeth Taylor for their own publicity. Beth Kummerfeld thought billionaire publisher Malcolm Forbes was one. In 1985, Forbes had divorced his wife, Roberta, mother of his five children. The marriage foundered on his voracious love of publicity, which his wife had disdained. He was also rumored to be gay, and, in fact, both he and Elizabeth always denied a romance, appearances to the contrary. Beth Kummerfeld, then a very active trustee of AmFAR ("I have probably given more money and raised more money than anybody else"), had her own company, which raised money for films and did some production. Kummerfeld, who had many Japanese contacts, took Taylor with her to Japan twice on brief fund-raising trips, the first in 1985. "She was on the wagon and had nothing to drink. Elizabeth paid her own expenses on both trips, including staff." On the first trip, Kummerfeld said the press mob "had been overwhelming. The press comes right at you, and I got bruised. That's why Elizabeth has to have bodyguards, to keep her from getting her back knocked off again." So on the second trip Kummerfeld "procured the former emperor's bodyguards for her."

On the second trip, in April 1988, Malcolm Forbes invited Taylor aboard his yacht, the *Highlander,* where guests were often greeted with bag pipes. Forbes and Elizabeth had been constant companions since September 1987, and Kirk Kerber, her waiter-friend from the Plaza Athenee, had designed some hand-painted purple sweatshirts she could wear on Forbes's motorcycle. According to Beth Kummerfeld, when Elizabeth arrived at Forbes's yacht, "there was the crew of Robin Leach and *Lifestyles of the Rich and Famous.* [Forbes] hadn't told her they would be filming." Kummerfeld said that Elizabeth told her, "Had I known they were going to be there, I never would have said yes." She thought it was a holiday. She agreed to cooperate with Leach's crew if he gave her an Erté painting. Kummerfeld suspected that "one of the reasons Malcolm got her in the first place was his promise that he would donate money to AIDS. In May, one of Kummerfeld's staff members took Forbes's call when he invited her to his upcoming anniversary party for *Forbes* magazine. The staffer told Forbes that Elizabeth was in Japan, "raising money for AIDS." According to Kummerfeld, Forbes answered, " 'Of course, we'll give her a donation, too.' " [The staffer] said, 'Well, you know she doesn't go for less than a million dollars,' and so he had to give a million dollars." Kummerfeld said that since Elizabeth's first trip to Japan also raised a million, "we started talking about 'the millionaires' club,' people who give a million dollars" to AmFAR.

The Passion line, a violet scent in containers that are various shades of purple, grosses around $70 million annually and is one of the top-ten best sellers among scents. It has recouped much of the income Elizabeth Taylor has lost since her days as a front-rank actress. Small wonder that she once remarked, "Success is a great deodorant." According to journalist Sharon Churcher, Chen Sam took credit for getting Taylor into the perfume business. Chen Sam continued to handle Taylor's public relations as well as her business involvement with Passion.

Before the line was unveiled, Taylor had a final meeting with Henry Wynberg, because she wanted to nullify their previous contract. Wynberg recalled: "Elizabeth had a small dinner party in her home in Bel Air. The food, which was excellent, was prepared by a friend of hers, Nicholas Grillo, who didn't participate in the dinner or in negotiations. He cooked the meal, poured some drinks, and left. The guests included the Lindsays, friends of mine from Los Angeles. After dinner, I presented Elizabeth with a perfume bottle and a fragrance which everyone passed around. Elizabeth sniffed it and claimed she liked it. She proposed a fifty-fifty split, as opposed to the original sixty-forty deal in my favor. I more or less agreed.

"Elizabeth had bought a fish tank and put it in her bedroom." This large hexagonal tropical fish tank could be viewed from all sides and stood about five feet from Elizabeth's bed. Wynberg said, "After the Lindsays left, she asked me to hang around and clean the tank. There were about five dead fish in the tank, which I removed. Afterwards I ended up spending the night with Elizabeth. We slept in her bed but didn't have sex. I left early in the morning."

Despite the verbal agreement between Taylor and Wynberg, they wound up in court, where Wynberg claimed that his former lover had made a good deal of money from his business efforts but had paid him nothing beyond an advance of $50,000 against expenses. In early December 1990, the suit reached the Superior Court of the State of California, County of Los Angeles. Wynberg said he took one look at the jury and realized he would "never win." The two sides settled, Elizabeth claiming exoneration and Wynberg claiming victory.

Passion's 1987 debut was backed by a $10 million promotion campaign, with Taylor making appearances in boutiques and department stores. She made numerous statements like "Passion is the ingredient in me that has made me who I am. It's my passion for life . . . my passion for passion that has made me never give up." She also purred, "I think [perfume] is more than just an accessory for a woman. It's part of her aura. I wear it even when I'm alone."

Photographer David McGough took lush Passion publicity shots of Elizabeth Taylor emerging from a purple pool against a red-and-purple sunset, with her hair wet and slicked back. In fact, she had to sit on "a special electronic chair because her back was so bad she couldn't get in the water properly."

Ogilvy & Mather, the advertising agency in charge of the Passion campaign, had hired Evitel, a graphics retouching and editing firm, to refinish the television advertising for the perfume. The job fell to Lisa Rubenstein, a young graphics designer, who spent more time retouching the Taylor project than she had spent on any other assignment. Rubenstein noted, "It's unusual to remake an entire TV film ad because it's so expensive. But I did it because ET looked terrible in the original version. Apparently she'd been drinking and gorging on food the night before, and her face was all bloated. Her skin was oily. It cost roughly $40,000 to retouch the film.

"She was a complete pain in the ass to work with. Everybody had to sign confidentiality agreements. She wouldn't get on an elevator unless a security guard checked it out first. It was an ordeal."

In October, Taylor went to Rome to work with director Franco Zeffirelli, who was making a movie about Toscanini, the great orchestra conductor. Malcolm Forbes accompanied her for part of the time—their first extended stay together. In January 1988, Taylor, now down to 122 pounds, began promoting her inspirational book, *Elizabeth Takes Off.* The book's publisher, G. P. Putnam's Sons, arranged a satellite tour for Taylor, but she stipulated that there were to be no questions about Aileen Getty, her daughter-in-law who was HIV-positive. In fact, Getty did not have full-blown AIDS, but by forbidding the press to ask about her, Taylor created the impression that Getty was sick. Taylor may have been angry at Getty for leaving Christopher Wilding. (For a time, Getty had also been very close to Michael Wilding.)

Even as she was promoting her book and advising America, Elizabeth was going downhill fast.

Chapter 28

In 1987, Franco Zeffirelli, the flamboyant Italian director known for lush staged productions and fabulous film versions of operas, including *Carmen, La Traviata,* and *Othello,* was planning a new film in the grand style of 1950s Hollywood epics: *Young Toscanini.* Focusing on an episode in the early life of the great conductor, the story takes place in Rio de Janeiro in 1886, where the eighteen-year-old Arturo Toscanini, in Brazil on an orchestra tour, is torn between an aging soprano attempting a comeback and a mistress his own age. The producers' candidates for the role of the temperamental diva, Russian soprano Nadina Bulichova, included Faye Dunaway, Barbra Streisand, and Shirley MacLaine. They felt that after all her TV movies Elizabeth Taylor was box-office poison. But Zeffirelli held out for the star he considered one of the few remaining cinematic divas. Twenty years earlier, he had directed Taylor in *The Taming of the Shrew.* "A film with Elizabeth Taylor costs a million dollars more," he said, "but I am convinced that it will be an excellent investment."

Because Taylor, now fifty-six and a grandmother of six, had not made a major film in seven years, Zeffirelli saw a parallel between her own situation and the role he had offered her in his at least $18-million project, a joint Italian-French production. Nadina has interrupted her stage career for the emperor of Brazil, played by distinguished French actor Philippe Noiret, who said gallantly that he had accepted the part for the sake of "Elizabeth Taylor's beautiful eyes." When Toscanini begins to coach his childhood idol for a return to the stage in *Aida,* Nadina has fallen into deep depression. The conductor is instrumental in her transformation: Her performance is a triumph, and she is back at the top of her art. Zeffirelli hoped that his production would do the same for Elizabeth and help restore her credibility in Hollywood.

Elizabeth's own interest in Toscanini may have gone back to Mike Todd, who had wanted to make his own film on the conductor and had even come up with a working title, *Maestro.* She had met Toscanini shortly before he died in 1957—"He was one of the most dynamic, flirtatious men I've ever met in my life, and he was ninety years old then"—but she had never been to the opera and had no interest in classical music. Zeffirelli had engaged soprano Aprile Millo to sing Elizabeth's arias in voice-over. Nevertheless, on trips to New York, where she went partying, hot-air ballooning, yachting, and motorcycling with Malcolm Forbes, Taylor spent some time studying opera-singing technique, including correct breathing, and the most important arias from *Aida.* One evening, she even went to the Metropolitan Opera for one act of *Turandot.* Retired soprano Birgit Nilson—Turandot had been one of her great roles—was in the audience. But it was Taylor who got applause as she sashayed down the aisle during the first intermission on her way out of the opera house. Millo said that Taylor had met with her for eight hours and had asked her, "Who is Aida?" Millo said later, "She listened to me sing and actually cried. . . . She went nuts over *Aida.*"

Screenwriter Bill Stadiem had been hired by Zeffirelli to rewrite the script of *Young Toscanini.* Zeffirelli persuaded Stadiem and one of the producers, Tarak Ben Ammar, to meet with Elizabeth themselves. On a hot, sunny day early in the summer of 1987 the two men drove out to Bel Air, and at a huge ornamental gate that reminded Stadiem of Versailles, they identified themselves into a squawk box. At the top of the driveway they found a very ordinary California ranch house with a pool. In the driveway was an Aston Martin Lagonda, for which Elizabeth had paid $153,000 on the spot one day when she had gone shopping for a Rolls. A young woman opened the door and said, "Hi, I'm Liz." It was Elizabeth Thorburn, a Scottish cordon bleu chef who used to work at Kensington Palace for Princess Margaret. Taylor kept her visitors waiting for a half hour, so they had time to look around. The living room opened into a game room, or den, and then into a dining room. The entire first floor was white, but looked, Stadiem thought, "like the Impressionist wing at the Metropolitan Museum of Art" in New York. Taylor's collection, mostly oil paintings, included a Modigliani, a Pissarro, a Monet, a Rouault, a Renoir, a Degas, Utrillos, and Vlamincks. Over the mantelpiece was a Frans Hals, bought for her by Mike Todd. Stadiem dubbed Taylor's den "the Stage Delicatessen Room," after the New York deli restaurant near Carnegie Hall, which is decorated with framed photos of famous diners. Her study held photos of her shaking hands or standing next to everybody who was anybody in politics and entertainment, including Presidents Eisenhower, Kennedy, Ford, and Reagan; Marshal Tito; Richard Burton and Noël Coward in gray top hats at Ascot; David Niven; and Princess Grace and Prince Rainier of Monaco. Elizabeth's two Oscars, for *Butterfield 8* and *Who's Afraid of Virginia Woolf?,* stood on bookshelves among a clutter of lesser awards. Her oval bedroom, upstairs in the two-story house, was an aerie with a patio looking out over treetops. Besides Alvin the parrot, Elizabeth had a Pekingese with a lavender bow and a Burmese cat.

When the diva finally appeared, she was wearing a one-piece bathing suit, high heels, and a turban. She looked slim, imposing, and taller than her actual five feet, four inches. She led Stadiem and Ben Ammar out back to the pool, where Stadiem saw a very beautiful young couple who were not introduced. The woman, who looked like a model, was topless, and her companion, who resembled a younger, handsomer George Hamilton, hardly moved the whole time Stadiem was present. This young man may have been one of Elizabeth's sons.

Taylor undid the straps of her bathing suit, telling her visitors, "Normally I would do this in the nude, but I don't know you well enough yet." The two men exchanged glances. Elizabeth seemed to be projecting a salty, down-to-earth, somewhat world weary manner, and her visitors had the impression she was rehearsing for her new role. She later explained that, in fact, she did not sunbathe in the nude on her property; there was a house above hers belonging to producer Keith Barish, and the occupants could see her. For the two hours she met with Stadiem and Ben Ammar, Elizabeth lay on a chaise longue and kept a sun reflector under her face. She explained that she needed to maintain a tan to set off her jewelry: She had just bought some new jewels from the estate of the duchess of Windsor and was going on tour to promote Passion.

At that point, Matthew Broderick was slated to play Toscanini. Taylor wanted to heat up their love scenes: "This Matthew Broderick is the cutest guy!" Stadiem and the producer explained that Zeffirelli's love scenes were usually very discreet. "Oh, I'll talk to Franco; don't worry about that," Taylor responded. "Let's go the distance with this." (In the end, a lesser actor played Toscanini, and Zeffirelli cut all the sex scenes.)

Elizabeth flew to Rome to begin filming, arriving in a bright violet suit and large matching hat and accompanied by a staff of four, two bodyguards, and innumerable pieces of Louis Vuitton luggage. Zeffirelli had asked her to put on ten pounds to play a well-padded opera star. "She said I was the only man she would do it for," Zeffirelli boasted. "Now she is bursting out of all her costumes." Before leaving for Rome, Elizabeth wolfed down her favorites, like fried chicken, mashed potatoes, and corn on the cob slathered in butter. On location in Rome and Bari, she had sweets for breakfast and for dinner, choices like fettucine with mushrooms, risotto with lobster, spaghetti marinara, and artichokes parmigiana.

But she was lonely and frustrated without a lover and gained more weight than necessary during filming. In the final version of the film, which wasn't shot in sequence, Stadiem said she goes from slim to fat and back again in an absurd way. During shooting, she enjoyed twitting her costar, C. Thomas Howell. When he twice flubbed a scene in which Nadina slaps Toscanini's face, she teased, "I guess you just like being slapped." Zeffirelli covered his camera lens with a piece of black nylon to blur Elizabeth's crow's-feet.

At one point, Elizabeth slipped on a wet marble bathroom floor and hurt her back. She stayed in her hotel room with Malcolm Forbes, who was visiting Rome en route from his palace in Morocco to his château in France. Elizabeth had not lost her love of presents—Forbes gave her an amethyst-and-diamond necklace and matching bracelet.

In September 1988, the film was unveiled at the Venice Film Festival, where it was booed at a press screening. Part of the problem was that Zeffirelli had condemned, sight unseen, another festival entry, Martin Scorsese's controversial *Last Temptation of Christ.* But *Young Toscanini* was hilariously awful. After impressing Stadiem and Ben Ammar during their meeting in Bel Air as saucy and sophisticated, Elizabeth was dead wood on-screen, seemingly embalmed. The Toscanini character was depicted as torn between Elizabeth in blackface singing the role of Egyptian slave Aida and an eighteen-year-old missionary, a sort of youthful Mother Teresa nursing Brazilian slaves. Elizabeth had the high point when she replicated a scene from Nadina's life and stepped forward onstage in the middle of one scene from *Aida,* holding hands with two black extras and pleading for the abolition of slavery. *Variety* reported that "the film perversely won supporters for its very *kitsch.*" Not enough of them, however, to persuade any American studio to distribute *Young Toscanini* in the United States, where it has never been distributed. The film was shown in Paris, where audiences laughed at the dialogue and the excessive sets.

According to Stadiem, Zeffirelli, badly in need of support in Venice, was very hurt that Elizabeth, pleading back problems, did not come to the premiere. In her place, she sent a young "personal representative" whom no one knew. She may have felt she had gained too much weight to appear in public, or she may have gotten wind that the film would be an embarrassment to her—far from the comeback vehicle that Zeffirelli had planned it would be.

In October, just a month after Zeffirelli's humiliation in Venice, Elizabeth, overcome by recurring drug and alcohol abuse, returned to the Betty Ford Center. She was slimmer when she entered, in preparation for promoting her weight-loss program in her book *Elizabeth Takes*

Off. The enterprising Alec Byrne snapped her before and after Betty Ford to document that she put on a good twenty-five pounds during her stay. Because of her back, she skipped the clinic's exercise sessions and often rode in a wheelchair. Her mother, Sara Taylor, then ninety-two, was hospitalized with bleeding ulcers in the Eisenhower Medical Center adjacent to Betty Ford. Elizabeth, her makeup perfect and her hair groomed daily by her own hairdresser, would visit her mother frequently, along with her brother, Howard. The hospital staff noticed that Elizabeth always seemed to show up at mealtime—so she could enjoy french fries and extra thick chocolate mousse, unavailable from the health-conscious kitchen at Betty Ford. Elizabeth often asked for seconds and supplemented her diet at night and at breakfast with secret stashes of fancy Italian chocolates.

Alec Byrne also got the first picture of a husky thirty-six-year-old fellow patient at Betty Ford pushing Elizabeth's wheelchair for her. Larry Fortensky was a former truck driver at construction sites who had been arrested at least twice for driving while intoxicated. His Teamsters Union insurance policy was covering his fees at Betty Ford. Like most rehabilitation programs for alcoholics and drug addicts, the Betty Ford Center discourages clients from forming intimate relationships immediately after giving up drink or narcotics. For almost a year after their stays at Betty Ford, Fortensky and Taylor remained friends and provided each other with support. As she had after her first sojourn at Betty Ford, Elizabeth continued to hold Alcoholics Anonymous meetings at her house, mostly with people she had met at Betty Ford, including Fortensky. As George Hamilton had been, Fortensky was forceful about persuading Elizabeth to give up her old habits and proved instrumental in getting her off alcohol and heavy medication.

Fortensky had grown up in Stanton, California, a working-class town of about thirty thousand in Orange County, about an hour south of Los Angeles. Stanton had a high crime rate, with many clashes between the white and Latino residents—a town where it was easy for young people to drift into drinking, drugs, and violence. The eldest of seven children—three boys and four girls—Fortensky had seen his parents divorce when he was five. His stepfather was an electrical superintendent. Fortensky himself had been married twice, both times to local women whom he had known in high school. When he first married, he was 19. According to his second wife, Karin Fleming, his first marriage lasted eighteen months and produced a daughter, Julie, now 25, married and living in Stanton. In 1972, he married Karin, an attractive woman who resembles a young Elizabeth Taylor. He was 22; Karin, seventeen.

Karin's mother had been opposed to her marriage because she knew Fortensky had been brought up in a family of heavy drinkers. In August 1991 photographer Alec Byrne followed Elizabeth and Fortensky to Fortensky's mother's funeral. (She was younger than Elizabeth when she died of cancer.) Byrne reported that while Taylor and Fortensky did not drink at the wake, the other relatives did—quite a bit. At one point during the wake, a truck drove up, delivering more beer. Byrne said that family members came out of the house to welcome the truck, waving beer cans.

"Believe it or not," Karin said, "Larry Fortensky was just about the coolest guy in Orange County—about 100,000 Heinekens ago." During his marriage to Karin, Fortensky would begin drinking, mostly beer, as soon as he came home from his construction jobs. He would continue drinking until he went to bed. If Karin pressured him to stop and threatened to leave him, he became violent and verbally abusive. Nevertheless, she felt he was "real people": honest, decent, humorous, and not especially materialistic. Because of his drinking and his slovenliness when he drank, she divorced him in 1979. Two years after their divorce, Fortensky wanted a reconciliation, but Karin already was dating someone else. She remarried and moved to Irvine, where Fortensky continued to call her about once a month.

Despite the differences in Fortensky and Taylor's backgrounds, they did have one bond besides a history of alcohol abuse: They both liked to eat. During the year Fortensky and Elizabeth spent as friends, they often drove to hamburger joints he knew in and around Stanton—Elizabeth in jeans and cowboy boots—where they ordered milk shakes and burgers with all the toppings.

✦ ✦ ✦

Throughout the spring and summer of 1989, Elizabeth continued her AIDS work, her perfume promotions, and her friendships with Malcolm Forbes and other escorts during frequent trips to New York. She launched a new perfume, White Diamonds, and a men's fragrance, Passion for Men. *London Daily Mail* editor Baz Bamigboye went to Paris for the Passion for Men announcement, at the Automobile Club on the Place de la Concorde. Taylor wore a navy shawl with a red border, reminiscent of her *Légion d'honneur* ribbon. Bamigboye found the event "quite a sad occasion. I thought, That's not a great actress. That's just a great movie personality."

Bamigboye asked Taylor, "What has inspired you to create this scent for men?"

Predictably, she replied, "My romances with the men in my life."

"Oh, that's kind of a gush," Bamigboye said dismissively.

Not realizing her questioner was Bamigboye, whom she was fond of, Taylor sniffed, "The tacky tabloids are here." Later, she apologized. But Bamigboye still felt "very sad. She could be doing so many other things."

Taylor returned to the United States to promote her men's cologne in stores and at bashes at, among other spots, a polo club called the Burbank Equestrian Center and the New York Stock Exchange, where she was escorted by Saudi arms dealer Adnan Khashoggi. Earlier in the year, Elizabeth had visited Khashoggi's house in Cannes, in the south of France, and in 1981 she had stayed at his home in Marbella, on Spain's Costa del Sol. There Khashoggi owned five thousand rolling acres several miles from the berth for his yacht. He kept a reserve of 70,000 pheasants for shoots and a stable of Arabian stallions that were shampooed daily. The house itself was Moorish, with mirrored ceilings and walls, gold sofas with lavender pillows—which must have delighted Elizabeth—and ten bathrooms, each decorated in a different marble. During the Passion for Men promotion, Beth Kummerfeld saw Elizabeth at a party at Khashoggi's palatial, $25-million apartment on two full floors of the Olympic Tower at 641 Fifth Avenue at Fifty-first Street in Manhattan, a very secure residence for tenants who wish to remain extremely private. Khashoggi's apartment—one of twelve residences he owned at the time—was equipped with an Olympic-sized swimming pool, a sauna, a Jacuzzi, a barber's chair, a bed ten feet wide and seven feet long, and part of an art collection worth $30 million. Spurred on by Elizabeth, Khashoggi had joined AmFAR's "millionaire's club."

When Elizabeth turned up at Khashoggi's party in New York, he was then under house arrest, free on $10 million bail after spending eight nights in jail in New York in July. He was awaiting trial for allegedly helping former Philippine president Ferdinand Marcos and his wife, Imelda, loot the Filipino treasury of millions. Beth Kummerfeld attributed Taylor's presence at Khashoggi's side to the fact that "she's very loyal to friends, especially when they're down and out. Take Rock Hudson, Peter Lawford. She'll help when they're down. One reason is that she herself is so sickly. She's never without pain." Nevertheless, photographer David McGough, who was photographing Taylor for the Passion for Men campaign, was asked by Taylor's staff not to photograph her at Khashoggi's.

In July 1989, Elizabeth, now fifty-seven, filmed her last TV movie, finally making good on her 1983 promise to the late Tennessee Williams by making a film version of his 1962 play *Sweet Bird of Youth.* The director was Nicolas Roeg, then best known for his idiosyncratic films like *Don't Look Now* and *The Man Who Fell to Earth.* Lucille Ball had turned down Taylor's role of an aging, alcoholic, and drug-addicted movie queen who thinks her comeback film has been a dud. Williams had told Taylor that he had written the part with her in mind. Elizabeth said, "I've played so many actresses . . . at least once a year I play a 'has-been' actress. . . . I'm a great success at 'has-beens.'" Her older son, actor Michael Wilding Jr., had a small part in the production as a producer.

Unlike Zeffirelli, the producer of *Sweet Bird of Youth* wanted Elizabeth to lose more weight. On location in Los Angeles, one of her aides saw her venture too close to the muffins and danish on the food table. "Have some fruit," she advised Elizabeth.

One of the crew members said, "She's a big girl and she can have anything she wants."

Elizabeth grinned and told him, "Yeah, big and getting bigger every minute." She settled for a slice of honeydew melon. Later, she held the wrap party at her home, serving ribs dripping barbecue sauce, hot dogs and hamburgers, corn on the cob, and salads.

Because Elizabeth was still overweight, her scenes in *Sweet Bird of Youth* were shot in dim lighting. Nevertheless, she looked bloated in her loose-fitting negligees and caftans. She insisted on keeping the mink coat made especially for her to wear in the part—it may have been some consolation for the film's poor reviews and poorer ratings.

By the time *Sweet Bird of Youth* aired, Larry Fortensky had moved into Elizabeth's Bel Air home, although he still supported himself doing construction work, leaving at dawn with his lunch pail and hard hat and coming home with his jeans, T-shirt, and work boots covered in dust. Reportedly, Elizabeth made him over à la *Pygmalion,* playing a female Henry Higgins to a male Eliza. She fed him gourmet meals as well as hamburgers, bought him fancy new Hollywood threads, had his hair streaked and styled by José Eber, and even paid for speech lessons. She herself gave him some lessons in good manners. Her friends who encountered him at parties found him very quiet, more like a bodyguard than an escort, and an even more unlikely lover than Dennis Stein, who at least had been familiar with Elizabeth's showbiz milieu. After her boasting about John Warner's attributes, some assumed that Elizabeth appreciated Fortensky as a stud, that he was especially well endowed. But Karin Fleming said that physically he was of normal size. At her home, decorated with amethyst crystals and purple orchids, Elizabeth built Fortensky a basketball court and a bachelor study downstairs with his own phone, where he could have privacy.

When he told Karin Fleming he was dating Elizabeth Taylor, she said, teasingly, "Larry, you've been drinking too much. Have you been hallucinating?"

He answered, "Well, I may be an alcoholic, but I know Elizabeth Taylor when I see her. Honest, it's true."

Fearful that Elizabeth would tire of him quickly and discard him, Karin asked, "Do you know what you're getting yourself into?"

Fortensky responded, "We'll just have to wait and see."

At home with Larry, Elizabeth maintained a down-home manner. Michael Patrick, a grandson of former vice president Hubert Humphrey, worked as her personal assistant for three months in 1989. When he arrived for his first day working for Elizabeth, his car stalled at the bottom of her steep driveway. She met him at her door, dressed in a T-shirt, stretch pants, and a bandanna.

"Did you walk all the way from Glendale?" she asked Patrick. Once he had explained his problem, she picked up a small whistle, a piece of jewelry, blew it, and yelled, "Hey, everybody, come on!"

The staff arrived. Elizabeth jumped in the driver's seat, explaining that because of her back, she'd steer; her staff helped Patrick push.

One day Elizabeth told Patrick she wanted him to take her shopping at Gelsen's, an upscale supermarket in the San Fernando Valley. She said she wanted to be "normal"—and besides, she was "dying" for a quarter pound of whipped cream cheese. So they went at midnight, and Elizabeth was surprised that more people didn't accost her.

Patrick also flew to Scottsdale with Elizabeth on Malcolm Forbes's private Boeing 727, the *Capitalist Tool.* Elizabeth wanted to know every detail of the arrangements: who would meet them, where they would stay, even the limo driver's name. When Elizabeth and Patrick settled into the limo in Scottsdale, she said to the driver, "Jack, I've got to tell you—in 1969, you picked up Richard Burton and me at this airport. Your wife was pregnant at the time. Her name was Evelyn. Just for the record, what did your wife have?" According to Patrick, the driver was blown away by this act of noblesse oblige.

For several days in mid-August, Elizabeth was a guest at Malcolm Forbes's lavish seventieth birthday party, at his nineteenth-century palace in Tangier, Morocco. Fortensky was not on the guest list, reportedly because Forbes was trying to persuade Taylor to marry him instead of the penniless construction worker, who made about $20 an hour, plus six or seven dollars in fringe benefits. Fortensky waited for Elizabeth to join him after the party at her home in Gstaad. It was his first trip to Europe.

Forbes commented that he thought Fortensky was "a nice fellow, but not the sort you would expect to be with Elizabeth, except for the fact that he had all the time in the world to devote to her. As far as I know, he didn't waste too much time in giving up the construction business for Elizabeth."

Forbes also found Fortensky "strange in certain ways. I remember when I visited him and Elizabeth in her suite at the Plaza Athenee. George Hamilton, Elizabeth's ex, was there, and they were flirting like mad. Larry couldn't have cared less, or at least he gave that impression. In Gstaad, when Elizabeth pulled the same stunt with John Warner vis-à-vis Richard Burton, the senator almost punched Burton out."

Meanwhile, the roughly six hundred rich or famous guests of Forbes's, including Henry Kissinger, Barbara Walters, Walter Cronkite, and three hundred CEOs of the Fortune 500, arrived in Tangier by chartered Concorde, Boeing 747, and DC-8, or on their own executive jets or private yachts. Three camels, plus hundreds of belly dancers, acrobats, jugglers, drummers, and Moroccan horsemen in full tribal gear greeted guests outside Forbes's Palais Mendoub. Inside, huge tents decorated with chandeliers had been set up in the palace gardens overlooking the Mediterranean. Guests dined on rack of lamb, pigeon pie, chicken and olives, exotic fruits, and a huge chocolate cake flown in from Beverly Hills. Beverly Sills sang "Happy Birthday," followed by a huge fireworks display.

Forbes made Elizabeth his hostess, and she appeared less than pleased at having to shake six hundred or more hands. Self-conscious about her weight, she wore a green-and-gold caftan. As usual, Forbes wore his dress kilt, and British publishing tycoon Robert Maxwell came dressed as a caliph, in towering turban and gold chains. Elizabeth gave Forbes a plaster sculpture that portrayed him riding a Harley-Davidson. Delighted, he took her on a shopping expedition in Tangier and bought her diamond earrings.

The "birthday party of the century"—Forbes was criticized afterward for one of the high-water marks of 1980s excess—had its shortcomings. The mid-August temperature in Tangier can exceed 100 degrees Fahrenheit—in the shade. "It was so hot," said columnist Cindy Adams, one of the invited multitude, "that guests were fainting in swimming pools."

Some extravagances were not noted in the numerous press accounts of the party. Drugs—especially hashish and marijuana—were so plentiful that dozens of electronic air purifiers had to be installed in Forbes's palace to diffuse the smell of the smoke. For some guests, the most distressing aspect of the party was Forbes's sexual predilection for young boys—a taste he could satisfy in Morocco—and leather gangs, an outgrowth of his fetish for sadomasochism. According to the late Doris Lilly, "Everyone knew about it, but nobody said a word. It was sad that he lacked the courage to come out of the closet. The hoax that he and Elizabeth Taylor attempted to perpetrate seemed ugly to me. They were never lovers. They used each other to enhance their public images."

Nevertheless, public relations expert James Mitchell recalled "an amusing incident that took place in Tangier. On the last day of the party I happened to be walking around the Casbah, and I spotted a taxicab that had pulled up next to a snake charmer. In the backseat of the taxi sat Elizabeth Taylor. She was dressed simply, in a little print outfit, and she was taking photographs out the cab window with a box camera that looked something like a Brownie Hawkeye. It was so cute, so touristy. She saw me walking and gave me a big smile and wave."

On February 24, 1990, Malcolm Forbes died in his sleep of a heart attack. Three days later, his memorial was held at St. Bartholomew's Church in Manhattan, on Park Avenue at Fifty-first Street. Outside the vast church, a lone bagpiper played beside one of Forbes's seventy-two motorcycles, a Harley-Davidson sporting Scottish and American flags and a vanity license plate that read "MSF." Elizabeth stole the show at the memorial. She arrived after the fourteen hundred other mourners were seated. In diamonds and mink, she took the seat of honor, in the front row on the aisle, next to former president Richard Nixon, who stood to greet her when she arrived. (Roberta Forbes, Malcolm's ex-wife, was buried in the middle of the row.) Outside, motorcycles roared as bikers arrived to pay tribute to "a damn good driver."

On March 26, Elizabeth lost another friend, one she had known for nearly twenty years: designer Halston died in San Francisco of AIDS. In early April, Elizabeth collapsed with viral pneumonia and was hospitalized for nine weeks. Fortensky and her children kept watch by her bedside during her near-fatal illness. Because word of Forbes's homosexuality had been made public and because of her well-documented friendships with Halston and Rock Hudson, rumors circulated that Taylor had AIDS. Through Chen Sam, Elizabeth refuted the whispers: "I feel it is important that people should not be afraid to be tested for AIDS. I have an annual physical and have been tested for the disease, and the test results are negative."

Since her hospitalization coincided with the Los Angeles County District Attorney's Office report on the investigation of her doctors on charges of overprescribing medication, there was also talk that her past alcohol and drug abuse had contributed to her severe illness. But at the end of June a thinner Taylor finally emerged from the hospital. Larry Fortensky gave her a kid—a baby miniature goat that lived with the couple in Bel Air. John Warner sent her a welcome-home meal via private jet: fried chicken, mashed potatoes and gravy, prepared by the cook they had had when they were married.* On behalf of AmFAR she made a brief public appearance to open the International Conference

*This was not the first time Warner had extended his largesse to Taylor since their marriage had ended. "To his embarrassment," according to his press secretary Phil Smith, "Senator John Warner in 1987 was asked by his former wife Elizabeth Taylor to introduce a private bill (S. 1919) for the relief of Elizabeth's son, Michael Wilding, allowing him to become an American citizen. Having been convicted in Great Britain of drug possession (and being a British subject), he faced deportment charges.

Billing himself as a musician (although he acted briefly, as did his mother, on the television soap opera *General Hospital*), Michael had been living with his girlfriend of the time, Johanna Lykke-Dahn, and had become the father of another daughter, Naomi.

Asked to perform roughly forty hours of community service as retribution for the drug conviction, Michael did approximately one-quarter of his service at the Scott Newman Drug and Rehabilitation Center in Los Angeles.

on AIDS in San Francisco. By the end of 1990, through Elizabeth's help, AmFAR had raised nearly $30 million.

According to Patricia Seaton, everyone who visited or wrote or sent gifts to Elizabeth while she was hospitalized received "*silly* little thank you notes" printed on blue paper from Cartier. They were form notes that said the friend's gesture "made me feel better and warm all over. Much love, Elizabeth." Even her name was printed, with only her initials in her handwriting.

One of Elizabeth's visitors in the hospital was her friend Michael Jackson. In June he was admitted to the same hospital with chest pains. He stayed on Elizabeth's floor, keeping his pet monkey with him. In the early 1980s, Michael had added Elizabeth to his friendships with older female stars, including Diana Ross, Sophia Loren, and Liza Minnelli. In his autobiography *Moonwalk,* Jackson wrote, "I love Elizabeth Taylor. I'm inspired by her bravery. She had been through so much and she is a survivor . . . I identify with her very strongly because of our experiences as child stars. When we first started talking on the phone, she told me she felt as if she had known me for years. I felt the same way."

In 1984, when Jackson was working on *Captain EO,* he and Elizabeth enjoyed being kids together. They ran up $3,000 a week in damages to Jackson's trailer, having messy food fights with each other. At his Neverland ranch near the tiny town of Los Olivos in the Santa Ynez Valley, Jackson installed a direct telephone "hot line" to Elizabeth's Bel Air home so that they could talk at all hours. In addition to going over the tribulations of early stardom and the attendant isolation and lack of privacy, the two discussed their pets, perfume, makeup, and hairdressers. A fellow ice cream junkie, Jackson considered investing in his own product, with a key ingredient of rhinoceros saliva. He also built a shrine to Elizabeth at Neverland: a room filled with posters, stills, books, and other Elizabeth Taylor memorabilia, as well as beanbag beds for her pets when she visited and shelves where her cats could stretch out. On a giant video screen Taylor's films played twenty-four hours a day. The wallpaper, which Jackson designed, was covered with her face. Michael's sister, Janet Jackson, told *France-Soir* that her brother had wanted walls the color of Elizabeth's eyes. "The painters never stopped mixing colors, but they never got it exactly right." Michael Jackson also briefly featured his Elizabeth Taylor shrine in one of his music videos.

Elizabeth and Michael frequently visited each other's homes. Michael also escorted her to various functions in Los Angeles and donated funds to fight AIDS. The rumor mill had it that Michael had proposed to Elizabeth. For public consumption she provided a pithy analysis of Jackson: "He's the least weird man I've ever known."

During her convalescence in the fall of 1990, Taylor rented a house in Santa Monica to be near the beach and reportedly considered moving there. In January 1991, just as she and Fortensky were leaving for Gstaad, she lost another good friend: Roger Wall, her secretary, had committed suicide at age forty-two because he had AIDS.

But the following July, Elizabeth opened a new chapter. She announced that in the fall she and Fortensky would marry. "This is it!" she exulted. Her announcement was very big news in Stanton, where one of Larry's aunts was planning an all-cotton wedding shower. She was going to give Elizabeth "a long T-shirt—like a nightdress—and they're gonna have a picture printed on it of Larry when he was real young, standing in front of his red convertible." Elizabeth had invited Larry's grandmother and his favorite aunt to Bel Air to go shopping. She had had them fitted with Nolan Miller dresses for the wedding and had bought each of them a pair of $400 shoes in Beverly Hills.

On October 5, Elizabeth and Fortensky were married under a gazebo at Michael Jackson's Neverland ranch before 160 guests. The wedding was originally planned for the sixth, but it was rescheduled to suit Nancy Reagan. Minister and Hollywood New Age guru Marianne Williamson, a self-described "spiritual psychotherapist," performed the brief ceremony. Elizabeth gave Larry a plain gold ring; hers was set with pavé diamonds. Elizabeth's wedding dress was three shades of yellow. In honor of the occasion, Michael Jackson wore *two* black gloves.

The best man was Elizabeth's hairdresser, José Eber, and Hollywood guests included Eva Gabor, Merv Griffin, President Ronald Reagan and Nancy Reagan, President Gerry Ford and Betty Ford, Elizabeth's mother, Carole Bayer Sager, Gregory and Veronique Peck, Barry Diller, and Diane von Furstenberg. There were also Elizabeth's children and grandchildren and Fortensky's relatives—though his father, whom he had not seen in twenty years, was not invited. The guests from Stanton loved the rides in Michael Jackson's amusement park.

Jackson footed the $1.5 million bill for the wedding. As a small thank-you, Elizabeth and Larry bought Michael a rare bird, an albino from the Amazon that cost $20,000, for his Neverland menagerie. They also paid the bird dealer's round-trip fare from New York to Los Angeles for special delivery to Michael's front door.

Proceeds from the sale of photographs of the Taylor-Fortensky wedding were to go to AIDS charities. Reportedly disenchanted with AmFAR management and dispersal of its funds, Elizabeth set up her own Elizabeth Taylor AIDS Foundation, which distributed the proceeds from the photos' sale.

In February 1992, to celebrate her sixtieth birthday, Taylor and Fortensky were feted at Disneyland by a thousand guests. Each of them received a T-shirt with Andy Warhol's portrait of Elizabeth printed on the front and back. On the plane back to New York a fellow passenger offered Chen Sam $500 for hers. Soon afterward, Elizabeth appeared on *Oprah,* where Oprah Winfrey showed footage of Taylor and Fortensky, both wearing jeans, arriving at Disneyland in a horse-drawn carriage and mounting a carousel together. "After everyone went home," Elizabeth told Oprah's audience, "I asked one of the [Disneyland] executives if they could keep it open [for an hour] for Larry and me. They did, and we went on every ride and just had a ball."

Oprah commented, "I heard you say on the news that you did this for the child in you. . . ."

Elizabeth answered, "Well, I worked all during my childhood, except for riding horses and getting away—I was at the studio amongst adults. My peers were all grown-ups. The child in me was really suppressed. I worked—and was paid. And it was on the screen, but it wasn't me."

Elizabeth then raised a fist and yelled, "Yeah! I feel great. I am happy. My life is wonderful. And I don't know what all the fuss about turning sixty is. . . . I never think about growing old. I barely think about growing up."

She went on to talk about Larry Fortensky: "Larry is so supportive. We were friends for a year before we got 'together' in that sense. I saw beneath his macho exterior a great sweetness. And a very astute understanding of people. And a very smart man."

In September 1994, Elizabeth's mother, Sara, died at the age of ninety-nine. Elizabeth had installed her in a condominium in Rancho Mirage. There were rosebushes outside and a view of a golf course and man-made lakes, garishly lit at night. Early in the morning, Sara would ride her oversized tricycle around the complex—a common form of exercise for older Californians. She belonged to a ladies' bridge group that included Jolie Gabor, the Gabor sisters' mother. Sara frequently went out with gay male escorts, mostly former M-G-M actors whom she had gotten to know in the complex. Elizabeth had hired a Chinese family—a couple and their baby girl—to look after Sara and had installed them in an adjoining condo. Sara's home was as much of a shrine to Elizabeth as Michael Jackson's was, and Sara herself maintained to the end that her daughter was perfect and that her whole life had been beautiful—a Hollywood movie. Sara was buried alongside Elizabeth's father, Francis. They occupy Crypt 16 and 17A in the Century of Peace section of Westwood Memorial Park in Los Angeles, a favorite Hollywood cemetery.

Elizabeth's brother, Howard Taylor, has pursued multiple careers, reportedly including oceanography and marine painting. In 1980 he and his family moved from Kauai, Hawaii, to Taos, New Mexico, where he opened a branch of the Taylor Art Gallery, his father Francis's business. But the gallery proved too confining for Howard. He sold it and bought twenty-eight acres of forest on a mountainside near Taos Ski Valley, where he built his own house. Maria, Howard's wife, worked as the manager of a Taos hotel. Already bearded, Howard pierced one ear. Elizabeth had her ears pierced, and brother and sister sported matching jewelry. Apart from his family, Howard's pride and joy is his collection of antique miniature stoves, for which he built a separate showcase in his new home.

Chapter 29

"I want my tombstone to say, 'She Lived,' Elizabeth Taylor proclaimed some years ago. Now, with much of her life behind her, any biographer assessing her career would have to agree that she has certainly accomplished her goal. The quintessential movie queen and last of the great actresses from the golden age of the Hollywood studio system, she has been one of the most watched, photographed, and gossiped-about personalities of our time. Her life has been more eventful and dramatic than any character she has portrayed on-screen, with the possible exception of Cleopatra, Queen of the Nile. Looking back on her decades in show business, Liz was recently quoted as saying, "Hollywood isn't what it used to be," which is perhaps the understatement of the century. She became a star, after all, when motion pictures treated their gods and goddesses with an otherworldly reverence rarely seen today. Her kind of glamour and privilege is an anomaly in the stripped-down reality show world of contemporary America. Yet, for what it's worth, she continues to thrive as if little has changed.

Or so it would seem. Elizabeth Taylor still resides in her capacious mansion behind tall electronic gates on exclusive Nimes Road in posh Bel Air, California, where even with our currently depressed economy, the smallest cottage sells for more than ten million dollars. Over the years she has added several wings to the original property and filled it with handcrafted, personalized furniture and furnishings as well as one of the most valuable private art collections in the country. Ensconced in the middle of her own little kingdom, Liz reigns over a household staff that includes maids, a butler, a chauffeur, a chef, a houseboy, a private secretary, a personal aide, a gardener, and a full-time maintenance man who doubles as a pool boy. Other employees come and go, including masseurs, personal trainers, physical therapists, acupuncturists, hair stylists, manicurists, money managers, accountants, and a battery of lawyers. It isn't as though Elizabeth can't afford to support her legion of helpers and advisors. By the beginning of 2011 she had amassed a fortune worth in excess of $600 million.

"The place is run like a corporation," said one of Taylor's staffers, "with Elizabeth Taylor as chief operating officer. There are all sorts of rules and regulations. Lateness is not tolerated. If you're two minutes late for a meeting with her, that's the last meeting you'll ever attend. At the same time she's a very generous boss. If you're sick, she sends you to her doctor. If you need personal time off and you ask for it in advance, she'll always grant it. If you have a problem, she'll discuss it with you. She gives regular cash bonuses and very expensive gifts at Christmas and Easter. As long as you don't cross her, she's enormously loyal. Several members of her staff have been with her for thirty years or more. Of course when you go to work for her you have to sign a nondisclosure agreement, but then that's common practice in today's Hollywood."

One reason Liz maintains such a large and all-encompassing household staff is that these days the preponderance of her time is spent at home. Despite occasional public appearances, she has become a rather remote and reclusive figure, a legend from the past, a superstar and icon whose legacy has already been written. Once one of the most prolific actresses in Hollywood, she no longer performs, though she would probably accept a role if offered the right one. After a brief appearance in *The Flintstones* in 1994, the last film project in which she participated was *Those Old Broads,* a 2001 made-for-television movie that also starred Shirley MacLaine, Joan Collins, and Taylor's old rival Debbie Reynolds, with whom she has now made her peace. Carrie

Fisher, the daughter of Debbie Reynolds and Eddie Fisher, wrote the script for the movie, and it was her idea to offer Elizabeth a role, realizing that her inclusion in the two-hour production would help draw a wide viewing audience.

One of the most remarkable aspects of Liz's life is that she's alive at all. It has been said before of her but it must be said again: she is truly the ultimate survivor, having outlived almost all her film contemporaries, particularly those like Natalie Wood, James Dean, Montgomery Clift, and Marilyn Monroe, who died tragically and at the height of their stardom. Ironically, Taylor consistently had the worst health of all of them, suffering dozens of illnesses and injuries requiring surgeries of all kinds and lengthy convalescences in hospitals and at home. According to medical reports, she has broken her back five times, had both hips replaced, and underwent brain surgery to remove a tumor that fortunately turned out to be benign. She has endured several skin cancer surgeries, has twice recovered from life-threatening bouts with pneumonia, and most recently has had to deal with complications attributable to osteoporosis as well as scoliosis, forcing her to make public appearances while restricted to a wheelchair.

In October 2009 Liz faced her most serious health problem to date, subjecting herself to a long and complicated heart operation, a procedure she had put off since 2004 when first diagnosed with congestive heart failure, a progressive condition that threatened her very existence. "She could barely move," remarked one of her household employees. "She fully understood the risks involved in undergoing heart surgery at a fairly advanced age. She was in her late seventies. But she'd become bedridden, an invalid, which for her represented a fate worse than death. As she saw it, she had no choice. It was do or die. And true to form, she came through it with flying colors." Several weeks after her heart surgery, she informed a reporter, "I feel as if I've been reborn."

Although no longer a movie queen, Taylor remained cognizant of the fact that she remained very much in the public eye. In May 2006, she appeared on *Larry King Live* to refute rumors that she was suffering from an advanced case of Alzheimer's disease. Three months later, while she vacationed on North Oahu, the press reported that she was on her deathbed and wanted to be buried in Hawaii. To counter this latest onslaught of misinformation, she boarded a 32-foot fishing vessel and went "swimming with the sharks." Covering the shark expedition, a local journalist disclosed that besides a couple of aides, she was traveling with Jason Winters, whom she described as "my manager and dear friend." Winters, a wealthy, self-made, forty-nine-year-old African American, had cofounded the Sterling/Winters Management Corporation, a Los Angeles–based talent agency whose client roster featured (among others) Janet Jackson, the sister of Liz's great buddy Michael Jackson. In addition to his firm, Winters reportedly controlled vast investments in real estate and industrial stock. When word spread that he and Taylor were in Hawaii, a whole new set of rumors were set in motion, suggesting that the couple, despite their nearly thirty-year age difference, were "madly in love" and about to marry.

One function fulfilled by Liz's affluent financier involved his ability to provide her with welcome advice concerning her fragrance business in addition to a newly developed jewelry line she had just begun to promote. By 2006 her perfume interests had grown into a major international consortium. Currently distributed by Elizabeth Arden, her leading brand names were still Passion and White Diamonds, both of which had been on the market for some fifteen years and had grossed an estimated billion dollars. Her latest scents—Black Pearls, Brilliant White Diamonds, Forever Elizabeth, and Violet Eyes—were all on the rise. Capitalizing on what remained Elizabeth's greatest asset, the last of the four brand names had been Jason's idea. By the same token he played an instrumental role in helping Liz launch the aptly named House of Taylor, her couture jewelry corporation. Because of the failing economy, her jewelry concern fared less well than the perfume company and within three years went bankrupt, though it led to the publication of *My Love Affair with Jewelry*, a book by Elizabeth showcasing her personal collection. "Husbands come and go," she proclaimed, "but diamonds are forever."

Business enterprises aside, by 2007 Jason and Liz were a bona fide item. They were seen out and about in both Los Angeles and Hawaii, where they jointly purchased a vacation retreat, a $10 million villa overlooking the sea. Early that year they were spotted at a seaside grille in Honolulu, feasting on caviar and lobster. A pair of burly security guards had been hired by Liz and stood nearby because she'd wanted to wear the 33-carat Krupp diamond given to her by Richard Burton. She also wore a floor-length satin gown and white mink stole, despite the tropical heat. As they sat watching a half-dozen Polynesian dancers and fire eaters, Liz tenderly stroked Jason's face and whispered into his ear. In Los Angeles they were sometimes seen together at the Abbey, a popular gay nightspot, and in the lounge at the Hotel Bel-Air, not far from Liz's estate. They attended Macy's Passport HIV/AIDS gala, an annual Los Angeles fund-raiser, which in 2007 honored Elizabeth by naming her Humanitarian of the Year. Winters was in the audience at the Paramount Pictures lot when Elizabeth acted on stage opposite James Earl Jones in a one-night AIDS benefit presentation of *Love Letters,* a play by A. R. Gurney, the proceeds from which were used to pay for a thirty-seven-foot AIDS "Care Van" and to help fund the recently established New Orleans AIDS Task Force. Jason and Liz watched the July Fourth fireworks together aboard a leased yacht off the beach at Santa Monica. The former actress later told New York gossip columnist Liz Smith that Winters "is one of the most wonderful men I've ever known, and that's why I love him so much." Pressed by Smith for further information, Taylor insisted she and Jason were just "close friends," an expression that in Hollywood can mean almost anything.

Rumors of an impending marriage continued to flourish, particularly in the tabloids. *Star* reported that Taylor had spent a million dollars on a bejeweled turban she intended to don on her wedding day. Liz emphatically denied the story, telling *USA Weekend* magazine, "Oh, God, no! I would never get married. I've gone down that road too many times to count." She had served as maid of honor (Michael Jackson had been best man) at Liza Minnelli's ill-fated 2002 marriage to concert promoter David Gest and was only too aware of the perils of a late-in-life betrothal. She spoke briefly in the *USA Weekend* interview of her previous vow to never walk down the aisle again, especially after her failed union with Larry Fortensky. Although she didn't say it, she no doubt must have wondered what had possessed her to marry Fortensky in the first place, a man twenty years her junior and with whom she had nothing in common save an alcohol abuse problem and a shared attraction to junk food.

Larry Fortensky had been the most unlikely of Liz's seven husbands. By the end of their marriage she had begun treating him more like a servant than a spouse. They slept in separate bedrooms and fought about almost everything. He complained that she snored like a truck driver; she lambasted him for smoking like a chimney, reportedly offering him a million dollars to give up cigarettes. He refused. He wanted to start his own construction company, but Taylor wouldn't have it; she wanted him to be available to travel with her and to escort her to celebrity bashes and charity events. Their daily schedules were also mutually incompatible: he was an early riser; she liked to stay up all night and spend her mornings in bed (an orthopedic model specially designed to accommodate her individual needs). An acquaintance of the superstar told a Fleet Street publication that Liz spent more time with her pet parrot—which she taught to say, "I love diamonds!"—than she did with her husband. When the London periodical called for a comment, one of Liz's entourage admitted that Taylor probably did spend more time with her parrot simply because the bird was more interesting than Larry Fortensky, "but don't quote me on that."

Larry Fortensky walked away from his four-year marriage to Taylor with a relatively healthy divorce settlement. His first purchases included a brand-new "fully loaded" black BMW and a luxury mobile home that he kept in the town of Hemet, an hour east of Los Angeles. However, according to newspaper reports, he was arrested in August 1996 for alleged drug use and again in 1998 for allegedly assaulting a girlfriend. In January 1999, he tumbled down a flight of stairs in a recently purchased San Juan Capistrano home, sustaining serious head and chest injuries. Barely breathing, he was taken to Mission Hospital

Regional Medical Center in Mission Viejo, California, where he underwent brain surgery. He remained in a coma for a month. A friend visited him at his home ninety days after the accident and encountered a bloated, shambling figure with barely enough cash on hand to buy groceries. The courts subsequently appointed Julie, a daughter from his first marriage, to be his "conservator" in order to protect what remained of his divorce settlement from Taylor. When his condition improved, he returned to court in an effort to regain control of his assets. Despite the fact that Liz failed to keep in touch with Larry (and apparently instructed her staff not to put through his telephone calls), she did not castigate him publicly. In her televised 2006 Larry King interview, she called Fortensky "a very sweet, gentle man, who wanted to experience life. . . . It just didn't work out between us."

Elizabeth Taylor's roller-coaster ride through life, for all its wondrous moments, afforded little peace and few dull moments. It seemed almost as if she thrived on excitement. In late 1995, with Taylor's marriage to Larry Fortensky coming apart, actress Sherilyn Fenn portrayed her in an NBC-TV miniseries about her life, *Liz: The Elizabeth Taylor Story* (based upon an earlier edition of this biography). When she learned that the miniseries had been scheduled to air in early 1996, Liz instructed her attorneys to seek an injunction against both NBC and Lester Persky, the film's producer. She claimed that she and she alone owned the rights to her life, and without her permission the film could not be broadcast. The case was dismissed. Being a worldwide celebrity, the details of Taylor's life were in the public domain. Anybody could write—or make a film—about her.

By strange coincidence Lester Persky lived next door to Taylor on Nimes Road. "My backyard looked out over her swimming pool," ventured Persky. "When she was alone she'd swim and sunbathe in the nude. She'd spread out across a chaise lounge, her flab hanging out over the sides of the chair. She eventually lost a lot of weight, but frankly I don't think she cared much what she looked like or what people thought of her. But that's a plus. She wasn't vain. She was gritty and tough. She'd once been America's glamour queen, but she fully accepted the process of aging. I don't think it really bothered her. She took life as it came."

As for the miniseries, Persky heard from a close friend of Liz's that she'd watched it on television. "Her friend told me she enjoyed it," remarked Persky. "She felt it was a fair depiction of her life. Of course she'd never admit as much to me."

In December 1999, the same month Queen Elizabeth II anointed Elizabeth Taylor a Dame Commander of the Order of the British Empire, she received a letter from former husband Eddie Fisher, asking her to meet with him. "After all that time," said Fisher (who died in 2010 at age eighty-two), "I wanted to see her and sort out all that had happened between us. Needless to say, she never responded. Looking back, I felt I'd gotten the short end of the stick. I can honestly say she was the love of my life. She was also my ruination. I basically gave up my singing career to be with her, and when she dumped me for Richard Burton, she made me out to be the bad guy. The press lauded her as nothing short of Joan of Arc at the same time that they condemned me for not immediately agreeing to a divorce, as if I were the one standing in the way of Elizabeth's happiness."

Regardless of what Elizabeth Taylor might have thought of Eddie Fisher, these were not her finest hours. By her own admission, the ten years between her divorce from Larry Fortensky and the beginning of her relationship with Jason Winters were among the most difficult she had ever faced. Her medical hardships and the scarcity of acting jobs were only part of the problem. Much of it had to do with her inability to find or sustain a meaningful love interest. From time to time she would date her old friend George Hamilton, but theirs was essentially a platonic relationship. Then there was actor Rod Steiger, whom she'd known for decades but with whom she'd never gone on a date. One day in 1999 he gave her a call and asked her out.

"I'd heard via the grapevine," recalled Steiger, who died in 2002, "that Elizabeth was rather depressed at this time. I'd been through about five years of clinical depression myself, so I thought perhaps I could help. I used to see her two or three times a week. I'd pick her up in my car and we'd go out for burgers and fried chicken. Or we'd visit friends. Other times we'd drive around the Santa Monica Mountains. When all else failed, we'd stay at home and play Scrabble. We wore matching gold pendants in the shape of the Little Prince from the fable by Antoine de Saint-Exupéry, which I bought at Tiffany. It wasn't a romance. We'd just talk and spend time together."

Steiger continued to see Elizabeth even though she'd become involved with actor Jeff Goldblum, whom she met at a party in Beverly Hills in April 2001. She was sixty-nine, and he was forty-eight. "Elizabeth asked me what I thought of Goldblum," said Steiger, "and I told her I barely knew the guy. 'What do you think of him?' I asked. 'Well,' she said, 'he makes me feel young, and he's crazy about me.' I must have rolled my eyes or something, because I didn't hear from her again for about a month. One day I read in the paper that they were going to marry, and a few days later I read that they'd broken up."

Taylor appeared at the Golden Globes ceremony in 2001, causing alarm when she hobbled onto the stage, seemingly disoriented and slurring her words. She'd been selected to present the Best Picture of the Year award. Instead of reading the names of the six nominees, she opened the envelope and announced *Gladiator* as the winning selection. The audience stirred. Taylor realized her mistake. Staring at the teleprompter, she recited the half-dozen nominees, then said, "And the winner is—*Gladiator!*" She then bid the audience farewell: "Good night to you all, y'all, y'all, y'all." Reporting the incident, the next day's *New York Post* accused the actress of apparently having been inebriated.

There were other bizarre episodes. Although she looked well in December 2002 when she appeared as one of five honorees at the twenty-fifth annual awards program at the John F. Kennedy Center in Washington, D.C., she seemed "out of it" several days later, according to a waiter, as she dined at La Dome in Los Angeles with her newest beau, Dr. Gary Schwartz, who happened to be her longtime dentist. The tabloids referred to Schwartz, ten years his companion's junior, as "the latest in a long line of Liz's boy-toy escorts" and with a touch of sophomoric wordplay inquired, "Which of the aging actress's many cavities is her dentist planning to fill?" No doubt distressed by the ridicule, Dr. Schwartz soon stopped seeing Elizabeth, at least socially.

Even more embarrassing was an event that took place in 2003 involving Taylor and members of her household staff. The would-be scandal, covered by London's *Daily Mail,* erupted when her landscape gardener, ordered by Taylor to create a "theme-park-style tropical garden" on her property, claimed she owed him money for the work and refused to pay. He sued. His court papers stipulated that not only hadn't he been properly recompensed, but that he'd been unjustly terminated. The gardener maintained that Taylor had attempted to coerce him into having sex with another male member of her staff, and that the other employee had been forced to have sex with Taylor. Liz's secret nickname (among employees), the gardener noted in his lawsuit, was "the old trampoline." If you refused "to jump the old trampoline," you risked being sacked. Although the case was settled out of court, the gardener's charges—whether true or not—left a permanent stain on Taylor's rapidly fading image.

Later in the year she and her entourage attended the Cannes Film Festival for a special screening of *Giant,* the 1956 film in which she'd played opposite Rock Hudson and James Dean. Exiting the theater after the show, she suffered what one French newspaper described as "a complete breakdown." She began weeping and couldn't stop. The next day as she came out of her hotel she was trailed by a pack of paparazzi. Suddenly wheeling around and facing them, she screamed, "If you want to take my picture, show me the fucking money." Alan Bouchard, one of the photographers in attendance that day, found the demand rather shocking. "Nobody knew what she meant," he said. "She kept insisting we fork up money before she'd agree to have her picture taken. 'Show me the money, show me the money,' she kept saying. But of course nobody needed her permission. It was the Cannes Film Festival, and she was there. And she was Elizabeth Taylor. After a long and heated debate, she finally explained herself. She wanted us to contribute to her AIDS Foundation. Then she'd pose for us. Okay, already. So somebody passed a hat around and we all anteed up a few bucks. She smiled. She seemed totally out of her mind. The thing is, I'd seen her in Paris years earlier when she and Burton were together. This was maybe a lifetime ago. She was so goddamn beautiful back then. Now this. She'd aged and not necessarily for the better. But she'd also lived. God, had she lived. And that's what it's all about."

Besides Jason Winters, one of Elizabeth Taylor's most sustaining relationships had been with Michael Jackson. When he died on June 25, 2009, of acute Propofol intoxication at age fifty, she issued an emotional tribute: "I loved Michael with all my soul and I can't imagine life without him. We had so much in common and we had such loving fun together. He will live in my heart forever, but it's not enough. My life feels so empty. I don't think anyone knows how much we loved each other. It was the purest, most giving love I've ever known."

Yet for all her passion, Taylor had been decidedly silent when Michael Jackson went on trial in 2005 for sexually abusing a minor, not the first time he'd faced such charges. Although acquitted, the pop star's reputation, already sullied in the eyes of the public, was forever tarnished. His most ardent supporters had to wonder. An incredibly talented entertainer, Jackson nevertheless had all the makings (and markings) of a child molester, a sexual deviant whose innocence in court had most probably been gained by virtue of an almost limitless bankroll. Even Elizabeth Taylor, for all her self-proclaimed love of the man, must have been revolted.

Taylor did not participate in the Staples Center memorial held for Jackson, instead issuing a statement that she wanted to conduct her mourning in complete privacy. Her absence from the memorial services gave rise to widespread rumors that the Jackson family didn't want her there and hadn't invited her. These rumors were never denied. Several members of the family evidently hadn't forgotten her notable lack of support during Michael's 2005 courtroom drama. Other family members, however, perhaps not wishing to create ill will, saw to it that Taylor was invited to Michael's funeral on September 3, 2009. After sitting through the ceremony at the Great Mausoleum in Los Angeles, with its magnificent stained-glass windows and replicas of Michelangelo's artworks, she told a friend, "I felt a sense of peace there that I've never experienced before."

Having lost many friends during the past decade, Elizabeth Taylor has gone to lengths to strengthen her ties to her own family, which at last count includes her four children, ten grandchildren, and four great-grandchildren. Her daughter Liza, a sculptress living in upstate New York, recently called Elizabeth "the great earth mother of all time." Elizabeth's son Michael has given up acting and, following in his half-sister's footsteps, has taken up art. His brother, Edward Wilding, continues as a film editor in California. Maria, Elizabeth's adopted daughter, after sampling a number of professions, is currently a philanthropist and resides in Idaho. The entire clan gathers at Taylor's Bel Air home twice a year—at Thanksgiving and on Liz's birthday.

For years another member of the family was Sugar, Liz's beloved white Maltese, whose life ended in 2005. The dog accompanied its owner everywhere. "I've never loved a dog this much," Taylor has said. "It's amazing. Sometimes I think there's a person in there." A few months after Sugar's demise, Liz transferred her love and affection to Daisy, another Maltese and a direct descendant of Sugar. Whenever the actress is seen in public with Jason Winters, they are invariably accompanied by a puff of white fur whose dog collar bears the name "Daisy Taylor."

Given the events and exigencies of Elizabeth Taylor's extraordinary eighty-year journey through life, it is nearly impossible to sum her up in words. Possibly it is her lifelong friend, actor Roddy McDowall, who came closest to placing her in some sort of meaningful context. Shortly before McDowall's death in October 1998, he spoke about Taylor, going back in time to their first meeting, in 1943, on the set of *Lassie Come Home.*

"I watched Elizabeth develop from a childhood star into one of

Hollywood's great street icons," he reminisced. "She is the living embodiment of luxury and style, the ultimate female screen close-up. She is the last living grande dame of the Hollywood studio system, and the first major actress to break away from that tradition in order to appear in films as an independent. She is also the first seven-figure contract player, the first actress paid a million dollars to appear in a film. She's the last great movie star to emerge from an era when Hollywood was the sacred Mecca of the movie industry, long before the age of special effects and comic book heroes and villains.

"But in reality, Elizabeth Taylor is much more than an actress. She's a personality. She was the first superstar to draw the world's attention to the plight of AIDS and at a point when such a stance was highly unpopular. She always swam against the current. She was never afraid to speak up for the underdog. She was loyal to her friends and relentless in her battles against the enemy.

"I don't know who can be compared to Elizabeth Taylor. Maybe Marilyn Monroe? They were both legends in their lifetime. The difference is Marilyn died in 1962, when she was only thirty-six. She remains frozen in our memory the way she looked at a relatively young age, still beautiful, still sexy, still the epitome of vulnerability and innocence. Liz, on the other hand, with her 'nine lives,' has become a mature woman. She has gained weight, suffered illness, gone through cycles of alcoholism and drug abuse, and has come out at the other end. It sounds trite to say so, but she is a survivor. She is by no means perfect. She is full of faults. But she is real. Despite her wealth and renown, she has endured many of the same struggles that most of us have had to face at one time or another."

Elizabeth Taylor died of congestive heart failure on March 23, 2011. She was seventy-nine years old.

CHAPTER NOTES

Whenever possible, the author has provided source within the body of the text. The following endnotes are included to supplement the textual references. And while it is not necessarily a complete list of sources, it provides the interested reader with some idea of the author's methodology. Also included are occasional comments of an extraneous but informative nature.

CHAPTER 1

Leonard Firestone and Betty Ford: The Laurance Rockefellers and Walter Annenbergs were also among the founders and funders of the Betty Ford Center, as were such Fortune 500 companies as Chevron, C.U.S.A., and Dart and Kraft, Inc.

"They'd never had a celebrity before," Dominick Dunne, "The Red Queen," *Vanity Fair,* December 1985.

"The Journal": "Elizabeth Taylor: Journal of a Recovery," by John Duka. *New York Times,* February 4, 1985.

The cases (D-4348; D-4350) against the three physicians herein named were instigated by John K. Van De Kemp, attorney general of the state of California, and William L. Marcus, deputy attorney general of the state of California. The results of the investigation were presented before the Division of Medical Quality, medical Board of California, state of California. In 1990, however, when the case went to the Los Angeles County district attorney's office, the latter refused to press criminal charges against any of the physicians and returned the case instead to the Medical Board of California. The lengthy records and inventories issued by the attorney general's office constitute the major source for specific medical information as contained in this chapter.

"The volume and variety": Vern Leeper, supervisor at the California Medical Board, stipulated in an interview with the author: "It's a wonder Elizabeth Taylor didn't overdose on all those drugs, but we have people who take unbelievable amounts of medication . . . it's because they've been taking them for years and they have a tolerance for medication that they survive. You and I would be dead in a minute."

Personal interviews for this chapter were conducted with Amy Porter, Barnaby Conrad, George Carpozi Jr., Tony Brenna, Patricia Seaton, Peter Lawford, Amy Tandem.

CHAPTER 2

Ladies Home Journal: Sara Taylor wrote a series of three autobiographical articles that ran in *Ladies' Home Journal* in April, May, and June 1954. The articles dealt substantially with Elizabeth Taylor. Sara later expressed the hope that the chapters could be expanded into a full-scale biography of Elizabeth. After writing one thousand pages, she circulated the book among agents and publishers, who deemed the manuscript unpublishable. Sara blamed the multiple rejections on her failure to delve into her daughter's sex life.

Elizabeth Taylor: An Informal Memoir, by Elizabeth Taylor, published by Harper & Row, 1965, is a skimpy whitewash of Elizabeth Taylor's life, with a few trenchant memories of her early childhood, which is its chief value as autobiography.

Nona Smith letter to Hedda Hopper, January 27, 1964. Hedda Hopper collection, Margaret Herrick Library, Academy of Motion Picture Arts and Sciences, Beverly Hills.

For further information on Victor Cazalet, see Robert Rhodes Jones, *Victor Cazalet: A Portrait.* London: Hamish Hamilton, 1976.

Elizabeth Taylor, by Elizabeth Taylor: Elizabeth Taylor also recorded in her memoir a ballet performance she gave with other students at Vacani in which the curtain fell but she continued to flutter about the stage while the other girls disappeared into the wings. Nobody associated with Vacani can recall this incident, which may or may not be a typical Taylor embroidery of actual events.

Personal interviews for this chapter were conducted with Thelma Cazalet-Keir, Kurt Stempler, Susan Licht, Ernest Lowy, Lady Diana Cooper, Betty Vacani, Olivia Raye-Williams, Jane Lynch, Charles R. Stephens, Allen T. Klots, Jerome Zerbe, Deborah Zygot, John Taylor, Roger Wall.

CHAPTER 3

According to M-G-M publicist Ann Straus, "There was a good deal of mutual resistance to Elizabeth Taylor at M-G-M. My uncle, Jack Cunnings, a prominent M-G-M producer, refused to give the child a screen test because he claimed he'd seen hundreds of beautiful young girls like Elizabeth, none of whom could act."

Dan Kelly memo: Universal Studios.

"She can't sing . . . ,": notes on Muhl-Selznick meeting February 5, 1932, Universal Studio Archives.

Television documentary: "Elizabeth Taylor: Film on Film," WNET-TV, January 27, 1990.

Conventional seven-year contract: see Alexander Walker, p. 39, *Elizabeth.*

Orson Welles: see Barbara Lemming, *Orson Welles,* pp. 259–60.

M-G-M: Covering 172 acres in Culver City, M-G-M boasted thirty soundstages,

150 ancillary buildings, a fully stocked zoo, woods, gardens, lakes, and some four thousand full-time employees.

Fred Zinnemann: letter from Fred Zinnemann to author's researcher, Susan Freedman, June 21, 1991.

Personal interviews for this chapter were conducted with Oscar De Mejo, Helen Ames Grobel, Helen Rose, Jane Hodges Grant, Charles Whalens, Judy Craven, Barbara Jackson, Samuel Marx, Clarence Brown, Lucille Rymann Carroll, Liz Whitney, Colonel Cloyce Tippett, Egon Merz, Ann Straus, Anne Revere.

CHAPTER 4

Lucille Carroll had been preparing to tour the country for talent when Elizabeth Taylor nominated herself for the role. Bill Grady had already auditioned several hundred Canadian hopefuls without much luck. Even young Katherine Hepburn had been briefly considered for the Taylor part.

Ate huge country breakfasts: eggs, pancakes, and home fries—at a place called Tibbs, in the hope that the added weight would increase her cleavage.

Fred Zinnemann letter to author's researcher, Susan Freedman.

Pandro Berman: interview with Pandro Berman, American Film Institute, Los Angeles, California, January 26, 1972.

Personal interviews for this chapter were conducted with Clarence Brown, Lucille Ryman Carroll, Egon Merz, Ann Straus, Anne Revere, Angela Lansbury, Chris Anderson, Mickey Rooney, Bob Salvatore.

CHAPTER 5

L. B. Mayer: In *Charmed Lives,* Michael Korda's memoir of his family, he recalls L. B. Mayer's "stultifying dinner parties" and L. B.'s "interminable monologues about how he had always been right and everybody else—Thalberg, Schenck, Goldwyn, his sons-in-law Goetz and Selzwick—had always been wrong, as well as disloyal and spineless."

Jean Porter: Jean Porter Oral History, SMU Archives.

William Ludwig: William Ludwig interview, Oral History, SMU Archives.

Elizabeth Taylor carried: Katherine Hepburn letter to author, March 21, 1990.

"The Love Game": Alexander Walker, *Elizabeth Taylor,* pp. 51–55.

"happily": see Diana Cary, *Hollywood's Children,* p. 234.

"pink and silver formal dress": Alexander Walker, *Elizabeth Taylor,* p. 65.

Memo: M-G-M Archives, n.d. L. B. Mayer to Howard Strickling.

Adrian (1903–1959). Gilbert Adrian was an American costume designer with M-G-M from 1927 to 1942 and is credited with the authentic images of Garbo, Shearer, Harlow, etc. He married Janet Gaynor in 1939 and later opened his own fashion establishment. They had one son, Robin, born July 6, 1940, now national sales manager at CBS-TV, Hollywood.

July 14, 1949: visits home of Alexander Warren.

Personal interviews for this chapter were conducted with John Taylor, Terry Moore, Laura Barringer, Mary MacDonald, Ava Gardner, Jane Powell, Kathryn Grayson, Lillian Burns Sydney, Anne Francis, Marshall Thompson, June Petersen, George Murphy, Jane Lydon, James Lydon.

CHAPTER 6

Jules Goldstone, Elizabeth Taylor's agent at the time, boasted of her beauty: "the most beautiful child since Venus de Milo."

Sixteenth birthday: see Walker, *Elizabeth Taylor,* 1946, pp. 61–62.

Smashed her car: statement made by Carole Baker (interview with Doris Lilly).

Despite her illness, Elizabeth prattled on about her crush on Peter Lawford, claiming that the moment she regained her health she intended to ask Lawford out on a date.

"Peter to me represented the first and last word on sophistication," Elizabeth told Sheron Hornby. "He's handsome and debonair," she added, "the kind of fellow you wouldn't mind introducing to your mother."

One of Elizabeth Taylor's many self-created fictions had to do with acting lessons. "I never had an acting lesson," she wrote in *Elizabeth Taylor: An Informal Memoir.* "I don't know how to act per se. I just developed as an actor." In truth, Lillian Burns Sidney spent hundreds of hours tutoring Taylor on her chosen craft.

Francis Taylor, Elizabeth's father, was also prone to exaggeration and fabrication. In an article, "My Daughter Elizabeth," which he wrote for *Parents* magazine (October 1944), he claimed: "Like most households, we have varied interests and we do not talk theatrical shoptalk." According to John Taylor, brother of Francis, "Shoptalk is all that Elizabeth and her mother engaged in. I never heard them discuss anything but the movies."

Glenn Davis: Glenn Davis played halfback for West Point and was known as "Mr. Outside." Army's other outstanding all-American that year was their fullback, Felix "Doc" Blanchard, whose sobriquet was "Mr. Inside."

Emily Torchia: Several of Ms. Torchia's comments come from the oral-history collection at SMU.

Personal interviews for this chapter were conducted with Ann Straus, Ann Cole, Jane Powell, Lillian Burns Sydney, John Taylor, Jane Ellen Wayne, Jim Schwartzberg, Glenn Davis, Leslie Rusch, Robert Kreis, Janet Leigh, June Allyson, Mary Astor, Larry Peerce, Patsy Kline, Hubie Kerns, Ralph Kiner, Joe Naar, Terry Moore, Earl Wilson, Johnny Meyers, Doris Lilly, Renee Helmer, Emily Torchia, Jackie Park.

CHAPTER 7

"I became intensely aware . . .": Elizabeth Taylor, *Elizabeth Takes Off,* p. 58.

"It is so strange . . ." Philippe Halsman, *Halsman, Sight and Insight.*

"I was absolutely terrified . . .": Academy of Motion Picture Arts and Sciences. George Stevens Jr. Collection. Filmed interview with Elizabeth Taylor held October 28, 1982, conducted by George Stevens Jr. and Susan Winslow, p. 1.

A Place in the Sun: A Place in the Sun was completed first, though it premiered after Elizabeth Taylor's next two films: *Father of the Bride* and *Father's Little Dividend,* made, respectively, in 1950 and 1951.

As Elizabeth recalled it: Academy of Motion Picture Arts and Sciences, George

Stevens Jr. Collection. Filmed interview with Elizabeth Taylor held October 28, 1982, conducted by George Stevens Jr. and Susan Winslow, p. 1.

Robert LaGuardia: Robert LaGuardia, *Monty,* p. 89.

Barron Hilton: The youngest son of Conrad Hilton Sr., Eric, handled the firm's personnel services and internal business affairs.

The Olive Wakeman letter from Elizabeth Taylor is located in the Conrad N. Hilton Archives, Conrad N. Hilton College of Hotel and Restaurant Management, University of Houston, Houston, Texas.

Personal interviews for this chapter were conducted with Yvonne Halsman, Eve Abbot Johnson, Ned Wynn, Mira Rostova, Luigi Luraschi, Patricia Bosworth, Billy LeMassena, Ashton Greathouse, Carole Doheny, Curt Strand, Zsa Zsa Gabor, Joan Bennett, Tom Irish, Doris Lilly, Ann Cole, Betty Sullivan Precht, Cathleen Huck.

CHAPTER 8

Quo Vadis: In the late 1940s, M-G-M had asked John Huston to direct the film, and Huston had considered placing Elizabeth Taylor and Gregory Peck in the lead roles. As Peck recalled the earlier planned version (letter to author, February 26, 1991): "I don't think I saw a finished script. I did have one or two conversations with Huston. He said he wanted to get completely away from the still earlier De Mille version. He wanted it to be primitive and rough-hewn.

"Somehow I went into the wardrobe department and tried on some Roman gear. It was apparent that my calves were too skinny and that boots would have to be devised. Later on, in *David and Bathsheba,* I wore such boots, and for the same reason."

The Plaza: According to her autobiography (*Elizabeth Taylor*) and other biographies that followed, the Plaza Hotel incident took place somewhat later, after Liz's romance had begun with Michael Wilding. According to the Plaza's records, however, the event is dated late January 1951.

annulment: Following their divorce, Elizabeth and Nicky met on several occasions to discuss the possibility of an annulment, once in New York and once at the Westport, Connecticut, home of Howard Young, who tried but failed to work out a resolution to the problem.

Personal interviews for this chapter were conducted with Geoff Miller, Jake Holmes, Garnet I. Sherman, Martha Reed, Larry Peerce, Marquise Emmita de la Falaise, Baron Alexis de Rede, Line Renaud, Claire Davis, Zsa Zsa Gabor, Joan Bennett, Stanley Donen, Betsy von Furstenberg, Patricia Hilton, Patricia Schmidlapp, Robert Quain, Penny Arum.

CHAPTER 9

Stewart Stern: letter to author, March 31, 1990. A less risqué limerick that Elizabeth Taylor used to recite at Hollywood dinner parties went:

> "What'll you have?" the waiter said,
> As he stood there picking his nose.

"Hard-boiled eggs, you son of a bitch!
You can't put your fingers in those!"

Benny Thau interoffice memo: M-G-M archives, Los Angeles, California.

Sapphire-ring story: Alexander Walker, *Elizabeth,* p. 137.

The menacing caller: FBI files, Washington, D.C.

Elizabeth had been exposed: ibid.

"What's Elizabeth got that I don't?": for another version of this anecdote see Steven Bach, *Marlene Dietrich,* pp. 351–52.

Marlene Dietrich: see also Maria Riva, *Marlene Dietrich,* pp. 62, 658. Following his divorce from Elizabeth Taylor, Michael Wilding again began dating Marlene Dietrich on and off.

Personal interviews for this chapter were conducted with Penny Arum, Marge Stengel, Leo Guild, Janet Leigh, Richard Thorpe, Stewart Stern, Stewart Granger, Zsa Zsa Gabor, Irene Mayer Selznick, Ava Gardner, Doris Lilly.

CHAPTER 10

"I can't. . . .": see Walker, *Elizabeth.*

Elephant Walk: It was H. N. Swanson, the legendary Hollywood agent, who first brought this Robert Standish vehicle to Elizabeth Taylor's attention. She initially wanted to acquire it as her own property for development purposes but later gave up the idea.

Peter Finch and Dana Andrews: Finch, Andrews, and Taylor ate lunch together each day at Lucy's El Adobe, a diner across the street from Paramount Studios. They were usually late returning to the set and formed what Finch dubbed "the Fuck-You Club," stressing his personal irreverence for Hollywood.

$47,000: Walker, *Elizabeth,* p. 148.

Pompous German director: see also Stewart Granger, *Sparks Fly Upward,* p. 299, for a similar version of this anecdote.

"I want somebody with guts": Warner Brothers archives.

Phyllis Gates: see Phyllis Gates and Bob Thomas, *My Husband, Rock Hudson,* p. 66.

Marla: see also Joseph C. Hamilton, "Liz and Me," *Texas Monthly,* December 1989.

Alexander Walker: Walker, *Elizabeth,* p. 163.

Elizabeth Taylor's health problems: Warner Brothers interoffice communications, USC.

"Iron lung . . .": see Walker, *Elizabeth,* p. 165.

The Glass Slipper, ibid., p. 164.

Elizabeth Taylor and Frank Sinatra: see Kitty Kelley, *His Way: The Unauthorized Biography of Frank Sinatra,* p. 215.

Personal interviews for this chapter were conducted with David Lewin, Armand Deutsch, H. N. Swanson, Stewart Granger, Dorismae Kerns, Oswald Morris, Richard Brooks, Ava Gabor, Kathryn Grayson, Joan Bennett, Dennis Hopper, Joseph C. Hamilton, Jeffrey Tanby, Terry Moore, James P. Knox, Lester Persky, Patricia Bosworth, Billy LeMassena, Joanna Casson, Jilly Rizzo, Gary Doctor, David McClintick, Miguel Ferreras.

CHAPTER 11

Phyllis Gates: Phyllis Gates and Bob Thomas, *My Husband, Rock Hudson,* p. 118.

"As she and Todd drove down": see Walker, *Elizabeth,* p. 170.

"The following afternoon": ibid.

"As she recounted the episode": Michael Todd Jr., *A Valuable Property,* p. 313.

"On hearing the words": ibid.

"I've lost a friend": ibid., pp. 313–14.

Personal interviews for this chapter were conducted with Mike Todd Jr., Kevin McCarthy, Dr. Rex Kennamer, Betsy Wolfe (Betsy Wolfe is a pseudonym, one of the few used in this book), Evelyn Keyes, Kurt Frings, Stewart Granger.

CHAPTER 12

"An Orthodox Jewish household": Chaym Goldbogen, Mike Todd's father, had always been identified by his son as a rabbi. Neither the rabbinical society of America nor the Jewish Theological Seminary lists a Rabbi Chaym Goldbogen in their voluminous files, suggesting that Todd invented the title for his father as a means of enhancing his own meager family background.

"Mike Todd Jr., the producer's son": Mike Todd Jr., *A Valuable Property,* p. 310.

"Guests making love": see Anne Chisholm and Michael Davie, *Lord Beaverbrook: A Life,* p. 498.

"Renoir, Pissarro, and Monet": Walker, *Elizabeth,* p. 175.

"Rolls-Royce Silver Cloud": ibid.

"Meals imported": ibid.

"Following the couple's return to California . . . :" Press reports of the day had it that Todd and Taylor flew to Acapulco, Mexico, to marry immediately upon her release from the Harkness Pavilion. Witnesses, however, stipulated that the couple first flew to Los Angeles (via Reno) to visit with Liz's sons prior to their marriage.

"$200,000": this anecdote supplied by Doris Lilly, who apparently heard it directly from Mike Todd.

"Fleeting premonition of tragedy": This phrase is supplied by Alexander Walker in his biography *Elizabeth,* p. 179.

"A girl": See Walker, *Elizabeth,* p. 183.

"The world's not ready for another Mike Todd": Elizabeth Taylor used Todd's line several weeks later when they returned to New York and appeared on Ed Morrow's TV show *Person to Person.*

Personal interviews for this chapter were conducted with Earl Wilson, Evelyn Keyes, Ed Dmytryk, Eva Marie Saint, Gwin Tate, Betsy Wolfe, Orson Bean, Phillip Dunne, Pia Lindstrom, David Anderson, Eddie Fisher, Patsy Kline, Doris Lilly, Joe Hyams, Ernesto Baer, Henry Woodbridge, Jean Murray Vanderbilt, José Maria Bayona, Di Bronn, Alexandre, Rosa Estoria, Marc Bohan, Simone Noir, Hebe Dorsey, Diana Vreeland, James Galanos, Art Buchwald.

CHAPTER 13

Cat on a Hot Tin Roof: Before Elizabeth Taylor showed interest, Grace Kelly was being seriously considered for Maggie the Cat. Kelly's subsequent marriage to Prince Rainier placed her out of contention, and the role went to Elizabeth Taylor.

Westport, Connecticut, house: The house belonged to the real estate agent who had been hired by the Todds to find them a residence in the area. After showing them a dozen unsatisfactory properties, the agent invited Elizabeth and Mike back to his house for a drink. When Elizabeth saw the agent's house, she told Todd, "This is the one I want." Todd subsequently paid the agent $50,000 for a one-year rental, and the agent and his family spent the next twelve months in Europe.

"incompatible with Paul Newman's": Joanne Woodward, wife of Paul Newman, told Edward Z. Epstein, coauthor of a Paul Newman biography, that Taylor and Newman's acting styles were completely different: "To say there was a difference in approach is the understatement of the century."

the *"Liz":* Most Elizabeth Taylor biographers have referred to Todd's leased airplane as the *Lucky Liz.* Photographs of the plane, however, make it clear that its proper name was the *Liz.* In any event, it proved highly unlucky for Mike Todd.

"Don Quixote": S. J. Perelman, who had received screen credit for having scripted *Around the World in 80 Days,* had already completed an acceptable version of Don Quixote. Because of Todd's death, the film was never made.

"dead at age forty-nine": Elizabeth sued Ayer Lease Plan, Inc. in Lyndon, New Jersey, for $5 million, charging them with negligence in the death of her husband. On February 20, 1962, federal court in New York awarded her a mere $40,000, the brunt of which (after legal fees) went into a trust fund for their daughter Liza Todd. The paltry award indicated that the court held Todd himself largely responsible for his own death.

Personal interviews for this chapter were conducted with Miguel Ferreras, Connie Wolf, Earl Wilson, Jack Smith, Jule Styne, Wayne C. Brockman, Marina Tal, Eddie Fisher, Truman Capote, Daphne Pereles, Kim Stanley, Burl Ives, Dame Judith Anderson, Meade Roberts, Richard Brooks, Kurt Frings, Bob Willoughby, Eva Guest.

CHAPTER 14

bronze casket: On March 3, 1959, a solemn Elizabeth Taylor returned to the Jewish Waldhern Cemetery to attend the dedication of the gravestone at Todd's burial site. The unpretentious stone was engraved: "Avrom Hirsch Goldbogen—Michael Todd—June 22, 1908–March 22, 1958. In June 1977, grave robbers ransacked Todd's casket and removed his remains, apparently in the belief that a $100,000 diamond ring had been buried with the cadaver. A body bag containing Todd's remains was located several days later outside the cemetery gates.

"On a couple of occasions": ibid., p. 360.

"The completion of the film": On finishing *Cat on a Hot Tin Roof,* Elizabeth became alarmed to learn that the IRS had launched an investigation into Mike Todd's recent income-tax returns, suggesting that he was guilty of income-tax fraud. Lasting a year, the investigation ended on an inconclusive note.

"Elizabeth, this is Hedda": Hedda Hopper, *The Whole Truth,* pp. 20–21.

Personal interviews for this chapter were conducted with Eva Guest, Dr. Rex Kennamer, Irene Sharaff, Daniel Stewart, Eddie Fisher, Richard Brooks, Eva Marie Saint, Burl Ives, Stewart Granger, Ken McKnight, Jane Ellen Wayne, Angela R. Sweeney, Rick Ingersoll, Mark Grossinger Etiss, Milton Lerner, Tania Grossinger, Al Melnick, Earl Wilson, Elaine Etess.

CHAPTER 15

"What about your children": see Debbie Reynolds, *Debbie: My Life,* pp. 189–90.

"prompting *Photoplay* to write": see Walker, *Elizabeth,* p. 208.

Vernon Scott: see Kitty Kelley, *Elizabeth Taylor,* p. 162. Kitty Kelley also provides a detailed account of Fisher-Taylor nuptials.

"gifts for Eddie": see Walker, *Elizabeth,* p. 211; see also various news reports of the day.

"evil and vicious tale": Gore Vidal letter to author, April 2, 1990.

"Monty's health had degenerated . . .": One evening after observing Monty's hopeless efforts on the set, Sam Spiegel said to Jack Hildyard, "We should have cast Monty as one of the mental patients in the film rather than as the doctor. He would have been perfect."

Eddie Fisher legally adopted Liza Todd. The adoption became a bone of contention during Elizabeth Taylor's divorce from Fisher; Taylor wanted Burton to be able to adopt her daughter. This was eventually accomplished, at considerable legal cost to Elizabeth. As for the Wilding boys, Michael Wilding would not permit them to be adopted by Fisher.

Parts of this chapter are based on the Walter Wanger papers, University of Wisconsin at Madison.

Two other versions of *Cleopatra* were also made. Claudette Colbert starred in Cecil B. De Mille's 1934 epic; Vivien Leigh, in a sumptuous 1945 offering that turned out to be Britain's costliest film ever.

"It sucks": see Walker, *Elizabeth,* p. 219.

"Now this is something": see Mike Stein, *Hollywood Speaks,* p. 175.

"The 'Bitch'": see Walker, *Elizabeth* pp. 219–20. Laurence Harvey and Elizabeth became better friends as the film progressed, but never quite as close as Taylor would have had others believe.

Personal interviews for this chapter were conducted with Lillian Burns Sydney, Eddie Fisher, Ken McKnight, Earl Wilson, Al Melnick, Rick Ingersoll, Fran Holland, Robert Serebrenik, Saul Lieberman, Bill Davidson, Ruth Nussbaum, Ann Straus, Dorismae Kerns, Gloria Luchenbill, Bob Willoughby, Truman Capote, Zsa Zsa Gabor, Jack Hildyard, Joseph L. Mankiewicz, Evelyn Keyes, Christopher Mankiewicz, Jean Murray Vanderbilt, Mary Jane Picard, David Brown, Daniel Mann, John Jiras.

CHAPTER 16

MCL Films, S.A.: Also known as MCL Films, S.A., the copartnership was created by attorney Martin Gang of Los Angeles. Fisher owned 147 shares of the capital stock, and Elizabeth Taylor had 148 shares. With a mailing address in Switzerland, the partnership was established to help save taxes on Elizabeth's huge earnings.

Shelley Winters: see Shelley Winters, *Shelley II,* pp. 342–47.

"During his absence": While Eddie Fisher was in Hollywood and Elizabeth in London, she received two kidnap threats against her children, who were staying with her at the Dorchester. The case was handled by Scotland Yard. No perpetrator was ever apprehended.

In February 1961, Eddie and Liz flew to Munich: see Walker, *Elizabeth,* p. 228, for a detailed account of the Seconal pill-taking incident.

Cedars of Lebanon Hospital: by 1961, the year of Elizabeth Taylor's fund-raising speech, Cedars of Lebanon-Mt. Sinai Hospital Medical Center. The dinner at which Elizabeth spoke was attended by a thousand guests and raised in excess of $7 million, a portion of which went toward medical research.

Max Lerner: see Kitty Kelley, *Elizabeth Taylor,* pp. 182–87.

Personal interviews for this chapter were conducted with Ronald Peters, John Valva, Rock Brynner, Ken McKnight, Lyle Stuart, Eddie Fisher, Tania Grossinger, Floyd Patterson, Lester Lanin, Art Buchwald, Charles Poletti, Dale Wasserman, Jackie Park, Jack Hildyard, Joanna Casson, Shelley Wanger, Max Lerner.

CHAPTER 17

First Taylor-Burton meetings: Burton himself describes his first meetings with Elizabeth in a slim volume he later published called *Meeting Mrs. Jenkins.*

Brad Geagley interviewed Tom Mankiewicz, Chris's younger brother, who took over Chris's position during the second half of *Cleopatra.*

"By mid-February 1962": Eddie Fisher threw a thirtieth birthday party for Elizabeth on February 27, 1962, at Alfredo's, one of Rome's best-known restaurants. Among others, he invited her parents, knowing that in their presence she would want to be on her best behavior. He hoped the presence of her parents might end the affair with Burton. It didn't.

Personal interviews for this chapter were conducted with Samuel Leve, Truman Capote, Eve Abbot Johnson, Eli Wallach, Douglas Kirkland, Mark Bohan, Donald Sanderson, Dr. Rex Kennamer, Patricia Seaton, George Carpozi Jr., Audrey Hepburn, Horst Haechler, Irene Sharaff, Richard Burton, Joseph L. Mankiewicz, Dr. Stanley Mirsky, Franz Fah, Hedi Donizetti-Mullener, Stewart Granger, Newton Steers Jr., Eddie Fisher, John Valva, Christopher Mankiewicz, David Lewin, Zsa Zsa Gabor, Eva Gabor, Brad Geagley, David Jenkins, Dale Wasserman, Phillip Dunne, Stephanie Wanger, Ken McKnight, Bert Stern.

CHAPTER 18

"Tempo": see Walker, *Elizabeth,* p. 253.

"Don't hate me, Tim": Melvyn Bragg, *Richard Burton,* p. 167.

John Morgan: ibid.

"compared Liz's brief stopover": Alexander Walker, *Elizabeth,* p. 261. Walker, who also apparently interviewed Graham Jenkins, was given basically the same comparison of Elizabeth's visit to Wales as representing a political campaign to garner votes on her own behalf.

"Elizabeth as is developed": *Don't Tread on Me: Selected Letters of S. J. Perelman,* p. 222.

near Philadelphia: The name of the institution in which Jessica was placed was the Deveroux Foundation, Devon, PA. Richard Burton later hired a public relations film to help raise funds for the foundation.

Montgomery Clift: see Gerald Clark, *Capote: A Biography,* p. 237.

Personal interviews for this chapter were conducted with John Valva, Michael Mindlin, Meade Roberts, Jerry Pam, Sue Lyons, John Huston, Ramon Castro, Sonia Rosenberg, Pico Pardo, Jane Ober, Stephen Birmingham, Budd Schulberg, Nelly Barquet, Guillermo Wulff, Lupe Wulff, Brad Geagley, Joseph L. Mankiewicz, Chris Mankiewicz, Elmo Williams, Franz Fah, David Jenkins, Graham Jenkins, Ava Gardner.

CHAPTER 19

"I arrived in the middle of an argument": Eddie Fisher, *Eddie Fisher,* p. 217.

New York Post: see *New York Post,* p. 6, July 14, 1994.

Rachel Roberts: the excerpts about Jordan Christopher are from unpublished sections of the diaries of actress Rachel Roberts. The diaries were provided courtesy of HarperCollins Inc.

"lazybones": production notes, Warner Brothers.

Personal interviews for this chapter were conducted with John Valva, Earl Wilson, Tom Snyder, Jack Smith, Meade Roberts, Gerald Clarke, Truman Capote, Richard Meryman, Eva Marie Saint, Martin Ransohoff, Edmund Kara, Rock Brynner, Hollis Alpert, Radie Harris, Rachel Roberts, David Lewin.

CHAPTER 20

Prof. Nevill Coghill: Nevill Coghill Papers: Oxford University.

Autobiography: Marlon Brando, *Songs My Mother Taught Me,* New York: Random House, 1994, pp. 254–56.

"I had a big struggle . . .": Michael Ciment, *Conversations with Losey,* pp. 280–81.

Personal interviews for this chapter were conducted with Robert Littman, Gerald Ayers, Truman Capote, Gisella Orchin, Robert Gardiner, Julie Harris, Robert Christedes, Francois de Lamothe, Francois Jevet, Jerry Vermilye, Baron Alexis de Rede, Tony Morgan, Sylvie Romain, Mia Farrow.

CHAPTER 21

"I tried it once": Bragg, *Richard Burton,* p. 258.

"La Peregina": see Bragg, *Richard,* p. 253.

"Elizabeth eventually played a cameo role": In so doing, she managed to make another female enemy—Charlotte Selwyn, a twenty-four-year-old British actress who was supposed to have made her debut in the cameo role that went to Taylor. Elizabeth, incidentally, didn't get a screen credit for her role. The producers called it "a fun thing."

Kitty Kelley: Kitty Kelley, *Elizabeth Taylor: The Last Star,* p. 257.

"through the intervention of a friend": The "friend" brought Elizabeth's photograph to Rose Stoler. Rose then read the tarot cards to predict Liz's future. The friend returned to Stoler's studio on two additional occasions with Elizabeth Taylor's photograph for supplementary tarot-card readings.

Margaret Leighton: By the time Leighton appeared in *Zee & Co.,* she was married to Michael Wilding, Elizabeth's second husband.

"white lace hot pants": see Kitty Kelley, *Elizabeth Taylor,* p. 279.

Ron Berkeley: Berkeley had once been married to fashion designer Vicky Tiel, whom the Burtons had helped set up by the financing of her couture atelier in the Saint-Germain-des-Prés section of Paris.

Personal interviews for this chapter were conducted with Jerry Vermilye, Meade Roberts, Roger Fillistorf, Hedi Donizetti-Mullener, Kevin McCarthy, Meryl Earl, Charles Jarrot, Ron Galella, John Valva, Rose Stoler, Nicole Valier, Ted H. Jordan, Billy Williams, Brian Hutton, Jerry Pam, Ed Dmytryk, J. Cornelius Crean, Leon Askin, Joseph Losey.

CHAPTER 22

"at Oxford": While Richard Burton lectured at Oxford, he and Liz stayed with her friend Sheran Cazalet, now married to Simon Horby, at their estate in Pusey, Oxfordshire.

Waris Husein: see also Paul Ferris, *Richard Burton,* pp. 224–28 for a somewhat altered version of the current author's interview with Husein.

"I told her to go": see Walker, *Elizabeth,* p. 319.

Personal interviews for this chapter were conducted with Linda Ashland, Andy Warhol, Jane Ober, Edward Dmytryk, George Barrie, Martin Poll, Stanley Eichelbaum, Billy Williams, Waris Husein, Larry Peerce, Dominick Dunne, Maurice Teynac, Monique Van Vooren, Raymond Vignali, Maureen Taylor.

CHAPTER 23

"This huge helicopter": see Dominick Dunne interview in James Spada, *Peter Lawford,* pp. 421–22.

"That woman will be . . .": Bob Colacello, *Holy Terror,* p. 152. Other references to Warhol in this section of the chapter occasionally derive from the same source.

"I believe in Santa Claus": Melvyn Bragg, *Richard Burton,* p. 419.

"Elizabeth Taylor similarly fled Oroville": Before leaving Oroville, Taylor befriended one of *The Klansman*'s minor cast members, namely, O. J. Simpson, who in 1974 was first making the transition from the gridiron to the silver screen.

"Alexander Walker": see Walker, *Elizabeth,* p. 323; see also Walker's description of the divorce session.

"Gwen Davis": see "Elizabeth Taylor: My Life Is a Little Complicated," *McCall's,* June 1976.

"the decorations": see Kitty Kelley, *Elizabeth Taylor,* p. 313.

"For $100": Document files in Los Angeles Superior Court, Civil Division, *Wynberg v. Taylor.* Passion Perfume Trial, December 1990.

"I know we": Walker, *Elizabeth,* p. 327.

"Maybe I'll": ibid.

Personal interviews for this chapter were conducted with Patricia Seaton, Henry Wynberg, Peter Lawford, Andy Warhol, Victor Bockris, Bob Colacello, Raymond Vignali, Gwen Davis, Phil Stearn, Truman Capote, Max Lerner, Richard Stanley, Ava Gardner, Jonas Gritzus, Paul Maslansky, Cindy Adams, Tony Brenna, Maya Plisetskaya, Marguerite Glatz, Chen Sam.

CHAPTER 24

"I turned around": Bragg, *Richard Burton,* p. 434.

"Alexander Walker": Walker, *Elizabeth,* p. 330.

Personal interviews for this chapter were conducted with Hedi Donizetti-Mullener, Henry Wynberg, Peter Lawford, Harvey Herman, Patricia Seaton, Halston, Doris Lilly, Ardeshir Zahedi, Firooz Zahedi, Dr. Louis Scarrone, Ronnie Stewart, Marian Christy, Frances Spatz Leighton, Claudia del Monte, Andy Warhol, Edward Carrachi, Sharon Churcher, Brigid Berlin, Bob Colacello, Allan Wilson, Lady Frances Ramsbotham, Teddy Vaughn, Gregg Risch, Rudy Maxa, Admiral Thomas Moorer, Chuck Conconi.

CHAPTER 25

Personal interviews for this chapter were conducted with Sen. John Warner, Stephen Bauer, George Coleman, Garry Clifford, Newton Steers Jr., Harriet Wasserman, James Mitchell, Stephen Sondheim, Heinz Lazek, Bette Davis, Zak Taylor, Gwin Tate, John Springer, Ina Ginsburg, Florence Klotz, Halston, Philip P. Smith, Rev. S. Nagle Morgan, Jackie Park, Joan Rivers, Lee Woolfert, Joyce Laabs, Felice Quinto, Steve Rubell, Steven Gaines, Sara Lithgow, Joel Broyhill, James Priddeaux, Oray, Henry Wynberg, Hannon Bell, Richard Stanley, Lester Persky, Sam Frank, Arthur Green, Cindy Adams, Michael Mullins, Harriet Meth, David McGough, Joey Adams, Dominique D'Ermo, Jerry Hieb, Wyatt Dickerson, Hank Lampey, Ronnie Stewart, Guy Hamilton.

CHAPTER 26

Burton's diaries record: Richard Burton's notebooks, entry for May 16, 1970.

Elizabeth Taylor: p. 195.

"As the overture was ending": Marie Brenner article in *New York* magazine, May 9, 1983.

"Hellman had said": Peter Feibleman, *Lilly: Reminiscences of Lillian Hellman,* p. 261.

"But when she was": Kitty Kelley, *The Last Star,* p. 399.

"Baby": *Elizabeth Takes Off,* p. 93.

"When Reagan was wounded": Nancy Reagan with William Novak, *My Turn.*

"By then, Elizabeth": Kitty Kelley, *The Last Star,* p. 40.

"To writer Charlotte Chandler": Charlotte Chandler, *The Ultimate Seduction,* pp. 27–28.

"From the bedroom": *Elizabeth Takes Off,* p. 103.

"very silent": Hebe Dorsey, "Burton Talks," *Vogue,* May 1983.

Taylor's 1982 ABC lawsuit: In 1994–95, Taylor had a similar reaction when producer Lester Persky acquired the television rights to this biography and sold them to NBC. Represented by her attorney, Neil Papiano, Taylor attempted on four separate occasions to sue NBC, the biography's author (C. David Heymann), the book's publisher (Carol Publishing Group), the screenwriter (Gerald Ayres), and Lester Persky Productions. Unable to obtain an injunction to prevent publication of the book or production and distribution of the miniseries, the feisty actress vowed to seek legal retribution once the NBC programs had aired.

"In May 1983": Elizabeth Taylor interview with Marie Brenner, *New York* magazine, May 9, 1983.

"On a white bathroom stool": Terry Oppenheimer, *Idol: Rock Hudson,* p. 247.

"under Sally Hay's care": see also Churcher, *New York Confidential,* p. 132.

"But Burton's journals record": Bragg, *Notebooks 1983,* entries for March 13–16, 20, 22, and 23.

"Burton himself was depressed": Graham Jenkins, *Richard Burton: My Brother,* pp. 237–39.

Personal interviews for this chapter were conducted with Austin Pendleton, Florence Klotz, Joseph Hardy, Hugh L. Hurd, Agnes Ash, Ed Safdie, A. Scott Berg, Felice Quinto, Richard Broadbent, Maureen Stapleton, Gwin Tate, Patricia Seaton, Elaine Young, Zak Taylor, Sharon Churcher, Susan Licht, Baz Bamigboye, Jonathan Gems, Sharon Nobel, Phil Blazer, Stanley Levy, Phil Blazer, Ronald Munchnick, Arnold Levy, Daphne Davis, Patti Taylor, Sarah Booth Convoy, Wendy Sahagen, Nancy Casey, Didi Drew, Dr. Rex Kennamer, Russell Turiak, and Stewart Granger.

CHAPTER 27

"Bufman told Sharon Churcher": Sharon Churcher, *New York Confidential,* p. 134.

"According to Burton's brother": Graham Jenkins, *Richard Burton: My Brother,* p. 242.

"Graham Jenkins": ibid., p. 245.

"Elizabeth's old friend": Patricia Seaton Lawford, *The Peter Lawford Story,* p. 227.

"At an AIDS benefit": Terry Oppenheimer, *Idol: Rock Hudson,* p. 220–22.

"Rock Hudson's memorial": Sara Davidson, *Rock Hudson: His Story,* p. 303.

"Taylor recalled working": Terry Oppenheimer, *Idol: Rock Hudson,* p. 241.

"chocolate martinis": Sara Davidson, *Rock Hudson: His Story,* p. 303.

"chocolate margaritas": Terry Oppenheimer, *Idol: Rock Hudson,* p. 241.

"The following spring": ibid., p. 247.

Personal interviews for this chapter were held with Peggy Lee, Russell Turiak, Jonathan Gems, Baz Bamigboye, Esme Chandler, Patricia Seaton, Frances Wall, Kirk Kerber, Zak Taylor, Elaine Young, Dennis Stein, Don Fauntleroy, Bob Guccione, Doris Lilly, Virginia Graham, Steven Gaines, Beverly Ecker, Gloria Rodriguez, Ben Smothers, Zsa Zsa Gabor, Judith van der Molen, Mart Crowley, Arthur Seidelman, Merrya Small, Liz Torres, Beth Kummerfeld, Wayne Anderson, Al Evans, Eve Abbott Johnson, Celia Lipton Farris, Ronnie Britt, Alec Byrne, Robert Rosenblum, Robert Woolley, Sharon Churcher, Henry Wynberg, David McGough, Lisa Rubenstein, Patti Taylor.

CHAPTER 28

"Fortensky had grown up": Judy Kessler, *Inside People,* p. 240.

"his home in Marbella": Ronald Kessler, *The Richest Man in the World,* p. 170.

"Khashoggi's palatial, $25 million apartment": ibid., pp. 168, 169, 171.

"In his autobiography": Michael Jackson, *Moonwalk,* p. 281.

"In 1984, when Jackson was working": Randy Taraborrelli, *Michael Jackson,* p. 390.

"Her announcement was very big news": Judy Kessler, *Inside People,* p. 241–42.

"The guests from Stanton": ibid., p. 246.

Personal interviews for this chapter were conducted with William H. Stadiem, Karin Fleming, Alec Byrne, Baz Bamingboye, Beth Kummerfeld, David McGough, Gerald Ayres, Malcolm Forbes, Cindy Adams, Doris Lilly, James Mitchell, Patricia Seaton, Christian Moulin, Hollis Alpert, Kathryn Livingston.

CHAPTER 29

This chapter did not appear in the original (1995) edition of *Liz.* The following articles were consulted in the preparation of this chapter: Daily Mail Online: "The Real Story Behind Liz Taylor's Plan to Marry Husband No. 9," by Paul Scott, September 29, 2007; Daily Mail Online: "Liz Taylor in Butler Sex Claim," article-19067/9/Liz Taylor-butler-sex-claim.ntiml; "Larry Fortensky Critically Injured in Fall," *Los Angeles Times,* January 29, 1999.

Personal interviews for this chapter were conducted with Eddie Fisher, Lester Persky, Alan Bouchard, Roddy McDowall.

BIBLIOGRAPHY

Adams, Edie, and Robert Windeler. *Sing a Pretty Song . . . : The "Offbeat" Life of Edie Adams.* New York: William Morrow, 1990.

Adams, Joey. *Here's to the Friars: The Heart of Show Business.* New York: Crown Publishers, 1976.

———. *Roast of the Town.* New York: Prentice-Hall, 1986.

Adams, Leith, and Keith Burns. *James Dean: Behind the Scene.* New York: Carol, 1990.

Adler, Bill. *Elizabeth Taylor, Triumphs and Tragedies.* New York: Ace Books, 1982.

Agee, James. *Agee on Film.* New York: McDowell-Obolensky, 1958.

All-Star Tribute to Elizabeth Taylor. CBS-TV, December 1, 1977.

Allan, John B. *Elizabeth Taylor.* Derby, Conn.: Monarch Books, 1961.

Alpert, Hollis. *Burton.* New York: G. P. Putnam's Sons, 1986.

Allyson, June, with Frances Spatz Leighton. *June Allyson.* New York: G. P. Putnam's Sons, 1982.

America's All-Star Tribute to Elizabeth Taylor. ABC-TV, March 9, 1989.

Andersen, Christopher. *Citizen Jane: The Turbulent Life of Jane Fonda.* New York: Henry Holt, 1990.

Angeli, Daniel, and Jean-Paul Dousset. *Private Pictures.* New York: Viking Press, 1980.

Anger, Kenneth. *Hollywood Babylon.* New York: Dell, 1975.

———. *Hollywood Babylon II.* New York: E. P. Dutton, 1984.

Astor, Mary. *My Story.* New York: Doubleday, 1959.

Atwan, Robert, and Bruce Forer, eds. *Bedside Hollywood: Great Scenes from Movie Memoirs.* New York: Nimbus Books, 1985.

Avedon, Richard. *Photographs: 1947–1977.* New York: Farrar, Straus & Giroux, 1978.

Bacall, Lauren. *By Myself.* New York: Ballantine Books, 1978.

Bach, Steven. *Marlene Dietrich: Life and Legend.* New York: William Morrow, 1992.

Bacon, James. *Hollywood is a Four-Letter Town.* Chicago: Henry Regnery, 1976.

Baker, Carroll. *Baby Doll: An Autobiography.* New York: Arbor House, 1983.

Barrett, Rona. *Miss Rona: An Autobiography.* Los Angeles: Nash, 1974.

Barrow, Andrew. *GOSSIP: A History of High Society from 1920–1970.* New York: Coward McCann & Geoghegan, 1979.

Bauer, Stephen M., with Frances Spatz Leighton. *At Ease in the White House: The Uninhibited Memoirs of a Presidential Social Aide.* New York: Birch Lane Press, 1991.

Behlmer, Rudy, and Tony Thomas. *The Movies About the Movies: Hollywood's Hollywood.* Secaucus, N.J.: Citadel Press, 1975.

Bell, Simon, Richard Curtis, and Helen Fielding. *Who's Had Who.* New York: Warner, 1990.

Bentley, Eric. *Are You Now or Have You Ever Been: The Investigation of Show Business by the Un-American Activities Committee, 1947–1958.* New York: Harper Colophon, 1972.

Bergen, Candice. *Knock Wood.* New York: Linden Press, 1984.

Berger, Marilyn. *The Beautiful People.* New York: Coward-McCann, 1967.

Birmingham, Stephen. *Duchess: The Story of Wallis Warfield Windsor.* Boston: Little, Brown, 1981.

———. *Jacqueline Bouvier Kennedy Onassis.* New York: Grosset & Dunlap, 1978.

Black, Shirley Temple. *Child Star: An Autobiography.* New York: McGraw-Hill, 1988.

Bloom, Claire. *Limelight and After: The Education of an Actress.* New York: Harper & Row, 1982.

Bockris, Victor. *The Life and Death of Andy Warhol.* New York: Bantam, 1989.

Boller, Paul F., Jr., and Ronald L. Davis. *Hollywood Anecdotes.* New York: Ballantine Books, 1987.

Bolton, Whitney. *The Silver Spade: The Conrad Hilton Story.* New York: Farrar, Straus & Young, 1954.

Bookbinder, Robert. *The Films of the Seventies.* Secaucus, N.J.: Citadel Press, 1982.

Bosworth, Patricia. *Montgomery Clift: A Biography.* New York: Harcourt Brace Jovanovich, 1978.

Bradshaw, Jon. *Dreams That Money Can Buy: The Tragic Life of Libby Holman.* New York: William Morrow, 1985.

Brady, Frank. *Citizen Welles: A Biography of Orson Welles.* New York: Charles Scribner's Sons, 1989.

———. *Onassis: An Extravagant Life.* Englewood Cliffs, N.J.: Prentice-Hall, 1977.

Bragg, Melvyn. *Richard Burton: A Life.* Boston: Little Brown, 1988.

Brando, Marlon, and Robert Lindsey. *Brando: Songs My Mother Taught Me.* New York: Random House, 1994.

Brochu, Jim. *Lucy in the Afternoon: An Intimate Memoir of Lucille Ball.* New York: William Morrow, 1990.

Brode, Douglas. *The Films of the Sixties: From La Dolce Vita to Easy Rider.* Secaucus, N.J.: Citadel Press, 1980.

———. *Lost Films of the Fifties.* Secaucus, N.J.: Citadel Press, 1988.

Brodsky, Jack, and Nathan Weiss. *The Cleopatra Papers: A Private Correspondence.* New York: Simon & Schuster, 1963.

Brough, James. *The Fabulous Fondas.* New York: David McKay, 1973.

Brouwer, Alexandra, and Thomas Lee Wright. *Working in Hollywood.* New York: Crown Publishers, 1990.

Brown, David. *Let Me Entertain You.* New York: William Morrow, 1990.

Brown, Eric. *Deborah Kerr.* New York: St. Martin's Press, 1978.

Brown, Peter Harry, and Pamela Ann Brown. *The MGM Girls: Behind the Velvet Curtain.* Edited by Toni Lopopolo. New York: St. Martin's Press, 1983.

Brown, Peter Harry. *Kim Novak: Reluctant Goddess.* New York: St. Martin's Press, 1986.

———. *Such Devoted Sisters—Those Fabulous Gabors.* New York: St. Martin's Press, 1985.

———, and Patte B. Barham. *Marilyn: The Last Take.* New York, Signet, 1992.

Brownlow, Kevin. *Hollywood: The Pioneers.* New York: Knopf, 1979.

Brynner, Rock. *Yul: The Man Who Would Be King: A Memoir of Father and Son.* New York: Simon & Schuster, 1989.

Buchwald, Art. *How Much Is That in Dollars?* Cleveland and New York: World, 1961.

———. *Son of the Great Society.* London: Weidenfeld & Nicolson, 1967.

Buckle, Richard, ed. *Self Portrait With Friends: The Collected Diaries of Cecil Beaton, 1926–1974.* New York: Times Books, 1979.

Burk, Margaret Tante. *Are the Stars Out Tonight?: The Story of the Famous Ambassador and Coconut Grove "Hollywood's Hotel."* Los Angeles: Round Table West, 1980.

Burton, Philip. *Early Doors: My Life and the Theatre.* New York: Dial Press, 1969.

Burton, Richard. *A Christmas Story.* London: Heinemann, 1965.

———. *Meeting Mrs. Jenkins.* New York: William Morrow, 1966.

Cafarakis, Christian. *The Fabulous Onassis: His Life and Loves.* New York: Pocket Books, 1973.

Caine, Michael. *What's It all About? An Autobiography.* New York: Turtle Bay Books, 1992.

Capote, Truman. *A Capote Reader.* New York: Random House, 1987.

Carey, Gary. *Katharine Hepburn: A Hollywood Yankee.* New York: St. Martin's Press, 1983.

———. *Marlon Brando: The Only Contender.* New York: St. Martin's Press, 1985.

Carpozi, George, Jr. *Poison Pen: The Unauthorized Biography of Kitty Kelley.* New York: Barricade Books, 1991.

———. *The Real Story: Liz Taylor.* New York: Manor Books, 1990.

Carter, Ernestine. *Magic Names of Fashion.* Englewood Cliffs, N.J.: Prentice-Hall, 1980.

Cary, Dianna Serra. *Hollywood's Children: An Inside Account of the Child Star Era.* Boston: Houghton-Mifflin, 1979.

Cassini, Igor, with Jeanne Molli. *I'd Do It All Over Again.* New York: G. P. Putnam's Sons, 1977.

Cazalet-Keir, Thelma. *From the Wings.* London: Bodley Head, 1967.

Cerasini, Marc. *O. J. Simpson: American Hero, American Tragedy.* New York: Pinnacle Books, 1994.

Chandler, Charlotte. *The Ultimate Seduction.* Garden City, N.Y.: Doubleday, 1984.

Chapin, Lauren, with Andrew Collins. *Father Does Know Best: The Lauren Chapin Story.* Nashville: Thomas Nelson, 1989.

Charisse, Cyd, and Tony Martin. *The Two of Us.* New York: Mason-Charter, 1976.

Chisholm, Anne, and Michael Davie. *Lord Beaverbrook: A Life.* New York: Knopf, 1993.

Churcher, Sharon. *New York Confidential.* New York: Crown Publishers, 1986.

Clark, Tom, with Dick Kleiner. *Rock Hudson: Friend of Mine.* New York: Pharos Books, 1989.

Clarke, Gerald. *Capote: A Biography.* New York: Simon & Schuster, 1988.

Cohn, Art. *The Nine Lives of Michael Todd.* New York: Random House, 1958.

Colacello, Bob. *Holy Terror: Andy Warhol Close Up.* New York: Harper Collins, 1990.

Cole, Gerald, and Wes Farrell. *The Fondas.* London: W. H. Allen, 1984.

Collier, Peter, and David Horowitz. *The Kennedys: An American Drama.* New York: Summit, 1984.

Collins, Joan. *Past Imperfect: An Autobiography.* New York: Simon & Schuster, 1984.

Collins, Nancy. *Hard to Get.* New York: Random House, 1990.

Conrad, Barnaby. *Time Is All We Have: Four Weeks at the Betty Ford Center.* New York: Arbor House, 1986.

Cook, Bruce. *Dalton Trumbo.* New York: Charles Scribner's Sons, 1977.

Considine, Shaun. *Bette and Joan: The Divine Feud.* New York: E. P. Dutton, 1989.

Cottrell, John, and Fergus Cashin. *Richard Burton: Very Close Up.* Englewood Cliffs, N.J.: Prentice-Hall, 1971.

Coursodon, Jean-Pierre, with Pierre Sauvage. *American Directors: Volume I.* New York: McGraw-Hill, 1983.

———. *American Directors: Volume II.* New York: McGraw-Hill, 1983.

Crist, Judith. *The Private Eye, the Cowboy and the Very Naked Girl: Movies From Cleo to Clyde.* New York: Holt, Rinehart & Winston, 1968.

Cronkite, Kathy. *On the Edge of the Spotlight.* New York: Warner Books, 1981.

Cronyn, Hume. *A Terrible Liar: A Memoir.* New York: William Morrow, 1991.

Crowther, Bosley. *Hollywood Rajah: The Life and Times of Louis B. Mayer.* New York: Henry Holt, 1960.

Culme, John, and Nicholas Rayner. *The Jewels of the Duchess of Windsor.* New York; Vencome Press, in association with Sotheby's, 1987.

Curti, Carlo. *Skouras: King of Fox Studios.* Los Angeles: Holloway House, 1967.

Curtis, Charlotte. *The Rich and Other Atrocities.* New York: Harper & Row, 1976.

Dabney, Thomas Ewing. *The Man Who Bought the Waldorf: The Life of Conrad N. Hilton.* New York: Duell, Sloan & Pierce, 1950.

Dalton, David. *James Dean: The Mutant King.* New York: St. Martin's Press, 1974.

Daniell, John. *Ava Gardner.* New York: St. Martin's Press, 1982.

D'Arcy, Susan. *The Films of Elizabeth Taylor.* Bembridge: BCW Publishing, 1977.

David, Lester, and Jhan Robbins. *Richard and Elizabeth.* New York: Funk & Wagnalls, 1977.

Davidson, Bill. *The Real and the Unreal.* New York: Harper Brothers, 1960.

———. *Spencer Tracy, Tragic Idol.* New York: E. P. Dutton, 1987.

Davis, Daphne. *Stars.* New York: Stewart, Tabori & Chang, 1983.

Davis, Ronald L. *Hollywood Beauty: Linda Darnell and the American Dream.* Norman, Oklahoma, and London: University of Oklahoma Press, 1991.

de Rothschild, Guy. *The Whims of Fortune: The Memoirs of Guy de Rothschild.* New York: Random House, 1985.

Deschner, Donald. *The Complete Films of Spencer Tracy.* Secaucus, N.J.: Citadel Press, 1968.

Deutsch, Armand. *Me and Bogie, and Other Friends and Acquaintances From a Life in Hollywood and Beyond.* New York: G. P. Putnam's Sons, 1991.

Dickens, Homer. *The Films of Barbara Stanwyck.* Secaucus, N.J.: Citadel Press, 1984.

———. *The Films of Katharine Hepburn.* Secaucus, N.J.: Citadel Press, 1971.

Dietz, Howard. *Dancing in the Dark.* New York: Quadrangle Books, 1974.

Dmytryk, Edward. *It's a Hell of a Life But Not a Bad Living.* New York: New York Times Books, 1978.

Doria, Luciano. *Burton-Taylor: Les Magnifiques.* Montreal: La Presse, 1973.

Douglas, Kirk. *The Ragman's Son: An Autobiography.* New York: Simon & Schuster, 1988.

Douglas, Peter. *Clint Eastwood Movin' On.* Chicago: Henry Regnery, 1974.

Dundy, Elaine. *Finch, Bloody Finch: A Life of Peter Finch.* New York: Holt, Rinehart & Winston, 1980.

Dunne, Philip. *Take Two: A Life in Movies and Politics.* New York: McGraw-Hill, 1980.

Eames, John Douglas. *The MGM Story.* New York: Crown Publishers, 1976.

Earley, Steven C. *An Introduction to American Movies.* New York: New American Library, 1978.

Eastman, John. *Retakes: Behind the Scenes of 500 Classic Movies.* New York: Ballantine Books, 1989.

Eddy, Mary Baker. *Science and Health With Key to the Scriptures.* Boston: First Church of Christ, Scientist, 1903.

Edelson, Edward. *Great Movie Spectaculars.* Garden City, N.Y.: Doubleday, 1976.

Edwards, Anne. *A Remarkable Woman: A Biography of Katharine Hepburn.* New York: William Morrow, 1985.

———. *Viven Leigh.* New York: Pocket Books, 1977.

Eells, George. *Hedda and Louella.* New York: G. P. Putnam's Sons, 1972.

———. *Malice in Wonderland.* New York: Lorevan, 1985.

———. *Robert Mitchum: A Biography.* New York: Franklin Watts, 1984.

Ehrlichman, John. *Witness to Power.* New York: Simon & Schuster, 1982.

Eisenhower, Julie Nixon. *Pat Nixon: The Untold Story.* New York: Simon & Schuster, 1986.

Ellison, Katherine. *Imelda: Steel Butterfly of the Philippines.* New York: McGraw-Hill, 1988.

Emal, Janet. *Light and Healthy Microwave Cooking.* Tucson, Ariz.: HP Books, 1986.

Englund, Steven. *Grace of Monaco.* New York: Kensington, 1984.

Ephron, Delia. *Funny Sauce.* New York: Penguin, 1986.

Epstein, Edward Jay. *The Rise and Fall of Diamonds: The Shattering of a Brilliant Illusion.* New York: Simon & Schuster, 1982.

Evans, Peter. *Ari: The Life and Times of Aristotle Socrates Onassis.* New York: Summit, 1986.

Fairchild, John. *Chic Savages.* New York: Simon & Schuster, 1989.

Farber, Stephen, and Marc Green. *Hollywood Dynasties.* New York: Delilah, 1984.

Faulkner, Trader. *Peter Finch: A Biography.* New York: Taplinger, 1979.

Feibleman, Peter. *Lilly: Reminiscences of Lillian Hellman.* New York: William Morrow, 1989.

Fein, Irving A. *Jack Benny: An Intimate Biography.* New York: G. P. Putnam's Sons, 1976.

Ferris, Paul. *Richard Burton.* New York: Coward-McCann, 1981.

Finch, Christopher. *Rainbow.* New York: Grosset & Dunlap, 1976.

Fisher, Carrie. *Postcards From the Edge.* New York: Pocket Books, 1987.

Fisher, Eddie. *Eddie: My Life, My Loves.* New York: Harper & Row, 1981.

Flamini, Roland. *Ava: A Biography.* New York: Coward-McCann, 1983.

Fontaine, Joan. *No Bed of Roses.* New York: William Morrow, 1978.

Fonteyn, Margot. *Margot Fonteyn: Autobiography.* New York: Warner Books, 1975.

Forbes, Malcolm, with Tony Clark, ed. *More Than I Dreamed: A Lifetime of Collecting.* New York: Simon & Schuster, 1989.

Ford, Betty, with Chris Chase. *Betty: A Glad Awakening.* Garden City, N.Y.: Doubleday, 1987.

Fordin, Hugh. *The World of Entertainment.* Garden City, N.Y.: Doubleday, 1975.

Francis, Anne. *Voices From Home: An Inner Journey.* Millbrae, Calif.: Celestial Age Arts, 1982.

Frank, Gerold. *Judy.* New York: Harper & Row, 1975.

———. *Zsa Zsa Gabor: My Story.* Cleveland and New York: World, 1960.

Fraser, Nicholas, Philip Jacobson, Mark Ottaway, and Lewis Chester. *Aristotle Onassis.* Philadelphia: Lippincott, 1977.

Freedland, Michael. *Jane Fonda: A Biography.* New York: St. Martin's Press, 1988.

———. *Katherine Hepburn.* London: W. H. Allen, 1984.

Frischauer, Willi. *Onassis.* New York: Meredith Press, 1968.

Gabler, Neal. *An Empire of Their Own: How the Jews Invented Hollywood.* Garden City, N.Y.: Doubleday, 1988.

Gaines, Steven. *Simply Halston: The Untold Story.* New York: G. P. Putnam's Sons, 1991.

Galella, Ron. *Off-Guard: Beautiful People Unveiled Before the Camera Lens.* New York: Greenwich House, 1983.

Gallagher, Elaine. *Candidly Caine.* London: Robson Books, 1990.

Gardner, Ava. *Ava: My Story.* New York: Bantam, 1990.

Gates, Phyllis, and Bob Thomas. *My Husband, Rock Hudson.* Garden City, N.Y.: Doubleday, 1987.

Geist, Kenneth L. *Pictures Will Talk: The Life and Films of Joseph L. Mankiewicz.* New York: Da Capo, 1978.

Geldorf, Bob. *Is That It?: The Autobiography.* New York: Ballantine Books, 1986.

Getty, J. Paul. *As I See It: My Life as I Lived It.* New York: Berkley, 1986.

Gillman, Peter, and Leni Gillman. *Alias David Bowie: A Biography.* London: Hodder & Stoughton, 1986.

Gish, Lillian, with Ann Pinchot. *Lillian Gish: The Movies, Mr. Griffith and Me.* Englewood Cliffs, N.J.: Prentice-Hall, 1969.

Givens, Bill. *Film Flubs: Memorable Movie Mistakes.* Secaucus, N.J.: Citadel Press, 1991.

Godfrey, Lionel. *Cary Grant: The Light Touch.* New York: St. Martin's Press, 1981.

Goodman, Ezra. *The Decline and Fall of Hollywood.* New York: Simon & Schuster, 1961.

Goodman, Walter. *The Committee: The Extraordinary Career of the House Committee on Un-American Activities.* New York: Farrar, Straus & Giroux, 1968.

Grady, Billy. *The Irish Peacock: The Confessions of a Legendary Talent Agent.* New Rochelle, N.Y.: Arlington House, 1972.

Graham, Sheilah. *Hollywood Revisited: A Fiftieth Anniversary Celebration.* New York: St. Martin's Press, 1985.

Granger, Stewart. *Sparks Fly Upward.* New York: G. P. Putnam's Sons, 1981.

Green, Bert, with Phillip Stephen Schulz. *Pity the Poor Rich.* Chicago: Contemporary Books, 1978.

Gregory, Adela, and Milo Speriglio. *Crypt 33: The Saga of Marilyn—The Final Word.* New York: Birch Lane Press, 1993.

Griffin, Merv, with Peter Barsocchini. *From Where I Sit: Merv Griffin's Book of People.* New York: Pinnacle Books, 1982.

———. *Merv: An Autobiography.* New York: Simon & Schuster, 1980.

Grobel, Lawrence. *Conversations With Capote.* New York: New American Library, 1985.

———. *The Hustons.* New York: Charles Scribner's Sons, 1989.

Grossinger, Tania. *Growing Up at Grossinger's.* New York: David McKay, 1975.

Guiles, Fred Lawrence. *Legend: The Life and Death of Marilyn Monroe.* New York: Stein and Day, 1985.

Guinness, Alec. *Blessings in Disguise.* New York: Knopf, 1986.

Gussow, Mel. *Don't Say Yes Until I Finish Talking: A Biography of Darryl F. Zanuck.* Garden City, N.Y.: Doubleday, 1971.

Haber, Mel. *Bedtime Stories of the Ingleside Inn.* Northridge, Calif.: Lord John Press, 1988.

Hadleigh, Boze. *Conversations With My Elders.* New York: St. Martin's Press, 1986.

Hall, William. *Raising Caine: The Authorized Biography.* Englewood Cliffs, N.J.: Prentice-Hall, 1981.

Halliwell, Leslie. *Halliwell's Filmgoer's Companion.* New York: Charles Scribner's Sons, 1988.

Halsman, Philippe. *Halsman Sight and Insight.* Garden City, N.Y.: Doubleday, 1972.

Hamblett, Charles. *The Hollywood Cafe.* New York: Hart, 1969.

Harmetz, Arjean. *The Making of the Wizard of Oz.* New York: Knopf, 1977.

Harris, Marlys J. *The Zanucks of Hollywood.* New York: Crown Publishers, 1989.

Harris, Radie. *Radie's World.* New York: G. P. Putnam's Sons, 1975.

Harris, Warren G. *Cary Grant: A Touch of Elegance.* New York: Doubleday, 1987.

———. *Natalie and R. J.: Hollywood's Star-Crossed Lovers.* New York: Dolphin Books, 1988.

Harrison, Rex. *A Damned Serious Business: My Life in Comedy.* New York: Bantam, 1991.

———. *Rex: An Autobiography.* New York: William Morrow, 1974.

Harvey, Stephen. *Directed by: Vincente Minnelli.* New York: Harper & Row, 1989.

Haskins, James. *Bricktop.* New York: Atheneum, 1983.

Hay, Peter. *Broadway Anecdotes.* New York: Oxford University Press, 1989.

Hayes, Helen, with Katherine Hatch. *My Life in Three Acts.* New York: Harcourt Brace Jovanovich, 1990.

Head, Edith, and Jane Kesner Ardmore. *The Dress Doctor.* Boston: Little, Brown, 1959.
Head, Edith, and Paddy Calistro. *Edith Head's Hollywood.* New York: E. P. Dutton, 1983.
Hepburn, Katharine. *Me: Stories of My Life.* New York, Knopf, 1991.
Hermann, Dorothy. *S. J. Perelman: A Life.* New York: G. P. Putnam's Sons, 1986.
Herndon, Venable. *James Dean: A Short Life.* Garden City, N.Y.: Doubleday, 1974.
Hersh, Burton. *The Mellon Family: A Fortune in History.* New York: William Morrow, 1978.
Hershey, Lenore. *Between the Covers: The Lady's Own Journal.* New York: Coward-McCann, 1983.
Heymann, C. David. *A Woman Named Jackie.* New York: Lyle Stuart, 1989.
———. *Poor Little Rich Girl: The Life and Legend of Barbara Hutton.* New York: Pocket Books, 1986.
Hickey, Des, and Gus Smith. *The Prince: Being the Public and Private Life of Larushka Mischa Skikne, a Jewish Lithuanian Vagabond Player, Otherwise Known as, Lawrence Harvey.* London: Leslie Frewin, 1975.
Higham, Charles. *Ava: A Life Story.* New York: Delacorte, 1974.
———. *Brando.* New York: New American Library, 1987.
———. *Hollywood at Sunset.* New York: Saturday Review Press, 1972.
———. *Howard Hughes: The Secret Life.* New York: G. P. Putnam's Sons, 1993.
———. *Kate: The Life of Katharine Hepburn.* New York: New American Library, 1975.
———. *Sisters: The Story of Olivia de Havilland and Joan Fontaine.* New York: Dell, 1984.
———, and Joel Greenberg. *The Celluloid Muse.* New York: Signet, 1969.
———, and Roy Moseley: *Cary Grant: The Lonely Heart.* New York: Harcourt Brace Jovanovich, 1989.
Hilton, Conrad N. *Be My Guest.* New York: Prentice-Hall, 1957.
Hirsch, Foster. *Elizabeth Taylor.* New York: Pyramid Publications, 1973.
———. *Joseph Losey.* Boston: Twayne Publishers, 1980.
Holden, Anthony. *Laurence Olivier.* New York: Atheneum, 1988.
Holmes, Nancy. *The Dream Boats.* Englewood Cliffs, N.J.: Prentice-Hall, 1977.
Holroyd, Michael. *Augustus John: A Biography.* New York: Holt, Rinehart & Winston, 1974.
Holt, Georgia, and Phyllis Quinn with Sue Russell. *Star Mothers.* New York: St. Martin's, 1989.
Hopper, Hedda, and James Brough. *The Whole Truth and Nothing But.* Garden City, N.Y.: Doubleday, 1963.
Hopper, Hedda. *From Under My Hat.* Garden City, N.Y.: Doubleday, 1952.
Hotchner, A. E. *Sophia: Living and Loving, Her Own Story.* New York: Bantam, 1979.
Houseman, John. *Front and Center.* New York: Simon & Schuster, 1979.
Howard, Jean, and James Watters. *Jean Howard's Hollywood: A Photo Memoir.* New York: Harry N. Abrams, 1989.
Howell, Georgina. *In Vogue: Sixty Years of Celebrities and Fashion From British Vogue.* New York: Penguin, 1978.
Howitt, Mary (1799–1888). *Poetical Works of Howitt, Milman, and Keats.* Philadelphia: Thomas, Cowperthwait, 1840.

Hudson, Rock, and Sara Davidson. *Rock Hudson: His Story.* New York: William Morrow, 1986.

Hughes-Hallett, Lucy. *Cleopatra: Histories, Dreams and Distortions.* New York: Harper & Row, 1990.

Huston, John. *An Open Book.* New York: Ballantine Books, 1980.

Israel, Lee. *Kilgallen.* New York: Delacorte, 1979.

Jackson, Michael. *Moon Walk.* New York: Doubleday, 1988.

James, Robert Rhodes. *Victor Cazalet.* London: Hamish Hamilton, 1976.

Jenkins, Graham. *Richard Burton, My Brother.* New York: Harper & Row, 1988.

Joesten, Joachim. *That Fabulous Greek!: Onassis.* New York: Tower, 1973.

Johnson, Dorris, and Ellen Leventhal. *The Letters of Nunnally Johnson.* New York: Knopf, 1981.

Johnson, Nora. *Flashback: Nora Johnson on Nunnally Johnson.* Garden City, N.Y.: Doubleday, 1979.

Junor, Penny. *Burton: The Man Behind the Myth.* London: Sidgwick & Jackson, 1985.

Kadish, Ferne, and Kathleen Kirtland. *Los Angeles on $500 a Day.* New York: Collier, 1976.

Kael, Pauline. *When the Lights Go Down.* New York: Holt, Rinehart & Winston, 1980.

Kaminsky, Stuart. *John Huston: Maker of Magic.* Boston: Houghton-Mifflin, 1978.

Kanin, Garson. *Tracy and Hepburn.* New York: Viking Press, 1971.

Kass, Judith M. *The Films of Montgomery Clift.* Secaucus, N.J.: Citadel Press, 1979.

Katz, Ephraim. *The Film Encyclopedia.* New York: Harper & Row, 1979.

Keenan, Brigid. *The Women We Wanted to Look Like.* New York: St. Martin's Press, 1977.

Kelley, Kitty. *Elizabeth Taylor: The Last Star.* New York: Simon & Schuster, 1981.

———. *His Way: The Unauthorized Biography of Frank Sinatra.* New York: Bantam Books, 1986.

———. *Nancy Reagan: The Unauthorized Biography.* New York: Simon & Schuster, 1991.

Kessler, Judy. *Inside People: The Stories Behind the Stories.* New York: Villard, 1994.

Kessler, Ronald. *The Richest Man in the World: The Story of Adnan Khashoggi.* New York: Warner Books, 1986.

Keyes, Evelyn. *Scarlet O'Hara's Younger Sister: My Life In and Out of Hollywood.* Secaucus, N.J.: Lyle Stuart, 1972.

Kiner, Ralph, with Joe Gergen. *Kiner's Korner: At Bat and on the Air—My Forty Years in Baseball.* New York: Arbor House, 1987.

Kirkland, Douglas. *Light Years: Three Decades Photographing Among the Stars.* New York: Thames and Hudson, 1989.

Kleiner, Dick. *Hollywood's Greatest Love Stories.* New York: Pocket Books; Simon & Schuster, 1976.

Kleiner, Dick (as told to by Mervyn Leroy). *Mervyn Leroy: Take One.* New York: Hawthorn Books, 1974.

Kleinfield, Sonny. *The Hotel: A Week in the Life of the Plaza.* New York: Simon & Schuster, 1989.

Kobal, John. *People Will Talk.* New York: Avrum Press, 1986.

Konolige, Kit. *The Richest Women in the World.* New York: Macmillan, 1985.

Koodynski, Andrzej. *Elizabeth Taylor.* Warszawa, Wydawn: Artystyczne i Filmowe, 1978.

Koskoff, David E. *The Mellons: The Chronicle of America's Richest Family.* New York: Thomas Y. Crowell, 1978.

Korda, Michael. *Charmed Lives: A Family Romance.* New York: Random House, 1979.

La Guardia, Robert. *Monty.* New York: Arbor House, 1977.

———, and Gene Arceri. *The Tempestuous Life of Susan Hayward.* New York: Macmillan, 1985.

Lasky, Jesse, Jr., with Pat Silver. *Love Scene: The Story of Laurence Olivier and Vivien Leigh.* New York: Thomas Y. Crowell, 1978.

Lawford, Lady, with Buddy Galon. *Bitch: The Autobiography of Lady Lawford.* Brookline, Mass.: Brandon Publishing, 1986.

Lawford, Patricia Seaton, with Ted Schwarz. *The Peter Lawford Story: Life With the Kennedys, Monroe and the Rat Pack.* New York: Carroll & Graf, 1988.

Leamer, Laurence. *Make Believe: The Story of Nancy and Ronald Reagan.* New York: Dell, 1983.

Leaming, Barbara. *Orson Welles.* New York: Viking, 1983.

Leclercq, Florence. *Elizabeth Taylor.* Boston: Twayne Publishers, 1985.

Leff, Leonard J., and Jerold L. Simmons. *The Dame in the Kimono: Hollywood, Censorship, and the Production Code from the 1920s to the 1960s.* New York: Grove Weidenfeld, 1990.

Leigh, Janet. *There Really Was a Hollywood.* Garden City, N.Y.: Doubleday, 1984.

Leigh, Wendy. *Speaking Frankly.* London: Frederick Muller, 1977.

Levant, Oscar. *The Importance of Being Oscar.* New York: Pocket Books, 1969.

Levy, Alan. *Forever Sophia.* New York: St. Martin's Press, 1979.

Liddell, Robert. *Elizabeth and Ivy.* London: P. Owen, 1986.

Likeness, George. *The Oscar People.* Mendota, Ill.: Wayside, 1965.

Lilly, Doris. *Those Fabulous Greeks: Onassis, Niarchos, and Livanos.* London: W. H. Allen, 1971.

Lofan, Joshua. *Movie Stars, Real People, and Me.* New York: Delacorte, 1978.

Loos, Anita. *Kiss Hollywood Good-by.* New York: Viking Press, 1974.

Loren, Sophia, with A. E. Hotchner. *Sophia: Living and Loving, Her Own Story.* New York: William Morrow, 1979.

Maass, Joachim. *The Gouffe Case.* New York: Harper Brothers, 1960.

McCambridge, Mercedes. *The Quality of Mercy.* New York: New York Times Books, 1981.

McCarty, John. *The Films of John Huston.* Secaucus, N.J.: Citadel Press, 1987.

McClelland, Doug. *Blackface to Blacklist: Al Jolson, Larry Parks, and "The Jolson Story".* Metuchen, N.J., and London: Scarecrow, 1987.

———. *Susan Hayward: The Divine Bitch.* New York: Pinnacle Books, 1973.

McDowall, Roddy. *Double Exposures.* New York: Delacorte, 1966.

———. *Double Exposure: Take Two.* New York: William Morrow, 1989.

McGilligan, Patrick. *George Cukor: A Double Life.* New York: St. Martin's Press, 1991.

McLellan, Diana. *Ear on Washington.* New York: Arbor House, 1982.

MacPherson, Myra. *The Power Lovers: An Intimate Look at Politicians and Their Marriages.* New York: G. P. Putnam's Sons, 1975.
Maddox, Brenda. *Who's Afraid of Elizabeth Taylor?* New York: M. Evans, 1977.
Madsen, Axel. *Chanel: A Woman of Her Own.* New York: Henry Holt, 1990.
Mailer, Norman. *Marilyn: A Biography.* New York: Grosset & Dunlap, 1972.
———. *Of Women and Their Elegance.* New York: Simon & Schuster, 1980.
Mansfield, Stephanie. *The Richest Girl in the World: The Extravagant Life and Fast Times of Doris Duke.* New York: G. P. Putnam's Sons, 1993.
Manso, Peter. *Mailer: His Life and Times.* New York: Simon & Schuster, 1985.
Manvell, Roger. *Love Goddesses of the Movies.* New York: Crescent, 1975.
Marion, Frances. *Off With Their Heads: A Serio-Comic Tale of Hollywood.* New York: Macmillan, 1972.
Marion, John L., with Christopher Anderson. *The Best of Everything: The Insider's Guide to Collecting—for Every Taste and Every Budget.* New York: Simon & Schuster, 1989.
Marx, Arthur. *The Nine Lives of Mickey Rooney.* New York: Stein and Day, 1986.
Marx, Samuel. *A Gaudy Spree: Literary Hollywood When the West Was Fun.* New York: Franklin Watts, 1987.
———. *Mayer and Thalberg, the Make-Believe Saints.* New York: Random House, 1975.
Massy, Baron Christian de, and Charles Higham. *Palace: My Life in the Royal Family of Monaco.* New York: Atheneum, 1986.
Maxwell, Elsa. *The Celebrity Circus.* New York: Appleton-Century, 1963.
Maychick, Diana. *Audrey Hepburn: An Intimate Portrait.* New York: Birch Lane Press, 1993.
———, and L. Avon Borgo. *Heart to Heart With Robert Wagner.* New York: St. Martin's Press, 1986.
Medved, Harry, and Michael. *The Hollywood Hall of Shame.* New York: G. P. Putnam's Sons, 1984.
Merman, Ethel, with George Eels. *Merman.* New York: Simon & Schuster, 1978.
Miller, Ann, and Norma Lee Browning. *Miller's High Life.* Garden City, N.Y.: Doubleday, 1972.
Milton, Frank. *Name Dropping.* New York: E. P. Dutton, 1985.
Minnelli, Vincente, and Hector Arce. *I Remember It Well.* Garden City, N.Y.: Doubleday, 1974.
Morella, Joe, and Edward Z. Epstein. *A Biography of Paul Newman and Joanne Woodward.* New York: Delacorte, 1988.
———. *The Complete Films and Career of Judy Garland.* Secaucus, N.J.: Citadel Press, 1969.
———. *Forever Lucy: The Life of Lucille Ball.* Secaucus, N.J.: Lyle Stuart, 1986.
———. *Rebels: The Rebel Hero in Films.* Secaucus, N.J.: Citadel Press, 1971.
Morley, Sheridan. *Elizabeth Taylor.* London: Pavilion, 1989.
———. *James Mason: Odd Man Out.* New York: Harper & Row, 1989.
———. *The Other Side of the Moon: The Life of David Niven.* London: Weidenfeld & Nicolson, 1985.

Mosley, Leonard. *Zanuck: The Rise and Fall of Hollywood's Last Tycoon.* Boston: Little, Brown, 1984.

Moseley, Roy, with Philip and Martin Masheter. *Rex Harrison: A Biography.* New York: St. Martin's Press, 1987.

Munn, Michael. *Hollywood Rogues.* New York: St. Martin's Press, 1991.

———. *Kirk Douglas.* New York: St. Martin's Press, 1985.

Nadelhoffer, Hans. *Cartier Jewelers Extraordinary.* London: Thames & Hudson, 1984.

Neagle, Anna. *Anna Neagle Says: "There's Always Tomorrow."* London: W. H. Allen, 1974.

Neal, Patricia, with Richard Deneut. *As I Am: An Autobiography.* New York: Simon & Schuster, 1988.

Nickens, Christopher. *Elizabeth Taylor: A Biography in Photographs.* Garden City, N.Y.: Doubleday, 1984.

———. *Natalie Wood: A Biography in Photographs.* Garden City, N.Y.: Doubleday, 1986.

Niven, David. *The Moon's a Balloon: Reminiscences by David Niven.* London: Coronet, 1971.

Nizer, Louis. *Reflections Without Mirrors: An Autobiography of the Mind.* New York: Berkley, 1979.

Nolan, William F. *John Huston: King Rebel.* Los Angeles: Sherborne, 1965.

Norman, Philip. *Tilt the Hourglass and Begin Again.* London: Elm Tree Books, 1985.

Oppenheimer, Jerry, and Jack Vitek. *Idol: Rock Hudson, The True Story of an American Film Hero.* New York: Villard, 1986.

O'Pray, Michael, ed. *Andy Warhol: Film Factory.* London: BFI, 1989.

Otis Skinner, Cornelia. *Life With Lindsay and Crouse.* Boston: Houghton-Mifflin, 1976.

Parish, James Robert. *The Hollywood Beauties.* New Rochelle, N.Y.: Arlington House, 1978.

———. *The MGM Stock Company.* New Rochelle, N.Y.: Arlington House, 1973.

Parker, John. *Five for Hollywood.* New York: Birch Lane Press, 1991.

Parsons, Louella. *Tell it to Louella.* New York: G. P. Putnam's Sons, 1961.

Payn, Graham, and Sheridan Morley, eds. *The Noël Coward Diaries.* Boston: Little, Brown, 1982.

Peary, Danny, ed. *Close-Ups: The Movie Star Book.* New York: Simon & Schuster, 1978.

Pepitone, Lena, and William Stadiem. *Marilyn Monroe Confidential.* London: Sedgwick & Jackson, 1979.

Perelman, S. J. *Chicken Inspector No. 23.* New York: Simon & Schuster, 1966.

———. *Don't Tread on Me: The Selected Letters of S. J. Perelman.* Edited by Prudence Crowther. New York: Viking Press, 1987.

Phillips, Julia. *You'll Never Eat Lunch in This Town Again.* New York: Random House, 1991.

Pomerantz, Joel. *Jennie and the Story of Grossinger's.* New York: Grosset & Dunlap, 1970.

Poter, Arthur. *Directory of Art and Antique Restoration.* San Francisco: s.n., 1975.

Powell, Jane. *The Girl Next Door and How She Grew.* New York: William Morrow, 1988.

Pye, Michael. *Moguls: Inside the Business of Show Business.* London: Temple Smith, 1980.

Quine, Judith Balaban. *The Bridesmaids.* New York: Weidenfeld & Nicolson, 1989.

Quirk, Lawrence J. *Fasten Your Seatbelts.* New York: William Morrow, 1990.

———. *The Films of Paul Newman.* Secaucus, N.J.: Citadel Press, 1971.

———. *The Films of Robert Taylor.* Secaucus, N.J.: Citadel Press, 1979.

———. *The Great Romantic Films.* Secaucus, N.J.: Citadel Press, 1974.

Reagan, Nancy, with William Novak. *My Turn.* New York: Random House, 1989.

Redfield, William. *Letters From an Actor.* New York: Viking Press, 1967.

Reed, Rex. *Big Screen, Little Screen.* New York: Macmillan, 1971.

———. *Valentines and Vitriol.* New York: Delacorte, 1972.

Reynolds, Debbie, and David Patrick Columbia. *Debbie: My Life.* New York: William Morrow, 1988.

Richie, Donald. *George Stevens: An American Romantic.* New York: Museum of Modern Art, 1970.

Riese, Randall. *The Unabridged James Dean: His Life and Legacy From A to Z.* Chicago: Contemporary Books, 1991.

———, and Neal Hitchens. *The Unabridged Marilyn: Her Life From A to Z.* New York: Congdon & Weed, 1987.

Right, Illiam. *All the Pain That Money Can Buy: The Life of Christina Onassis.* New York: Simon & Schuster, 1991.

Riva, Maria. *Marlene Dietrich.* New York: Knopf, 1993.

Rivers, Joan, with Richard Meryman. *Still Talking.* New York: Turtle Bay Books, 1991.

Roberts, Rachel, and Alexander Walker, ed. *No Bells On Sunday: The Rachel Roberts Journals.* New York: Harper & Row, 1984.

Robin-Tani, Marianne. *The New Elizabeth.* New York: St. Martin's Press, 1988.

Rollyson, Carl. *Lillian Hellman: Her Legend and Her Legacy.* New York: William Morrow, 1988.

Romero, Gerry. *Sinatra's Women.* New York: Manor Books, 1976.

Rooney, Mickey. *I. E. An Autobiography.* New York: Bantam Books, 1966.

———. *Life is Too Short.* New York: Villard, 1991.

Roosevelt, Selwa ("Lucky"). *Keeper of the Gate.* New York: Simon & Schuster, 1990.

Rosen, Marjorie. *Popcorn Venus: Women, Movies and the American Dream.* New York: Coward-McCann, 1973.

Rosenberg, Bernard, and Harry Silverstein. *The Real Tinsel.* London: Macmillan, 1970.

Ross, Lillian. *Picture.* London: Victor Gollancz, 1953.

Ruskin, Cindy. *The Quilt.* New York: Pocket Books, 1988.

Sackett, Susan. *The Hollywood Report Book of Box Office Hits.* New York: Watson-Guptill, 1990.

Sakol, Jeannie, and Caroline Latham. *About Grace: An Intimate Notebook.* Chicago: Contemporary Books, 1993.

Sarrlot, Raymond, and Fred E. Basten. *Life at the Marmont.* Santa Monica, Calif.: Roundtable, 1987.

Scavullo, Francesco, with Sean Byrnes. *Scavullo Women.* New York: Harper & Row, 1982.

Schary, Dore. *Heyday, An Autobiography.* Boston: Little, Brown, 1979.

Schatz, Thomas. *The Genius of the System.* New York: Pantheon, 1988.

Schickel, Richard, and Sid Avery. *Hollywood at Home: A Family Album, 1950–1965.* New York: Crown Publishers, 1990.

Schulberg, Budd. *Moving Pictures: Memories of a Hollywood Prince.* New York: Stein and Day, 1981.

Segaloff, Nat. *Hurricane Billy: The Stormy Life and Films of William Friedkin.* New York: William Morrow, 1990.

Sellers, Michael, with Sarah and Victoria Sellers. *P.S. I Love You: an Intimate Portrait of Peter Sellers.* New York: E. P. Dutton, 1982.

Selznick, Irene Mayer. *A Private View.* New York: Knopf, 1983.

Seward, Ingrid. *Diana: An Intimate Portrait.* Chicago: Contemporary Books, 1988.

Shank, Theodore J., ed. *A Digest of 500 Plays.* New York: Collier, 1963.

Shapiro, Doris, with Alan Jay Lerner. *We Danced All Night: My Life Behind the Scenes.* New York: William Morrow, 1990.

Sharaff, Irene. *Broadway and Hollywood: Costumes Designed by Irene Sharaff.* New York: Van Nostrand Reinhold, 1976.

Shaw, Arnold. *Sinatra: Twentieth-Century Romantic.* New York: Holt, Rinehart & Winston, 1968.

Sheppard, Dick. *Elizabeth: The Life and Career of Elizabeth Taylor.* Garden City, N.Y.: Doubleday, 1974.

Sherman, Len. *The Good, the Bad and the Famous.* New York: Lyle Stuart, 1990.

Shevey, Sandra. *The Marilyn Scandal: Her True Life Revealed By Those Who Knew Her.* New York: Jove, 1987.

Shilts, Randy. *And the Band Played On.* New York: Viking Press, 1987.

Silverman, Debora. *Selling Culture.* New York: Pantheon Books, 1986.

Silverman, Stephen M. *The Fox That Got Away: The Last Days of the Zanuck Dynasty at 20th Century-Fox.* Secaucus, N.J.: Lyle Stuart, 1988.

Sinclair, Andrew. *Speigel: The Man Behind the Pictures.* Boston: Little, Brown, 1987.

Skinner, Cornelia Otis. *Life with Lindsay and Crouse.* Boston: Houghton-Mifflin, 1976.

Skolsky, Sidney. *Don't Get Me Wrong—I Love Hollywood.* New York: G. P. Putnam's Sons, 1975.

Smith, Ronald L. *Sweethearts of '60s TV.* New York: St. Martin's Press, 1989.

Smolla, Rodney A. *Swing the Press: Libel, the Media, and Power.* New York: Oxford University Press, 1986.

Sobol, Louis. *The Longest Street.* New York: Crown Publishers, 1968.

Spada, James. *Grace.* Garden City, N.Y.: Doubleday, 1987.

———. *Peter Lawford: The Man Who Kept the Secrets.* New York: Bantam, 1991.

———. *Shirley and Warren.* New York: Macmillan, 1985.

Spoto, Donald. *The Kindness of Strangers: The Life of Tennessee Williams.* Boston: Little, Brown, 1985.

Springer, John, and Jack Hamilton. *They Had Faces Then—Annabella to Zorina: The Superstars, Stars and Starlets of the 1930s.* Secaucus, N.J.: Citadel Press, 1978.

Stack, Robert, with Mark Evans. *Straight Shooting.* New York: Macmillan, 1980.

Stassinopoulos, Arianna. *Maria Callas: The Woman Behind the Legend.* New York: Ballantine Books, 1981.

Stein, Mike. *Hollywood Speaks: An Oral History.* New York: G. P. Putnam's Sons, 1974.

Steinberg, Cobbett. *Reel Facts: The Movie Book of Records.* New York: Vintage Books, 1981.

Stern, Mike. *A Look at Tennessee Williams.* New York: Hawthorn, 1969.

Stine, Whitney. *"I'd Love to Kiss You . . .": Conversations With Bette Davis.* New York: Pocket Books, 1990.

———. *Stars and Star Handlers: The Business of Show.* Santa Monica, Calif.: Roundtable, 1985.

Stone, Paulene, with Peter Evans. *One Tear Is Enough: My Life With Laurence Harvey.* London: Michael Joseph, 1975.

Strasberg, Susan. *Bittersweet.* New York: G. P. Putnam's Sons, 1980.

Stuart, Sandra Lee. *The Pink Palace: Behind Closed Doors at the Beverly Hills Hotel.* Secaucus, N.J.: Lyle Stuart, 1978.

Sudjic, Deyan. *Cult Heroes: How to Be Famous for More Than Fifteen Minutes.* New York: W. W. Norton, 1990.

Summers, Anthony. *Goddess: The Secret Lives of Marilyn Monroe.* New York: Macmillan, 1985.

Swanson, H.N. *Sprinkled with Ruby Dust.* New York: Warner, 1989.

Swindell, Larry. *Spencer Tracy . . . A Biography.* New York: New American Library, 1969.

Taraborrelli, J. Randy. *Call Her Miss Ross: The Unauthorized Biography of Diana Ross.* New York: Birch Lane Press, 1989.

———. *Laughing Till It Hurts: The Complete Life and Career of Carol Burnett.* New York: William Morrow, 1988.

———. *Michael Jackson: The Magic and the Madness.* New York: Birch Lane Press, 1991.

Taylor, Elizabeth. *Elizabeth Takes Off.* New York: G. P. Putnam's Sons, 1987.

———. *Elizabeth Taylor: An Informal Memoir by Elizabeth Taylor.* New York: Harper & Row, 1965.

———. *Nibbles and Me.* New York: Duell, Sloan & Pearce, 1946.

Taylor, S. J. *Shock Horror: Tabloids in Action.* New York: Bantam Books, 1991.

Theodoracopulos, Taki. *Princes, Playboys and High-Class Tarts.* New York: Karz-Cohl Publishing, 1984.

Thomas, Tony, and Aubrey Solomon. *The Films of 20th Century-Fox.* Secaucus, N.J.: Citadel Press, 1985.

Thomas, Tony. *The Films of Marlon Brando.* Secaucus, N.J.: Citadel Press, 1973.

———. *The Films of the Forties.* Secaucus, N.J.: Citadel Press, 1975.

———. *Howard Hughes in Hollywood.* Secaucus, N.J.: Citadel Press, 1985.

Thorndike, Joseph J., Jr. *The Very Rich: A History of Wealth.* New York: American Heritage, 1976.

Tierney, Gene, with Mickey Herskowitz. *Self-Portrait.* New York: Wyden, 1979.

Todd, Michael, Jr., and Susan McCarthy Todd. *A Valuable Property.* New York: Arbor House, 1983.

Tomkies, Mike. *The Robert Mitchum Story.* Chicago: Henry Regnery, 1972.

Tornabene, Lyn. *Long Live the King: A Biography of Clark Gable.* New York: G. P. Putnam's Sons, 1976.

Turner, Lana. *Lana: The Lady, the Legend, the Truth.* New York: E. P. Dutton, 1982.
Tyler, Parker. *A Pictorial History of Sex in Films.* Secaucus, N.J.: Citadel Press, 1974.
Tynan, Kathleen. *The Life of Kenneth Tynan.* New York: William Morrow, 1987.
Ustinov, Peter. *Dear Me.* Boston: Little, Brown, 1977.
Valentine, Tom, and Patrick Mahn. *Daddy's Duchess: An Unauthorized Biography of Doris Duke.* Secaucus, N.J.: Lyle Stuart, 1987.
Van Doren, Mamie, with Art Aveilhe. *Playing the Field.* New York: G. P. Putnam's Sons, 1987.
Vermilye, Jerry, and Mark Ricci. *The Films of Elizabeth Taylor.* Secaucus, N.J.: Citadel Press, 1976.
Vickers, Hugo. *Cecil Beaton: A Biography.* Boston: Little, Brown, 1985.
———. *Vivien Leigh.* Boston: Little, Brown, 1988.
Walker, Alexander. *The Celluloid Sacrifice: Aspects of Sex in the Movies.* New York: Hawthorn, 1966.
———. *Elizabeth.* London: Weidenfeld & Nicolson, 1990.
———. *Peter Sellers.* New York: Macmillan, 1981.
———. *Vivien: The Life of Vivien Leigh.* New York: Weidenfeld & Nicolson, 1987.
Wallis, Hal, and Charles Highar. *Starmaker: The Autobiography of Hal Wallis.* New York: Macmillan, 1980.
Wander Bonanno, Margaret. *Angela Lansbury: A Biography.* New York: St. Martin's Press, 1987.
Wanger, Walter. *My Life With Cleopatra.* New York: Bantam Books, 1963.
Warhol, Andy. *The Philosophy of Andy Warhol.* New York: Harcourt Brace Jovanovich, 1975.
Warhol, Andy, and Pat Hackett, ed. *The Andy Warhol Diaries.* New York: Warner, 1989.
———. *Popism: The Warhol 60s.* New York: Harcourt Brace Jovanovich, 1980.
Watcham, Maurice. *Watcham's Office Practice.* London: McGraw-Hill, 1979.
Wayne, Jane Ellen. *Ava's Men: The Private Life of Ava Gardner.* New York: St. Martin's Press, 1990.
———. *Crawford's Men.* Englewood Cliffs, N.J.: Prentice-Hall, 1988.
———. *Grace Kelly's Men.* New York: St. Martin's Press, 1991.
———. *Robert Taylor.* New York: St. Martin's Press, 1973.
Webb, Michael, ed. *Hollywood: Legend and Reality.* Boston: Little, Brown, 1986.
Wilcox, Herbert. *Twenty-five Thousand Sunsets.* London: Bodley Head, 1961.
Wilding, Michael, as told to Pamela Wilcox. *Apple Sauce: The Story of My Life.* London: Allen & Unwin, 1982.
Wiley, Mason, and Damien Bona. *Inside Oscar: The Unofficial History of the Academy Awards.* New York: Ballantine Books, 1987.
Wilkerson, Tichi, and Marcia Borie. *The Hollywood Reporter: The Golden Years.* New York: Coward-McCann, 1984.
Williams, Tennessee. *Five O'Clock Angel: Letters of Tennessee Williams to Maria St. Just, 1948–1982.* New York: Knopf, 1990.
———. *Memoirs.* New York: Bantam Books, 1976.
———. *Where I Live: Selected Essays.* New York: New Directions, 1978.

Wilson, Earl. *Hot Times: True Tales of Hollywood and Broadway.* Chicago: Contemporary Books, 1984.

———. *Sinatra: An Unauthorized Biography.* New York: Signet, 1976.

Winans, Christopher. *Malcolm Forbes: The Man Who Had Everything.* New York: St. Martin's Press, 1990.

Winters, Shelley. *Shelley: Also Known as Shirley.* New York: William Morrow, 1980.

———. *Shelley II: The Middle of My Century.* New York: Simon & Schuster, 1989.

Woodward, Ian. *Audrey Hepburn.* New York: St. Martin's Press, 1984.

———. *Glenda Jackson: A Study in Fire and Ice.* London: Weidenfeld & Nicolson, 1985.

Wright, William. *Lillian Hellman: The Image, the Woman.* New York: Simon & Schuster, 1986.

Wynn, Ned. *We Will Always Live in Beverly Hills: Growing Up Crazy in Hollywood.* New York: William Morrow, 1990.

Zadan, Craig. *Sondheim & Co.* New York: Harper & Row, 1989.

Zee, Donald. *Marvin: The Story of Lee Marvin.* New York: St. Martin's Press, 1980.

Zeffirelli, Franco. *Zeffirelli: The Autobiography of Franco Zeffirelli.* New York: Weidenfeld & Nicolson, 1986.

Zimmer, Jill Schary. *With a Cast of Thousands: A Hollywood Childhood.* New York: Stein and Day, 1963.

Zumwalt, Elmo, Jr. *On Watch: A Memoir.* New York: Quadrangle Books, 1976.

FILMOGRAPHY

1942
THERE'S ONE BORN EVERY MINUTE
Hugh Herbert, Tom Brown, Peggy Moran, Guy Kibbee, Catherine Doucet, Edgar Kennedy, Carl "Alfalfa" Switzer, Elizabeth Taylor (Gloria Twine)
Universal
Associate Producer: Ken Goldsmith
Director: Harold Young
Screenwriters: Robert B. Hunt, Brenda Weisberg

1943
LASSIE COME HOME
Roddy McDowall, Donald Crisp, Edmund Gwenn, Dame May Whitty, Nigel Bruce, Elsa Lanchester, Elizabeth Taylor (Priscilla)
M-G-M
Producer: Samuel Marx
Director: Fred M. Wilcox
Screenwriter: Hugh Butler

1944
JANE EYRE
Orson Welles, Joan Fontaine, Margaret O'Brien, Peggy Ann Garner, Agnes Moorehead, Elizabeth Taylor (Helen)

Twentieth Century-Fox
Producer: William Goetz
Director: Robert Stevenson
Screenwriters: Aldous Huxley, Robert Stevenson, John Houseman

1944
THE WHITE CLIFFS OF DOVER
Irene Dunne, Alan Marshal, Frank Morgan, Roddy McDowall, Dame May Whitty, Peter Lawford, Van Johnson, June Lockhart, Elizabeth Taylor (Betsy, age ten)
M-G-M
Producer: Sidney Franklin
Director: Clarence Brown
Screenwriters: Claudine West, Jan Lustig, George Froeschel

1944
NATIONAL VELVET
Mickey Rooney, Donald Crisp, Elizabeth Taylor (Velvet Brown), Anne Revere, Angela Lansbury
M-G-M
Producer: Pandro S. Berman
Director: Clarence Brown
Screenwriters: Theodore Reeves, Helen Deutsch

1946
COURAGE OF LASSIE
Elizabeth Taylor (Kathie Merrick), Frank Morgan, Tom Drake, Selena Royle
M-G-M
Producer: Robert Sisk
Director: Fred M. Wilcox
Screenwriter: Lionel Hauser

1947
CYNTHIA
Elizabeth Taylor (Cynthia Bishop), George Murphy, S. Z. Sakall, Mary Astor, Gene Lockhart
M-G-M
PRODUCER: Edwin H. Knopf
DIRECTOR: Robert Z. Leonard
SCREENWRITERS: Harold Buchman, Charles Kaufman

1947
LIFE WITH FATHER
William Powell, Irene Dunne, Elizabeth Taylor (Mary Skinner), Edmund Gwenn, ZaSu Pitts
Warner Brothers
PRODUCER: Robert Buckner
DIRECTOR: Michael Curtiz
SCREENWRITER: Donald Ogden Stewart

1948
A DATE WITH JUDY
Wallace Beery, Jane Powell, Elizabeth Taylor (Carol Pringle), Carmen Miranda, Xavier Cugat, Robert Stack, Selena Royle
M-G-M
PRODUCER: Joe Pasternak
DIRECTOR: Richard Thorpe
SCREENWRITERS: Dorothy Cooper, Dorothy Kingsley

1948
JULIA MISBEHAVES
Greer Garson, Walter Pidgeon, Peter Lawford, Cesar Romero, Elizabeth Taylor (Susan Packett), Lucile Watson, Nigel Bruce
M-G-M
PRODUCER: Everett Riskin

Director: Jack Conway
Screenwriters: William Ludwig, Harry Ruskin, Arthur Wimperis

1949
LITTLE WOMEN
June Allyson, Peter Lawford, Margaret O'Brien, Elizabeth Taylor (Amy March), Janet Leigh, Rossano Brazzi, Mary Astor
M-G-M
Producer/Director: Mervyn LeRoy
Screenwriters: Andrew Solt, Sarah Y. Mason, Victor Heerman

1950
CONSPIRATOR
Robert Taylor, Elizabeth Taylor (Melinda Greyton), Robert Flemyng
M-G-M
Producer: Arthur Hornblow Jr.
Director: Victor Saville
Screenwriter: Sally Benson

1950
THE BIG HANGOVER
Van Johnson, Elizabeth Taylor (Mary Belney), Percy Waram, Leon Ames, Edgar Buchanan, Selena Royle, Gene Lockhart
M-G-M
Producer/Director/Screenwriter: Norman Krasna

1950
FATHER OF THE BRIDE
Spencer Tracy, Joan Bennett, Elizabeth Taylor (Kay Banks), Don Taylor, Billie Burke
M-G-M
Producer: Pandro S. Berman
Director: Vincente Minnelli
Screenwriters: Frances Goodrich, Albert Hackett

1951
FATHER'S LITTLE DIVIDEND
Spencer Tracy, Joan Bennett, Elizabeth Taylor (Kay Dunstan), Don Taylor, Billie Burke
M-G-M
PRODUCER: Pandro S. Berman
DIRECTOR: Vincente Minnelli
SCREENWRITERS: Frances Goodrich, Albert Hackett

1951
A PLACE IN THE SUN
Montgomery Clift, Elizabeth Taylor (Angela Vickers), Shelley Winters, Anne Revere, Raymond Burr
Paramount
PRODUCER/DIRECTOR: George Stevens
SCREENWRITERS: Michael Wilson, Harry Brown

1951
CALLAWAY WENT THATAWAY
Fred MacMurray, Dorothy McGuire, Howard Keel.
Guest Stars: June Allyson, Clark Gable, Elizabeth Taylor, Esther Williams, Dick Powell.
M-G-M
PRODUCER/DIRECTOR/SCREENWRITERS: Norman Panama, Melvin Frank

1952
LOVE IS BETTER THAN EVER
Larry Parks, Elizabeth Taylor (Anastacia Macaboy), Josephine Hutchinson, Tom Tully
M-G-M
PRODUCER: William H. Wright
DIRECTOR: Stanley Donen
SCREENWRITER: Ruth Brooks Flippen

1952
IVANHOE
Robert Taylor, Elizabeth Taylor (Rebecca), Joan Fontaine, George Sanders, Emlyn Williams
M-G-M
PRODUCER: Pandro S. Berman
DIRECTOR: Richard Thorpe
SCREENWRITER: Noel Langley

1953
THE GIRL WHO HAD EVERYTHING
Elizabeth Taylor (Jean Latimer), Fernando Lamas, William Powell, Gig Young, James Whitmore
M-G-M
PRODUCER: Armand Deutsch
DIRECTOR: Richard Thorpe
SCREENWRITER: Art Cohn

1954
RHAPSODY
Elizabeth Taylor (Louise Durant), Vittorio Gassman, John Ericson, Louis Calhern, Michael Chekhov
M-G-M
PRODUCER: Lawrence Weingarten
DIRECTOR: Charles Vidor
SCREENWRITERS: Fay and Michael Kanin

1954
ELEPHANT WALK
Elizabeth Taylor (Ruth Wiley), Dana Andrews, Peter Finch, James Donald, Rosemary Harris
Paramount
PRODUCER: Irving Asher

Director: William Dieterle
Screenwriter: John Lee Mahin

1954
BEAU BRUMMELL
Stewart Granger, Elizabeth Taylor (Lady Patricia), Peter Ustinov, Robert Morley
M-G-M
Producer: Sam Zimbalist
Director: Curtis Bernhardt
Screenwriter: Karl Tunberg

1954
THE LAST TIME I SAW PARIS
Elizabeth Taylor (Helen Ellswirth), Van Johnson, Walter Pidgeon, Donna Reed, Eva Gabor, Roger Moore
M-G-M
Producer: Jack Cummings
Director: Richard Brooks
Screenwriters: Julius J. Epstein, Philip G. Epstein, Richard Brooks

1956
GIANT
Elizabeth Taylor (Leslie Lynnton Benedict), Rock Hudson, James Dean, Carroll Baker, Jane Withers, Chill Wills, Mercedes McCambridge
Warner Brothers
Producers: George Stevens, Henry Ginsberg
Director: George Stevens
Screenwriters: Fred Guiol, Ivan Moffat

1957
RAINTREE COUNTY
Montgomery Clift, Elizabeth Taylor (Susanna Drake), Eva Marie

Saint, Nigel Patrick, Lee Marvin, Rod Taylor, Agnes Moorehead
M-G-M
PRODUCER: David Lewis
DIRECTOR: Edward Dmytryk
SCREENWRITER: Millard Kaufman

1958
CAT ON A HOT TIN ROOF
Elizabeth Taylor (Maggie Pollitt), Paul Newman, Burl Ives, Jack Carson, Judith Anderson, Madeleine Sherwood
M-G-M
PRODUCER: Lawrence Weingarten
DIRECTOR: Richard Brooks
SCREENWRITERS: Richard Brooks, James Poe

1959
SUDDENLY, LAST SUMMER
Elizabeth Taylor (Catherine Holly), Katharine Hepburn, Montgomery Clift, Albert Dekker, Mercedes McCambridge
Columbia Pictures
PRODUCER: Sam Spiegel
DIRECTOR: Joseph L. Mankiewicz
SCREENWRITERS: Gore Vidal, Tennessee Williams

1960
SCENT OF MYSTERY (HOLIDAY IN SPAIN)
Denholm Elliott, Peter Lorre, Paul Lukas, Elizabeth Taylor (the Real Sally Kennedy)
A Michael Todd Jr. Release
PRODUCER: Michael Todd Jr.
DIRECTOR: Jack Cardiff
SCREENWRITER: William Roos

1960
BUTTERFIELD 8
Elizabeth Taylor (Gloria Wandrous), Laurence Harvey, Eddie Fisher, Dina Merrill, Mildred Dunnock
M-G-M
Producer: Pandro S. Berman
Director: Daniel Mann
Screenwriters: Charles Schnee, John Michael Hayes

1963
CLEOPATRA
Elizabeth Taylor (Cleopatra), Richard Burton, Rex Harrison, Hume Cronyn, Roddy McDowall, Martin Landau
Twentieth Century-Fox
Producer: Walter Wanger
Director: Joseph L. Mankiewicz
Screenwriters: Joseph L. Mankiewicz, Ranald MacDougall, Sidney Buchman

1963
THE V.I.P.S
Elizabeth Taylor (Frances Andros), Richard Burton, Louis Jourdan, Elsa Martinelli, Margaret Rutherford, Maggie Smith, Orson Welles
M-G-M
Producer: Anatole deGrunwald
Director: Anthony Asquith
Screenwriter: Terence Rattigan

1965
THE SANDPIPER
Elizabeth Taylor (Laura Reynolds), Richard Burton, Eva Marie Saint, Charles Bronson, Robert Webber
M-G-M
Producer: Martin Ransohoff

DIRECTOR: Vincente Minnelli
SCREENWRITERS: Dalton Trumbo, Michael Wilson

1966
WHO'S AFRAID OF VIRGINIA WOOLF?
Elizabeth Taylor (Martha), Richard Burton, George Segal, Sandy Dennis
Warner Brothers
PRODUCER: Ernest Lehman
DIRECTOR: Mike Nichols
SCREENWRITER: Ernest Lehman

1967
THE TAMING OF THE SHREW
Elizabeth Taylor (Katharina), Richard Burton, Michael York, Cyril Cusack
Columbia Pictures
PRODUCERS: Richard Burton, Elizabeth Taylor, Franco Zeffirelli
DIRECTOR: Franco Zeffirelli
SCREENWRITERS: Paul Dehn, Suso Cecchi D'Amico, Franco Zeffirelli

1967
DOCTOR FAUSTUS
Elizabeth Taylor (Helen of Troy), Richard Burton, Andreas Teuber, Elizabeth O'Donovan
Columbia Pictures
PRODUCERS: Richard Burton, Richard McWhorter
DIRECTORS: Richard Burton, Nevill Coghill
SCREEN ADAPTATION: Nevill Coghill

1967
REFLECTIONS IN A GOLDEN EYE
Elizabeth Taylor (Leonora Penderton), Marlon Brando, Brian Keith, Julie Harris

Warner Brothers—Seven Arts
Producer: Ray Stark
Director: John Huston
Screenwriters: Chapman Mortimer, Gladys Hill

1967
THE COMEDIANS
Elizabeth Taylor (Martha Pineda), Richard Burton, Alec Guinness, Peter Ustinov, Lillian Gish
M-G-M
Producer/Director: Peter Glenville
Screenwriter: Graham Greene

1968
BOOM!
Elizabeth Taylor (Flora "Sissy" Goforth), Richard Burton, Noël Coward
Universal Pictures
Producers: John Heyman, Norman Priggen
Director: Joseph Losey
Screenwriter: Tennessee Williams

1968
SECRET CEREMONY
Elizabeth Taylor (Leonora), Mia Farrow, Robert Mitchum
Universal Pictures
Producers: John Heyman, Norman Priggen
Director: Joseph Losey
Screenwriter: George Tabori

1970
THE ONLY GAME IN TOWN
Elizabeth Taylor (Fran Walker), Warren Beatty, Charles Braswell, Hank Henry

Twentieth Century-Fox
Producer: Fred Kohlmar
Director: George Stevens
Screenwriter: Frank D. Gilroy

1971
UNDER MILK WOOD
Elizabeth Taylor (Rosie Probert), Richard Burton, Peter O'Toole, Vivien Merchant, Glynis Johns
The Rank Organisation
Producers: Hugh French, Jules Buck
Director: Andrew Sinclair
Screenwriter: Andrew Sinclair

1972
ZEE & CO. (X Y AND ZEE)
Elizabeth Taylor (Zee Blakeley), Michael Caine, Susannah York, Margaret Leighton
Columbia Pictures
Producers: Jay Kanter, Alan Ladd, Jr.
Director: Brian G. Hutton
Screenwriter: Edna O'Brien

1972
HAMMERSMITH IS OUT
Elizabeth Taylor (Jimmie Jean Jackson), Richard Burton, Beau Bridges, Peter Ustinov, Leon Ames
Cinerama Releasing Corporation
Producer: Alex Lucas
Director: Peter Ustinov
Screenwriter: Stanford Whitmore

1973
NIGHT WATCH
Elizabeth Taylor (Ellen Wheeler), Laurence Harvey, Billie Whitelaw
Avco Embassy
PRODUCERS: Martin Poll, George W. George, Barnard S. Straus
DIRECTOR: Brian G. Hutton
SCREENWRITER: Tony Williamson

1973
ASH WEDNESDAY
Elizabeth Taylor (Barbara Sawyer), Henry Fonda, Helmut Berger, Keith Baxter, Monique Van Vooren
Paramount Pictures
PRODUCER: Dominick Dunne
DIRECTOR: Larry Peerce
SCREENWRITER: Jean-Claude Tramont

1974
THAT'S ENTERTAINMENT!
Narrators: Fred Astaire, Bing Crosby, Gene Kelly, Peter Lawford, Liza Minnelli, Donald O'Connor, Debbie Reynolds, Mickey Rooney, Frank Sinatra, James Stewart, Elizabeth Taylor
M-G-M/United Artists
EXECUTIVE PRODUCER: Daniel Melnick
PRODUCER/DIRECTOR/WRITER: Jack Haley Jr.

1974
IDENTIKIT (THE DRIVER'S SEAT)
Elizabeth Taylor (Lise), Ian Bannen, Guido Mannari, Mona Washbourne, Maxence Mailfort
Avco Embassy
PRODUCER: Franco Rossellini
DIRECTOR: Giuseppe Patroni Griffi
SCREENWRITERS: Raffaele La Capria, Giuseppe Patroni Griffi

1976
THE BLUE BIRD
Elizabeth Taylor (Mother/Maternal Love/Witch/Light), Jane Fonda, Ava Gardner, Cicely Tyson, Robert Morley
Twentieth Century-Fox
Executive Producer: Edward Lewis
Producer: Paul Maslansky
Director: George Cukor
Screenwriters: Hugh Whitemore, Alfred Hayes, Alexei Kapler

1977
A LITTLE NIGHT MUSIC
Elizabeth Taylor (Desiree Armfeldt), Diana Rigg, Len Cariou, Lesley-Anne Down, Hermione Gingold
New World Pictures
Executive Producer: Heinz Lazek
Producer: Elliott Kastner
Director: Harold Prince
Screenwriter: Hugh Wheeler

1979
WINTER KILLS
Jeff Bridges, John Huston, Anthony Perkins, Sterling Hayden, Eli Wallach, Dorothy Malone, Elizabeth Taylor (Lola Comante)
Embassy Pictures
Producers: Leonard J. Goldberg, Robert Sterling
Director/Screenwriter: William Richert

1980
THE MIRROR CRACK'D
Angela Lansbury, Geraldine Chaplin, Tony Curtis, Rock Hudson, Kim Novak, Elizabeth Taylor (Marina Rudd)
EMI/Associated Film
Producers: John Brabourne, Richard Goodwin

Director: Guy Hamilton
Screenwriters: Jonathan Hales, Barry Sandler

1981
GENOCIDE (DOCUMENTARY)
Narrators: Elizabeth Taylor, Orson Welles
A Simon Wiesenthal Center Release
Producer/Director: Arnold Schwartzman
Screenwriters: Arnold Schwartzman, Martin Gilbert, Rabbi Marvin Hier

1988
IL GIOVANE TOSCANINI (YOUNG TOSCANINI)
C. Thomas Howell, Elizabeth Taylor (Nadina Bulichoff), Sophie Ward, Pat Heywood, John Rhys-Davies, Franco Nero
Carthago Films/Canal Plus/Italian International
Producers: Fulvio Lucisano, Tarak Ben Ammar
Director: Franco Zeffirelli
Screenwriter: William H. Stadiem

1994
THE FLINTSTONES
John Goodman, Rick Moranis, Elizabeth Perkins, Rosie O'Donnell, Kyle MacLachlan, Halle Berry, Elizabeth Taylor
Hanna-Barbera/Amblin Entertainment/Universal
Producers: William Hanna, Joseph Barbera, Kathleen Kennedy, David Kirschner, Gerald R. Molen
Director: Brian Levant
Screenwriters: Tom S. Parker, Jim Jennewein, Steven E. deSouza

MOVIES MADE FOR TELEVISION

1973
DIVORCE; HIS/DIVORCE; HERS
Elizabeth Taylor (Jane Reynolds), Richard Burton, Carrie Nye
ABC-TV
Executive Producer: John Heyman
Producers: Terence Baker, Gareth Wigan
Director: Waris Hussein
Screenwriter: John Hopkins

1976
VICTORY AT ENTEBBE
Helmut Berger, Theodore Bikel, Linda Blair, Richard Dreyfuss, Kirk Douglas, Elizabeth Taylor (Edra Vilnofsky), Helen Hayes, Anthony Hopkins, Burt Lancaster
ABC-TV
Executive Producer: David L. Wolper
Producer: Robert Guenette
Director: Marvin J. Chomsky
Screenwriter: Ernest Kinoy

1978

RETURN ENGAGEMENT

Elizabeth Taylor (Dr. Emily Loomis), Joseph Bottoms, Allyn Ann McLerie, Peter Donat

NBC-TV

PRODUCERS: Franklin R. Levy, Mike Wise

DIRECTOR: Joseph Hardy

SCREENWRITER: James Prideaux

1983

BETWEEN FRIENDS (NOBODY MAKES ME CRY)

Elizabeth Taylor (Deborah Shapiro), Carol Burnett, Barbara Bush, Henry Ramer

HBO

EXECUTIVE PRODUCERS: Robert Cooper, Marian Rees

PRODUCERS/WRITERS: Shelley List, Jonathan Estrin

DIRECTOR: Lou Antonio

1985

MALICE IN WONDERLAND (THE RUMOR MILL)

Elizabeth Taylor (Louella Parsons), Jane Alexander, Richard Dysart, Joyce Van Patten

CBS-TV

EXECUTIVE PRODUCER: Judith A. Polone

PRODUCER: Jay Benson

DIRECTOR: Gus Trikonis

SCREENWRITERS: Jacqueline M. Feather, David Seidler

1985

NORTH AND SOUTH (MINISERIES)

Kirstie Alley, David Carradine, Leslie-Anne Down, Genie Francis, Patrick Swayze, Elizabeth Taylor (special guest star)

ABC-TV

EXECUTIVE PRODUCERS: David L. Wolper, Chuck McLain

PRODUCER: Paul Freeman
DIRECTOR: Richard Heffron
SCREENWRITERS: Douglas Heyes, Paul F. Edwards, Kathleen A. Shelley, Patricia Green

1986
THERE MUST BE A PONY
Elizabeth Taylor (Marguerite Sydney), Robert Wagner, James Coco, William Windom
ABC-TV
EXECUTIVE PRODUCER: Robert Wagner
PRODUCER: Howard Jeffrey
DIRECTOR: Joseph Sargent
SCREENWRITER: Mart Crowley

1987
POKER ALICE
Elizabeth Taylor (Alice Moffett), George Hamilton, David Wayne, Richard Mulligan
CBS-TV
EXECUTIVE PRODUCER: Harvey Matofsky
PRODUCER: Renée Valente
DIRECTOR: Arthur Allan Seidelman
SCREENWRITER: James Lee Barrett

1989
SWEET BIRD OF YOUTH
Elizabeth Taylor (Alexandra Del Lago—the Princess Kosmonopolis), Mark Harmon, Rip Torn, Valerie Perrine
NBC-TV
EXECUTIVE PRODUCERS: Donald Kushner, Peter Locke, Linda Yellen
DIRECTOR: Nicholas Roeg
SCREENWRITER: Gavin Lambert

STAGE APPEARANCES

1981
THE LITTLE FOXES by Lillian Hellman
Novella Nelson, Joe Seneca, Maureen Stapleton, Joe Ponazecki, Dennis Christopher, Elizabeth Taylor (Regina Giddens), Humbert Allen Astredo, Anthony Zerbe, Ann Talman, Tom Aldredge
Martin Beck Theatre, New York
Director: Austin Pendleton
Settings: Andrew Jackness
Costumes: Florence Klotz
Lighting: Paul Gallo
Presented by: Zev Bufman, Donald C. Carter, Jon Cutler

1983
PRIVATE LIVES by Noël Coward
Kathryn Walker, Richard Burton, John Cullum, Elizabeth Taylor (Amanda Prynne), Helena Carroll
Lunt-Fontanne Theatre, New York
Director: Milton Katselas
Settings: David Mitchell
Costumes: Theoni V. Aldredge
Lighting: Tharon Musser
Presented by: the Elizabeth Theater Group, Zev Bufman and Elizabeth Taylor

ACKNOWLEDGMENTS

Liz would not have been possible without the help of countless individuals and institutions. First acknowledgment must go to Steven Schragis, the publisher of this book. Then I would like to thank my editor, Bruce Shostak, as well as Bruce Bender, president of the firm; my literary agents, Georges and Anne Borchardt and Cindy Klein; and Allan Wilson, Marcy Swingle, Ben Petrone, Meryl Earl, Hillel Black, Donald Davidson, Frank Lavena, Cheryl Moch, and others at the Carol Publishing Group who helped and encouraged me. I am likewise indebted to my literary attorney, Eugene L. Girden, for his scrupulous reading and vetting of the manuscript, as well as Mel Wulf, who performed the same task on behalf of the publisher.

I am particularly grateful to a first-rate staff of researchers and interviewers that included Pat Maniscalco, Esq., Ann Marie Cunningham, Jeanne Lunin Heymann, Roberta Fineberg, June Petersen, Joanne Green-Levine, Devon Jackson, Arlene Kayatt, Esq., Mark Alvey, Carl Schultz, Laura Birely, Warren Chang, Leni Gilman, Suzanne Freedman, Barbara Frank, Jeff Hoyt, Beth Judy, Anthony Mazzaschi, Michelle Rugo, Mary Grace Sinnott, Marisa Steffers, Marlan Warren, Annath White, Garret Weyr, and others I may have inadvertently forgotten to mention.

Much research was conducted in various archives, libraries, newspaper morgues, and government agencies. Among these were the Library for the Performing Arts at Lincoln Center; Margaret Herrick Library, Academy of Motion Picture Arts and Sciences; the American Film Institute; M-G-M Studios; Hilton Hotels Corporation; Motion Picture and Television Fund; Special Collections, Boston University Library system; Special Collections, New York Public Library; Special Collections, Columbia University Library system; Museum of Modern Art Film Archives; *Star* magazine archives; *San Francisco Examiner* Archives; Parallalax Productions; Celebrity Services, Inc.; Special Collections, University of Virginia Library system; Cleveland Public Library; Directors Guild of America; UCLA Libraries; USC Libraries; Special Collections, Duke University Library system; U.S. Department of Justice, Federal Bureau of Investigation; Carlton Institute; Library of Congress; Los Angeles Superior Court Archives and Records Department; U.S. Department of Navy; Theater Collection, Harvard College Library; University of Houston Library; *Lake Superior* magazine; Time Inc.; Audio-Visual Center, Indiana University; Special Collections, the University of Tennessee Library system; Minneapolis Public Library and Information Center; Turner Communications; the Museum of Broadcasting; U.S. Department of State; U.S. Naval Institute; the Lawrence & Lee Theatre Research Institute; Special Collections, Yale University Library system; Oxford University Library; Special Collections, University of Wisconsin (Madison) Library system; Oral History Collection, Southern Methodist University; University of Texas Humanities Research Center; the Riviera Country Club; Palm-Aire Spa Resort; Photofest; Shake Books & Magazine Archive Service; Metropolitan Toronto Reference Library; Harry S. Truman Presidential Library; British Ministry of Agriculture, Fisheries and Food; Willenborg Productions; American Heritage Center Development, University of Wyoming; NBC-TV; the Wisconsin Center for Film and Theater Research, the Wesleyan Cinema Archives; State Historical Society of Wisconsin; British Information Service; the British Museum.

I must also mention my mother, Renée K. Vago Heymann, who repeatedly encouraged me to complete this project.

And finally I thank the thousand individuals who agreed to be interviewed for this book or who answered questions in writing. While a few requested anonymity, many did not. Among the latter are:

Stephen Abel, Avi Ben Abraham, Cindy Adams, Joey Adams, Leith Adams, Ronald Adamson, Edward Albee, Alexandre (Louis Albert Alexandre Rimon), Arthur Allene, June Allyson, Hollis Alpert, Sarah Altshul, Ellis Ambern, Wendell Amos, Chris Anderson, David Anderson, Dame Judith Anderson, Melinda Anderson, Robert Anderson, Wayne Anderson, Jane Ardmore, Peter Arlington, Marcia Armstrong, Robert ("Tito") Arias, Penny Arum, Agnes Ash, Eleanor Ashe, Linda Ashland, Larry Ashmead, Leon Askin, Ed Asiano, Mary Astor, Humbert Allen Astredo, Edith Atkins, Jack Atlas, Richard Avedon, Sid Avery, Gerald Ayers.

Jean Babette, Anna-Marie Baer, Ernesto Baer, Gayle Baizer, Baz Bamigboye, Charles Barile, Nelly Barquet, Rona Barrett, George Barrie, Laura Barringer, David Barrison, Cora Bartlett, Stephen M. Bauer, José María Bayona, Orson Bean, Marie-Therese Beaumier, Tanya Bearer, Gretchen Begruygen, Hannon Bell, Melvin Belli, Jane Halsman Bello, Laslo Benedek, Joan Bennett, Terri Bennett, Helen Bentley, A. Scott Berg, Gretchen P. Berg, Brigid Berlin, Carl Bernstein, Gary Bernstein, Mashey Bernstein, Natalie Best, Juanita Bevelaequia, Alain Beverini, Susan Biloxi, Stephen Birmingham, Earl Blackwell, Richard ("Mr. Blackwell") Blackwell, Amanda Blake, Julian Blaustien, Phil Blazer, John Block, David Blundy, Victor Bookris, Rosemary Bogley, Marc Bohan, Phyllis Borea, Peter C. Borsari, Peter Bosch, Marie-Therese Bosque, Patricia Bosworth, Nathalie Boudin, Rudy Bower, Frank Brady, Susan Braudy, Tony Brenna, Lindsay Brice, Ronnie Britt, Richard Broadhurst, Wayne C. Brockman, Richard Brooks, Clarence Brown, David Brown, Di Bronn, Joel Broyhill, Arthur Bruckel, Patty Brundage, Molly Brush, Rock Brynner, Art Buchwald, Guido Bulanini, Richard Burton, Sally Hay Burton, Jerry Buss, Alec Byrne.

Daniel Cahen, Steve Cahill, Sammy Cahn, Jan Calder, Louisa Campbell, Eileen Capeda, Malbert J. Caplan, Truman Capote, Edward Caracchi, George Carpozi Jr., Lucille Rymann Carroll, Nancy Casey, Joanna Casson, Jean Castel, Ramon Castro, Edward Catacchi,

Thelma Cazalet-Keir, Marge Champion, Charles Champlin, Charlotte Chandler, Robert Chen, Judy Chisholm, Robert Christedes, Camille T. Christie, George Christie, Marian Christy, Sharon Churcher, Jane Churchman, Gerald Clarke, Garry Clifford, Bill Cling, Sherry Suib Cohen, Roy Cohn, Robert ("Bob") Colacello, Ann Cole, George Coleman, Charles Collingwood, Josephine Collins, Stephen Collins, David Patrick Columbia, Chuck Conconi, Barnaby Conrad, Peter Conrad, Sarah Booth Conroy, Lady Diana Cooper, Roger Copeland, Christina Cranford, Judy Craven, J. Cornelius Crean, Jane Hodges Crest, Kay Croker, Hume Cronyn, Mart Crowley, Priscilla Cunningham, Kent Cunow, Charlotte Curtis.

Eric Dahler, Jean Dalrymple, Timothy Daly, Cesare Danova, Phyllis Dantagnan, Bob Davidoff, Claire Davids, Bill Davidson, Bette Davis, Daphne Davis, Glenn Davis, Gwen Davis, Ronald L. Davis, Craig Dawson, Hilary Dealey, Philip Dealey, Jane Dean, Emile de Antonio, Harley Decorret, Marquise Emmitta de la Falaise, Anne de Gasperi, Francois de Lamothe, Oscar de la Renta, Claudia del Monte, Bonnie Ann DeMeio, Dr. Joseph L. DeMeio, Oscar De Mejo, Juanita de Muñoz, Kitty Dennis, Sandy Dennis, Baron Alexis de Rede, Countess Jacqueline de Ribes, Dominique D'Ermo, Julian de Rothschild, Debby Destri, Armand Deutsch, Curtis de Witz, Wyatt Dickerson, Tandy Dickinson, Howard Diller, Kathleen Di Toro, Edward Dmytryk, Gwen Dobson, Gary Doctor, Carole Wells Doheny, Ken Dolan, Brigitte Domani, Stanley Donen, Hedi Donizetti-Mullener (Olden), William V. Donovan, Casper Dooley, Carol Dorian, Anne d'Ornano, Hebe Dorsey, Kirk Douglas, Valerie Douglas, Didi Drew, Diana DuBois, Francoise Ducout, Angela Fox Dunn, Dominick Dunne, Irene Dunne, Philip Dunne.

Meryl Earl, Beverly Ecker, Alice Edwards, Peter Edwards, Stanley Eichelbaum, William P. Elder, R. D. Eno, Delia Ephron, Rosa Estoria, Arnunco Estrada, Elaine Grossinger Etess, Mark Grossinger Etess, Michelle Etienne, Al Evans.

Zev Faber, Franz Fah, John Fahrnsworth, Douglas Fairbanks, Jr., Celia Lipton Farris, Mia Farrow, Don Fauntleroy, Peter Feibleman, Georges Fenster, Dennis Ferrara, Miguel Ferreras, Bruce Fesier, Roger Fillistorf, Larry Fina, Richard Fina, Richard Finn, Eddie Fisher, Edward J. Fitzgibbon, Karin Fleming, Lilly Fonda, Joan Fontaine, Bryan Forbes, Malcolm S. Forbes, Stanley S. Formosa, Irene Frain, Anne Francis, Sam Frank, Martha Frankl, Joe Franklin, Muriel Freeman, Elizabeth ("Betty") Fretz, Julie Freund, Leonard Friedman, Kurt Frings, Mrs. Aaron Frosch.

Eva Gabor, Zsa Zsa Gabor, Danielle Gain, Steven Gaines, James Galanos, Ron Galella, Robert David Lyon Gardiner, Ava Gardner, Renee Garnett, Louise Gault, Jackie Gayle, Brad Geagley, Jan Geidt, Jeremy Geidt, Jonathan Gems, Sandy Gibbons, Stefan Gierasch, Mary Gimble, Ina Ginsburg, Peter Givens, Garrett Glaser, Marguerite Glatz, Claire Goldman, Karina Golumbie, Teresa Gonzales, Virginia Graham, Stewart Granger, Phyllis Grann, James Grant, Albert Grasselli, Kathryn Grayson, Ashton W. Greathouse, Arthur Green, Joann Green, Gloria Greer, Gene Griessley, Kathy Griffen, Gary M. Griffin, Jonas Gritzus, Tanya Griskind, Nelson Gross, Tania Grossinger, Bob Guccione, Eva Guest, Leo Guild, Gloria Gunsberg.

Mel Haber, Pat Hackett, Horst Haechler, Irene Halsman, Jane Halsman, Yvonne Halsman, Halston, Anne Hamilton, Guy Hamilton, Jack Hamilton, Joseph C. Hamilton, Darlene Hammond, Tom Harding, Joseph Hardy, Mary Harrington, Julie Harris, Radie Harris, Rex Harrison, Stephen Harvey, Gene Hawkins, Sen. Paula Hawkins, Rod Helm, Renee Helmer, Peter Henrich, Katharine Hepburn, Harvey Herman, Jerry Herman, Lenore Hershey, Jerry Hieb, Jack Hildyard, Francesca Hilton, Patricia Hilton, Philip Hodson, Richard Hoffman, Jerry Hogan, Fran Holland, Tom Hollatz, Jake Holmes, Steven Holt, Catherine (Mrs. Thomas) Hook, Dennis Hopper, A. E. Hotchner, Jeffrey Hoyt, Cathleen Huck, Ross Hunter, Hugh L. Hurd, George Hurrell, Waris Hussein, John Huston, Brian Hutton, Joe Hyams.

Lenny Ickton, Christopher Idines, Le'Ann Ince, Rick Ingersoll, Tom Irish, Burl Ives, Ruth Jacobson, Barbara Jackson, Charles Jarrott, Françoise Javet, Marion Javitz, Dorothy Jeakins, Patrice Jean, David Jenkins, Graham Jenkins, Eloise Jensen, Rick Jewell, Alexandra Jew-ett, John Jiras, Jean-Claude Jitrois, Glynis Johns, Eve Abbot Johnson, Melissa C. Johnson, David Jones, Fred Jones, Ted H. Jordan, Dany Jucaud.

Meir Kahane, Nathan Kahn, John Kaperonis, Dick Kaplan, Edmund Kara, Judith M. Kass, Barry Andrew Kearsley, Pepi Kelman, Dr. Rexford ("Rex") Kennamer, Kirk Kerber, Dorismae Kerns, Hubie Kerns, Evelyn Keyes, Michael Kilian, Ralph Kiner, Ernest Kinoy, David Kirby, Douglas Kirkland, James Kirkwood, Kay Kline, Patsy Kline, Kenny Kling, Allen T. Klots, Florence Klotz, J. Z. Knight, James P. Knox, Cecilia Kover, Robert Kreis, Jean Kriegel, Werner Kuchler, Brigitte Kueppers, Beth Kummerfeld, Asan Tirobi Kwan.

Joyce Laabs, Skip Lackey, Eleanor Lambert, Hank Lampey, Phil Landon, Louise Lane, Lester Lanin, Angela Lansbury, Richard Lasko, Philip Lathrop, Laurent, Peter Lawford, Heinz Lazek, Larry Leamer, Joanna Lee, Nancy Lee, Peggy Lee, Vern Leeper, Kenneth Leffers, Mr. Xavier Le Grand, Janet Leigh, Wendy Leigh, Frances Spatz Leighton, William ("Billy") LeMassena, Jean Leon, Masha Leon, Margot Lerner, Max Lerner, Milton Lerner, Samuel Leve, Bruce Levitt, Arnold Bruce Levy, Stanley Levy, David Lewin, Werner Lewin, Susan Licht, Bob Lieberman, Sol Lieberman, Doris Lilly, Pia Lindstrom, Gerrol Lipsky, Sarah Lithgow, Robert Littman, Anne Livet, Kathryn Livingston, Toni LoCicero, Bronnyn Long, Richard Long, Mario Lopez, Joseph Losey, Merrill Lowell, Ernest Lowy, Gloria V. Luchenbill, Luigi Luraschi, Renee Luttgen, James Lydon, Jane Lynch, Jeffrey Lyons, Sue Lyons, Mary MacDonald, Jim Mahoney, Norman Mailer, Hormoz Maleki, Leonard Maltin, Rouben Mamoulian, Chris Mankiewicz, Joseph L. Mankiewicz, Paul Mankin, Daniel Mann, Stephanie Mansfield, Peter Manso, John Marion, Rosa Marshall, Vita Marshall, Jack Martin, Liberty ("Female") Martine, Samuel Marx, Paul Maslansky, Ginger Mason, Morgan Mason, Pamela Mason, Ichiro Masuda, Harvey Matofsky, Rudy Maxa, Felice Ferreras Mayer, Roger Mayer, Floyd Mayfield, Fran McArthur, Dan McCall, Betty McCann, Rebecca McCann, Kevin McCarthy, Sarah McClendon, David McClintick, Constance McCormick, Sandra McElwaine, Ethel McGinnis, David McGough,

Dorothy McGuire, F. Kenneth ("Ken") McKnight, Diana McLellan, Ailene ("Suzy") Mehle, Al Melnick, Stuart Melville, Bill Merchant, Sam Merrill, Richard Meryman, Egon Merz, Harriet Meth, Johnny Meyers, Hywel Miles, Sylvia Miles, Dick Millais, Ann Miller, Geoff Miller, Adm. Gerald E. Miller, Nolan Miller, Michael Mindlin, Lee Minnelli, Stanley Mirsky, M.D., James H. Mitchell, Morton Mitosky, Minna Mittleman, Terry Moore, Wendy Moore, Thelma Moorehouse, Adm. Thomas Moorer, Rev. S. Nagle Morgan, Tony Morgan, Jane Morgis, Jane Mullen, Sheridan Morley, Oswald Morris, Debby Moss, Doug Motel, Christian ("Mr. Christian") Moulin, Yves Mourousi, Lesley Mullener, Mollie Mulligan, Michael Mullins, Robert Munchnick, George Murphy, Jimmy Murphy.

Joe Naar, Aubrey Nabor, May Najem, Norma Nathan, Sally Nelson-Harb, Knoi Nguyen, Christopher Nickens, Madeleine Nicklin, Bill Nieves, Sharon Nobel, Simone Noir, Philip Norman, Millard P. North, Ruth Nussbaum.

Jane Ober, Christina Onassis, Jerry Oppenheimer, Oray, Gisella Orkin, Xavier Orozsco, Hilda Owen.

Jerry Pam, Pico Pardo, Jackie Park, Nadine Parker, Michael Patrick, Floyd Patterson, Dan Paul, Amy Peake, Gregory Peck, Larry Peerce, Austin Pendleton, Daphne Pereles, Anna Perez, Dorothy Perkins, Sally Perle, Lester Persky, Ronald Peters, June Petersen, Donna Peterson, Ben Petrone, Michele Petti, Olga Petrov, Albert Pfeiffer, Mary Jane Picard, Ann Pickford, Harriet F. Pilpel, W. Pitts, Maya Plisetskaya, Hal Polaire, Charles Poletti, Martin Poll, Joe Ponazecki, Cyril Porter, William Post Jr., Larry Postman, Michael Powazinik, Jane Powell, Betty Sullivan Precht, James Prideaux, Lisa Pritzker.

Robert Quain, Anthony Quayle, Judith Balaban Quine, Ann C. Quinn, Felice Quinto.

Irving Raff, Lady Frances Ramsbotham, Ambassador Peter E. Rambsbotham, Martin Ransohoff, Count Lanfranco Rasponi, Olivia Raye-Williams, Francois Reboul, Martha Reed, Karen E. Reist, Line Renaud, Pierre Reval, Anne Revere, Patrick Reynolds, Michael Rich, Bill Richert, Gregg Risch, Martin Ritt, Paul Riva, Joan Rivers, Jilly

Rizzo, Dr. Leon Robb, Meade Roberts, Gloria Rodriguez, Ambassador Joseph Rogers, Peter Rogers, Sylvie Romain, Mrs. Jan Chamberlin Rooney, Mickey Rooney, Franklin D. Roosevelt Jr., Selwa ("Lucky") Roosevelt, Joel Rose, Kate Rose, Helen Rosen, Sonia Rosenberg, Robert Rosenblum, Richard Rosenthal, Mrs. Richard Rosenthal, Mira Rostova, Billy Royal, Alan Rubenstein, Lisa Rubenstein, Cecilia Rupprechter, Leslie Rusch, George Rush.

Ed Safdie, Wendy Sahagen, Eva Marie Saint, Tim Sallow, Bob Salvatore, Jack Salzman, Chen Sam, Mark Samuels, Donald Sanderson, Carlos ("Coco") Santoscoy, Joseph Sargent, Dr. Louis A. Scarrone, Thomas Schatz, Mary Louise Scheid, Jean Scherrer, Marina Schiano, Patricia Schmidlapp, Ian Schrager, Stephen Schragis, Budd Schulberg, Erna Schulhofer, Steven Schwartz, Jim Schwartzberg, Vernon Scott, Patricia Seaton (Lawford), Arthur Seidleman, David Seidler, Bonnie Selfe, Walter Seltzer, Irene Mayer Selznick, Marcelle Senesi, Rabbi Robert Serebrenik, Angie Shafkin, Mark Shap, Irene Sharaff, Wilfred Sheed, Garnet I. Sherman, Jean Shilling, Robert A. Sideman, Lillian Burns Sidney, Michelangelo Signorile, Stephen M. Silverman, Iselin Simon, Kathy Simons, Phil Sinclair, Thomas Skow, Robert Slatzer, Larry Sloan, Merrya Small, David Smith M.D., Jack Smith, Liz Smith, Nona Smith, Philip Smith, Ben Smothers, Tom Snyder, Walter Sobel, Stephen Sondheim, Helena Sorrell, Barbara P. Soy, James Spada, Nancy G. Speer, Paul Spindler, Doris Lee Spring, John Springer, Peter Stackpole, William H. Stadiem, Jack Stallworth, Kim Stanley, Richard Stanley, Barbara Stanwyck, Maureen Stapleton, Ray Stark, Francine Statler, Newton Steers Jr., Pat Steger, Dennis Stein, Kurt Stempler, Marge Stengel, Charles R. Stephens, Bert Stern, Phil Stern, Stewart Stern, Eilene Stevens, Daniel K. Stewart, Jane Stewart, Marian Stewart, Ronald Stewart, Tricia Stiles, John Stockwell, Rose Stoler, Jacob Stone, Roger Stone, Larry Storm, Curt Strand, Ann Straus, Marianne Strong, Carole Stuart, Lyle Stuart, Jule Styne, Brian Sullivan, H. N. Swanson, Angela R. Sweeney.

Michael Tabori, Marina Tal, Jeffrey Tanby, Amy Tandem, J. Randy Taraborrelli, Jeff Tarentino, Gwin Tate, John Taylor,

Noreen Taylor, Patti Taylor, Zak Taylor, Patrick Terrail, Maurice Teynac, Bob Thomas, Craig Thomas, Moira Thomas, Marshall Thompson, Richard Thorpe, Col. Cloyce Tippett, James Toback, Michael Todd Jr., Emily Torchia, Francine Torrent, Liz Torres, Roy E. Traband, Stanley Tretick, Marisa Trimble, Dr. Randolph Troques, Edward M. Tsercover, Russell Turiak.

Tony Unger, Carol Upper.

Betty Vacani, Nicole Valier, John Valva, Jean Murray Vanderbilt, Judith Van der Molen, June Van Dyck, Joyce Van Patten, Julio Vargas, Teddy Vaughen, Jerry Vermilye, Carol Vernier, Bill Vickers, David Victor, Gore Vidal, Raymond Vignale, Jean-Pierre Villon, Bernard Voisin, Sandra Ritter Voluck, Betsy von Furstenberg, Trudy von Trotha, Monique van Vooren, Diana Vreeland.

Malvin Wald, Carla Wall, Frances Wall, Roger Wall, Eli Wallach, Paul Wallach, Shelley Wanger, Stephanie Wanger, Mrs. Willard Ware, Andy Warhol, Sen. John Warner, Dale Wasserman, Harriet Wasserman, Jane Ellen Wayne, John Wayne, Robin Weir, Haskell Wexler, Charles Whalens, John Whaley, Hugh Wheeler, Liz Whitney, Tom Wicky, Billy Wilder, Barbara Williams, Billy Williams, Rev. Eric Williams, Elmo Williams, Bob Willoughby, Allan Wilson, Earl Wilson, Jeri Wilson, Lee Wohlfert, Connie Wolf, Renée Wood, Henry Woodbridge, Danny Woodruff, Betsy Wolfe, Robert Woolley, Jane Woolrich, Guillermo Wulff, Lupe Wulff, Henry Wynberg, Ned Wynn.

Alex Yalaia, Tom Yaroschulc, Elaine Young, Terence Young.

Ardeshir Zahedi, Firhooz Zahedi, John Zavala, Jerome Zerbe, Melvyn Zerman, Fred Zinnemann, Adm. Elmo R. Zumwalt Jr., Irving Zussman, Deborah Zygot.